Lecture Notes in Computer Science

Edited by G. Goos and J. Hartmanis
Series: GI, Gesellschaft für Informatik e. V.

48

Theoretical Computer Science 3rd GI Conference

Darmstadt, March 28–30, 1977

Edited by
H. Tzschach, H. Waldschmidt, H. K.-G. Walter
on behalf of the GI

Springer-Verlag
Berlin · Heidelberg · New York 1977

Program Committee
Prof. Dr. J. Berstel
Prof. Dr. K.-H. Böhling
Prof. Dr. W. Brauer
Prof. Dr. E. Engeler
Prof. Dr. G. Hotz
Prof. Dr. C.-P. Schnorr

Editors
Prof. Dr. Hans Tzschach
Prof. Dr. Helmut Waldschmidt
Prof. Dr. Hermann K.-G. Walter
Institut für Theoretische Informatik
Technische Hochschule Darmstadt
Magdalenenstr. 11
6100 Darmstadt/BRD

AMS Subject Classifications (1970): 68-XX, 94-XX, 02-xx, 02Dxx, 02EXX, 02Fxx, 05-04
CR Subject Classifications (1974): 5, 1

ISBN 3-540-08138-0 Springer-Verlag Berlin · Heidelberg · New York
ISBN 0-387-08138-0 Springer-Verlag New York · Heidelberg · Berlin

Printed in Germany
Printing and binding: Beltz Offsetdruck, Hemsbach/Bergstr. 2145/3140-543210

VORWORT

Die 3. GI-Fachtagung Theoretische Informatik setzt die Reihe der Vorgängertagungen über Automatentheorie und Formale Sprachen fort. Wie an den hier zusammengefaßten Berichten erkennbar ist, ist mit der Namensänderung eine gewisse Ausweitung der Themenkreise verbunden. Hier sind als Beispiel die Arbeiten über die Deadlock-Problematik zu nennen. Die Arbeiten lassen ferner die derzeitigen Schwerpunkte der Forschung auf dem Gebiet der Theoretischen Informatik erkennen. Der Tagungsband faßt die Vorträge zusammen, die auf der dritten Fachtagung vom 28. - 30. März 1977 an der Technischen Hochschule Darmstadt gehalten werden. Da wie schon bei den Vorgängertagungen an der Form der Tagung ohne Parallelsitzungen festgehalten wurde, mußte aus der erfreulich großen Anzahl von Anmeldungen eine Auswahl getroffen werden, die dem Programmkomitee in vielen Fällen schwergefallen ist.

An dieser Stelle danken die Veranstalter den Vortragenden, Teilnehmern, Helfern und allen, die zum Gelingen der Tagung beigetragen haben, herzlich. Das Bundesministerium für Forschung und Technologie hat durch seine finanzielle Förderung die Durchführung der Tagung ermöglicht. Für großzügige Unterstützung danken wir der Technischen Hochschule Darmstadt und den Spendern aus der Industrie. An den organisatorischen Arbeiten und der Vorbereitung dieses Bandes haben die Herren Dr. H. Becker und Dipl.-Math. P. Ochsenschläger tatkräftig mitgewirkt. Ihnen gilt unser Dank ebenso wie dem Springer Verlag und den Herausgebern der Reihe Lecture Notes in Computer Science für die Aufnahme des Tagungsberichts in diese Reihe.

Darmstadt, im März 1977

H. Walter
H. Waldschmidt
H. Tzschach

INHALTSVERZEICHNIS

HAUPTVORTRÄGE

VORTRÄGE IN DER REIHENFOLGE DES PROGRAMMS

On polynomial time isomorphisms of complete sets

L. Berman - J. Hartmanis

In this note we show that the recently discovered NP complete sets arising in number theory, the PTAPE complete sets arising in game theory and EXPTAPE complete sets arising from algebraic word problems are polynomial time isomorphic to the previously known complete sets in the corresponding categories.

1. Introduction

The investigation of lower level computational complexity and of analysis of algorithms has been strongly influenced by the study of efficient reducibilities and the resulting discovery of complete problems in various complexity classes, [1,4,5]. The investigation of the complexity classes NP, PTAPE, and EXPTAPE has shown that they are fundamental to a real understanding of complexity theory and that complete problems for those classes appear naturally in computer science, operations research, and also in many branches of mathematics such as number theory, game theory, and abstract algebra. As a matter of fact a bewildering variety of complete problems have been found for these classes. In particular, the families NP and PTAPE have yielded suprisingly many complete problems.

In [3] polynomial time computable isomorphism (p-isomorphism) was investigated, and necessary and sufficient conditions were

+This research has been supported in part by National Science Foundation Research Grant DCR 75-09433.

discovered that guarantee that a given NP complete set is polynomial time isomorphic to a standard NP complete set, say the conjunctive normal form satisfiability problem for Boolean functions. Using these methods it was shown that all the well known NP complete problems are isomorphic under p-time mappings. This established that inspite of the different origins and attempted simplifications all the classical NP complete problems are essentially identical. Similar p-isomorphism results were obtained for the well known PTAPE complete sets, again showing them to be essentially the same set [3].

Since then several other interesting problems have been shown to be complete for the classes NP, PTAPE, and EXPTAPE. At the Eighth Annual ACM Symposium on Theory of Computation (1976) it was shown that

(a) NP complete problems arise naturally in number theory [7],

(b) a large number of problems about winning strategies in game theory are PTAPE complete [10],

(c) certain word problems in algebra (equivalently, certain problems concerning properties of Petri nets) are complete in EXPTAPE [2].

At the FOCS (1976) it was shown that numerous questions related to divisibility of sparse polynomials are NP complete [9].

The purpose of this paper is to show that these new complete problems are polynomial time isomorphic to the corresponding classical complete problems in their respective classes.

2. Isomorhisms of NP Complete Sets

We recall that

NP = {L|L is accepted by a non-deterministic Turing machine in polynomial time}

PTAPE = {L|L is accepted by a deterministic Turing machine in polynomial tape}

EXPTAPE = {L|L is accepted by a deterministic Turing machine in 2^{cn} tape, for some c>0, and n = length of input}.

We say that A, $A \subseteq \Sigma^*$, is NP complete if and only if A is in NP and for every L in NP there exists a polnomial time computable function f such that

$$x \in L \text{ if and only if } f(x) \in A.$$

PTAPE complete and EXPTAPE complete sets are defined similarly.

The notion of polynomial completeness has been of enormous use in classifying recursive sets; however, it does have its limitations. The class of NP complete sets contains many sets of practical importance; and so, it is natural to study these sets more closely in an attempt to gain greater insight into whatever structural properties they possess which make them hard.

As an attempt to capture the notion of "polynomial structural identity" we have made the following defintions

Definition: Two sets A and B are polynomial time isomorphic (p-isomorphic) if there is a function f satisfying the following properties:

1. f is 1-1 and onto;
2. $x \in A$ iff $f(x) \in B$
3. both f anf f^{-1} can be computed in p-time.

One should note the similarity between this definition and the definition of recursively isomorphic.

Let CNF-SAT designate the set of all satisfiable Boolean formulas in conjuncture normal form. It is known that CNF-SAT is a NP complete set [1]. From Theorems 7 and 8 in [3] we can derive the following result.

Theorem NP: An NP complete set B is p-isomorphic to CNF-SAT if and only if there exist two p-time computable functions S_B and D_B such that

1. $(\forall x,y)[S_B(x,y) \in B \text{ iff } x \in B]$
2. $(\forall x,y)[D_B(S_B(x,y))=y]$.

Thus to determine whether an NP complete set B is p-isomorphic to the classic NP complete sets [5], such as CNF-SAT, we just have to check whether the set B admits the two p-time computable functions S_B and D_B. The function S_B is a polynomial time padding function which encodes arbitrary strings y in x while preserving the membership in the set B, and the function D_B must reverse this process by determining in polynomial time what string was encoded into x. It should be pointed out that these are very simple conditions and in part the purpose of this paper is to demonstrate how easily these conditions can be verified for different sets.

We illustrate this with an interesting new NP complete set arising from quadratic Diophantine equations. In [7] it was shown that the set

$$\text{DIOPH} = \{ax^2+by-c \mid a,b,c\geq 0 \text{ are integers and there are positive integers } x_o,y_o \text{ such that } ax_o^2+by_o-c=0\}$$

is NP complete (where ax^2+by-c is encoded in standard binary form).

Corollary: DIOPH is p-isomorphic to CNF-SAT.

Proof: From [7] we know that DIOPH is an NP complete set. Therefore, from our previous theorem we just have to verify that there exist two p-time functions S and D satisfying the two conditions of the theorem.

Define the encoding function $S((a,b,c),n)$ as follows:
Let $\hat{n}$ = the integer obtained by concatenating 1 and n treating the

resulting binary string as an integer. Let n_i be the $i^{\underline{th}}$ digit of $\hat{n}$ when $\hat{n}$ is expressed in binary.

If $b \neq 0$ then

begin find smallest prime so that p does not divide b

let $j = 2\cdot(\lfloor \log_p b\rfloor+1)(\lfloor \log_2 \hat{n}\rfloor+1)$

$$n' = \left[\sum_{i=0}^{\lfloor \log_2 \hat{n}\rfloor} n_i p^{2i(\lfloor \log_p b\rfloor+1)}\right] + p^{j-(\lfloor \log_p b\rfloor+1)}$$

$a' = p^j a$

$b' = b$

$c' = p^j c+bn'$

end

if $b = 0$ then

begin if there are natural number solutions

then begin for any p-time pairing function f

$a' = 1$

$b' = 0$

$c' = [f(f(a,c),n)]^2$

end

else begin $a' = 1$

$b' = 0$

$c' = 1 + [f(f(a,c),n)]^2$

end

end

We must now show that the above function $S(-,-)$ has the desired properties. If $b = 0$, the correctness of S is clear since square roots can be performed in p-time and both f and f^{-1} are in p-time by assumption.

If $b \neq 0$ the situation is less immediate. First, notice that p, the smallest prime not dividing b, can be found in p-time since for large n the product of primes less than n is $O(2^{2^n})$. Therefore, there is a prime $p < \lfloor \log \log b \rfloor$ which does not divide b and these can all be checked in time polynomial in log b. This establishes that S(–,–) can be computed in p-time. Note also that given S((a,b,c),n) we can recover b and therefore also p.

The following observations will be useful in showing that S(–,–) preserves membership in DIOPH:

1) $p^j > bn'$

2) n' is a sequence of blocks of $(\lfloor \log_p b \rfloor + 1)$ digits

when expressed in base p. It is also self delimiting, i.e. given

n' =

		$\lfloor \log_p b \rfloor + 1$	

p and b and any string which ends in bn', n' can be recovered from the end of the string. Therefore given S((a,b,c),n), we can compute n. This guarantees that the decoding function D exists and so, if S(–,–) preserves membership, we are done.

Let $(x_\circ, y_\circ)$ be a solution to $ax^2+by-c+0$ then $(x_\circ, p^j y_\circ + n')$ is a solution to $p^j ax^2 + by - (p^j c + bn')$.

If (x_1, y_1) is a solution to

$$ap^j x^2 + by - (p^j c + bn') = 0$$

then we claim that $(x_1, \frac{y_1 - n'}{p^j})$ is a natural number solution to

$$ax^2 + by - c = 0.$$

First, notice that p^j divides $b \cdot (y_1 - n')$ and p does not divide b so p^j divides $(y_1 - n')$.

$$p^j [ax_1^2 + b(\frac{y_1 - n'}{p^j}) - c] = ap^j x_1^2 + by_1 - (p^j c + bn') = 0.$$

So $(x_1, \frac{y_1-n'}{p^j})$ is an integer solution and it merely remains to show that $y_1-n' \geq 0$, or equivalently that $ax_1^2-c \leq 0$. Now

$$p^j(ax_1^2-c) = b(n'-y_1)$$

if $ax_1^2-c>0$ then since $y_1>0$ and $b>0$ $p^j \leq b(n'-y_1) < bn'$ a contradiction to observation 1.

Therefore, the function $S(-,-)$ satisfies the requirements of the NP Theorem and by observation 2 the needed $D(-)$ function exists. Thus

$$ax^2 + by - c \in \text{DIOPH iff } S[ax^2 + by-c,d] \in \text{DIOPH}.$$

Therefore, the two p-time computable functions D and S have the required properties for DIOPH and we conclude from Theorem NP that DIOPH is p-isomorphic to CNF-SAT, as was to be shown.

The above problem is unusual only in that the encoding and decoding functions are difficult to compute. This, no doubt, reflects the complexity of the reduction used to show the problem NP-complete. Our next example is again drawn from questions in classical mathematics; however, our isomorphism results apply in a much more direct manner.

We consider the set

$$\text{DIV} = \{(\alpha_1,\ldots,\alpha_{k1};\beta_1,\ldots,\beta_{k2}) \mid \prod_{j=1}^{k2}(x^{\alpha_j}-1) \text{ is not a factor of } \prod_{j=1}^{k2}(x^{\beta_j}-1)\}.$$

In [9] it was shown that this set is NP-complete. We now show:

Theorem: DIV is p-isomorphic to CNF-SAT.

Proof: Consider the map $S(w,y)$ defined as

$$S((\alpha_1,\ldots,\alpha_{k1};\beta_1,\ldots,\beta_{k2}),y) = (\alpha_1,\ldots,\alpha_{k1},y;\beta_1,\ldots,\beta_{k2},y)$$

It is immediate that $S(w,y) \in \text{DIV} \iff w \in \text{DIV}$. Letting $D(-)$ be the obvious function shows us that DIV satisfies the hypothesis of Theorem NP and our theorem is established.

We should also note that many sets which are not known to be NP complete do have our D and S function and will therefore be isomorphic to CNF-SAT if they turn out to be NP complete.

Theorem: **If Graph Isomorphism is NP hard then it is isomorphic to CNF-SAT.**

Proof: Graph isomorphism admits the S and D function and is in NP. If it should be NP hard, (i.e. if every NP set could be many one reduced to it) the hypothesis of Theorem NP would be satisfied.

Theorem: If NP = PSPACE then INEQ(0,1,+,·,*,),(,) is p-isomorphic to CNF-SAT.

Pf: If NP = PSPACE then INEQ is NP complete and so the hypothesis of theorem NP are satisfied

In a similar fashion, our results apply almost immediately to every natural set we know of which is not known to be in P.

3. Isomorphisms of PTAPE Complete Sets

From Theorems 7 and 11 in [3] we can derive a result for p-isomorphisms of PTAPE complete sets, similar to the previous result for NP complete sets.

It is known that

$$L_{\Sigma^*}=\{R|R \text{ is regular expression over } \Sigma,(,),\cdot,\cup,* \text{ and } L(R)=\Sigma^*\}$$

is a PTAPE complete set [8].

Theorem PTAPE: A PTAPE complete set B is p-isomorphic to $L_{\Sigma}*$ if and only if there exist two p-time computable functions S_B and D_B such that

1. $(\forall x,y)[S_B(c,y) \in B$ iff $x \in B]$

2. $(\forall x,y)[D_B(S_B(x,y)) = y]$.

In [10] a large number of new sets arising from decision problems based on finite two-person perfect-information games were shown to be PTAPE complete. We will select a few representatives of these sets and show that they are p-isomorphic to L_{Σ^*}. The reader should be able to supply similar proofs for all other PTAPE complete sets in [10]. Note that in [10] it is shown that these sets are PTAPE complete under log-tape reducability. Since log-tape computations can be performed in polynomial time we know that these sets are also complete under polynomial time reductions, as defined in this paper.

For all the games described below we say that there exists a winning strategy iff there exists a winning strategy for the player who starts the game. The players alternate in successive moves. We assume that the games are encoded by a simple and straight forward method, and for the sake of brevity, we will describe them without always referring to thse encodings.

1. Input is a graph. Each player on his move places a marker on an unoccupied node which is not adjacent to any occupied node. Loser is first player unable to move. $L_1=\{G|G$ is a graph with winning strategy$\}$.
2. Input is a positive (i.e. no negations are present) CNF Boolean formula A. Each player on his move chooses a variable in A which has not yet been chosen. After all variables have been chosen the starting player wins iff A is true when all the variables chosen by him are set to true and those chosen by his opponent to false.

   $L_2 = \{A|A$ CNF formula with a winning strategy$\}$.

3. Input is two collections of finite sets of integers. $\mathbf{A} = \{Ai \mid 1 \le i \le m\}$ and $\mathbf{B} = \{Bi \mid 1 \le i \le n\}$. The players take turns choosing integers from the union of all the unoccupied sets Ai and Bi. A set is said to be occupied if some integer in it has been played. The starting player wins if all sets in $\mathbf{A}$ are occupied before all sets in $\mathbf{B}$ are occupied. Any player who simultaneously occupies the last unoccupied sets of $\mathbf{A}$ and $\mathbf{B}$ loses.

   $L_3 = \{(\mathbf{A},\mathbf{B}) \mid \text{starting player has winning strategy}\}$

<u>Corollary</u>: The sets L_1, L_2 and L_3 are all p-isomorphic to $L_{\Sigma *}$.

<u>Proof</u>: By the previous theorem we just have to show that each of these sets, L_i, admits two p-time computable functions D_i and S_i, $1 \le i \le 3$, satisfying the conditions of the theorem.

To show that such functions exist for L_1, we consider three graphs which consist of a simple cycle through four, five and six nodes, respectively. It is easily seen that for each of these graphs the second player has a winning strategy. He can pick a node so that no further play is possible in the graph. We use this fact to construct the function S_1 as follows:

let G be a description of a graph and $y \in \{0,1\}^*$, then $S_1(G,Y) = G^1$, where G^1 is a description of the graph G followed by (descriptions of) a six-cycle graph (as a marker) followed by a sequence of (descriptions of) four and five-cycle graphs encoding the digits of y (a four-cycle denotes a "one" and five-cycle denotes a "zero"). The function S_1 is p-time computable (for any straight forward encoding of graphs) and, furthermore, G is in L_1 iff $S_1(G,y)$ is in L_1. To see this we just have to observe that if there is a winning strategy in G then there is one in $S_1(G,y)$, since the first player starts in G and any attempt to use the additional graphs (by the second player) results in a two move sequence which cannot change the outcome of the game. If G is not in L_1, then neither is $S_1(G,y)$ since starting in or entering any of the added graphs just delays the outcome of the game in G by an even number of moves. Finally, we note that there exists a p-time function D_1 such that $D_1[S_1(G,y)] = y$. D_1 just checks the highest numbered nodes for four or five-cycles until it detects a six-cycle or detects that the graph is not of the form $S_1(G,y)$. This completes the proof that L_1 is p-isomorphic to $L_{\Sigma*}$.

We now show that there exist two p-time computable functions, D_2 and S_2, satisfying the required conditions for L_2 to be p-isomorphic to $L_{\Sigma*}$. For input A and y, $y \in \{0,1\}^*$, $S_2(A,y) = A^1$, where A^1 has enough new variables to add a conjuction of two new variables (as a marker) followed by conjuctions of three and four variables, respectively (always using distinct variables) encoding the zeros, and ones of the sequence y. Clearly, S_2 is p-time computable and it is seen that

$$S_2(A,y) \in L_2 \text{ iff } A \in L_2$$

since if A can be made true by the first player then so can A^1 and vica versa. Finally, it is also clear that a p-time computable function D_2 exists such that $D_2[S_2(A,y)] = y$.

In the following we construct the required functions D_3 and S_3 for L_3. For given $\mathbb{A}, \mathbb{B}$ and y

$$S_3[(\mathbb{A},\mathbb{B}),y] = (\mathbb{A}^1, \mathbb{B}^1),$$

where $\mathbf{A}^1$ and $\mathbf{B}^1$ are the old $\mathbf{A}$ and $\mathbf{B}$ augmented by new sets of integers longer than those used in $\mathbb{A}$ and $\mathbb{B}$. Exactly the same size sets are added to $\mathbb{A}$ and $\mathbb{B}$ and in the same order, but they are over different integers; the first two new (marker) sets have one element each followed by pairs of sets of two and three (new integers) encoding the digits of y. Clearly, S_3 is p-time computable and

$$(A^1, B^1) \text{ is in } L_3 \text{ iff } S_3[(A, B), y] \text{ is in } L_3,$$

since the added sets just prolong the game but cannot change the outcome. It is also seen that the required p-time computable D_3 exists. This completes the proof that L_1, L_2 and L_3 all are p-isomorphic to $L_{\Sigma*}$.

4. EXPTAPE Complete Problems

We will now show that a recently discovered EXPTAPE complete problem associated with the uniform word problem for commutatative semipromps is p-isomorphic to previously known EXPTAPE complete problems.

Let $M_{i,n}$ be an enumeration of Turing machines which run on 2^{kn} tape. We can start with a standard enumeration of all Turing machines M_1, M_2,... and get $M_{i,k}$ for each integer $k, k \geq 0$, by adding a subroutine to M_i which lays off 2^{nk} tape for inputs of length n and if M_i tries to use more than 2^{kn} tape it is stopped and the input is rejected, otherwise $M_{i,n}$ does the same as M_i. let

$$L_{EXP} = \{M_{i,k}\#CODE(x_1x_2...x_n) \mid M_i \text{ accepts input } x_1, x_2...x_n \text{ on } 2^{kn} \text{ tape}\}$$

where for $M_{i,k}$ $CODE(x_1x_2...x_n)$ is a straight forward symbol by symbol encoding of the sequence $x_1, x_2...x_n$ such that the length of $CODE(x_1x_2...x_n) = k \cdot c \cdot n$, where c is the number of tape squares needed to encode a tape symbol of M_i (we assume a uniform length encoding). The set L_{EXP} is acceptable on 2^n tape since $M_{i,k}$ operated in $2^{k \cdot n}$ tape and the simulation of $M_{i,k}$ on $x_1x_2...x_n$ can be carried out on $2^{c \cdot k \cdot n}$ tape squares. Furthermore it is seen that L_{EXP} is a complete language in EXPTAPE, since for any L accepted by $M_{i,k}$ the p-time mapping

$$f(x_1 \ldots x_n) = M_{i,k}\#CODE(x_1 x_2 \ldots x_n)$$

is such that

$$x_1 \ldots x_n \text{ is in L iff } M_{i,k}\#CODE(X_1 x_2 \ldots x_n) \text{ is in } L_{EXP}.$$

From Theorems 7 and 11 in [3] we easily get the following result

Theorem EXPTAPE: An EXPTAPE tape complete set L is p-isomorphic to L_{EXP} iff there exist two p-time computable functions D and S such that

$$(\forall xy)[\ D(x,y) \in L \text{ iff } x \in L]$$

$$(\forall xy)[\ S(D(x,y) = y].$$

Recently [2] it has been shown that the uniform word problem for commutative semi groups (UWCS) is an EXTAPE complete language and that equivalently the reachability problem in Petri sets is also complete in EXPTAPE. We now give the definition of the UWCS. Let

Σ be a finite set of generators

and let

$$\mathbf{S} = \{w_i \equiv v_i \mid w_i, v_i \in \Sigma^*,\ 1 \le i \le k\}$$

be a finite set of equivalences including ab = ba for all a,b in Σ. Note that the associativity of concatenation automatically guarantees that we have an associative and commutative operation.

Then define

$$\alpha \equiv \beta(\mathbb{S}), \text{ for } \alpha,\beta\in\Sigma^*,$$

iff by a finite number of applications of the equivalences from $\mathbb{S}$ to substrings in α we can transform α into β. let

$$UWCS = \{<\alpha,\beta,\mathbb{S}>|\alpha\equiv\beta(\mathbb{S})\}.$$

Corollary: UWCS is p-isomorphic to L_{EXP}.

Proof: In [2] it was shown that UWCS is an EXPTAPE complete set under logn-tape reductions. Thus UWCS is EXPTAPE complete under p-time reductitions. Therefore we just have to show that UWCS admits two p-time computable functions D and S satisfying Theorem EXPTAPE.

We construct D as follows:

$$S(<\alpha,\beta,\mathbb{S}>,y) = <\alpha\bar{y},\beta\bar{y},\mathbb{S}^1>,$$

where we have added two new symbols to Σ, a_0 and a_1, and $\bar{y} = h(y)$ where h is defined by $h(0) = a_0$ and $h(1) = a_1$ and extended to sequences by induction $h(\epsilon) = \epsilon$ and $h(wx) = h(w)h(x)$; the only new relations added to $\mathbb{S}$ to get $\mathbb{S}^1$ are the ones defining commutativety, for all x in Σ $xa_0 = a_0x$ and $xa_i = ax_1$. It is seen that S is p-time computable and that

$S(<\alpha,\beta,\mathbb{S}>) \in$ UWCS iff $<\alpha\bar{y},\beta\bar{y},\mathbb{S}^1>\in$ UWCS,

since

$$\alpha\equiv\beta(\mathbb{S}) \text{ iff } \alpha\bar{y}\equiv\beta\bar{y}(\mathbb{S}^1).$$

Finally we note that there exists a p-time computable function S such that

$$D[S(<\alpha,\beta,\mathbb{S}>y)] = y.$$

Thus UWCS is p-isomorphic to L_{EXP}, as was to be shown.

At the 17th STOC, Chandra and Stockmeyer presented numerous new games which are complete for EXPTAPE, the techniques of the last section show immediately that the new sets are p-time isomorphic to L_{EXP}.

References

1. Cook, S. "The Complexity of Theorem Proving Procedures", Proceedings Third Annual ACM Symposium an Theory of Computing, May 3-5, 1971, pp 151-158.
2. Cordova, E., R. Lipton and A.R. Meyer, "Exponential Tape Complete Problems for Petri Nets and Commutative Semigraphs; Preliminary Report", Proceedings Eighth Annual ACM Symposium on Theory of Computing, May 3-5, 1976, pp. 50-54.
3. Hartmanis, J and L. Berman, "On Isomorphisms and Density of NP and other Complete Sets," Proceedings Eighth Annual ACM Symposium on Theory of Computing, May 3-5, 1976, pp 30-40.
4. Hartmanis, J. and J. Simon, "on the Structure of Feasible Computations in Advances in Computers, Vol 14 (eds. M. Rubinoff and M.C. Yovits) Academic Press, New York, 1976, pp 1-43.
5. Karp, R. "Reducabilities Among Combinatorial Problems", In "Complexity of Computer Computations" (R. Miller and J. Thatcher eds) pp 85-104 Plenum Press New York. 1972.
6. Ladner, R.E. "On the Structure of Polynomial Time Reducibility" JACM, vol. 22, No. 1, January 1975, pp. 155-171.
7. Manders, K. and L. Adleman, "NP-Complete Decision Problems for Quadratic Polynomials," Proceeding Eighth Annual ACM Symposium on Theory of Computing, May 3-5, 1976 pp. 23-29.
8. Meyer, A.R. and L. Stochmeyer, "The Equvalence Problem for Regular Expressions with Squaring Requires Exponential Space", IEEE 13th Annual Symposium on Switching and Automata Theory, 1972, pp. 125-129,
9. Plaisted, D.A. "More NP-Hard and NP-Complete Problems Involving Polynomials and Integers", IEEE 17the FOCS, 1976.
10. Schaefer, T.J. "Complexity of Decision Problems Based in Finite Two-Person Perfect-Information Games", Proceedings Eighth Annual ACM Symposium on Theory of Computing, May 3-5, 1976, pp. 41-49.

NEW BOUNDS ON FORMULA SIZE

M. S. Paterson

Abstract. A variety of theorems bounding the formula size of rather simple Boolean functions are described here for the first time. The principal results are improved lower and upper bounds for symmetric functions.

1. Introduction.

In preparing my presentation to this 1977 GI-Conference I have borne in mind the high level of knowledge and expertise in the audience at such a meeting. I resolved that it would be most appropriate to talk about some of the most recent research upon which I have been engaged. The results to be described have been obtained by myself usually in collaboration with others, notably Mike Fischer, Albert Meyer and Bill McColl, during the past year or so. One was completed only a few days ago and none has yet appeared in published form.

Boolean function complexity is a key area of theoretical computer science. Questions of actual and potential efficiency in computation appear here in their ultimately refined form. It is the sticking-place for many problems arising from circuit design, algorithmic analysis and automata theory. The principal measures of complexity for Boolean functions are circuit size, formula size and depth. While the first must be regarded as the most fundamental measure, it is an unhappy historical fact that no lower bound non-linear in the number of arguments has yet been proved for the circuit size of an explicitly described function. This can be juxtaposed with the classical result that all but a vanishing fraction of Boolean functions have exponential circuit size. In contradistinction several lower bound theorems have liberated formula size from this "linear strait-jacket", disclosing a richer structure of function complexities. It is to be hoped that the present exploration into formula size will be overtaken within the next decade by similar developments with respect to circuit size.

The technical nature of the results presented here makes it reasonable to assume that the interested reader has some previous knowledge of the definitions and basic results, so for example I shall not define "formula" explicitly. For a brief survey of the field may I suggest [Pat 76]; for a very full account, [Sav 76] is to be recommended.

2. Definitions.

Let $B_n = \{h : \{0,1\}^n \to \{0,1\}\}$ be the set of n-argument Boolean functions. We consider formulae for such functions composed of argument variables $x_1,\ldots,x_n$ and arbitrary binary connectives from the full set B_2. We find it convenient to account the size of a formula as the number of occurrences of variables in it. (The alternative count of the number of connectives would result in a size of exactly one less.) The formula size $F(h)$ of a function $h \in B_n$ is defined to be the size of the shortest formula representing h.

Our choice of the whole of B_2 as the set of connectives is important in that two kinds of complete basis for B_n can be distinguished. Strong ones contain either '$\oplus$' (not-equivalence, sum modulo 2) or '$\equiv$' (equivalence), and weak ones contain neither. Examples of minimal strong and weak bases are $\{\oplus,\to\}$ and {NAND} respectively. Pratt [Pra 75] has demonstrated that, to within a constant factor in formula size, there are just two equivalence classes of complete bases, the strong and the weak, and has quantified the maximum disparity between them. For the results presented here, we could as well choose any strong complete basis.

The set S_n of symmetric functions contains just those functions in B_n which depend only on the number of 1's among their arguments. Equivalently, $h \in B_n$ is symmetric if and only if there is a function $\chi_h : \{0,\ldots,n\} \to \{0,1\}$, the characteristic function of h, such that for all x,

$h(x) = \chi_h(\sum_i x_i)$. Hence we have $|S_n| = 2^{n+1}$, as compared with $|B_n| = 2^{2^n}$.

To express lower and upper complexity bounds more succinctly the following notation is convenient. Let f(n), g(n) be non-negative-valued functions from the natural numbers. We write

$f(n) = O(g(n))$ if $\exists a>0$ such that $f(n) \leq a.g(n)$
for all sufficiently large n

$f(n) = \Omega(g(n))$ if $g(n) = O(f(n))$

$f(n) = \Theta(g(n))$ if $f(n) = O(f(n))$ and $f(n) = \Omega(g(n))$.

3. Neciporuk's theorem and corollaries.

A simple yet powerful theorem yielding lower bounds of up to $\Theta(n^2/\log n)$ on formula size is implicit in [Nec 66]. Suppose the arguments of some $h \in B_n$ to be partitioned into blocks $R_1,\ldots,R_p$. When for some i, the arguments in all the blocks R_j, $j \neq i$, are fixed to 0 or 1 in some way, the result is a restriction of h to R_i, a function h' depending only on R_i. Let m_i be the number of different such h' for all possible fixations of the other variables. In this notation the theorem is concisely expressed.

Theorem (Neciporuk) $\quad F(h) = \Omega\left(\sum_{i=1}^{p} \log m_i\right)$.

This result establishes lower bounds for a variety of functions of interest. Most applications have been to functions with a rather combinatorial nature such as 'determinant' [Klo 66], 'marriage problem' [HaS 72] or indirect addressing schemes [Nec 66], [Pau 75]. Two corollaries of a somewhat different character have emerged recently.

If we identify the $n = t^r$ cells of a $\overleftrightarrow{t \times \ldots \times t}^{\,r}$ array in r dimensions with the arguments $x_1,\ldots,x_n$, then any predicate on patterns of black and white colourings of the cells corresponds with a function in B_n. Of particular appeal are those predicates of a geometric or topological natue. The predicate $CONN_r^{(n)} \in B_n$ which is true if and only if the black cells of the r-dimensional array are connected has been considered by Hodes [Hod 70].

Theorem (Paterson & Fischer) $F(CONN_r^{(n)}) = \Omega(n \log n)$ for $r \geq 2$.

The proof uses Neciporuk's theorem applied with blocks of size $2s = \Theta(n^{1/(2r)})$. By embedding arbitrary permutation connections between s of these cells and the other s, we can show that at least s! restrictions are possible for each block. In the case r = 1, it is an easy observation that $F(CONN_r^{(n)}) = \Theta(F(T_2^{(n)}))$, where T_2 is the threshold function defined in the next section.

With a similar correspondence we can identify a set of binary strings of length n with a function of B_n. For any $L \subseteq \Sigma^*$, where $\Sigma = \{0,1\}$, we define $g_L^{(n)} \in B_n$ to be the function corresponding to the set $L \cap \Sigma^n$. The lower bounds on context-free language recognition proved by Hotz [Hot 75] and Mehlhorn [Meh 76] can be improved slightly as follows.

Theorem There is a context-free language L such that

$$F(g_L^{(n)}) = \Omega(n^2/\log n).$$

The language used in the proof is defined by

$$L = \{0^* \, 1 \, w \, 00 \, \Sigma^* \, w^R \, \Sigma^* \mid w \in \Sigma^*\}.$$

The stated bound results from Neciporuk's theorem when we choose the arguments for each block and set the other arguments to impose a form

$$0^* \, 1 \, b_1 \, 1 \, b_2 \, \ldots \, 1 \, b_m \, 1 \, 00 \, \Sigma^*$$

where $b_1, \ldots, b_m$ are the block variables, and $m \sim 2 \log_2 n$. Each block in turn is thus forced into the rôle of 'w' in the definition of L.

An upper bound of $O(n^2 \log n)$ for $F(g_L^{(n)})$, encouragingly close to the lower bound proved, is demonstrable with a formula which is a disjunction of O(n) formulae, each corresponding to 'folding' the string about some position. Each string of L is detected by a formula where the fold is at the centre of symmetry of w, w^R.

4. Bounds for symmetric functions.

Since $|S_m| = 2^{m+1}$, Neciporuk's theorem produces only trivial bounds when applied to symmetric functions. The first non-linear lower bounds for any function in S_n were proved by Hodes and Specker [HoS 68]. They are corollaries of the following general result. We write $\bigvee Y$ for $\bigvee_{x_i \in Y} x_i$ and similarly for $\bigoplus$.

Theorem (Hodes & Specker) There is a (very rapidly growing) function G such that for all c,m, if $n \geq G(m,c)$ and ϕ is any formula of size less than cn with argument set $X = \{x_1,\ldots,x_n\}$, then there is a subset $Y \subseteq X$ with $|Y| = m$ and constants b_o, b_1, b_2 such that the restricted formula ϕ_Y of m arguments got by setting the variables of $X \backslash Y$ to 0 is equivalent to

$$b_o \ .\oplus.\ b_1 \wedge \neg \bigvee Y \ .\oplus.\ b_2 \wedge \bigoplus Y$$

This theorem has been applied [Hod 70] to prove non-linear lower bounds for some geometric and topological predicates as considered earlier and also for some symmetric functions. The statement of the theorem is somewhat complicated, but for application to S_n only, a considerable simplification is possible. The following corollary appears not to have been stated previously.

Theorem (Meyer & Paterson) For all $c > o$, for n sufficiently large,

only 16 functions of S_n have formula size less than cn.

The sixteen functions are characterized by the property of the characteristic function that

$$\chi(r) = \chi(r+2) \text{ for } 1 \leq r \leq n-3.$$

The threshold functions $T_k^{(n)}$ are defined by

$$\chi_{T_k}(r) = 1 \leftrightarrow r \geq k$$

so $F(T_k^{(n)})$ is certainly nonlinear in n for any fixed $k \geq 2$.

It is shown by Khasin [Kha 69] and Pippenger [Pip 75] that

$F(T_k^{(n)}) = O(n \log n)$ for all fixed k, but only existence proofs are given. Elementary recursion using dichotomy generates explicit formulae with sizes which are $\Theta(n(\log n)^{k-1})$ for fixed k. McColl and Paterson have deferred this growth rate initially by using increasingly tortuous identities[McC 76].

<u>Theorem</u> For $2 \leq k \leq 6$, $F(T_k^{(n)}) = O(n.\log n\ (\log\log n)^{k-2})$.

Our method is to partition the n arguments into $n^{\frac{1}{2}}$ blocks of size $n^{\frac{1}{2}}$. The predicate that at least r blocks satisfy $T_s^{(n^{\frac{1}{2}})}$ is abbreviated as $T_r(T_s)$. Then for example, our recursive construction for T_3 uses the identity.

$$T_3^{(n)} = T_3(T_1) \vee T_1(T_3) \vee (T_2(T_1) \wedge T_1(T_2)).$$

With the aim of raising the very slowly increasing lower bounds of Hodes' and Specker's theorem, Fischer, Meyer and Paterson weakened somewhat the conclusion of the theorem and proved lower bounds of $\Omega(n.\log n/\log\log n)$ [FMP 75]. Recent improvements in both the scope of functions covered and the bound attained provide a theorem analogous to Hodes' and Specker's, with the following corollary for symmetric functions.

<u>Theorem.</u> For any $h \in S_n$, if $\chi_h(k) \neq \chi_h(k+2)$ for some $k = k(n)$, then

$$F(h) = \Omega(n.\log k).$$

For example, lower bounds of $\Omega(n.\log n)$ are established for threshold functions $T_{\theta n}^{(n)}$ where θ is constant, $0 < \theta < 1$, and for the congruence functions $C_k^{(n)}$, k fixed, $k > 2$, where C_k is defined by

$$\chi_{C_k}(r) = 1 \text{ if and only if } r \text{ is a multiple of } k.$$

Our especial favourite is C_4 since we now have

$$F(C_4^{(n)}) = \Theta(n.\log n).$$

The upper bound is shown using the identity

$$C_4^{(n)} = \neg D_1^{(n)} \wedge \neg D_o^{(n)}$$

where $D_o, D_1, D_2, \ldots$ represent successive digits (lowest first) of the binary representation of the sum of the arguments. The D's are expressed recursively by constructing the D's for each of two equal halves of the argument set and performing a binary addition on the results. Thus

$$D_r^{(1)}(x) = x \text{ if } r = 0$$
$$\quad = 0 \text{ if } r > 0$$

$$D_o^{(2n)}(\underset{\sim}{x}, \underset{\sim}{y}) = D_o^{(n)}(\underset{\sim}{x}) \oplus D_o^{(n)}(\underset{\sim}{y})$$

$$D_1^{(2n)}(\underset{\sim}{x}, \underset{\sim}{y}) = D_1^{(n)}(\underset{\sim}{x}) \oplus D_1^{(n)}(\underset{\sim}{y}) \oplus \left(D_o^{(n)}(\underset{\sim}{x}) \wedge D_o^{(n)}(\underset{\sim}{y})\right)$$

Since $F(D_o^{(n)}) = n$, we have $F(D_1^{(n)}) = O(n.\log n)$.

An arbitrary function of S_n is representable as some function of $D_o, D_1, \ldots, D_m$ where $m = \lceil \log(n+1) \rceil - 1$, and may be expressed in a formula using just one occurrence of D_m, two of D_{m-1}, four of D_{m-2}, et cetera. Small formulae for the D's yield therefore small formulae for all S_n. Using approximately this method Pippenger [Pip 74] has determined that

$$F(S_n) \underset{\text{def}}{=} \max \{F(h) \mid h \in S_n\} = O(n^{\alpha})$$

where $\alpha = \log_2(6 + 4\sqrt{2}) \doteq 3{\cdot}54$.

In his binary adder Pippenger uses "full adders" to compute each new digit d of the sum and new carry digit c from two digits d', d'', of the summands and the previous carry c'. He employs the formula pair

$$d = d' \oplus d'' \oplus c'$$

$$c = (c' \wedge (d' \vee d'')) \vee (d' \wedge d'').$$

A small refinement in the construction is to replace the latter formula by

$$c = d' \oplus ((c' \oplus d') \wedge (d'' \oplus d'))$$

and split the argument set into two unequal parts at each stage. Optimization of the ratio of this split (with the help of Colin Whitby-Strevens and the Warwick University Burroughs 6700 computer) decreases the exponent.

<u>Theorem</u>. $F(S_n) = O(n^{\beta})$ where $\beta < 3{\cdot}41866705572$.

5. Conclusion.

A number of new bounds for symmetric, or otherwise fairly simple, functions are sketched here in a preliminary form. I hope that by the time of the GI meeting at least some may be available in a more polished and complete version.

I should like to acknowledge the cooperation and encouragement derived from many other people than those named explicitly, and the valuable stimulation provided by such international meetings as this.

References

[FMP 75] M.J. Fischer, A.R. Meyer and M.S. Paterson. "Lower bounds on the size of Boolean formulas: preliminary report", Proc. 7th Ann. ACM Symp. on Th. of Computing (1975), 45-49.

[HaS 72] L.H. Harper and J.E. Savage. "On the complexity of the marriage problem", Advances in Mathematics 9, 3 (1972), 299-312.

[Hod 70] L. Hodes. "The logical complexity of geometric properties in the plane", J. ACM 17, 2 (1970), 339-347.

[HoS 68] L. Hodes and E. Specker. "Lengths of formulas and elimination of quantifiers I", in Contributions to Mathematical Logic, K. Schutte, ed., North Holland Publ. Co., (1968), 175-188.

[Hot 75] G. Hotz. "Untere Schranken für das Analyseproblem kontext-freier Sprachen", Techn. Bericht, Univ. des Saarlandes, 1976.

[Kha 69] L.S. Khasin. "Complexity bounds for the realization of monotone symmetrical functions by means of formulas in the basis $\vee$, &, $\neg$.", Eng. trans. in Soviet Physics Dokl., 14 12 (1970),1149-1151; orig. Dokl. Akad. Nauk SSSR, 189, 4 (1969), 752-755.

[Klo 66] B.M. Kloss. "Estimates of the complexity of solutions of systems of linear equations", Eng. trans. in Soviet Math Dokl. 7, 6 (1966), 1537-1540; orig. Dokl. Akad. Nauk SSSR, 171, 4 (1966), 781-783.

[McC 76] W.F. McColl. "Some results on circuit depth", Ph.D. dissertation, Computer Science Dept., Warwick University, 1976.

[Meh 76] K. Mehlhorn. "An improved bound on the formula complexity of context-free recognition". Unpublished report, 1976.

[Nec 66] E.I. Neciporuk. "A Boolean function", Soviet Math. Dokl. 7, 4 (1966), 999-1000, orig. Dokl. Akad. Nauk SSSR 169, 4 (1966), 765-766.

[Pat 76] M.S. Paterson. "An introduction to Boolean function complexity". Stanford Computer Science Report STAN-CS-76-557 Stanford University, 1976; to appear in Astérisque.

[Pau 75] W. Paul. "A 2.5 N lower bound for the combinational complexity of Boolean functions", Proc. 7th Ann. ACM Symp. on Th. of Comp. Albuquerque (1975), 27-36.

[Pip 74] N. Pippenger. "Short formulae for symmetric functions", IBM Research Report RC-5143, Yorktown Hts., 1974.

[Pip 75] N. Pippenger. "Short monotone formulae for threshold functions". IBM Research Report RC 5405, Yorktown Hts., 1975.

[Pra 75] V.R. Pratt. "The effect of basis on size of Boolean expressions". Proc. 16th Annual IEEE Symposium on Foundations of Computer Science, 119-121.

[Sav 76] J.E. Savage. The Complexity of Computing, Wiley-Interscience, New York, 1976.

[Sha 49] C.E. Shannon. "The synthesis of two-terminal switching circuits", Bell System Technical Journal 28 (1949), 59-98.

INFORMATIQUE ET ALGEBRE LA THEORIE DES CODES A LONGUEUR VARIABLE

J.-F. Perrot

INTRODUCTION

Nos connaissances sur les codes ayant fait ces dernières années des progrès sensibles, il a semblé utile de replacer dans la perspective générale de la théorie quelques résultats récents. Mais il a fallu se restreindre à un seul point de vue, considéré comme essentiel : l'adéquation de méthodes algébriques, au premier rang desquelles l'utilisation du monoïde syntactique, à la solution de problèmes de nature entièrement différente, adéquation qui n'est effective que sous l'hypothèse que les codes envisagés sont rationnels et les monoïdes syntactiques finis. C'est ce phénomène surprenant que nous avons tenté de mettre en lumière dans le cadre de la théorie générale des codes, celle dont traitait Nivat en 1965 [16], par opposition à la théorie des codes préfixes, voire bipréfixes, qui mérite un exposé à part. Nous avons aussi dû laisser de côté les aspects probabilistes, pourtant fondamentaux, nous n'avons pas abordé les décompositions des codes ni le théorème-clé sur l'irréductibilité du polynôme associé à un code complet fini [29].

Reprenant pour l'essentiel la démarche de Schützenberger en 1956 [26] [27], nous présentons d'abord les notions intuitives touchant au déchiffrement des codes, et nous les illustrons par des exemples et des propriétés à caractère élémentaire. Puis nous introduisons les sous-monoïdes libérables, les monoïdes syntactiques et les caractérisations par matrices à éléments 0 et 1.

Enfin, sous l'hypothèse que nos codes sont complets, nous voyons reparaître les notions de synchronisation et de délai de déchiffrage en liaison avec la structure des monoïdes syntactiques.

Aucun des résultats que nous exposons n'est original, et les quelques démonstrations que nous esquissons ont pour but d'aider à la compréhension. Nous espérons ainsi faciliter à nos lecteurs l'accès d'un des domaines les plus fascinants de l'Informatique théorique.

Je tiens à remercier D. Perrin pour ses précieuses indications et sa collaboration à la rédaction de ce texte.

I - PROBLEMES DE DECHIFFREMENT

a) L'unique déchiffrabilité

Etant donné deux alphabets X et Y, coder Y sur X consiste à associer un mot $c(a) \in X^*$ à chaque lettre $a \in Y$, et à chaque mot $m \in Y^*$, $m = a_1 a_2 \ldots a_k$, le mot $c(m) = c(a_1)\, c(a_2) \ldots c(a_k)$. On souhaite alors que la connaissance de c(m) détermine entièrement le "message original" m, ce qui se traduit par l'implication : $c(a_1)\, c(a_2) \ldots c(a_k) = c(a'_1)\, c(a'_2) \ldots c(a'_h) \Rightarrow k = h$ et $a_i = a'_i$ pour $i = 1,2,\ldots k$. En introduisant le sous-ensemble-image $A = c(Y) \subset X^*$, cette implication se scinde en deux conditions indépendantes :

- l'application c est une bijection de Y sur A ;
- tout mot w du sous-monoïde A^* engendré par A dans X^* admet une factorisation et une seule en produit de mots de A.

Dans la tradition de la théorie de l'information, cette dernière condition est appelée condition d'unique déchiffrabilité, (cf. le traité de Ash [1]). En théorie des langages, on dira que A engendre A^* de manière non-ambiguë. L'application c est un homomorphisme injectif, ou monomorphisme de Y^* dans X^*: par exemple, chez Hashiguchi et Honda [10] [11], les homomorphismes qui conservent différentes propriétés des langages rationnels (hauteur d'étoile, "local testability")sont tous des monomorphismes. Du point de vue algébrique, A^* est un sous-monoïde libre du monoïde libre X^* [6] [20] ,etc..

Définition 1 : Un code sur un alphabet X est une partie A du monoïde libre X^*, telle que le sous-monoïde A^* soit librement engendré par A.
Une façon simple de construire un code est de prendre un ensemble de mots de même longueur : on obtient ainsi un code à longueur constante (en anglais "block-code"). Lorsqu'on n'impose pas cette restriction, on parle de codes à longueur variable ("variable-length codes" [9]) : comme il ne sera question ici que de ces derniers, nous dirons simplement codes.

Exemples : Nous prendrons toujours pour X l'alphabet binaire

$X = \{x, y\}$

$A_1 = \{y, xy, yxx, xyxx, xxxx\}$ est un code

$A_2 = \{y, xy, xxy, xyyx\}$ n'est pas un code

$A_3 = \{xx, xy, xxy, yyx\}$ est un code

$A_4 = \{xy, yx\}(\{xx, yy\})^*$ est un code.

Remarque : L'image-miroir $\tilde{A}$ d'un code A est encore un code.

Codes formés de deux mots : Si le sous-monoïde engendré par deux mots $a, b \in X^*$ n'est pas libre, c'est qu'il existe deux mots différents $f, f' \in \{A,B\}^*$, où A et B sont deux nouveaux symboles, tels que $c(f) = c(f')$ avec $c(A) = a$ et c(B) = b ; le couple (a, b) est donc une solution de <u>l'équation à deux variables</u> f = f'.

Or un résultat général de la théorie des équations dans les monoïdes libres affirme que toute solution d'une équation propre à n variables est représentable dans un monoïde libre à au plus n-1 générateurs ([14] Thm.1.3.19). Par conséquent, pour deux variables, une solution quelconque est de la forme $a = u^p$, $b = u^q$ pour un certain mot $u \in X^*$. La réciproque étant immédiate, nous avons le résultat suivant, qui a été trouvé indépendamment par de nombreux auteurs [2] [10] [15] :

<u>Théorème 1</u> : <u>Deux mots</u> a <u>et</u> b <u>forment un code ssi ils ne sont pas puissances d'un même troisième mot.</u>

Ce résultat sert, par exemple, dans la démonstration que, pour $|Y| = 2$, tout monomorphisme de Y^* dans un autre monoïde libre conserve la hauteur d'étoile des expressions rationnelles [10].

b) <u>Délai de déchiffrage, codes préfixes</u>

Etant donné un code A et un mot $w \in A^*$, on cherche la factorisation de w en mots de A en lisant w de gauche à droite : on constate alors que pour certains codes, la détermination du premier facteur même peut nécessiter la lecture du mot w tout entier, si long soit-il. Ainsi pour le code A_1, le premier facteur de $w' = xy\,x^{4n}y$ est $xy \in A_1$, mais celui de $w'' = xyx^{4n+2}y$ est xyxx : on dira que le délai de déchiffrage de A_1 est infini.

<u>Définition 2</u> : <u>Le délai de déchiffrage</u> d'un code A est le plus petit entier d, s'il existe, tel que, si un mot $w \in A^*$ possède un facteur gauche $a_o a_1 \ldots a_d \in A^{d+1}$, alors le premier facteur de l'unique décomposition de w sur A est a_o. En d'autres termes, si $a_o a_1 \ldots a_d u = a'_o v \in A^*$ pour quelques $u \in X^*$, $v \in A^*$ et $a'_o \in A$, alors $a_o = a'_o$.

<u>Exemple</u> : le délai de déchiffrage du code A_3 est 1, ainsi que celui du code A_4.

Le délai de déchiffrage d'un code est 0 ("instantaneous code" [1]) ssi aucun mot du code n'est facteur gauche d'un autre mot du code, condition qui suffit d'ailleurs à assurer l'unique déchiffrabilité. Un tel code est appelé un <u>code préfixe</u>. Les codes préfixes jouent un rôle particulièrement important dans la théorie, à cause de leurs remarquables propriétés intrinsèques mais aussi parce qu'il sont très faciles à construire : tout code préfixe se représente en effet par un arbre, les mots du code correspondant aux sommets pendants (ou feuilles) de l'arbre.

Exemples : A_5 =

{ xxx, xxyx, xxyy
xy, yxx, yxyx
yxyy, yyx, yyy }

$\tilde{A}_4$ est un code préfixe, représentable par un arbre infini

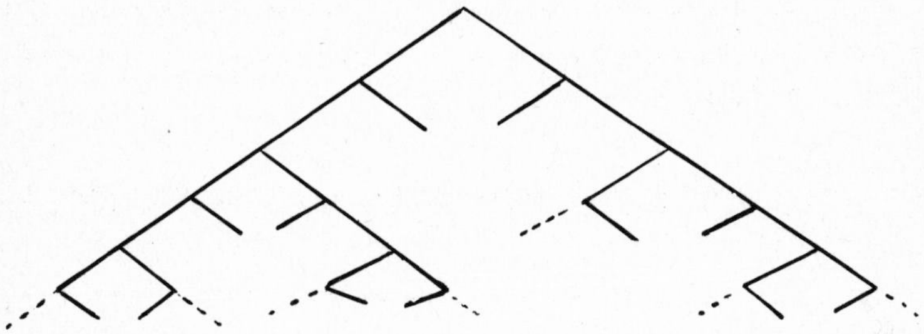

En renversant le sens de lecture, on pourra parler du délai de déchiffrage de droite à gauche d'un code A, qui est le délai de déchiffrage (de gauche à droite) de son image-miroir $\tilde{A}$, et des codes suffixes, qui sont les images-miroir des codes préfixes.

Exemples : le délai de déchiffrage de droite à gauche de A_1 est infini, ainsi que celui de A_3. A_4 est un code suffixe.

Un code qui est à la fois préfixe et suffixe, i.e. dont le délai de déchiffrage est nul des deux côtés, est appelé code bipréfixe. Tout code à longueur constante est naturellement bipréfixe, mais il existe d'autres codes bipréfixes, par exemple A_5.

c) Synchronisation :

Définition 3 : Etant donné un code A, deux mots $f, g \in A^*$ forment une paire synchronisante si, quels que soient u et $v \in X^*$, $ufgv \in A^*$ entraîne $uf \in A^*$ et $gv \in A^*$.

Exemples : (y, y) est une paire synchronisante pour A_1.
A_4 ne possède point de paire synchronisante, A_5 non plus.

Intuitivement, l'apparition d'une paire synchronisante fg dans un mot $ufgv \in A^*$ permet de décoder ce mot à partir de la "scansion" uf, gv, indépendamment de toute autre information.

Définition 4 : Le délai de synchronisation d'un code A est le plus petit entier s, s'il existe, tel que pour tout $f, g \in A^s$, (f,g) soit une paire synchronisante. Si un tel entier n'existe pas, le délai de synchronisation est infini.

Le délai de déchiffrage d'un code est toujours inférieur ou égal à son délai de synchronisation :

Si s est fini, pour tout $g \in A^s$, $a, a' \in A$, $u \in X^*$ et $v \in A^*$, $agu = a'v \in A^*$ entraîne $a = a'$ car, en prenant $f \in A^{s-1}$ a il vient $fgu \in A^*$ donc $gu \in A^*$ puisque (f,g) est une paire synchronisante, d'où, par unicité de la factorisation, $a = a'$.

Le délai de synchronisation étant défini de manière symétrique, ceci vaut également pour le délai de déchiffrage de droite à gauche.

Exemple : A_1 et A_3 ont tous deux un délai de synchronisation infini. Pourtant, quelque soit $f \in A_3^*$, (f, yyx) est une paire synchronisante pour A_3.

On voit par ces exemples que la finitude du délai de synchronisation est une contrainte extrêmement forte. Pour une discussion de différentes conditions équivalentes, cf. [25].

Les codes à délai de synchronisation fini apparaissent dans les descriptions de diverses variétés (au sens d'Eilenberg [8]) de langages rationnels (Schützenberger [30] , [31]). Nous allons les retrouver dans une perspective tout à fait différente.

d) Pureté et conjugaison

Dans une terminologie empruntée à la théorie des groupes, un sous-monoïde P d'un monoïde M est dit pur lorsque, pour tout entier k et tout élément $m \in M$, $m^k \in P \Rightarrow m \in P$. Un code $A \subset X^*$ est appelé pur si A^* est un sous-monoïde pur de X^*.

Exemple : Aucun des codes que nous avons envisagés jusqu'ici n'est pur : pour A_1, A_3, A_4 et A_5 cela résulte de la présence de puissances d'une lettre dans le code ; pour A_4 on peut prendre $(yxy)^2 \in A_4^*$ et $yxy \notin A_4^*$.

Soient à présent deux mots $a, b \in X^*$ qui forment un code. Si ce code est pur, aucun mot u apppartenant à $a^* b$ n'est puissance d'un autre mot v, car on aurait $v \in \{a, b\}^*$ et deux factorisations différentes pour u. La réciproque est beaucoup plus difficile à établir : elle fait l'objet du théorème 5 de [15].

Théorème 2 (Lentin et Schützenberger) : Un code formé de deux mots $a, b \in X^*$ est pur ssi pour tout mot $u \in a^* b \cup ab^*$, $u = v^k$ implique $k = 1$.

Un sous-monoïde P d'un monoïde M est dit très pur (Restivo) ou sans conjugaison externe (Spehner) lorsque, pour tout $m', m'' \in M$, $m'm'' \in P$ et $m'' m' \in P$ impliquent $m' \in P$ et $m'' \in P$. Tout sous-monoïde très pur est également pur (car, pour $k > 1$, $m^k \in P$ s'écrit $m\, m^{k-1} = m^{k-1} m \in P$, d'où

$m \in P$). De même, on appelle code très pur tout code engendrant un sous-monoïde très pur.

Il résulte d'une observation de [15], § 3.5, qu'un code pur formé de deux mots a, b est très pur ssi les mots a et b ne sont pas conjugués, i.e. s'ils ne se mettent pas sous la forme $a = uv$, $b = vu$ pour quelques $u, v \in X^*$

Exemple : $A_6 = \{xy, yx\}$ est pur, mais non pas très pur.

Le résultat que nous avons annoncé est le suivant :

Théorème 3 (Restivo [23]) : Tout code à délai de synchronisation fini est très pur. Réciproquement, si A est un code rationnel vérifiant $A \cap X^* A^p X^* = \emptyset$ pour quelque entier p, et si A est très pur, alors son délai de synchronisation est fini et ne dépasse pas $2p(s + 1)$ où s est le nombre d'états de l'automate réduit reconnaissant A^*.

Les codes très purs apparaissent notamment dans les factorisations des monoïdes libres, en liaison avec la construction des bases des algèbres de Lie libres (cf. Viennot [36] [37]). Nous retrouverons les codes finis très purs , qui sont aussi, d'après le théorème de Restivo, les codes finis à délai de synchronisation fini, à propos de questions touchant les monoïdes syntactiques ("strict local testability").

e) Algorithmes

L'algorithme de Sardinas et Patterson (cf. [1]) a fait l'objet de nombreuses variations (cf. [13], [25]). Les résultats les plus récents sont ceux de Spehner [33] [34]. Il s'agit essentiellement de ceci :

Soit A une partie finie de X^*, dont on veut savoir si c'est un code. Nous supposerons donc, pour simplifier, que A vérifie $A \cap A A^* = \emptyset$. On construit un graphe G dont les sommets sont les mots de X^*, avec un arc joignant le mot u au mot v ssi on peut trouver $w \in A^*$ et $a \in A$ tels que uw et wv soient non-vides et que $uwv = a$. En désignant par 1 le mot vide de X^*, il vient :

(i) A est un code ssi G ne contient aucun circuit passant par 1.

(ii) Le délai de déchiffrage de A est fini ssi G ne contient aucun circuit passant par un descendant de 1.

(iii) Le délai de synchronisation de A est fini ssi G est sans circuit.

Exemples : A_2 : $xy\,y \in A_2^*$ et de $xy \in A_2$ on tire un circuit

$$1 \xrightarrow{xyy} x \xrightarrow{y} 1$$

$\tilde{A}_1$: le sous-graphe formé par les descendants de 1 se dessine ainsi

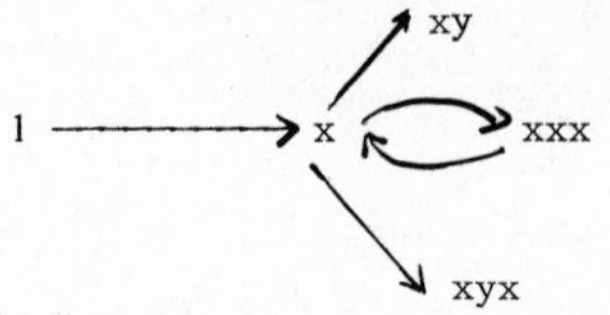

avec un circuit.

A_3 : de même

$$1 \xrightarrow{xx} y \xrightarrow{1} yx \qquad \text{sans circuit}$$

mais le sommet x porte une boucle: 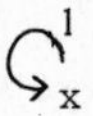

Il est clair que, A étant supposé fini, la partie utile du graphe G est aussi finie. Il reste à en extraire les renseignements cherchés de la manière la plus économique : c'est ce à quoi s'attache Spehner [34], en utilisant notamment un algorithme de Tarjan pour calculer les composantes fortement connexes. Il conclut que ce travail peut être réalisé en temps et en espace polynomiaux par rapport à la somme des longueurs des mots de A. De plus, lorsque A n'est pas un code, il donne la base du plus petit sous-monoïde libre contenant A^* [33] ainsi que diverses autres extensions [34].

II - SOUS-MONOIDES LIBERABLES

a) Définitions :

Un sous-monoïde P d'un monoïde M est appelé unitaire à gauche [6] lorsque, pour tout $p \in P$ et $m \in M$, $pm \in P$ entraîne $m \in P$. On vérifie sans difficulté qu'un sous-monoïde d'un monoïde libre X^* est engendré par un code préfixe ssi il est unitaire à gauche dans X^*.

De même, disons avec Schützenberger [26] qu'un sous-monoïde P d'un monoïde M est libérable lorsque, pour tout $p,q \in P$ et $m \in M$, $pm \in P$ et $mq \in P$ entraînent $m \in P$. On vérifie qu'un sous-monoïde d'un monoïde libre X^* est lui-même libre, i.e. engendré par un code, ssi il est libérable dans X^* (Théorème de Schützenberger, cf. [26], [16] et en dernier lieu [7]).

Il est clair que l'intersection d'une famille quelconque de sous-monoïdes libérables (resp. unitaires) d'un monoïde M est encore un sous-monoïde libérable (resp. unitaire) de M. Etant donné un sous-ensemble quelconque A de M, il existe donc un plus petit sous-monoïde libérable (resp. unitaire) contenant A. Dans le cas particulier où M est libre, ce résultat a été retrouvé par Tilson [35], et la base du plus petit sous-monoïde libre contenant $A \subset X^*$ est calculée par Spehner [33] [34].

b) Homomorphismes, monoïde syntactique

Soit h un homomorphisme de M sur un autre monoïde M', et P' un sous-monoïde libérable (resp. unitaire) de M' : son image inverse $h^{-1}(P')$ est un sous-monoïde libérable (resp. unitaire) de M.

D'autre part, soit P un sous-monoïde de M vérifiant $h^{-1}h(P) = P$: si P est libérable dans M, son image h(P) est un sous-monoïde libérable de M'.

Rappelons que le monoïde syntactique Synt(L) d'un langage $L \subset X^*$ est par définition la plus petite image homomorphe de X^* par un homomorphisme h vérifiant $h^{-1} h(L) = L$. (cf. [26] [8]).

Le théorème de Schützenberger permet alors d'énoncer :

Théorème 4 : Une partie P d'un monoïde libre X^* est un sous-monoïde libre (resp. engendré par un code préfixe) ssi son image dans son monoïde syntactique est un sous-monoïde libérable (resp. unitaire à gauche) de Synt(P).

Etant donné un code $A \subset X^*$, le monoïde syntactique de A^* est fini ssi A est une partie rationnelle de X^*, et notamment lorsque A est fini. C'est principalement à ce dernier cas que nous nous intéresserons désormais: l'étude des propriétés du monoïde syntactique de A^* donne alors des renseignements très précis sur les questions que nous avons évoquées dans la première section de ce travail (délai de déchiffrage, synchronisation, pureté), comme l'indiquait Schützenberger dès 1956.

A titre d'exemple, montrons que si un code rationnel A est tel que A^* soit un langage apériodique, i.e. que tous les sous-groupes de $\mathrm{Synt}(A^*)$ soient triviaux, alors A est un code pur :

Soit $f \in X^*$ tel que $f^k \in A^*$; on a $f^{kp} \in A^*$ pour tout entier p. Soit $m = h(f)$ l'image de f dans $\mathrm{Synt}(A^*)$: l'hypothèse d'apériodicité entraîne l'existence d'un entier r tel que $m^r = m^{r+1} = m^{r+q}$ pour tout entier q, donc $m^r \in h(A^*)$. L'image de A^* étant libérable, en écrivant $m^{r+1} \in h(A^*)$ sous la forme $m\, m^r \in h(A^*)$ et $m^r\, m \in h(A^*)$ il vient $m \in h(A^*)$ et par suite, $f \in h^{-1}(m) \subset A^*$, C.Q.F.D.

La réciproque n'est pas vraie en général, comme le montre l'exemple du code préfixe $(x^2)^*y$. Elle est vraie si A est fini [21] et plus généralement si A est lui-même un langage apériodique, en vertu d'un résultat de Schützenberger sur certaines variétés de langages rationnels [32].

Théorème 5 (Restivo) : Un code fini A est pur ssi A^* est un langage apériodique.

Par conséquent, le théorème 2 nous fournit un critère permettant de savoir si le sous-monoïde engendré par un code formé de deux mots est apériodique ou non : ainsi, A_6 engendre un monoïde apériodique.

Ce résultat de Restivo a été retrouvé indépendamment par Hashiguchi et Honda ([11], Cor. 3.2.) qui démontrent qu'un homomorphisme c de Y^* dans X^* (avec X et Y finis) conserve le caractère apériodique ou localement testable des langages rationnels ssi c est un monomorphisme tel que le sous-monoïde libre $c(Y^*)$ soit lui-même apériodique (donc engendré par un code fini pur) ou localement testable. Ils établissent au passage que $c(Y^*)$ est localement testable ssi il est strictement localement testable, et Restivo [22] a d'autre part montré que sous-monoïde engendré par un code fini A était strictement localement testable ssi le délai de synchronisation de A était fini. Nous pouvons donc énoncer :

Théorème 6 : Pour un code fini A, les trois conditions suivantes sont équivalentes :

(i) le délai de synchronisation de A est fini ;

(ii) A est très pur ;

(iii) A^* est localement testable.

Exemple : Soit $A_7 = \{xy, yxy\}$: A_7^* est localement testable, mais A_6^* ne l'est pas.

c) Caractérisations

On sait depuis longtemps qu'un sous-monoïde P d'un monoïde M est unitaire à gauche ssi il existe une représentation de M par applications d'un ensemble S dans lui-même, M opérant à droite dans S, tel que P soit le stabilisateur de quelque $s \in S$, $P = \{m \in M ; s.m = m\}$; en écrivant ces applications sous forme matricielle, on obtient ainsi une représentation de M par matrices à éléments 0 et 1, monomiales en ligne (i.e. ayant au plus un élément non nul par ligne). De même, à tout sous-monoïde Q unitaire à droite(i.e. dans le cas d'un monoïde libre, sous-monoïde engendré par un code suffixe) correspond une représentation de M par matrices à éléments 0,1 monomiales en colonne. Notons qu'il s'agit ici de monoïdes de matrices carrées à éléments entiers, la condition d'être monomiales suffisant à assurer que ces éléments ne sortent pas de l'ensemble { 0,1}. D'une manière générale, on sait que la contrainte, pour un monoïde de matrices à éléments entiers, que tous les éléments de ces matrices soient 0 ou 1 est une contrainte très forte : on peut considérer de tels monoïdes comme des monoïdes de relations d'un type particulier, appelées "relations non-ambiguës" par J.M. Boé [3].

Théorème 7 ([3] [4]) : Un sous-monoïde P d'un monoïde M est libérable ssi il existe une représentation r de M par matrices à éléments 0,1 telle que $P = \{m \in M \; ; \; r(m)_{1,1} = 1\}$

Corollaire (Schützenberger) : **Un sous-monoïde** rationnel P d'un monoïde libre X^* est libre ssi il existe une représentation r de X^* par matrices carrées de dimension finie à éléments 0,1 telle que

$$P = \{w \in X^* \; ; \; r(w)_{1,1} = 1\}$$

En effet, si la dimension est finie le monoïde de matrices est fini et P est donc rationnel ; réciproquement, si P est rationnel son monoïde syntactique est fini, l'image de P est un sous-monoïde libérable de Synt(P), d'où une représentation de dimension finie.

Signalons à ce sujet que, contrairement au cas des sous-monoïdes unitaires, pour lesquels le monoïde syntactique admet une représentation minimale unique (celle que donne l'automate réduit), le monoïde syntactique d'un sous-monoïde libre "général" peut avoir plusieurs représentations matricielles "irréductibles" non équivalentes. Pour plus de détails sur la structure de ces représentations voir Boé [3] et Césari [5].

III - MAXIMALITE ET COMPLETUDE

a) Codes maximaux

Toute partie d'un code étant encore un code, il est naturel d'appeler maximal tout code qui n'est contenu strictement dans aucun autre. Le critère suivant, pour savoir si un code donné est maximal ou non, est classique :

Soit A un code sur un alphabet X à q lettres : on a

$$\Sigma \{ q^{-|a|} \; ; \; a \in A \} \leqslant 1$$ (inégalité de Kraft-Macmillan, [1]);

si la somme est égale à 1 le code est maximal, et réciproquement si A est rationnel (voir notamment [8]).

Exemples : Les codes A_1, A_4, A_5 sont maximaux, A_3, A_6 et A_7 ne le sont pas. $A_3 \cup \{xyy, yyy\}$ est un code maximal à délai de déchiffrage infini.

La famille des codes étant $\cup$-inductive, l'axiome de Zorn affirme que tout code est contenu dans un code maximal. Lorsque le code donné est fini, on peut espérer qu'un code maximal le contenant sera aussi fini : il n'en est rien, en général, et Restivo [24] montre que le code non-maximal $A_8 = \{ x^5, x^2y, x^2yx, y, yx \}$ n'est contenu dans aucun code maximal fini.

b) Codes complets

Un sous-monoïde quelconque P d'un monoïde M sera dit complet (resp. complet à droite, à gauche) s'il rencontre tous les idéaux bilatères (resp. à droite, à gauche) de M. La complétude se conservant par homomorphisme, l'image de P rencontre alors tous les idéaux bilatères de son monoïde syntactique, donc l'idéal minimal s'il existe. Lorsque P n'est pas complet le monoïde syntactique possède un zéro, image commune de tous les idéaux de M ne rencontrant pas P; ce zéro est alors l'idéal minimal de Synt(P), lequel ne rencontre pas l'image de P. Si P est un sous-monoïde rationnel de X^*, Synt(P) est fini et contient donc un idéal minimal.

Proposition : Un sous-monoïde rationnel $P \subset X^*$ est complet ssi son image dans Synt(P) rencontre l'idéal minimal du monoïde syntactique. Si P est incomplet Synt(P) possède un zéro et l'image de P rencontre l'idéal 0-minimal, qui est unique.

L'unicité de l'idéal 0-minimal, pour P incomplet, se vérifie ainsi : Si Synt(P) possédait deux idéaux 0-minimaux distincts, chacun d'entre eux contiendrait au moins un élément de l'image de P, et où serait le produit de ces deux éléments ?

Un code $A \subset X^*$ sera dit complet (resp. complet à droite, à gauche) ssi le sous-monoïde libre A^* est complet (resp. complet à droite, à gauche) dans X^*. D'autres auteurs [16] appellent complets les codes maximaux, d'autres [8] appellent denses les sous-monoïdes que nous appelons complets. Ces différences de terminologie sont sans grande conséquence vu le résultat suivant (cf. par exemple [8]).

Théorème 8 : Tout code maximal est complet ; tout code complet rationnel est maximal. Les trois conditions suivantes sont équivalentes pour un langage rationnel $A \subset X^*$:

(i) A est un code complet à droite (resp. à gauche) ;

(ii) A est un code préfixe (resp. suffixe) complet à droite (resp. à gauche) ;

(iii) A est un code préfixe (resp. suffixe) complet.

L'hypothèse "A rationnel" n'est pas superflue, comme le montre l'exemple du code $\{ x^{1+|w|} y w \ ; \ w \in \{x, y\}^* \}$ qui est un code préfixe complet qui n'est ni maximal ni complet à droite, car on peut lui adjoindre y.

Pour un code préfixe A, on vérifie facilement, grâce au fait que A^* est unitaire à gauche, que A est complet à droite ssi A est maximal en tant que code préfixe. Le théorème 8 entraîne donc qu'un code préfixe rationnel maximal en tant que code préfixe est aussi maximal en tant que code. Or, la maximalité en tant que code préfixe se voit immédiatement sur l'arbre représentant le code : elle correspond à la présence de q successeurs pour chaque sommet non terminal, où q est le nombre de lettres de l'alphabet. On voit ainsi que A_5 est maximal, mais non A_6 ni A_7 :

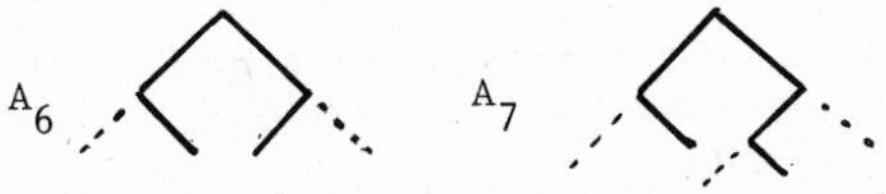

Les codes incomplets ont été moins étudiés que les codes complets : citons la famille de tous les codes finis sur $\{x, y\}$ contenus dans $x^* \cup x^*y\,x^*$, décrite par Restivo [24] au moyen de factorisations des polynômes cyclotomiques, à laquelle appartient le code A_8, et, pour les codes préfixes finis, ceux dont les monoïdes syntactiques sont inversifs, étudiés par Keenan et Lallement [12]. Nous ne traiterons plus que de codes complets.

c) Codes synchronisants. Groupe d'un code complet.

Définition 5 : Un code est appelé synchronisant lorsqu'il est complet et possède des paires synchronisantes.

Exemple : A_1 est un code synchronisant (mais son délai de synchronisation est infini).

Proposition : Un code préfixe rationnel $A \subset X^*$ est synchronisant ssi il existe un mot $w \in X^*$, appelé mot synchronisant, tel que $X^*w \subset A^*$.

La présence d'un mot synchronisant assure la complétude du code et donne des paires synchronisantes (w, w') quel que soit $w' \in A^*$. Réciproquement, si A préfixe complet a une paire synchronisante (f, g), pour tout mot u on peut trouver v tel que $ufgv \in A^*$ (car A est complet à droite d'après le théorème 8), d'où $uf \in A^*$ et par conséquent f est un mot synchronisant.

Corollaire : Si un code bipréfixe $A \subset X^*$ est synchronisant, alors $A = X$.

En effet, A^* est alors unitaire à droite, et la présence d'un mot synchronisant entraîne $A^* = X^*$. Le code A_5 nous donne donc un exemple de code complet non synchronisant.

Définition 6 : Pour un code rationnel complet A, on appelle groupe du code A, noté G(A), le groupe de structure de l'idéal minimal du monoïde syntactique de A^*.

On trouvera en [3] une démonstration du résultat suivant :

Théorème 9 : Un code rationnel complet est synchronisant ssi son groupe est trivial.

Pour un code préfixe synchronisant, la trivialité du groupe résulte du fait que les éléments de l'idéal minimal sont des applications de rang 1 dans la représentation du monoïde syntactique évoquée en II c), images, entre autres, des mots synchronisants. Le groupe d'un code non préfixe est moins facile à appréhender (voir [3] ,[5]).

Soulignons que "presque tous les codes" sont synchronisants. On peut classer ceux qui ne le sont pas selon la nature de leur groupe : pour les codes préfixes complets finis on dispose de quelques informations [19], on connaît mieux encore ceux des codes bipréfixes (complets finis) [18], mais on sait depuis peu que les codes bipréfixes ne sont pas les seuls à "fabriquer des groupes" [17].

d) Monoïdes syntactiques des codes complets finis.

Le but de ce dernier paragraphe est de présenter une interprétation du

Théorème de Markov-Schützenberger [28] : Soit A un code complet fini : ou bien A est préfixe, ou bien son délai de déchiffrage est infini.

L'interprétation en question, due à D. Perrin, fait observer la présence ou l'absence d'un élément idempotent "au-dessus" d'un certain idéal à droite de Synt(A^*) : si un tel idempotent apparaît, le délai de déchiffrage est infini, s'il n'apparaît pas le code est préfixe.

Nous supposons connue la théorie classique des équivalences de Green dans les monoïdes finis (cf [6]).

Lemme fondamental : Soit A une partie finie de X^* engendrant un sous-monoïde complet : l'image de A^* dans son monoïde syntactique contient au moins un idempotent de chaque D-classe régulière.

Preuve : Soit $u \in X^*$ ayant une image idempotente dans Synt (A^*): nous pouvons choisir u plus long que tous les mots de A. Avec $k > |u|$, u^k a la même image que u ; A^* étant complet, pour quelques f, $g \in X^*$ on a $fu^k g \in A^*$, et il est certain que chaque facteur u contient au moins une scansion de la factorisation sur A, et qu'au moins deux de ces facteurs se décomposent de la même manière u = u' u". Ecrivons $fu^k g = fu^{k'} u'u''u^{k''} u' u''u^{k'''} g$ avec $k = k' + k'' + k''' + 2$ et $u''u^{k''}u' \in A^*$, d'où syntactiquement $u'' u' \in A^*$. Or, l'image de u" u', mot conjugué de u, est un idempotent appartenant à la même D-classe que u. Q.E.D.

Soit alors A un code complet fini. Dire que son délai de déchiffrage est d signifie que pour tout mot $b \in A^d$, pour tout $a \in A$, et $u \in X^*$, $a\,b\,u \in A^*$ implique $bu \in A^*$, et par suite que l'ensemble A^d est tout entier contenu dans l'idéal à droite P de X^* ainsi défini :

$$P = \{ f \in X^*;\ f' \in X^*,\ w \in A^*,\ w\,ff' \in A^* \text{ impliquent } ff' \in A^* \}.$$

Un délai de déchiffrage fini interdit donc la présence d'une D-classe régulière qui ne rencontrerait pas P, i.e. située au dessus de P : en effet, A^* contiendrait l'image inverse d'un des idempotents de cette D-classe, d'après le Lemme fondamental, et cette image inverse contiendrait des produits arbitrairement longs de mots de A qui ne seraient pas dans P. En d'autres termes, un délai de déchiffrage fini entraîne que $P = B\,X^*$ où B est un ensemble fini. Et Schützenberger démontre, par un argument purement combinatoire, que cette dernière hypothèse a pour conséquence que A est complet à droite, donc préfixe ([29], Observation _in fine_).

BIBLIOGRAPHIE

1. ASH, R. : Information theory, Interscience - Wiley ,1965.

2. BLUM, E.K. : A note on free subsemigroups with two generators, Bull. American Math. Soc. 71 (1965) 678-679.

3. BOE, J-M. : Représentations des monoïdes : Applications à la théorie des codes, Thèse 3ème cycle, Montpellier 1976.

4. BOE, J-M., J. BOYAT, Y. CESARI, A. LACHENY et M. VINCENT : Automates et monoïdes syntaxiques des sous-monoïdes libres, à paraître dans Information and Control.

5. CESARI, Y. : Sur l'application du théorème de Suschkewitsch à l'étude des codes rationnels complets, in Automata, Languages, and Programming, 2nd Colloquium, J. Loeckx, Ed., (Lecture Notes in Computer Science, n°14), Springer 1974, p. 342-350.

6. CLIFFORD, A.H. and G.B. PRESTON : The Algebraic Theory of Semigroups, American Math. Soc. Vol 1 : 1961, Vol. 2 : 1967.

7. DE LUCA, A. : A Note on Variable Length Codes, Information and Control 32 (1976) 263-271.

8. EILENBERG, S. : Automata, Languages and Machines, Academic Press, Vol. A : 1974, Vol. B : 1976.

9. GILBERT, E.N. and E.F. MOORE : Variable-Length Binary Encodings, Bell System Tech. J. 38 (1959) 933-967.

10. HASHIGUCHI, K. and N. HONDA : Homomorphisms that Preserve Star height, Information and Control 30 (1976) 247-266.

11. HASHIGUCHI, K. and N. HONDA : Properties of Code Events and Homomorphisms over Regular Events, J. Comput. System Sci. 12 (1976) 352-367.

12. KEENAN, M. and G. LALLEMENT : On certain Codes admitting inverse semigroups as Syntactic monoids, Semigroup Forum 8 (1974) 312-331.

13. LANDI, D.M. : Variable-length encodings, Ph. D. Thesis, North-western University, 1966.

14. LENTIN, A. : Equations dans les monoïdes libres, Gauthier-Villars / Mouton, 1972.

15. LENTIN, A. et M.P. SCHÜTZENBERGER : A combinatorial Problem in the Theory of Free Monoids, in Combinatorial Mathematics and its Applications, Bose and Dowling, eds., University of North Carolina Press, 1969, p.128-144.

16. NIVAT, M. : Eléments de la théorie générale des codes, in Automata Theory, E. R. Caianiello, Ed., Academic Press 1966, p. 278-294.

17. PERRIN, D. : Codes asynchrones, à paraître au Bulletin de la Société Mathématique de France.

18. PERRIN, D. : La transitivité du groupe d'un code bipréfixe fini, à paraître dans Math. Zeitschrift.

19. PERROT, J-F. : Groupes de permutations associés aux codes préfixes finis, in Permutations, Actes d'un Colloque réunis par A. Lentin, Gauthier-Villars/Mouton, 1974, p. 19-35.

20. POLLAK, G. : On free Subsemigroups of free semigroup, Studia Sci. Math. Hungarica 7(1972) 317-319.

21. RESTIVO, A. : Codes and aperiodic languages, in 1. Fachtagung über Automatentheorie und formale Sprachen, Lecture Notes in Computer Science n°2, Springer 1973, 175-181.

22. RESTIVO, A. : On a Question of Mc Naughton and Papert, Information and Control 25(1974) 93-101.

23. RESTIVO, A. : A Combinatorial Property of Codes having finite Synchronization Delay, Theoretical Computer Science 1 (1975) 95-101.

24. RESTIVO, A. : On a Family of Codes related to factorization of Cyclotomic polynomials, in Automata, Languages, and Programming 3rd Int. Colloquium, S. Michaelson and R. Milner, Eds., Edinburgh University Press, 1976, p. 38-44.

25. RILEY, J.A. : The Sardinas/Patterson and Levenshtein theorems, Information and Control 10 (1967) 120-136.

26. SCHUTZENBERGER, M.P. : Une théorie algébrique du codage, Séminaire Dubreil-Pisot, Année 1955/56, Exposé n°15, 24p. (Institut Henri Poincaré, Paris), et C.R. Acad. Sci. Paris 242 (1956) 862-864.

27. SCHUTZENBERGER, M.P. : On an application of Semigroup methods to some problems in coding, I.R.E. Trans. on Information theory, I.T.2, (1956) 47-60.

28. SCHUTZENBERGER, M.P. : On a Question concerning Certain Free submonoids, J. Comb. Theory 1(1966) 437-442.

29. SCHUTZENBERGER, M.P. : Sur certains sous-monoïdes libres, Bull. Soc. Math. France 93 (1965) 209-223.

30. SCHUTZENBERGER, M.P. : Sur les monoïdes finis dont les groupes sont commutatifs, R.A.I.R.O R-1, 1974, 55-61.

31. SCHUTZENBERGER, M.P. : Sur certaines opérations de fermeture dans les langages rationnels, Symposia Mathematica XV(1975).

32. SCHUTZENBERGER, M.P. : Sur certaines pseudo-variétés de monoïdes finis, Rapport IRIA-Laboria n°62, 1974.

33. SPEHNER, J-C. : Quelques constructions et algorithmes relatifs aux sous-monoïdes d'un monoïde libre, Semigroup Forum 9 (1975) 334-353.

34. SPEHNER, J-C. : Quelques problèmes d'extension, de conjugaison et de présentation des sous-monoïdes d'un monoïde libre, Thèse Sc.Math, Univ. Paris VII, 1976.

35. TILSON, B.: The intersection of free submonoids of a free monoid is free, Semigroup Forum 4 (1972) 345-350.

36. VIENNOT, G. : Algèbres de Lie libres et monoïdes libres, Thèse Sc.Math., Univ. Paris VII, 1974.

37. VIENNOT, G. : Un problème combinatoire sur les mots ne se chevauchant pas, in Journées de Combinatoire et Informatique, Univ. Bordeaux 1, 1975, p. 341-351.

On a DESCRIPTION OF TREE-LANGUAGES BY LANGUAGES

B. Courcelle

Introduction :

The classical notion of a language can be generalized into that of a tree-language or set of finite trees. Automata and grammars can be defined to generate tree-languages. A lot of authors have studied this generalization among them we quote Fischer [4], Rounds [7], Engelfriet [2], [3], Hossley [6].

We are interested in decision problems for tree-languages and their possible applications to program schemes. But tree-languages are not easy to handle. It seems reasonnable to use one's experience in dealing with languages to study them (as much as possible). As in the case of context-free languages, a lot of decision problems are undecidable. But it is interesting to search for decidable subcases as it has been widely done for context-free languages.

A first possibility is to encode finite trees as words using for instance polish notation. But it is known from [4] that context-free tree-languages become indexed languages through this encoding. We would prefer to describe context-free tree-languages by context-free languages. An other possibility is explored here. We represent a tree by a finite language : basically the set of its branches. Certain tree-languages can be characterized by the set of branches of their elements. We call them closed.

Our main results are the following ones :

A recognizable tree language is closed iff it is recognized by a deterministic top-down finite state automaton . One can decide whether a recognizable tree-language is closed.

Simple deterministic tree-languages (the obvious generalization of simple deterministic languages) are closed. But whereas the equivalence problem for simple deterministic grammars is decidable, its generalization to tree grammars is interreductible with the (still open) equivalence problem for DPDA's. (See Valiant [8] for decidable subcases).

Some of these results are proved in [1],[9].

We now give some more details.

Let F be a finite alphabet, each element f of which is given with an <u>arity</u> $\rho(f) \geq 1$. Let $V_k = \{v_1,\ldots,v_k\}$ be a set of symbols of arity 0. Let $M(F,V_k)$ be the set of terms on $F \cup V_k$ and well formed with respect to arities. Such a term is called a <u>tree</u>.

<u>Example 1</u> : $F = \{f,g\}$, $\rho(f) = 3$, $\rho(g) = 2$.

Then $t = f(g(v_1,v_3),v_2,f(v_1,v_2,v_4))$ is an element of $M(F,V_4)$. A tree-like pictorial representation is :

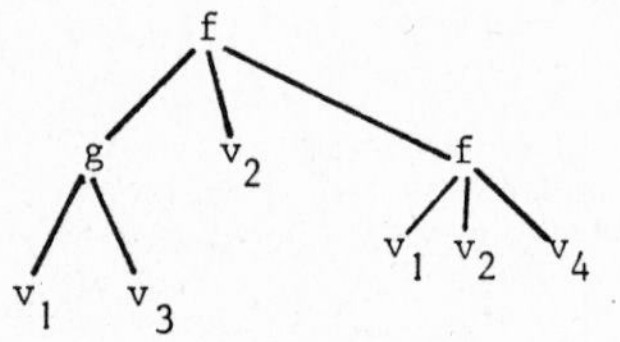

A tree language is a subset of some $M(F,V_k)$.

We associate to F the new alphabet $F_{spl} = \{[f,i] \,/\, f \in F$ and $1 \leq i \leq \rho(f)\}$. For $t \in M(F,V_k)$ the <u>set of branches</u> of t is the language $B(t) \subset (F_{spl} \cup V_k)^*$ inductively defined by :

$$\begin{cases} B(v_i) = \{v_i\} \\ B(f(t_1,\ldots,t_n)) = \bigcup_{1 \leq i \leq n} [f,i]B(t_i) \\ \text{for } f \in F,\ \rho(f) = n \text{ and } t_1,\ldots,t_n \in M(F,V_k) \end{cases}$$

For t defined in example 1 we get :

$B(t) = \{f_1g_1v_1, f_1g_2v_3, f_2v_2, f_3f_1v_1, f_3f_2v_2, f_3f_3v_4\}$ (where f_i stands for $[f,i]$).

Clearly, for $t,t' \in M(F,V_k)$, $B(t) = B(t')$ iff $t = t'$.

For $L \subset M(F,V_k)$ let $B(L) = \bigcup\{B(t) \,/\, t \in L\}$ and $\bar{L} = \{t \in M(F,V_k) \,/\, B(t) \subset B(L)\}$. We call $\bar{L}$ the <u>closure</u> of L and say that L is <u>closed</u> if $L = \bar{L}$.

<u>Proposition</u> : <u>For closed tree languages L and L', B(L) = B(L') iff L = L'</u>.

<u>Example 2</u> : If $L = \{t\}$ then L is closed. The following tree language L_0

is not closed :

$$L_0 = \left\{ f(g(v_1), g(v_1)),\ f(h(v_1), h(v_1)) \right\}$$

(because $f(g(v_1),h(v_1))$ belongs to $\bar{L}_0 - L_0$).

Recognizable tree-languages.

Several notions of finite-state tree-automata can be defined (we refer to Engelfriet [2] for notations) : top-down or bottom-up nondeterministic automata (respectively denoted t-fsa and b-fsa) together with deterministic ones (respectively dt-fsa and db-fsa). It is known [6] that t-fsa's, b-fsa's and db-fsa's have the same power : they accept the recognizable tree-languages (let Rec denote this family). Rec is a boolean algebra. It enjoys a lot of the properties of the family of recognizable languages.

On the other hand dt-fsa's define a proper subfamily of Rec. We call it DRec, the family of deterministic recognizable tree-languages ; it is closed by intersection but neither by union nor difference.

We get the following results :

Theorem 1 : Let $L = T(A)$ for some fsa A.

1) If A is a dt-fsa then L is closed.
2) One can built a dt-fsa $\bar{A}$ such that $T(\bar{A}) = \bar{L}$.
3) One can decide whether $L \in$ DRec (i.e whether L is closed).
4) $B(L)$ is a regular language.

Hint : We can assume that A is a t-fsa. One builds $\bar{A}$ by the determinization procedure for ordinary finite state automata.

We also get :

Corollary : Let L be a closed tree language. Then $L \in$ Rec iff $L \in$ DRec iff $B(L)$ is a regular language.

Context-free tree grammars.

Formal definitions can be found in [3].

Example 3 :

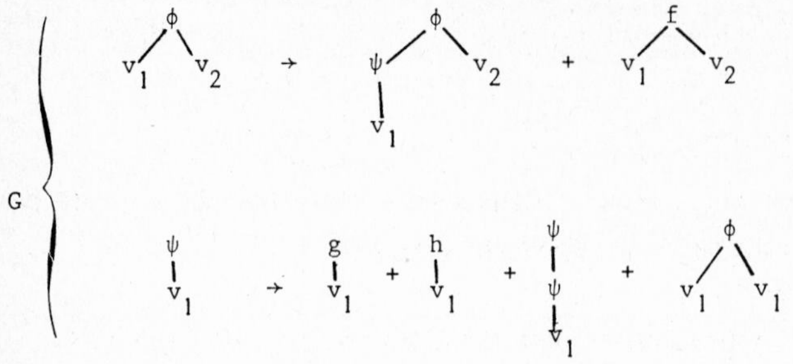

In this grammar, ϕ and ψ are non terminal function symbols. Rather than a formal definition we give a typical derivation (where the derived symbol is marked by +) :

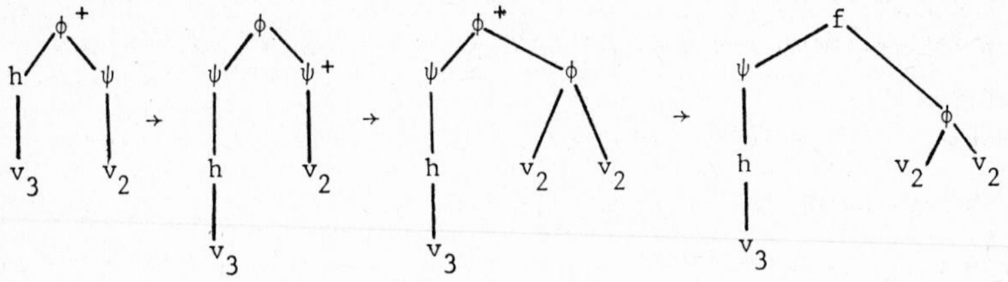

Given G and some starting tree $t_0 \in M(F \cup \{\phi,\psi\}, V_k)$, let

$L(G) = L(G,t_0) = \{t \in M(F,V_k) \ / \ t_0 \overset{*}{\rightarrow} t\}$.

A context-free tree-language is such L(G).

Theorem 2 : 1. Let L = L(G) be a context-free tree-language. Then B(L) is a context-free language.

2. There exists a context-free tree-language L such that B(L) is regular but $L \notin$ Rec.

3. One cannot decide whether a context-free tree-language is closed.

Let us give the context-free grammar G' which generates B(L(G)) where G is defined in example 3 with $\psi(v_1)$ as starting tree :

$$G' \left\{ \begin{array}{l} \phi_1 \rightarrow \phi_1\psi_1 + f_1 \\ \phi_2 \rightarrow \phi_2 \quad + f_2 \\ \psi_1 \rightarrow g_1 + h_1 + \psi_1\psi_1 + \phi_1 + \phi_2 \end{array} \right.$$

$$S \rightarrow \psi_1 v_1$$

The start symbol of G' is S.

This grammar has been built in such a way that $L(G',\phi_i) = \{u \in F^*_{spl} \,/\, uv_i \in B(L(G,\phi(v_1,v_2)))\}$ for $i = 1,2$,

and $L(G',\psi_1) = \{u \in F^*_{spl} \,/\, uv_1 \in B(L(G,\psi(v_1)))\}$.

Simple deterministic tree-languages

Simple deterministic grammars [5] generate a proper subfamily of the deterministic languages. They have a decidable equivalence problem. Let us recall the definition.

A grammar G is simple deterministic iff it is in Greibach Normal Form and for all S (non terminal symbol) and a (terminal symbol) there exists at most one word m such that $S \to am$ is a rule of G. Analogously :

A tree grammar G is simple deterministic iff :

1. for every non terminal symbol ϕ and terminal symbol of $f \in F$ there exists at most one rule of the form $\phi(v_1,\ldots,v_n) \to f(t_1,\ldots,t_r)$ and
2. every rule is of this form.

The following tree grammar is simple deterministic.

Example 4 :

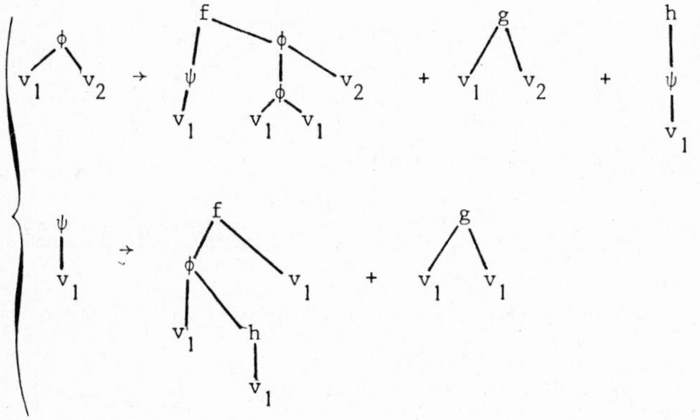

We get the following theorems

Theorem 3 : Let L = L(G) be a simple deterministic tree language :

1) L is closed.
2) B(L) is a deterministic language.
3) One can decide whether L is recognizable.

Theorem 4: For any prefix-free deterministic language L one can construct a simple deterministic grammar G s.t. $B(L(G)) = Lv_1$. The equivalence problems

<u>for DPDA's (deterministic pushdown automata) and simple deterministic tree grammars are interreductible</u>.

<u>Conclusion</u> :

The description of a tree-language L by the language B(L) is suitable when one deals with closed tree-languages.

Two main problems are left open :

1) How to describe $\overline{L(G)}$ for an arbitrary context-free tree grammar G.

2) Extend the notion of simple deterministic tree grammar into a notion of <u>deterministic</u> tree grammar, for which the equivalence problem reduces to the equivalence problem of DPDA's.

<u>References</u> :

[1] B. Courcelle, Sur les ensembles algébriques d'arbres et les langages déterministes, quelques applications à la théorie des schémas de programmes, Thèse, Université de Paris-7, (1976).

[2] J. Engelfriet, Bottom-up and top-down tree transformations - a comparison, Math. System Theory, vol. 9 (1975) pp. 199-231.

[3] J. Engelfriet, E.M. Schmidt, IO and OI, Report PB-47, Aarhus University, Danemark, (1975).

[4] M. Fischer, Grammars with macro-like instructions, Proc. of the 9th Annual Symp. on Switching and Automata Theory (1968) pp. 131-142.

[5] J.E. Hopcroft, A.J. Korenjak, Simple deterministic languages, Proc. of the 7th Symposium on Switching and Automata Theory, Berkeley (1966) pp. 36-46.

[6] R. Hosseley, Finite tree automata and ω-automata, Report MAC TR-102 (1972).

[7] W.C. Rounds, Mappings and grammars on trees, Math. Systems Theory 4 (1970) pp. 257-287.

[8] L.G. Valiant, Decision procedures for families of deterministic push-down automata, Report n°7, Computer Centre of Warwick University, Coventry, England (1973).

[9] B. Courcelle, A Representation of Trees by Languages, submitted for publication.

HIGHER TYPE PROGRAM SCHEMES AND THEIR TREE LANGUAGES

W. Damm

abstract

We introduce classes of program schemes, which generalize the notion of a recursive program scheme in the sense of Nivat [8], by allowing recursion on higher functional types. The equivalence class of such a scheme can be characterized by an infinite tree and by a tree language. We extend the concept of schematic tree grammars (Nivat [7,8]) and prove, that this allows to generate new tree languages. With this result we prove, that the class of schemes introduced is not translatable into the class of recursive program schemes.

1. introduction

A recursive program scheme in the sense of Nivat [8], abstracts the control structure of a certain class of recursive procedures in order to investigate their common properties. These procedures take only data elements as parameters and do not allow procedures as parameters, as e.g. in ALGOL 68. In this paper, we investigate such higher type procedures. We can prove, that the auxiliary use of recursion on higher functional domains increases the computational power of a programming language. To this purpose we introduce a family $(R_n(\Sigma) \mid n \in \mathbb{N})$ of program scheme classes with recursion of functional degree n, Σ denoting the basic set of function symbols.

As an example, consider the following scheme $S \in R_2(\Sigma)$:

$$S \quad \begin{cases} \rightarrow F(x) = \varphi(g,h)(x) \\ \varphi(F_1,F_2)(x) = f(\varphi(F_1 o g, F_2 o h)(x), F_1(F_2(x))) \end{cases}$$

Here, we assume $\Sigma = \{f^{(2)}, g^{(1)}, h^{(1)}\}$. F is the main procedure, which has one formal parameter of functional type 0 . The procedure φ is recursively defined and is of functional type 2 : it expects two monadic functions of type 1 and yields a monadic function of type 1 . The solution of S in some continuous interpretation $\underset{\sim}{A}$ of Σ is the first component of the least fixpoint of the function in

$$[[A \to A] \times [[A \to A]^2 \to [A \to A]] \quad \to \quad [A \to A] \times [[A \to A]^2 \to [A \to A]]]$$

induced by S , and is thus a monadic function. In fact, there is an interpretation $\underset{\sim}{A}$, such that this function cannot be programmed by any recursive program over $\underset{\sim}{A}$ in the sense of Nivat [8].

The classes $R_n(\Sigma)$ have many properties in common with the special cases $R_0(\Sigma)$ of regular program schemes with parameters [1], [7] , and $R_1(\Sigma)$ of recursive program schemes [8]. In fact, we obtain the results for $R_n(\Sigma)$ as consequences of easy provable corresponding theorems for regular schemes.

We prove a Mezei-Wright-like theorem, which essentially says, that one can first compute symbolically on trees and then interpret, or directly compute in the domain of interpretation. From this theorem, we obtain the existence of a Herbrand interpretation and a characterization of a scheme by an infinite tree.

As with recursive program schemes, we can associate with each scheme a schematic tree grammar, which generates approximations of this infinite tree:

Let S be as above. The following derivation steps indicate, how S can be used as a tree grammar:

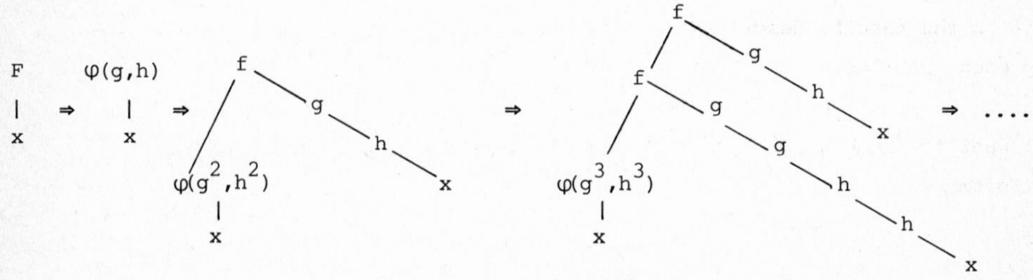

Intuitively, it should be clear, that S generates approximations of t . It is this tree, which characterizes the equivalence class of S .

t =

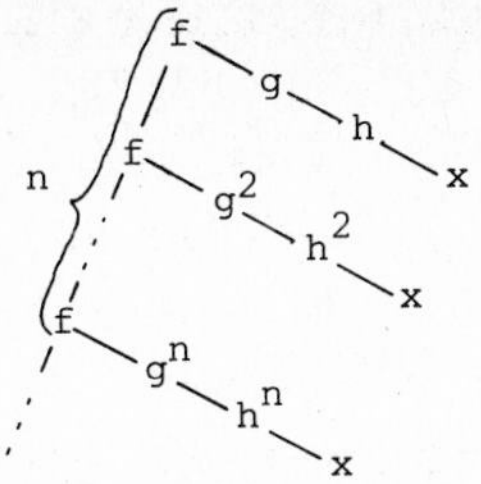

These tree grammars generalize the concept of a schematic context free tree grammar [8]. Let $\mathcal{S}_n(\Sigma)$ be the class of tree languages obtained from $R_n(\Sigma)$. We prove, that these classes form a hierarchy, i.e. $\mathcal{S}_n(\Sigma) \subseteq \mathcal{S}_{n+1}(\Sigma)$ for all $n \in \mathbb{N}$. Moreover, we can generate new languages: $\mathcal{S}_0(\Sigma) \subsetneqq \mathcal{S}_1(\Sigma) \subsetneqq \mathcal{S}_2(\Sigma)$.

We then prove, that all schemes have an equivalent normal form, such that this normalform generates <u>all</u> approximations of its infinite tree. Thus we can apply the results on schematic tree languages to obtain $R_n(\Sigma) \rightsquigarrow R_{n+1}(\Sigma)$ and $R_2(\Sigma) \not\rightsquigarrow R_1(\Sigma) \not\rightsquigarrow R_0(\Sigma)$, where "$\rightsquigarrow$" stands for translatable. This proves, that recursion on higher functional types allows to define new functions at the base level.

The formalization of the topic in the setting of deterministic program schemes was suggested by K. Indermark. In [5] he introduces typed combinator schemes, which include fixpoint combinator schemes at any functional level. Then he shows, how to reduce the subclass, which, when interpreted define functions of type 1 , to certain standard forms. By a normal form theorem of Wand [9], these coincide with the classes $R_n(\Sigma)$ introduced in this paper.

Engelfriet and Schmidt define in [4] the corresponding nondeterministic hierarchy of schemes, and prove, that the regular, context-free and macro string languages may be obtained as solutions over a particular interpretation at level 0,1, and 2, respectively.

In [10], Wand indicates a proof of a similar result. He uses a categorical generalization of his concept of a μ-clone of an algebra [9], to define a hierarchy of string languages, which starts with the regular, context-free and indexed languages.

This paper consists of five sections. The algebraic background is given in section 2 . In section 3 , we review simple recursive schemes. Section 4 contains the results described in the introduction. The last section mentions some open problems.

I want to thank Klaus Indermark for his constant support and helpful criticism.

2. algebraic background

An algebraic definition of the semantic of higher type schemes requires heterogeneous continuous rather than ordinary algebras as interpretations. In this section, we define these algebras and summarize some properties. The reader is refered to [1] for details.

Let I be a set of sorts, and I^* be the set of strings over I. For $w \in I^*$, $l(w)$ denotes the length of w. If $l(w) = n > 0$, we write $w = w(1)\cdots w(n)$. The empty string will be denoted by e.

An I-sorted alphabet is a family $\Sigma = \langle \Sigma^{\langle w,i\rangle} \rangle_{\langle w,i\rangle \in I^* \times I}$. The elements of $\Sigma^{\langle w,i\rangle}$ are called base function symbols of arity $\langle w,i\rangle$. If $X = \langle X^i \rangle_{i \in I}$ is a family with domain I, then $\Sigma(X)$ is the I-sorted alphabet defined by $\langle e,i\rangle \mapsto \Sigma^{\langle e,i\rangle} \cup X^i$, $w \neq e \Rightarrow \langle w,i\rangle \mapsto \Sigma^{\langle w,i\rangle}$.

A Σ-algebra is a pair $\underset{\sim}{A} = (A, \varphi_A)$, where A is a family of sets $\langle A^i \rangle_{i \in I}$, and φ_A assigns each $f \in \Sigma^{\langle w,i\rangle}$ a function over A of correct arity, i.e. $\varphi_A(f) : A^w \to A^i$. Here, A^w denotes the generalization of the cartesian product defined by $A^e := \{\perp\}$ - $\perp$ is a new symbol - , and $A^{wi} := A^w \times A^i$.

A family of mappings $h = \langle h^i : A^i \to B^i \rangle_{i \in I}$ between carriers of Σ-algebras $\underset{\sim}{A}$ and $\underset{\sim}{B}$ is a Σ-homomorphism iff $\forall f \in \Sigma^{\langle w,i\rangle}$ $h^i(\varphi_A(f)(a_1,..,a_n)) = \varphi_B(f)(h^{w(1)}(a_1),..,h^{w(n)}(a_n))$. If h is a homomorphism, then we write $h : \underset{\sim}{A} \to \underset{\sim}{B}$.

In addition to the Σ-structure, we require the algebras to have some order structure.

A Σ-algebra is ordered iff each A^i is a partially ordered set with minimal element $\perp_{A^i}$ and all operations $\varphi_A(f)$ are monotone.

$\underset{\sim}{A}$ is continuous iff $\underset{\sim}{A}$ is ordered, each directed subset $D \subseteq A^i$ has a least upper bound $\bigsqcup D \in A^i$, and all operations are continuous, i.e. if $f \in \Sigma^{\langle w,i\rangle}$ and $D_j \subseteq A^{w(j)}$ is directed, then $\varphi_A(f)(\bigsqcup D_1,..,\bigsqcup D_n) = \bigsqcup \varphi_A(f)(D_1,..,D_n)$.

A directed subset $D \subseteq A^i$ is an ideal iff $d \in D \wedge a \leq d \Rightarrow a \in D$. Let $\underline{alg}_\Sigma$, P-$\underline{alg}_\Sigma$ and Δ-$\underline{alg}_\Sigma$ denote the class of Σ-algebras, ordered Σ-algebras, and continuous Σ-algebras, respectively. In each of these classes there exists an algebra, which is initial in a sense to be defined below. We repeat here the construction of an initial continuous algebra given in [1].

Let $\underset{\sim}{CT}_\Sigma = (CT_\Sigma, \varphi_{CT_\Sigma})$ be the Σ-algebra defined as follows:
The carrier of sort i is the set of all partial mappings $t : \mathbb{N}^* \to \Sigma$ such that

(o) $e \in dom(t) \Rightarrow t(e) \in \Sigma^{<u,i>}$ for some $u \in I^*$

(1) $\gamma \in \mathbb{N}^* \wedge \nu \in \mathbb{N} \wedge \gamma\nu \in dom(t)$

$$\Rightarrow \begin{cases} \gamma \in dom(t) \\ t(\gamma) \in \Sigma^{<u,s>} \text{ for some } s \in I \Rightarrow o \leq \nu < m = l(u) \end{cases}$$
$$\wedge\ t(\gamma\nu) \in \Sigma^{<w,u(\nu+1)>} \text{ for some } w \in I^* .$$

The assignment function φ_{CT_Σ} is given by

$$a \in \Sigma^{<e,i>} \Rightarrow \varphi_{CT_\Sigma}(a)(\underline{\perp}) := \{(e,a)\}$$
$$f \in \Sigma^{<w,i>} \wedge o < n = l(w) \Rightarrow \varphi_{CT_\Sigma}(f)(t_1,..,t_n) := \{(e,f)\} \cup \bigcup_{o \leq \nu < n} \{(\nu u,g) \mid (u,g) \in t_{\nu+1}\}$$

Intuitively, we can think of $t \in CT_\Sigma^{\ i}$ as of an infinite $\Sigma_\perp := \Sigma(<\perp_i \mid i \in I>)$-tree, where $\perp_i$ is the totally undefined partial mapping in $CT_\Sigma^{\ i}$. The order relation is induced from set ordering of partial functions; with this ordering, $\underset{\sim}{CT}_\Sigma$ is a continuous algebra. Moreover, $\underset{\sim}{CT}_\Sigma$ is <u>initial</u> in Δ-<u>alg</u>$_\Sigma$:

<u>2.1 theorem</u> (ADJ [1])

Let $\underset{\sim}{A} \in \Delta$-<u>alg</u>$_\Sigma$. Then there exists a unique strict continuous Σ-homomorphism $h_{\underset{\sim}{A}} : \underset{\sim}{CT}_\Sigma \to \underset{\sim}{A}$.

Let $\underset{\sim}{T}_\Sigma^{\leq}$ be the subalgebra of $\underset{\sim}{CT}_\Sigma$ obtained by restricting the carrier to partial mappings with finite domain . Then $\underset{\sim}{T}_\Sigma^{\leq}$ is ordered and initial in P-<u>alg</u>$_\Sigma$. It is isomorphic to the usual $\Sigma_\perp$-word algebra, where the order relation is defined by

$$t \leq t' \text{ iff } \exists \alpha_j \in \Sigma_\perp^* \ \exists t_j \in T_\Sigma^{\leq i_j} \ t = \alpha_o \perp_{i_1} \alpha_1 \cdot\cdot \alpha_{n-1} \perp_{i_n} \alpha_n \wedge t' = \alpha_o t_1 \alpha_1 \cdots \alpha_{n-1} t_n \alpha_n .$$

$\underset{\sim}{T}_\Sigma$ denotes the subalgebra of $\underset{\sim}{T}_\Sigma^{\leq}$ obtained by restricting the carrier to total mappings. It is well known, that $\underset{\sim}{T}_\Sigma$ is initial in <u>alg</u>$_\Sigma$.

In order to define derived operations of terms, we have to introduce variables. Let, for $w \in I^*$, $Y_w := \{y_{1,w(1)},..,y_{n,w(n)}\}$, and $Y_e := \emptyset$. The set of variables of sort i , $Y_w^{\ i}$, is $\{y_{j,w(j)} \mid 1 \leq j \leq l(w) \wedge w(j) = i\}$. The free continuous Σ-algebra generated by Y_w, $\underset{\sim}{CT}_\Sigma(Y_w)$, has as carrier of sort i $CT_{\Sigma(Y_w)}^{\ i}$. As $\underset{\sim}{CT}_{\Sigma(Y_w)}$ is initial in Δ-<u>alg</u>$_{\Sigma(Y_w)}$, each term induces a derived operation over $\underset{\sim}{A}$:

Let $t \in CT_{\Sigma}(Y_w)^i$ and $\underset{\sim}{A} \in \Delta\text{-}\underline{alg}_{\Sigma}$.
Then $\underline{derop}_{\underset{\sim}{A}}(t) : A^w \to A^i$ is given by

$$a = (a_1,..,a_n) \mapsto h_{\underset{\sim}{A(a)}}(t) \ ,$$

where $\underset{\sim}{A(a)}$ is the $\Sigma(Y_w)$-algebra obtained from $\underset{\sim}{A}$ by letting $y_{j,w(j)}$ name a_j .

Note, that for $w = e$, $\underline{derop}_{\underset{\sim}{A}}(t)(\underline{\perp}) = h_{\underset{\sim}{A}}(t)$.

Term substitution is a special case of a derived operation:
if $t \in CT_{\Sigma}(Y_w)^i$, $(t_1,..,t_n) \in CT_{\Sigma}(Y_v)^w$, then $\underline{derop}_{\underset{\sim}{CT_{\Sigma}(Y_v)}}(t)(t_1,..,t_n)$ is the term obtained from t by simultaneously substituting t_j for $y_{j,w(j)}$ in t .

When interpreting terms over some algebra, term substitution corresponds to functional substitution.

2.2 lemma (ADJ [1])

Let $\underset{\sim}{A} \in \Delta\text{-}\underline{alg}_{\Sigma}$, $t \in CT_{\Sigma}(Y_w)^i$, $(t_1,..,t_n) \in CT_{\Sigma}(Y_v)^w$.

$$\underline{derop}_{\underset{\sim}{A}}(\underline{derop}_{\underset{\sim}{CT_{\Sigma}(Y_v)}}(t)(t_1,...,t_n)) = \underline{derop}_{\underset{\sim}{A}}(t) \circ (\underline{derop}_{\underset{\sim}{A}}(t_1);..;\underline{derop}_{\underset{\sim}{A}}(t_n))$$

This implies, that term substitution is associative.

3. regular schemes

A regular scheme over Σ is a system of regular equations with parameters [1],[7]. In section 5 , we will define higher type schemes as regular schemes over alphabets derived from Σ . Most theorems will follow by algebraically extending similar results for regular schemes, which will be reviewed in this section.

3.1 definition (regular scheme over Σ , $R(\Sigma)$)

$R(\Sigma) := \langle R(\Sigma)^{\langle w,i\rangle} \rangle_{\langle w,i\rangle \in I^* \times I}$. The set of regular schemes of sort $\langle w,i\rangle$, $R(\Sigma)^{\langle w,i\rangle}$, is the set of all mappings $S : X_v \to T^{\leqslant}_{\Sigma(Y_w)}(X_v)$ for some $v \in I^*$, such that $\forall 1 \leqslant j \leqslant l(v)\ S(x_{j,v(j)}) \in T^{\leqslant}_{\Sigma(Y_w)}(X_v)^{v(j)} \wedge v(1) = i$.
Such a scheme can be written as m equations $x_{j,v(j)} = S(x_{j,v(j)})$.
The elements of Y_w are called parameters.

Given some continuous interpretation $\underset{\sim}{A} = (A,\varphi_A)$ of Σ , $S \in R(\Sigma)^{<w,i>}$ is intended to compute a function $A^w \to A^i$. This function is obtained from S by first substituting the argument $a = (a_1,..,a_n)$ into the parameters and then taking the first component of the least fixpoint of the function $A^v \to A^v$ induced by S and a .

3.2 definition (interpretation of S over $\underset{\sim}{A}$, $[\![(S,\underset{\sim}{A})]\!]$)

Let $\underset{\sim}{A} \in \Delta\text{-}\underline{alg}_\Sigma$ and S as above. Then $[\![(S,\underset{\sim}{A})]\!] : A^w \to A^i$ is given by

$$[\![(S,\underset{\sim}{A})]\!](a) := \underline{pr}_1^{(m)}\Big(\bigsqcup_{k\in\mathbb{N}} (\underline{derop}_{\underset{\sim}{A}(a)}(S(x_{1,v(1)}));..;\ \underline{derop}_{\underset{\sim}{A}(a)}(S(x_{m,v(m)})))^k (\bot_{A^{v(1)}},..,\bot_{A^{v(m)}})\Big)$$

Two schemes S and S' are equivalent ($S\sim S'$) iff they compute the same functions under all interpretations:

$S\sim S' \Leftrightarrow \forall \underset{\sim}{A} \in \Delta\text{-}\underline{alg}_\Sigma\ [\![(S,\underset{\sim}{A})]\!] = [\![(S',\underset{\sim}{A})]\!]$.

This extends to classes of schemes $R,R' \subseteq R(\Sigma)$:

R is translatable into R' ($R \rightsquigarrow R'$) $\Leftrightarrow \forall S \in R\ \exists S' \in R'\ \ S\sim S'$;

R is equivalent to R' ($R\sim R'$) $\Leftrightarrow R \rightsquigarrow R' \wedge R' \rightsquigarrow R$.

The equivalence class of a regular scheme $S \in R(\Sigma)^{<w,i>}$ is characterized by its infinite tree $\underline{T(S)} := [\![(S,\underset{\sim}{CT}_\Sigma(Y_w))]\!](y_{1,w(1)},..,y_{n,w(n)})$.
This characterization follows as a corollary from a Mezei-Wright-like theorem: given an algebra $\underset{\sim}{A}$, one can alternatively take the derived operation of T(S) over $\underset{\sim}{A}$, or interpret S directly over $\underset{\sim}{A}$.

3.3 theorem (ADJ, [1])

$$[\![(S,\underset{\sim}{A})]\!] = \underline{derop}_{\underset{\sim}{A}}(T(S))$$

3.4 corollary

$$S\sim S' \Leftrightarrow T(S) = T(S')$$

Alternatively, one can characterize equivalence operationally. Following Nivat [7], we can view a regular scheme as a schematic regular tree grammar.

3.5 definition (language generated by S , $L(S)$)

Let S be as in definition 3.1 , and let $\tau,\tau' \in T^{\leqslant}_{\Sigma(Y_w)}(X_v)$.
τ' derives directly from τ in S ($\tau \underset{S}{\Rightarrow} \tau'$) iff $\exists \alpha,\alpha' \in (\Sigma_\perp \cup Y_w \cup X_v)^*$
$\exists j \in \{1,..,l(v)\}$ $\tau = \alpha x_{j,v(j)}\alpha'$ $\wedge$ ((i) $\tau' = \alpha \perp_{v(j)}\alpha'$ $\vee$ (ii)$\tau' = \alpha S(x_{j,v(j)})\alpha'$)
Let $\overset{*}{\underset{S}{\Rightarrow}}$ denote the transitive reflexive closure of $\underset{S}{\Rightarrow}$. The language generated by S is defined by $L(S) := \{t \in T^{\leqslant}_{\Sigma}(Y_w)^i \mid x_{1,v(1)} \overset{*}{\underset{S}{\Rightarrow}} t\}$.

Note, that S allows two kinds of substitution: either (ii) a right hand side of S is substituted for a variable, or (i) the undefined symbol of correct sort is substituted.

example 1

Let $f \in \Sigma^{<ii,i>}$ for some $i \in I$, and let $S_o \in R(\Sigma)^{<i,i>}$ be the scheme
$x_1 = f(x_1,y_1)$, where we abbreviate x_1 for $x_{1,i}$ and y_1 for $y_{1,i}$.
An example of a derivation is

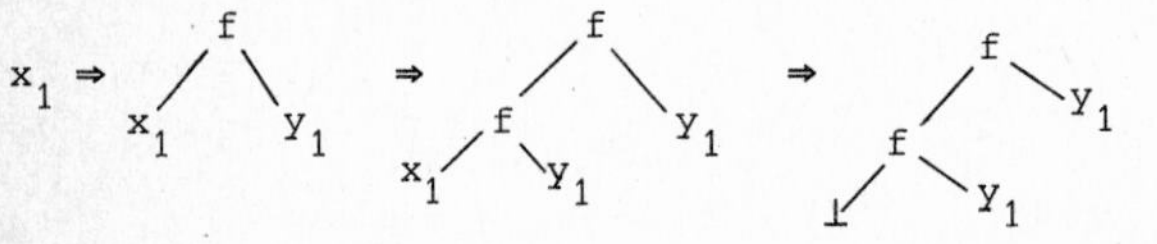

. Let t_n =

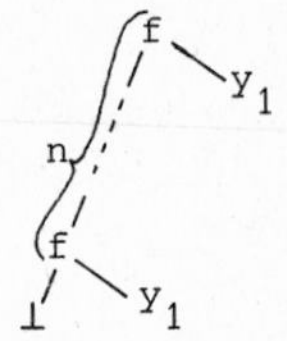

Then $L(S_o) = \{t_n \mid n \in \mathbb{N}\}$ is directed and $\bigsqcup L(S_o) = T(S_o) =$

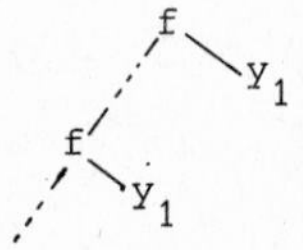

Nivat proves in [7], that $L(S)$ is directed. In fact, its join equals $T(S)$:

3.6 theorem (Courcelle [2])

$$\bigsqcup L(S) = T(S)$$

This result says, that S generates arbitrary exact finite approximations of its infinite tree. However, in order to characterize $T(S)$ and thus equivalence, $L(S)$ has to contain <u>all</u> finite approximations. A tree language generated by a scheme in weak normalform has this property.

<u>3.7 definition</u> (weak normal form)

Let S be as in definition 3.1 . S is in weak normalform iff

$$\forall 1 \leqslant j \leqslant l(v) \qquad S(x_{j,v(j)}) = \begin{cases} a \in \Sigma_\perp^{<e,i>} & \text{for some } i \in I \\ \text{or } \; y_{r,w(r)} & \text{for some } r \in \{1,..,l(w)\} \\ \text{or } \; f\, x_{1,u(1)} \ldots x_{r,u(r)} & \text{for some } f \in \Sigma^{<u,s>}, \\ & \text{some } <u,s> \in I^* \times I . \end{cases}$$

<u>wnf</u> $(R(\Sigma))$ denotes the class of regular schemes in weak normal form.

A direct modification of a lemma proved by Mezei and Wright in [6] shows, that for any S one can effectively construct an equivalent scheme <u>wnf</u>(S) in weak normal form.

<u>3.8 corollary</u>

$$\underline{\text{wnf}}\ (R(\Sigma)) \sim R(\Sigma)$$

Moreover, the language generated by such a scheme is an ideal.

<u>3.9 lemma</u>

$$S \in \underline{\text{wnf}}(R(\Sigma)) \Rightarrow L(S) \text{ is an ideal}$$

proof:

Let $S : X_v \to T^{\leqslant}_{\Sigma(Y_w)}(X_v)$, and let $t \in L(S)$, $t' \in T^{\leqslant}_{\Sigma}(Y_w)$ be such, that $t' \leqslant t$. Then $t' = \alpha_o \perp_{i_1} \alpha_1 \ldots \alpha_{r-1} \perp_{i_r} \alpha_r$ and $t = \alpha_o t_1 \alpha_1 \ldots \alpha_{r-1} t_r \alpha_r$ for some $\alpha_j \in (\Sigma_\perp \cup Y_w)^*$, $t_j \in T^{\leqslant}_{\Sigma}(Y_w)$. Without loss of generality, we may assume $r = 1$.

As S is in weak normal form, at most one "terminal" symbol in $(\Sigma_\perp \cup Y_w)^*$ is introduced in one derivation step, thus the root $f := t_1(e) \in \Sigma^{<u,i_1>} \cup Y_w^{i_1}$ of the subtree t_1 is introduced by some rule $x_{j,v(j)} \mapsto f\, x_{1\mu(1)} \ldots x_{r,u(r)}$ (some $u \in I^*$) . This implies, that the derivation of t is of the form

$$x_{1,v(1)} \overset{*}{\Rightarrow} \beta_o x_{j,v(j)} \beta_1 \Rightarrow \beta_o f\, x_{1,u(1)} \ldots x_{r,u(r)} \beta_1 \overset{*}{\Rightarrow} t ,$$

where $\beta_o , \beta_1 \in (\Sigma_\perp \cup Y_w \cup X_v)^*$ are such, that

$$\beta_o \overset{*}{\Rightarrow} \alpha_o , \; f\, x_{1,u(1)} \ldots x_{r,u(r)} \overset{*}{\Rightarrow} t_1 , \; \beta_1 \overset{*}{\Rightarrow} \alpha_1 .$$

But then we can "cut down" t to t' by substituting $\perp_{i_1}$ for $x_{j,v(j)}$ and obtain

$$x_{1,v(1)} \overset{*}{\Rightarrow} \beta_o\, x_{j,v(j)} \quad \beta_1 \Rightarrow \beta_o \perp_{i_1} \beta_1 \overset{*}{\Rightarrow} t' ,$$

thus $t' \in L(S)$ □

Since the language of a scheme in weak normal form is uniquely determined by its join, we have derived an operational characterization of equivalence.

3.10 corollary

$$S \sim S' \Leftrightarrow L(\underline{wnf}(S)) = L(\underline{wnf}(S'))$$

4. regular schemes on higher types

The concept of recursion on higher types suggests the construction of a series of algebras, which have as carrier functions, functions of functions, ... , etc., and as operations functional substitution and projections, up to the appropriate level, starting with the base functions. Then "recursion on higher types" can be defined as interpreting a regular scheme involving symbols for substitution, projections, and base functions in such an algebra, called derived algebra.

4.1 definition (derived index set, $D^n(I)$, derived alphabet, $D^n(\Sigma)$)

The derived index set of order n is inductively defined by

$$D^o(I) := I \quad , \quad D^{n+1}(I) := D^n(I)^* \times D^n(I) \; .$$

The derived alphabet of order n , $D^n(\Sigma)$, is the $D^n(I)$-sorted alphabet defined inductively by $D^o(\Sigma) := \Sigma$; $D(\Sigma)$ is the $D(I)$ - sorted alphabet given by

(i) $f \in D(\Sigma)^{\langle e,\langle w,i\rangle\rangle}$ for $f \in \Sigma^{\langle w,i\rangle}$

(ii) $\pi^w_j \in D(\Sigma)^{\langle e,\langle w,w(j)\rangle\rangle}$ for $w \in I^*$, $1 \leq j \leq l(w)$

(iii) $\$^v_{\langle w,i\rangle} \in D(\Sigma)^{\langle\langle v,i\rangle\langle w,v(1)\rangle\ldots\langle w,v(m)\rangle,\langle w,i\rangle\rangle}$ for $w,v \in I^*$, $i \in I$.

Finally, $D^{n+1}(\Sigma) := D(D^n(\Sigma))$.

Consider the class $R(D^n(\Sigma))$ of regular schemes over $D^n(\Sigma)$. Among these schemes, there are some, which are of sort $\langle e,\langle\ldots,\langle e,\langle w,i\rangle\rangle\ldots\rangle\rangle$ and thus, after successive applications to $\perp$, define a function of arity $\langle w,i\rangle$. Let $\underline{b}_n : I^* \times I \rightarrow D^n(I)$ be the mapping, which picks out the sorts, we are interested in:

$$\underline{b}_o\langle w,i\rangle := i \; , \; \underline{b}_1\langle w,i\rangle := \langle w,i\rangle \; , \; \underline{b}_{n+1}\langle w,i\rangle := \langle e,\underline{b}_n\langle w,i\rangle\rangle \; .$$

Then the class of regular schemes of order n is the class of regular schemes over $D^n(\Sigma)$, which are of sort $\underline{b}_{n+1}\langle w,i\rangle$ for some $\langle w,i\rangle \in I^* \times I$.

4.2 definition (regular scheme of order n , $R_n(\Sigma)$)

$R_n(\Sigma) = \langle R_n(\Sigma)^{<w,i>} \rangle_{<w,i> \in I^* \times I}$. The class of regular schemes of order n and sort $<w,i>$ is given by $R_n(\Sigma)^{<w,i>} := R(D^n(\Sigma))^{b_{n+1}<w,i>}$.

example 2

Let Σ be given by $<ii,i> \mapsto \{f\}$, $<i,i> \mapsto \{g,h\}$, and let $X_{<i,i>} = \{x_{1,<i,i>}\}$. Then the following scheme S_1 is in $R_1(\Sigma)^{<i,i>}$:

$$x_{1,<i,i>} = \$^{ii}_{<i,i>}(f,\$^{i}_{<i,i>}(x_{1,<i,i>},\$^{i}_{<i,i>}(g,\pi^{i}_{1})),\ \$^{i}_{<i,i>}(g,\pi^{i}_{1}))$$

As $I = \{i\}$, we can view Σ as a ranked alphabet. Moreover, the arity of the substitution symbol is clear from the context, thus we may informally write

$$F_1 = \$(f,\ \$(F_1,\ \$(g,\pi_1)),\ \$(g,\pi_1))$$

for S_1 . We used F_1 for $x_{1,<i,i>}$ to stress, that x_1 has sort $<i,i>$ and is thus a function variable. Intuitively, the term on the right hand side says: substitute into f as first argument the composition of F_1 and g and as second argument g , thus the right hand side may be "translated" to $f(F_1(g(y_1)),g(y_1))$. This argument can be formalized to prove, that any scheme in $R_1(\Sigma)$ is equivalent to a recursive program scheme over Σ in the sense of Nivat [8] (see [3], [4]) . In particular, S_1 is equivalent to

$$F(y_1) = f(F_1(g(y_1)),g(y_1)) .$$

By definition 3.2 , $S \in R_n(\Sigma)$ could be interpreted over any $\underset{\sim}{B} \in \Delta\text{-}\underline{alg}_{D^n(\Sigma)}$, but in general, we are interested in interpretations, which respect the intended meaning of the $'s and π's . To this end, we define for any $\underset{\sim}{A} \in \Delta\text{-}\underline{alg}_{\Sigma}$ the derived algebra of order n , $D^n(\underset{\sim}{A})$.

4.3 definition (derived algebra of order $n, D^n(\underset{\sim}{A})$)

The derived algebra of order $n, D^n(\underset{\sim}{A})$, is inductively defined by $D^o(\underset{\sim}{A}) := \underset{\sim}{A}$; $D(\underset{\sim}{A})$ is the $D(\Sigma)$-algebra $(D(A),\varphi_{D(A)})$, which has the set of all continuous functions from $A^w \to A^i$ as carrier of sort $<w,i>$ (i.e. $D(A)^{<w,i>} := [A^w \to A^i]$) . The assignment function $\varphi_{D(A)}$ is defined by

(i) $\varphi_{D(A)}(f)(\underline{\perp}) := \varphi_A(f)$ for $f \in \Sigma^{<w,i>}$

(ii) $\varphi_{D(A)}(\pi^w_j)(\underline{\perp}) := \lambda(a_1,..,a_n)\ a_j$

(iii) $\varphi_{D(A)}(\$^v_{<w,i>})(g,g_1,..,g_m) := g \circ (g_1;..;g_m)$ (; denotes target tupling)

(iv) $\varphi_{D(A)}(\$^e_{<v,i>})(a) := \lambda(a_1,..,a_m)\ a(\underline{\perp})$

Finally, $D^{n+1}(\underset{\sim}{A}) := D(D^n(\underset{\sim}{A}))$.

Derived algebras are also introduced by Engelfriet and Schmidt [4], to define semantics for nondeterministic higher type equations. In this case, additional restrictions must be imposed on the class of interpretations.

Let $D^n(\Delta\text{-}\underline{alg}_\Sigma) := \{D^n(\underset{\sim}{A}) \mid \underset{\sim}{A} \in \Delta\text{-}\underline{alg}_\Sigma\}$ be the class of all derived algebras of order n. It is routine to prove, that $D(\underset{\sim}{A})$ with the pointwise order on $[A^w \to A^i]$ is a continuous algebra, thus $D^n(\Delta\text{-}\underline{alg}_\Sigma) \subseteq \Delta\text{-}\underline{alg}_{D^n(\Sigma)}$.
We denote by $\underline{ap}^{(n)}_{<w,i>}$ the function, which sends an element of $D^{n+1}(\underset{\sim}{A})^{\underline{b}_{n+1}<w,i>}$ to the function in $[A^w \to A^i]$ given by

$$\underline{ap}^{(n)}_{<w,i>}(f) := f \underbrace{(\perp)\dots(\perp)}_{n\text{-times}}$$

Then we say, that two schemes are equivalent iff they compute, up to applications to $\perp$, the same function in all derived algebras. Let $S \in R_n(\Sigma)^{<w,i>}$, $S' \in R_m(\Sigma)^{<w,i>}$.

4.4 definition (equivalence, $\sim$)

$$S \sim S' \Leftrightarrow \forall \underset{\sim}{A} \in \Delta\text{-}\underline{alg}_\Sigma \;\; \underline{ap}^{(n)}_{<w,i>}([\![(S,D^n(\underset{\sim}{A}))]\!]) = \underline{ap}^{(m)}_{<w,i>}([\![(S',D^m(\underset{\sim}{A}))]\!])$$

For $n=m=o$, $R_o(\Sigma) = R(\Sigma)$ and the above definitions coincide with the definitions given in section 3. However, if $n > o$, then $\sim$ differs from the equivalence relation characterized in section 3, as we compare schemes only with regard to the subclass $D^n(\Delta\text{-}\underline{alg}_\Sigma)$ of all possible interpretations. Thus $T(S) = [\![(S,\underset{\sim}{CT}_{D^n(\Sigma)})]\!](\perp) \in CT_{D^n(\Sigma)}^{\underline{b}_n<w,i>}$ no longer characterizes $\sim$, but using the translation indicated in example 2, we can transform $T(S)$ into a tree $\underline{yield}^{(n)}_{<w,i>}(T(S)) \in CT_\Sigma(Y_w)^i$, by taking into account the meaning of all $'s and π's in $T(S)$, and this tree characterizes S.

More formally, we define this translation as a $D(\Sigma)$-homomorphism by imposing a $D(\Sigma)$-structure on $CT_\Sigma(Y)$. Let $\underset{\sim}{DCT}_\Sigma(Y)$ be the $D(\Sigma)$-algebra, where the carrier of sort $<w,i>$ is $CT_\Sigma(Y_w)^i$, and where the assignment function is given by

$$\varphi_{DCT_\Sigma(Y)}(f)(\perp) := f\, y_{1,w(1)} \dots y_{n,w(n)} \quad \text{for} \quad f \in \Sigma^{<w,i>}$$
$$\varphi_{DCT_\Sigma(Y)}(\pi^w_j)(\perp) := y_{j,w(j)}$$
$$\varphi_{DCT_\Sigma(Y)}(\$^v_{<w,i>})(t,t_1,\dots,t_m) := \underline{derop}_{\underset{\sim}{CT}_\Sigma(Y_w)}(t)(t_1,\dots,t_m),\; \varphi_{DCT_\Sigma(Y)}(\$^e_{<w,i>})(t) = t$$

thus $\$^v_{<w,i>}$ denotes term substitution. As $\underset{\sim}{DCT}_\Sigma(Y) \in \Delta\text{-}\underline{alg}_{D(\Sigma)}$, there exists a unique homomorphism $\underline{yield}_1 : \underset{\sim}{CT}_{D(\Sigma)} \to \underset{\sim}{DCT}_\Sigma(Y)$.

example 3

Let S_1 be the scheme defined in example 2. Consider the approximation of $T(S_1)$, which contains $\perp$ instead of... , and call this tree t. We will informally compute $\underline{yield}_1(t)$. Recall, that $\underline{yield}_1(\pi_1) = y_1$, and that \$ means term substitution, thus $\underline{yield}_1(\$(g,\pi_1)) = g(y_1)$.

$T(S_1) =$ 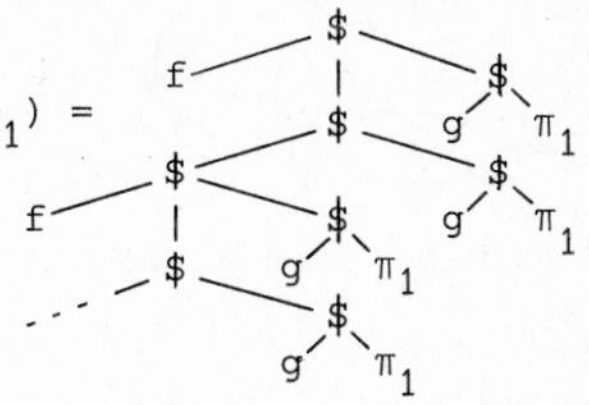

As $\perp$ is a constant, $\underline{yield}_1(\$(\perp,\$(g,\pi_1))) = \perp$.
Now let $t' := \$(f,\$(\perp,\$(g,\pi_1)),\$(g,\pi_1))$, then $\underline{yield}_1(t') = f(\perp,g(y_1))$. As t' occurs as first argument of a substitution symbol, $\underline{yield}_1$ of the second argument is to be substituted for each occurence of y_1 in $\underline{yield}_1(t')$, thus $\underline{yield}_1(\$(t',\$(g,\pi_1))) = f(\perp,g(g(y_1)))$, and $\underline{yield}_1(t) = f(f(\perp,g(g(y_1))), g(y_1))$.

$\underline{yield}_1(T(S_1)) =$ 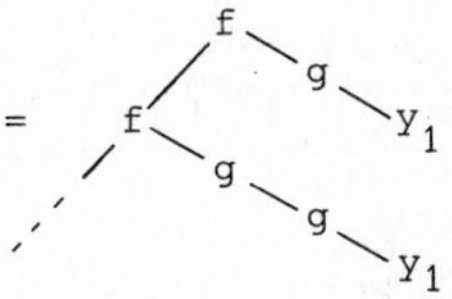

In general, we can define a $D^{n+1}(\Sigma)$-structure on $CT_{D^n(\Sigma)}(Y)$ and thus define $\underline{yield}_{n+1}$ to be the unique $D^{n+1}(\Sigma)$-homomorphism $\underset{\sim}{CT}_{D^{n+1}(\Sigma)} \to \underset{\sim}{DCT}_{D^n(\Sigma)}(Y)$; in particular,

$$\underline{yield}_{n+1}^{\underline{b}_{n+1}<w,i>} : CT_{D^{n+1}(\Sigma)}^{\underline{b}_{n+1}<w,i>} \to CT_{D^n(\Sigma)}^{\underline{b}_n<w,i>} .$$

This allows to combine the mappings $\underline{yield}_n^{\underline{b}_n<w,i>}$ to a single mapping

$$\underline{yield}_{<w,i>}^{(n+1)} : CT_{D^{n+1}(\Sigma)}^{\underline{b}_{n+1}<w,i>} \to CT_\Sigma(Y_w)^i$$

defined by $\underline{yield}_{<w,i>}^{(o)} := \underline{id}_{CT_\Sigma(Y_w)^i}$, $\underline{yield}_{<w,i>}^{(n+1)} := \underline{yield}_{<w,i>}^{(n)} \circ \underline{yield}_{n+1}^{\underline{b}_{n+1}<w,i>}$.

In order to prove, that $\underline{yield}_{<w,i>}^{(n)}(T(S))$ characterizes S, we show first a Mezei-Wright-like theorem. Engelfriet and Schmidt prove in [4] a similar result for nondeterministic equations. Let $S \in R_n(\Sigma)^{<w,i>}$.

4.5 theorem

$$\underline{ap}^{(n)}([\![(S,D^n(\underset{\sim}{A}))]\!]) = \underline{derop}_{\underset{\sim}{A}}(\underline{yield}^{(n)}(T(S)))$$

proof:

For $n=0$, theorems 4.5 and 3.3 coincide. Now let $n=k+1$, and consider the following diagram:

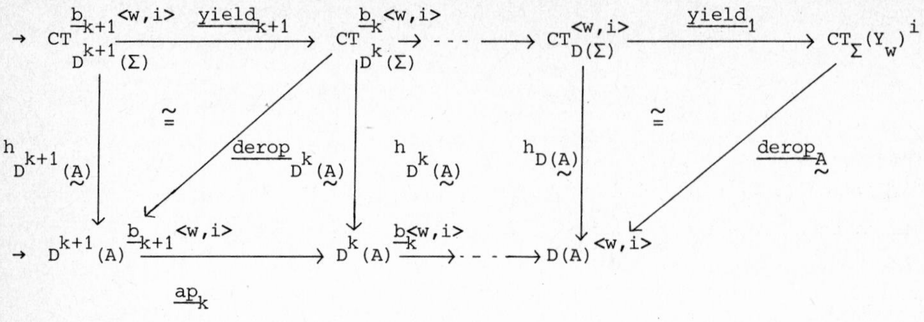

Here, $\underline{ap}_k^{<e,\alpha>} : D^{k+1}(A)^{<e,\alpha>} \to D^k(A)^{\alpha}$ sends f to $f(\perp)$. One can check, that $\underline{derop}_{D^k(\underset{\sim}{A})}$ is a strict continuous $D^{k+1}(\Sigma)$-homomorphism, thus by theorem 2.1 , the diagrams marked $\cong$ commute. By definition of $\underline{derop}$, we have

$$(*) \quad \underline{ap}_k^{<e,\underline{b}_k<w,i>>} \circ \underline{derop}_{D^k(\underset{\sim}{A})}^{<e,\underline{b}_k<w,i>>} = h_{D^k(\underset{\sim}{A})}^{\underline{b}_k<w,i>} .$$

With $(*)$ we can prove by induction on k , that

$$(1) \quad \underline{derop}_{\underset{\sim}{A}} \circ \underline{yield}^{(k+1)} = \underline{ap}^{(k)} \circ h_{D^{k+1}(\underset{\sim}{A})} \qquad \text{holds.}$$

By theorem 3.3,

$$(2) \quad [\![(S,D^{k+1}(\underset{\sim}{A}))]\!] = \underline{derop}_{D^{k+1}(\underset{\sim}{A})}(T(S)) .$$

As $T(S) \in CT_{D^{k+1}(\Sigma)}^{\underline{b}_{k+1}<w,i>}$, $\underline{derop}_{D^{k+1}(\underset{\sim}{A})}^{\underline{b}_{k+2}<w,i>}(T(S)) \in D^{k+2}(A)^{\underline{b}_{k+2}<w,i>}$. Thus we can apply $\underline{ap}^{(k+1)}$ to both sides of (2) and obtain

$$\underline{derop}_{\underset{\sim}{A}}(\underline{yield}^{(k+1)}(T(S)))$$

by (1)
$$= \underline{ap}^{(k)}(h_{D^{k+1}(\underset{\sim}{A})}(T(S)))$$

by $(*)$
$$= \underline{ap}^{(k)}(\underline{ap}_{k+1}(\underline{derop}_{D^{k+1}(\underset{\sim}{A})}(T(S)))) = \underline{ap}^{(k+1)}(\underline{derop}_{D^{k+1}(\underset{\sim}{A})}(T(S)))$$

by (2)
$$= \underline{ap}^{(k+1)}([\![(S,D^{k+1}(\underset{\sim}{A}))]\!]) \quad \square$$

From this it follows, that $D^n(\underset{\sim}{CT}_\Sigma(Y_w))$ is a Herbrand interpretation. Let $S \in R_n(\Sigma)^{<w,i>}$, $S' \in R_m(\Sigma)^{<w,i>}$.

<u>4.6 corollary</u>

$$S \sim S' \;\Leftrightarrow\; \underline{ap}^{(n)}([\![(S, D^n(\underset{\sim}{CT}_{\Sigma}(Y_w)))]\!]) = \underline{ap}^{(m)}([\![(S, D^m(\underset{\sim}{CT}_{\Sigma}(Y_w)))]\!])$$

As by theorem 4.5

$$\underline{ap}^{(m)}([\![(S', D^m(\underset{\sim}{CT}_{\Sigma}(Y_w)))]\!])(y_{1,w(1)},\ldots,y_{n,w(n)}) = \underline{yield}^{(m)}(T(S')) ,$$

this tree characterizes the equivalence class of S' .

<u>4.7 corollary</u>

$$S \sim S' \;\Leftrightarrow\; \underline{yield}^{(n)}(T(S)) = \underline{yield}^{(m)}(T(S'))$$

In section 3 we have shown, how to associate a tree language to a regular scheme. As a scheme $S \in R_n(\Sigma)^{<w,i>}$ has sort $\underline{b}_{n+1}<w,i>$, it may be interpreted as a schematic tree grammar, which defines a tree language in $T^{\leqslant}_{\Sigma}(Y_w)^i$ obtained as the image under $\underline{yield}^{(n)}$ of $L(S) \subseteq T^{\underline{b}_n<w,i>}_{D^n(\Sigma)}$. Then, for increasing n , we can define increasingly complex tree languages.

<u>4.8 definition</u> (schematic tree language of order n, $\mathcal{S}_n(\Sigma)$)

$\mathcal{S}_n(\Sigma) = <\mathcal{S}_n(\Sigma)^{<w,i>}>_{<w,i> \in I^* \times I}$. The set of schematic tree languages of order n and sort $<w,i>$ is given by

$$\mathcal{S}_n(\Sigma)^{<w,i>} := \{L \subseteq T^{\leqslant}_{\Sigma}(Y_w)^i \mid L = \underline{yield}^{(n)}(L(S)) \wedge S \in R_n(\Sigma)^{<w,i>}\}$$

The following examples will illustrate the definition. For the sake of simplicity, we consider the $\{i\}$-sorted (ranked) case. Let $\Sigma = \{f^{(2)}, g^{(1)}, h^{(1)}\}$.

<u>example 4</u>

Let S_1 be the scheme of example 2:

$F_1 = \$(f,\$(F_1,\$(g,\pi_1)), \$(g,\pi_1))$

Then $\underline{yield}^{(1)}(L(S_1)) = \{t_n \mid n \in \mathbb{N}\}$.

As an example, consider the following derivation:

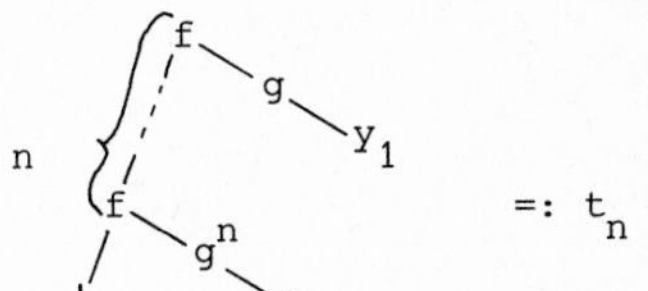

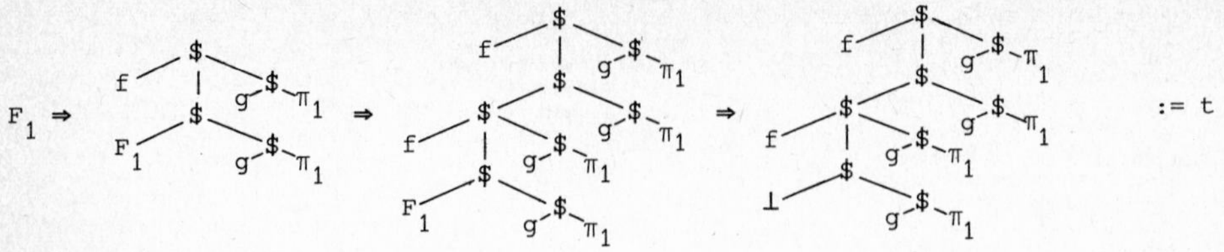

In example 3, we have demonstrated, that $\underline{\text{yield}}^{(1)}(t) = \underline{\text{yield}}_1(t) = t_2$.

<u>example 5</u>

For the sake of simplicity, we give an example of a recursive scheme S'_2 over $D(\Sigma)$, which is equivalent to $S_2 \in R_2(\Sigma)$ defined in 4.10 .

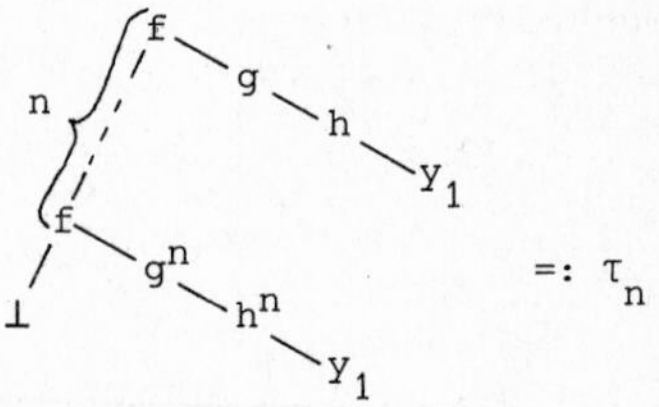

$$S'_2 \begin{cases} \to F = \varphi(g,h) \\ \varphi(F_1,F_2) = \$(f,\varphi(\$(F_1,g)\ ,\$(F_2,h)),\$(F_1,F_2)) \end{cases}$$

S'_2 is equivalent to the macro scheme S over Σ defined in the introduction. The following derivation indicates, that $\underline{\text{yield}}^{(1)}(L(S'_2)) = \{\tau_n \mid n \in \mathbb{N}\}$. In fact $\underline{\text{yield}}^{(2)}(L(S_2)) = \underline{\text{yield}}^{(1)}(L(S'_2))$, thus $\{\tau_n \mid n \in \mathbb{N}\} \in \mathcal{Y}_2(\Sigma)$.

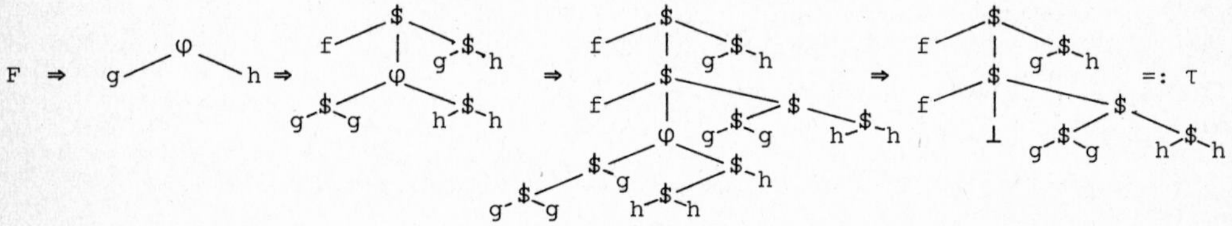

Let $\tau' := \$(\$(g,g),\$(h,h))$.

As $\underline{\text{yield}}_1(g) = g(y_1), \underline{\text{yield}}_1(\tau') = g(g(h(h(y_1))))$, thus $\underline{\text{yield}}_1\ (\tau) = \tau_2$.

Using $\underline{yield}_1$, one can show, that $\mathcal{S}_1(\Sigma)$ equals the class of IO-context-free schematic languages (see [3]). Engelfriet and Schmidt [4] prove this for non-deterministic IO-grammars. The regular and context-free schematic languages are only the first two steps in a hierarchy of tree languages:

<u>4.9 theorem</u>

$$\forall n \in \mathbb{N} \qquad \mathcal{S}_n(\Sigma) \subseteq \mathcal{S}_{n+1}(\Sigma)$$

proof:

Let $S : X_\beta \to T^{\leqslant}_{D^n(\Sigma)(Y_\alpha)}(X_\beta)$. We will define a scheme $\underline{comb}_{n+1}(S) \in R_{n+1}(\Sigma)$, such that $\underline{yield}^{(n+1)}(L(\underline{comb}_{n+1}(S))) = \underline{yield}^{(n)}(L(S))$. The translation is described by a mapping

$$\underline{comb}^{<\alpha,\nu>}_{n+1} : CT_{D^n(\Sigma)(Y_\alpha)}(X_\beta)^\nu \to CT_{D^{n+1}(\Sigma)}(X_\gamma)^{<\alpha,\nu>}$$

$$(\gamma := <\alpha,\beta(1)>\ldots<\alpha,\beta(m)>) .$$

$\underline{comb}_{n+1}$ is defined by structural induction:

$$\underline{comb}^{<\alpha,\nu>}_{n+1}(x_{j,\beta(j)}) := x_{j,<\alpha,\beta(j)>} \quad \text{for } 1 \leqslant j \leqslant m := l(\beta)$$

$$\underline{comb}^{<\alpha,\nu>}_{n+1}(y_{j,\alpha(j)}) := \pi^\alpha_j \quad \text{for } 1 \leqslant j \leqslant l(\alpha)$$

$$\underline{comb}^{<\alpha,\nu>}_{n+1}(a) := \$^e_{<\alpha,\nu>}(a) \quad \text{for } a \in D^n(\Sigma)^{<e,\nu>}$$

$$\underline{comb}^{<\alpha,\nu>}_{n+1}(\bot_\nu) := \bot_{<\alpha,\nu>}$$

$$\underline{comb}^{<\alpha,\nu>}_{n+1}(f(t_1,..,t_r)) := \$^\delta_{<\alpha,\nu>}(f,\underline{comb}^{<\alpha,\delta(1)>}_{n+1}(t_1),..,\underline{comb}^{<\alpha,\delta(r)>}_{n+1}(t_r))$$

$$\text{for } f \in D^n(\Sigma)^{<\delta,\nu>}, (t_1,..,t_r) \in CT_{D^n(\Sigma)(Y_\alpha)}(X_\beta)^\delta .$$

One can easily check, that $\underline{yield}_{n+1} \circ \underline{comb}_{n+1} = \underline{id}_{CT_{D^n(\Sigma)}}$.

Moreover, substitution and $\underline{comb}_{n+1}$ commute in the following way:

if $t \in CT_{D^n(\Sigma)(Y_\alpha)}(X_\delta)^\nu$, $(t_1,..,t_r) \in CT_{D^n(\Sigma)(Y_\alpha)}(X_\beta)^\delta$, then

$$(*)\left\{\begin{aligned} &\underline{comb}^{<\alpha,\nu>}_{n+1}(\underline{derop}_{\underset{\sim}{CT}_{D^n(\Sigma)(Y_\alpha)}}(X)(t)(t_1,..,t_r)) \\ &= \underline{derop}_{\underset{\sim}{CT}_{D^{n+1}(\Sigma)}}(X)(\underline{comb}^{<\alpha,\nu>}_{n+1}(t))(\underline{comb}^{<\alpha,\delta(1)>}_{n+1}(t_1),..,\underline{comb}^{<\alpha,\delta(r)>}_{n+1}(t_r)) .\end{aligned}\right.$$

This assertion is proved by induction on t . It says, that one can first substitute terms at the $D^n(\Sigma)$-level and then apply $\underline{comb}_{n+1}$, or equivalently first apply $\underline{comb}_{n+1}$ and then substitute.

Now define $\underline{comb}_{n+1}(S) : X_\gamma \to T^{\leqslant}_{D^{n+1}(\Sigma)}(X_\gamma)$

by

$$\underline{comb}_{n+1}(S)(x_{j,<\alpha,\beta(j)>}) := \underline{comb}^{<\alpha,\beta(j)>}_{n+1}(S(x_{j,\beta(j)})).$$

Then (*) implies $\underline{comb}_{n+1}(L(S)) = L(\underline{comb}_{n+1}(S))$. But then $\underline{yield}^{(n)}(\underline{yield}_{n+1}(L(\underline{comb}_{n+1}(S)))) = \underline{yield}^{(n)}(L(S))$ □

In fact, term substitution on higher types allows to define new languages. Let Σ contain $f \in \Sigma^{<ii,i>}, g,h \in \Sigma^{<i,i>}$ for some $i \in I$.

4.10 theorem

$$\mathcal{S}_o(\Sigma) \subsetneqq \mathcal{S}_1(\Sigma) \subsetneqq \mathcal{S}_2(\Sigma)$$

proof:

Let, for $L \subseteq T^{\leqslant}_{\Sigma}(Y_w)^i$, $\underline{br}(L)$ denote the set of branches of all terms in L , where leaves are omitted. It is routine to show, that for $L \in \mathcal{S}_o(\Sigma)$, $\underline{br}(L)$ is a regular (string) language. Moreover, Courcelle proves in [2], that $\underline{br}(L)$ for a schematic context-free tree language is context-free. Now consider the scheme S_1 of example 4 . As $\underline{br}(\underline{yield}^{(1)}(L(S_1))) = \{f^n g^n \mid n \in \mathbb{N}\} \cup \{f\}^*$, $\underline{yield}^{(1)}(L(S_1)) \notin \mathcal{S}_o(\Sigma)$. Now let $S_2 \in R_2(\Sigma)^{<i,i>}$ be given by

$$z_1 = \$^{<i,i><i,i>}_{<e,<i,i>>}(z_2, g, h)$$

$$z_2 = \$^{<ii,i><i,i><i,i>}_{<<i,i><i,i>,<i,i>>}(\$^{ii}_{<i,i>}, \$^{e}_{<<i,i><i,i>,<ii,i>>}(f), \$^{<i,i><i,i>}_{<<i,i><i,i>,<i,i>>}(z_2,$$

$$\$^{<i,i><i,i>}_{<<i,i><i,i>,<i,i>>}(\$^{i}_{<i,i>}, \pi_1^{<i,i><i,i>}, \$^{e}_{<<i,i><i,i>,<i,i>>}(g))$$

$$\$^{<i,i><i,i>}_{<<i,i><i,i>,<i,i>>}(\$^{i}_{<i,i>}, \pi_2^{<i,i><i,i>}, \$^{e}_{<<i,i><i,i>,<i,i>>}(h)),$$

$$\$^{<i,i><i,i>}_{<<i,i><i,i>,<i,i>>}(\$^{i}_{<i,i>}, \pi_1^{<i,i><i,i>}, \pi_2^{<i,i><i,i>})).$$

Here $z_1 \in X_{<e,<i,i>>}$ and $z_2 \in X_{<<i,i><i,i>,<i,i>>}$.

Then $\underline{yield}^{(2)}(L(S_2)) = \underline{yield}^{(1)}(L(S'_2))$, where S'_2 is defined in example 5.

As $\underline{br}(\underline{yield}^{(2)}(L(S_2))) = \{f^n g^n h^n \mid n \in \mathbb{N}\} \cup \{f\}^*$, $\underline{yield}^{(2)}(L(S_2)) \notin \mathcal{S}_1(\Sigma)$ □

As we want to apply these results to schemes, we have to characterize equivalence by tree languages. In general, $\underline{yield}^{(n)}(L(\underline{wnf}(S)))$ will not have this property, since the image of an ideal $L \subseteq T_{D^n(\Sigma)}$ under $\underline{yield}_n$ is not necessarily an ideal. To repair this, we modify $\underline{wnf}$ slightly to a normalform $\underline{nf}$.

To define this normalform, we need to iterate $\underline{comb}$ from some level $k-1 \leqslant n$ to n. Let $\underline{b}_n^k : D^k(I) \to D^n(I)$ be given by $\underline{b}_k^k\langle\gamma,\nu\rangle := \langle\gamma,\nu\rangle$, $\underline{b}_n^k\langle\gamma,\nu\rangle := \langle e,\underline{b}_{n-1}^k\langle\gamma,\nu\rangle\rangle (o < k \leqslant n)$.

Define $\underline{comb}^{[k,n]}_{\langle\gamma,\nu\rangle} : CT_{D^{k-1}(\Sigma)}(Y_\gamma)^\nu \to CT_{D^n(\Sigma)}^{\underline{b}_n^k\langle\gamma,\nu\rangle}$ by

$$\underline{comb}^{[k,k]}_{\langle\gamma,\nu\rangle} := \underline{id}_{CT_{D^{k-1}(\Sigma)}(Y_\gamma)^\nu}, \quad \underline{comb}^{[k,n]}_{\langle\gamma,\nu\rangle} := \underline{comb}_k^{\underline{b}_n^k\langle\gamma,\nu\rangle} \circ \underline{comb}^{[k,n-1]}_{\langle\gamma,\nu\rangle} .$$

4.11 <u>definition</u> (normal form of S, $\underline{nf}(S)$)

Let $S \in R_n(\Sigma)$. If $n=0$, then $\underline{nf}(S) := \underline{wnf}(S)$. For $n \geqslant 1$, we define $\underline{nf}(R_n(\Sigma)) \subseteq \underline{wnf}(R_n(\Sigma))$ by $S \in \underline{nf}(R_n(\Sigma))$ iff $\exists S_1 \in \underline{wnf}(R_n(\Sigma))$

$$S_1 : X_\alpha \to T^{\leqslant}_{D^n(\Sigma)}(X_\alpha) \wedge S = \underline{wnf}(S_2),$$

where

$$S_2 : X_\alpha \to T^{\leqslant}_{D^n(\Sigma)}(X_\alpha)$$

is defined by

$$S_2(x_{j,\alpha(j)}) := \begin{cases} \underline{comb}^{[k,n]}_{\langle\gamma,\nu\rangle}(f(y_{1,\gamma(1)},\dots,y_{m,\gamma(m)})) & \text{iff } \alpha(j) = \underline{b}_n^k\langle\gamma,\nu\rangle \\ \wedge\, l(\gamma) = m > 0 \wedge S_1(x_{j,\alpha(j)}) = f \in D^{k-1}(\Sigma)^{\langle\gamma,\nu\rangle} & \\ S_1(x_{j,\alpha(j)}) & \text{otherwise} \end{cases}$$

Thus, to obtain a normalform $\underline{nf}(S)$ of S, we take $S_1 = \underline{wnf}(S)$ and replace any right hand side $f \in D^{k-1}(\Sigma)^{\langle\gamma,\nu\rangle}$ of S_1 by $\underline{comb}^{[k,n]}(f(y_{1,\gamma(1)},\dots,y_{m,\gamma(m)}))$. As these terms have depth >2, we replace S_2 by its weak normal form. Since $\underline{yield} \circ \underline{comb} = \underline{id}$, we have the following corollary:

4.12 <u>corollary</u>

$$\underline{nf}(R_n(\Sigma)) \sim R_n(\Sigma)$$

Moreover, the image under $\underline{yield}^{(n)}$ of a scheme in normalform is an ideal.

4.13 <u>lemma</u>

$$S \in \underline{nf}(R_n(\Sigma)) \Rightarrow \underline{yield}^{(n)}(L(S)) \text{ is an ideal}$$

The proof of lemma 4.13 is technical and omitted. These results allow, to characterize a scheme operationally. Let $S \in R_n(\Sigma)$, $S' \in R_m(\Sigma)$.

4.14 theorem

$$S \sim S' \Leftrightarrow \underline{yield}^{(n)}(L(\underline{nf}(S))) = \underline{yield}^{(m)}(L(\underline{nf}(S')))$$

proof: $S \sim S'$

by 4.12

$$\Leftrightarrow \quad \underline{nf}(S) \sim \underline{nf}(S')$$

by 4.7

$$\Leftrightarrow \quad \underline{yield}^{(n)}(T(\underline{nf}(S))) = \underline{yield}^{(m)}(T(nf(S')))$$

by 3.6

$$\Leftrightarrow \quad \underline{yield}^{(n)}(\bigsqcup L(\underline{nf}(S))) = \underline{yield}^{(m)}(\bigsqcup L(\underline{nf}(S')))$$

by continuity of yield

$$\Leftrightarrow \quad \bigsqcup \underline{yield}^{(n)}(L(\underline{nf}(S))) = \bigsqcup \underline{yield}^{(m)}(L(\underline{nf}(S')))$$

by 4.13

$$\Leftrightarrow \quad \underline{yield}^{(n)}(L(\underline{nf}(S))) = \underline{yield}^{(m)}(L(\underline{nf}(S'))) \qquad \square$$

Because of theorem 4.9 , this implies, that the classes $R_n(\Sigma)$ form a hierarchy.

4.15 corollary

$$\forall n \in \mathbb{N} \qquad R_n(\Sigma) \rightsquigarrow R_{n+1}(\Sigma)$$

Thus recursion on level n can always be simulated by recursion on level $n+1$. In general, the converse is not true. Let Σ contain $f \in \Sigma^{<ii,i>}$, $g,h \in \Sigma^{<i,i>}$. Then the first two steps of the hierarchy are strict.

4.16 theorem

$$R_2(\Sigma) \not\rightsquigarrow R_1(\Sigma) \not\rightsquigarrow R_o(\Sigma)$$

proof:

Consider some normalform $\underline{nf}(S_1)$ of S_1 as defined in example 5 , and suppose $S \sim \underline{nf}(S_1)$ for some $S \in R_o(\Sigma)$. By corollary 4.11 , we may assume, that S is in normalform, thus, by theorem 4.14 , $L(S) = \underline{yield}^{(1)}(L(\underline{nf}(S_1))) =: L_1$. As $\underline{br}(L_1) = \{f^n g^m \mid n \geq m\}$ is not regular, $L_1 \notin \mathcal{S}_o(\Sigma)$, contradicting $L(S) = L_1$, thus $R_1(\Sigma) \not\rightsquigarrow R_o(\Sigma)$.

Now let $L_2 := \underline{yield}^{(2)}(L(\underline{nf}(S_2)))$, where S_2 is defined in 4.10, and suppose $S \sim \underline{nf}(S_2)$ for some $S \in \underline{nf}(R_1(\Sigma))$; then, by theorem 4.14, $\underline{yield}_1(L(S)) = L_2$. By an argument similar to the proof of the pumping lemma,

$\underline{br}(L_2) = \{f^{n_1} g^{n_2} h^{n_3} \mid n_1 \geq n_2 \geq n_3\}$ is not context-free. But then $L_2 \notin \mathcal{Y}_1(\Sigma)$, contradicting $L_2 = \underline{yield}_1(L(S))$. Thus $R_2(\Sigma) \not\hookrightarrow R_1(\Sigma)$.

This proves, that the auxiliary use of recursion on higher types allows to define new functions at the base level. In particular [3], $[\![(S_2, D^2(\underset{\sim}{CT}_\Sigma(Y_i)))]\!]$ cannot be programmed by any recursive program scheme in the sense of Nivat [8].

5. outlook

We have established a hierarchy of tree languages and a hierarchy of schemes, and demonstrated, how these are related. Moreover, we proved, that new objects are definable by allowing recursion on higher types.

Yet another hierarchy can be defined. Let V be some alphabet, and let Σ be the $\{i\}$-sorted alphabet $\{+^{(2)}, \underline{v}^{(1)}, \underline{e}^{(o)} \mid v \in V\}$. Consider the Σ-algebra $\underset{\sim}{L(V)} = (P(V^*), \varphi_{L(V)})$, where $\varphi_{L(V)}(+)(L_1, L_2) := L_1 \cup L_2$, $\varphi_{L(V)}(\underline{v})(L) := \{vl \mid l \in L\}$, and $\varphi_{L(V)}(\underline{e})(\perp) := \{e\}$. Then we obtain classes of string languages over V by

$$\mathcal{L}_n(V) := \{\underline{ap}^{(n)}([\![(S, D^n(\underset{\sim}{L(V)}))]\!])(\perp) \mid S \in R_n(\Sigma)^{<e,i>}\}$$

Because of theorem 4.15, $\mathcal{L}_n(V) \subseteq \mathcal{L}_{n+1}(V)$. One can show, that this hierarchy coincides with the OI-hierarchy of string languages defined by Engelfriet and Schmidt in [4], and with the hierarchy defined by Wand in [10].

We conjecture, that the set of branches of a tree language in $\mathcal{Y}_n(\Sigma)$ is a string language in $\mathcal{L}_n(\Sigma)$. Moreover, we conjecture, that all discussed hierarchies are strict for all $n \in \mathbb{N}$.

6. references

[1] ADJ: GOGUEN, J.A./THATCHER, J.W./WAGNER, E.G./WRIGHT, J.B.
Initial algebra semantics
IBM-Report RC 5701, 1975

[2] COURCELLE, B. Ensembles Algébriques d'Arbres et Langages Déterministes; quelques applications aux Schémas de Programme
IRIA report 1975

[3] DAMM, W. Higher type schemes and their tree languages
to appear

[4] ENGELFRIET, J./SCHMIDT, E.M. IO and OI
Datalogisk Afdelning report, DAIMI PB-47, Aarhus University, Denmark, 1975

[5] INDERMARK, K. Schemes with recursion on higher types
in: Mathematical foundations of Computer Science, Proc. 5th conference in Gdansk, Polen, Lecture Notes in Computer Science, 45, 1976

[6] MEZEI, J./WRIGHT, J.B. Algebraic automata and context-free sets
Inf. and Control, 11, 1967

[7] NIVAT, M. Langages algêbriques sur le magma libre et sêmantique des schêmas de programme
in: Automata, Languages and Programming, ed. M. Nivat, North-Holland Publishing Company, Amsterdam, 1972

[8] NIVAT, M. On the interpretation of recursive program schemes
Symposia Matematica, Atti del convegno d'Informatica teorica, Roma, 1973

[9] WAND, M. A concrete approach to abstract recursive definitions
in: Automata, Languages and Programming, ed. M. Nivat, North-Holland Publishing Company, Amsterdam, 1972

[10] WAND, M. An algebraic formulation of the Chomsky hierarchy
in: Category theory applied to computation and control, Lecture Notes in Computer Science, 25, 1975

Das Äquivalenzproblem für spezielle Klassen von Loop-1-Programmen

H. Huwig und V. Claus

Abstract: Diese Arbeit sucht den Grund für das Auftreten von Nichtentscheidbarkeiten bei Loop-1-Programmen mit angereichertem Befehlsvorrat im gelichzeitigen Auftreten der algorithmischen Sprachelemente "Loop X" und "Abfrage auf Null" zusammen mit Funktionen, die verhindern, Abfragen aus Schleifen "herauszuziehen".

Wir beweisen daher:

- Das Äquivalenzproblem für Loop-1-Programme bleibt lösbar, falls man den Befehlsvorrat um die Vorgängerfunktion erweitert.
- Es bleibt lösbar, falls man die Abfrage auf Null hinzunimmt.
- Nach Erweiterung des Befehlsvorrates um die Abfrage auf Null und die Vorgängerfunktion ist das Äquivalenzproblem nicht mehr lösbar.

Prof. Dr. B. Monien sind wir wegen zahlreicher Diskussionen zu Dank verpflichtet.

Der Übergang von der üblichen Notation von Loop-1-Programmen zu einer kategoriellen Schrittweise beruht auf der Beobachtung

- daß man Speicherplätze mit Hilfe von Produkten
- und Loop-Schleifen mit Hilfe von Gleichungen darstellen kann.

Der höhere formale Aufwand macht sich bezahlt zum einen durch die klare Formulierung des Äquivalenzproblems, zum anderen durch den Anschluß an die Theorie der heterogenen Algebren, der für wietergehende Untersuchungen der hier betrachteten Funktionen von Nutzen sein sollte.

Der Befehlsvorrat für Loop-O-Programme spaltet auf in einen Teil, der die Manipulation von Produkten gestattet, dessen Elemente also stets als Dialogisierung, Vertauschung oder Projektion interpretiert werden müssen, und einen anderen, der die Symbole für die Grundbefehle enthält, deren Interpretation völlig frei ist bis auf die Beachtung gewisser Quelle- und Zielbedingungen. Von der Theorie besteht kein Anlaß, auf die in Programmiersprachen gebräuchliche Typisierung von Funktionssymbolen zu verzichten. Wir definieren daher:

Def 1: $\tau = (Q,Z)$ heißt Befehlsvorrat <==>

$Q,Z: \Omega \longrightarrow A^*$ sind Abbildungen von

$\Omega = \Omega_A + \Omega_B$, einer Menge von Funkionssymbolen,

in das freie von der Menge A der Typensymbole erzeugte Monoid, wobei gilt:

i) $\Omega = \{d_a | a \varepsilon A\} \cup \{v_{a,b} \mid a,b \varepsilon A\} \cup \{p_A \mid a \varepsilon A\}$

mit

α) $a \varepsilon A \Longrightarrow Q p_a = Q d = a \wedge Z d_a = aa \wedge Zp_a = e$

und

β) $a,b \varepsilon A \Longrightarrow Q v_{a,b} = ab \wedge Zv_{a,b} = ba$

ii) $w \varepsilon \Omega_B \Longrightarrow Z w \varepsilon A$.

Def 2: $\mathbb{L}_o(\tau)$ sei die freie von τ erzeugte X-Kategorie (strikt monoidale Kategorie). Sei heißt die Kategorie der Loop-O-Programme zu τ.

$\pi_o(\tau)$ bezeichnet die freie von τ erzeugte heterogene Theorie. (D-Kategorie).

Ein X-Funktor $\mathfrak{I}$: $\mathbb{L}_o(\tau) \longrightarrow$ Set heißt

Semantik <==> $\mathfrak{I}$ faktorisiert über den kanonischen Projektionsfunktor $\pi : \mathbb{L}_o(\tau) \longrightarrow \pi_o(\tau)$.

In obiger Definition steht Set für die Kategorie aller Mengen, wobei wir Produkte auf kanonische Art und Weise bilden. Definition 2 stellt dann sicher, daß für jede Semantik $\mathfrak{I} = (\mathfrak{I}_0, \mathfrak{I}_1)$ ($\mathfrak{I}_0$ die Objekt- und

und ϕ_1 die Morphismenabbildung) gilt:

i) $a \in A \Longrightarrow \Phi_1 d_a : \Phi_0 a \longrightarrow \Phi_0 a \times \Phi_0 a$
$x \longrightarrow (x,x)$

ii) $a \in A \Longrightarrow \Phi_1 p_a : \Phi_0 a \longrightarrow \underline{1}$

iii) $a,b \in A \Longrightarrow \Phi_1 v_{a,b} : \Phi_0 a \times \Phi_0 b \longrightarrow \Phi_0 \times \Phi_0 a$
$(x,y) \longrightarrow (y,x)$.

Zu vorgegebener Semantik $\Phi : \mathbb{L}_0(\tau) \longrightarrow \underline{Set}$

lautet das Äquivalenzproblem:

Gegeben $x,y \in \mathbb{L}_0(\tau)$ gilt $\Phi x = \Phi y$?

<u>Bez 1</u> Sei $\Omega_0 = \{d,v,p\} \cup \{A,\nu,+,\dot{-}\} \cup \{mod_k \mid k \in \mathbb{N}\} \cup \{div_k \mid k \in \mathbb{N}\}$

$Q_0, Z_0 : \Omega_0 \longrightarrow \mathbb{N} = 1^*$ so gewählt, daß sich $w \in \Omega_0$ auf die übliche Art und Weise interpretieren läßt. (A stehe für die Abfrage auf Null und ν für die Nachfolgerfunktion).

Sei $\tau_0 = (Q_0, Z_0)$ und $\Phi_0 : \mathbb{L}_0(\tau_0) \longrightarrow \underline{Set}$, die Semantik, die jedes $w \in \Omega_0$ in naheliegender Weise interpretiert. Insbesondere:

$$\Phi_0 A : \mathbb{N}_0^3 \longrightarrow \mathbb{N}_0$$

$$(x,y,z) \mapsto \begin{cases} x & \text{falls } z = 0 \\ y & \text{falls } z \neq 0 \end{cases}$$

Es gilt dann:

<u>Satz 1</u> Das Äquivalenzproblem für Φ_0 ist lösbar.

<u>Bew</u> Siehe [T].

Dieser Satz ist sehr nützlich, um die Entscheidbarkeit spezieller Loop-1-Semantiken zu zeigen.

<u>Def 3:</u> Sei $\tau = (Q,Z)$ ein Befehlsvorrat mit $\zeta, \nu \in \Omega_B$ und $Q\zeta = Z\zeta = Z\nu = a \in A$.

Definiere einen Befehlsvorrat τ' durch:

i) $\Omega' = \Omega \cup \{ f^+ \mid f \in \mathbb{L}_0(\tau)$ mit

$$Q_{\mathbb{L}_0(\tau)} f = Z_{\mathbb{L}_0(\tau)} f \}$$

ii) $Q' : \Omega' \to A^*$

$$g \to \begin{cases} Qg & \text{falls } g \in \Omega \\ (Q_{\mathbb{L}_0(\tau)} g)\, a & \text{falls } g = f^+ \in \mathbb{L}_0(\tau) \end{cases}$$

iii) $Z' : \Omega' \to A^*$

$$g \to \begin{cases} g Z & \text{falls } g \in \Omega \\ f Z_{\mathbb{L}_0(\tau)} & \text{falls } g = f^+ \in \mathbb{L}_0(\tau) \end{cases}$$

$\mathbb{L}_1(\tau) := \mathbb{L}_0(\tau')$ heißt die Kategorie der Loop-1-Programme zu τ.

$\pi(\tau) := \pi_0(\tau', E)$ sei die freie von τ' bezüglich den Relationen E erzeugte Theorie.

Dabei ist $E = \{ (id_f \times p_a), f^+ \circ (id_{Qf} \times \zeta)) \mid f \in \mathbb{L}_0(\tau)$

$$Qf = Zf \} \cup$$

$$\{ (f \circ f^+, f \overset{+}{\circ} (id_{Qf} \times \nu)) \mid f \in \mathbb{L}_0(\tau)$$

$$Qf = Zf \}.$$

Ein Funktor $\Phi : \mathbb{L}_1(\tau) \to$ Set heißt Loop-1-Semantik $\iff$ Φ faktorisiert über den kanonischen Projektionsfunktor

$$\pi : \mathbb{L}_1(\tau) \to \pi_1(\tau).$$

Durch Iteration dieses Prozesses und Übergang zum Colimes erhält man die primitiv rekursiven Funktionen zu einem beliebigen Typ τ !

Satz 2 Vor $\Omega_1 = \{ d, v, p \} \cup \{ \nu, \zeta, V \}$

$Q_1 Z_1 : \Omega_1 \to \mathbb{N}_0$ so gewählt, daß die folgende Interpretation $\Phi_1 : \mathbb{L}_1(\tau) \to$ Set möglich ist

$$\Phi_1 \nu : \mathbb{N}_0 \to \mathbb{N}_0 \qquad \phi_1 V : \mathbb{N}_0 \to \mathbb{N}_0$$
$$n \mapsto n+1 \qquad\qquad n \mapsto n \dot{-} 1$$

$$\Phi_1 \zeta : \mathbb{N}_0 \to \mathbb{N}_0$$
$$n \mapsto 0$$

Beh Das Äquivalenzproblem für Φ_1 ist lösbar.

Bew [Wö,B] Die Idee ist völlig analog zu der, die wir in Satz 3 benutzen.

Bez 2 $\Omega_2 = \{d,v,p\} \cup \{\nu,\zeta,A\}$

$Q_2, Z_2 : \Omega_2 \longrightarrow \mathbb{N}_0$ so gewählt, daß $\Phi_2\ \nu$ als Nachfolgerfunktion Φ_2 als die konstante Funktion Null und Φ_2 als Abfrage auf Null interpretieren kann.

Unser Ziel ist es zu zeigen: Das Äquivalenzproblem für Φ_2 ist lösbar.
Die Beweisidee beruht darauf einen Funktor $I: \mathbb{L}_1(\tau_2) = \mathbb{L}_0(\tau_2') \longrightarrow \mathbb{L}_0(\tau_0)$ zu konstruieren, so daß gilt: Das Diagramm

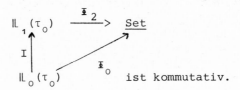

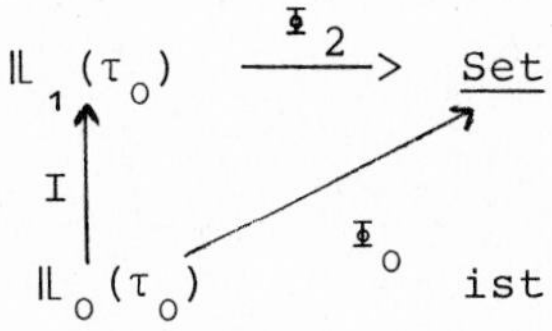

ist kommutativ.

Es gilt dann $x,y \in \mathbb{L}_1(\tau_0)$ so folgt:

$I_2 x = \Phi_2 y \iff (\Phi_0 \circ I)\, x = (\Phi_0 \circ I)\, y \iff$

$\Phi_0(Ix) = \Phi_0(I_y)$.

und damit ist das Äquivalenzproblem von Φ_2 auf das von Φ_0 zurückgeführt.
Wir legen I auf Ω_2 und damit auf $\mathbb{L}_0(\tau_2)$ fest durch:
$IA = A \quad I\nu = x \quad I\zeta = \dot{-} \circ d$. Es verbleibt I auf $\overline{\mathbb{L}_0(\tau_2)} :=$
$\{ f^+ \mid f \in \mathbb{L}_0(\tau_2)$ mit $Qf = Zf \}$ und damit auf ganz $\mathbb{L}_1(\tau_2)$ festzulegen. Hierzu berechnen wir mit Hilfe einiger Normalformensätze für $f^+ \in \mathbb{L}_0(\tau_2)$ $\Phi_2 f^+$ danach ist klar, wie man I wählen muß.

Bez 2 Mit $\langle X \rangle$ bezeichnen wir für eine Menge $X \subset \mathbb{L}_0(\tau_2)$ die von X erzeugte objektgleiche Unter-X-Kategorie von $\mathbb{L}_0(\tau_2)$.

H.S.1 $f \in \mathbb{L}_0(\tau_2) \Longrightarrow$

$\exists^1 f_0 \in \langle \{d,v,p\} \rangle,\ f_1 \in \langle \{\nu,\zeta\} \rangle$ und $f_2 \in \langle A \rangle$

mit $f\phi_2 = (f_2 \circ f_1 \circ f_0)\, \phi_2$.

Bew Da man in $\mathbb{L}_o(\tau_2)$ sequentielle Normalformen herstellen kann, zeigen die Gleichungen

$$\Phi_2(d_{fZ} \circ f) = \Phi_2((f\times f) \circ d_{fQ})$$

$$\Phi_2(v_{Z(f\times g)} \circ (f\times g)) = \Phi_2((g\times f) \circ v_{fQgQ})$$

$$\Phi_2(c \circ f) = \Phi_2(c)$$

$$\Phi_2(p \circ f) = \Phi_2(p_{fQ})$$

$$\Phi_2(f \circ A) = \Phi_2(A \circ (f\times f\times id))$$ die Behauptung.

Bem 1 $f^+, g^+ \in \mathbb{L}_o(\tau_2)$ mit $\Phi_2 f \neq \Phi_2 g$
$\Longleftrightarrow \Phi_2 f^+ \neq \Phi_2 g^+$

Bew Die Abbildung die einer Funktion ihre Iterierte zuordnet ist bijektiv (Man beachte die Komponente $(x,1)$).

Bez 3 Sei $\sim_1$ die auf $\mathbb{N}_o$ durch $x \sim_1 y \Longleftrightarrow$
$(x = o \wedge y = o) \vee (x \neq o \wedge y \neq o)$ definierte Äquivalenzrealtion
$\sim_r$ die komponentenweise Fortsetzung von $\sim_r$ auf $\mathbb{N}_o^r$.

Bem 2 $f \in \mathbb{L}_o(\tau_2)$ mit $\Phi_2 f\colon \mathbb{N}_o^r \longrightarrow \mathbb{N}_o^s \Longrightarrow$
$(x \sim_r y \Longrightarrow (\Phi_2 f)\, x \sim_s (\Phi_2 f)\, g)$

Bew Da man in $\mathbb{L}_o(\tau_2)$ sequentielle Normalformen herstellen kann, genügt es die Behauptung auf Ω_2 nachzuprüfen. Dort ist sie aber trivial.

Bem 3 $f \in \mathbb{L}_o(\tau_2)$ mit $\Phi_2 f\colon \mathbb{N}_o^r \longrightarrow \mathbb{N}_o^r$
und $\pi_r\colon \mathbb{N}_o^r \longrightarrow \mathbb{N}_{o/\sim r}^r$ die natürliche Projektion. Dann gilt
$^1\delta_f\colon \mathbb{N}_{o/\sim r}^r \longrightarrow \mathbb{N}_{o/\sim r}^r$ mit $\delta_f \circ \pi_r = \pi_r \circ \Phi_2 f$.

Bew Mit $\Phi_2 f$ ist auch $\pi_r \circ \Phi_2 f$ mit $\sim_r$ verträglich.

H.S. 2 Vor wie in Bem 3, zusätzlich:

$$w_r\colon \mathbb{N}_o^{r\,\mathbb{N}_o^r} \times \mathbb{N}_o^r \longrightarrow \mathbb{N}_o^r$$
$$(f,x) \longmapsto fx$$

Beh $\exists \Psi : \mathbb{N}_0^r /_{\sim r} \longrightarrow \mathbb{N}_0^{r\,\mathbb{N}_0^r}$ mit

$\Phi_2 f = w_r \circ (\Psi \times id) \circ (\pi_r \times id) \circ \Phi_2 d_r$.

Bew Zu vorgegebenen $f \in \mathbb{L}_0(\tau_2)$ konstruiere man eine Normalform f' gemäß H.S.1. Zu $x \in \{0,1\}^r \subset \mathbb{N}_0^r$ konstruiere man $g_{\bar{x}} \in \langle \{d,v,p\} \rangle \circ \langle \{\nu, \zeta\} \rangle$

mit $y \in \mathbb{N}_0^r \; y \sim_r x \Longrightarrow (\Phi_2 g_{\bar{x}})\, y = (\Phi_2 f')\, y = (\Phi_2 f)\, y$

Da jede Äquivalenzklasse durch ein $x \in \{0,1\}^r$ repräsentiert wird, leistet die Festsetzung

$$x \in \{0,1\}^r \Rightarrow \Psi\bar{x} = \Phi_2 g_{\bar{x}}$$

das Gewünschte.

H.S.3 Vor wie in H.S.2

Beh $n \in \mathbb{N}_0 \Longrightarrow f\overset{n}{x} = ((\Psi\, \delta_f^{n-1}\, \bar{x}) \circ \ldots \circ \Psi(\bar{x}))\, x$

Bew Mittels vollständiger Induktion unter Beachtung von H.S.2.

Satz 3 Das Äquivalenzproblem für Φ_2 ist lösbar.

Bew Es verbleibt den Funktor I auf $\overline{\mathbb{L}_0(\tau_2)}$ festzulegen. Zu vorgegebenen $f \in \overline{\mathbb{L}_0(\tau_2)}$ bestimme man zunächst eine Normalform f' mit $f\Phi_2 = f'\Phi_2$ gemäß H.S.1. Hieraus berechne man $\delta := \delta_{f'}$ und Ψ. Da δ auf einer endlichen Menge operiert gibt es $i,k \in \mathbb{N}_0 (k>0)$ mit $\delta^i = \delta^{i+k}$, (und solch ein Paar kann man effektiv finden). Damit gilt dann aber: Für $n \geq i$ folgt:

$$\Psi\,\delta^n \bar{x} \circ \ldots \circ \Psi\bar{x} = \Psi\,\delta^{i+mod_k\,(n \dot{-} i)}\bar{x} \circ \ldots \circ \Psi\,\delta^{i+1}\bar{x}$$

$$\circ (\Psi\,\delta^{i+k-1}\bar{x} \circ \ldots \circ \Psi\bar{x}).$$

Nach H.S.2 kann man zu $\bar{x} \varepsilon \{0,1\}^r$ ein $g_{\bar{x}} \varepsilon <\{d,v,p,\zeta,\nu\}>$ finden mit $\Psi\bar{x} = \Phi_2 g_{\bar{x}}$. Da $\beta\bar{x}: = (\Psi\,\delta^{i+k-1}\bar{x} \circ \ldots \Psi\delta^{i}\bar{x})$ ein endliches Produkt solcher Funktionen darstellt, gibt es auch ein $g'_{\bar{x}} \varepsilon <\{d,v,p,\nu,\zeta\}>$ mit $\Psi\bar{x} = I_2 g'_{\bar{x}}$. Nach Satz 2 kann man also ein $h_{\bar{x}} \varepsilon \mathbb{L}_0(\tau_0)$ finden mit:

$$\Phi_2 g'^{+}_{\bar{x}} = \Phi_0 h_{\bar{x}}.$$

Die Anzahl der Rekursionsschritte n läßt sich mit Hilfe eines Ausdrucks in div_k korrigieren. (Man beachte: "1 Schritt für $g'_{\bar{x}}$ entspricht k Schritten von $g_{\bar{x}}$"). Für Funktionen $\beta_{\bar{x},j}: = \Psi\,\delta^{i+j}\,\bar{x} \circ \ldots \circ \Psi\delta^{i+1}\bar{x}$

$j = 1,\ldots,k-1$ lassen sich Ausdrücke $h_{\bar{x},j} \varepsilon <\{d,v,p,\nu,\zeta\}>$ als insbesondere $h'_{\bar{x},j} \varepsilon \mathbb{L}_0(\tau_0)$ finden mit

$$\beta_{\bar{x},j} = \Phi_2\, h_{\bar{x},j} = \Phi\, h'_{\bar{x},j}.$$

Welcher dieser Korrekturausdrücke anzuwenden ist, läßt sich mit Hilfe von mod_k feststellen. Analog verfährt man mit $\Psi\,\delta^{j}\bar{x} \circ \ldots \circ \Psi\bar{x}$ mit $j \leq i-1$.

Die so gewonnenen Ausdrücke lassen sich mit Hilfe der Fallentscheidung durch Prädikate der Form $y \,\varepsilon\, \bar{x}$ zu einem Ausdruck a mit $\Phi_2 f^{+} = \Phi_2 f'^{+} = \Phi_0 a$ zusammensetzen.

Definiere nun einen Funktor $I: \mathbb{L}_1(\tau_2) \longrightarrow \mathbb{L}_0(\tau_0)$ der jedem $f \,\varepsilon\, \mathbb{L}_0(\tau_2)$ ein $f' \varepsilon\, \mathbb{L}_0(\tau_0)$ wie oben zuordnet. Das betrachtete Diagramm ist dann kommutativ und somit das Äquivalenzproblem von $\mathbb{L}_1(\tau_2)$ auf $\mathbb{L}_0(\tau_0)$ zurückgeführt und somit entscheidbar.

<u>Bez 8</u> $\Omega_3 = \{p,d,v\} \cup \{A,\nu,V,\zeta\}$

τ_3 und $\Phi_3: \mathbb{L}_1(\tau_3) \longrightarrow$ <u>Set</u> seien so gewählt, daß Φ_3 jedes $\omega \varepsilon \Omega_3$ in naheliegender Weise interpretiert.

Da das Halteproblem für Registermaschinen nicht lösbar ist, genügt es, das Äquivalenzproblem für $\mathfrak{I}_3$ auf das Halteproblem für Registermaschinen zurückzuführen, um seine Unlösbarkeit nachzuweisen.

Satz Das Äquivalenzproblem für $\mathfrak{I}_3$ ist nicht lösbar.

Bew Die Definition für Registermaschinen sei so getroffen, daß sie nach Erreichen des Endzustandes in diesem verbleibt und die Registerinhalte nicht mehr verändert. Zu vorgegebener Registermaschine R mit Überfrüfungsfunktion δ konstruiert man einen Ausdruck $\Delta \in \mathbb{L}_o(\tau_3)$ für dessen Interpretation $\mathfrak{I}_3 \Delta : \mathbb{N}_o^{r+2} \longrightarrow \mathbb{N}_o^{r+2}$ gilt: Die erste Komponente simuliert das Zustandsverhalten von R, die nächsten r Komponenten nehmen die Registerinhalte auf und in der letzten Komponente wird genau dann eine '1' notiert, wenn R ein Endzustand ist, eine 'O' sonst. In $\mathbb{L}_o(\tau_3)$ konstruiere man Ausdrücke q mit $\mathfrak{I}_3 q : \mathbb{N}_o^{r+2} \longrightarrow \mathbb{N}_o$ ist die Projektion auf die letzte Komponente, sowie für $x \in \mathbb{N}_o^r$ Ausdrücke a_x mit $\mathfrak{I}_3 a_x : \mathbb{N}_o \longrightarrow \mathbb{N}_o^{r+3}$

$$z \longrightarrow (q_o, x, o, z)$$

Es gilt dann:

$\mathfrak{I}_3 (q \circ \Delta^+ \circ a_x) = \mathfrak{I}_3 \zeta \iff$ R angesetzt auf $x = (x_1, \ldots, x_r)$ hält nicht an. Also ist das Äquivalenzproblem für $\mathfrak{I}_3$ nicht lösbar.

Literatur

[B] H. Beck, Zur Entscheidbarkeit der funktionalen Äquivalenz, Automata Theory and Formal Languages 2nd GI Conference, Springer Lecture Notes 33, 1975.

[C] V. Claus, Crossing Functions I, Berichtsreihe der Abteilung Informatik an der Universität Dortmund 11/75.

[Hu] H. Huwig, Beziehungen zwischen beschränkter syntaktischer und beschränkter primitiver Rekursion, Dissertation.

[Ho] G. Hotz, Schaltkreistheorie, Walter de Gruyter, 1974.

[Wö] K. Wöhl, Untersuchungen über das Äquivalenzproblem einfacher Programme, Dissertation (in Vorbereitung).

[T] D. Tsichritzis, The equivalence problem of simple programs, JACM 17 (1970)

A COMPARATIVE STUDY OF ONE-COUNTER IANOV SCHEMES

Tadashi AE, Toru Kikuno and Norio Tamura

1. Introduction

Most of extensions from Ianov schemes are apt to make the scheme equivalence problem undecidable, although it would be desirable to be decidable for further researches of program schemes (e.g., the normal form of programs). For convenience we classify these extensions into two categories as follows;

i) many variable schemes, i.e., flowchart schemes, and

ii) recursion schemes.

(In general, i) and ii) are not disjoint, and therefore ii) implies here the "monadic" case.) As for i) the strong equivalence problem is undecidable for most cases (even for the case of two variables). On the other hand, it is expected to be decidable for rather large subclasses of ii) (even for the whole class).

With respect to Ianov schemes with one counter, namely, one-counter Ianov schemes, the direction of extension lies between i) and ii), and the strong equivalence problem of these schemes becomes decidable by Valiant's result of deterministic one-counter automata[1]. In Section 3 we shall state this proof and, in Section 4, it is shown that the class of one-counter Ianov schemes is properly contained by the class of two-variable-independent flowchart schemes with an equality test. Moreover, in Section 5, it is proved that the class of one-counter Ianov schemes is imcomparable with the class of monadic recursion schemes.

As a similar extension to ours, Indermark's scheme[8] is already known, and its strong equivalence problem is decidable[9]. However, these two schemes (Indermark's and ours) belong to different classes of schemes.

2.Definitions

We define an n-variables monadic flowchart scheme (shortly, flowchart scheme) as follows;

1. Start statement; START($x_1,\ldots,x_n$), where $x_1,\ldots,x_n$ are variables.
2. Function statement; $x_j=f_k(x_i)$, where $1\leq i,j\leq n$, and $\{f_k\}$ is the finite set of function symbols.
3. Predicate statement; $P_\ell(x_i)$, where $1\leq i\leq n$, and $\{P_\ell\}$ is the finite set of predicate symbols.
4. Loop statement; LOOP.
5. Halt statement; HALT($x_1,\ldots,x_n$).

A flowchart scheme S over a finite set Σ_s of the above symbols (statements) is a finite flow diagram constructed from statements over Σ_s with one Start symbol.

If S is a flowchart scheme such that any function statement is allowed for the case of i=j only, then S is said to be a varible-independent flowchart scheme. An interpretation I defines a set D, the domain, and assigns a mapping from D to D, for each function symbol f_k, and a mapping from D to $\{T, F\}$, for each predicate symbol P_ℓ . Only the variables in the start symbol have initial values ξ defined by I. After the computation had a regular halt, the value of $\langle S,I,\xi\rangle$(shortly, val $\langle S,I,\xi\rangle$) is the value of contents of variables in the halt statement. A scheme S_a is strongly equivalent to a scheme S_b if and only if val $\langle S_a,I,\xi\rangle$= val $\langle S_b,I,\xi\rangle$ for any interpretation I and any initial value ξ . (ξ is often omitted when no confusion arises.) If there exists a scheme in a class $\mathcal{L}_b$ which is strongly equivalent to any scheme in a class $\mathcal{L}_a$, then $\mathcal{L}_a$ is said to be translatable into $\mathcal{L}_b$, and otherwise to be not translatable into $\mathcal{L}_b$. If $\mathcal{L}_a$ and $\mathcal{L}_b$ are not translatable to each other, then $\mathcal{L}_a$ (or $\mathcal{L}_b$) is said to be imcomparable with $\mathcal{L}_b$ (or $\mathcal{L}_a$).

A monadic recursion scheme (shortly, S_{RS}) is a finite list of definitional equations;

$F_1(x)$:= if $P_1(x)$ then $\alpha_1(x)$ else $\beta_1(x)$

$\vdots$

$F_n(x)$:= if $P_n(x)$ then $\alpha_n(x)$ else $\beta_n(x)$,

where $F_1,\ldots,F_n$ are new defined functional variables (symbols), $P_1,\ldots,P_n$ are (not necessarily distinct) predicates, and $\alpha_1, \beta_1,\ldots\ldots,\alpha_n, \beta_n$ are (possibly empty) strings of defined and basis function symbols.
We denote by $\mathcal{L}_{RS}$ the class of all monadic recursion schemes.

Besides S_{RS} and $\mathcal{L}_{RS}$, we introduce following definitions and notations;

$\mathcal{L}_1$; the class of one-variable flowchart schemes, i.e., Ianov schemes (shortly, S_1).

$\mathcal{L}_{1C}$; the class of Ianov schemes with one counter, i.e., one-counter Ianov schemes (shortly, S_{1C}), where the counter is a variable with fixed interpretation such that possible assignments are C=C+1 and C=C-1 , and the possible test is " if C=0 " . (Initially, C is set to be 0.)

$\mathcal{L}_{2E}$; the class of two-variable-independent flowchart schemes with an equality test (shortly, S_{2E}) such as " if $x_1=x_2$ " , where x_1 and x_2 are variables.

(About more definitions, see e.g.[2,3 and 12].)

3.Strong Equivalence problem of S_{1C}

The following proposition is proved by Valiant[1].

Proposition 1. The problem whether any two deterministic one-counter automata (shortly, doca) are equivalent or not is decidable.

This proposition implies that it is also decidable whether, for any S_a and S_b in $\mathcal{L}_{1C}$, S_a is strongly equivalent to S_b or not. Using a standard technique we shall state its proof. For an S_{1C} in $\mathcal{L}_{1C}$ we denote by $P_1,\ldots,P_\ell$ the predicate symbols, and by $f_1,\ldots,f_k$ the function symbols. The interpreted value of S_{1C} under a free interpretation I (shortly, $val^{\#}_I(S_{1C})$) [3] is given as a sequence such as $[xP_{01}\ldots P_{0\ell}][f_1P_{11}\ldots P_{1\ell}][f_2P_{21}\ldots P_{2\ell}]\ldots$ $[f_kP_{k1}\ldots P_{k\ell}]$, where val $\langle S_{1C},I\rangle=f_k\ldots f_2f_1$ and P_{ij} is identical to the value

(T or F) of $P_j(f_i \dots f_2 f_1)$ under I. The interpreted value language $L^{\#}(S)$ is defined as the set of $val_I^{\#}(S)$ under all free interpretations I [3].

Then , we shall show a construction of the doca $A(S_{1C})$ which accepts exactly $L^{\#}(S_{1C})$. In $A(S_{1C})$, $[xP_{01} \dots P_{0\ell}]$ or $[f_i P_{i1} \dots P_{i\ell}]$ is an input symbol. If S_{1C} executes START, then $A(S_{1C})$ reads $[xP_{01} \dots P_{0\ell}]$, advances one step on the input tape and memorizes $P_{01} \dots P_{0\ell}$ by an internal state. At that time, the content of the counter is empty. (The counter is said to be "zero".) In general, $A(S_{1C})$ memorizes $P_{i1} \dots P_{i\ell}$ by an internal state, if its input head is in the symbol $[f_{i+1} P_{(i+1)1} \dots P_{(i+1)\ell}]$ after having read $[xP_{01} \dots P_{0\ell}] \dots [f_i P_{i1} \dots P_{i\ell}]$. According to the execution of S_{1C} , $A(S_{1C})$ behaves as the following way.

(1) If x=f(x) (a function statement is executed in S_{1C}) and f is identical to f_{i+1} , then $A(S_{1C})$ reads $[f_{i+1} P_{(i+1)1} \dots P_{(i+1)\ell}]$, advances the input head, and memorizes newly $P_{(i+1)1} \dots P_{(i+1)\ell}$ by an internal state.

(2) If $P_j(x)$=T or F (a predicate statement is executed in S_{1C}), then $A(S_{1C})$ checks whether P_{ij}=T or F. At that time, $A(S_{1C})$ makes ε-move and does not change the internal state.

(3) If HALT is executed in S_{1C} , then $A(S_{1C})$ checks whether the counter is zero or not, and if it is zero, then $A(S_{1C})$ accepts the input tape. (Without loss of generality, we can assume that any S_{1C} arrives at HALT in " zero " counter.)

(4) If LOOP is executed in S_{1C} , then $A(S_{1C})$ rejects the input tape.

From (1) to (4), the content of the counter is invariant.

(5) If C=C+1 in S_{1C} , then $A(S_{1C})$ increases the counter by one.

(6) If C=C-1 in S_{1C} , then $A(S_{1C})$ decreases the counter by one except for the case where the counter is zero.

(7) If C=0 test is executed in S_{1C} , then $A(S_{1C})$ checks whether the counter is zero or not. At that time, the content of the counter is invariant.

From (5) to (7), $A(S_{1C})$ makes ε-moves without changing the internal state.

The doca $A(S_{1C})$ constructed as the above accepts exactly $L^{\#}(S_{1C})$. Therefore, for any S_a and S_b in $\mathcal{L}_{1C}$, S_a is strongly equivalent to S_b if and only if $A(S_a)$ is equivalent to $A(S_b)$.

Proposition 2. The strong equivalence problem of S_{1C} is decidable.

4.Relation between $\mathcal{L}_{1C}$ and $\mathcal{L}_{2E}$ –

If $\mathcal{L}_a$ and $\mathcal{L}_b$ are translatable to each other, then $\mathcal{L}_a$ is said to be identical to $\mathcal{L}_b$. It is already known that the class of (monadic) flowchart schemes with one counter is identical to the class of those without counter[4]. However, if we obtain a flowchart scheme without counter which is strongly equivalent to a flowchart scheme with one counter, then the number of increased variables is finite but unbounded. The situation is same for S_{1C} and therefore an S_{1C} is translated into a (monadic) flowchart scheme, generally, with more than two variables. To obtain a more compact result, we introduce an additional programming feature,i.e., an equality test such as " if $x_1=x_2$ " , and define S_{2E} and $\mathcal{L}_{2E}$ as in Section 2. Then we obtain the following.

Theorem 1. $\mathcal{L}_{1C}$ is properly contained by $\mathcal{L}_{2E}$.

Outline of proof. For any S_{1C} in $\mathcal{L}_{1C}$ we can construct an S_{2E} to simulate exactly S_{1C} . We explain it using an example, since the formal proof requires too many pages[5].

step i) Transform S_{1C} (e.g. Fig.1) into the graphical representation G_{1C} (as in Fig.2).

Two variables x_1 and x_2 of S_{2E} follow the variable x of S_{1C} , but both are limited as follows;

* x_1 can follow x, independently of x_2 , if the associated value† of x is +1

†) We call the associated value of x to be c , if the statement to x is represented as an edge label (f,c) in G_{1C} , where f may be a (T or F) predicate.

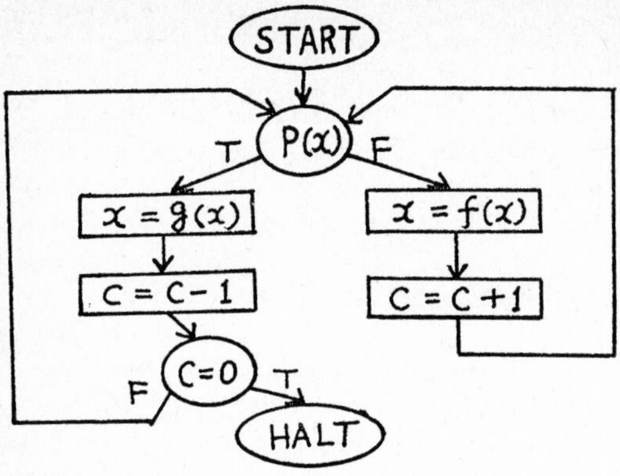

Fig.1. A one-counter Ianov scheme
(In figures the variables of START or HALT are omitted.)

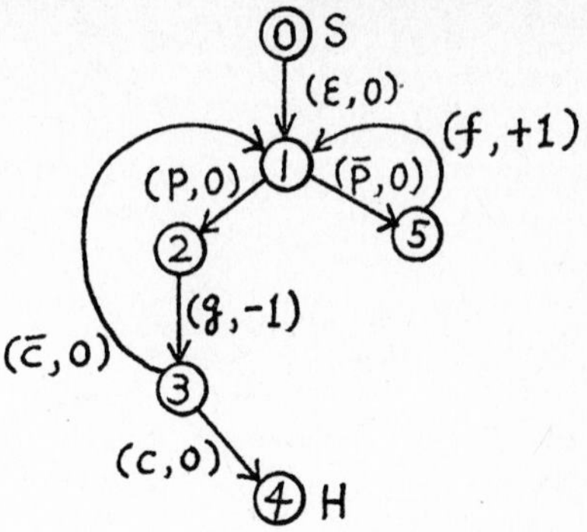

Fig.2. The graphical representation G_{1C} of the scheme in Fig.1.

or 0, but can follow x whose associated value is -1 if and only if x_2 can follow x whose associated value is +1.

** x_2 can follow x independently of x_1 , if the associated value of x is -1 or 0, but can follow x whose associated value is +1 if and only if x_1 can follow x whose associated value is -1. (The latter is the same condition of * .)

For this purpose we introduce the graphical representation G_{2E} which corresponds to S_{2E} .

step ii) Transform G_{1C} into G_{2E} . (G_{1C} in Fig.2 is transformed into G_{2E} in Fig.3.)

step iii) Transform G_{2E} into S_{2E} . (G_{2E} in Fig.3 is transformed into S_{2E} in Fig.4.)

The correctness of this procedure can be proved formally[5]. Then, there exists an S_{2E} which is strongly equivalent to any S_{1C} .

The class of value languages† of S_{1C} is context-free, but there exists a scheme S_{2E} whose value language is context-sensitive. For example, the scheme in Fig.5 has the value language $\{ h^n g^n f^n / \ n \geq 1 \}$. Two schemes

---

†) The value language of a scheme S is defined as the set of val $\langle S,I \rangle$ under all free interpretations I [3].

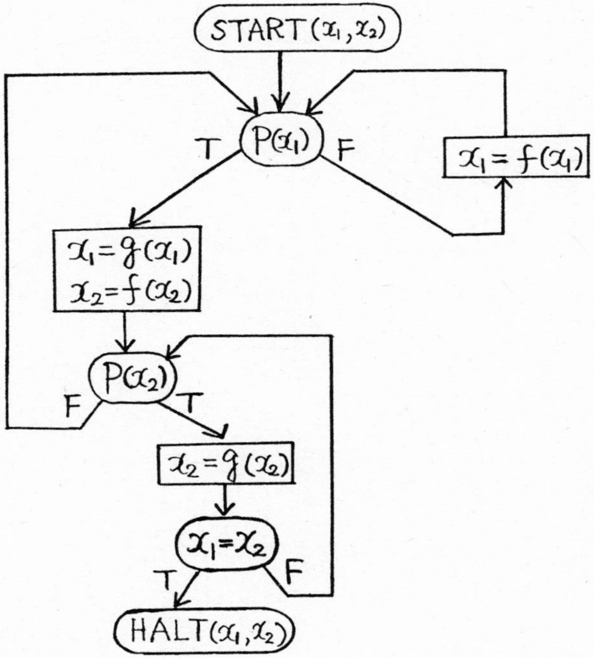

Fig.4. A scheme S_{2E} which is strongly equivalent to the scheme in Fig.1.

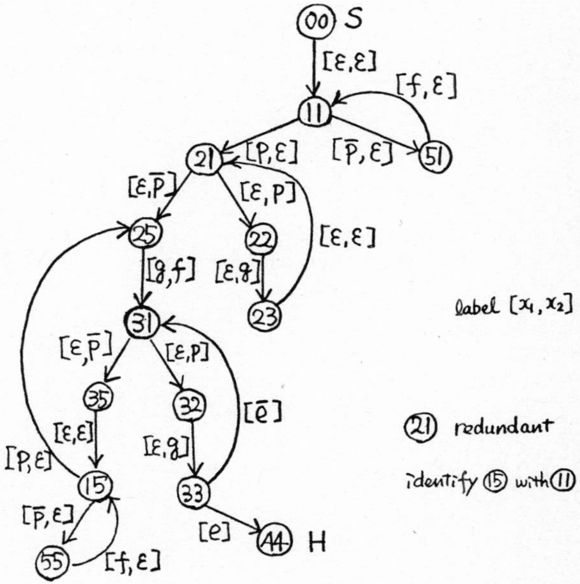

Fig.3. The graphical representation G_{2E} which simulates G_{1C} in Fig.2.

which have distinct value languages cannot be strongly equivalent[3].

Therefore we conclude that $\mathcal{L}_{1C}$ is properly contained by $\mathcal{L}_{2E}$.

q.e.d.

Since the flowchart scheme with the equality test is no longer monadic, the three-variable-independent flowchart scheme with the equality test can trivially simulate S_{1C} . Then, the theorem 1 implies that " two variables " are enough to simulate S_{1C} , if we allow an equality test to be used.

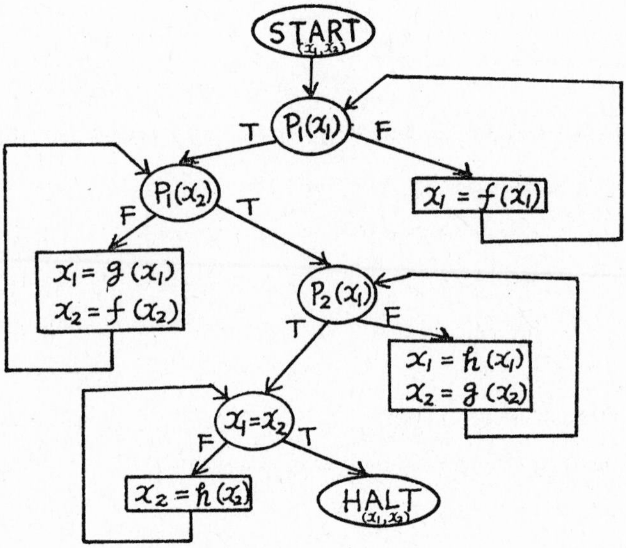

Fig.5. A scheme S_{2E} which is not strongly equivalent to any one-counter Ianov schemes.

5.Comparison with Monadic Recursion Schemes

It is already known that there exists an S_{RS} which is not strongly equivalent to any (n-variables) monadic flowchart scheme with one counter [3,4]. Then, we shall prove the opposite part in the case of S_{1C} .

Theorem 2. There exists an S_{1C} which is not strongly equivalent to any S_{RS} .

Proof. We shall prove that the scheme S_d of Fig.6 is not strongly equivalent to any S_{RS} . For S_d we define two sets of free interpretations $\{I_n^*\}$ and $\{H_n^*\}$ ($n \geq 1$) as follows;

$$I_n^* : \quad \begin{array}{ll} P_1(f^i(x))=T & (\ 0 \leq i < n\ ) \\ P_1(f^i(x))=F & (\ n \leq i\ ) \\ P_2(f^i(x))=F & (\ i \neq n\ ) \\ P_2(f^n(x))=T & \end{array}$$

and

$$H_n^* : \quad \begin{array}{ll} P_1(f^i(x))=T & (\ 0 \leq i < n\ ) \\ P_1(f^i(x))=F & (\ n \leq i\ ) \\ P_2(f^i(x))=F & (\ \text{for all } i\ ) \end{array} .$$

Then, we obtain that val $\langle S_d , I_n^* \rangle = f^{2n}$ and val $\langle S_d , H_n^* \rangle = f^n$. Suppose that there exists an S_{RS} which is strongly equivalent to S_d . Then, the computation of $\langle S_{RS} , H_n^* \rangle$ is shown as

$$\alpha_0 \rightarrow \alpha_1 \rightarrow \cdots\cdots\cdots \rightarrow \alpha_m = \alpha f^n \rightarrow \cdots\cdots\cdots \rightarrow f^n \quad ,$$

where α is a nonnull string of functional variables, and α_m is the term αf^n which appears for the first time. It should be noticed that only the interpretation $P_r(f^n(x))=F$ ($r=1,2$) is applied to each functional variable F_i of α on the computation of $\alpha f^n \rightarrow \cdots \rightarrow f^n$. Even for $f^j(x)$ ($j>n$) we obtain that $\alpha f^j \rightarrow \cdots \rightarrow f^j$ if $P_r(f^j(x))=F$ ($r=1,2$).

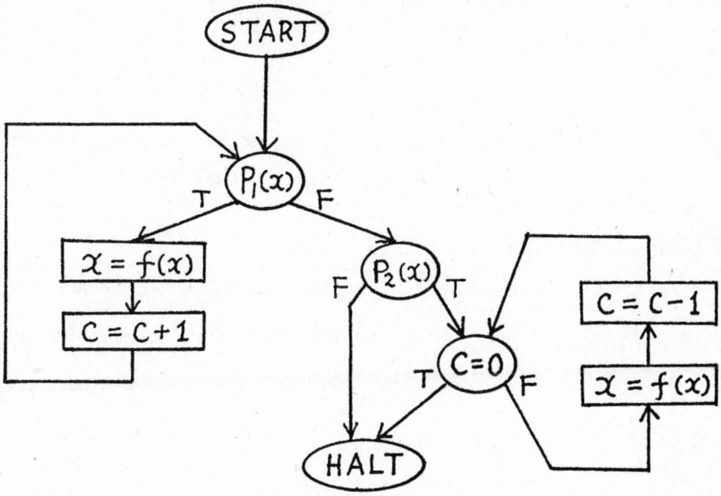

Fig.6. A one-counter Ianov scheme S_d which is not strongly equivalent to any monadic recursion scheme.

Since S_{RS} cannot distinguish I_n^* from H_n^* for $f^i(x)$ ($i<n$), the computation of $\langle S_{RS}, I_n^* \rangle$ is

$$\alpha_0 \rightarrow \alpha_1 \rightarrow \cdots\cdots \rightarrow \alpha_m = \alpha f^n \rightarrow \cdots\cdots \rightarrow f^{2n} \quad ,$$

where $\alpha = F_{m_1} F_{m_2} \ldots F_{m_k}$. Let us consider the computation of $F_{m_1} F_{m_2} \ldots F_{m_k} f^n \rightarrow \cdots \rightarrow f^{2n}$. If $F_{m_{(\ell+1)}} F_{m_{(\ell+2)}} \ldots F_{m_k} f^n \rightarrow \cdots \rightarrow f^n$ and $F_{m_\ell} F_{m_{(\ell+1)}} \ldots F_{m_k} f^n \rightarrow \cdots \rightarrow f^i f^n$ ($0 < i \leq n$) , then $F_{m_1} F_{m_2} \ldots F_{m_k} f^n \rightarrow \cdots \rightarrow F_{m_1} F_{m_2} \ldots F_{m_\ell} f^n \rightarrow \cdots \rightarrow F_{m_1} F_{m_2} \ldots F_{m_{\ell-1}} f^{i+n} \rightarrow \cdots \rightarrow f^{i+n}$ is derived, using the definition of I_n^* and the fact that $j=i+n$. Then we have that $i=n$.

Since the number of functional variables of S_{RS} is finite, there exist two distinct natural numbers n_1 and n_2 such that $F_{m_\ell(n_1)} = F_{m_\ell(n_2)}$, where $F_{m_\ell(n_1)}$ or $F_{m_\ell(n_2)}$ is the functional variable of $\alpha_{m(n_1)} = \alpha_{(n_1)} f^{n_1}$ or, of $\alpha_{m(n_2)} = \alpha_{(n_2)} f^{n_2}$, respectively. Then, the computation from $\alpha_{m(n_1)}$ under the interpretation $I_{n_1}^*$ is same as the computation from $\alpha_{m(n_2)}$ under the interpretation $I_{n_2}^*$. Namely, we obtain that val$\langle S_{RS}, I_{n_1}^* \rangle = f^i f^{n_1}$ and val$\langle S_{RS}, I_{n_2}^* \rangle = f^i f^{n_2}$.

Therefore, either val$\langle S_{RS}, I_{n_1}^* \rangle \neq f^{2n_1}$ or val$\langle S_{RS}, I_{n_2}^* \rangle \neq f^{2n_2}$ must hold, since $n_1 \neq n_2$. However, this is a contradiction.

q.e.d.

It is also known that there exists a monadic flowchart scheme with one counter which is not strongly equivalent to any S_{RS} . Then, the theorem 2 implies a stronger case of that.

Corollary. $\mathcal{L}_{1C}$ is imcomparable with $\mathcal{L}_{RS}$.

Moreover, it is easy to show that $\mathcal{L}_{1C} \cap \mathcal{L}_{RS}$ contains properly $\mathcal{L}_1$ (the class of Ianov schemes). In the remainder of this section we shall refer to a subclass of $\mathcal{L}_{1C} \cap \mathcal{L}_{RS}$ which contains properly $\mathcal{L}_1$.

A well-formed one-counter Ianov scheme (shortly, S_w) is an S_{1C} which halts in "zero" counter and satisfies the following condition;

If the outgoing edge of lavel T (true) is cut for each C=0 test statement, then

(i) each elementary loop includes at most one C=C-1 assignment, and

(ii) for each C=C+1 assignment (say, C^{+1}), all elementary loops including C=C-1 assignment which are reachable from C^{+1} return to the same point.

We denote by $\mathcal{L}_W$ the class of S_W and show the following proposition without proof. (The details are in [6].)

Proposition 3. $\mathcal{L}_W$ is translatable into $\mathcal{L}_{RS}$ and properly contains $\mathcal{L}_1$.

Since $\mathcal{L}_{1C}$ is identical to $\mathcal{L}_{r\ell RSC}$, where $\mathcal{L}_{r\ell RSC}$ is the class of (monadic) right-linear recursion schemes with one counter, $\mathcal{L}_{1C} \cap \mathcal{L}_{RS}$ is identical to $\mathcal{L}_{r\ell RSC} \cap \mathcal{L}_{RS}$.

From the theorem 1 and the corollary of the theorem 2, $\mathcal{L}_{2E}$ is not translatable into $\mathcal{L}_{RS}$. We shall consider the opposite relation, namely, whether $\mathcal{L}_{RS}$ is translatable into $\mathcal{L}_{2E}$ or not.

The value language of S_{RS} is context-free and there exists a scheme S_{RS} whose value language is $L_B = \left\{ f^{m_1} g f^{m_2} g f^{m_3} g g f^{m_3} g f^{m_2} g f^{m_1} \;/\; m_1, m_2, m_3 \geq 1 \right\}$. On the other hand, the value language of S_{2E} is identical to the language L which is accepted by a deterministic two-head finite automaton which can sense the coincidence of positions of two heads. Moreover L_B does not belong to the class of all L .† Hence, L_B does not belong to the class of value languages of S_{2E} . Since two schemes which have distinct value languages cannot be strongly equivalent[3], $\mathcal{L}_{RS}$ is not translatable into $\mathcal{L}_{2E}$.

Proposition 4. $\mathcal{L}_{2E}$ is imcomparable with $\mathcal{L}_{RS}$.

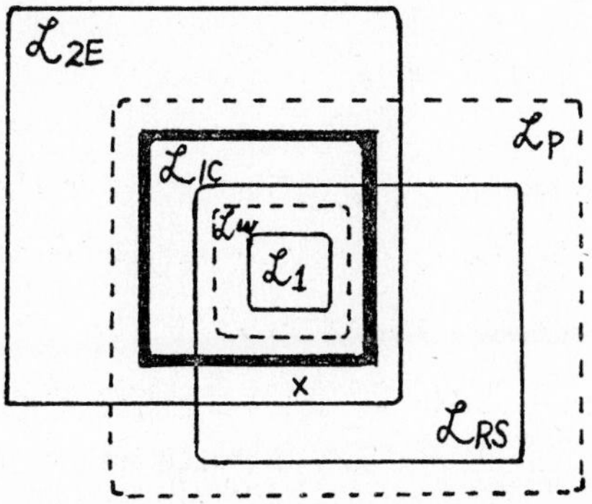

Fig.7. Relation of $\mathcal{L}_{1C}$ with other classes of schemes.

†) This proof depends on Rosenberg's paper ("On multi-head finite automata", IBM.J.R&D,10,p.388(1966)) which Ibarra et al. point out its intuitivism.

6. Summary

We summarize a comparative study of $\mathcal{L}_{1C}$ as in Fig.7, where $\mathcal{L}_{P}$ is the class of Ianov schemes with one pushdown variable and it is yet unknown whether there exists a scheme in the point **x** .

It can be easily proved just as in the case of two-variables flowchart schemes[7] that the strong equivalence problem of S_{2E} is undecidable. As is well known, the decidability of the scheme equivalence problem is yet unknown with respect to $\mathcal{L}_{RS}$ as well as $\mathcal{L}_{P}$. It is, however, known that there exists some subclass of $\mathcal{L}_{P}$ whose scheme equivalence problem is decidable. It is Indermark's scheme[8] or its extended scheme (Tokura et al.[9]), which is imcomparable with $\mathcal{L}_{1C}$ [11].

The effect of more than one counter is also discussed[10]. In this paper, however, we restrict our attention to one-counter case, because of the decidability of the scheme equivalence problem.

The complexity of S_{1C}'s equivalence problem remains as a further research. It seems, however, difficult to find an efficient algorithm, considering the result of Ianov schemes or linear recursion schemes[13].

References

[1] Valiant,L.G.,Deterministic one-counter automata, JCSS 10 (1975)340-350.

[2] Manna,Z.,Mathematical theory of computation, McGraw-Hill Inc.(1974)Chap.4.

[3] Garland,S.J.and D.C.Luckham,Program schemes, recursion schemes, and formal languages, JCSS 7 (1973)119-160.

[4] Plaisted,D.A.,Flowchart schemata with counters, Proc.4th Annual ACM Symp. on Theory of Computing (1972)44-51.

[5] Ae,T.,T.Kikuno and N.Tamura,Ianov schemes with one counter (to appear in Japanese).

[6] Tamura,N.,T.Kikuno and T.Ae,On Ianov schemas augmented by one counter - comparison with recursive schemas -, Tech.Report on IECE of Japan AL75-68 (1976) (in Japanese).

[7] Luckham,D.C.,D.M.R.Park and M.S.Paterson,On formalized computer programs, JCSS 4 (1970)220-249.

[8] Indermark,K.,On Ianov schemas with one memory location, Lecture Notes in Computer Science 2, Springer-Verlag (1973)284-293.

[9] Tokura,N.,T.Kasami and S.Furuta,Ianov schemas augmented by a pushdown memory, Proc.15th Annual Symp. on SWAT (1974)84-94.

[10]Weihrauch,K.,Program schemata with polynomial bounded counters, Information Processing Letters 3 (1975)91-96.

[11]Tamura,N.,Some problems on program schemes, Master thesis, Dept. of Electronics, Hiroshima University (1976)(in Japanese).

[12]Chandra,A.K.and Z.Manna,Program schemas with equality, Proc.4th Annual ACM Symp. on Theory of Computing (1972)52-64.

[13]Constable,R.L.,H.B.Hunt III, and S.Sahni,On the computational complexity of scheme equivalence, Tech. Report prepared for Cornell University (1974).

GROBSTRUKTUREN FÜR KONTEXTFREIE GRAMMATIKEN

E.-W. Dieterich

In allen höheren Programmiersprachen gibt es Zeichenkombinationen, durch die ein Programm grob strukturiert wird, z.B. begin...end, if...then...else...fi oder case...of [5,6,7]. Solche Zeichenkombinationen legen eine sog. "Grobstruktur" (GS) einer Grammatik fest. Ein Programmierer versucht, sich mit Hilfe von GS-Zeichen einen groben Überblick über den syntaktischen Aufbau eines Programmes zu verschaffen. Dadurch wird ein Programm in kleinere Teile zerlegt, die i.a. einfacher analysiert werden können.

Auch Algorithmen zur syntaktischen Fehlerbehandlung stützen sich häufig auf intuitiv bestimmte Grobstrukturen ab [3,4]. Ferner treten bei Untersuchungen über inkrementell übersetzbare Sprachen gewisse vorgegebene Zeichenkombinationen auf, welche die änderbaren Programmteile festlegen [2]. Automatisch strukturierende Schönschreibprogramme orientieren sich ebenfalls an charakteristischen Zeichenkombinationen.

All diese Beispiele legen es nahe, den intuitiven Begriff "Grobstruktur" einer formalen Behandlung zugänglich zu machen. Bei der Definition wird dabei besonderer Wert auf die Konstruierbarkeit von Grobstrukturen für eine gegebene kontextfreie Grammatik gelegt.

1. Einfache Grobstrukturen

Eine kontextfreie Grammatik ist ein Quadrupel $G = (V,T,P,Z)$ mit dem Vokabular V, dem terminalen Alphabet $T \subset V$, der Produktionenmenge P und dem Axiom $Z \in V-T$. $S(G) := \{x \in V^* \,/\, Z \Rrightarrow x\}$ heißt Menge der Satzformen von G. Dabei bezeichnet $\Rrightarrow$ die transitive und reflexive Hülle der Ableitungsrelation $\dashrightarrow$, V^* die Menge aller Wörter über V, ε das leere Wort und $V^+ := V^*-\{\varepsilon\}$.

Als mögliche Kandidaten für Alphabete von GS-Zeichen definieren wir:
$K \subset V$ heißt *Kernalphabet* von G :$\Leftrightarrow$ für jede Produktion $N::=x \in P$ mit $N \in K$ gilt $h_K(x) \neq \varepsilon$. Dabei ist h_K ein Homomorphismus mit

$$h_K(X) = \begin{cases} X, \text{ falls } X \in K \\ \varepsilon \quad \text{sonst.} \end{cases}$$

Die Elemente eines Kernalphabets heißen *Kernzeichen*. Durch ein Kernalphabet K ist die Menge der *Kern-Produktionen* $P_K := \{ N::=x \in P \,/\, h_K(x) \neq \varepsilon \}$ festgelegt.

Nach Definition ist sichergestellt, daß jedes nichtterminale Kernzeichen in einem Strukturbaum direkt oder über weitere Kernzeichen mit einem terminalen Kernzeichen verbunden ist.

Beispiel 1: Wir betrachten als Beispiel-Grammatik G_P einen leicht modifizierten Auszug aus der Pascal-Grammatik [7]. Das Axiom von G_P ist <program>, das terminale Alphabet besteht aus den nur rechts auftretenden Zeichen, und die Produktionen von G_P sind:

p_1 <program> ::= <type def part> <compound> .
p_2, p_3 <type def part>::= ε |<type part>
p_4, p_5 <type part> ::= type <id> = <type> ;| <type part> <id> = <type> ;
p_6 <type> ::= <record type>| ...
p_7 <record type> ::= record <field list> end
p_8 <field list> ::= <id> : <type> <variant part> | ...
p_9 <variant part> ::= <vcase> <variant list>
p_{10} <vcase> ::= case <id> : <id> of
p_{11} <compound> ::= begin <stlist> end
p_{12}, p_{13} <stlist> ::= <statement>|<stlist> ; <statement>
p_{14}, p_{15} <statement> ::= <compound>|<case st>| ...
p_{16} <case st> ::= <scase> <case field> esac
p_{17} <scase> ::= case <expr> of

Kernalphabete von G_P sind z.B.

K_1 = {record, begin, end},
K_2 = {record, begin, end, type, <type part>, case, of, <scase>, esac}.

Wegen der leeren rechten Seite von p_2 kann kein Kernalphabet <type def part> enthalten. /□/

Tritt in einem Pascal-Programm ein Teilwort record x end auf, wobei in x kein weiteres Kernzeichen aus K_1=K vorkommt, so kann man dies nach <record type> reduzieren, falls x nach <field list> (ohne Anwendung einer Kern-Produktion) reduzierbar ist; oder formal

(record x end <--- <record type> und x ∈ S_f(<field list>)).

Dabei ist für ein $u \in (V-K)^*$ $S_f(u)$ die Menge der Satzformen der *grobstrukturfreien Grammatik* $G_f(u)$ für u, die wie folgt definiert ist:

$G_f(u) = (V\cup\{Z_u\}, T_f, P_f, Z_u)$ mit $P_f := (P-P_K)\cup\{Z_u ::= u\}$, $Z_u \notin V$, $T_f := T\cup\{N \,/\, \exists N::=n \in P_K\}$.

Man beachte, daß $S_f(\varepsilon) = \{\varepsilon\}$. Es folgt unmittelbar:

Lemma 1: $S_f(u) \subset (V - K)^*$.

Die *K-Grobstruktur* GS(G,K) von G bzgl. des Kernalphabets K ist ein System von Regeln

$$R := \{(x_oA_1x_1\ldots A_nx_n \longleftarrow N \text{ und } x_\nu \in S_f(u_\nu),\ o\leq\nu\leq n)\ /$$
$$N::=u_oA_1u_1\ldots A_nu_n \in P_K,\ A_1A_2\ldots A_n \in K^+,\ u_ou_1\ldots u_n \in (V\text{-}K)^*\}$$
$$\cup\ \{(\$x\$ \longleftarrow Z' \text{ und } x \in S_f(Z))\}.$$

Dabei sei $\$, Z' \notin V$. Die Zeichenreihe $A_1A_2\ldots A_n \in K^+$ heißt *Kernmuster* von $p = (x_oA_1x_1\ldots A_nx_n \longleftarrow N \text{ und } x_\nu \in S_f(u_\nu),\ o\leq\nu\leq n) \in R$.

$v \in V^*$ ist in GS(G,K) nach $w \in V^*$ *reduzierbar*, i.Z. $v \underset{GS}{\longleftarrow} w$:⇔ es gibt eine Regel $(x_oA_1x_1\ldots A_nx_n \longleftarrow N \text{ und } x_\nu \in S_f(u_\nu), o\leq\nu\leq n) \in R$, $v = av_oA_1v_1\ldots A_nv_nb$ mit $v_\nu \in S_f(u_\nu)$, $o\leq\nu\leq n$, $w = aNb$. Mit $\underset{GS}{\Longleftarrow}$ werde die transitive und reflexive Hülle von $\underset{GS}{\longleftarrow}$ bezeichnet.

Lemma 2: $x \in S(G) \Rightarrow \$x\$ \underset{GS}{\Longleftarrow} Z'$.

Beispiel 2: Die K_1-Grobstruktur $GS(G_p,K_1)$ der Grammatik aus Beispiel 1 besteht aus folgenden Regeln:

R_1 := {(record x end <--- <record type> und x ∈ S_f(<field list>)),
(begin x end <--- <compound> und x ∈ S_f(<stlist>)),
($ x $ <--- Z' und x ∈ S_f(<program>))}.

$G_f(K_1$,<field list>) enthält z.B. die Regeln

{$Z_{\text{<field list>}}$::=<field list>,p_8,p_9,p_{10}}. □

Der intuitiven Vorstellung von Grobstrukturen folgend werden K-Grobstrukturen wie folgt eingeschränkt:

Eine K-Grobstruktur heißt *überschiebungsfrei* :⇔ sie enthält keine zwei (nicht notwendig verschiedenen) Regeln mit Kernmuster a bzw. b derart, daß

(i) $a = lbr$ mit $l, r \in K^+$ oder

(ii) $a = lc$, $b = cr$ mit $c, l, r \in K^*$ und $c \neq \varepsilon$, $lr \neq \varepsilon$.

Eine K-Grobstruktur ist insbesondere dann nicht überschiebungsfrei, wenn sie eine Regel mit Kernmuster aba, $a \neq \varepsilon$, enthält.

Die Überschiebungsfreiheit stellt sicher, daß die Kernmuster in einem Satz ohne Kontextbetrachtungen erkannt werden können [1].

Eine überschiebungsfreie K-Grobstruktur heißt *deterministisch* :⇔

(i) für jede Regel $(x_oA_1x_1\ldots A_nx_n \longleftarrow N \text{ und } x_\nu \in S_f(u_\nu), o\leq\nu\leq n)$ gilt: $u_o = u_n = \varepsilon$ (und damit $x_o = x_n = \varepsilon$) *(Kern-Randbedingung)*

(ii) es gibt keine zwei verschiedenen Regel in R mit demselben Kernmuster *(Invertierbarkeit)*.

Man beachte, daß es entscheidbar ist, ob ein $K \subset V$ ein Kernalphabet von G ist und ob eine K-Grobstruktur deterministisch ist.

Beispiel 3: Die in Beispiel 2 angegebene K_1-Grobstruktur $GS(G_p,K_1)$ ist deterministisch. $\square$

Eine Regel einer (deterministischen) K-Grobstruktur kann man nur anwenden, wenn alle ihre Bedingungen $x_\nu \in S_f(u_\nu)$ verifiziert sind. Bei der "Grobanalyse" ist jedoch die syntaktische Struktur der Wörter zwischen zwei Kernzeichen noch nicht von Interesse. Mit dem Ergebnis aus Lemma 1 definieren wir:

Ersetzt man die Bedingungen $x_\nu \in S_f(u_\nu)$ der Regeln einer deterministischen K-Grobstruktur durch die schwächeren Bedingungen $x_\nu \in (V\text{-}K)^*$, so erhält man die *K-Struktur* St(G,K) von G bzgl. K. Die Relation $\underset{St}{\leftarrow}$ ergibt sich aus $\underset{GS}{\leftarrow}$ entsprechend.

Jeder Regel p der K-Struktur ist genau eine Regel z(p) der K-Grobstruktur zugeordnet.

Die Regeln einer K-Struktur, deren Bedingungen leicht zu überprüfen sind, dienen der Erkennung von GS-Phrasen; die zugehörigen Regeln der K-Grobstruktur enthalten die für die (nachträgliche) Feinanalyse notwendige Information. Es gilt [1]:

Satz 3: Sei GS(G,K) eine deterministische K-Grobstruktur und St(G,K) die zugehörige K-Struktur von G.

(a) Für jede Satzform s von G gilt $\$s\$ \underset{St}{\Leftarrow} Z'$.

(b) Ist s Satzform von G und $\$s\$ \underset{ST}{\leftarrow} \$s'\$$, so ist auch s' Satzform von G.

(c) Sei p eine Regel der K-Struktur und $s, s' \in (V \cup \{\$,Z'\})^*$.

  (i) Ist s vermöge z(p) nach s' reduzierbar, so ist s auch vermöge p nach s' reduzierbar.

  (ii) Ist s vermöge p nach s' reduzierbar und werden (nachträglich) für die Wörter zwischen den Kernzeichen der Phrase die Bedingungen von z(p) verifiziert, so ist s auch vermöge z(p) nach s' reduzierbar.

In den grobstrukturfreien Grammatiken kann es neue Grobstrukturen geben.

Beispiel 4: In der K_1-Grobstruktur $GS(G_p,K_1)$ aus Beispiel 2 definiert das Teilalphabet $K_3 = \{$case, of$\}$ in $G_f(K_1,$<field list>$)$ sowie in $G_f(K_1,$<stlist>$)$ eine deterministische K_3-Grobstruktur. $\square$

2. Erweiterte Grobstrukturen

Neben Kernzeichen gibt es in höheren Programmiersprachen auch Zeichen, die nur in einem bestimmten Kontext für eine Grobstruktur relevant sind. Betrachten wir dazu folgendes Beispiel:

Beispiel 5: (a) Eine K-Grobstruktur von G_P mit Kernzeichen case und of verletzt die Invertierbarkeit, da ":" als Kernzeichen ungeeignet ist. Jedoch entscheidet das Fehlen bzw. Auftreten eines ":" zwischen case und of, ob ein GS-Muster für <scase> bzw. <vcase> vorliegt. Andere Auftreten von ":" wie etwa nach Marken werde dabei nicht betrachtet.
(b) Das Schlüsselwort type ist für die Produktion p_4 charakteristisch. Jedoch kann die Kern-Randbedingung nicht erfüllt werden, da ";" kein geeignetes Kernzeichen ist. Trotzdem bestimmt das erste Auftreten eines ";" nach type das Phrasenende. /̲7̲

Zur Behandlung von solchen kontextabhängigen Zeichen führen wir den Begriff der Fragmentzerlegung ein.

Sei $s \in V^*$ und $F \subset T \cup \{\varepsilon\}$ eine nichtleere Menge von sog. *Fragmenten*.
$s_L(F) := s_0;X;s_1$ heißt *L-Fragmentzerlegung* von s bzgl. F :⇔
$s = s_0 X s_1$, $X \in F$, $s_0 \in (V-F)^*$ und mit $X = \varepsilon$ ist auch $s_1 = \varepsilon$.

$s_L(F)$ ist nicht für jedes s und F definiert. Falls $s_L(F)$ definiert ist, so ist es eindeutig bestimmt und leicht aufzubauen, indem man von links das erste Auftreten eines Zeichens aus F sucht.

R-Fragmentzerlegungen $s_R(F)$ werden durch Vertauschen der Bedingungen für s_0 und s_1 definiert. Eine allgemeinere Definition der Fragmentzerlegung, wo als Fragmente Zeichenmuster anstelle einzelner Zeichen zugelassen werden, findet man in [1].

Wir erweitern nun die Regeln einer überschiebungsfreien (nicht deterministischen) K-Grobstruktur um geeignete Fragmente, um so ohne Feinanalyse
(a) zwei Regeln mit gleichem Kernmuster unterscheiden und
(b) die Phrasenränder bestimmen zu können.

In Beispiel 5 wurden dafür charakteristische Zeichen in den grobstrukturfreien Zwischenwörtern $x_\nu \in S_f(u_\nu)$ der Regeln angegeben.

Sei GS(G,K) eine überschiebungsfreie K-Grobstruktur von G. Jeder Regel

$$(1)\quad p = (x_0 A_1 x_1 \ldots A_n x_n \;\text{<---}\; N \text{ und } x_\nu \in S_f(u_\nu),\ 0 \leq \nu \leq n)$$

von GS(G,K) seien Fragmente $f(p,\nu) \in T \cup \{\varepsilon\}$ von u_ν zugeordnet, $0 \leq \nu \leq n$.

Ersetzt man jede Regel (1) durch

(2) $p' = (x_o A_1 x_1 \ldots A_n x_n$ <--- N und (FR) und (FL))

mit (FR) $u_{o,R}(f(p,u_o)) = u_o^o \; ; \; f(p,o) \; ; \; u_o^1$ und

$x_o = x_o^o \; f(p,o) \; x_o^1$ mit $x_o^\mu \in S_f(u_o^\mu)$, $o \leq \mu \leq 1$;

(FL) $u_{\nu,L}(f(p,\nu)) = u_\nu^o \; ; \; f(p,\nu) \; ; \; u_\nu^1$ und

$x_\nu = x_\nu^o \; f(p,\nu) \; x_\nu^1$ mit $x_\nu^\mu \in S_f(u_\nu^\mu)$, $o \leq \mu \leq 1$, $1 \leq \nu \leq n$;

so erhält man die *(K,f)-Grobstruktur* GS(G,K,f) von G bzgl. K und f. Die Zeichenreihe $f(p,o)A_1 f(p,1)\ldots A_n f(p,n)$ heißt *Muster* von p'.

Beispiel 6: Für die Grammatik G_P betrachten wir das in Beispiel 1 angegebene Kernalphabet K_2. Als Fragmente, die wir auf die Kern-Produktionen P_{K_2} beziehen, wählen wir

$f(p_4,1) = f(p_5,1) = \;;$ $\qquad f(p_{1o},1) = \;:$

Alle anderen Fragmente seien ε.

Dann besteht $GS(G_P,K_2,f)$ aus den Regeln

(record x end	<--- <record type>	und	x ∈ S_f(<field list>)),
(begin x end	<--- <compound>	und	x ∈ S_f(<stlist>)),
(case x : x' of	<--- <vcase>	und	x,x' ∈ S_f(<id>)),
(case x of	<--- <scase>	und	x ∈ S_f(<expr>)),
(<scase> x esac	<--- <case st>	und	x ∈ S_f(<case list>)),
(type x ;	<--- <type part>	und	x ∈ S_f(<id> = <type>)),
(<type part> x ;	<--- <type part>	und	x ∈ S_f(<id> = <type>)),
(\$ x \$	<--- Z'	und	x ∈ S_f(<program>)) .

Hier kann wieder esac durch end ersetzt werden, um so die Form von <case st> wie in der Original-Grammatik zu haben [7]. /̸7

Wie bei deterministischen K-Grobstrukturen verlangen wir für (K,f)-Grobstrukturen Invertierbarkeit und eine Randbedingung:

Eine (K,f)-Grobstruktur heißt *invertierbar* :⇔ es gibt keine zwei verschiedenen Regeln mit gleichem Muster.

Für $a = A_1 \ldots A_n \in K^+$ definieren wir die Menge der ν-ten Fragmente
$F_\nu(a) := \{ f(p,\nu) \;/\; a \text{ ist Kernmuster von } p\}$, $o \leq \nu \leq n$.

Eine (K,f)-Grobstruktur erfüllt die *Randbedingung* :⇔

(i) für alle Regeln der Form (2) gilt $u_o^o = u_n^1 = \varepsilon$;

(ii) für alle $a = A_1 \ldots A_n \in K^+$ gilt: falls $\varepsilon \in F_\mu(a)$, so ist $F_\mu(a) = \{\varepsilon\}$ für $\mu \in \{o,n\}$.

Durch die Bedingung (ii) ist eindeutig bestimmt, ob links von A_1 bzw. rechts von A_n ein nichtleeres Fragmentzeichen zu suchen ist.

Beim Auftreten eines Kernmusters $a = A_1 \ldots A_n$ ist i.a. noch nicht bekannt, welche GS-Regel mit diesem Kernmuster anzuwenden ist. Dies soll durch Fragmentzerlegungen bzgl. der $F_\nu(a)$ auf die grobstrukturfreien Zwischenwörter $s_\nu \in S_f(u_\nu)$ bestimmt werden. Dazu benötigen wir noch die folgende Bedingung:

Eine invertierbare (K,f)-Grobstruktur, die die Randbedingung erfüllt, heißt *deterministisch* :⇔ für jede Regel (2) mit $a = A_1 \ldots A_n$ gilt:

(DR) Ist $u_{o,R}(f(p,o)) = u_o^o \,;\, X \,;\, u_o^1$, so ist

$\forall s \in S_f(u_o)$: $s_R(F_o(a)) = s^o \,;\, X \,;\, s^1$ mit $s^\mu \in S_f(u_o^\mu)$, $o \leq \mu \leq 1$;

(DL) Ist $u_{\nu,L}(f(p,\nu)) = u_\nu^o \,;\, X \,;\, u_\nu^1$, so ist

$\forall s \in S_f(u_\nu)$: $s_L(F_\nu(a)) = s^o \,;\, X \,;\, s^1$ mit $s^\mu \in S_f(u_\nu^\mu)$, $o \leq \mu \leq 1, 1 \leq \nu \leq n$.

Satz 4: Es ist entscheidbar, ob eine (K,f)-Grobstruktur von G deterministisch ist.

Beweis: Die Invertierbarkeit und die Randbedingung ergeben sich direkt aus der Angabe von GS(G,K,f). Zur Determiniertheit betrachtet man für jede Regel der Form (2) die reduzierte grobstrukturfreie Grammatik $G_f(k,u_\nu^o) = (V_f, T_f, P_f, Z_{u_\nu^o})$, $1 \leq \nu \leq n$. (DL) ist genau dann erfüllt, wenn $T_f \cap F_\nu(a) = \emptyset$. Symmetrisch argumentiert man mit $G_f(K,u_o^1)$ für (DR). /7

Um bei der Grobanalyse wieder die syntaktische Struktur der grobstrukturfreien Zwischenwörter nicht überprüfen zu müssen, ordnen wir einer deterministischen (K,f)-Grobstruktur eine *(K,f)-Struktur* zu, indem wir die Bedingungen (FR) und (FL) der Regeln (2) ersetzen durch

(FR') $x_o \in (V-K)^*$ und $x_{o,R}(F_o(a)) = \varepsilon \,;\, f(p,o) \,;\, x_o^1$

(FL') $x_\nu \in (V-K)^*$ und $x_{\nu,L}(F_\nu(a)) = x_\nu^o \,;\, f(p,\nu) \,;\, x_\nu^1$ für $1 \leq \nu \leq n$.

Damit ist wie in Abschnitt 2 jeder Regel der (K,f)-Struktur genau eine Regel der (K,f)-Grobstruktur zugeordnet.

Aus der Invertierbarkeit folgt, daß durch das gefundene Muster die anzuwendende Regel eindeutig bestimmt ist. Zur Konstruktion der Fragmentzerlegungen braucht man nur die entsprechenden Fragmentmengen, aber nicht das Kernmuster zu kennen, in dem gerade gearbeitet wird. Dadurch könnte es vorkommen, daß man in zwei Zwischenwörtern eines Kernmusters Fragmente findet, die in keinem Muster gemeinsam vorkommen können. (DR) und (DL) stellen jedoch sicher, daß bei syntaktisch korrekten Satzformen nur Muster aufgebaut werden können und aus der zugeordneten Regel der (K,f)-Grobstruktur die korrekte Information für die Feinanalyse erhalten wird.

Man kann Satz 3 auf (K,f)-Grobstrukturen und (K,f)-Strukturen erweitern.

Beispiel 7: Die (K_2,f)-Grobstruktur ist deterministisch: sie ist offensichtlich invertierbar und erfüllt die Randbedingung. Ferner tritt in G_f(<id>) kein ":" auf und in G_f(<id> = <type>) kein ";". Die (K_2,f)-Struktur $St(G_P,K_2,f)$ enthält u.a. die Regeln

(case x of <--- <vcase> und $x \in (V-K_2)^*$, $x_L(\{:\}) = x' \; ; \; : \; ; \; x''$),

(case x of <--- <scase> und $x \in (V-K_2)^*$, $x_L(\{:\}) = x \; ; \; \varepsilon \; ; \; \varepsilon$). □

In [1] wird ein Algorithmus zur Konstruktion von K- und (K,f)-Strukturen für kontextfreie Grammatiken angegeben. Dabei wird berücksichtigt, daß für die Fehlerbehandlung Grobstrukturen mit möglichst vielen GS-Zeichen erwünscht sind, während man zur Vereinfachung der syntaktischen Analyse Grobstrukturen mit so wenigen GS-Zeichen sucht, daß gerade noch gewisse "kritische" Produktionenpaare getrennt werden.

3. Automatenmodell

Die Zweistufigkeit der Analyse mit Hilfe einer Grobstruktur spiegelt sich in einem Automatenmodell darin wieder, daß ein spezieller Automat die Grobanalyse erledigt und Information über die auszuführende Feinanalyse an Kellerautomaten weitergibt, die aus den grobstrukturfreien Grammatiken konstruiert werden. Die einzelnen Automaten werden durch einen übergeordneten *Steuerautomaten* angestoßen.

Der Automat zur Grobanalyse nach einer K-Struktur muß gezielt die Kernzeichen betrachten können, die in einer Satzform weit verstreut auftreten. Dazu verallgemeinern wir das Konzept eines (bottom-up-)Kellerautomaten zu einem sog. *K^*-Automaten*, der als Kellerelemente wieder Keller besitzt und nur die obersten Zeichen der einzelnen Keller betrachten kann. Die Keller werden dabei so aufgebaut, daß die obersten Elemente Kernzeichen sind.

Nach dem Einlesen eines Kernzeichens können zwei Fälle auftreten: falls die obersten Elemente der obersten Keller kein Kernmuster bilden, wird ein neuer Keller erzeugt und weiter eingelesen (Beispiel 8b); sonst wird das Kernmuster durch das zugehörige Nonterminal ersetzt (Beispiel 8d). Über den Steuerautomaten werden außer der angewendeten Produktion die zu löschenden Keller zusammen

Beispiel 8: Wir betrachten die K_1-Grobstruktur aus Beispiel 2. In den Konfigurationen eines K^*-Automaten bezeichnet $ den untersten Keller sowie das Ende der Eingabe; die Zustände sind im Beispiel irrelevant. Man beachte, daß die Kellerelemente spiegelbildlich zu lesen sind. x^s bezeichne das Spiegelbild von x.

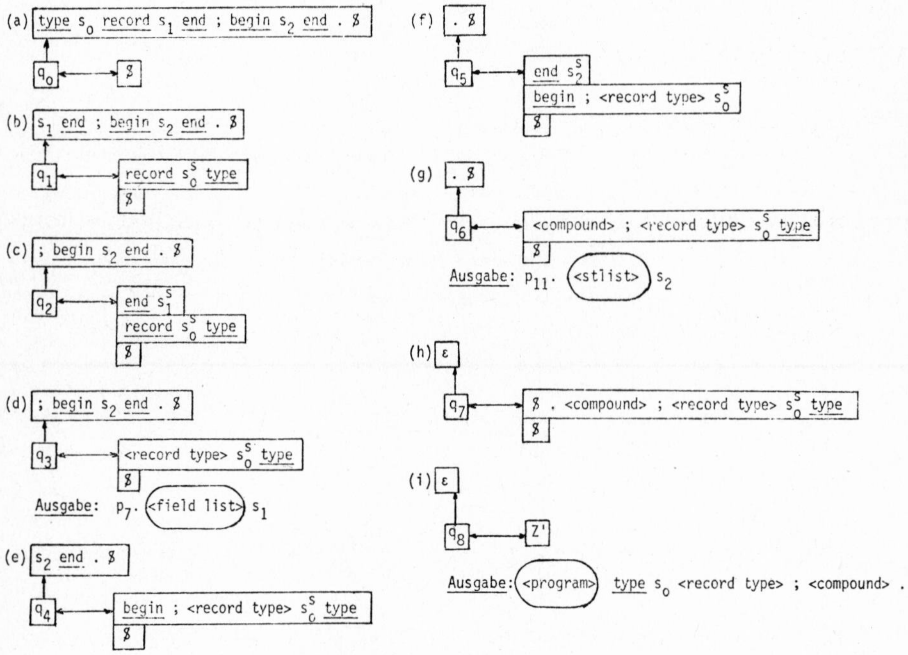

================================

mit einer Verschlüsselung ihrer Axiome ausgegeben, die bei der Reduktion bestimmt werden. Die Verschlüsselung wird bei der Feinanalyse so interpretiert, daß der zugehörige Analyse-Automat gestartet wird.

Es läßt sich zeigen, daß ein K^*-Automat durch einen deterministischen linear beschränkten Automaten (DLBA) simuliert werden kann [1].

Zur Konstruktion der Fragmentzerlegung einer (K,f)-Struktur erweitern wir den K^{*}-Automaten um Aktionen, welche einen Keller bei Auftreten eines Fragmentzeichens in zwei Keller zerlegen. Auch dieser erweiterte K^{*}-Automat kann durch einen DLBA simuliert werden.

Naturgemäß liefert die Analyse mit Hilfe einer Grobstruktur keine strenge Links-Rechts-Ableitung, die oft erwünscht ist - etwa zur Behandlung der Semantik parallel zur Syntaxanalyse. Deshalb hat der Steuerautomat neben der Koordination der Teilanalyse noch die Aufgabe, nach außen eine strenge Links-Rechts-Ableitung zu simulieren [1].

Literaturverzeichnis

[1] DIETERICH,E.-W.: Grobstrukturen kontextfreier Grammatiken. Fachbereich Mathematik der TU München, Dissertation, 1976

[2] EARLEY,J., CAIZERGUES,P.: A method for incrementally compiling languages with nested statement structure. CACM 15, 1972, 1o4o-1o44

[3] McKEEMAN,W.M., HORNING,J.J.,WORTMAN,D.B.: A compiler generator. Prentice Hall, Inc., Englewood Cliffs, N.J., 1969

[4] MEERTENS,L.G.Th., VAN VLIET,J.C.: Repairing the paranthesis skeleton of Algol 68 programs. Stichting mathematisch centrum. Amsterdam, IW2/73, 1973

[5] NAUR,P.(ed.): Revised report on the algorithmic language Algol 6o. Num. Math. 4, 1969, 79-218

[6] VAN WIJNGAARDEN,A.(ed.): Report on the algorithmic language Algol 68. Num. Math. 14, 1969, 79-218

[7] WIRTH,N.: The programming language Pascal. Acta Informatica 1, 1971, 35-63

STRUKTURELLE UNTERSUCHUNGEN ZUR SCHWERSTEN KONTEXTFREIEN SPRACHE

K. Estenfeld

Abstract :In this paper the grammatical structure of the "Hardest contextfree language" L_0 of Sh. Greibach 4 is analyzed and the following result is obtained :

There exists a grammar G_0 for L_0, such that for each c.f. language L and for each c.f. grammar G in Greibach-Normalform generating L the set of derivations of words of L in G is mapped functorially into the set of derivations of the words of L_0 in G_0.

Einleitung : In [4] hat Sh. Greibach eine "schwerste kontextfreie Sprache" L_0 definiert und gezeigt,daß jede k.f.Sprache L als invers-homomorphes Bild von L_0 dargestellt werden kann. Diese Sprache L_0 ist für Komplexitätsbetrachtungen interessant, da durch diese Darstellung die Zeitkomplexität zum Erkennen von L_0 obere Schranke für die Zeitkomplexität zum Erkennen der kontextfreien Sprachen ist.

Die Sprache L_0 ist eine nichtdeterministische Version der Dycksprache. Zu jeder Ableitung in einer beliebigen k.f. Grammatik G für die Sprache L korrespondiert ein Dyckwort mit vorgesetztem Sonderzeichen ¢, das Konkatenation von Teilwörtern aus einem Wort aus L_0 ist. Diese Korrespondenz ist injektiv [2].

In dieser Arbeit wird nun die grammatikalische Struktur der Greibachsprache L_0 betrachtet. Aus der Definition der Greibachsprache und der Kodierungsfunktion für die Produktionen einer beliebigen Grammatik [4] wird eine spezielle Grammatik G_0 für L_0 konstruiert. Diese Grammatik G_0 hat die Eigenschaft, daß die

Zeichen einer beliebigen Grammatik G in Greibachnormalform in Zeichenreihen aus G_0 so kodiert werden können, daß eine Produktion in G in eine Folge von Produktionen in G_0 überführt wird. Diese Zuordnung ist ein Funktor [6], d.h. daß die Ableitung p' in G_0, die zu einer Ableitung p in G korrespondiert, gerade das Wort w' aus L_0 erzeugt, welches das Bild des von p erzeugten Wortes w unter der von Sh. Greibach benützten Kodierung ist.

Nach einigen Definitionen wird zuerst die Grammatik G_0 für L_0 angegeben.Danach konstruieren wir eine Längenfunktion, die zu einem Wort w aus L(G) die Länge des korrespondierenden Wortes w' aus L_0 berechnet.Daran anschließend geben wir den Funktor an, der die oben beschriebenen Eigenschaften hat.

Wir beginnen mit folgender Definition :

Definition 1 Eine ε-freie kontextfreie Grammatik G=(T,NT,P,S)
mit T= endliche Menge der terminalen Zeichen
NT= endliche Menge der nichtterminalen Zeichen
P= endliche Menge der Produktionen
S= Axiom

liegt in *Greibachnormalform (GNF)* vor, falls gilt :
in G existieren nur Produktionen der Form $A \to a\alpha$ mit $A \in NT, a \in T$ und $\alpha \in NT^*$.
Wenn im folgenden von Grammatiken in Standardform gesprochen wird,so bedeutet das,daß G in GNF vorliegt,wobei auf der rechten Seite der Produktionen nicht das Axiom auftreten darf.
Die Ableitungen seien immer leftmost erzeugt.
Beides stellt keine Einschränkungen dar.
Die Produktionen einer kontextfreien Grammatik seien durchnummeriert,d.h. $P=\{p_1,\ldots,p_n\}$, n=Anzahl der Produktionen,so daß im folgenden die Ableitung eines Wortes $w=w_1\ldots w_k \in L(G)$ mit dem String $p=p_{w_1}\ldots p_{w_k} \in P^*$ identifiziert wird.

Definition 2 Sei $D_k := \{a_1,\dots,a_k,\bar{a}_1,\dots,\bar{a}_k\}$;

Sei $G_D := (\{S\}, D_k, P, S)$ eine kontextfreie Grammatik, wobei $P = \{S \to SS, S \to a_i S \bar{a}_i, i=1,\dots,k, S \to \varepsilon\}$

Dann heißt die von G_D erzeugte kontextfreie Sprache $D := L(G_D)$ *Dyck - Menge* über D_k.

Die Elemente der Dyck - Menge lassen sich noch folgendermaßen charakterisieren :

Definition 3 Sei $D_k := \{a_1,\dots,a_k,\bar{a}_1,\dots,\bar{a}_k\}$ und sei

$$R = \{a_i \bar{a}_j \equiv \begin{cases} 1 & \text{falls } i=j \\ 0 & \text{falls } i \neq j \end{cases}\}$$ ein

Relationensystem, wobei 1 die Einheit in D_k^* ist, und für alle $w \in D_k^*$ gilt : $0 \cdot w = 0$.

Dann ist $D = \{w \in D_k^*, w \equiv 1 \bmod R\}$ die Dyck - Menge über D_k.

Die Elemente aus D werden im folgenden Dyckwörter genannt. Die $a_i, i=1,\dots,k$ stehen für öffnende Klammern verschiedenen Typs, die $\bar{a}_i$ für die entsprechenden schließenden Klammern. Im folgenden benötigen wir nur noch zwei Klammertypen a_1 und a_2 (bzw. $\bar{a}_1$ und $\bar{a}_2$). Mit diesen beiden Klammertypen werden die Produktionen einer kontextfreien Grammatik in Standardform kodiert.

Definition 4 *(Greibachsprache)*

Sei $T := D_2 \cup \{c, ¢\}$ mit $D_2 \cap \{c, ¢\} = \emptyset$

D sei die Dyckmenge über D_2 , sei d ein neues Symbol, dann ist

$L_0 := \{x_1 c y_1 c z_1 d \dots d x_n c y_n c z_n d, n \geq 1, y_1 \dots y_n \in ¢D, x_i, z_i \in T^*$ für alle i, $y_i \in D_2^*$ für $i \geq 2\} \cup \{\varepsilon\}$

die Greibachsprache.

(Nichtdeterministische Version der Dyck - Menge).

L_o wählt ein Teilwort aus jeder durch d begrenzten Gruppe in der Art, daß die Konkatenation der ausgewählten Teilwörter in der Reihenfolge der d - Blöcke zu $\not{c}D$ gehört. Ein solches Wort wird auch Dyckwort genannt. Es dürften keine Verwechselungen möglich sein.

Bemerkung L_o kodiert die Ableitungen einer kontextfreien Grammatik G=(NT,T,P,S) in Standardform folgendermaßen:

Die Nichtterminalen von G seien beliebig durchnummeriert, so daß $NT=\{A_1,\dots,A_N\}$, wobei ohne Einschränkung $A_1=S$ das Axiom sei.

Definition 5 ξ und $\bar{\xi}$ seien wie folgt definierte Funktionen :

$$P \longrightarrow \{a_1,a_2,\bar{a}_1,\bar{a}_2,\not{c}\}^*$$

die folgendermaßen auf den Produktionen wirken:

Sei $p \in P$ die Produktion $A_i \to a, a \in T$

dann: $\bar{\xi}\,(A_i \to a) := \bar{a}_1\bar{a}_2^{\,i}\bar{a}_1$;

sei $p \in P : A_i \to aA_{i_1}\dots A_{i_m}$, $A_i, A_{i_l} \in NT$, $l=1,\dots,m$

dann: $\bar{\xi}\,(A_i \to aA_{i_1}\dots A_{i_m}) := \bar{a}_1\bar{a}_2^{\,i}\bar{a}_1 a_1 a_2^{\,i_m} a_1 \dots a_1 a_2^{\,i_1} a_1$;

Ist $i \neq 1$, dann gilt :

$$\xi(p) := \bar{\xi}(p)$$

für $i=1$ gilt :

$$\xi(p) := \not{c}a_1a_2a_1\bar{\xi}(p)\ .$$

Wenn nun $p_{i_1}\dots p_{i_n}$ die Ableitung für $w=w_1\dots w_n$ ist, so ist die kodierte Ableitung $\xi(p_{i_1}\dots p_{i_n}) := \xi(p_{i_1})\dots\xi(p_{i_n})$ gerade ein Dyckwort, das sich unter R zu $\not{c}1$ kürzen läßt.

Definition 6 Mit P_a sei die Menge aller Produktionen in P bezeichnet, die auf der rechten Seite mit dem terminalen Zeichen a beginnen.

Sei also $P_a = \{p_{a_1},\dots,p_{a_l}\}$ diese Menge.

Dann sei $\tilde{\xi}(a) := c\xi(p_{a_1})c\ldots\xi(p_{a_1})cd$ ein Homomorphismus.
Einem Wort $w \in L(G)$ ordnet man ein Wort $w' \in \{a_1, a_2, \bar{a}_1, \bar{a}_2, c, \bar{c}\}^*$ zu in folgender Weise :
sei $w = w_1 \ldots w_n$,dann ist $w' = \tilde{\xi}(w_1) \ldots \tilde{\xi}(w_n)$

Es existiert nun folgender

Satz 7 (Greibach)

Ist L eine kontextfreie Sprache,dann existiert ein Homomorphismus h ,so daß $L - \{\varepsilon\} = h^{-1}(L_0 - \{\varepsilon\})$.
der oben definierte Homomorphismus $\tilde{\xi}$ leistet das gewünschte.

Um die Produktionen einer kontextfreien Grammatik G mit Hilfe von ξ kodieren zu können,um so das Greibachwort zu erhalten, müssen die Produktionen in Standardform vorliegen.Da es ja das Ziel dieser Arbeit ist,einen Strukturvergleich zwischen den Ableitungen in G, die zu einem Wort $w \in L(G)$ führen, und den Ableitungen, die das zugehörige Greibachwort w' erzeugen, müssen die Produktionensysteme gleiche Struktur besitzen.
Es soll nun eine Grammatik in Standardform für L_0 angegeben werden.
Hierzu wird zunächst eine Grammatik in GNF angegeben zur Erzeugung der Dyckmenge über beliebiger Anzahl Klammertypen.

Definition 8 Sei G_{D_k} die kontextfreie Grammatik folgenden Aussehens :

$G_{D_k} := (NT_{D_k}, T_{D_k}, P_{D_k}, S)$ mit

$NT_{D_k} = \{S, B_i\}$ $i = 1, \ldots, k$

$T_{D_k} = \{a_i, \bar{a}_i\}$ $i = 1, \ldots, k$

$P_{D_k} = \{p_1, \ldots, p_4\}$ mit

p_1: $S \to a_i B_i$

p_2: $B_i \to \bar{a}_i S$

p_3: $S \to a_i S B_i$

p_4: $B_i \to \bar{a}_i$ $i = 1, \ldots, k$

Wir werden uns im folgenden auf zwei verschiedene Klammertypen beschränken, jedoch lassen sich alle Aussagen leicht auf eine größere Anzahl Klammertypen verallgemeinern.

Wir werden also die Grammatik G_{D_2} betrachten.

Es gilt nun :

Lemma 9 G_{D_2} erzeugt die Dyckmenge über zwei Klammertypen

Der Beweis ist unmittelbar einsichtig.

Bem. Die Grammatik ist vom Typ LL.

In [2] werden nun mehrere Schritte angegeben, die zur Grammatik G_o führen.

Definition 10 Sei $G_o=(NT_o,T_o,P_o,\sigma_o)$ folgende kontextfreie Grammatik :

$NT_o:=\{\sigma_o,\sigma,S_o,S,X,P,B_1,B_2,A_1\}$

$T_o :=\{a_1,a_2,\bar{a}_1,\bar{a}_2,c,\not{c},d\}$

$P_o :=\{p_1,\dots,p_{24}\}$ mit :

$p_1 : \sigma_o \to cXS_o\sigma$	$p_{13} : B_i \to \bar{a}_i\sigma XS$
$p_2 : \sigma_o \to cS_o\sigma$	$p_{14} : B_i \to \bar{a}_i S$
$p_3 : \sigma_o \to \varepsilon$	$p_{15} : S \to a_i\sigma XS\sigma XB_i$
$p_4 : S_o \to \not{c}A_1\sigma XB_1$	$p_{16} : S \to a_i S\sigma XB_i$
$p_5 : S_o \to \not{c}A_1B_1$	$p_{17} : S \to a_i\sigma XSB_i$
$p_6 : S_o \to \not{c}A_1\sigma XS\sigma XB_1$	$p_{18} : S \to a_i SB_i$
$p_7 : S_o \to \not{c}A_1S\sigma XB_1$	$p_{19} : B_i \to \bar{a}_i$
$p_8 : S_o \to \not{c}A_1\sigma XSB_1$	$p_{20} : \sigma \to cP$
$p_9 : S_o \to \not{c}A_1SB_1$	$p_{21} : P \to tP$
$p_{10} : A_1 \to a_1$	$p_{22} : P \to d$
$p_{11} : S \to a_i\sigma XB_i$	$p_{23} : X \to tX$
$p_{12} : S \to a_iB_i$	$p_{24} : X \to c$

$i=1,2$

Bemerkung t steht für ein beliebiges Element aus $T_o \setminus \{d\}$

Erläuterungen zu den Produktionen :

p_1 bis p_3 beginnen mit dem Axiom und dienen dazu, den ersten d - Block des Greibachwortes zu erzeugen. Aus S_0 leitet sich mit Hilfe der Produktionen p_4 bis p_{19} das zu einer Ableitung in der kontextfreie Grammatik G korrespondierende Dyckwort ab. Durch die Nichtterminalen $_\sigma X$ wird die Aufspaltung des Dyckwortes an den "richtigen" Stellen ermöglicht. Durch die Produktionen p_{20} bis p_{24} werden die Kodierungen der Produktionen, die zu dem gleichen d - Block wie das Dyckteilwort gehören (d.h. sie beginnen mit dem gleichen terminalen Zeichen auf der rechten Seite), erzeugt. P_{20} bis p_{22} erzeugen immer das Ende eines d - Blockes ($cz_i cd$ - Teil in Def. von L_0), und p_{23} und p_{24} den Anfang eines d - Blockes ($x_i c$ - Teil in Def. von L_0).

Das Produktionensystem von G_0 liegt in Standardform vor

Es gilt nun :

Satz 11 G_0 erzeugt die Greibachsprache L_0

Definition 12 Sei l_p eine Funktion, die zu jeder Produktion einer kontextfreien Grammatik G in Standardform die Länge der Kodierung angibt.

Durch Fallunterscheidung nach der angewendeten Produktion definieren wir $l_p : P_G \to \mathbb{N}_0$ wie folgt :

i) $p : S \to aA_{i_1} \ldots A_{i_s}$ sei die Produktion,

$i_j \in \{2,\ldots,NT\}$, $j=1,\ldots,s$

NT=Anzahl der Nichtterminalen in G

dann : $$l_p(p) := 7 + \sum_{i=2}^{NT} \delta_{pi} \cdot (i+2)$$

mit $\delta_{pi} := \begin{cases} 0 & \text{auf der rechten Seite der Produktion p kommt nicht } A_i \text{ vor }, i \in \{2,\dots,NT\} \\ k & \text{auf der rechten Seite der Produktion p kommt } A_i \text{ k mal vor, } k \geq 1 \end{cases}$

ii) $p : A_i \to aA_{i_1} \dots A_{i_r}$ sei die Produktion, $i > 1$

dann : $l_p(p) := j+2+ \sum_{j=2}^{NT} \delta_{pj} \cdot (j+2)$

δ_{pj} wie oben definiert.

Die Wohldefiniertheit von l_p folgt direkt aus der Konstruktion der Kodierung.

Wir können mit Hilfe der Funktion l_p nun die Länge des zu einer Ableitung korrespondiernden Dyckwortes berechnen.

Es ergibt sich folgendes

Lemma 13 Sei $w \in L(G), |w| = n$.

Für die Länge l_D des zu der Ableitung von w korrespondierenden Dyckwortes $\tilde{w}$ gilt :

$l_D(\tilde{w}) = \sum_{i=1}^{n} l_p(p_{w_i})$,wobei p_{w_i} die in der Ab - leitung von w als ite angewendete Produktion ist.

Bew. (Induktion nach n)

Es gilt :die Anzahl der Produktionen, um w mit $|w|=n$ abzuleiten,ist gleich n.

n=1 : $w=a \in T$, dann gibt es die Produktion $S \to a$ und $l_D(a) = l_p(a) = |{\not c} a_1 a_2 a_1 \bar{a}_1 \bar{a}_2 \bar{a}_1| = 7$ $\Rightarrow$Beh.

n>1 : Sei $w = w_1 \dots w_n \in L(G)$ .Da jedes w_i genau durch eine Produktion p_{w_i} erzeugt wird,und die Kodierung von p_{w_i} im Dyckwort gerade nach Konstruktion das ite

Teilwort ist,müssen nur die Längen der kodierten Produktionen der Ableitung addiert werden.

d.h. $\sum_{i=1}^{n} l_p(p_{w_i}) = l_D(\tilde{w}) \Rightarrow$ Beh.

Die Länge des Greibachwortes bestimmen wir dadurch, daß wir die Längen der einzelnen d - Blocks addieren. Die Länge des iten d - Blocks ergibt sich dadurch, daß wir die Längen aller einzelnen kodierten Produktionen in dem d - Block und deren Anzahl+2 addieren.

Formal : Sei d_i der ite d - Block von w'

dann :

$$l(d_i) = \sum_{p_{w_i} \in P_{w_i}} (l_p(p_{w_i})+1)+2$$

wobei p_{w_i} eine Produktion,deren terminales Zeichen w_i ist.Wir summieren also über alle Produktionen,deren terminales Zeichen w_i ist (ihre Kodierungen gehören nach Konstruktion gerade in den iten d - Block).Die Addition der 1 zu jeder Kodierung steht für das c vor jeder Kodierung,die Addition der 2 steht für das letzte cd des d - Blockes.

Es ergibt sich also als abschließendes

Korollar 14 Sei $w \in L(G), |w|=n$.

Dann gilt für die Länge(Anzahl der Produktionen) $l_{GR}(w')$ des Greibachwortes w', das zur Ableitung von w korrespondiert :

$$l_{GR}(w') = \sum_{i=1}^{n} l(d_i)$$

Wir wollen nun mit Hilfe von G_0 einen Funktor konstruieren, der der Ableitung eines Wortes $w \in L(G)$ die Ableitung des zugehörigen Greibachwortes $\in L(G_0)$ zuordnet.Dieser Funktor kann natürlich nicht längenerhaltend sein, da wir gesehen haben

(mit Hilfe der Funktion l_{GR}), daß das korrespondierende Greibachwort sehr viel länger ist als das Wort in der kontextfreien Sprache.

Funktoren dienen dazu,Kategorien miteinander vergleichen zu können.Es sind strukturerhaltende Abbildungen zwischen Kategorien.Man kann leicht jede Grammatik als Kategorie beschreiben. Diese Konstruktion wird genau in [6] beschrieben.

Wir geben nun die Definition eines Funktors.

Definition 15 Seien K_1 und K_2 x-Kategorien.
$\Phi=(\phi_1,\phi_2)$ heißt ein *Funktor* von K_1 in K_2,
wenn gilt :

(F1) $\phi_1 : Obj(K_1) \longrightarrow Obj(K_2)$ und
$\phi_2 : Mor(K_1) \longrightarrow Mor(K_2)$ sind Monoidhomomorphismen

(F2) Das Diagramm

$$\begin{array}{ccc} Mor(K_1) & \xrightarrow{Q_1,Z_1} & Obj(K_1) \\ \downarrow \phi_2 & & \downarrow \phi_1 \\ Mor(K_2) & \xrightarrow[Q_2,Z_2]{} & Obj(K_2) \end{array}$$

ist kommutativ

(F3) Für alle $w \in Obj(K_1)$ gilt :
$\phi_2(1_w) = 1_{\phi_1(w)}$

(F4) Für alle $f,g \in Mor(K_1)$ mit $Q(f) = Z(g)$ gilt :
$\phi_2(f o g) = \phi_2(f) o \phi_2(g)$

Ein Funktor heißt injektiv,surjektiv oder bijektiv,falls ϕ_1 und ϕ_2 injektiv,surjektiv oder bijektiv sind.

Wir können in Abhängigkeit des Wortes $w \in L(G)$ und der Grammatik G ein Greibachwort w' zu w angeben.Wir können also vor der Erzeugung (Ableitung) des Greibachwortes die Positionen der Dyckteilwörter in jedem d-Block des Greibachwortes festlegen, so daß jeder d-Block eindeutig bestimmt ist.

Dies bedeutet keine Einschränkung.
Wir können also den Funktor eindeutig bestimmen.

ϕ_1 wirkt auf den terminalen und nichtterminalen Zeichen der kontextfreien Grammatik, ϕ_2 wirkt auf den einzelnen Produktionen.

Wir wollen im folgenden immer annehmen, daß $L_0 \neq \{\varepsilon\}$, da der Fall $L_0 = \{\varepsilon\}$ trivial ist. (Produktion p_3 in G_0 muß angewendet werden)

Es soll nun im folgenden der gewünschte Funktor konstruiert werden und seine Korrektheit bewiesen werden.

Sei also $G=(NT,T,P,A_1)$ mit $NT=\{A_1,...,A_N\}$ eine beliebige kontextfreie Grammatik in Standardform und G_0 die Grammatik für die Greibachsprache.

Definition 16 Sei $\Phi = (\phi_1,\phi_2) : G \longrightarrow G_0$ wie folgt definiert :

$\phi_1 : Obj(G) \longrightarrow Obj(G_0)$ mit :

$\phi_1(A_1) := \sigma_0$ (Axiom in G_0)

$\phi_1(A_i) := XB_1B_2^iB_1\sigma$, $i \geq 2$

$\phi_1(t) := \tilde{\xi}(t)$ (d - Block zu t)

$\phi_2 : Mor(G) \longrightarrow Mor(G_0)$ mit :

Sei $p : A_i \rightarrow w$, $w=a\alpha$ mit $a \in T$, $\alpha \in NT^*$,

dann wählen wir als

$\phi_2(p) = \phi_2(A_i \rightarrow w)$ einen speziellen Morphismus aus $Mor(\phi_1(A_i),\phi_1(w))$, der im folgenden durch Fallunterscheidungen der Produktionen aus P angegeben wird.

Wir müssen folgende 4 Fälle von Produktionen in einer Ableitung unterscheiden :

1. $p : A_1 \rightarrow a$, A_1=Axiom, $a \in T$

2. $p : A_1 \to aA_{1_1} \dots A_{1_k}$ $, 1_s \in \{2,\dots,N\}$ $, s=1,\dots,k, k\geq 1$

3. $p : A_i \to a$ $, i\geq 2$

4. $p : A_i \to aA_{i_1} \dots A_{i_k}$ $, i\geq 2, k\geq 1, i_s \in \{2,\dots,N\}$

Für jeden dieser Fälle wird der Morphismus explizit angegeben.

ϕ_1 wird auf $w \in \{T \cup NT\}^+$ wie folgt definiert :

Sei $w=w_1\dots w_n \in \{T \cup NT\}^+$,dann

$\phi_1(w) = \phi_1(w_1\dots w_n) := \phi_1(w_1)\dots\phi_1(w_n)$

ϕ_2 wird wie folgt auf Ableitungen fortgesetzt :

Seien p_i und p_j Produktionen,wobei ohne Einschränkung p_j in einer Ableitung nach p_i ausgeführt wird.

Wir definieren : $\phi_2(p_i o p_j) := \phi_2(p_i) o \phi_2(p_j)$,

wobei zunächst $\phi_2(p_i)$ ausgeführt wird und dann der in $Z(\phi_2(p_i))$ am weitesten links (kanonisch!) erzeugte $XB_1B_2^iB_1\sigma$ - Block $Q(\phi_2(p_j))$ ist.

Wir erweitern ϕ_2 auf Produktionenfolgen wie folgt :

$\phi_2(p_{i_1}\dots p_{i_k}) := \phi_2(p_{i_1}) o \dots o \phi_2(p_{i_k})$ in der oben beschriebenen Art.

Wir sehen sofort,daß diese Definition die Axiome eines Funktors erfüllt.

Im folgenden sollen nun die verschiedenen Fälle der Morphismen $\phi_2(p)$ in G_o angegeben werden,so daß die Existenz des Funktors nachgewiesen ist.

Wir müssen immer eine Produktionenfolge angeben,die aus $\phi_1(Q(p))$ $\phi_1(Z(p))$ erzeugt.Diese Produktionenfolge wählen wir dann als $\phi_2(p)$.

<u>1. Fall</u> : $p : A_1 \to a$

Wir müssen zeigen : es existiert eine Produktionenfolge

aus $\mathrm{Mor}(\phi_1(A_1),\phi_1(a)) = \mathrm{Mor}(\sigma_0,\tilde{\xi}(a))$, wobei

$\tilde{\xi}(a)=Wc\xi(p)cVd = Wc¢a_1a_2a_1\bar{a}_1\bar{a}_2\bar{a}_1cVd$ mit

$W \in c\{a_1,a_2,a_1,a_2,c,¢\}^*$ und $V \in \{a_1,a_2,a_1,a_2,c,¢\}^*c$

W und V sind die Kodierungen der restlichen Produktionen, in denen a als terminales Zeichen vorkommt, getrennt durch c (sie lassen sich in G_0 regulär erzeugen).

<u>Behauptung</u> :

$\sigma_0 \overset{*}{\Rightarrow} Wc¢a_1a_2a_1\bar{a}_1\bar{a}_2\bar{a}_1cVd$!

i) falls $W=c \Rightarrow$ 1. anzuwendende Produktion p_2

ii) falls $W=cw$, $w \in \{a_1,a_2,\bar{a}_1,\bar{a}_2,c,¢\}^+ \Rightarrow$ erste anzuw. Produktion p_1. Wir betrachten o.E. Fall ii)

$$\sigma_0 \underset{p_1}{\rightarrow} cXS_0\sigma \underset{p_{23}^s}{\overset{*}{\Rightarrow}} cwXS_0\sigma \underset{p_{24}}{\Rightarrow} cwcS_0\sigma \underset{p_9}{} cwc¢A_1SB_1\sigma \underset{p_{10}}{\Rightarrow}$$

$$cwc¢a_1SB_1\sigma \underset{p_{18}}{\Rightarrow} cwc¢a_1a_2SB_2B_1\sigma \underset{p_{12}}{\Rightarrow} cwc¢a_1a_2a_1B_1B_2B_1\sigma \underset{p_{19}^3}{\overset{*}{\Rightarrow}}$$

$$cwc¢a_1a_2a_1\bar{a}_1\bar{a}_2\bar{a}_1\sigma \underset{p_{20}}{\Rightarrow} cwc¢a_1a_2a_1\bar{a}_1\bar{a}_2\bar{a}_1cP \underset{p_{21}^j}{\overset{*}{\Rightarrow}}$$

$$cwc¢a_1a_2a_1\bar{a}_1\bar{a}_2\bar{a}_1cvcP' \underset{p_{22}}{\Rightarrow} cwc¢a_1a_2a_1\bar{a}_1\bar{a}_2\bar{a}_1cvcd$$

Wir erhalten: $\tilde{p}=p_1p_{23}^sp_{24}p_9p_{10}p_{18}p_{12}p_{19}^3p_{20}p_{21}^jp_{22}$ erzeugt $\phi_1(a)$ aus $\phi_1(A_1)$.

also $\phi_2(p) := \tilde{p} \Rightarrow$ 1. Fall

<u>*Bemerkung*</u> Es gilt : $|\tilde{\xi}(a)| = s+j+|\xi(p)|+3$, s und j sind abhängig von der kontextfreien Grammatik.

<u>2. Fall</u> : $p : A_1 \rightarrow aA_{1_1}\ldots A_{1_k}$

Wir müssen zeigen : es existiert eine Produktionenfolge aus $\mathrm{Mor}(\phi_1(A_1),\phi_1(aA_{1_1}\ldots A_{1_k})) =$

$\mathrm{Mor}(\sigma_0,\tilde{\xi}(a)\phi_1(A_{1_1})\ldots\phi_1(A_{1_k}))$ mit

$\tilde{\xi}(a) = Wc\xi(p)cVd = Wc¢a_1a_2a_1\bar{a}_1\bar{a}_2\bar{a}_1a_1a_2^{1_k}a_1\ldots a_1a_2^{1_1}a_1cVd$

und

$$\phi_1(A_{1_s}) = XB_1B_2^{1_s}B_1\sigma, s=1,\dots,k;$$

W und V analog zu 1.Fall ,sei W=cw und V=vc

Behauptung :

$$\sigma_0 \overset{*}{\Rightarrow} Wc\not{c}a_1a_2a_1\bar{a}_1\bar{a}_2\bar{a}_1a_1a_2^{1_k}a_1\dots a_1a_2^{1_1}a_1cVdXB_1B_2^{1_1}B_1\sigma\dots XB_1B_2^{1_k}B_1\sigma \quad !$$

$$\sigma_0 \underset{p_1}{\Rightarrow} cXS_0\sigma \underset{p_{23}^{s}}{\overset{*}{\Rightarrow}} cwXS_0\sigma \underset{p_{24}}{\Rightarrow} cwcS_0\sigma \underset{p_9}{\Rightarrow} cwc\not{c}A_1SB_1\sigma \underset{p_{10}}{\Rightarrow}$$

$$cwc\not{c}a_1SB_1\sigma \underset{p_{18}}{\Rightarrow} cwc\not{c}a_1a_2SB_2B_1\sigma \underset{p_{12}}{\Rightarrow} cwc\not{c}a_1a_2a_1B_1B_2B_1\sigma \underset{p_{19}^{2}}{\overset{*}{\Rightarrow}}$$

$$cwc\not{c}a_1a_2a_1\bar{a}_1\bar{a}_2B_1\sigma \underset{p_{14}}{\Rightarrow} cwc\not{c}a_1a_2a_1\bar{a}_1\bar{a}_2\bar{a}_1S\sigma \underset{p_{18}}{\Rightarrow}$$

$$cwc\not{c}a_1a_2a_1\bar{a}_1\bar{a}_2\bar{a}_1a_1SB_1\sigma \underset{p_{18}^{1_k}}{\overset{*}{\Rightarrow}} cwc\not{c}a_1a_2a_1\bar{a}_1\bar{a}_2\bar{a}_1a_1a_2^{1_k}SB_2^{1_k}B_1\sigma \underset{p_{16}}{\Rightarrow}$$

$$cwc\not{c}a_1a_2a_1\bar{a}_1\bar{a}_2\bar{a}_1a_1a_2^{1_k}a_1S\sigma XB_1B_2^{1_k}B_1\sigma \underset{p_{18}^{1_{s-1}+1}\ p_{16}}{\overset{*}{\Rightarrow}} ,s=k,\dots,3$$

$$cwc\not{c}a_1a_2a_1\bar{a}_1\bar{a}_2\bar{a}_1a_1a_2^{1_k}a_1\dots a_1a_2^{1_2}a_1S\sigma XB_1B_2^{1_2}B_1\sigma\dots XB_1B_2^{1_k}B_1\sigma$$

$$\underset{p_{18}^{1_1+1}}{\overset{*}{\Rightarrow}}$$

$$cwc\not{c}a_1a_2a_1\bar{a}_1\bar{a}_2\bar{a}_1a_1a_2^{1_k}a_1\dots a_1a_2^{1_1}SB_2^{1_1}B_1\sigma X\dots XB_1B_2^{1_k}B_1\sigma$$

$$\underset{p_{11}}{\Rightarrow}$$

$$cwc\not{c}a_1a_2a_1\bar{a}_1\bar{a}_2\bar{a}_1a_1a_2^{1_k}a_1\dots a_1a_2^{1_1}a_1\sigma XB_1B_2^{1_1}B_1\sigma\dots XB_1B_2^{1_k}B_1\sigma$$

$$\underset{p_{20}}{\Rightarrow}$$

$$cwc\not{c}a_1a_2a_1\ldots a_1a_2^{1_1}a_1cPXB_1B_2^{1_1}B_1\sigma\ldots XB_1B_2^{1_k}B_1\sigma$$

$$\underset{p_{21}^j\ p_{22}}{\overset{*}{\Rightarrow}}$$

$$cwc\not{c}a_1a_2a_1\ldots a_1a_2^{1_1}a_1cvcdXB_1B_2^{1_1}B_1\sigma\ldots XB_1B_2^{1_k}B_1\sigma$$

Wir setzen $\phi_2(p)$ als den so erhaltenen Morphismus, der $\phi_1(aA_{1_1}\ldots A_{1_k})$ aus $\phi_1(A_1)$ erzeugt $\Rightarrow$ 2.Fall

3. Fall : $p : A_i \to a \quad, i \geq 2$

Wir müssen zeigen : es existiert eine Produktionenfolge aus $Mor(\phi_1(A_i),\phi_1(a)) = Mor(XB_1B_2^iB_1\sigma,\tilde{\xi}(a))$ mit

$$\tilde{\xi}(a) = Wc\bar{a}_1\bar{a}_2^i\bar{a}_1cVd$$

Behauptung :

$XB_1B_2^iB_1\sigma \overset{*}{\Rightarrow} Wc\bar{a}_1\bar{a}_2^i\bar{a}_1cVd$!

$$XB_1B_2^iB_1\sigma \underset{p_{23}}{\Rightarrow} cXB_1B_2^iB_1\sigma \underset{p_{23}^j}{\overset{*}{\Rightarrow}} cwXB_1B_2^iB_1\sigma \underset{p_{24}}{\Rightarrow} cwcB_1B_2^iB_i\sigma \underset{p_{19}^{i+2}}{\overset{*}{\Rightarrow}}$$

$$cwc\bar{a}_1\bar{a}_2^i\bar{a}_1\sigma \underset{p_{20}}{\Rightarrow} cwc\bar{a}_1\bar{a}_2^i\bar{a}_1cP \underset{p_{21}^s}{\overset{*}{\Rightarrow}} cwc\bar{a}_1\bar{a}_2^i\bar{a}_1cvcP \underset{p_{22}}{\Rightarrow}$$

$$cwc\bar{a}_1\bar{a}_2^i\bar{a}_1cvcd$$

Wir erhalten : $\tilde{p} = p_{23}^{j+1}p_{24}p_{19}^{i+2}p_{20}p_{21}^sp_{22}$ erzeugt $\phi_1(a)$ aus $\phi_1(A_i)$,

also $\phi_2(p) := \tilde{p}$ $\Rightarrow$ 3.Fall

Wir müssen nun noch den letzten Fall betrachten.

4 . Fall : $p : A_i \to aA_{i_1} \ldots A_{i_k}$, $i \geq 2$

Wir müssen zeigen : es existiert eine Produktionenfolge aus $Mor(\phi_1(A_i), \phi_1(aA_{i_1} \ldots A_{i_k})) =$
$Mor(XB_1B_2^iB_1\sigma, \tilde{\xi}(a)\phi_1(A_{i_1}) \ldots \phi_1(A_{i_k}))$ mit

$$\tilde{\xi}(a) = Wc\bar{a}_1\bar{a}_2^i\bar{a}_1a_1a_2^{i_k}a_1 \ldots a_1a_2^{i_1}a_1cVd$$

Behauptung :

$$XB_1B_2^iB_1\sigma \overset{*}{\Rightarrow} Wc\bar{a}_1\bar{a}_2^i\bar{a}_1a_1a_2^{i_k}a_1 \ldots a_1a_2^{i_1}a_1cVdXB_1B_2^{i_1}B_1\sigma \ldots XB_1B_2^{i_k}B_1\sigma \quad !$$

$$XB_1B_2^iB_1\sigma \underset{p_{23}^s\, p_{24}}{\overset{*}{\Rightarrow}} WcB_1B_2^iB_1\sigma \underset{p_{19}^{i+1}}{\overset{*}{\Rightarrow}} Wc\bar{a}_1\bar{a}_2^iB_1\sigma \underset{p_{14}}{\Rightarrow} Wc\bar{a}_1\bar{a}_2^i\bar{a}_1S\sigma$$

$$\overset{*}{\Rightarrow} Wc\bar{a}_1\bar{a}_2^i\bar{a}_1a_1a_2^{i_k}SB_2^{i_k}B_1\sigma \overset{*}{\Rightarrow} Wc\bar{a}_1\bar{a}_2^i\bar{a}_1a_1a_2^{i_k}a_1S\sigma XB_1B_2^{i_k}B_1\sigma$$

$$\overset{*}{\Rightarrow} Wc\bar{a}_1\bar{a}_2^i\bar{a}_1a_1a_2^{i_k}a_1 \ldots a_1a_2^{i_1}SB_2^{i_1}B_1\sigma \ldots XB_1B_2^{i_k}B_1\sigma$$

$p_{18}^{i_{m-1}+1}$ p_{16} $m=k,..,3$ $p_{18}^{i_1+1}$

$$\underset{p_{11}}{\Rightarrow} Wc\bar{a}_1\bar{a}_2^i\bar{a}_1a_1a_2^{i_k}a_1 \ldots a_1a_2^{i_1}a_1\sigma XB_1B_2^{i_1}B_1\sigma \ldots XB_1B_2^{i_k}B_1\sigma$$

$$\underset{p_{20}}{\Rightarrow} Wc\bar{a}_1\bar{a}_2^i\bar{a}_1a_1a_2^{i_k}a_1 \ldots a_1a_2^{i_1}a_1cPXB_1B_2^{i_1}B_1\sigma \ldots XB_1B_2^{i_k}B_1\sigma$$

$$\underset{p_{21}^j\, p_{22}}{\overset{*}{\Rightarrow}} Wc\bar{a}_1\bar{a}_2^i\bar{a}_1a_1a_2^{i_k}a_1 \ldots a_1a_2^{i_1}a_1cVdXB_1B_2^{i_1}B_1\sigma \ldots XB_1B_2^{i_k}B_1\sigma$$

Wir erhalten also :

$\tilde{p} = p_{23}^s p_{24} p_{19}^{i+1} p_{14} p_{18}^{i_k+1} p_{16} \ldots p_{18}^{i_1+1} p_{11} p_{20} p_{21}^j p_{22}$ erzeugt

$\phi_1(aA_{i_1} \ldots A_{i_k})$ aus $\phi_1(A_i)$

also $\phi_2(p) := \tilde{p}$ $\Rightarrow$ 4.Fall

Wir haben also für alle vier Fälle einen Morphismus $\phi_2(p)$ angegeben. Die Länge eines jeden Morphismus läßt sich mit der angegebenen Längenfunktion l_{GR} berechnen. Wir erhalten nun also aus dem vorigen folgendes Ergebnis :

SATZ 17 Sei G eine beliebige kontextfreie Grammatik in Standardform, G_0 die Grammatik für die Greibachsprache.

Es existiert ein Funktor $\Phi = (\phi_1, \phi_2) : G \longrightarrow G_0$,der jeder Ableitung $\tilde{p}$ in G,die ein Wort w $\in$ L(G) erzeugt, eine Ableitung $\tilde{p}'$ in G_0 zuordnet,die das zu w korrespondierende Greibachwort w' $\in L_0$ erzeugt.

Bew. folgt aus dem obigen.

Literaturverzeichnis :

[1] Aho,Ullman The Theory of Parsing,Translation and Compiling Vol. I Parsing,Prentice-Hall

[2] Estenfeld Ein funktorieller Zusammenhang zwischen einer beliebigen kontextfreien Sprache und der Greibachsprache Diplomarbeit,Saarbrücken 1976

[3] Greibach A new Normalform Theorem for Contextfree Phrase Structure Grammars JACM 12,1965

[4] Greibach Remarks on Context-Free Languages and Polynomial Time Recognition Dep. ofSystem Science University of California, Los Angeles

[5] Hopcroft-Ullman Formal Languages and their Relation to Automata Addison Wesley 1969

[6] Hotz,Claus Automatentheorie und formale Sprachen Band III Formale Sprachen , BI-Hochschulskripten

EINE UNTERE SCHRANKE FÜR DEN PLATZBEDARF BEI DER ANALYSE BESCHRÄNKTER KONTEXTFREIER SPRACHEN

H. Alt

1. Einleitung

Die Untersuchung von Algorithmen zur Analyse formaler Sprachen ist sowohl in der theoretischen als auch in der praktischen Informatik (Compilerbau) ein wichtiges Problem.

Der Wunsch, ein Maß für die Güte eines solchen Algorithmus zu haben, führt zu Komplexitätsbetrachtungen. Neben der Zeitkomplexität (Laufzeit eines Algorithmus in Abhängigkeit von der Länge der Eingabe) ist der Platzbedarf eines Algorithmus das meist untersuchte Komplexitätsmaß.

Für deterministische Analysealgorithmen kontextfreier Sprachen sind folgende <u>obere Schranken</u> für den Platzbedarf bekannt :

Generell ist jede kontextfreie Sprache mit $O((\log n)^2)$ Platz (n=Länge der Eingabe) analysierbar. Ein entsprechender Algorithmus wurde von Lewis, Hartmanis, Stearns [1o] angegeben. Dieser hat jedoch wegen zu großer Laufzeit $(O(n^{\log n}))$ keine praktische Bedeutung.

Es ist ein offenes Problem, ob jede kontextfreie Sprache mit $O(\log n)$ Platz analysierbar ist. Es dürfte auch sehr schwierig sein, einen solchen Algorithmus zu finden. Nach Resultaten von Monien [14] und Sudborough [17] würde nämlich daraus folgen, daß jede kontextsensitive Sprache mit einem <u>deterministischem</u> lba erkennbar ist, d.h. das lba-Problem wäre gelöst.

Für Teilklassen der kontextfreien Sprachen wurde $O(\log n)$ als obere Schranke bereits nachgewiesen, z.B. für die Dycksprachen (Hotz, Messerschmidt [9], Ritchie, Springsteel [15]) oder die Klammersprachen (Mehlhorn [13], Lynch [11]).

Eine generelle <u>untere Schranke</u> für den Platzbedarf bei der Analyse nichtregulärer Sprachen ist bekannt, nämlich $O(\log \log n)$ (Hartmanis, Stearns [1o]).

Man kann zeigen (siehe [10]), daß der Platzbedarf einer Turingmaschine, die eine beliebige nichtreguläre Sprache erkennt mindestens mit log log n wächst. Es wird in [10] auch eine nichtreguläre, kontextfreie Sprache angegeben, die mit O (log log n) Platz erkennbar ist, und damit ist diese untere Schranke für die kontextfreie Analyse nicht mehr zu verbessern. Beschränkt man sich jedoch auf gewisse Teilklassen der kontextfreien Sprachen, so lassen sich stärkere untere Schranken nachweisen. Erste Ergebnisse in dieser Richtung finden sich in [2] und [1], wo die Ergebnisse von [2] verallgemeinert werden. Diese Arbeit ist eine Kurzfassung von [1], wo auch die exakte Fassung der Beweise zu finden ist, die hier meist nur angedeutet sind. Wir zeigen log n als untere Schranke für den Platzbedarf beim Erkennen von Sprachen gewisser Teilklassen der kontextfreien Sprachen.

2. Hauptergebnisse

Als erstes erhalten wir;

Satz 1: Ist $\{a_1,\dots,a_k\}$ ein Alphabet und $L \subset \{a_1\}^* \dots\dots \{a_k\}^*$ kontextfrei und nichtregulär, so benötigt man zum Erkennen von L mindestens logarithmischen Platz.

(das soll heißen: Für eine deterministische Turingmaschine, die L erkennt und Platzbedarf $S : \mathbb{N}_0 \to \mathbb{N}_0$ hat, gilt: $0 < \limsup_{n \to \infty} \frac{S(n)}{\log n} \leq \infty$)

Dabei soll eine Turingmaschine aus einem Eingabeband mit einem 2-Weg-Lesekopf, einer endlichen Kontrolle und einer endlichen Anzahl von Arbeitsbändern, auf denen Lese-Schreibköpfe arbeiten, bestehen. Zum Platzbedarf sollen nur die auf den Arbeitsbändern benutzten Zellen beitragen.

Beweisidee: Wir identifizieren Worte $a_1^{n_1} \dots\dots a_k^{n_k}$ mit $(n_1,\dots,n_k) \in \mathbb{N}_0^k$. Damit unterscheiden wir nicht mehr zwischen Teilmengen von $\{a_1\}^* \dots \{a_k\}^*$ und den entsprechenden von $\mathbb{N}_0^k$. Es ist somit klar, was wir unter regulären, kontextfreien etc. Teilmengen von $\mathbb{N}_0^k$ verstehen. Nach dem Satz von Parikh ist jede kontextfreie Teilmenge $L \subset \mathbb{N}_0^k$ halblinear, d.h. L ist endliche Vereinigung linearer Mengen.

Dabei soll eine Menge $L' \subset \mathbb{N}_0^k$ linear heißen, wenn es Vektoren

$\alpha, \beta_1, \ldots, \beta_s \in \mathbb{N}_o^k$ ($s \geq 1$) gibt mit

$$L' = \{\alpha + k_1\beta_1 + \ldots + k_s\beta_s \mid k_1, \ldots, k_s \in \mathbb{N}_o\}$$

Bsp. für k = 2, s = 2:

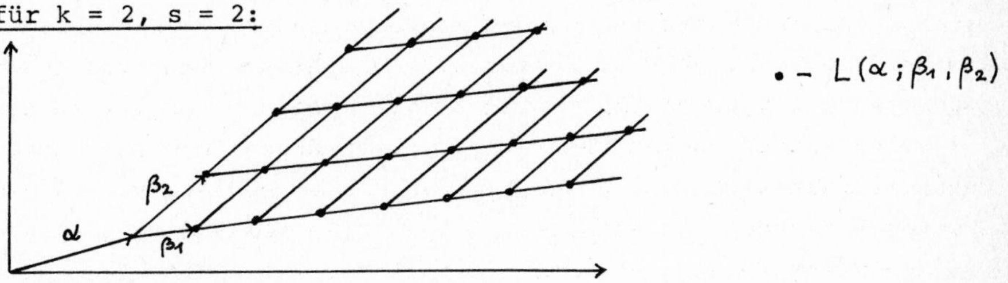

Unter einem Gitter in $\mathbb{N}_o^k$ verstehen wir eine Teilmenge der Form

$$G(\alpha; r_1, \ldots, r_k) = \{\alpha + (p_1r_1, \ldots, p_kr_k) \mid p_1, \ldots, p_k \in \mathbb{N}_o\}$$
mit $\alpha \in \mathbb{N}_o^k$; $r_1, \ldots, r_k \in \mathbb{N}$

Bsp. für k = 2

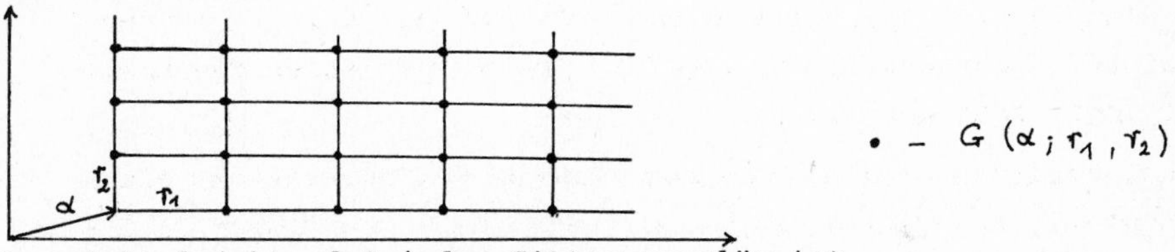

Man sieht leicht, daß jedes Gitter regulär ist.

Ein Kegel in $\mathbb{N}_o^k$ ist eine Teilmenge der Form

$$K(\alpha; \beta_1, \ldots, \beta_s) = \{\alpha + r_1\beta_1 + \ldots + r_s\beta_s \mid r_1, \ldots, r_s \in \mathbb{Q}_+\}$$
($\mathbb{Q}_+$ - Menge der positiven rationalen Zahlen)

Bsp. für k = 2

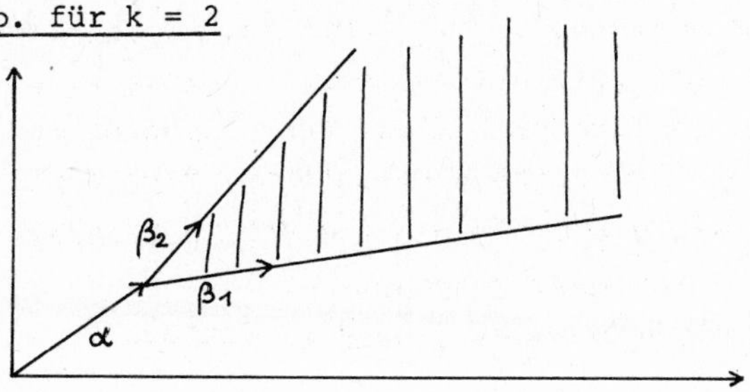

$K(\alpha; \beta_1, \beta_2)$

Wir nennen eine Menge $M \subset \mathbb{N}_o^k$ <u>ausgedehnt</u>, falls es in M eine unendliche Folge $\gamma_1, \gamma_2, \ldots$ von Vektoren gibt, bei denen keine Komponente wesentlich stärker wächst als die anderen, d.h. es gibt Zahlen $c_1, \ldots, c_k > o$ mit:

$$\sum_{l=1}^{k} \gamma_{jl} \leq c_i \gamma_{ji} \text{ für alle } j \in \mathbb{N},\ 1 \leq i \leq k$$

(dabei soll sein: $\gamma_j = (\gamma_{j1}, \ldots, \gamma_{jk})$ für alle $j \in \mathbb{N}$.)

Es läßt sich nun zeigen:

1. Ist eine nichtreguläre, halblineare, ausgedehnte Sprache $L \subset \mathbb{N}_o^k$ selbst oder ihr Komplement mit weniger als logarithmischem Platz erkennbar, so gibt es ein Gitter $G \subset L$.

2. Zu jeder halblinearen Sprache $L \subset \mathbb{N}_o^k$ gibt es eine reguläre Menge $R \subset \mathbb{N}_o^k$ und einen Kegel $K \subset \mathbb{N}_o^k$, so daß gilt:

$$L \cap K = R \cap K$$

Beh. 1 zeigt man folgendermaßen: steht geringerer als logarithmischer Platz zur Verfügung, so gibt es wegen der Ausgedehntheit von L eine Eingabe $a_1^{n_1} \ldots a_k^{n_k} \in L$, bei der sich ein Maschinenzustand (=(Zustand der endlichen Kontrolle, Speicherinhalt, Stellung der Köpfe im Speicher)) innerhalb eines a_i-Bereiches mindestens einmal wiederholt. Mann kann dann zeigen, daß auch die Eingabe $a_1^{n_1} \ldots a_{i-1}^{n_{i-1}} a_i^{n_i + s n!} a_{i+1}^{n_{i+1}} \ldots a_k^{n_k}$ für alle $S \in \mathbb{N}_o$ akzeptiert wird, und da dies für alle $1 \leq i \leq k$ gilt liegt auch das ganze Gitter $G((n_1, \ldots, n_k); n_1!, \ldots, n_k!)$ in L.

Zum Beweis von Beh. 2. legt man zunächst ein Gitter über L. Dann zeigt man, daß die Anzahl der Punkte aus L in einer Gittermasche um so größer ist, je weiter "rechts oben" sich diese Masche befindet, d.h. je größer ihre Punkte bzgl. der partiellen Ordnung auf $\mathbb{N}_o^k$ sind.

Da jede Gittermasche nur endlich viele Punkte enthält, kommt man schließlich zu einem Bereich, in dem alle Maschen die gleichen Punkte mit L gemeinsam haben. Daher hat in diesem Bereich L die gleichen Punkte wie eine reguläre Menge R.

Nehmen wir nun an, die Beh. von Satz 1 sei falsch, d.h. es gebe eine nichtreguläre, halblineare Sprache L, die mit weniger als logarithmischem Platz erkennbar ist. Wir zeigen durch Induktion über k, daß dies nicht möglich ist.
Ist k = 1, so ist jede halblineare Menge auch regulär und ein solches L kann nicht existieren.

Induktionsschritt:
Seien R,K die nach 2. zu L gehörigen Mengen.
Dann betrachten wir $L_1 = L \setminus R$
und $L_2 = R \setminus L$

Beide sind mit weniger als logarithmischem Platz erkennbar, beide sind halblinear (siehe [5]) und wegen $L = L_1 \cup (R \setminus L_2)$ ist mindestens eine davon nichtregulär. Ist diese nicht ausgedehnt, so läßt sich zeigen, daß es eine halblineare, nichtreguläre Menge $L' \subset \mathbb{N}_0^{k-1}$ gibt, die mit gleichem Platzbedarf erkennbar ist, was nach Induktionsvoraussetzung nicht möglich ist.
Ist sie ausgedehnt, so folgt nach 1., daß sie ein Gitter enthält, was nach 2. aber nicht möglich ist, da

$$L_i \cap K = \emptyset \quad \text{für } i = 1,2$$

aber $$K \cap G = \emptyset \quad \text{für jedes Gitter } G \subset \mathbb{N}_0^k$$

Haben wir nun eine nichtreguläre, beschränkte Sprache $L \subset w_1^* \ldots w_k^*$ ($w_1, \ldots, w_k \in \Sigma^*$, wobei Σ endl. Alphabet), so folgt daraus, daß man für

$$L' = \{a_1^{i_1}, \ldots, a_k^{i_k} \mid w_1^{i_1}, \ldots, w_k^{i_k} \in L\}$$

mindestens logarithmischen Platz benötigt, das gleiche Resultat für L. Man hat also:

<u>Satz 2:</u> Das Erkennen nichtregulärer beschränkter Sprachen erfordert mindestens logarithmischen Platz.

Man kann leicht zeigen (siehe auch [15]), daß jede beschränkte Sprache mit logarithmischem Platz erkennbar ist und somit ist unsere untere Schranke exakt.

Eine Sprache $L \subset \Sigma^*$ heißt <u>strikt nichtregulär</u>, wenn es Worte u,v,w, $x,y \in \Sigma^*$ gibt, so daß

$$\{u\}\{v\}^*\{w\}\{x\}^*\{y\} \cap L \quad \text{kontextfrei und nichtregulär ist.}$$

Zu einer strikt nichtregulären Sprache L betrachten wir

$$L' = \{a_1^{i_1}\ a_2^{i_2} \mid u\ v^{i_1}\ w\ x^{i_2}\ y \in L\}$$

und folgern wie oben aus logarithmischem Platzbedarf für L' mindestens logarithmischen Platzbedarf für L. Wir erhalten also:

Satz 3: Das Erkennen strikt nichtregulärer Sprachen erfordert mindestens logarithmischen Platz.

In [16] hat Stearns gezeigt, daß jede nichtreguläre, deterministische, kontextfreie Sprache strikt nichtregulär ist. Damit folgt aus Satz 3:

Satz 4: Das Erkennen nichtregulärer, deterministischer, kontextfreier Sprachen erfordert mindestens logarithmischen Platz.

Die Sätze 3 und 4 benutzen nur das Ergebnis von Satz 1 für den Fall k = 2 und werden bereits in [2] gezeigt.

3. Abschließende Bemerkungen

1. Beh. 1. gilt auch für nichtdeterministische Turingmaschinen. Aus dem Beweis von Satz 1 folgt daher:

Satz 5: Ist L eine Sprache aus einer der in den Sätzen 1-4 erwähnten Klassen, so erfordert das Erkennen von L oder das des Komplements von L auf einer nichtdeterministischen Maschine mindestens logarithmischen Platz.

Satz 5 gilt für beide Definitionen für Platzbedarf bei nichtdeterministischen Maschinen, die üblich sind

a) Mindestens eine akzeptierende Rechnung für jede akzeptierte Eingabe hat die Platzschranke zu erfüllen.

b) Jede mögliche Rechnung für jede beliebige Eingabe hat die Platzschranke zu erfüllen.

Liegt Definition a) zugrunde, so gilt die Aussage von Satz 1 nicht für nicht deterministische Maschinen. Ein Gegenbeispiel ist die Sprache $\{a^n b^m | n \neq m\}$, die dann mit Platz O (log log n) erkennbar ist (vgl. [2]). Es ist ein offenes Problem, ob Satz 1 für nichtdeterministische Maschinen gilt, wenn Definition b) zugrunde liegt. Für alle Sprachen, von denen man weiß, daß sie kein Gitter enthalten, gilt obige Aussage, z.B. für

$\{a^n b^n c^n | n \in \mathbb{N}\}$ oder für
$\{a^n b^m \quad | m \geq n\}$

2. Der Beweis der Beh. 1. (Seite 4) hängt nur von der Anzahl der möglichen Speicherzustände ab und nicht von der Art des Speichers oder des Speicherzugriffs etc. Damit gelten die Ergebnisse auch für andere Maschinenmodelle, wie z.B. RAM's (1- oder 2-Weg), Turingmaschinen mit mehrdimensionalem Speicher usw. Sie gelten sogar für das allgemeinste denkbare Modell, den in [1] definierten "allgemeinen Automaten".

3. Aus [3], [4] und [7] wissen wir, daß die Bedingung "kontextfrei" in Satz 1 nicht weggelassen werden kann, z.B. ist die Sprache

$\{a^n |$ die kleinste Zahl, die n nicht teilt, ist Zweierpotenz$\}$
mit Platz O (log log n) erkennbar.

4. Aus [10] wissen wir, daß es nichtreguläre, kontextfreie Sprachen gibt die mit Platz O (log log n) erkennbar sind, z.B.

$\{0,1,\#\}^* \setminus \{\#\,\mathrm{bin}(1)\#\,\mathrm{bin}(2)^R\# \ldots \#\,\mathrm{bin}(n)^{(R)}\# \;|$
$n \in \mathbb{N}\}$

wobei bin (i) die Binärdarstellung der Zahl i ist und w^R das Spiegelbild des Wortes w. Damit gilt unsere untere Schranke also nicht für alle nichtregulären kontextfreien Sprachen.

5. Unsere untere Schranke ist für halblineare und beschränkte Sprachen scharf wie in [1] und [15] gezeigt wurde, wo entsprechende Algorithmen des Platzbedarfs O (log n) angegeben wurden. Es ist ein offenes Problem, ob alle deterministischen kontextfreien Sprachen mit Platz O (log n) erkennbar sind.

LITERATURVERZEICHNIS

[1] Alt,H.: Eine untere Schranke für den Platzbedarf bei der Analyse beschränkter kontextfreier Sprachen, Dissertation, Saarbrücken 1976

[2] Alt, H. / Mehlhorn, K. : Lower Bounds for the Space Complexity of Contextfree Recognition, erscheint im Tagungsband des 3rd Coll. on Automata, Languages and Programming, 1976

[3] Alt, H. / Mehlhorn, K.: A Language over a Single Letter Alphabet requiring only O(log log n) Space, SIGACT NEWS, Vol. 7, 1975

[4] Freedman, A.R. / Ladner, E.R. : Space Bounds Processing Contentless Inputs, ICSS, 1976.

[5] Ginsburg, S.: The Mathematical Theory of Context-Free Languages, McGraw-Hill, 1972

[6] Greub, W.H.: Linear Algebra, Springer-Verlag, 1967.

[7] Hartmanis, J. / Berman, L.: A Note on Tape Bounds for SLA Language Processing, 16th FOCS Symposium, Berkeley, 1975

[8] Hopcroft, J.W. / Ullmann, J.D.: Formal Languages and their Relation to Automata, Addison-Wesley, Reading, Mass. 1969

[9] Hotz, G. / Messerschmidt, J.: Dyck-Sprachen sind in Bandkomplexität log n analysierbar, TB Univ.d.Saarlandes, 1974

[1o] Lewis, P.M. / Hartmanis, J. / Stearns, R.E.: Memory Bounds for the Recognition of Context-Free and Context-Sensitive Languages,IEEE Conference Record on Switching Circuit Theory and Logical Design, 179-2o2, 1965

[11] Lynch, N.: Log Space Recognition and Translation of Paranthesis Languages, USC, 1975 - July

[12] Mehlhorn, K.: Komplexitätstheorie, Vorlesungsskript WS 1975/76, Univ.d.Saarlandes

[13] Mehlhorn, K.: Bracket Languages are Recognizable in Logarithmic Space, TB Univ.d.Saarlandes, 1975

[14] Monien, B.: About the Deterministic Simulation of Nondeterministic (log n)-Tape Bounded Turing Machines, 2-te GI Fachtagung, Kaiserslautern, 1975

[15] Springsteel / Ritchie : Language Recognition by Marking Automata, Information & Control, 1972, Nr.4, May, 313-33o

[16] Stearns, R.E.: A Regularity Test for Pushdown-Machines, Information & Control, 11, 1967, 323-34o

[17] Sudborough, I.H.: On Tape Bounded Classes and Multi-head Finite Automata, 14th SWAT Symposium, 1973, 138-144

On one-way Auxiliary pushdown automata

F.-J. Brandenburg

ABSTRACT:

A class of machines called one-way auxiliary pushdown automata, 1-APDA, is introduced. These machines differ from the well-known auxiliary pushdown automata by their input tape, which is one-way only. We restrict ourselves to f-tape-bounded 1-APDA with $f(n) \leqslant n$ and investigate some of their properties. In particular, it is shown:

i) $\log \log n$ is a lower bound for the tape complexity of 1-APDA to accept non-context-free languages, and this is a sharp bound.

ii) If $f(n) <\cdot n$, i.e. if $\lim f(n) / n = 0$, then $\{w_1 c w_2 c \overleftarrow{w}_1 c \overleftarrow{w}_2 / w_1, w_2 \in \{o,1\}^*, \ |w_1| = |w_2|\}$ is not accepted by any f-tape-bounded 1-APDA.

iii) For every f with $f(n) <\cdot n$, nondeterministic f-tape-bounded 1-APDA are strictly more powerful than deterministic f-tape-bounded 1-APDA. This is in opposition to (two-way) auxiliary pushdown automata and to f-tape-bounded 1-APDA with $f(n) \geqslant c \cdot n$.

INTRODUCTION:

In recent years, automata theorists have devoted a great deal of effort to the study of one-way and two-way acceptors. Examples of such devices include the finite state automata, pushdown automata, stack automata, time- and tape-bounded Turing machines, and extensions of these models with several heads or auxiliary storage tapes.

The question asked most of all for each of these devices is the question of determinism versus nondeterminism. There are only a few cases where an answer is known. (See Book 75). For the two extreme cases of finite state automata and arbitrary Turing machines and for f-tape-bounded (two-way) auxiliary pushdown automata with $f(n) \geqslant \log n$, nondeterminism adds nothing to the power of acceptance. On the other hand, the family of deterministic context-free languages, defined by deterministic (one-way) pushdown automata,

is a proper subfamily of the family of context-free languages, defined by nondeterministic (one-way) pushdown automata, and the complexity classes of deterministic, tape-bounded on-line Turing machines below linear tape complexity are smaller than the corresponding nondeterministic complexity classes. (See Hopcroft, Ullman 69 b).
In this paper it is shown that nondeterministic f-tape-bounded one-way auxiliary pushdown automata with $f(n) \lessdot n$ are strictly more powerful than their deterministic counterparts. Thus, the question of determinism versus nondeterminism is completely settled for f-tape-bounded one-way and two-way auxiliary pushdown automata, provided $f(n) \geqslant \log n$. Furthermore, for the simulation of nondeterministic f-tape-bounded auxiliary pushdown automata by deterministic auxiliary pushdown automata, the two-way mechanism is absolutely necessary.

PRELIMINARIES:

Definition 1:

A one-way auxiliary pushdown automaton, 1-APDA, $M = (K,\Sigma,\Gamma_1,\Gamma_2,\delta,p_o,Z_o,F)$ is a 8-tuple, where K and F are the sets of states and final states, Σ,Γ_1 and Γ_2 are the input alphabet, the Turing tape alphabet and the pushdown tape alphabet. p_o is the initial state and Z_o the initial pushdown symbol. The transition relation δ is a mapping from $K \times \Sigma \cup \{e\} \times \Gamma_1 \times \Gamma_2$ into the finite subsets of $K \times \Gamma_1 \times \{-1,o,1\} \times \Gamma_2^*$.

The notions of configurations, moves, computations, acceptance, and equivalence for 1-APDA are defined in the same way as for Turing machines or auxiliary pushdown automata.

A 1-APDA M is deterministic, iff in each configuration M has at most one choice of move.

If f is a function on the natural numbers and L is a subset of Σ^*, then we say M accepts L within tape-bound f iff M accepts L, and for each $w \in L$, $|w| = n$, M accepts w in a computation using no more than $f(n)$ squares on any Turing tape.
Now, M is said so be a f-tape-bounded 1-APDA.

Informally, each f-tape-bounded 1-APDA is a combination of a f-tape-bounded on-line Turing machine and a one-way pushdown automaton. Thus, a 1-APDA can be considered as an on-line Turing machine with an additional pushdown tape or as an extended pushdown automaton, which has an external memory of $f(n)$ storage cells.

Obviously, there is a "linear Speed-up Theorem" for tape-bounded 1-APDA. Furthermore, we can restrict ourselves to 1-APDA with one Turing tape only.

2. HALTING 1-APDA

In the view of this paper, writing pushdown automata, introduced and studied by Mager, are equivalent to linear tape-bounded 1-APDA and to linear tape-bounded (two-way) auxiliary pushdown automata. These automata define the largest complexity class, we will consider. Many properties of writing pushdown automata are also due to f-tape-bounded 1-APDA with $f(n) \leqslant n$. Especially, we can rewrite Mager's proof, that writing pushdown automata may use only a bounded amount of pushdown storage and may halt for all inputs.

Lemma 1:

For each f-tape-bounded (deterministic) 1-APDA M with $f(n) \geqslant \log n$ there is an equivalent f-tape-bounded (deterministic) 1-APDA M', such that for any input of length n, the length of the pushdown tape of M' does not grow beyond $c' \cdot 2^{c \cdot f(n)}$ for some $c, c' > o$.

Theorem 1:

If M is a f-tape-bounded 1-APDA and $\log n \leqslant f(n)$ for all n, then there is an equivalent f-tape-bounded 1-APDA M'' that halts for all inputs. Furthermore, if M is deterministic, then so is M''.

Corollary 1:

For each computable function f, and each f-tape-bounded 1-APDA M, the set of strings accepted by M is recursive.

This corollary can also be obtained from the fact, that auxiliary pushdown automata simulate 1-APDA and that f-tape-bounded auxiliary pushdown automata define recursive sets, provided f is computable.

Corollary 2:

The families of sets accepted by f-tape-bounded deterministic 1-APDA are closed under complementation, provided $f(n) \geqslant \log n$.

Proof:
The usual construction of interchanging the sets of accepting and non-accepting states of a halting, deterministic 1-APDA M yields a 1-APDA M', which accepts the complement of the set of strings, accepted by M.

3. LOWER COMPLEXITY BOUNDS

We first develop a "pumping lemma" for 1-APDA and then show that log log n is a lower complexity bound. Finally, the example, which proves that "log log n" is a sharp lower bound, illustrates the efficient mechanism of interactions of the Turing tape and the pushdown tape of a 1-APDA to compute and store integers on least possible squares of the Turing tape.

Lemma 2:

Let $M = (K,\Sigma,\Gamma_1,\Gamma_2,\delta,p_o,Z_o,F)$ be a 1-APDA. Assume that M writes at most l symbols on its pushdown tape in one step, i.e. $\delta(p,a,A,Z) \ni (p',B,d,\gamma)$ implies $|\gamma| \leqslant 1$. Furthermore, let $x \in \Sigma^*$ be accepted by M and assume that M uses k squares of its Turing tape for an accepting computation of x.

Define the set of "external states" of M on x by

$Q_x := \{q = (p,\alpha\uparrow\beta) \ / \ \ p \in K, \ \alpha\uparrow\beta \in \Gamma_1^*\uparrow\Gamma_1^*, \ |\alpha\beta| \leqslant k\}$. Then $|Q_x| \ \leqslant \ |K| \cdot \sum_{i=1}^{k} i \cdot |\Gamma_1|^i \ \leqslant \ |K| \cdot (k+1) \cdot |\Gamma_1|^{k+1}$, where $|Q_x|$ denotes the number of elements of the set Q_x.

If the length of x is greater than $l^{|Q_x|^2 \cdot |\Gamma_2|}$, then x can be written as $x = uvwyz$ with $|vy| \geqslant 1$ and for each $i \geqslant 0$, $x_i = uv^i wy^i z$ is accepted by M too, such that M does not use more than k squares of its work tape.

Proof:
The proof is just the pumping lemma, written in terms of pushdown automata or 1-APDA.

Theorem 2:

If M is a f-tape-bounded 1-APDA, where f is not bounded above by a constant, then $\limsup f(n) / \log\log n > 0$.

Proof:

For each integer k, let n_k be the smallest n such that $f(n) \geq k$, and let x be an input of length n_k to M, using at least k cells of the Turing tape.

Because of Lemma 2, $n_k \leq 1^{|Q_X|^2 \cdot |\Gamma_2|}$.

Hence, for some constant $c > o$, $n_k \leq 2^{2^{c \cdot k}}$ and $\log \log n_k \leq c \cdot k$.

Thus, for the infinity of n which are n_k for some k, we have $1/c \leq f(n) / \log \log n$.

This proves the theorem.

Corollary 3:

For f-tape-bounded 1-APDA, if f is a tape function such that $\limsup f(n) / \log \log n = o$, then only context-free languages are accepted.

Theorem 3:

There exists a log log n tape-bounded deterministic 1-APDA M that accepts the non-context-free language $\{a^{2^{2^k}} / k \geq o\}$.

Proof:

Informally, M operates as follows.

Each integer i can uniquely be represented as $i = 2^{t_1} + 2^{t_2} + \ldots + 2^{t_r}$, where $t_1 > t_2 > \ldots > t_r \geq o$. Let $\tilde{t}_j$ denote the binary expansion of the integer t_j and let ¢ be a new symbol. If M has read i a's from the input tape, then the pushdown tape contains the string $\tilde{t}_{r-1}$ ¢ ... ¢ $\tilde{t}_1 Z_o$ where $\tilde{t}_{r-1}$ is on the top of the pushdown tape and the Turing tape contains $\tilde{t}_r$. Each t_j is less or equal to 2^k. Hence, each $\tilde{t}_j$ has length less or equal to k+1.

If M reads the i+1 st a, it successively computes the binary representation of i+1, using the contents of the pushdown tape and at most $\lceil \log \log i+2 \rceil$ squares of the Turing tape.

M starts with an empty Turing tape and with Z_o on its pushdown tape. M accepts, iff the pushdown tape contains Z_o and the Turing tape contains a string of the form $1o^k$, $k \geq o$.

Notice, that for each input a^n, M uses precisely $\lceil \log \log n+1 \rceil$ storage cells to decide, whether n is of the form 2^{2^k}

4. DETERMINISM VERSUS NONDETERMINISM

We define a language L which can only be accepted by linear tape-bounded 1-APDA and therefrom we deduce some relations between deterministic and nondeterministic 1-APDA.

Theorem 4:

If $\lim f(n) / n = o$, then the language
$L = \{w_1 c w_2 c \overleftarrow{w}_1 c \overleftarrow{w}_2 \; / \; w_1 w_2 \in \{o,1\}^*, |w_1| = |w_2| = n, n \geq o\}$
is not accepted by any f-tape-bounded 1-APDA.

Proof:
Suppose, there is some f-tape-bounded 1-APDA M that accepts L. Without loss of generality let $f(n) \geq \log n$, and assume that M does not increase its pushdown tape beyond $c_1 \cdot 2^{c_2 \cdot f(n)}$ and halts for all inputs. Furthermore, M has exactly one final state q_f and accepts in q_f with blanks on its Turing tape and with the initial pushdown symbol Z_o on its pushdown tape.

A storage state of M is any triple $q = (p, \alpha\uparrow\beta, z) \in K \times \Gamma_1^* \uparrow \Gamma_1^* \times \Gamma_2$, where p is a state of M, $\alpha \uparrow \beta$ is the contents of the Turing tape and z is the topmost symbol of the pushdown tape. $q_o = (p_o, \uparrow b, z_o)$ is the initial storage state and $q_f = (p_f, \uparrow b, z_o)$ is the only accepting storage state.
Now, a configuration of M is any pair (q,γ) where q is a storage state and γ is a string on the pushdown tape below the topmost symbol. For any input string x and all configurations (q,γ) and (q',γ') we write $x : (q,\gamma) \vdash (q',\gamma')$, if M starting in (q,γ) and processing x will enter (q',γ'). Thus, x is accepted by M iff $x : (q_o, e) \vdash (q_f, e)$.

For any configuration (q,γ) of M, if there is a string $y = y_1 c y_2 c y_3 c y_4$ (or $y = y_1 c y_2 c y_3$) with $y_i \in \{o,1\}^*$ such that $y : (q,\gamma) \vdash (q_f, e)$, then there is at most one $x \in \{o,1\}^*$ (or $x \in \{o,1\}^* c \{o,1\}^*$) such that $x : (q_o, e) \vdash (q,\gamma)$ and xy is in the form required by L, or M would accept a string not in L.
Thus, for each string $x \in \{o,1\}^* \cup \{o,1\}^* c \{o,1\}^*$, if $x : (q_o,e) \vdash (q,\gamma)$ and if there is some y with $y : (q,\gamma) \vdash (q_f, e)$, then x is identified by (q,γ).

Moreover for any $w_1, w_1' \in \{o,1\}^*$ $(w_1 c w_2', w_2''$ with $|w_1| = |w_2' w_2''|)$ there must be some configuration (q,γ) which is accessible from the initial configuration when $w_1(\overleftarrow{w_1}\, c\, w_2')$ is the initial portion of the input string, and $w_1'\ c\ w_2\ c\ \overleftarrow{w_1 w_1'}\ c\ \overleftarrow{w}_2 : (q,\gamma) \vdash (q_f,e)$ holds $(w_2'\ c\ \overleftarrow{w}_1\ c\ \overleftarrow{w_2' w_2''} : (q,\gamma) \vdash (q_f,e))$.

Let us consider a computation of M, on an input string $w_1 c w_2 c \overleftarrow{w}_1 c \overleftarrow{w}_2$, $|w_1| = |w_2| = n$, if M finally enters the accepting storage state.
In the first phase, on input $w_1 c$, M enters some configuration (q_1, γ_{w1}) which identifies w_1.
In the second phase M processes an initial part u of w_2. In this phase, M may enlarge the pushdown storage first, but finally it erases some symbols from γ_{w2} and enters some configuration $(q_2, \gamma_{w_1'})$.
In the third phase, on input vc with $uv = w_2$, M never reads symbols from $\gamma_{w_1'}$ and enters some configuration $(q_3, \gamma_v\ \gamma_{w_1'})$.
In the fourth phase, on input $\overleftarrow{w}_1 c$, there are two cases for the operations of M. M either erases γ_v on the pushdown tape and reads a part of $\gamma_{w_1'}$ or M does not read anything of $\gamma_{w_1'}$.
In the first case, M tries to compare w_1 and $\overleftarrow{w}_1$, but it erases γ_v and forgets v. Now, phase four ends, if M will read the topmost symbol of $\gamma_{w_1'}$ in the next step. Then M has processed j symbols from $\overleftarrow{w}_1 c$ and is in a configuration $(q_4, \gamma_{w_1'})$.
In the second case, M may compare w_1 and $\overleftarrow{w}_1$ by its storage states only. It processes $\overleftarrow{w}_1 c$ and enters some configuration $(q_5, \gamma_{\overleftarrow{w}_1 v}\ \gamma_{w_1'})$.
In the fifth phase, if case 1 holds true in phase four, M processes the remaining n-j symbols of $\overleftarrow{w}_1$ and $c\overleftarrow{w}_2$ and ends up in the accepting storage state.
If case 2 holds true in phase four, after an initial part of w_2 of length e, M will read the topmost symbol of $\gamma_{w_1'}$ in the next step, being in some configuration $(q_6, \gamma_{w_1'})$. M completes this phase by processing the remaining part of $\overleftarrow{w}_2$ and ends up in the accepting storage state.
The following picture illustrates the movements of M on its pushdown tape, when additional zigzag movements are omitted.

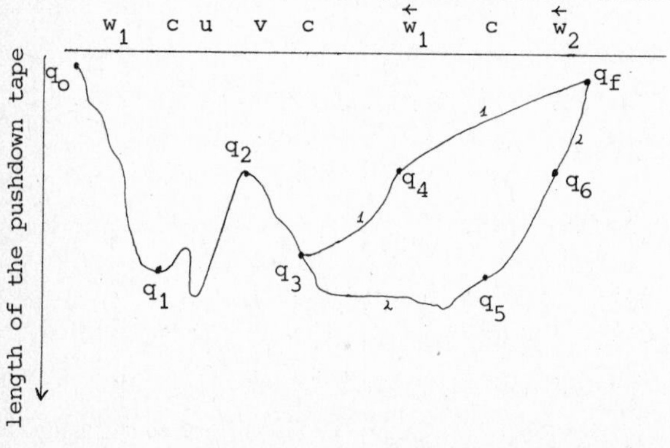

We will now investigate a quantitative analysis of the five phases of the computations of M. It turns out that M cannot compare both w_1, $\overleftarrow{w}_1$ and w_2, $\overleftarrow{w}_2$ and thus accepts strings which are not in L.

For each n, the set of storage states M may use for any accepting computation of an input string of length 4n+3 is defined by

$Q_n = \{q \mid q = (p, \alpha \uparrow \beta, Z) \in K \times \Gamma_1^* \uparrow \Gamma_1^* \times \Gamma_2, \ |\alpha\beta| \leq f(4n+3)\}$.

Thus, the number of elements of Q_n is bounded by

$$|Q_n| \leq |K| \cdot f(4n+3) \cdot |\Gamma_1|^{f(4n+3)}$$

$$\leq c_3 \cdot 2^{c_4 \cdot f(4n+3)} \leq 2^{k' \cdot f(4n+3)} \quad \text{for some constants}$$

$c_3, c_4, k' > o$ and all $n > n_o$ for some n_o.

For each storage state $q_1 \in Q_n$ define

$S_1(q_1) = \{w_1 \in \{o,1\}^n \mid w_1 c : (q_o, e) \vdash (q_1, \gamma_{w_1})$ and there exists w_2 such that $w_2 c \overleftarrow{w}_1 c \overleftarrow{w}_2 : (q_1, \gamma_{w_1}) \vdash (q_f, e)\}$

and for each $q_1 \in Q_n$ and each $w_1 \in S_1(q_1)$ let

$S_2(q_1, w_1) = \{w_2 \in \{o,1\}^n \mid w_1 c : (q_o, e) \vdash (q_1, \gamma_{w_1})$ and $w_2 c \overleftarrow{w}_1 c \overleftarrow{w}_2 : (q_1, \gamma_{w_1}) \vdash (q_f, e)\}$.

Claim 1:

There exists a storage state $q_1 \in Q_n$ such that

$$\left|\{w_1 \in S_1(q_1) / |S_2(q_1, w_1)| \geq 2^{n/2} / |Q_n|\}\right| \geq 2^{n/2} / |Q_n|.$$

Proof:

Assume the contrary. Then M accepts less than $2 \cdot 2^{3n/2}$ strings $w_1 c w_2 c \overleftarrow{w}_1 c \overleftarrow{w}_2$, $|w_1| = |w_2| = n$, but there are 2^{2n} strings of this form in L.

For each $q_1 \in Q_n$ and each $w_1 \in S_1(q_1)$ let

$S_2'(q_1, w_1) = \{u \in \{o,1\}^* \mid$ there is a string v with $uv = w_2 \in S_2(q_1, w_1)$, such that $w_1 c : (q_o, e) \vdash (q_1, \gamma_{w_1})$, $\gamma_{w_1} = \gamma_{w_1'} \gamma_{w_1''}$,

$u : (q_1, \gamma_{w_1''}) \vdash (q_2^u, e)$ and $vc: (q_2^u, e) \vdash (q_3^{uv}, \gamma_v)\}$.

$S_2''(q_1, w_1) = \{v \in \{o,1\}^* \mid$ there is $u \in S_2'(q_1, w_1)$ and $uv \in S_2(q_1, w_1)\}$.

Claim 2:

For each $q_1 \in Q_n$ and each $w_1 \in S_1(q_1)$ $|S_2'(q_1, w_1)| \leq |Q_n| \cdot |\gamma_{w_1}|$, or M accepts strings which are not in L.

Proof:

If M erases a further symbol from γ_{w_1} it has at most $|Q_n|$ different choices of storage states. Thus, the above relation holds.

Because of claim 1 and $S_2(q_1, w_1) \subseteq S_2'(q_1, w_1) \cdot S_2''(q_1, w_1)$ there exists a storage state q_1 such that for all $w_1 \in S_1(q_1)$

$|S_2''(q_1,w_1)| \geq 2^{n/2} / |Q_n|^2 \cdot |\gamma_{w_1}|.$

Now we fix the storage state q_2^u and define

$S(w_1,q_1,q_2) = \{v \in S_2''(q_1,w_1) \mid$ there is a string $u \in S_2'(q_1,w_1)$
such that $w_1 c : (q_o,e) \vdash (q_1,\gamma_1''\gamma_1')$,
$u : (q_1,\gamma_1'') \vdash (q_2,e)$ and $vc: (q_2,e) \vdash (q_3^v,\gamma_v)\}$.

Then there are storage states q_1,q_2 such that

$|S(w_1,q_1,q_2)| \geq 2^{n/2} / |Q_n|^3 \cdot |\gamma_{w_1}|$ and

$|\{w_1 / |S(w_1,q_1,q_2)| \geq 2^{n/2} / |Q_n|^3 \cdot |\gamma_{w_1}|\}| \geq 2^{n/2} / |Q_n|^2.$

Claim 3:

Let $w_1 \in \{o,1\}^*$ and $q_1,q_2 \in Q_n$. If there is some $i > |Q_n|$ such that there are i strings $w_2^i \in S_2(q_1,w_1)$, $w_2^i = u_i v_i$, $v_i \in S(w_1,q_1,q_2)$, $q_4^i \in Q_n$ and $w_1 = x_i y_i$ with
$w_1 c : (q_o,e) \vdash (q_1,\gamma_{w_1''}\gamma_{w_1'})$, $u_1 : (q_1,\gamma_{w_1''}) \vdash (q_2,e)$,
$v_i c\overleftarrow{y}_i : (q_2,e) \vdash (q_4^i,e)$ and $\overleftarrow{x}_i c w_2^i : (q_4^i,\gamma_{w_1'}) \vdash (q_f,e)$, then for some $i \neq j$ and $w_2^i \neq w_2^j$, $q_4^i = q_4^j$ holds true.

Thus M accepts both strings $w_1 c u_i v_i c \overleftarrow{y}_i \overleftarrow{x}_i c \overleftarrow{w}_2$ and $w_1 c u_i v_j c \overleftarrow{y}_j \overleftarrow{x}_i c \overleftarrow{w}_2$, the latter of which is not in L.

The claim is evident, since there are only $|Q_n|$ different choices of q_4^i.

Claim 4:

Suppose for some $i > |Q_n|$ and $q_1,q_2 \in Q_n$ there are strings $w_1^i \in S_1(q_1)$ such that for each w_1^i there exist
$w_2^i \in S_2(q_1,w_1)$ and $q_6^i \in Q_n$ with $w_2^i = u_i v_i$, $v_i \in S(w_1^i,q_1,q_2)$, $w_2^i = x_i y_i$ and $w_1^i c u_i : (q_o,e) \vdash (q_2,\gamma_{w_1^i})$,
$v_i c \overleftarrow{w}_1^i c \overleftarrow{y}_i : (q_2,e) \vdash (q_6^i,e)$, $\overleftarrow{x}_i : (q_6^i,\gamma_{w_1^i}) \vdash (q_f,e)$, then for some $i \neq j$ and $w_1^i \neq w_1^j$, $q_6^i \neq q_6^j$ holds true.

Thus, M accepts both strings

$w_1^i c u_i v_i c \overleftarrow{w}_1^i c \overleftarrow{y}_i \overleftarrow{x}_i \in L$ and $w_1^i c u_i v_j c \overleftarrow{w}_1^j c \overleftarrow{y}_j \overleftarrow{x}_i \notin L$.

Claim 5:

Consider the set

$S(q_1,q_2) = \{w_1 \mid |S(w_1,q_1,q_2)| \geq 2^{n/2} / |Q_n|^3 \cdot |\gamma_{w_1}|\}$

where $|S(q_1,q_2)| \geq 2^{n/2} / |Q_n|^2$ for some $q_1,q_2 \in Q_n$.

If both $2^{n/2} / |Q_n|^3 \cdot |\gamma_{w_1}| > |Q_n|$ and $2^{n/2} / |Q_n|^2 > |Q_n|$ then $S(q_1,q_2)$ satisfies the presuppositions of at least one of claim 3 or claim 4.

Since $\lim f(n) / n = o$, for all $k > o$ there exists n_o such that for all $n > n_o$, $k \cdot f(n) < n$. Let $k/2 = 4 \cdot 5k' + 5k''$, where k''

is obtained from the bound on the length of the pushdown tape of M, namely $c_1 \cdot c^{c_2 \cdot f(4n+3)} \leqslant 2^{k'' f(4n+3)}$.

Now, $|Q_n|^4 \cdot |\gamma_w| \leqslant 2^{4k' \cdot f(4n+3)} \cdot 2^{k'' f(4n+3)} < 2^{n/2}$.

Hence, the pressupposition of claim 5 are satisfied, and the theorem is proven.

Definition 2:

Let Σ be an alphabet and $a \notin \Sigma$.

For each rational number r with $r \geqslant 1$ we define

$f_r : \Sigma^* \to \Sigma^*\{a\}^*$

$\quad x \to x a^m$, where $m = [|x|^r - |x|]$.

$g_r : \mathbb{N} \to \mathbb{N}$ and

$\quad n \to [n^r]$

$h_r : \mathbb{N} \to \mathbb{N}$

$\quad n \to \max\{[n^{1/r}], [\log n]\}$, where $[p]$ denotes the greatest integer less or equal to p.

Notice, that f_r, g_r and h_r are computable by on-line log n-tape-bounded deterministic Turing machines.

The functions f_r pad the length of a string by a polynomial amount, and for $\log n \leqslant n^{1/r}$, g_r is the inverse function of h_r, and vice versa.

The following results can be easily obtained from theorem 3 and theorem 4.

Theorem 5:

For each rational number $r, r \geqslant 1$, there is a h_r-tape-bounded 1-APDA M_r that accepts $L_r := f_r(L)$.

Theorem 6:

Let p,q be rationals with $p,q \geqslant 1$.

If L_p is accepted by some h_q-tape-bounded 1-APDA M_q, then there is a $h_q(g_p(n))$-tape-bounded 1-APDA that accepts L.

Theorem 7:

For all rationals p,q with $1 \leqslant p < q$, the language L_q is not contained in the family of languages accepted by h_p-tape-bounded 1-APDA.

Hence, there are infinite hierarchies of families of languages defined by h_r-tape-bounded 1-APDA, deterministic and nondeterministic.

Theorem 8:

The language $L = \{w_1 c w_2 c \overleftarrow{w}_1 c \overleftarrow{w}_2 \ / \ w_1, w_2 \in \{o,1\}^*, \ |w_1| = |w_2|\}$ can be expressed as the intersection of the context-free languages $L_1 = \{w_1 c x c \overleftarrow{w}_1 c y \ / \ x,y,w_1 \in \{o,1\}^*\}$, $L_2 = \{x c w_2 c y c \overleftarrow{w}_2 \ / \ x,y,w_2 \in \{o,1\}^*$.
$L_3 = \{w_1 c w_2 c w_3 c w_4 \ / \ w_i \in \{o,1\}^*, \ |w_1| = |w_2|\}$.
The complement of L is a context-free language.

Corollary 4:

For every f with $f(n) <\cdot n$,
the families of languages accepted by f-tape-bounded nondeterministic 1-APDA are neither closed under complementation nor under intersections of context-free languages.

Theorem 9:

For every f with $f(n) <\cdot n$,
nondeterministic f-tape-bounded 1-APDA are strictly more powerful than deterministic f-tape-bounded 1-APDA.

Proof:

The complement of the language L is context-free. Thus, for any f there is some nondeterministic 1-APDA accepting it. Because of corollary 2, if there is a f-tape-bounded deterministic 1-APDA accepting it, then there is a $\max\{f(n), \log n\}$ - tape-bounded deterministic 1-APDA, accepting L. For $f(n) <\cdot n$, this contradicts theorem 4.

Thus, it is evident that the complement of the language L is an inherently nondeterministic language.

Cook has shown that for every f with $f(n) \geqslant \log n$, deterministic and nondeterministic two-way f-tape-bounded auxiliary pushdown automata have the same accepting power.

Since f-tape-bounded 1-APDA with $c \cdot f(n) \geqslant n$ can simulate f-tape-bounded two-way auxiliary pushdown automata, and vice versa, nondeterminism adds nothing to the power of acceptance in this case.

Finally, the language L can be accepted by deterministic two-way pushdown automata, i.e. by deterministic two-way f-tape-bounded auxiliary pushdown automata with $f(n) = o$ for all n. Hence, we obtain.

Theorem 1o:

For every f with $f(n) \lessdot n$, (deterministic or nondeterministic) f-tape-bounded two-way auxiliary pushdown automata are strictly more powerful than (deterministic or nondeterministic resp.) f-tape-bounded 1-APDA.

Theorem 11:

For every f with $f(n) \lessdot n$, (deterministic or nondeterministic) f-tape-bounded 1-APDA are strictly more powerful than (deterministic or nondeterministic resp.) f-tape-bounded on-line Turing machines.

This stems from the fact, that the deterministic context-free language $\{w c \overleftarrow{w} \;/\; w \in \{o,1\}^*\}$ is not accepted by any nondeterministic f-tape-bounded on-line Turing machine, unless $f(n) > k \cdot n$. (See Hopcroft, Ullman 69 b).

Theorem 12:

For every $c > o$ and every f with $f(n) \lessdot n$, $c \cdot n$-tape-bounded deterministic or nondeterministic 1-APDA are strictly more powerful than f-tape-bounded nondeterministic 1-APDA.

In order to accept the language L and its complement by deterministic auxiliary pushdown automata, either the two-way mechanism, or at least a linear amount of Turing tape are necessary. In this case, there is no difference in the accepting power of one-way and two-way devices. Thus, for the simulation of nondeterministic auxiliary pushdown automata by deterministic auxiliary pushdown automata, the two-way mechanism is absolutely necessary.

5. REFERENCES

Book, R.V. (1975). Formal Language Theory and Theoretical Computer Science. Proceedings 2nd GI Conference, Automata Theory and Formal Languages, Kaiserslautern (1975), 1-16. Lecture Notes in Computer Science, No. 33.

Book, R.V. (1976). Translational Lemmas, Polynomial Time, and $(\log n)^j$-Space. Theoretical Computer Science 1 (1976), 215 - 226.

Cook, S.A. (1971). Characterizations of Pushdown Machines in Terms of Time-Bounded Computers. JACM 18 (1971), 4 - 18.

Hopcroft, J.E., Ullman, J.D. (1969 a). Formal Languages and their Relation to Automata. Addison-Wesley Publishing Company.

Hopcroft, J.E., Ullman, J.D. (1969 b). Some Results on Tape-Bounded Turing Machines. JACM 16 (1969), 168 - 177.

Mager, G. (1969). Writing Pushdown Automata. JCSS 3 (1969), 276 - 318.

Verbeek, R. (1976). private communication.

Un langage algebrique non-generateur

L. Boasson

Abstract

We give an example of a context-free language L_o which is not a full generator of the CFL's family though it is expansive and meeting the IRS condition [9]. We get then a counter-example to a conjecture of S. Greibach [9] which can be compared to a positive result dealing with the same questions concerning parenthesis languages [5].

La théorie des langages a particulièrement donné lieu à des travaux concernant les langages algébriques (ou "context-free") dont le rôle apparaît comme crucial en Informatique Théorique. L'introduction de la théorie des AFL's [7] a donné naissance à une série de nouvelles questions concernant la famille Alg. de ces langages. Celles-ci sont le plus souvent traitées en utilisant les transductions rationnelles et leur caractérisation algébrique en terme de morphisme, morphisme inverse et intersection rationnelle [11]. Le fait que la famille Alg. soit un "full AFL" résulte de propriétés de clôture classiques. Le caractère principal [7] de ce "full AFL" apparaît comme une reformulation du théorème de Chomsky-Schützenberger [6] utilisant le fait qu'un langage de Dyck peut-être codé par $D_2'^*$, le langage de Dyck sur deux paires de parenthèses. Si l'on considère les choses de ce point de vue, deux remarques sont alors naturelles.

1. Les seules opérations d'AFL utilisées sont les transductions rationnelles, ce qui fait que $D_2'^*$ peut-être considéré aussi bien comme un générateur du "full AFL" que du cône rationnel [4] Alg. On sait bien que cette propriété vaut pour tout générateur de Alg [4], si bien que nous utiliserons le terme de *générateur* pour un langage L sans préciser s'il s'agit d'un générateur du full AFL ou du cône rationnel.

2. Le langage $D_1'^*$, langage de Dyck sur une paire de parenthèse semble avoir un statut particulier. Ce problème est maintenant résolu: on sait que le cône rationnel engendré par $D_1'^*$ est celui des *langages à un compteur* Ocl, qui constitue une sous-famille propre de Alg. [2].

Très tôt dans l'étude des grammaires algébriques, il a été établi que les grammaires linéaires engendraient une sous-famille propre de Alg., la famille Lin des *langages linéaires*. Il se trouve que Lin constitue aussi un cône rationnel principal. Muni ainsi de deux sous-familles de Alg., il était naturel de considérer le plus petit "full AFL" les contenant toutes les deux et qui soit fermée par substitution; on obtient ainsi la famille Gre des *langages de Greibach*. On sait, en vertu de résultats généraux [8], que ce full AFL n'est pas principal et qu'il constitue donc une sous-famille propre de Alg. On a longtemps pensé que Gre était le full AFL maximal strictement inclu dans Alg., c'est-à-dire celui constitué de tous les *langages algébriques qui ne sont pas générateur* de Alg., noté Nge. On sait [3] maintenant qu'il n'en est rien et la question reste ouverte de savoir si Nge est principal ou non.

C'est dans cette situation que S. Greibach a été conduite à proposer deux conjectures dont le principe est de restreindre la classe des langages considérés de telle sorte que, si possible, Nge et Gre coincident sur cette sous-classe de Alg. La première consistait à proposer d'établir ce résultat pour les langages parenthétiques ce qui a été fait dans [5]. C'est la seconde qui nous intéresse ici:

Un langage algébrique ne contenant aucun langage rationnel infini est-il soit générateur, soit langage de Greibach?

Nous nous proposons de donner ici un contre-exemple à cette conjecture.

Si l'on considère le langage algébrique L_o engendré par la grammaire $S \longrightarrow aSSa + aSSb + b$, on établit successivement

a) Le langage L_o ne contient aucun rationnel infini.

b) Le langage L_o n'est pas quasi-rationnel (ou est expansif) [6].

Ce point est prouvé en montrant que toute grammaire engendrant L_o est expansive, ce qui résulte d'applications répétées du lemme d'Ogden [12] (exactement comme pour prouver que $D_1'^*$ n'est pas quasi-rationnel).

Notons alors que l'on en déduit que L_o n'est pas un langage de la famille Gre. En effect, on sait qu'un langage à un compteur ne contenant aucun rationnel infini est quasi-rationnel. Il ne nous reste donc plus à montrer que

c) L_o n'est pas un générateur de Alg.

La preuve est assez technique et repose sur le

Théorème [1]: *Le langage algébrique* L *sur l'alphabet* X *est générateur de* Alg. *si et seulement si il existe un langage rationnel* K *sur* Y = {a,b,c,d,x,y} *est un morphisme* ψ *de* Y* *dans* X* *tels que*:
$\psi^{-1}L \cap K = x\, E_1\, y$
(où E_1 est le langage engendré par $S \longrightarrow aSbSc + d$).

On montre d'abord que si L_1 est une partie de L_o, soit L_1 est contenue dans un quasi-rationnel inclus dans L_o, soit il existe des mots de L_1 tels que $g = \alpha u \beta \in L_1$ et pour tout mot v de même longueur que u = $\alpha v \beta \in L_1$. On en déduit que si L_o était générateur, on pourrait à partir des éléments fournis par le théorème précédent trouver un mot $h = \alpha_1 u_1 \beta_1$ dans E_1 tel que $\alpha_1 v_1 \beta_1$ soit aussi dans E_1 avec $|u_1|_a < |u_1|_c$ et $|v_1|_a > |v_1|_c$ ce qui est impossible.

Des points a), b), et c) découle donc la

<u>Proposition:</u> Il existe des langages expansifs ne contenant aucun langage rationnel infini qui ne sont pas générateurs de la famille Alg.

Ce résultat peut même être précisé si l'on note que le contre-exemple proposé et non seulement déterministe, mais aussi simple déterministe [10]. Le rapprochement de cette situation avec celle obtenue dans le cas des langages parenthétiques [5] fait apparaître alors une différence de nature essentielle entre ces deux classes de langages déterministes.

<u>Remerciements:</u> Je tiens à remercier ici tout particulièrement B. Courcelle qui est à l'origine de tous ces résultats puisque c'est lui qui m'a proposé le langage L_o dans le cadre d'un travail commun en cours sur les schémas de programme.

Bibliographie

1. Beauquier, J.: Générateurs Algébriques Non-Ambigus. In: Automata, Languages and Programming. 3rd Colloquium. Edimbourg (1976), p. 66-73
2. Boasson, L.: An Iteration Theorem for One-Counter Languages. 3rd Annual ACM Symposium on Theory of Computing (1970), p. 116-120
3. Boasson, L.: The Inclusion of the Substitution Closure of Linear and One-Counter Languages in the Largest Sub. AFL of the Family of CFL's is proper. Information Processing Letters, 2, No. 5 (1973), p. 135-140
4. Boasson, L., Nivat, M.: Sur Diverses Familles de Languages Fermées par transduction Rationnelle. Acta Informatica 2 (1973), p. 180-188
5. Boasson, L., Nivat, M.: Parenthesis Generators. 17th Annual Symposium on Foundations of Computer Sciences (SWAT) - Octobre 1976
6. Ginsburg, S.: The Mathematical Theory of CFL's. McGraw-Hill (1966)
7. Ginsburg, S.: Algebraic and Automata Theoretic Properties of Formal Languages. North-Holland (1975)
8. Greibach, S.: Chains of Full AFL's. Math. System Theory 4, No. 3 (1970), p. 231-242
9. Greibach, S.: One-Counter Languages and the IRS Condition. J. of Computer and System Sciences 10 (1975), p. 237-247
10. Hopcroft, J.E., Korenjack, A.J.: Simple Deterministic Languages. 7th IEEE Symposium on Swisthing and Automata Theory (1966), p. 36-46
11. Nivat, M.: Transduction des Langages de Chomsky. Anales de l'Institut Fourier 18 (1968), p. 339-456
12. Ogden, W.: A Helpful Result for Proving Inherent Ambiguity. Math. System Theory 2 (1967), p. 191-194

Cylindres de langages simples et pseudo-simples

J.-M. Autebert

ABSTRACT : There is a simple language S such that every realtime context-free language can be obtained by an inverse g.s.m. mapping from S. Hence the family of realtime context-free languages is a principal A.F.D.L.

We show here that the cylinder (closure under inverse homomorphism and intersection with regular sets) of realtime languages is principal and then we get easily the result.

KEY WORDS : Deterministic context-free, realtime and simple deterministic languages, cylinder, principality.

1. INTRODUCTION

Un cylindre est une famille de langages fermée par homomorphisme inverse et par intersection avec des rationnels. Un tel cylindre est dit principal s'il peut être généré par une sous-famille réduite à un seul élément. Cette notion est voisine de la notion d'A.F.D.L. (famille fermée pour les opérations de "g.s.m. mapping" (1) inverse, l'union et l'étoile marquées, et suppression des marqueurs de fin). En effet un homomorphisme inverse est un g.s.m. mapping inverse particulier et les deux notions généralisent la notion d'homomorphisme inverse grâce à un contrôle d'états finis. Outre l'intérêt purement algébrique de la question de principalité, elle débouche directement sur la question de complexité de reconnaissance de la famille considérée. Ainsi S. Greibach montre que l'A.F.D.L. des langages context-free est principal [3] exhibant un "hardest language" pour cette famille, et que les langages context-free déterministes ne forment pas un A.F.D.F. principal [4]. D'autre part nous montrons par ailleurs que le cylindre des langages à compteur n'est pas principal [1] et L. Boasson et M. Nivat montrent que celui des langages linéaires ne l'est pas lui non plus [2]. Nous nous penchons ici sur le cas de familles de langages dont l'importance a été soulignée par l'étude des schémas de programmes : les langages pseudo-simples ("context-free realtime") qui sont les langages reconnus par des automates à pile déterministes sans ε-transition et qui forment un cylindre, et les langages simples qui sont reconnus par des automates à pile déterministes sans états.

S. Greibach conjecture que l'A.F.D.L. des context-free realtime n'est pas principal [4]. Nous montrons ici qu'il l'est, en exhibant un langage simple générateur du cylindre des langages pseudo-simples et qui est également générateur de cette famille en tant qu'A.F.D.L.

(1) Un g.s.m. est un sextuple $M = <Q, X, Y, \delta, \lambda, q_0>$ où Q, X et Y sont des ensembles finis d'états, d'entrée et de sortie, δ est la fonction de transition, fonction de $Q \times X$ dans Q , λ est la fonction de sortie, fonction de $Q \times X$ dans Y^* et $q_0 \in Q$. δ et λ étant étendues canoniquement pour $Q \times X^*$, on définit pour un mot $f \in X^*$ $M(f) = \lambda(q_0,f)$ et pour un langage L , $M(L) = \{M(f) | f \in L\}$ et $M^{-1}(L) = \{f | M(f) \in L\}$ $M(L)$ et $M^{-1}(L)$ sont respectivement des g.s.m. mapping et g.s.m. mapping inverse de L .

2. RESULTATS

Nous donnons ici les principaux résultats nouveaux.

Théorème 1 : Le plus petit cylindre contenant les langages simples est le cylindre des langages pseudo-simples.

Théorème 2 : Le cylindre des langages pseudo-simples est principal.

Théorème 3 : L'A.F.D.L. des langages pseudo-simples (les context-free realtime) est principal.

3. RAPPELS

Un automate à pile déterministe est un septuplet

$$\mathcal{A} = < X, Q, Z, q_0, z_0, Q_T, \lambda>$$

où X est l'alphabet d'entrée

Q est l'ensemble des états

Z est l'alphabet de pile

$q_0 \in Q$ est l'état initial

$z_0 \in Z$ est le symbole initial de pile

$Q_T \subseteq Q$ est l'ensemble des états terminaux

λ est une application partielle de $(X \cup \{\varepsilon\}) \times Q \times Z$ dans $Q \times Z^*$ telle que

$\forall (q,z) \in Q \times Z$ ou bien $\lambda(\varepsilon,q,z)$ n'est pas définie

ou bien $\lambda(\varepsilon,q,z)$ est définie et $\forall x \in X$

$\lambda\ (x,q,z)$ n'est pas définie.

Une ε-transition est un triple (ε,q,z) pour lequel λ est définie.

Un automate à pile pseudo-simple est un automate à pile déterministe dans lequel il n'y a pas d'ε-transition

Un automate à pile simple est un automate à pile déterministe sans états.

Un langage déterministe (respectivement pseudo-simple, simple) est un langage tel qu'il existe un automate à pile déterministe (respectivement pseudo-simple, simple) le reconnaissant.

Nous utiliserons dans la suite le fait que l'on ne réduit pas la généralité des langages reconnus par des automates à pile simples si l'on n'autorise pas d'ε-transitions.

4. DEFINITION DE QUELQUES FAMILLES DE LANGAGES

a) Soit D_n^* le langage de sémi-Dyck sur l'alphabet $Z_n = \{z_i, \bar{z}_i | i = 1,\ldots, n\}$ et soit Σ_n l'ensemble des lettres non barrées.

Soit $X_n = Z_n \cup \{a,c,\#\}$ où $a,c,\# \notin Z_n$

Appelons Θ l'homomorphisme de X_n^* dans Z_n^* qui efface les lettres a, c et $\#$.

Posons $E_n = a\,\bar{z}_1\,\Sigma_n^*\,c^{i_1}\,a\,\bar{z}_2\,\Sigma_n^*\,c^{i_2}\,a \ldots a\,\bar{z}_n\,\Sigma_n^*\,c^{i_n}$ et considérons les rationnels

$K_{n,p} = ((E_n)^p\#)^*$ dans lequel toutes les puissances de la lettre c sont comprises entre 1 et p.

Un facteur d'un mot de $K_{n,p}$ de la forme $a\,\bar{z}_j\,f\,c^i$ où $f \in \Sigma_n^*$ et $i \in \{1,\ldots, p\}$ et $j \in \{1,\ldots, n\}$ sera dit élémentaire.

Notons que pour un mot non vide de $K_{n,p}$ il y a exactement $n\,p$ facteurs élémentaires avant le premier $\#$ et entre 2 $\#$ consécutifs.

Définissons l'application de X_n^* dans X_n^*, baptisée chemin, définie pour des mots de $K_{n,p}$ de la façon suivante :

si $f \in K_{n,p}$, chemin(f) est le mot obtenu, s'il existe, en effectuant la concaténation d'un facteur élémentaire pris parmi les $n\,p$ précédant chaque lettre $\#$ du mot f, ce choix obeissant aux règles suivantes :

- le premier est le premier facteur élémentaire
- le k+1 *ième* est choisi en fonction des k premiers $h_1, h_2,\ldots, h_k$: si i est la puissance de la lettre c dans h_k, il est pris parmi les n facteurs élémentaires constituant le *ième* facteur E_n; c'est celui qui commence par $a\,\bar{z}_j$ si $\Theta\,(h_1 h_2 \ldots h_k\,\bar{z}_j)$ appartient à $\bar{z}_1\,D_n^*\,\Sigma_n^*$

b) Nous pouvons désormais définir les familles de langages suivantes :

$$\mathcal{PS} = \{PS_{n,p} | n \in \mathbb{N}, p \in \mathbb{N}\}$$

où $\forall n, \forall p\ PS_{n,p} = \{f \in K_{n,p} | \Theta(\text{chemin}(f)) \in \bar{z}_1 D_n^*\}$

posons $S_n = PS_{n,1}$

$$\mathcal{S} = \{S_n | n \in \mathbb{N}\}$$

5. PROPRIETES INTERMEDIAIRES

Lemme 1 : Si L est un langage pseudo-simple, alors il existe $(n,p) \in \mathbb{N}^2$, il existe un homomorphisme φ tels que $L = \varphi^{-1}(PS_{n,p})$

Lemme 2 : Si L est un langage simple, alors il existe un entier n et un homomorphisme φ tels que $L = \varphi^{-1}(S_n)$

La preuve s'effectue en construisant dans les deux cas l'homomorphisme φ à partir de la donnée d'un automate reconnaissant L. On étend tout d'abord l'application λ en une application totale par adjonction d'un nouveau symbole de pile qu'aucune règle ne permet de dépiler. Si n est alors le nombre de symboles de pile et p le nombre des états de l'automate, à chaque lettre x de l'alphabet d'entrée correspond $n\,p$ règles de l'automate et l'on associe à chacune des règles $x, q, z_i \to q', g$ le facteur $a\,\bar{z}_i\,g\,c^t$ où t est un numéro correspondant à l'état q'. $\varphi(x)$ peut alors être décrit comme le produit de tous ces $n\,p$ facteurs rangés par ordre sur les numéros des états du membre gauche des règles, puis par ordre sur les lettres de l'alphabet de pile. Le fonctionnement de l'automate à pile lorsqu'il reconnait un mot f est décrit par le chemin de $\varphi(f)$.

Lemme 3 : Tous les langages de $\mathcal{PS}$ sont pseudo-simples.

Lemme 4 : Tous les langages de $\mathcal{S}$ sont simples.

La preuve se fait par la donnée explicite pour chaque langage de $\mathcal{PS}$ (resp. de $\mathcal{S}$) d'un automate pseudo-simple (resp. simple) qui le reconnaît.

Des lemmes 1 et 3 vient :

Proposition 1 : La famille $\mathcal{PS}$ génère le cylindre des langages pseudo-simples

Lemme 5 : $\forall (n,p) \in \mathbb{N}^2$, $\exists \ell \in \mathbb{N}$, $\exists K$ rationnel, $\exists\, \varphi$ homomorphisme tels que $PS_{n,p} = \varphi^{-1}(S_\ell) \cap K$

Des lemmes 4 et 5 et de la proposition 1 on déduit le théorème 1

Proposition 2 : La famille $\mathcal{S}$ génère le cylindre des langagas pseudo-simples.

Lemme 6 : $\exists n_0 \in N$ tel que $\forall n \in N$, $\exists K$ rationnel, $\exists \varphi$ homomorphisme tels que $S_n = \varphi^{-1} (S_{n_0}) \cap K$

Dans notre preuve n_0 vaut 6.

De tout ceci on déduit le théorème 2

Un examen attentif des rationnels utilisés pour montrer les lemmes 5 et 6 permet de se rendre compte que ceux-ci jouent un rôle très faible et en fait les deux opérations cylindriques peuvent être faites ici par g.s.m. mapping inverse. Ce qui établit le théorème 3.

REFERENCES

[1] J.M. AUTEBERT Non-principalité du cylindre des langages à compteur. à paraître dans Mathematical Systems Theory

[2] L. BOASSON et M. NIVAT Le cylindre des langages linéaires n'est pas principal
2.G.I. Fachtagung Automaten Theorie und Formale Sprachen (1975) p 16-19

[3] S. GREIBACH The hardest Context-Free language
S.I.A.M. Journal 2 (1973) p 304-310

[4] S. GREIBACH Jump PDA's and hierarchies of deterministic Context-Free languages.
S.I.A.M. Journal 3 (1974) p 111-127

FAMILLES DE LANGAGES FERMEES PAR CROCHET ET CROCHET OUVERT

F. Rodriguez

ABSTRACT

In this paper we present a new unary operator, the open bracket, which resemble the operator bracket of [1]. We derive from it the characterization of some families of checking Automata Languages.

INTRODUCTION

Caractériser algébriquement les familles de langages a connu une première solution par le développement de la théorie des familles agréables de langages (FAL dans [2], full AFL dans [5]). Or cet outil puissant ne permet pas de définir, par exemple, l'ensemble des langages linéaires : ceux-ci ne forment pas une FAL mais un cône rationnel [11].

La théorie des cônes rationnels, essentiellement développée par M. NIVAT [2], [1], permet donc d'appréhender des structures algébriques beaucoup plus fines que celles définies par les FAL. Toutefois cela ne permet pas encore de définir algébriquement le cône rationnel des langages linéaires ou celui des langages ultralinéaires de rang p [3].

Dans l'article "Familles de Langages Translatables et fermées par crochet" [1] BOASSON, CRESTIN et NIVAT présentent une solution à ce problème en introduisant deux nouveaux opérateurs unaires, la translation et le crochet. Ces opérateurs qui associent, à des transductions rationnelles près, à tout langage L, le langage $L' = \{w\ell\tilde{w} \mid w \in X^*, \ell \in L\}$, préservent la famille des langages algébriques. En outre, ces opérateurs ne sont pas des opérateurs syntaxiques tels que les définit GREIBACH dans [10].

Cette démarche nous a conduit naturellement à définir un nouvel opérateur, le crochet ouvert, qui, à des transductions rationnelles près, associe à L le langage $L'' = \{w\ell w \mid w \in X^*, \ell \in \mathcal{L}\}$ et à étudier la famille de langages la plus classique fermée pour cet opérateur : la famille des langages Vérifiables [13] [14] (Checking Automata Languages dans [8]).

Les langages vérifiables sont reconnus par une sous-classe propre des "one way stack Automata" [8] : les accepteurs vérificateurs (Checking Automata).

Ces automates disposent d'une mémoire sur laquelle ils peuvent écrire un mot, qui sitôt que l'on en a examiné le contenu ne peut plus être modifié.

La classe des langages vérifiables présente de nombreuses analogies structurelles avec celle des langages algébriques : toutes deux forment des FAL principales et fermées par substitution. On peut y définir une hiérarchie infinie de cônes rationnels semblable à celle de GREIBACH pour les algébriques [7] en considérant le fonctionnement des accepteurs vérificateurs : mouvements bornés en mémoire, mot mémoire appartenant à un langage borné [13], [14].

Il n'est donc pas surprenant que l'opérateur crochet ouvert joue pour les langages vérifiables un rôle analogue à celui du crochet pour les algébriques. En outre nous pensons que ce sont de telles techniques qui permettrons de conclure à l'incomparabilité de classes de langages : ainsi montrons-nous que le cône rationnel des linéaires, engendré par $S_2 = \{wc\tilde{w} | w \in X^*\}$ est incomparable au cône des carrés, engendré par $C_1 = \{wcw | w \in X^*\}$.

Le problème de l'incomparabilité des familles de langages algébriques et vérifiables reste cependant ouvert et, par ce fait, la conjecture de S. GREIBACH [9] suivant laquelle le cône rationnel maximal contenu dans les algébriques serait l'intersection de ces deux familles.

Plus précisément nous montrons dans cet article que les résultats présentés en [1] par BOASSON, CRESTIN et NIVAT, sont vrais pour l'opérateur crochet ouvert.

Nous établissons alors un théorème (théorème 4) sur la fermeture par crochet (resp. crochet ouvert) des cônes rationnels principaux.

Le théorème 6 définit une hiérarchie infinie croissante de langages vérifiables C_i, tels qu'il n'existe aucune transduction rationnelle τ vérifiant $\tau(C_i) = C_{i+1}$. Ce résultat est établi en utilisant un théorème d'itération [15] pour les langages vérifiables reconnus par les accepteurs vérificateurs à mouvements bornés de degré i [13], [14], [15].

Ce théorème permet alors de montrer que le plus petit cône rationnel fermé par crochet ouvert est vérifiable, non algébrique et non principal.

Enfin nous établissons que les langages $S_2 = \{wc\tilde{w} | w \in X^*\}$ et $C_1 = \{wcw | w \in X^*\}$ sont rationnellement incomparables.

Nous ne donnerons, en général, qu'une idée des preuves le plus souvant très techniques. Nous utiliserons les notations définies dans [1] :

Tous les monoïdes libres considérés seront finiment engendrés et ε désignera l'élément neutre. Toutes les familles de langages $\mathcal{L}$ considérées vérifieront :

$\forall L \in \mathcal{L}$, il existe un alphabet fini X_L tel que $L \subset X_L$.
désignera l'alphabet dénombrable des X_L.

1. NOTATIONS ET DEFINITIONS

Définition 1 :

Un homomorphisme φ d'un monoïde libre X^* dans l'ensemble des parties d'un monoïde Y^* (muni de la structure de monoïde induite par celle de Y^*) est une $\mathcal{L}$-substitution si et seulement si pour tout $x \in X$, $\varphi(X) \in \mathcal{L}$.

Nous noterons par $\mathcal{L} \square \mathcal{L}'$ la famille de langages définie par :

$$\mathcal{L} \square \mathcal{L}' = \{\varphi(L) | L \in \mathcal{L} \text{ et } \varphi \text{ est une } \mathcal{L}'\text{-substitution}\}.$$

Ainsi si Fin désigne la famille des langages finis et Rat la famille des langages rationnels ("regular languages") :

- Fin $\square$ $\mathcal{L}$ est la plus petite famille de langages contenant $\mathcal{L}$ et fermée par union et produit.

- Rat $\square$ $\mathcal{L}$ est la plus petite famille de langages contenant $\mathcal{L}$ et fermée par union, produit et étoile.

Nous désignerons par $\mathcal{C}(\mathcal{L})$ le <u>cône rationnel</u> engendré par $\mathcal{L}$ [2], c'est-à-dire :

$$\mathcal{C}(\mathcal{L}) = \{\tau(L) | L \in \mathcal{L} \text{ et } \tau \text{ est une transduction rationnelle}\}.$$

$\mathcal{C}^U(\mathcal{L})$ désignera la fermeture par union de $\mathcal{C}(\mathcal{L})$ ("semi AFL" engendré par $\mathcal{L}$ dans [6]. La FAL (Famille Agréable de Langages, "full AFL" dans [5]) engendrée par $\mathcal{L}$ n'est autre que :

$$\text{Rat} \,\square\, \mathcal{C}(\mathcal{L})$$

plus petit cône rationnel contenant $\mathcal{L}$, fermé par union, produit et étoile.

De même Fin $\square$ $\mathcal{C}(\mathcal{L})$ est le plus petit cône contenant $\mathcal{L}$ et fermé par union et produit.

Rat_2 désignera la famille des parties rationnelles du produit cartésien de deux monoïdes libres [4]. Il est connu [11] que la partie A de $X^* \times Y^*$ est rationnelle si et seulement si il existe un monoïde libre Z^*, un langage rationnel $K \subset Z^*$ et deux homomorphismes φ et ψ dans X^* et Y^* respectivement tels que :

$$A = \{(\varphi(w), \psi(w)) | w \in K\}.$$

<u>Définition 2</u> :

Pour tout $A \in Rat_2$ et pour tout langage L :

. Le <u>crochet</u> de L par A, noté [A,L] est l'ensemble

$$[A,L] = \{a_1 w \tilde{a}_2 | (a_1,a_2) \in A, w \in L\}$$

où $\tilde{a}_2$ est l'image miroir de a_2. ([1])

. Le <u>crochet ouvert</u> de L par A, noté [A,L[est l'ensemble :

$$[A,L[= \{a_1 w a_2 | (a_1,a_2) \in A, w \in L\}$$

Une famille de langages $\mathcal{L}$ est dite fermée par crochet (resp. crochet ouvert) si et seulement si $A \in Rat_2$, $L \in \mathcal{L}$ impliquent $[A,L] \in \mathcal{L}$ (resp. $[A,L[\in \mathcal{L}$).

Nous désignerons par $[\mathcal{L}]$ (resp. $[\mathcal{L}[$) le plus petit cône rationnel fermé par union et crochet (resp. crochet ouvert) contenant $\mathcal{L}$.

$\mathcal{L}_{[[}$ désignera le plus petit cône rationnel fermé par union et contenant la famille $\mathcal{L}''$ des crochets ouverts de $\mathcal{L}$:

$$\mathcal{L}'' = \{[A,L[\mid A \in Rat_2,\ L \in \mathcal{L}\}.$$

Si l'on définit de même la famille $\mathcal{L}'$ des crochets de $\mathcal{L}$:

$$\mathcal{L}' = \{[A,L] \mid A \in Rat_2,\ L \in \mathcal{L}\},$$

on peut énoncer :

Théorème 1 : Si $\mathcal{L}$ est un cône rationnel,

a) $[\mathcal{L}]$ est identique à la fermeture par union de $\mathcal{L}'$. ([1])

b) $\mathcal{L}_{[[}$ est identique à la fermeture par union de $\mathcal{L}''$.

Démonstration :

Celle de a) est donnée dans [1]. On démontre de façon identique que la fermeture par union de $\mathcal{L}''$ est un cône rationnel. Mais en général, nous le verrons plus loin, ce cône n'est pas fermé par crochet ouvert. □

Aussi introduirons-nous la notation :

$$\mathcal{L}_{[[^1} = \mathcal{L}_{[[}$$

et $\forall i \leq 1$ $\quad \mathcal{L}_{[[^{i+1}} = (\mathcal{L}_{[[^i})_{[[}$

Définition 3 : ([2])

Une famille de langages $\mathscr{L}$ est dite translatable si et seulement si pour tout couple de symboles a et b $\in \Sigma$ et tout langage $L \in \mathscr{L}$, le crochet $[(a,b)^*,L]$ appartient à $\mathscr{L}$.

Remarquons que :

$$[(a,b)^*,L] = \{a^n \ell b^n | n \in \mathbb{N}, \ell \in L\} = [(a,b)^*,L[$$

$<\mathscr{L}>$ désignera le plus petit cône rationnel translatable et fermé par union contenant $\mathscr{L}$.

Contrairement à ce qui se passe pour $[\mathscr{L}]$, il est faux que $<\mathscr{L}>$ soit la fermeture par union de la famille des translatés de $\mathscr{L}$ [1] :

$$\mathscr{L}''' = \{[(a,b)^*,L],\ a,b \in \Sigma,\ L \in \mathscr{L}\}.$$

2. PROPRIETES DES FAMILLES DE LANGAGES TRANSLATABLES, FERMEES PAR CROCHET ET CROCHET OUVERT

Nous retrouvons pour les cônes rationnels fermés par union et contenant les crochets ouverts d'une famille de langages les mêmes propriétés que celles énoncées par BOASSON, CRESTIN et NIVAT dans [1] pour l'opérateur crochet. Les preuves sont semblables aussi ne les referons-nous pas.

Théorème 1 : ([2])

Si $\mathscr{L}$ est un cône rationnel fermé par union, $L \subset X^*$ un langage quelconque et a et b deux lettres n'appartenant pas à X :

$$[(a,b)^*,L] \in \text{Rat} \,\square\, \mathscr{L} \text{ implique } L \in \mathscr{L}$$

Il en découle immédiatement

Corollaire 1 : (a,b,c,d sont prouvés dans [1])

a) $<\mathcal{L}> \subsetneq \mathrm{Fin} \,\square <\mathcal{L}> \Rightarrow \mathrm{Fin} \,\square <\mathcal{L}> \subsetneq <\mathrm{Fin} \,\square <\mathcal{L}>>$

b) $<\mathcal{L}> \subsetneq \mathrm{Rat} \,\square <\mathcal{L}> \Rightarrow \mathrm{Rat} \,\square <\mathcal{L}> \subsetneq <\mathrm{Rat} \,\square <\mathcal{L}>>$

c) $[\mathcal{L}] \subsetneq \mathrm{Fin} \,\square\, [\mathcal{L}] \Rightarrow \mathrm{Fin} \,\square\, [\mathcal{L}] \subsetneq [\mathrm{Fin} \,\square\, [\mathcal{L}]]$

d) $[\mathcal{L}] \subsetneq \mathrm{Rat} \,\square\, [\mathcal{L}] \Rightarrow \mathrm{Rat} \,\square\, [\mathcal{L}] \subsetneq [\mathrm{Rat} \,\square\, [\mathcal{L}]]$

e) $\mathcal{L}_{[[} \subsetneq \mathrm{Fin} \,\square\, \mathcal{L}_{[[} \Rightarrow \mathrm{Fin} \,\square\, \mathcal{L}_{[[} \subsetneq (\mathrm{Fin} \,\square\, \mathcal{L}_{[[})_{[[}$

f) $\mathcal{L}_{[[} \subsetneq \mathrm{Rat} \,\square\, \mathcal{L}_{[[} \Rightarrow \mathrm{Rat} \,\square\, \mathcal{L}_{[[} \subsetneq (\mathrm{Rat} \,\square\, \mathcal{L}_{[[})_{[[}$

Théorème 2 :

Si $\mathcal{L}$ est un cône rationnel fermé par union, L_1 et L_2 deux langages sur des alphabets disjoints X_1 et X_2, les conditions $L_1 L_2 \in [\mathcal{L}]$ et $L_1 L_2 \in \mathcal{L}_{[[}$ impliquent chacune que L_1 ou L_2 appartient à $\mathcal{L}$.

($L_1 L_2 \in [\mathcal{L}] \Rightarrow L_1$ ou $L_2 \in \mathcal{L}$ est prouvé dans [1]).

Du théorème 2 on tire immédiatement :

Corollaire 2 :

Si $\mathcal{L}$ est un cône fermé par union :

a) $\mathcal{L} \subsetneq [\mathcal{L}] \Rightarrow [\mathcal{L}] \subsetneq \mathrm{Fin} \,\square\, [\mathcal{L}]$ ([1])

b) $\mathcal{L} \subsetneq <\mathcal{L}> \Rightarrow <\mathcal{L}> \subsetneq \mathrm{Fin} \,\square\, [\mathcal{L}]$ ([1])

c) $\mathcal{L} \subsetneq \mathcal{L}_{[[} \Rightarrow \mathcal{L}_{[[} \subsetneq \mathrm{Fin} \,\square\, \mathcal{L}_{[[}$.

De même les théorème 1 et 2 permettent d'établir :

Théorème 3 :

Soit $\mathcal{L}$ un cône rationnel fermé par union. Les conditions :

a) $<\mathcal{L}> \subsetneq \mathrm{Fin} \,\square <\mathcal{L}>$

b) $<\mathcal{L}> \subsetneq \mathrm{Rat} \,\square <\mathcal{L}>$

c) $[\mathcal{L}] \subsetneq \mathrm{Fin} \,\square\, [\mathcal{L}]$

d) $[\mathcal{L}] \subsetneq \mathrm{Rat} \,\square\, [\mathcal{L}]$

e) $\mathcal{L}_{[[} \subsetneq \mathrm{Fin} \,\square\, \mathcal{L}_{[[}$

f) $\mathcal{L}_{[[} \subsetneq \mathrm{Rat} \,\square\, \mathcal{L}_{[[}$

impliquent respectivement :

a') Le plus petit cône rationnel translatable fermé par union et produit contenant $\mathcal{L}$ est non principal.

b') La plus petite FAL translatable contenant $\mathcal{L}$ est non principale.

c') Le plus petit cône rationnel fermé par union, produit et crochet contenant $\mathcal{L}$ est non principal.

d') La plus petite FAL fermée par crochet et contenant $\mathcal{L}$ est non principale.

e') Le plus petit cône rationnel fermé par union, produit et crochet ouvert contenant $\mathcal{L}$ est non principal.

f') La plus petite FAL fermée par crochet ouvert et contenant $\mathcal{L}$ est non principale.

Démonstration :

a $\Rightarrow$ a' ... d $\Rightarrow$ d' sont prouvés dans [1].

Pour e $\Rightarrow$ e' et f $\Rightarrow$ f', il suffit de remarquer que si

$$\mathcal{C}_1 = \mathcal{L}_{[[}$$

$$\forall p > 1 \qquad \mathcal{C}_p = (\mathrm{Fin} \,\square\, \mathcal{C}_{p-1})_{[[}$$

alors en vertu du corollaire 2, on montre par récurrence que $\mathcal{C}_p \subsetneq \mathcal{C}_{p+1}$.

Soit alors $\mathcal{C}_\infty = \bigcup_{p \geq 1} \mathcal{C}_p$. $\mathcal{C}_\infty$ est un cône rationnel fermé par union et produit. Montrons qu'il est fermé par crochet ouvert.

Soit $L \in \mathcal{E}_\infty$, alors il existe p tel que $L \in \mathcal{E}_p$. Alors pour tout $A \in Rat_2$, $[A,L[\in \mathcal{E}_{p+1} \subset \mathcal{E}_\infty$. La preuve s'achève alors comme dans [1]. □

Dans le cas où $\mathcal{L}$ est un cône rationnel principal, nous pouvons en outre énoncer :

Théorème 4 :

Si $\mathcal{L}$ est un cône rationnel principal et L un générateur de $\mathcal{L}$, si X est un alphabet d'au moins deux lettres, disjoint de celui de L, alors :

- $[\mathcal{L}]$ est un cône rationnel principal dont $[\{(w,w) | w \in X^*$, L] est un générateur.

- $\mathcal{L}_{[[}$ est un cône rationnel principal dont $[\{(w,w) | w \in X^*\}, L[$ est un générateur.

Démonstration :

Celles pour $[\mathcal{L}]$ et $\mathcal{L}_{[[}$ sont identiques. Il est clair que $L' = [\{(w,w) | w \in X^*\},L]$ appartient à $[\mathcal{L}]$.

Réciproquement pour montrer que $L_0 \in [\mathcal{L}]$ est image par transduction rationnelle de L' il suffit, puisque $[\mathcal{L}]$ et $\mathcal{L}$ sont fermés par union, de montrer que pour tout $A \in Rat_2$ et tout $M \in \mathcal{L}$, on a :

$$L_1 = [A,M] \in \mathcal{E}(L').$$

On peut supposer en outre que les alphabets X_A et X_M sont disjoints puisque $\mathcal{L}$ et $[\mathcal{L}]$ sont des cônes rationnels.

Soit alors τ une transduction rationnelle telle que $M = \tau(L)$. D'autre part d'après [11] il existe deux homomorphismes alphabétiques φ et ψ, un langage rationnel K tels que :

$$A = \{(\varphi(w),\psi(w)) | w \in K\}.$$

Nous supposerons $K \subset X^*, X \cap X_L = \emptyset$, où X est un alphabet d'au moins deux lettres. Alors il existe une transduction rationnelle τ_1 telle que

$$L_1 = [A,M] = \tau_1(L)$$

En effet, soit τ_1 qui n'accepte que les chaînes dans $K . X_L^* . K$ et transforme leur facteur gauche appartenant à K comme φ, le facteur inclus dans X_L^* comme τ et le facteur droit dans K comme ψ. Cette transduction rationnelle répond bien à la question.

□

Corollaire 3 :

Un cône rationnel principal $\mathcal{L}$ est fermé par crochet (resp. crochet ouvert) si et seulement si pour tout générateur L de $\mathcal{L}$:

$$[\{(w,w) | w \in X^*\}, L] \in \mathcal{L}$$

$$(\text{resp. } [\{(w,w) | w \in X^*\}, L \in \mathcal{L})$$

où X est disjoint de X_L.

Corollaire 4 :

Soit $\mathcal{L}$ un cône rationnel principal dont L est un générateur.

Alors $\forall i \in \mathbb{N}$, $\mathcal{L}_{[[^i}$ est un cône rationnel principal dont

$$L_i = \{w_1 c w_2 c \ldots w_i \ell w_i \ldots c w_2 c w_1 | w_p \in X^*, 1 \leq p \leq i, \ell \in L\}$$

est un générateur si X est un alphabet d'au moins deux lettres, disjoint de X_L et $c \notin X$.

3. APPLICATIONS

Dans [1] BOASSON, CRESTIN et NIVAT identifient, à l'aide des opérateurs $\langle\ \rangle$ et [ ] un certain nombre de familles de langages algébriques. L'opérateur crochet ouvert permet, de façon analogue, de définir des familles de langages non plus algébriques mais vérifiables [14] ("Checking Automata Languages" dans [8]). En particulier les langages vérifiables sont fermés par crochet ouvert tandis que les langages algébriques ne le sont pas. Soit alors X un alphabet d'au moins deux lettres et c et d deux symboles n'appartenant pas à X. Les langages :

$$\forall i \geq 1 \quad C_i = \{w_i c w_{i-1} \ldots c w_1 d w_1 c \ldots w_{i-1} c w_i \mid w_p \in X^*,\ 1 \leq p \leq i\}$$

sont vérifiables et non algébriques.

Du théorème 4 et du corollaire 4 on déduit immédiatement puisque {d} est un générateur de Rat :

Théorème 5 :

$$[\mathrm{Rat}] = \mathscr{C}\{wd\tilde{w} \mid w \in X^*\} = \mathrm{Lin} \quad [12]$$

$$\mathrm{Rat}_{[[^i} = \mathscr{C}\{w_i c w_{i-1} \ldots c w_1 d w_1 c \ldots w_{i-1} c w_i \mid w_p \in X^*,\ 1 \leq p \leq i\}.$$

où Lin désigne le cône des langages linéaires.

Nous pouvons alors montrer que si $\mathscr{L}$ est un cône rationnel non fermé par crochet ouvert, alors $\mathscr{L}_{[[}$ n'est pas nécessairement fermé par crochet ouvert. En effet nous avons :

Théorème 6 :

Il n'existe pas de transduction rationnelle τ telle que :

$$C_{i+1} = \tau\,(C_i),\ \forall i \geq 1$$

Démonstration :

Ce théorème est établi par des techniques totalement différentes. On montre, en utilisant le lemme 1 de [15], que le langage C_{i+1} n'est accepté par aucun accepteur vérificateur à mouvement borné de degré i [14] et donc que C_{i+1} n'est pas image de C_i par transduction rationnelle. □

Il en résulte :

Corollaire 5 :

$$[\mathrm{Rat}[= \bigcup_{i \geq 1} \mathscr{C}(C_i) \text{ est un cône rationnel non principal.}$$

Démonstration :

On a clairement $[\mathrm{Rat}[= \bigcup_{i \geq 1} \mathcal{C}(C_i)$, $[\mathrm{Rat}[$ est donc un cône rationnel qui contient une suite infinie strictement croissante de cônes rationnels $\mathcal{C}(C_i)$. D'après [10],$[\mathrm{Rat}[$ est donc non principal.

Par contre nous avons, si C_∞ désigne le langage vérifiable :

$$C_\infty = \{w_p c w_{p-1} \ldots c w_1 d w_1 c \ldots w_{p-1} c w_p \mid p \in \mathbb{N},\ w_i \in X^*,\ 1 \leq i \leq p\} \quad \square$$

Corollaire 6 :

$\mathcal{C}(C_\infty)$ est un cône rationnel principal fermé par crochet ouvert.

Démonstration :

On a clairement :

$$[\{(w,w) \mid w \in X^*\},\ cC_\infty c[= C_\infty$$

et le résultat découle du corollaire 3. $\square$

Nous pouvons enfin montrer que :

Théorème 7 :

$\{wc\tilde{w} \mid w \in X^*\}$ et $\{wcw \mid w \in X^*\}$ sont rationnellement incomparables si $c \notin X$ et $|X| \geq 2$.

Démonstration :

$C_1 = \{wcw \mid w \in X^*\}$ est bien connu pour être vérifiable et non algébrique. Donc il n'existe pas de transduction rationnelle τ telle que $\tau\{wc\tilde{w}\} = C_1$.

Réciproquement si l'on suppose que $S_2 = \{wc\tilde{w} \mid w \in X^*\}$ appartient au cône rationnel engendré par C_1, soit $\mathrm{Rat}_{[[}$, si l'on considère les décompositions possibles de tout mot $wc\tilde{w}$ en $a_j\ m_j\ b_j$ tels que $(a_j,b_j) \in A_j \in \mathrm{Rat}_2$, $m_j \in M_j$ rationnel, avec $S_2 = \bigcup_j [A_j,M_j[$, on montre qu'on aboutit à une contradiction.

$\square$

Corollaire 7 :

[Rat] et $Rat_{[[}$ sont incomparables.

Ces résultats nous conduisent alors à poser les trois conjectures suivantes :

Conjecture 1 :

$\mathscr{C}(C_\infty)$ est le plus petit cône rationnel principal fermé par crochet ouvert.

Conjecture 2 :

Si $\mathscr{L}$ est un cône rationnel tel que

$\mathscr{L} \subsetneq \mathscr{L}_{[[}$ alors $\mathscr{L}_{[[^i} \subsetneq \mathscr{L}_{[[^{i+1}}$, $\forall i \geq 1$

Conjecture 3 :

$[Rat] \cap Rat_{[[} = \mathscr{C}(\{a^n b^n | n \in \mathbb{N}\})$

soit $\mathscr{C}(\{wc\tilde{w}\}) \cap \mathscr{C}\{(wcw)\} = \mathscr{C}\{a^n b^n\}$.

BIBLIOGRAPHIE

1. BOASSON L., CRESTIN J.P., NIVAT M.
Familles de Langages Translatables et Fermées par Crochet
Acta Informatica 2, 383-393 (1973).

2. BOASSON L., NIVAT M.
Sur Diverses Familles de Langages Fermées par Transduction Rationnelle
Acta Informatica 2, 180-188 (1973).

3. CRESTIN J.P.
Sur un Langage quasi-rationnel d'ambiguïté non bornée
Thèse de 3ème cycle - Faculté des Sciences de TOULOUSE (1967) (Miméographiée)

4. ELGOT C., MEZEI J.
On Relations Defined by Generalized Finite Automata
IBM Journal of R. and D. 9, 47-68 (1965).

5. GINSBURG S., GREIBACH S.
Abstract Families of Languages
Memoirs Amer. Math. Soc. 87, 1-32 (1969).

6. GINSBURG S., GREIBACH S.
Principal AFL
J. Computer and System Sciences 4, 308-338 (1970).

7. GREIBACH S.
An Infinite Hierarchy of Context-free Languages
J. Assoc. Comput. Mach. 16, 91-106 (1969).

8. GREIBACH S.
Checking Automata and One Way Stack Languages
J. Computer and System Sciences 3, 196-217 (1969).

9. GREIBACH S.
Chain of Full AFL's
Math. Syst. Theory 4 n°3, 231-242 (1970).

10. GREIBACH S.
Syntactic Operators on full semi AFL's
J. Computer and System Sciences 6, 30-76 (1972).

11. NIVAT M.
Transduction des Langages de Chomsky
Annales de l'Institut Fourier 18, 339-456 (1968).

12. NIVAT M.
Transduction des Langages de Chomsky
Chapitre VI - These de Doctorat, Paris (1967) (Miméographiée).

13. RODRIGUEZ F.
Une Hiérarchie Infinie de cônes d'Accepteurs Vérificateurs
in 1. Fachtagung über Automatentheorie und Formale Sprachen, Lecture Notes in Computer Sciences, Springer Verlag, 81-87 (1973).

14. RODRIGUEZ F.
Cônes d'Accepteurs - Application à l'étude d'une Hiérarchie Infinie de Cônes Rationnels de Langages d'Accepteurs Vérificateurs
Thèse Docteur-Ingénieur, TOULOUSE (1973).

15. RODRIGUEZ F.
Une Double Hiérarchie Infinie de Langages Vérifiables
RAIRO R1, 5-20, (1975).

Eine Klasse geordneter Monoide und ihre Anwendbarkeit in der Fixpunktsemantik

V. Lohberger

Abstract

Taking ordered monoids, which obey some extra axioms that concern the relation-ship between order relation and monoid structure we topologize them by means of the order relation and investigate the resulting spaces. They turn out to be fixpoint-spaces.

Proceeding to function spaces in which the elements are not only monoid operable, that means they can be added, but also structurable, that means components of elements can be selected and compound elements can be contructed from simpler ones, the axiomatic properties of the original spaces turn over to the latter ones;the algebraic operations are continous and thus fixpoint-equations with these operations can be solved.

Zusammenfassung

Geordnete Monoide, die einigen zusätzlichen Forderungen genügen, was das Zusammenspiel von Ordnungsrelation und Monoid-Struktur betrifft, werden mit Hilfe der Ordnung topologisiert und die sich ergebenden Räume untersucht. Es sind Fixpunkträume.

Beim Übergang zu Funktionen-Räumen, in denen die Elemente (Objekte) nicht nur mittels Monoid-Operation addierbar sind, sondern auch strukturierbar, d.h. Teilobjekte können selektiert und Verbundobjekte können aus einfacheren konstruiert werden, bleiben die axiomatisch geforderten Eigenschaften der ursprünglichen Räume erhalten; die algebraischen Operationen sind stetig und daher Fixpunktgleichungen mit diesen Operationen lösbar.

Inhalt

1. Einführung

Es ist bekannt, daß Funktionen mit minimalen Fixpunkten in halbgeordneten Mengen zur Festlegung der Semantik rekursiv definierter Objekte (z.Beispiel Mengen, Datenstrukturen, rekursive Prozeduren) geeignet sind. In vielen dieser Untersuchungen sind die Trägermengen vollständige Verbände (z.Beispiel Scott (/S75/),(/S72/), Indermark (/I75/)), in anderen vollständige Halbordnungen (Z.Beispiel Loeckx (/L74/), Ehrich (/E76/)). Als hinreichende Bedingung für die Existenz und Eindeutigkeit und effektive Approximierbarkeit der minimalen Fixpunkte wird von den Funktionen Vertauschbarkeit von Funktions-Evaluation und Grenzwertbildung im Sinne der Ordnung gefordert und diese Eigenschaft in Analogie zur Begriffsbildung der reellen Analysis Stetigkeit genannt. Insbesondere von Scott wurden bestimmte vollständige Verbände untersucht, in denen die von einer geeigneten Umgebungsbasis erzeugte Topologie gerade diejenigen Funktionen stetig gemacht, welche das obige Kriterium erfüllen. Die meisten Autoren nehmen allerdings den Stetigkeitsbegriff im ersten Sinne als gegeben.

Hier setzen wir an und geben eine Struktur axiomatisch, indem wir halbgeordnete Monoide, welche einigenzusätzlichenForderungen genügen, als elementare Objekt-Räume (E-Räume) bezeichnen. Diese Forderungen umfassen Atomizität der Ordnung, Zusammenspiel von Monoid-Addition und Ordnung, Vollständigkeit. Wir geben einige Beispiele; die üblicherweise betrachteten Vollständigen Verbände sind E-Räume, aber wir geben auch einfache E-Räume an, die keine Verbände sind. Zur Erzeugung einer Standard-Topologie rüsten wir die Räume mit einem System von Basis-Mengen aus, die ähnlich wie bei Scott durch Elemente nahe dem minimalen Element bestimmt sind und mit einem Element alle größeren enthalten.

E-Räume werden bezüglich ihrer algebraischen, topologischen und Ordnungsstruktur beleuchtet und Zusammenhänge zwischen den drei Strukturen hergestellt. Insbesondere ist das eingangs erwähnte (Ketten-)Stetigkeitskriterium hier notwendig und hinreichend, aber auch einige andere Kriterien, die wir in der Literatur häufig finden, (Z.Beispiel Netz-Kriterium, ε- δ- Kriterium). Der Fixpunktsatz sichert Existenz,

Eindeutigkeit und effektive Approximierbarkeit eines minimalen Fixpunktes für jede stetige Funktion in E-Räumen. Wir befassen uns auch damit, welche Entartungen durch Verzicht auf einige Axiome entstehen können.

Beim Übergang zu dem Raum der Funktionen aus einem freien Monoid in einen E-Raum bleiben alle Axiome erfüllt, so daß der Ergebnisraum auch E-Raum ist; dieser Übergang lässt sich iterieren. Die resultierenden Räume (in Anlehnung an Ehrich als D-Räume bezeichnet) lassen sich mit weiteren algebraischen Operationen ausrüsten, welche Verallgemeinerungen der Selektion undKonstruktion aus der Wiener Methode sind, so wie anderen interessanten Operationen. Diese Funktionen erweisen sich als stetig in der Topologie, welche die D-Räume als E-Räume haben, und die wir auch durch andere äquivalente Forderungen charakterisieren können. So besitzen rekursive Gleichungssysteme mit diesen Operatoren durch den Fixpunktsatz angebbare Lösungen.

Wir besehen uns nun Konstrukte in Programmiersprachen, hier ALGOL 68, welche wir als rekursive Gleichungssysteme in D-Räumen auffassen können, wobei die Verknüpfungen sich als die vertrauten stetigen algebraischen Operatoren in D-Räumen interpretieren lassen, so daß wir die gewünschten Fixpunkte kontruktiv angeben und zur Festlegung der Semantik heranziehen können. Für freie Monoide sind die Lösungsalgorithmen bekannt, die Lösungen erlauben eine Darstellung, die bei Datenstrukturen nach Art der ALGOL 68 - Modes im Wesentlichen die Menge der Selektionswege als reguläre Mengen ausweist, was sich Algorithmen zur Konsistenzprüfung etc. zu Nutze machen können.

Ein Teil der Ergebnisse ist bereits in einem vorläufigen Technischen Bericht (/L76/) enthalten, auf den wir uns des öfteren beziehen, um uns knapp zu fassen.

2. E - Räume

Die Bezeichnung "E-Raum" geschieht in Anlehnung an die Terminologie der "elementaren Objekte" der Wiener Methode. So werden wir die Bezeichnungen "Objekt" und "Element" eines E-Raumes synonym verwenden. Objekte von E-Räumen, welche Information tragen (hier in einem intuitiven Sinn) lassen sich verknüpfen, wobei das Ergebnis der Operation mindestens soviel Information beinhaltet wie die Operanden. Es gibt auch ein Objekt mit minimaler Information, welches bei der Verknüpfung keinen Beitrag zu leisten vermag. Daher benötigen wir wenigstens ein geordnetes Monoid (meist additiv geschrieben) mit Nullelement. Ist ein Element größer als ein anderes ("enthält es mehr Information ") so soll es ein drittes geben, welches die Differenz beitragen kann ("die fehlende Information zu liefern vermag").

Die Atomizität ist ein Mittel, zwischen endlichen (effektiven, erreichbaren) und unendlichen (uneffektiven, unerreichbaren) Objekten gegebenenfalls zu unterscheiden.

Aus technischen Gründen werden wir von einem Ketten-vollständigem Bereich ausgehen. Die Approximierbarkeit schließt Räume aus, in denen es Elemente gibt, denen man nicht durch Addition vieler endlicher Elemente beliebig nahe kommen kann.

Der Sinn des Einordbarkeitsaxioms wird später klar, wie auch die Forderung, welche die Stetigkeit der Addition sicherstellt.

Diese Intuition präzisieren wir wie folgt:

Def $(E,+,\leq,0,A)$ ist E-Raum

$:\Longleftrightarrow$

E	Trägermenge	(elementare Objekte)
+	assoziative binäre Operation	(Addition)
$\leq$	reflexive Ordnung	(Ordnung)
0	Neutrales der Addition	(Neutrales)
A	Teilmenge von $E-\{0\}$ mit $e \leq a \in A \Rightarrow e=0 \vee e=a$	(Atome)

wobei:

(Zur Vereinfachung der Bezeichnungen nennen wir solche Objekte endlich, die als endliche Summe von Atomen dargestellt werden können, dazu die Null, andere unendlich)

(M) $\forall e \in E : 0 \leq e$ (Minimalität)

(I) $\forall e,f,g \in E$:
$(e \leq f \Rightarrow e+g \leq f+g \wedge g+e \leq g+f)$ (Isotonie)

(C) Jede Kette
$e_1 \leq e_2 \leq \ldots \leq e_i \leq \ldots$
mit Elementen aus E hat ein Supremum in E (Ketten-Vollständigkeit)

(R) Jedes Element $e \in E$ ist Supremum einer Kette endlicher Elemente (Approximierbarkeit)

(S) $e \leq f \Rightarrow \exists\, d_l, d_r \in E$:
$(d_l + e = f \wedge e + d_r = f)$ (partielle Lösbarkeit)

(Q) Für jede Kette
$x_1 \leq x_2 \leq \ldots \leq x_i \leq \ldots$ in E und für jedes endliche Element $f \in E$ mit $f \leq supr(x_i)$ gibt es ein Mitglied
x_j der Kette mit $f \leq x_j$. (Einordbarkeit)

(CT) $\forall x,p \in E$: Wenn k endlich ist und

$k \le x+p$ ist, dann gibt es endliche
Elemente h_1, h_2 mit
$h_1 \le x$, $h_2 \le p$, $h_1 + h_2 \ge k$. (Stetigkeit)

Zur Notation

Wie "$\le$", so werden wir in sinnfälliger Weise "$\ge$", "$<$", "$>$", "$\sim$", "$\nsim$" benutzen.
Für Ketten $e_1 \le e_2 \le \ldots \le e_i \le \ldots$
verwenden wir die Schreibweise (e_i) . $a_j \in (e_i)$ heißt: a_i kommt in der Kette vor; für supr $(e_i)=e$ sagen wir auch "(e_i) konvergiert gegen e" u.ä.

F bezeichne die Menge der endlichen Elemente in E.
Wie üblich, werden wir die E-Räume schlicht durch die Trägermenge bezeichnen, sofern über die Bedeutung von $+, \le, 0, A$ Konsens besteht. Um Wiederholungen zu vermeiden, gelte für die Sätze dieses Abschnittes die Generalvoraussetzung:
E ist E-Raum mit $+, \le, 0, A$, sofern nichts anderes spezifiziert.

Topologisierung

E-Räume sind für uns mit einer Standard-Topologie ausgerüstet, welche durch folgende Basis erzeugt wird: Die Basismengen sind die

$$U(f) := \{e \mid f \le e\} \subseteq E \quad \text{für} \quad f \in F \quad .$$

Die erzeugte Topologie heißt $\mathcal{E}$, wie üblich der zugehörige topologische Raum $(E, \mathcal{E})$.

Beispiele

1. Potenzmengenverbände abzählbarer Mengen, z.B. Scotts $(P\omega, \cup, \subseteq, \emptyset, \omega)$
2. "flache" Verbände wie $(\omega \cup \{\top, \bot\}, \cup, \subseteq, \emptyset, \omega)$

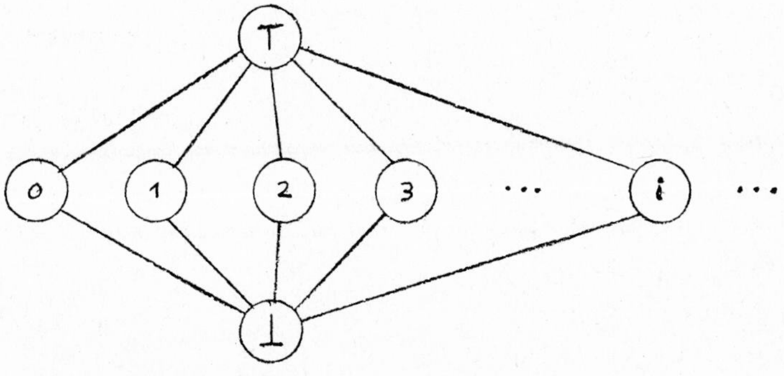

3. Auch nicht-idempotente Bereiche wie $(\omega \cup \{T\}, +, \leq, 0, \{1\})$, wobei + arithmetische Addition ist.
4. Die Menge der "Bags" ("Multi-Sets") über abzählbaren Mengen.
5. Halbordnungen wie durch die Skizze angedeutet:

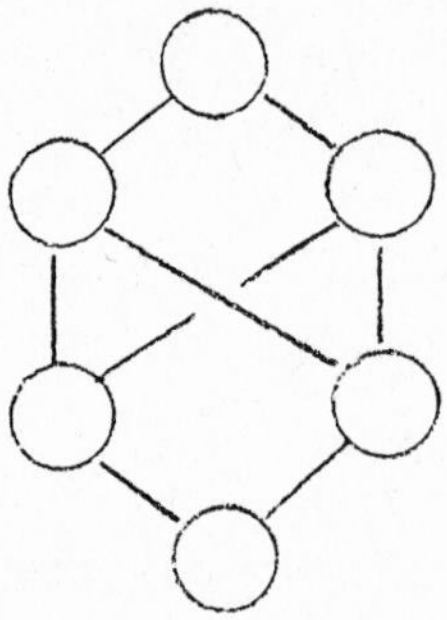

(Kein Verband)

6. Auch nicht-kommutative Strukturen. Daher sollten die Sätze (wie die Axiome) zweiseitig gegeben werden, wie auch die Beweise. Zur Vermeidung von Redundanz betreiben wir unsere Untersuchungen nur ein-seitig, des zwei-seitigen Charakters bewußt.

<u>Lemma</u> (i) Jede nichtleere offene Menge enthält ein endliches Element

(ii) Jede offene Menge enthält mit jedem unendlichen Element x eine Kette (f_i) endlicher Elemente mit supr $(f_i) = x$.

(iii) $x \leq y \Longleftrightarrow$ y ist in jeder Umgebung von x enthalten

(iv) $x \not\leq y \Longleftrightarrow$ Es gibt eine offene Menge, die x enthält, aber nicht y

(v) $x \not\leq y \Longleftrightarrow$ Es gibt ein endliches Element f mit $f \leq x$ aber $f \not\leq y$

(vi) $x \not\leq y \Longleftrightarrow \{d \mid x+d=y\} = \{d \mid d+x=y\} = \emptyset$

<u>Beweis</u> Die Beweise bieten keine besonderen Schwierigkeiten und können daher hier übergangen werden. Allerdings bedarf "$\Longleftarrow$" in (iii) einiger Überlegung ///.

<u>Lemma</u> (i) $(E, \mathfrak{E})$ ist ein zusammenhängender topologischer Raum.
(ii) $(E, \mathfrak{E})$ ist ein T_0-Raum, aber nicht T_1-Raum.

<u>Beweis</u> kann übergangen werden. ///.

Nachdem wir uns mit einfachen Eigenschaften von E-Räumen vertraut gemacht haben, befassen wir uns nun mit dem Verhalten stetiger Funktionen in E-Räumen. Der Stetigkeitsbegriff ist hier der durch die Topologie gegebene: Eine Funktion heißt stetig, wenn ihre Urbilder offener Mengen wieder offen sind.

Lemma (i) jede stetige Funktion $g:E \to E$ ist isoton

(ii) jede isotone Funktion $g:F \to F$ ist im Unterraum F stetig

Beweis einfach ///.

Insbesondere fallen also Stetigkeit und Isotonie in endlichen E-Räumen sowie solchen mit endlicher Höhe zusammen. Im allgemeinen fallen die Begriffe aber nicht zusammen, wie man am Beispiel der Funktion

$$g(x) := \begin{cases} 1 & \text{für } x \not\geq 5 \\ 9 & \text{für } 5^{\infty} > x \geq 5 \\ 36 & \text{für } x \geq 5^{\infty} \end{cases}$$

im E-Raum vom Beispiel 4 sehen kann.

Wir wissen (/S75/), daß das ε-δ-Stetigkeitskriterium der reellen Analysis ein Analogon im Verband aller Teilmengen von ω hat. Eine entsprechende Formulierung ist auch in E-Räumen möglich, wir zeigen, daß das Kriterium hier notwendig und hinreichend ist. Das gleiche gilt für ein zweites Kriterium: der Vertauschbarkeit von Grenzprozeß und Funktions-Evaluation. Dieses Kriterium wird auch in (/S75/) gegeben, seine Notwendigkeit dort gezeigt. Viele Autoren gehen davon aus, daß diese Eigenschaft mit Stetigkeit gleichwertig sein soll, so greifen z.B. Ehrich (/E76/), Loeckx (/L74/), Indermark (/I75/) und Scott in früheren Papieren diese Eigenschaft auf, um Stetigkeit in diversen vollständigen Halbordnungen zu definieren.

Wir zeigen, daß diese Eigenschaft, von manchen Autoren auch "Kettenstetigkeit" oder "ω-Stetigkeit" genannt, in E-Räumen mit Stetigkeit äquivalent ist. Ebenso ist ein drittes Kriterium, das "Netz"-Kriterium, hier für abzählbare Netze, mit Stetigkeit äquivalent.

Satz (ε-δ-Stetigkeitskriterium)

Eine Funktion $g: E \to E$ ist stetig

$\Longleftrightarrow$ für alle $x \in E$ und $f \in F$ gilt:

$f \leq g(x) \Leftrightarrow \exists h \in F : h \leq x \wedge f \leq g(h)$

Beweis (i) (Hinreichende Seite) g erfülle das Kriterium.

Sei B Basismenge mit $B=U(f)$ für ein $f \in F$.

Wir zeigen, daß $g^{-1}(B)$ offen ist.

Falls $g^{-1}(B)$ leer ist, so ist die Behauptung gezeigt; sei also $x \in g^{-1}(B)$. Das bedeutet, $g(x) \in B$. Wegen $B=U(f)$ ist daher $f \leq g(x)$.

Das Kriterium ("$\Longrightarrow$") sichert die Existenz eines endlichen Elements $h \leq x$ mit $f \leq g(h) \varepsilon B$ und $h \varepsilon g^{-1}(B)$. Somit gibt es für jedes $x \varepsilon g^{-1}(B)$ ein endliches Element $h \varepsilon g^{-1}(B)$ mit $h \leq x$. Wir schließen daher

$$g^{-1}(B) \subseteq \bigcup_{h \varepsilon F \cap g^{-1}(B)} U(h)$$

Sei andererseits $h \varepsilon g^{-1}(B)$ und $x \varepsilon E$ mit $h \leq x$. Wegen $h \varepsilon g^{-1}(B)$ gilt $f \leq g(h)$. Wegen des Kriteriums ("$\Longleftarrow$") ist dann $f \leq g(x)$, daher $g(x) \varepsilon B$ und $x \varepsilon g^{-1}(B)$, was die Inklusion in der Gegenrichtung beweist. Damit ist das g-Urbild jeder Basismenge selbst Vereinigung von Basismengen und somit g stetig.

(ii) (notwendige Seite) Sei g stetig.
Seien $x \varepsilon E$ und $f \varepsilon F$ vorgegeben.
"$\Longrightarrow$") Sei $f \leq g(x)$.
Annahme: $\forall h \varepsilon F$: $h \leq x \wedge f \nleq g(h)$
Falls $x \varepsilon F$, so nehme man $h := x$ zum Widerspruch.
Sei also $x \varepsilon E - F$.
Man betrachte die Basismenge $U(f)$. Wegen $g(x) \varepsilon U(f)$ ist $x \varepsilon g^{-1}(U(f))$, welches offene Menge sein muß und daher ein endliches Element h mit $h \leq x$ besitzen muß. Wegen der Annahme, für alle diese endlichen h gelte $f \nleq g(h)$, so folgt $g(h) \notin U(f)$, was einen Widerspruch ergibt.
"$\Longleftarrow$") Sei $h \varepsilon f$ und $h \leq x$ und $f \leq g(h)$. Wegen der Isotonie von g erhalten wir $g(h) \leq g(x)$, somit $f \leq g(x)$. ///.

<u>Satz</u> (Ketten - Stetigkeitskriterium)
Eine Funktion $g : E \to E$ ist stetig
$\Longleftrightarrow$ für alle Ketten (a_i) mit Elementen aus E gilt $g(\text{supr}(a_i)) = \text{supr}(g(a_i))$

<u>Beweis</u> (i) (hinreichende Seite) g erfülle das Kriterium.
Durch Kontraposition sehen wir, daß g isoton ist. Nun zeigen wir, daß das Urbild jeder offenen Menge offen ist.
Sei $B = U(f)$ Basismenge.
Falls $g^{-1}(B)$ leer ist, so reicht uns das.
Sei also $x \varepsilon g^{-1}(B)$, d.h. $g(x) \varepsilon B$ und somit $g(x) \geq f$.
Wegen Axiom (R) gibt es eine Kette (x_i) mit $x_i \varepsilon F$ für alle i und $\text{supr}(x_i) = x$. Wegen der oben festgestellten Isotonie von g ist damit auch $(g(x_i))$ Kette und wegen des Kriteriums ist $\text{supr}(g(x_i)) = g(\text{supr}(x_i)) = g(x)$. Wegen Axiom (Q) gilt für ein $x_j \varepsilon (x_i)$ nun $g(x_j) \geq f$ (und erst

recht für die Kettenglieder mit höherer Nummer). Somit gibt es für jedes x aus dem Urbild von B ein endliches $h = x_j \leq x$ im Urbild. Wir schließen wie im Beweis des vorigen Satzes, daß

$$g^{-1}(B) \subseteq \bigcup_{h \in F \cap g^{-1}(B)} U(h)$$

Andererseits, sei nun $h \in g^{-1}(B) \cap F$, $x \in E$ mit $h \leq x$. Wegen $h \in g^{-1}(B)$ wissen wir, daß $f \leq g(h)$. Wegen der Isotonie ist dann auch $f \leq g(h) \leq g(x)$, also $g(x) \in B$, d.h. $x \in g^{-1}(B)$. So gilt die Inklusion auch in der Gegenrichtung und daher ist g stetig.

(ii) (notwendige Seite) Sei g stetig.
Sei (a_i) beliebige Kette und $a = \mathrm{supr}(a_i)$. Eines unserer Lemmata garantiert uns die Isotonie von g, damit ist $(g(a_i))$ auch Kette und muß ein Supremum haben, das wir s nennen.
Wegen Isotonie ist ferner $g(a) \geq s$.
Wir müssen nun zeigen, daß $g(a) \leq s = \mathrm{supr}(g(a_i))$.
Sei $f \in F$ mit $f \leq g(a)$. Wegen des ε-δ-Kriteriums gibt es nun ein $h \in F$ mit $h \leq a$ und $f \leq g(h)$. Weil h endlich ist, wenden wir Axiom (Q) an und erhalten ein $a_j \in (a_i)$ mit $h \leq a_j$.
Wegen der Isotonie von g ist dann $g(h) \leq g(a_j)$, also $f \leq g(h) \leq g(a_j) \leq s$, im Ganzen also: $f \leq g(a)$ impliziert $f \leq s$. Wegen der Eigenschaft des Supremums schließen wir $g(a) \leq s$. ///.

Bemerkung: Ohne die Forderung nach Atomizität wäre das Kettenkriterium hier kein notwendiges Kriterium. Man prüfe dieses für die Struktur $(\mathbb{R}_0^+ \cup \{\infty\}, +, \leq, 0)$, die die Axiome mit Ausnahme der Atomizität erfüllt, und die Funktion

$$g(x) := \begin{cases} 10 & \text{für } x < 10 \\ 20 & \text{für } x \geq 10 \end{cases}$$

In einigen Publikationen (/z.B.I75/) wird auch das sogenannte Netz-Kriterium für die Definition von Stetigkeit in Halbordnungen herangezogen. Wir zeigen, daß dieses Kriterium für abzählbare Netze (abzählbare gerichtete Mengen) in E-Räumen ebenfalls notwendig und hinreichend ist.

Satz (Netz - Stetigkeitskriterium)
Eine Funktion $g : E \to E$ ist stetig
$\Longleftrightarrow$ Für alle abzählbaren Netze $N \subseteq E$ gilt $g(\mathrm{supr}(N)) = \mathrm{supr}(g(N))$
(die Suprema existieren und die Werte sind gleich).

Beweis Über Zurückführung auf das Ketten - Kriterium, siehe (/L76/). ///.

Mit Hilfe der Kriteria bekommen wir den Fixpunktsatz, der für viele Arten von Halbordnungen wohlbekannt ist.

Korollar (Fixpunktsatz)
Jede stetige Funktion $g:E \to E$ hat einen kleinsten Fixpunkt.
Dieser ist

$$supr(g^i(0))$$

wobei g^i die i-malige Komposition von g ist.

Beweis Unsere Struktur erfüllt die Bedingungen von Loeckx (/L74/), das Kettenkriterium sagt uns, daß unsere stetigen Funktionen Ketten-stetig im Sinne von Loeckx sind, so daß wir den dortigen Fixpunktsatz anwenden können.
In (/L76/) ist ein Beweis gegeben, der im Sinne von Scott (/S75/) verläuft.

Der nichtkonstruktive Teil des Satzes kann nun auch so formuliert werden:
Jeder E-Raum ist Fixpunktraum.

Ohne Beweis geben wir noch einige Resultate, welche die Rolle der Addition beleuchten:

Lemma Die Addition eines festen Elements ist stetig.

Bemerkung Axiom (CT) ist hierfür notwendig. Man vergleiche für eine gegen Bsp.4 geänderte Multiset-Operation $a+b := u(a) \cdot u(b)$ mit
$u(x) = (x \varepsilon F \to x,\ T \to x \cdot x)$.

Lemma (i) Jedes unendliche Element kann als Limes einer unendlichen Reihe dargestellt werden.

(ii) f ist genau dann endliches Objekt, wenn es keine streng monoton wachsende Reihe gibt, die f darstellt.

Bemerkung hier ist Axiom (Q) notwendig.

3. D-Räume

Von den E-Räumen, wo an algebraischen Operationen nur die Addition vorausgesetzt wird, wollen wir nun durch Produktbildung zu Räumen strukturierter Objekte kommen, deren algebraische Eigenschaften z.B. in (/E76/) diskutiert sind. Diese Räume sind mit zwei weiteren grundlegenden Operationen ausgerüstet: der Selektion von Teilobjekten und der Konstruktion von Verbundobjekten. Die strukturierten Objekte sind Verallgemeinerungen der Wiener Objekte, wie auch die entsprechenden Operationen. Man kann mit Hilfe dieser Grundoperationen nämlich eine Amputation (Abschneiden eines Teilobjektes) sowie den dreistelligen μ-Operator als zusammengesetzte Operationen definieren, was aber hier außer Betracht bleibt.

Der Bereich der strukturierten Objekte, in Anlehnung an Ehrich als D-Objekte bezeichnet, ist hier der Raum der Funktionen eines freien Monoids S in den Raum der E-Objekte. Standardmäßig veranschaulichen wir uns D-Objekte als Wurzelbäume mit Kantenmarkierungen aus S und Knotenmarkierungen aus E, S wird auch als das Alphabet der Selektoren, S^* als die Menge der Selektionswege bezeichnet (λ leeres Wort):

D-Objekt d:

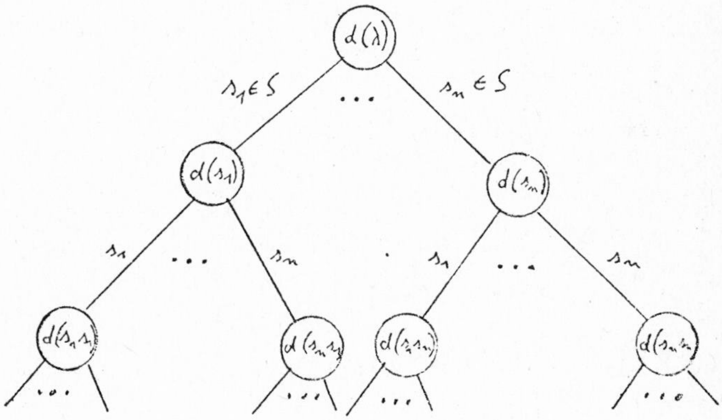

In der graphischen Darstellung können Teilobjekte fortgelassen werden, für deren sämtliche Selektionswege x gilt $d(x) = 0 \in E$. Periodizitäten können durch Zyklen in Graphen dargestellt werden.

Unsere Vorstellungen präzisieren wir nun wie folgt:

Def. $D = (D, +_D, \leq_D, 0_D, A_D)$ ist D-Raum

$:\Longleftrightarrow$ Es existiert ein E-Raum $E = (E, +, \leq, 0, A)$ und eine Menge S von

Selektoren mit

(i) $D = E^{S^*}$ (Funktionenraum)

(ii) $\forall x \in S^* \forall d_1, d_2 \in D : d_1 +_D d_2(x) = d_1(x) + d_2(x)$ (Komponentenweise Additi

(iii) $d_1 \leq_D d_2 \Leftrightarrow \forall x \in S^* : d_1(x) \leq d_2(x)$ (Komponentenweise Ordnun

(iv) $\forall x \in S^* : 0_D(x) = 0$ (Nullfunktion)

(v) $A_D = \{d \mid d \in D : \exists x \in S^* : (d(x) \in A \wedge \forall y \in S^* : y \neq x \Rightarrow d(y) = 0)\}$
(Atomizität)

Sofern aus dem Kontext ersichtlich ist, ob wir $+_D$ oder $+$, $\leq_D$ oder $\leq$ etc. betrachten, werden wir den Index fortlassen. D-Räume seien wie folgt mit den Operationen Konstruktion und Selektion ausgerüstet:

$\forall x \in S^* \; \forall d \in D \quad \forall z \in S^*$:

$x{:}d(z) := (z=xy \rightarrow d(y),\ T \rightarrow 0)$ (Konstruktion)

$d.x(z) := d(xz)$ (Selektion)

Für eine algebraische Darstellung von D-Objekten können wir uns bequem an die Schreibweise des Ringes der formalen Potenzreihen

$$E(/\ S\ /)$$

über nichtkommutativen Variablen aus S mit E-Objekten als Koeffizienten anlehnen, für $d \in D$ wollen wir schreiben

$$d = \sum_{x \in S^*} x{:}d(x)$$

wobei wir Nullen als Komponenten weglassen und somit endliche Objekte eine multinomiale Darstellung haben. Man beachte: wir schreiben $x{:}d(x)$ statt $d(x)x$. Es gibt eine Reihe von Beziehungen zu Polynom- und Potenzreihenringen, die hier aber nicht betrachtet werden.
In der Schreibweise wollen wir zwischen E und $\lambda{:}E$ nicht unterscheiden.

Wir weisen darauf hin, daß zwar die Definition von D-Räumen axiomatisch ist, aber eine Kontruktionsweise enthält, so daß wir zu vorgegebenen E-Raum und Sektorbereich S stets den D-Raum über E und S konstruieren können.

Zunächst stellen wir fest:

Lemma (i) jeder E-Raum ist D-Raum

(ii) jeder D-Raum ist E-Raum

Beweis (i) jeder E-Raum kann als D-Raum über sich selbst und dem leeren Selektoralphabet mit dem freien Monoid $\emptyset^* = \{\lambda\}$ aufgefaßt werden. Wichtiger ist (ii).

(ii) Die Konstruktion des Produktraumes respektiert die E-Axiome ///.

So haben wir für D-Räume in natürlicher Weise endliche und unendliche Objekte, Topologie, Stetigkeitskriterien, den Fixpunktsatz u.a.m.

Lemma Die Topologie, welche ein D-Raum als E-Raum hat, ist die Produkttopologie.

Beweis Man vergleiche die Basismengen der Produkttopologie und der E-Topologie von D. Es sind die gleichen. ///.

Theorem (Stetigkeit der algebraischen Operationen)

(i) Die Selektion durch ein festes Selektorwort ist stetig.

(ii) Die Konstruktion mit einem festen Selektorwort ist stetig.

(iii) Die Addition eines festen D-Objektes ist stetig.

Beweis Wir wissen aus der Topologie, daß eine Funktion in einem Produktraum genau dann stetig ist, wenn sie es in jeder Komponente ist. Nun betrachten wir die y-Komponente für ein beliebig vorgegebenes Selektorwort $y \varepsilon S^*$, indem wir die Projektion P_y anwenden, und wir sehen, daß für beliebige aber feste d, $e \varepsilon D$ und $x \varepsilon S^*$:

(i) $P_y\ (d.x) \equiv P_{xy}(d)$

(ii) $P_y\ (x{:}d) \equiv (y{=}xz \rightarrow P_z(d),\ T \rightarrow 0)$

(iii) $P_y\ (e{+}d) \equiv P_y(e) + P_y(d)$

Die rechts stehenden Funktionen sind stetig, weil sie entweder Projektionen oder E-Summen von Projektionen sind (Die Fallunterscheidung in (ii) geschieht ohne Ansehen des Arguments). ///.

Nun sind wir in der Lage, (rekursive) Gleichungssysteme in D-Räumen zu lösen, welche syntaktisch korrekt aus den Operationen Konstruktion, Selektion, Addition von Bekannten und Unbekannten aufgebaut sind.

Betrachten wir ein Beispiel aus ALGOL 68 (In ALGOL 68 ist allerdings echte Rekursion in der mode-Definition nicht erlaubt, sondern nur Rekursion über Referenzen, das Beispiel eröffnet uns dennoch einen Zugang):

$\underline{\text{mode}}$ u = $\underline{\text{struct}}$ ($\underline{\text{bool}}$ r,u s, w t)

$\underline{\text{mode}}$ w = $\underline{\text{struct}}$ (u s, $\underline{\text{int}}$ t)

Eine Datenstruktur (mode) ist eine Funktion, die bei Angabe von Selektionswegen (Argumenten) Teilobjekte oder auch Werte liefert. Es liegt nahe, die Gleichungen in einem D-Raum zu interpretieren, wobei sich die Operatoren struct wie $\sum$ und Angabe von Selektoren wie Konstruktion verhalten:

$$u = r : \text{bool} + s : u + t : w$$

$$w = \qquad s : u + t : \text{int}$$

Die Lösung im D-Raum der Typen ist dann (durch den Fixpunktsatz)

$$u = \sum_{x \varepsilon (s \vee ts)^*} xr{:}\text{bool} + \sum_{x \varepsilon (s \vee ts)^*} xtt : \text{int} \quad .$$

d.h. ein unendliches (reguläres) Objekt, welches wir auch durch andere äquivalente mode-Definitionen erhalten hätten.
Nun dürfen wir aber struct und andere Operatoren nicht so wie oben verwenden, wohl aber z.B.

$\underline{\text{mode}}$ b = $\underline{\text{struct}}$ ($\underline{\text{struct}}$ ($\underline{\text{int}}$ i, $\underline{\text{ref}}$ $\underline{\text{int}}$ ri) s,
$\underline{\text{ref}}$ $\underline{\text{struct}}$ ($\underline{\text{int}}$ i, $\underline{\text{ref}}$ b rb) $_{rs}$)

Die Bedeutung des ref und die daraus ableitbare Semantik von Namensnamen, unfreien Selektionswegen und anderer Erscheinungen muß weiter Exposition vorbehalten bleiben (/L76.b/), wir bemerken hier nur, daß wir die Eigenschaft von D-Räumen nutzen, selbst wieder E-Räume zu sein, um zu immer reicher ausgestatteten höheren D-Räumen aufzusteigen. Referenzieren und Dereferenzieren übernehmen dabei die Rollen der Funktionsbildung zum Aufsteigen und der Applikation zum Absteigen.

4. Schluß

Aus der Motivation heraus, das algebraische Konzept der D-Räume (/E76/) zu übernehmen und dadurch zu bereichern, daß ein sinnvolles hinreichendes Kriterium für den Fixpunktsatz, gemeinhin Stetigkeit genannt, mit dem topologischen Begriff Stetigkeit zusammenfalle, verschob sich zunächst der Schwerpunkt der Untersuchung von den Räumen strukturierter Objekte zu den Räumen elementarer Objekte. Deren Axiome konnten so gewählt werden, daß die gängigen Stetigkeitskriterien den gleichen Begriff bestimmten.

So konnte eine begriffliche Grundlage geschaffen werden, um die gewünschten Manipulationen in den strukturierten Bereichen (von Bäumen ähnlich Wiener Objekte) vorzunehmen, indem z.B. rekursive mode-Deklarationen als Fixpunktgleichungen angesehen und gelöst werden. Gleichzeitig ergibt sich die Möglichkeit, zu höher strukturierten Räumen aufzusteigen, zwecks formaler Klärung der Semantik anderer Sprachmittel, was aber weiteren Betrachtungen vorbehalten bleibt.

Literaturangaben

(/E 76/) Ehrich, H.-D.: Outline of an algebraic theory of structured objects. Proc. 3rd International Colloquium on Automata, Languages, and Programming, Edingburgh University Press, Edinburgh 1976.

(/I 75/) Indermark, K.: Gleichungsdefinierbarkeit in Relationalstrukturen, Bericht Nr. 98, Gesellschaft für Mathematik und Datenverarbeitung, 1975.

(/L 74/) Loeckx, J.: The fixpoint-theorem and the Principle of Computational Induction. Bericht A 74/08 Universität Saarbrücken, Fachbereich Informatik, 1974.

(/Lo76/) Lohberger, V.: Axioms for Ordered Monoids that are Fixpoint-Spaces According to a suitable Topology. TR 28/76 Abteilung Informatik, Universität Dortmund, July 1976.

(/Lo76.b/) Lohberger, V.: Spaces of Structured Objects and Applications to the Semantics of Data Structures. TR 36/76 Abteilung Informatik, Universität Dortmund, in Prep.

(/S 72/) Scott, D.: Continous Lattices. In: Topology, algebraic Geometry and Logic. Lecture Notes in Mathematics, Nr. 274. Springer, Berlin 1972.

(/S 75/) Scott, D.: Data Types and Lattices. In: Müller,G.H. (ed): Proceedings of the International Summer Institute and Logic Colloquium, Kiel 1974, Springer Lecture Notes 499, Berlin 1975.

SYSTEMES SCHEMATIQUES GENERALISES

L. Kott

Abstract We extend algebraic semantics introduced by M.Nivat #5,6# in order to construct a semantics of an ALGOL-like computer language which give us answers to the problems of call-by-value,assignment statements and initialization of local variables.With this semantics and an inductive method (related to our formalism) so powerful as computionnal induction we justify the inductive assertion method of C.A.Hoare #1#.Hence we extend results of Z.Manna and J.Vuillemin #4# to a strictly larger family of programs.

1.Introduction.Un exemple.

"The purpose of a mathematical semantics is to give a correct and meaningful correspondence between programs and mathematical entities in a way that is entirely independant of an implementation "#7#.La définition d'une sémantique d'ALGOL doit faire ressortir les caractéristiques de ce langage et,plus particulièrement,la structure en blocs des programmes ALGOL;structure qui conduit à distinguer,dans un programme,entre variables globales et variables locales.

Ces dernières,déclarées dans un sous-bloc d'un programme,doivent,bien sûr, être initialisées et cette opération ne va pas sans problèmes:ainsi,dans le travail de Z.Manna et J.Vuillemin #4# par exemple,on constate que cette initialisation est transcrite comme la substitution à la variable locale de l'expression qui calcule cette valeur initiale;or,ceci est une opération purement syntaxique dont il convient de montrer la validité sémantique.

C'est ce problème qui nous a amené à construire une nouvelle sémantique d'un langage très voisin d'ALGOL (cf. #2#) qui permet,en outre,de rendre compte de phénomènes analogues et plus généraux comme l'existence d'instructions d'affectation et l'appel par la valeur des arguments d'une procedure.Cette construction étend celle de M.Nivat #5,6#,qui n'a pour ambition que la représentation des procédures ALGOL et non du langage lui-même,et permet de retrouver les résultats obtenus par les constructions antérieures.

Un exemple va bien montrer la nécessité de formuler une sémantique tenant compte des phénomènes décrits ci-dessus.Soit P le programme:

```
BEGIN INTEGER PROCEDURE FACT(Z);INTEGER Z;
      FACT:=IF Z=0 THEN 1 ELSE Z*FACT(Z-1);
      INTEGER X;
      READ(X);
      BEGIN INTEGER Y;
            Y:=FACT(X);
            X:=IF X=(X÷2)*2 THEN 1 ELSE (X↑Y)+Y;
      END;
      WRITE(X);
END
```

qui calcule sur $\mathbb{Z}$ la fonction:

$n \to \omega$ si $n<0$ (ω=indéfini)

$n \to 1$ si $n\geq 0$ et n pair

$n \to n^{n!}+n$ si $n\geq 0$ et n impair

Suivant la méthode décrite dans #4#, à ce programme est associé le système de fonctionnelles

$$\begin{cases} H(x) \leftarrow \underline{si}\ x=0\ \underline{alors}\ 1\ \underline{sinon}\ x.H(x-1) \\ F(x) \leftarrow \underline{si}\ x \text{ est pair } \underline{alors}\ 1\ \underline{sinon}\ x^{H(x)} + x \end{cases}$$

et la fonction calculée par le programme est égale au plus petit point fixe de la seconde fonctionnelle. Or ce plus petit point fixe est la fonction:

$n \to 1$ si n est pair

$n \to \omega$ si n est impair et $n<0$

$n \to n^{n!}+n$ si n est impair et $n\geq 0$

qui est distincte de celle qui est effectivement calculée par le programme P. La raison de cette différence se trouve dans le traitement de l'instruction Y:=FACT(X) qui dans #4# est traitée par l'opération syntaxique de substitution ce qui s'avère non valide sur le plan sémantique.

Nous allons développer un formalisme faisant bien le partage entre syntaxe et sémantique en étendant celui défini par M.Nivat #5,6#. Rappelons qu'un programme est donné par un schéma de programme -qui fait abstraction de la signification des fonctions de base- et une interprétation -qui restitue leur sens aux symboles de fonction de base-. Un schéma de programme est considéré comme un système d'équations sur un magma (ensemble des termes bien formés grossièrement parlant) dont la solution est un langage qui permet, une interprétation étant donnée, de définir la fonction calculée par le schema. Cependant cette théorie ne peut être utilisée sans précautionset nous sommes, donc, amenés à définir des systèmes de réécriture, dits systèmes schématiques généralisés (S.S.G.), dans lesquels, au moment d'interpréter le langage solution, la distinction entre variables globales et locales se retrouvera: les variables globales seront valuées tandis que les variabes locales seront calculées.

Dans notre formalisme, au programme P est associé le S.S.G., Σ, suivant:

$$\Sigma \begin{cases} \eta(u) = c(p(u),a,g(u,\eta(h(u)))) + \Omega \\ \phi(u) = \psi(u,w) + \Omega \\ \psi(u,v) = c(q(u),a,f(u,v)) + \Omega \\ w = \eta(u) \end{cases}$$

dans lequel la première équation représente la procédure FACT; la seconde exprime que la fonction calculée par le programme P se déduit de la fonction à deux arguments calculée par le sous-bloc du programme; la quatrième décrit l'instruction Y:=FACT(X).

Σ est considéré comme une grammaire algébrique dont les non-terminaux sont ϕ, ψ et η et ϕ est l'axiome. Dans un premier temps on calcule le langage $L(\Sigma,\phi)$ qui est égal à

$\{\Omega,\underline{t}\}$ avec $\underline{t} = c(q(u),a,f(u,w))$

Ici w est considéré comme un non-terminal.

Soit I l'interprétation de domaine $\mathbb{Z}\cup\{\omega\}$ telle que c_I soit le conditonnel usuel, a_I la constante 1, f_I l'application qui à (x,y) associe x^y+y, g_I la multiplication, h_I la fonction prédécesseur et Ω_I la constante ω. Pour définir la fonction calculée par Σ, sous l'interprétation I, il faut interpréter les mots de $L(\Sigma,\phi)$ et, plus particulièrement, le mot t; or ceci oblige à calculer, sous I, la valeur de w pour une valeur donnée de u.

En analogie avec les cas concrets (ALGOL par exemple) la valeur de t est différente de ω seulement si la valeur de w est elle-même distincte de ω. Ce calcul de w se fait par la technique habituelle de la règle de recopie #6# et définit pour valeur de w:

ω si u est valué par un entier strictement négatif

n! si u est valué par un entier positif ou nul

Si bien que le mot t aura pour valeur ω si $n<0$ et $c_I(p_I(n),a_I,f_I(n,n!))$ si $n\geq 0$. Il en résulte que la fonction calculée par (Σ,ϕ) sous l'interprétation I est

$n \to \omega$ si $n<0$

$n \to 1$ si $n\geq 0$ et n pair

$n \to n^{n!}+n$ si $n\geq 0$ et n impair

qui constitue la sémantique correcte du programme P.

2. Présentation des résultats.

La définition formelle des S.S.G. est donnée plus bas. On obtient les résultats suivants dont on trouvera les preuves dans #2#.

Théorème 1 Il existe un algorithme qui à tout programme écrit en ALGOL associe un S.S.G. et une interprétation permettant de définir la fonction calculée par ce programme.

Théorème 2 Il existe une règle d'induction qui permet de tester si un S.S.G. vérifie un prédicat admissible (au sens de #3#).

Corollaire Les règles de la vérification de programme introduites par C.A. Hoare #1# sont sémantiquement valides.

On étend ainsi les résultats de #4# à une classe strictement plus grande de programmes ainsi que le montre l'exemple du §1.

3. Systèmes schématiques généralisés.

3.0. Définitions

Soient les ensembles suivants:

- Φ ensemble de symboles dits "symboles de fonction inconnue";
- F ensemble de symboles dits "symbole de fonction de base";
- V ensemble de variables;
- W ensemble de variables locales (notées v.l.)

Soit ρ une application de Φ F dans N appelée arité. $M(\Phi\cup F, V\cup W)$ désigne le magma libre (cf. #6#) engendré par $V\cup W$ i.e. l'ensemble des mots ainsi obtenus:

$V\cup W \subseteq M(\Phi\cup F, V\cup W)$

si $t_1,\ldots,t_{\rho(f)}$ sont dans $M(\Phi\cup F, V\cup W)$ et f dans $\Phi\cup F$ alors le mot

$f(t_1,\ldots,t_{\rho(f)})$ appartient au magma.

Un système schématique généralisé (S.S.G.) est un ensemble fini d'équations sur le magma $M(\Phi\cup F, V\cup W)$ de la forme

$$\begin{cases} \phi^i(v_1,\ldots,v_{\rho_i}) = \tau^i + \Omega; \tau^i \in M(\Phi \cup F, \{v_1,\ldots,v_{\rho_i}\} \cup \{w^{i,1},\ldots,w^{i,\sigma_i}\}) \\ w^{i,j} = \tau^{i,j}; \tau^{i,j} \in M(\Phi \cup F, \{v_1,\ldots,v_{\rho_i}\}) \end{cases}$$

où $i \in \{1,2,\ldots,N\}, j \in \{1,2,\ldots,\sigma_i\}$ et ρ_i est une abréviation de $\rho(\phi^i)$.

La définition d'une sémantique des S.S.G. se fait en trois étapes.

3.1. Construction d'un système infini simulant un S.S.G..

Cette construction est fondée sur le principe suivant:soit g l'application de Z dans Z définie par

$$\forall x \in \mathbf{Z} \;\; g(x) \equiv \underline{\text{si}} \; x=0 \; \underline{\text{alors}} \; 1 \; \underline{\text{sinon}} \; g(x+1)$$

g peut être considérée,pour une interprétation précise,comme étant calculée par le système infini suivant noté Σ^∞

$$\Sigma^\infty \begin{cases} \phi^0(v) = c(p(v),a,\phi^1(s(v))) + \Omega \\ \phi^1(v) = c(p(v),a,\phi^2(s(v))) + \Omega \\ \vdots \quad \vdots \quad \vdots \\ \phi^n(v) = c(p(v),a,\phi^{n+1}(s(v))) + \Omega \\ \vdots \quad \vdots \quad \vdots \end{cases}$$

Σ^∞ n'est que la concrétisation de toutes les réécritures possibles dans la définition de g et peut être condensé sous la forme

$$\begin{cases} \phi_m(v) = c(p(v),a,\phi_{m\alpha}(s(v))) + \Omega \\ m \in \{\alpha\}^* \end{cases}$$

en utilisant un symbole spécial α.

C'est dans l'esprit de cet exemple qu'à tout S.S.G.,Σ,nous associons un système infini,$\Sigma_{\alpha,\beta}$,qui le simule.Utilisant A et B,deux ensembles de lettres,pour indexer les symboles de fonction inconnue et les variables locales,$\Sigma_{\alpha,\beta}$ est de la forme

$$\Sigma_{\alpha,\beta} \begin{cases} \phi^i_m(v_1,\ldots,v_{\rho_i}) = \tau^i_m + \Omega; \tau^i_m \in M(\Phi_{\alpha,\beta} \cup F, V \cup W_{\alpha,\beta}) \\ w^{i,j}_m = \tau^{i,j}_m; \tau^{i,j}_m \in M(\Phi_{\alpha,\beta} \cup F, V) \\ m \in (A \cup B)^* \end{cases}$$

où $\Phi_{\alpha,\beta} = \{\phi^i_m | \phi^i \in \Phi$ et $m \in (A \cup B)^*\}$et $W_{\alpha,\beta} = \{w^{i,j}_m | w^{i,j} \in W$ et $m \in (A \cup B)^*\}$

Nous appellerons Σ_α le système infini qui simule le comportement du S.S.G. Σ sans tenir compte du caractère spécifique des variables locales et qui s'écrit

$$\Sigma_\alpha \begin{cases} \phi^i_m(v_1,\ldots,v_{\rho_i}) = \tau^i_m + \Omega \\ m \in A^* \end{cases}$$

3.2. "Résolution" des variables locales.

La valeur de chaque v.l. est obtenu,au moment de l'interprétation,par l'intermédiaire d'une expression de M(F,V);connaître ces expressions c'est "résoudre" les v.l..

A chaque variable locale,$w^{i,j}$,nous associons l'ensemble des mots-index de $(A\;B)^*$ qu'il se voit attribuer par le fonctionnement de $\Sigma_{\alpha,\beta}$ comme système de réécriture.Cet ensemble Θ^i_j est un arbre fini ou non;par suite à chaque S.S.G. est associée une famille d'arbres dits arbres de v.l..

Soit F l'ensemble $\{T_j^i | i \in \{1,\ldots,N\}, j \in \{1,\ldots,\sigma_i\}\}$ tel que chaque T_j^i soit un sous-arbre initial fini de Θ_j^i. $\Sigma_{\alpha,\beta}$ étant un système de réécriture dans lequel la dérivation associée à F est celle qui conduit à réécrire en Ω tout symbole de fonction inconnue introduisant une v.l. dont l'index n'est pas un noeud d'un T_j^i pour quelque i et quelque j.

Nous avons alors le résultat, technique, mais très important suivant:

Théorème *L'ensemble F étant donné, il est toujours possible d'associer à chaque v.l. dont l'index est un noeud d'un élément de F un mot du magma* M(F,V).

3.3. Interprétation et sémantiques

Soit Σ_α le système associé au S.S.G. Σ (cf. § 3.1. in fine). une interprétation discrète de Σ_α sur le magma M(F,V) est donnée par:

- un domaine discret D_I muni d'un plus petit élément ω,
- pour chaque symbole f de F une application de $D_I^{(f)}$ dans D_I,
- et un ensemble F de sous-arbres initiaux finis des arbres de v.l.

Une telle interprétation est notée (I,F). ν étant une valuation (i.e. une application de V dans D_I), on définit une application de $M(F,V\ W_\alpha)$ dans D_I par:

$$(I,F,\nu)[\Omega] = \omega ; (I,F,\nu)[v] = \nu(v);$$

$$(I,F,\nu)[f(t_1,\ldots,t_{\rho(f)})] = \begin{cases} \omega \text{ si dans quelque } t_i \text{ apparait une v.l. dont l'index n'est pas un noeud de } F. \\ \omega \text{ si dans quelqur } t_i \text{ il existe une v.l., w par exemple, d'index dans } F \text{ telle que } val(w)=\omega. \\ f_I((I,F,\nu)[t_1],\ldots,(I,F,\nu)[t_{\rho(f)}]) \text{ sinon.} \end{cases}$$

où val(w) est l'élément de D_I ainsi obtenu: w, ayant son index dans un élément de F, est "soluble" (cf. Th. § 3.2.); il lui est donc associé un mot de M(F,V) qui, I et étant données, définit un élément de D_I que nous notons, justement, val(w).

Le théorème central est alors atteint.

Théorème *Si $L(\Sigma_\alpha)$ est le langage engendré par Σ_α et si (I,F) est une interprétation de Σ_α alors, t et t' étant deux mots de $L(\Sigma_\alpha)$, $(I,F,\nu)[t]\neq\omega$ et $(I,F,\nu)[t']\neq\omega$ impliquent $(I,F,\nu)[t] = (I,F,\nu)[t']$.*

D'où découle immédiatement la définition de la sémantique de Σ_α. Une interprétation (I,F) étant donnée on définit l'application $Val_{I,F}\Sigma_\alpha$, pour toute valuation ν, par

$$Val_{I,F}\Sigma_\alpha(\nu) = \begin{cases} d \text{ si il existe t de } L(\Sigma_\alpha) \text{ tel que } (I,F,\nu)[t] = d \neq \omega \\ \omega \text{ sinon} \end{cases}$$

3.4. Sémantiques d'un S.S.G. Σ.

Une première sémantique, dite "concréte", vient immédiatement des résultats du paragraphe précédent; on pose tout simplement

$$Val_{I,F}\Sigma = Val_{I,F}\Sigma_\alpha$$

où (I,F) est une interprétation de Σ comme de Σ_α.

Pour la seconde sémantique, dite "abstraite", on considère des interprétations discrètes au sens habituel #5,6#; soit I une telle interprétation, nous définissons l'application calculée par Σ, sous I, en posant pour toute valuation ν

$$\mathrm{Val}_I\Sigma(\nu) = \begin{cases} d & \text{si il existe un ensemble } F \text{ de sous-arbres initiaux finis des arbres de v.l. tel que } \mathrm{Val}_{I,F}\Sigma_\alpha(\nu) = d \neq \omega \\ \omega & \text{sinon} \end{cases}$$

La cohérence de cette définition est assurée par la propriété suivante

Proposition Soient F et F' deux ensembles de sous-arbres initiaux finis des arbres de v.l. tels que chaque élément de F soit un sous-arbre d'un élément de F', alors $\mathrm{Val}_{I,F}\Sigma_\alpha$ est une application moins définie que $\mathrm{Val}_{I,F'}\Sigma_\alpha$.

Il suffit alors de donner l'équation associée, dans notre formalisme, à chaque instruction ALGOL pour définir la sémantique de ce langage et obtenir, ainsi, le Théorème 1 annoncé au §2. Le théorème 2, quant à lui, exige l'introduction de notions et de propriétés qu'il n'est pas possible de développer ici. Le lecteur intéressé pourra se rapporter à #2#.

Bibliographie

#1# C.A. Hoare "Procedures and parameters:An axiomatic approach" in Lectures Notes in Mathematics 188 (E.Engeler Ed.)pp.102-116,Springer-Verlag,Berlin(1971).

#2# L. Kott "Approche par le magma d'un langage de programmation type ALGOL:sémantique et vérifications de programme" Thèse de 3° cycle,Université Paris VII (1976).

#3# Z. Manna,S. Ness et J. Vuillemin "Inductive methods for proving properties of programs" C.ACM 16 pp.491-502 (1973).

#4# Z. Manna et J. Vuillemin "Fixpoint approach to the theory of computation" C.ACM 15 pp.528-536 (1972).

#5# M. Nivat "Sur l'interprétation des schémas de programme monadiques" Rapport IRIA-Laboria n°1 (1972).

#6# M. Nivat "On the interpretation of recursive polyadic schemas" Instituto Nazionale di Alta Matematica,Symposia Matematica, Volume XV (1974).

#7# D. Scott et C. Strachey "Toward a mathematical semantics for computer languages" Tech. Monography PRG-6,Oxford University,Oxford (1971).

Formale Korrektheitsbeweise für While-Programme

J. Loeckx

Einleitung

In den letzten Jahren hat man einige Erfahrung gesammelt in der Durchführung formaler Korrektheitsbeweise, die auf axiomatische oder denotationnelle Semantik aufbauen (vgl. z.B. [1,2]). Dabei hat sich herausgestellt, daß die Formeln, die während eines solchen Beweises auftreten, schnell unübersichtlich werden; dies erschwert dem Benutzer die Interpretation dieser Formeln und somit die Durchführung des Beweises. Ein Grund dafür ist die Tatsache, daß die benutzten Semantikbeschreibungen so allgemein sind, daß sie auch auf nicht-triviale Programmiersprachen anwendbar sind (vgl. z.B. [3,4]).

Dieser Bericht beschränkt sich auf eine Klasse von while-Programmen. Für diese Programme wird eine einfache axiomatische Semantikbeschreibung eingeführt; der Grundgedanke dabei ist, jeder Variablen eine Funktion zuzuordnen, deren Argumente die Anzahl der Durchläufe der verschiedenen Schleifen zählen. Die Semantikbeschreibung sowie der Korrektheitsbeweis eines Programms werden dann relativ einfach und übersichtlich.

Der hier eingeführte Formalismus hat große Ähnlichkeiten mit LUCID [5,6,7], aber er unterscheidet sich von ihm unter anderem aus folgenden Gründen. Erstens werden den Variablen Funktionen statt unendlicher Vektoren zugeordnet; diese Tatsache zusammen mit den dem λ-Kalkül entnommenen Notationen vereinfacht die Schreibweise sowie einige Ableitungsregeln. Zweitens ist das Ziel dieser Arbeit nicht die Einführung einer neuen Programmiersprache sondern die Behandlung von while-Programmen.

1. While-Programme

While-Programme (siehe z.B. [8], p. 203) bestehen essentiell aus einer Folge von Anweisungen; jede Anweisung besteht entweder aus einer Zuweisung oder einer while-Anweisung.

Ein while-Programm heißt *elementar*, wenn alle while-Anweisungen geschachtelt sind. Genauer ausgedrückt, ein elementares while-Programm wird definiert von E zusammen mit den kontext-freien Produktionen

E ::= <u>begin</u> P <u>end</u>;

P ::= Q; <u>while</u> B <u>do</u> P <u>od</u>; Q | Q

Q ::= Q;S | ε ,

wobei S eine Zuweisung, B ein boolescher Ausdruck und ε das leere Wort darstellt. Ein elementares while-Programm entspricht daher dem in Fig. 1 angegebenen Flußdiagramm; dabei sind $Q_0, Q_1, \ldots, Q_{n-1}$, $R_0, R_1, \ldots, R_n$, bzw. $B_1, B_2, \ldots, B_n$, Elemente der syntaktischen Klasse Q, bzw. B. Die *Schachtelungstiefe* eines Blocks Q_i, R_i oder B_i $(0 \le i \le n)$ ist die Zahl i.

Ein elementares while-Programm heißt *normalisiert*, wenn jede Variable höchstens zweimal im linken Glied einer Zuweisung vorkommt; außerdem muß im Fall zweier solcher Vorkommen die erste Zuweisung in einem Block Q_i und die zweite in einem Block R_{i+1} auftreten $(0 \le i \le n-1)$; Beispiele für solche normalisierten while-Programme findet man in Fig. 2 und 3. Eine Variable, die nicht in einem linken Glied einer Zuweisung vorkommt, heißt *Eingabevariable*. Eine Variable, die nur einmal im linken Glied einer Zuweisung auftritt, wird benutzt zur Speicherung eines Zwischenresultats und heißt deshalb *Hilfsvariable*; eine Variable, die zweimal im linken Glied einer Zuweisung auftritt, kann an der Steuerung einer while-Schleife teilnehmen und heißt deshalb *Kontrollvariable*. Die *Schachtelungstiefe* einer Hilfsvariablen ist die Schachtelungstiefe des Blocks, zu der die entsprechende Zuweisung gehört; die Schachtelungstiefe einer Kontrollvariablen ist die Schachtelungstiefe des Blocks, zu der die zweite Zuweisung gehört.

In diesem Bericht werden nur normalisierte elementare while-Programme betrachtet. Daß diese Einschränkungen nicht wesentlich sind, geht aus folgenden Überlegungen hervor. Erstens gibt es einen Algorithmus, der ein beliebiges elementares while-Programm in ein normalisiertes while-Programm überführt [9]; die Wirkung dieses Algorithmus beruht im wesentlichen auf der Einführung zusätzlicher Variablen. Zweitens ist es ohne große Schwierigkeiten möglich, die Resultate auf (nicht-elementare) while-Programme zu verallgemeinern.

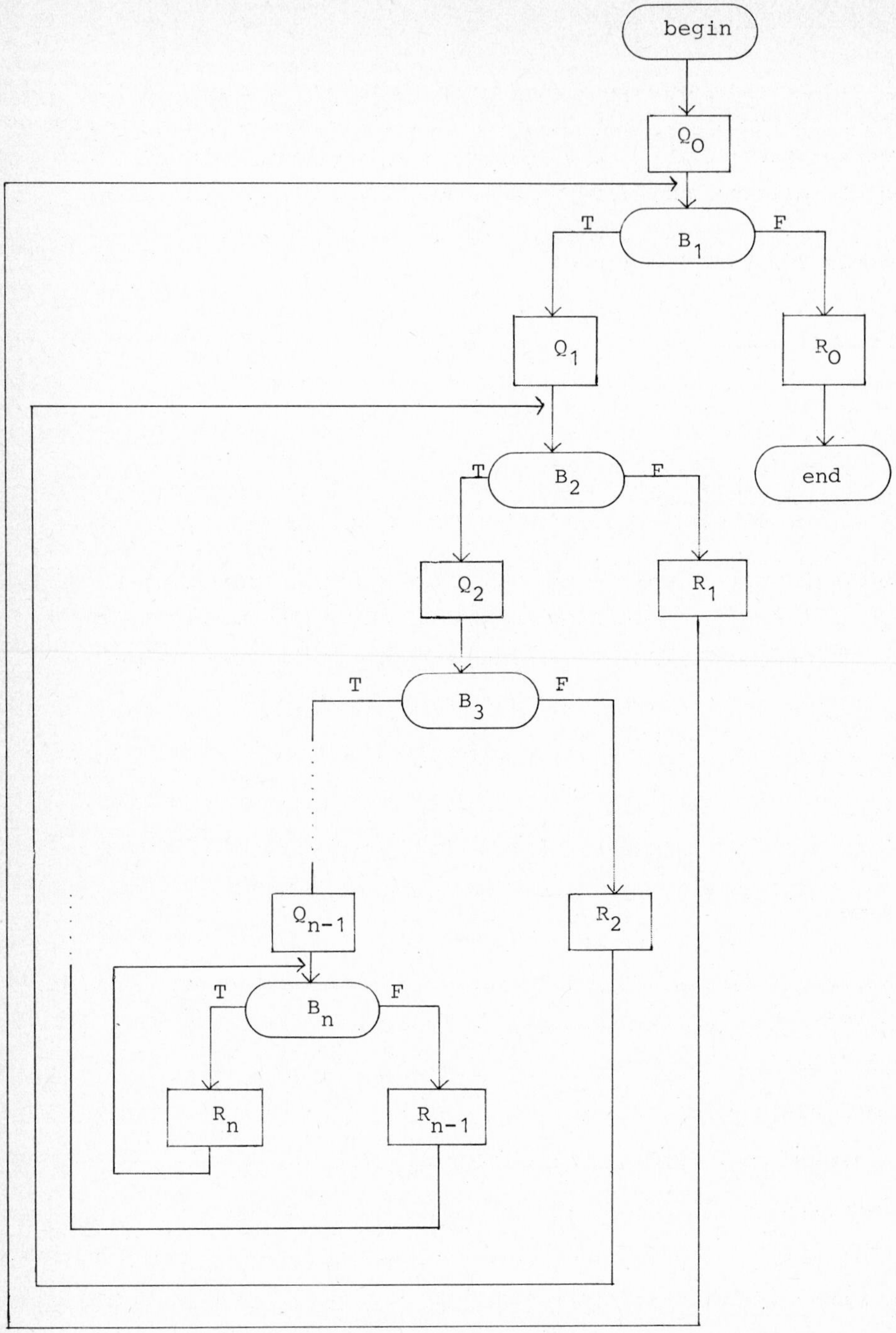

Figur 1: Das Flußdiagramm eines elementaren while-Programms ($n \geq 0$); R_i, $1 \leq i \leq n$, bezeichnet einen Block, der vor einem Rücksprung ausgeführt wird.

2. Notationen für Funktionen

Sei $\underline{D}$ die Vereinigung der Bereiche der Variablen eines while-Programms (einschließlich {$\underline{\text{true}}$,$\underline{\text{false}}$}) und sei $\underline{N}$ die Menge aller nicht-negativen ganzen Zahlen. Es werden jetzt einige Notationen eingeführt, von denen die meisten dem λ-Kalkül entnommen sind.

In Absatz 3 werden Funktionen

$$\underbrace{\underline{N} \to (\underline{N} \to (\underline{N} \to \ldots (\underline{N}}_{n\text{-mal}} \to \underline{D}))\ldots)$$

und

$$\underbrace{\underline{N} \to (\underline{N} \to (\underline{N} \to \ldots (\underline{N}}_{n\text{-mal}} \to \underline{N}))\ldots)$$

eingeführt $(n \geq 1)$; n heißt der *Rang* einer solchen Funktion. Zur Verdeutlichung wählt man im weiteren Verlauf für eine Funktion vom Rang n einen Identifikator wie fn oder gn, der den Rang n explizit angibt.

Statt z.B.

$$(f2(t))(s)$$

darf man

$$f2(t)(s)$$

schreiben.

Die klassischen Funktionen und Prädikate werden in der üblichen Weise erweitert:

$$f2 + g2$$

wird definiert durch

$$(\forall s,t)((f2+g2)(s)(t) = f2(s)(t)+g2(s)(t)) \;;$$

ähnlich gilt

$$f2 = g2$$

genau dann, wenn

$$(\forall s,t)(f2(s)(t) = g2(s)(t))$$

gilt.

Wenn $n \geq 1$ und $m=n-1$, dann ist

$$fn(gm)$$

die Funktion von Rang m, die aus der Komposition der Funktionen fn und gm erhalten wird; etwas präziser: wenn z.B.

$$f3 : \underline{N} \rightarrow (\underline{N} \rightarrow (\underline{N} \rightarrow \underline{D}))$$

und $g2 : \underline{N} \rightarrow (\underline{N} \rightarrow \underline{N})$,

dann ist die Funktion

$$f3(g2) : \underline{N} \rightarrow (\underline{N} \rightarrow \underline{D})$$

definiert durch

$$(\forall s,t)((f3(g2))(s)(t) = f3(g2(s)(t))(s)(t).$$

Man beachte insbesondere, daß gemäß dieser Definition im Fall n=1

$$f1(g0)$$

die übliche Notation für den Wert der Funktion f1 für das Argument g0 ist.

Schließlich darf ein Ausdruck wie

$$f2 + [\lambda t.g2] + [\lambda t,s.1] \quad (*)$$

einfachheitshalber geschrieben werden als

$$f2 + g1 + 1 ;$$

es gilt also z.B.

$$(f2+g1+1)(s) = f2(s)+g1+1$$

oder

$$(f2+g1+1)(s)(t) = f2(s)(t)+g1(t)+1 .$$

(*) Es wird vorausgesetzt, daß t nicht frei in g vorkommt.

3. Die Semantik eines while-Programms

Der Grundgedanke der Semantikbeschreibung besteht darin, jeder Variablen mit Schachtelungstiefe n eine Funktion

$$fn : \underline{N} \rightarrow (\underline{N} \rightarrow \ldots (\underline{N} \rightarrow \underline{D}))\ldots)$$

vom Rang n zuzuordnen. Dabei ist diese Funktion so definiert, daß z.B.

$$f2(3)(4)$$

der Wert der entsprechenden Variablen ist zum Zeitpunkt des dritten Durchlaufs der inneren while-Schleife innerhalb des vierten Durchlaufs der äußeren while-Schleife. Um diese Gedanken präzisieren zu können, werden die Funktionale S und M und die booleschen Variablen τ_i eingeführt.

Das Funktional S bildet eine Funktion vom Rang n, n≥1, in eine Funktion gleichen Ranges ab; dabei ist z.B. der Wert

$$S[f2]$$

von S für das Argument f2 eine Funktion, die durch

$$(\forall s,t)(S[f2](s)(t) = f2(s+1)(t))$$

definiert wird. Man beachte, daß S distributiv bezüglich der klassischen Operationen ist; es gilt also z.B.

$$S[fn+gn] = S[fn] + S[gn]$$

oder

$$S[\neg \underset{\cdot\cdot}{g}n] = \neg S[\underset{\cdot\cdot}{g}n] .$$

Das Funktional M bildet ein Prädikat vom Rang n, n≥1, in eine Funktion

$$\underline{N} \rightarrow (\underline{N} \rightarrow (\underline{N} \rightarrow \ldots (\underline{N} \rightarrow \underline{N}))\ldots)$$

vom Rang n-1 ab; dabei ist z.B. der Wert

$$M[\underset{\cdot\cdot}{g}3]$$

von M für das Argument $\underset{\cdot\cdot}{g}3$ eine Funktion, die durch

$$(\forall s,t)(M[\underset{\cdot\cdot}{g}3](s)(t)) = \begin{cases} w & \text{falls } \underset{\cdot\cdot}{g}3(v)(s)(t) = \underline{true} \text{ für jedes } v, \\ & 0 \le v < w, \text{ und } \underset{\cdot\cdot}{g}3(w)(s)(t) = \underline{false} \\ \text{undefiniert sonst} & \end{cases}$$

definiert ist. Man beachte die Ähnlichkeit mit der Theorie der rekursiven Funktionen: S - oder genauer S[f](t) - entspricht der Notation

$$f(t+1)$$

in einem Rekursionsschema; M entspricht dem Minimalisierungsoperator.

Einem while-Programm mit maximaler Schachtelungstiefe n (vgl. Fig. 1) werden n boolesche Variablen τ_i, $1 \leq i \leq n$, zugeordnet, deren Wert das Terminieren des entsprechenden Programmteils ausdrückt. Etwas genauer:

> τ_i = <u>true</u> $\Leftrightarrow$ wenn während der Ausführung des while-Programms der Block B_i erreicht wird, dann wird es - möglicherweise nach einigen Durchläufen der i. Schleife - über seinen F-Ausgang verlassen.

Die Semantikbeschreibung des while-Programms aus Fig. 1 besteht dann aus drei Teilen, wie von den Figuren 2 und 3 illustiert wird:

(1°) einige Axiome, die den Zuweisungen des while-Programms entsprechen und die gleich näher besprochen werden;

(2°) die Liste der booleschen Ausdrücke p_i der Blöcke B_i, $1 \leq i \leq n$;

(3°) die Spezifikation der Schachtelungstiefe der Variablen bzw. des Ranges der Funktionen.

Die Axiome erhält man, indem man jede Zuweisung in eine Gleichung zwischen Funktionen transformiert; dabei entspricht einer Variablen j mit Schachtelungstiefe k eine Funktion j mit Rang k, $0 \leq k \leq n$. Etwas genauer: jede Zuweisung aus einem Block Q_i, $0 \leq i \leq n$, oder aus dem Block R_n führt zu einem Axiom

$\vdash$Gleichung ;

jede Zuweisung aus einem Block R_i, $0 \leq i \leq n-1$, führt zu einem Axiom

$\tau_i \vdash$ Gleichung .

Dabei wird die Gleichung aus der Zuweisung abgeleitet mit Hilfe der folgenden Regeln, die für jedes Vorkommen der Variablen j die entsprechende "Übersetzung" in die Funktion j angibt; sie wird illustriert von den Figuren 2 und 3:

1. Fall: Vorkommen im linken Glied einer Zuweisung

(1°) wenn j Hilfsvariable ist: j

(2°) wenn j Kontrollvariable ist:

- erstes Vorkommen: j(O)
- zweites Vorkommen: S[j]

2. Fall: Vorkommen im rechten Glied einer Zuweisung eines Blocks mit Schachtelungstiefe m; dabei ist k die Schachtelungstiefe der Variablen j

(1°) wenn $m \geq k$: j

Ausnahme: j ist eine Kontrollvariable und das Vorkommen tritt im Block R_k nach der zweiten Zuweisung auf: S[j]

(2°) wenn $m<k$: $j(M[p_k])(M[p_{k-1}])\ldots(M[p_{m+1}])$,
wobei $p_k, p_{k-1}, \ldots, p_{m+1}$ die Funktionen sind, die den booleschen Ausdrücken der Blöcke $B_k, B_{k+1}, \ldots, B_{m+1}$ entsprechen.

3. Fall: Vorkommen im booleschen Ausdruck eines Blocks B_k (*)

Ähnlich wie im 2. Fall

Man beachte, daß die Reihenfolge, in der die erhaltenen Axiome geschrieben werden, irrelevant ist.

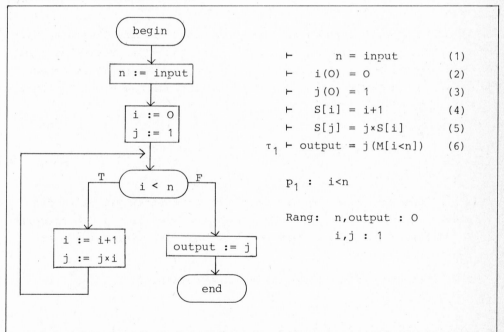

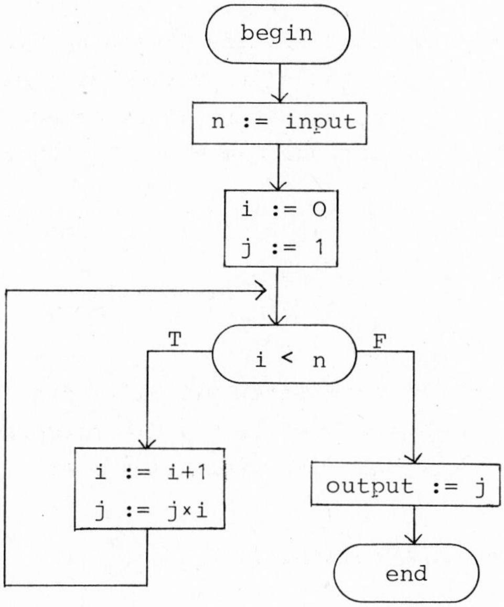

	⊢	n = input	(1)
	⊢	i(0) = 0	(2)
	⊢	j(0) = 1	(3)
	⊢	S[i] = i+1	(4)
	⊢	S[j] = j×S[i]	(5)
τ_1	⊢	output = j(M[i<n])	(6)

p_1 : i<n

Rang: n,output : 0
i,j : 1

Figur 2: Ein while-Programm und seine Semantik; das Programm berechnet (input)!

(*) Diese booleschen Ausdrücke treten in der Übersetzung nur als Argumente auf (siehe 2. Fall, m<k).

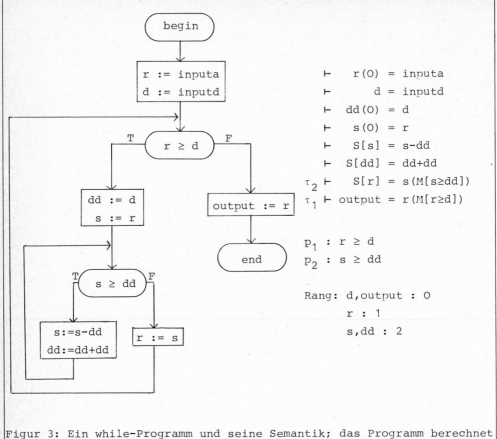

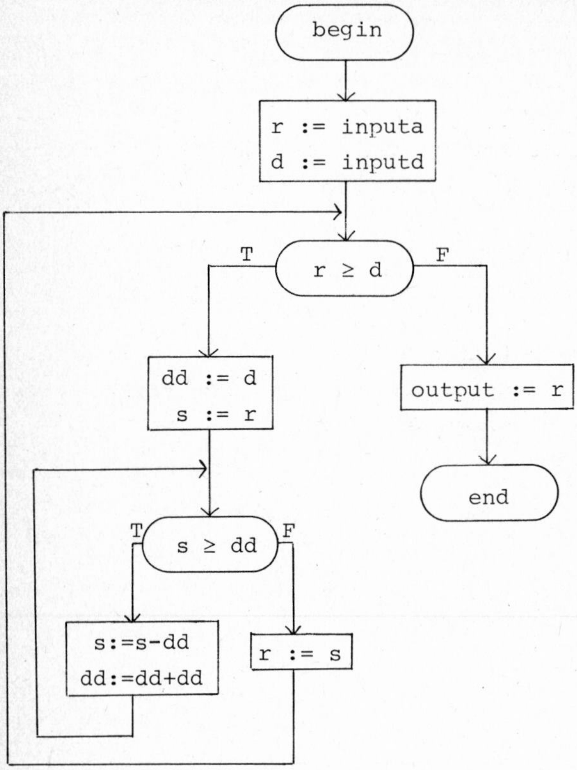

$\vdash \; r(0) = inputa$

$\vdash \; d = inputd$

$\vdash \; dd(0) = d$

$\vdash \; s(0) = r$

$\vdash \; S[s] = s\text{-}dd$

$\vdash \; S[dd] = dd+dd$

$\tau_2 \vdash \; S[r] = s(M[s \geq dd])$

$\tau_1 \vdash \; output = r(M[r \geq d])$

p_1 : $r \geq d$

p_2 : $s \geq dd$

Rang: d,output : 0
r : 1
s,dd : 2

Figur 3: Ein while-Programm und seine Semantik; das Programm berechnet (inputa)mod(inputd) (siehe Dijkstra, "A discipline of programming", Prentice-Hall, 1976 (p. 59)).

4. Die partielle Korrektheit (*)

4.1. Prinzip

Der Grundgedanke eines Beweises der partiellen Korrektheit ist folgender: die Axiome, die die Semantik eines while-Programms beschreiben, werden zusammen mit einigen zusätzlichen Ableitungsregeln in den Prädikatenkalkül eingebettet. Um zu beweisen, daß ein Programm partiell

(*) Der Begriff "partielle Korrektheit" wird benutzt im Sinne von [8], p. 165.

korrekt bezüglich des Ausgabeprädikats q ist, genügt es dann, den Satz

$$\tau_1 \vdash q$$

abzuleiten.

Zur Durchführung solcher Beweise werden zusätzlich nur drei Ableitungsregeln und zwei Axiome benötigt. Die erste Ableitungsregel ist eine Induktionsregel:

$$\frac{\vdash q(0) \quad \vdash q \supset S[q]}{\vdash q} \tag{R1}$$

Die zweite Ableitungsregel bezieht sich auf das Verlassen einer while-Schleife; sie benutzt ein Funktional H, das ein Prädikat in ein Prädikat gleichen Rangs abbildet und dessen Wert durch die beiden folgenden Axiome definiert wird:

$$\vdash H[q](0) = \underline{\text{true}} \tag{A1}$$

$$\vdash S[H[q]] = H[q] \wedge q \tag{A2}$$

(siehe Figur 4). Die zweite Ableitungsregel ist dann:

$$\frac{\vdash (\neg p_i) \wedge H[p_i] \supset q}{\tau_i \vdash q(M[p_i])} \quad (1 \le i \le n) \tag{R2}$$

(siehe Figur 4); dabei ist p_i das Prädikat aus Block B_i. Schließlich ist

Argument	0	1	2	3	4	...
p_1	true	true	false	.....		
$H[p_1]$	true	true	true	false	false	...
$(\neg p_1) \wedge H[p_1]$	false	false	true	false	false	...

Figur 4: Illustration der Werte von $H[p_1]$ und $(\neg p_1) \wedge H[p_1]$

die dritte Ableitungsregel

$$\frac{\vdash \tau_i}{\vdash \tau_{i+1}} \quad (1 \le i \le n-1) \;; \tag{R3}$$

diese Regel wird z.B. benötigt um aus einem Satz

$$\tau_2, \tau_1 \vdash q$$

den Satz

$$\tau_1 \vdash q$$

ableiten zu können.

4.2. Beispiel

Zur Illustration folgt der Beweis der partiellen Korrektheit des while-Programms aus Figur 2. Zu beweisen ist:

$$\tau_1 \vdash output = (input)! \qquad (a)$$

Zuerst wird bewiesen:

$$\vdash j = i! \qquad (b)$$

Dazu wird die Ableitungsregel (R1) benutzt. Es genügt also zu beweisen:

$$\vdash (j=i!)(0) \qquad (b1)$$

und $\vdash (j=i!) \supset S[j=i!]$ (b2)

(b1) gilt, denn

$$\vdash (j=i!)(0) = (j(0)=(i(0))!)$$

wegen der in Absatz 2 definierten Erweiterung der klassischen Funktionen

$$= (1=0!)$$

wegen Figur 2, Axiome (2) und (3) ;

(b2) gilt genau dann, wenn

$$\vdash (j=i!) \supset S[j] = S[i]!$$

wegen der Eigenschaft der Distributivität von S

oder $\vdash (j=i!) \supset j \times S[i] = (i+1)!$

wegen Figur 2, Axiome (5) und (4)

oder $\vdash (j=i!) \supset j \times (i+1) = (i+1)!$

wegen Figur 2, Axiom (4).

Die Gültigkeit dieses letzten Satzes ist evident.

Da

$$\vdash n = input$$

und $\tau_1 \vdash output = j(M[i<n])$

gilt (a) genau dann, wenn

$\tau_1 \vdash j(M[i<n]) = n!$

gilt. Gemäß der Ableitungsregel (R2) genügt es zu beweisen, daß

$\vdash_\neg (i<n) \wedge H[i<n] \supset j = n!$

oder, wegen (b), daß

$\vdash (i \geq n) \wedge H[i<n] \supset i = n.$

Dazu wird die Ableitungsregel (R1) benutzt; es genügt also zu beweisen, daß

$$\vdash ((i \geq n) \wedge H[i<n] \supset (i=n))(O) \qquad (a1)$$

und $\vdash ((i \geq n) \wedge H[i<n] \supset i=n)$
$\supset S[(i \geq n) \wedge H[i<n] \supset (i=n)]$. (a2)

(a1) gilt genau dann, wenn

$\vdash (i(O) \geq n) \wedge H[i<n](O) \supset (i(O)=n)$

oder $\vdash (O \geq n) \wedge \underline{\text{true}} \supset O=n)$
wegen Figur 2, Axiom (2) und wegen Axiom (A1).

Die Gültigkeit dieses Satzes ist evident, da (oder genauer: wenn) n eine ganze nicht-negative Zahl ist.

(a2) gilt genau dann, wenn

$\vdash (i(O) \geq n) \ldots) \supset (S[i] \geq n) \wedge S[H[i<n]] \supset (S[i] = n))$
wegen der Eigenschaft der Distributivität von S(*) ,

oder $\vdash (\ldots) \supset ((i+1 \geq n) \wedge H[i<n] \wedge (i<n) \supset (i+1 = n))$
wegen Figur 2, Axiom (4) und wegen Axiom (A2) ,

oder $\vdash (\ldots) \supset \underline{\text{true}}$
weil $i+1 \geq n$ und $i<n$ implizieren, daß $i+1 = n$.

Die Gültigkeit dieses letzten Satzes ist evident.

Ein weiteres Beispiel findet man im Anhang.

(*) Man erinnere sich dabei daran, daß z.B. $(i \geq n)$ eine verkürzte Notation für $(i \geq \lambda t.n)$ ist; deshalb gilt $S[i \geq n] = (S[i] \geq n)$.

5. Das Terminieren

Um zu beweisen, daß das while-Programm aus Fig. 1 terminiert, genügt es, den Satz

$$\vdash \tau_1$$

zu beweisen. Dieser Satz kann aus den folgenden n Sätzen abgeleitet werden:

$$\vdash \tau_n$$

und

$$\tau_{i+1} \vdash \tau_i \qquad (1 \le i \le n-1) \ .$$

Um diese Sätze zu beweisen, wird nur eine einzige zusätzliche Ableitungsregel benötigt:

$$\frac{\vdash P_i \supset (t > S[t]) \qquad \vdash P_{i-1} \supset (t \le 0 \supset \neg p_i)}{\vdash \tau_i} \qquad (1 \le i \le n) \ , \qquad \text{(R4)}$$

dabei sind:

$P_j = p_1 \wedge p_2 \wedge \ldots \wedge p_j$, $i-1 \le j \le i$;

p_j die booleschen Ausdrücke der Blöcke B_j, $1 \le j \le i$;

t eine beliebige Funktion von Rang i, deren Wertbereich (eine Teilmenge der) Menge der ganzen Zahlen ist.

Das Terminieren des while-Programms aus Fig. 2 kann z.B. folgenderweise bewiesen werden. Man wähle

$$t = n-i \ .$$

Entsprechend der Ableitungsregel (R4) genügt es zu beweisen

$$\vdash (i<n) \supset (n-i > S[n-i]) \qquad \text{(a)}$$

und $\vdash (n-i \le 0) \supset \neg (i<n)$ (b)

(a) gilt genau dann, wenn

$$\vdash (i<n) \supset (n-i > n-(i+1))$$

wegen Fig. 2, Axiom (4)

oder $\vdash (i<n) \supset (1>0)$;

die Gültigkeit dieses letzten Satzes ist evident. Schließlich gilt (b) trivialerweise. Ein weiteres Beispiel findet man im Anhang.

Man bemerke noch, daß aus der partiellen Korrektheit

$\tau_1 \vdash q$

eines while-Programms und aus seinem Terminieren

$\vdash \tau_1$

seine totale Korrektheit

$\vdash q$

folgt.

Man bemerke auch, daß das Nicht-Terminieren eines while-Programms bewiesen ist, wenn man

$\tau_1 \vdash \underline{\text{false}}$

bewiesen hat.

Anhang: Beweis der totalen Korrektheit des while-Programms von Fig. 3

Es wird angenommen, daß inputa $\geq$ 0 und inputd > 0. Zu beweisen ist:

$\vdash$ output = inputa mod inputd .

A1. Hilfssatz: $\vdash$ s mod d = r mod d $\wedge$ dd mod d = 0

Beweis

Wegen (R1) genügt es, zu beweisen:

$\vdash$ s(0) mod d = r mod d $\wedge$ dd(0) mod d = 0 (a)

und

$\vdash$(s mod d = r mod d $\wedge$ dd mod d = 0) $\supset$
(S[s] mod d = r mod d $\wedge$ S[dd] mod d = 0) (b)

(a) gilt, denn

$\vdash$ r mod d = r mod d $\wedge$ d mod d = 0

(b) gilt, denn

$\vdash$ (s mod d = r mod d $\wedge$ dd mod d = 0) $\supset$
(s mod d - dd mod d = r mod d $\wedge$ 2dd mod d = 0) ┘

A2. Hilfssatz: $\tau_2 \vdash$ r mod d = inputa mod d

Beweis

Wegen (R1) genügt es, zu beweisen:

$\tau_2 \vdash$ r(0) mod d = inputa mod d (a)

und

$\tau_2 \vdash (r \underline{mod}\ d = inputa\ \underline{mod}\ d) \supset (S[r]\ \underline{mod}\ d = inputa\ \underline{mod}\ d)$ (b)

(a) gilt, denn

$\vdash inputa\ \underline{mod}\ d = inputa\ \underline{mod}\ d$

Um zu beweisen, daß (b) gilt, genügt es, zu beweisen:

$\tau_2 \vdash (r\ \underline{mod}\ d = inputa\ \underline{mod}\ d) \supset (s(M[s \geq dd])\ \underline{mod}\ d = inputa\ \underline{mod}\ d)$ (b1)

Wegen (R2) genügt es zu beweisen:

$\vdash \neg(s \geq dd) \wedge H[s \geq dd] \supset$
$(r\ \underline{mod}\ d = inputa\ \underline{mod}\ d \supset s\ \underline{mod}\ d = inputa\ \underline{mod}\ d)$

oder, wegen Hilfssatz A1:

$\vdash \ldots \supset (r\ \underline{mod}\ d = inputa\ \underline{mod}\ d \supset r\ \underline{mod}\ d = inputa\ \underline{mod}\ d)$ ┘

A3. Hilfssatz: (partielle Korrektheit): $\tau_1 \vdash output = inputa\ \underline{mod}\ inputd$

Beweis

Es genügt zu beweisen:

$\tau_1 \vdash r\ (M[r \geq d]) = inputa\ \underline{mod}\ d$

oder, wegen (R3):

$\tau_1, \tau_2 \vdash r\ (M[r \geq d]) = inputa\ \underline{mod}\ d$

oder, wegen (R2):

$\tau_2 \vdash \neg\ (r \geq d) \wedge H[r \geq d] \supset r = inputa\ \underline{mod}\ d$

oder, wegen Hilfssatz A2:

$\tau_2 \vdash r<d \wedge H[r \geq d] \supset r = r\ \underline{mod}\ d$.

Dieser Satz gilt wegen der Definition von mod. ┘

A4. Hilfssatz: $\vdash d > 0 \wedge dd > 0$

Beweis

Wegen (R1) genügt es, zu beweisen

$\vdash d>0 \wedge dd(0) > 0$ (a)

und

$\vdash d>0 \wedge dd>0 \supset d>0 \wedge S[dd] > 0$ (b)

(a) gilt, weil $dd(0) = d = inputd > 0$

(b) gilt, weil

$\vdash dd > 0 \supset dd+dd > 0$ ┘

A5. Hilfssatz: $\vdash r > s - dd$

Beweis

Wegen (R1) genügt es, zu beweisen:

$\vdash r > s(0) - dd(0)$ (a)

und

$\vdash r > s - dd \supset r > S[s] - S[dd]$ (b)

(a) gilt, wenn

$\vdash r > r - d$ (a1)

(a1) gilt wegen Hilfssatz A4.

(b) gilt, wenn

$\vdash r > s - dd \supset r > s - 3dd$ (b1)

(b1) gilt wegen Hilfssatz A4. ┘

A6. Hilfssatz (Terminieren der inneren Schleife): $\vdash \tau_2$

Beweis

Man nehme $t = 2s+dd+1$

Wegen (R4) genügt es, zu beweisen:

$\vdash r \geq d \wedge s \geq dd \supset 2s+dd > S[2s+dd]$ (a)

und

$\vdash r \geq d \supset (s+dd<0 \supset \neg (s \geq dd))$ (b)

Um (a) zu beweisen, genügt es, zu beweisen:

$\vdash r \geq d \wedge s \geq dd \supset 2s+dd > 2s - 2dd + 2dd$

oder

$\vdash \ldots \supset dd > 0$

Dies gilt wegen Hilfssatz A4.

Um (b) zu beweisen, genügt es, zu beweisen:

$\vdash r \geq d \supset (s+dd<0 \supset s < dd)$.

Dies gilt, denn wenn $s+dd<0$, dann ist $s-dd<0$, da $dd>0$ gilt wegen Hilfssatz A4. ┘

A7. Hilfssatz (Terminieren der äußeren Schleife): $\tau_2 \vdash \tau_1$

Beweis

Man nehme $t = r-d+1$

Wegen (R4) genügt es, zu beweisen:

$\tau_2 \vdash r \geq d \supset r-d > S[r] - d$ (a)

und

$\tau_2 \vdash r-d<0 \supset \neg (r \geq d)$. (b)

Um (a) zu beweisen, genügt es, zu beweisen:

$\tau_2 \vdash r \geq d \supset r > s(M[s \geq dd])$

oder, wegen (R2):

$\vdash s < dd \wedge H[s \geq dd] \supset (r \geq d \supset r > s)$ (a1)

Um (a1) zu beweisen, genügt es wegen (R1), daß

$\vdash s(0) < dd(0) \wedge \underline{true} \supset (r \geq d \supset r > s(0))$ (a11)

und

$\vdash (s < dd \wedge H[s \geq dd] \supset (r \geq d \supset r > s))$
$\supset (S[s] < S[dd] \wedge s \geq dd \wedge H[s \geq dd]$
$\supset (r \geq d \supset r > S[s]))$

oder

$\vdash (\ldots) \supset (\ldots \supset (r \geq d \supset r > s - dd))$ (a12)

(a11) gilt, denn

$\vdash r < d \supset (r \geq d \supset r > r)$

(a12) gilt wegen Hilfssatz A5

(b) gilt trivialerweise. ┘

A8. Satz (totale Korrektheit): $\vdash$ output = inputa mod inputd

Beweis

Gilt wegen Hilfssatz A6, A7 und A3. ┘

Bedankung: Für verschiedene Diskussionen bin ich u.a. W. Barth verpflichtet.

Referenzen

[1] S. Igarashi, R.L. London, D.C. Luckham, "Automatic program verification", Acta Informatica 4,2 (1975)

[2] R. Milner, "Implementation and applications of Scott's Logic for Computable Functions", Proc. ACM Conf. on Proving Assertions about Programs, SIGPLAN Notices 7,1 (1972)

[3] C.A.R. Hoare, N. Wirth, "An axiomatic definition of the programming language PASCAL", Acta Informatica 2,4 (1973)

[4] L. Aiello, M. Aiello, R. Weyrauch, "The semantics of PASCAL in LCF", Artif. Intell. Memo 221, Stanford Univ. (1974)

[5] E.A. Ashcroft, W.W. Wadge, "LUCID, a formal system for writing and proving programs", SIAM J. Comp. 5,3 (1976)

[6] E.A. Ashcroft, W.W. Wadge, "LUCID, a non-procedural language with iteration", Comm. ACM, to appear

[7] E.A. Ashcroft, W.W. Wadge, "Program proving without tears", Colloque de l'IRIA sur la construction, l'amélioration et la vérification de programmes, Arc-et-Senans, 1-3 juillet 1975

[8] Z. Manna, "Mathematical theory of computation", McGraw-Hill, 1975

[9] S. Lehmann, J. Loeckx, "An algorithm normalizing elementary while-programs", Bericht Nr. A 76/14, Fachbereich 10, Universität des Saarlandes (Saarbrücken), Dezember 1976

TOWARDS AUTOMATION OF PROOFS BY INDUCTION

F.W. von Henke

Introduction. In proving theorems about recursively defined functions the most difficult task is the appropriate instantiation of the induction rule. Usually, once, the induction is set up properly, the remainder of the proof can be carried out in an almost straightforward manner, unless it requires further inductions.

This paper presents some heuristics for automating proofs by induction. The logical framework is the Logic for Computable Functions (LCF) /5,6/, which originates in D.Scott's work and, in the form used here, was developed and implemented in an interactive proving system by R.Milner. This logic is very well suited to express recursive functions and to reason about them. A central rule of inference of LCF is Scott's rule for computational induction, also called "Scott's induction". It is the only form of induction provided by the LCF system; accordingly, the heuristics are developed to deal primarily with computational induction. However, it is well known (cf. /4/) that other forms of induction can be simulated by computational induction. We shall briefly explain below how to express structural induction in this framework and indicate how the heuristics for computational induction can also handle structural induction.

The heuristics are intended to reflect and formalize the common experience in generating induction proofs. Though developed in the framework of LCF, they are largely independent of the idiosynchrasies of the underlying logic.

Preliminaries. We use the language of LCF terms which, roughly speaking, consists of the expressions of the λ-calculus (identifiers, applications or 'combinations' s(t), and abstractions $\lambda x.t$), augmented by conditional expressions $p \Rightarrow q,r$ ('if p then q else r') and least fixed points $\alpha F.t$ ('least fixed point of the functional $\lambda F.t$'). Atomic well-formed formulae are built up from terms by means of the relation symbols $\sqsubseteq$ (inequivalence) and $\equiv$ (equivalence). For a well-formed formula P and a recursive definition $f \equiv \alpha F.t(F)$, the inference rule for computational induction states that from the truth of P(UU) (UU being the undefined element) and the truth of P(t(F)) assuming P(F), we can infer truth of $P(\alpha F.t(F))$.

In the following we use the terminology of the LCF proving system. The 'goal' is the statement to be proved (an atomic well-formed formula in LCF). A 'tactic' is a (possibly derived) rule of inference which is used for generating subgoals from a goal.

The basis for the heuristics is a syntactic analysis of the goal and the recursive definitions of identifiers (function names) occurring in the goal. The standard form of a recursive definition is assumed to be an equivalence $f \equiv \alpha F. \lambda x_1 \ldots x_n . t$ where the term t usually contains occurrences of F and the parameters $x_1,\ldots,x_n$; f will be called a 'recursive function' for short. We distinguish between three kinds of parameters of recursive functions:

(a) case-controlling parameters, which occur in the condition term of a conditional expression;

(b) recursion parameters, which are modified in a 'recursive call';

(c) constant parameters, which are passed down the recursion without being changed.

For example, in the recursive definition

$$f \equiv \alpha F. \lambda x\ y\ z.\ p(x) \Rightarrow g(y),\ h(x,\ F(k(x),\ y,\ m(x,z)))$$

x is case-controlling and recursion parameter, y is a constant parameter and z is a recursion parameter. In general, a case-controlling parameter is also a recursion parameter; otherwise, a recursion may never terminate.

Heuristics for Induction. The heuristics attempt to catch the basic ideas that are behind induction proofs. Most of them derive directly or indirectly from the following rather obvious principle:

(P) An assumption that has been made in order to prove a goal has to be used whenever possible in the course of the proof.

This principle applies, in particular, to the assumptions that are an integral part of a proof rule as, e.g., the hypothesis in the induction rule. For if an induction hypothesis is not used in the course of a proof, induction is obviously the wrong tactic to try in proving the goal under consideration, either because it will fail to lead to a complete proof, or because the goal can be proved in a simpler way which does not involve induction (by symbolic evaluation, for example).

In the following the basic heuristics for dealing with induction are listed. We assume that the goal under consideration contains occurrences of one or more (names of) recursive functions and that we are considering induction on (some occurrences of) the recursive function f. The heuristics are stated as 'rules' which determine whether - and on which occurrences - induction on f is possible and reasonable.

(R1) Universal quantification of arguments: All recursion arguments of the occurrences of f to be inducted on have to be universally quantified.

(R2) Minimal recursion terms: Induct only on those occurrences of f which correspond to minimal recursion terms in the goal. (A term $f(t_1,..,t_n)$ is called <u>minimal recursion term</u> if no recursion argument t_i of f contains recursively defined identifiers.)

(R3) Match of arguments: If induction is to be done on more than one occurrence of f, then the corresponding arguments have to match as follows:

(a) Case-controlling arguments have to match literally.

(b) Recursion arguments have to contain the same variable; e.g. h(y) matches y and g(x,y).

(c) Constant arguments can be arbitrary terms (no match is required).

(R4) Second level analysis: If the rules (R1) - (R3) do not yield an unambiguous decision on the instantiation of induction then analysis continues at the next higher level in the term structure of the goal; those (properly matching) occurrences of f are selected for induction which themselves form recursion arguments of (the occurrences of) the recursive function selected by second level analysis (cf. the example below).

(R5) Inequivalences: Induction only on the right hand side of an inequivalence is never necessary.

(R6) Equivalences: Induction on only one side of an equivalence does not lead to a proof, unless the other side is a constant term.

Discussion. The central rule is (R1), in spite of its apparent simplicity. It is an immediate consequence of the basic principle (P): the induction hypothesis can be instantiated, that is it will match corresponding terms in the conclusion (at some stage of proof generation) only if the arguments that get changed (i.e. the recursion arguments) can be instantiated properly. Note that a quantified formula like $\forall x.\ r(x) \equiv s(x)$ is just an alternative notation for $\lambda x.\ r(x) \equiv \lambda x.\ s(x)$. Obviously, only bound variables can be instantiated (via β-conversion). Universal quantification may involve a kind of 'generalization' in that a term is being replaced by a 'fresh' variable.

The rules (R2) and (R3), in turn, are direct consequences of (R1). If a recursion argument contains a defined identifier, then this argument cannot be universally quantified without creating a generalized subgoal that may not be true. In addition, condition (a) in rule (R3) is justified as follows. If the arguments that control the cases are not identical, case analysis has to be done for each argument separately; this will generally lead to subgoals for 'cross-cases' which are not provable.

As an example, consider associativity of the function defined by

$$f \equiv \alpha F.\ \lambda x\ y\ .\ p(x) \Rightarrow y,\ h(x,\ F(k(x),\ y)).$$

Here x is case-controlling and recursion parameter and y a constant parameter. In the goal

$$\forall\ x\ y\ z.\ \ f(x,\ f(y,z)) \equiv f(f(x,y),\ z)$$

all occurrences of f except the third correspond to minimal recursion terms. Furthermore, the first and fourth occurrences match in the sense of (R3); therefore, these are the occurrences to be inducted on. Similarly, in the goal

$$\forall\ x.\ \ n(n(x)) \equiv n(x)$$

where $n \equiv \alpha N.\ \lambda x.\ p(x) \Rightarrow x,\ N(h(x))$, the rules determine the second and third occurrences of n for induction.

The following example will illustrate rule (R4). Let

$$a \equiv \alpha A.\ \lambda x\ y.\ t_a, \qquad m \equiv \alpha M.\ \lambda x\ y.\ t_m, \qquad n \equiv \alpha N.\ \lambda x.\ t_n$$

such that x is always a case-controlling and recursion argument and y is a constant argument. In the goal

$$(1) \quad \forall\ x\ y\ z.\ \ m(n(x),\ a(n(y),n(z))) \equiv a(m(n(x),\ n(y)),\ m(n(x),\ n(z)))$$

there are three groups of matching occurrences of n. Second level analysis means reducing goal (1) to

$$(2) \quad \forall\ u\ v\ w.\ \ m(u,\ a(v,w)) \equiv a(m(u,v),\ m(u,w))$$

Now, by applying rules (R1) - (R3) all three occurrences of m are selected, thus induction is done on all occurrences of n with argument x in goal (1).

The rules (R1) - (R4) are more or less heuristic in the sense that they possibly admit 'counterexamples'. In contrast, the last two rules, which concern the relation symbols of LCF, are lemmas of the proof theory of LCF, that is, they can be proved in the context of LCF. Consider an inequivalence which contains occurrences of a recursive function f only on the right hand side. In an attempted proof by induction on f, a proof of the base case implies a proof of the original goal, by an argument involving monotonicity. Thus, if the inequivalence is provable at all, it can be proved by other means without using induction. If rule (R6) prevents a direct proof of an equivalence by induction, the equivalence may have to be split into two inequivalences (as subgoals). Complete proofs of (R5) and (R6) can be found in /3/.

Structural Induction. Structural induction can be simulated in LCF by introducing a recursive function that characterizes the data structure and then applying computational induction to this function. We have chosen to use identity functions for representing structures; for example, the function which is defined by

$$\text{Num} \equiv \alpha N.\ \lambda x.\ \text{is-zero}(x) \Rightarrow 0,\ \text{suc}(N(\text{pred}(x)))$$

characterizes the type of non-negative integers, together with suitable axioms about the primitives 0, suc (successor), pred (predecessor) etc. (cf. /2/). Obviously, for a non-negative integer n we have $\text{Num}(n) \equiv n$.

A variable x can be restricted to this type by replacing all occurrences of x in the goal by Num(x). By means of the heuristics presented above a set of matching occurrences of the function representing the type is selected; this corresponds to choosing a variable for structural induction. The actual 'structural induction' is then carried out in the course of proving the induction step. (As an alternative, variables can also be restricted by a relativizing recursive type predicate (cf. /6/).)

Note that for this kind of proofs second level analysis may be essential. Consider, for example, addition and multiplication on non-negative integers as defined by

$$\text{add} \equiv \alpha A.\ \lambda x\ y.\ \text{is-zero}(x) \Rightarrow y,\quad \text{suc}(A(\text{pred}(x), y))$$
$$\text{mul} \equiv \alpha M.\ \lambda x\ y.\ \text{is-zero}(x) \Rightarrow 0,\quad \text{add}(y, M(\text{pred}(x), y))$$

Then the goal

$$\forall\ x\ y\ z.\ \ \text{mul}(\text{Num}(x), \text{add}(\text{Num}(y), \text{Num}(z)))$$
$$\equiv \text{add}(\text{mul}(\text{Num}(x), \text{Num}(y)), \text{mul}(\text{Num}(x), \text{Num}(z)))$$

stating distributivity of multiplication is just an instantiation of the goal (1) discussed above, so analysis will result in induction on Num(x).

<u>A Theorem Prover for LCF</u>. The rules dealing with induction constitute the core of a proving algorithm for LCF. The algorithm also comprises heuristics for handling the other tactics provided in the LCF system (abstraction and application, substitution, simplification, case-splitting etc.). For most of the tactics the associated heuristics are rather straightforward; in essence, the top-most combinator in the left-hand-side term of the goal determines the tactic to be applied next. A particular problem arises in connection with substitution. As a recursive definition can be used for substitution as well as for induction, the algorithm has to decide which of these tactics is to be applied. As a general rule, induction is always attempted first, and only if this fails (e.g. because of the rules discussed above) substitution is applied. However, there are exceptions to this rule; substitution is always prefered to induction if an induction would interfere with a hypothesis of a previous induction being used later on in the proof. For example, the remaining occurrence of n in the goal $\forall x.\ n(n(x)) \equiv n(x)$ discussed above will cause a substitution of the defining term into the subgoal rather than a second induction.

The proving algorithm has been implemented in form of a prover module for the LCF interactive proving system (presently only at the Stanford Artificial Intelligence Laboratory). The prover automates the routine part of proof generation and, without requiring user interaction, generates complete proofs for standard problems of the size and complexity of the McCarthy-Painter algorithm for compiling arithmetical expressions. Heuristics, proving algorithm and prover are described in greater detail in /3/.

Related Work. To the author's knowledge, the only attempt to automate induction proofs which has been described in the literature is the work by R. Boyer and J Moore /1/ on proving theorems about LISP functions by structural induction. Apart from the differences as regards the underlying logic, the approach discussed here differs from theirs in several ways (which the author considers advantages):

- It handles computational induction as well as structural induction.
- It does not depend on a particular underlying structure, thus being applicable at a schematic level where no data structure is assumed.
- It is not restricted to functions for which a primitive recursive definition is given (the exact class of functions and problems the algorithm is able to handle is not known as yet).
- Some problems concerning generalization do not come up in this context; the techniques allow us to solve also some problems in which logically independent variables have been identified.

References

/1/ R.B. Boyer and J S. Moore: Proving theorems about LISP functions. Journal of the ACM 22 (1975), 129-144.

/2/ F. W. von Henke: On the representation of data structures in LCF. Memo AIM-267, Stanford University, 1975.

/3/ F. W. von Henke: Notes on automating theorem proving in LCF. Technical report, GMD Bonn, 1976.

/4/ Z. Manna: Mathematical Theory of Computation. McGraw-Hill, 1974.

/5/ R. Milner: Logic for computable functions - description of an implementation. Memo AIM-169, Stanford University, 1972.

/6/ R. Milner: Implementation and applications of Scott's logic for computable functions. Proc. ACM Conference on Proving Assertions about Programs, Las Cruces, N.M., 1972, 1-6.

A SYNTACTIC CONNECTION BETWEEN PROOF PROCEDURES AND REFUTATION PROCEDURES

W. Bibel

Abstract. It is constructively shown that there is a common improvement of both proof procedures and refutation procedures.

Introduction

Theoretically, theorem proving can be done by proof procedures which demonstrate the validity of a formula, as well as by refutation procedures which demonstrate the unsatisfiability of the negation of a formula. Practically, almost all procedures are of the latter type for the following reason.

Both types involve transformation to normal form, specifically to *conjunctive* normal form in the first case and clause form or conjunctive normal form of the negation of the formula which corresponds to the *disjunctive* normal form of the unnegated formula, in the second case. Most theorems considered so far in the field of theorem proving are much "closer" to disjunctive than to conjunctive normal form. This experience definitely favors refutation procedures since transformation from one normal form to the other may increase the length of the formula exponentially.

Proof procedures, on the other hand, have their virtues as well. By definition they represent the most direct way for proving theorems; they are much easier to be well understood; and last not least, they allow a considerably simpler implementation (cf. [MB]). So they still seem worthwhile to be studied seriously [STP]. This definitely is the case after it has been succeeded to overcome their only deficiency mentioned in the last paragraph by avoiding transformation to any normal form whatsoever [PSG].

But a huge amount of efforts have been invested in refutation procedures; can proof procedures profit from all these results? They can, even in a very direct sense as we show in this paper. Roughly spoken, the argument is the following. If refutation procedures are improved by avoiding transformation to normal form in an analogue way as it has been described in [PSG] for proof procedures then the distinction in fact becomes meaningless: any refutation procedure of that type is a proof procedures as well and vice versa.

It should be noticed that this includes a proof for the fact that avoiding normal form offers an advantage for any kind of procedures and thus is a major step forward for theorem proving as a whole.

Complementary formulas

The result of this paper concerns exclusively the propositional logic part or theorem proving procedures. Therefore it is possible to restrict the discussion to formulas of propositional logic (see also conclusions) which are defined in the usual way using (propositional) variables or atoms, denoted by V, and the connectives $\neg$, $\wedge$, and $\vee$. It is assumed that $\wedge$ has higher rank than $\vee$ in order to omit some of the parentheses. A, B, C, D denote formulas. The *length* $l(A)$ of a formula A is the number of occurrences of variables and connectives in it. $\equiv$ denotes identity of strings.

1.D. For any formula A the formula $\bar{A}$ is defined inductively as follows.
   a. If $A \equiv V$ then $\bar{A} \equiv \neg V$
   b. If $A \equiv \neg V$ then $\bar{A} \equiv V$
   c. If $A \equiv \neg\neg B$ then $\bar{A} \equiv \bar{B}$
   d. If $A \equiv \neg B$ and not of the form b. or c. then $\bar{A} \equiv \neg\bar{B}$
   e. If $A \equiv B \wedge C$ or $A \equiv B \vee C$ then $\bar{A} \equiv \bar{B} \vee \bar{C}$ or $\bar{A} \equiv \bar{B} \wedge \bar{C}$, respectively.

2.L. $\bar{A}$ and $\neg A$ are equivalent.
   Proof by induction on $l(A)$ using de Morgan's laws.

Because of this lemma we can further assume that negation signs do not occur within a formula except immediately before variables. Thus it makes sense to talk of an unnegated or *positive* and of a negated or *negative* variable in a formula.

Cancellation of a variable V in a formula A means cancellation of V and of those connectives and parentheses in A such that the result again is a formula.

3.D. A *partial formula* B of a formula A is the substring of A which is obtained from A by cancellation of zero or more variables in A .

Each *subformula* in the usual sense thus is a partial formula, but the converse is not true; e.g. $A \vee B$ is a partial formula but not a subformula of $A \vee B \wedge C$. Our interest is focussed especially on those partial formulas B of A such that B and A are equivalent.

4.D. d-*clauses* (d from disjunctive) in a formula A are defined inductively as follows.

a. If $A \equiv V$ or $A \equiv \neg V$ then A is the only d-clause in A

b. If $A \equiv B \wedge C$ then each d-clause in B or in C is also a d-clause in A

c. If $A \equiv B \vee C$ and D_1 , D_2 are d-clauses in B and C , resp., then $D_1 \vee D_2$ is a d-clause in A .

The definition of c-*clauses* (c from conjunctive) is obtained from that for d-clauses by exchanging $\wedge$ and $\vee$ and by substituting "d-clause" by "c-clause".

For example $(V_1 \vee V_2) \wedge V_3$ contains exactly the d-clauses $V_1 \vee V_2$ and V_3 and the c-clauses $V_1 \wedge V_3$ and $V_2 \wedge V_3$. Obviously, d- and c-clauses are partial formulas. If A is in conjunctive (disjunctive) normal form then the d- (c-) clauses are just the clauses of A . The following lemma is easily proved.

5.L. If B is the conjunctive (disjunctive) normal form of A then for each d- (c-) clause of A there is an identical d- (c-) clause in B and vice versa.

6.D. Two (occurrences of) variables V_1 , V_2 in A are called *complementary* in A if $V_1 \equiv V_2$ and one is positive, the other negative in A . A formula A is called *complementary* if for each variable in A there is also a complementary variable in A . A partial formula B of A is called p-*complementary* (n-*complementary*) in A (p from positive, n from negative) if B is complementary and for each d- (c-) clause C in A there are two complementary variables occurring (at the same position) in C and in B . Moreover B is called *minimal* if there is no *proper* partial formula B' of B , i.e. $l(B') < l(B)$, which is p- (n-) complementary in A .

For example $V_1 \vee \neg V_1 \wedge (V_2 \vee \neg V_2 \wedge \neg V_2)$ is a minimal p-complementary partial formula of
$V_1 \vee \neg V_1 \wedge (V_2 \vee V_3 \vee \neg V_2 \wedge \neg V_2) \vee V_4$.

The results

In the following the reader should notice that all proofs and thus all statements are constructive. We begin with the part concerning proof procedures.

7.T. A formula A contains a p-complementary partial formula iff the conjunctive normal form of A contains a p-complementary partial formula.

Proof by induction on the number n of $\wedge$'s in A which occur in a subformula of A of the form $D_1 \vee D_2$. If $n = 0$ then the statement is trivial since A itself is in conjunctive normal form.

Let $n > 0$ and $C_1 \wedge C_2$ be a subformula of A which occurs within a subformula of A of the form $D_1 \vee D_2$ but in none of the form $D_1' \wedge D_2'$. Further let A_1 and A_2 result from A by cancellation of (all variables in) C_2 and C_1, respectively.

a. Assume, B is p-complementary in A, and B_1 and B_2 result from B by cancellation of those parts of C_2 and C_1, resp., which occur in B; then $B_1 \wedge B_2$ is p-complementary in $A_1 \wedge A_2$ and the induction hypothesis is now applicable.

b. Conversely, by induction hypothesis there is a p-complementary partial formula of $A_1 \wedge A_2$ which necessarily is of the form $B_1' \wedge B_2'$ where B_i' is a partial formula of A_i, $i = 1,2$. Each variable in $A_1 \wedge A_2$ occurs at a corresponding position in A; thus $B_1' \wedge B_2'$ uniquely determines a corresponding partial formula B of A, which contains exactly those variables in A which correspond to those in $B_1' \wedge B_2'$. (Observe that $B_1 \wedge B_2$ constructed from this partial formula B according to a. not necessarily would be identical with $B_1' \wedge B_2'$.) B obviously is p-complementary since $B_1' \wedge B_2'$ has this property.

8.C. A is valid iff A contains a p-complementary partial formula.

Proof. According to 7. it can be assumed that A is in conjunctive normal form for which the statement is trivial.

Next we handle the part concerning refutation procedures.

9.T. A contains a n-complementary partial formula iff the conjunctive normal form of A contains a n-complementary partial formula.

The proof is literally the same as that for 7. with the only exception that p-complementary now reads n-complementary.

10.L. If B is a n-complementary partial formula of a formula A in conjunctive normal form then B contains a formula B' which is n-complementary and consists of a conjunction of d-clauses of A which do not contain complementary variables.

Proof by induction on the number n of d-clauses in A which contain both, variables from B and not from B, or which contain complementary variables.

If $n = 0$ then the assertion is trivially satisfied with $B' \equiv B$.

Let $n > 0$ and C be a d-clause in A of that type. Let D be a literal in C which does not belong to B or for which there is a complementary literal in C. Each c-clause in A by definition contains two complementary variables from B; this applies especially for those containing D and under the assumptions it can be assumed that D is different from these variables. The two variables are also contained in each c-clause which are obtained from c-clauses containing D by substituting D by any other literal from C. Therefore the variables from C are superfluous in B and thus can be cancelled, resulting in a n-complementary partial formula B" of A to which the induction hypotheses now is applicable.

11.T. Let A be a formula in conjunctive normal form; then A contains a n-complementary partial formula B iff there is a derivation (by resolution) of the empty clause from d-clauses of A which does not contain d-clauses with complementary variables.

Proof. Assume, there is a derivation of the empty clause. Let C be the conjunction of all initial clauses of the derivation and C_1, C_2 two of them which are resolved upon the variable V with resolvent $C_1' \vee C_2'$. By induction hypotheses we assume that the formula C' which derives from C by substitution of the subformula $C_1 \wedge C_2$ by $C_1' \vee C_2'$, is n-complementary in itself. Then also C is n-complementary in itself, because each c-clause in C contains two complementary variables which are resolved upon or a c-clause of C' ; if $C_1' \vee C_2'$ already is the empty clause then C obviously is n-complementary in C . Let B be the partial formula of A consisting of those d-clauses of A which occur in C . Then obviously B is n-complementary in B since this holds for C . Thus by definition B is n-complementary in A .

Conversely, assume that A contains a n-complementary partial formula B . Then by definition and 5. this means that each c-clause in the disjunctive normal form of A contains two complementary variables which says that the normal form and thus A itself is unsatisfiable. By the completeness theorem for resolution (see [LTP], theorem 5.3., e.g.) which is constructive as far as propositional logic is concerned, it follows that there is a derivation of the empty clause from d-clauses of A , even from those of B because of 10., which satisfies the required condition.

12.C. A is unsatisfiable iff A contains a n-complementary partial formula.
On the basis of the completeness theorem and of 9. and 11. the proof is now trivial.

Finally, we combine the two results 8. and 12. by the following theorem.

13.T. B is a p-complementary partial formula of A iff $\bar{B}$ is a n-complementary partial formula of $\bar{A}$.
The proof follows immediately from the definitions.

The reader might ask whether the p- (n-) complementary partial formulas of A are of real importance in the sense that they can be determined *without* the use of a normal form of A . Therefore the rest of the section is devoted to giving a rough description of such an algorithm which even determines a minimal formula of that type.

14.D. Let the *depth* of (an occurrence of) a variable V in a formula A be the number of different subformulas of the form $B \wedge C$ which contain this occurrence of V . The *depth* of A is the maximal depth of its variables.

15.A. (Algorithm which tests whether there is a p-complementary partial formula B of a given formula A and in case of a positive answer returns such a minimal B)

a. For i from 0 until the depth of A do the following: For each d-clause compare each variable of depth i with each variable of depth j , $0 \leq j \leq i$, whether they are complementary; if this is the case with $V^{(i)}$ and $V^{(j)}$ then all other variables of depth $k \geq i$ in d-clauses which contain both $V^{(i)}$ and $V^{(j)}$ can be cancelled, and $V^{(i)}$ and $V^{(j)}$ will be marked; else if there is none such pair, STOP (A is not a theorem).

b. A is a theorem and a minimal B is obtained by cancelling all non-marked variables.

Conclusions

By our constructive results 7. or 9.,10.,11. for any traditional proof or refutation procedure, resp., there is a corresponding procedure which operates on the given formula instead of its normal form. Such a procedure obviously is more efficient compared with the original one, even in the strong sense (relation $\ll\!\triangleleft$ in [EVB]) since the search space is concentrated considerably while the actions essentially are the same. (Recently I learned that this advantage also has been used in an implementation of a resolution procedure [ITP].) At this level, however, a distinction between proof and refutation procedures is meaningless according to 13. since there is only a trivial difference between B and $\bar{B}$, thus unifying both approaches in a most satisfactory way (these results already have been announced in 3.4. of [MB]).

Strictly speaking, sofar these results are obtained only for propositional logic. But they are generalized to first-order logic in a straightforward way, because one can assume that both types of procedures operate in exactly the same way as far as first-order logic constructs are concerned thus reducing their difference to what has been discussed in this paper; for example, one might assume that both use Skolem-functions, unification, etc. in the usual way.

Comparison of *different* approaches to handling the first-order constructs is yet another issue which is independent from that discussed in this paper. But it may seem appropriate to remark that such a comparison between the usual Skolem-function approach and the relational approach as described in [PSG], which is based on a relation rather than on Skolem-functions, has been indicated in section 5 of

[PSG] considering splitting rules known since 1971. Together with the results of the present paper this yields a closer connection between resolution procedures and Gentzen-type procedures than that described in [RAH]. But in the meantime the splitting rules have been improved [UTP]; therefore a detailed comparison now might show complete equivalence between the relational approach and the Skolem-function approach with improved splitting.

Similarly as with the first-order constructs the transformation from normal form procedures to the new ones saves all other results obtained sofar in theorem proving such as search strategies, etc.. But probably it is a promising task to study algorithms checking for p-complementary partial formulas, and their implementations independently. The procedure PAIR in [PSG] and algorithm 15. in this paper are first steps in that direction.

A further improvement could be achieved by allowing other logical connectives. Especially in the case of $\longleftrightarrow$ this seems to be very promising since its usual replacement again causes exponential growth.

Let us conclude with the remark that so far in the history of theorem proving any important general improvement was accompanied by the achievement of invariance against a certain logically valid transformation (see also [MB]). This time we were concerned with the transformation between proving and disproving. Are there any remaining logically valid transformations against which the procedures obtained so far are not invariant?

References

[STP] Bibel, W.: An approach to a systematic theorem proving procedure in first-order logic. Computing 12, 43-55 (1974).

[EVB] Bibel, W.: Effizienzvergleiche von Beweisprozeduren. GI '74, Lect. Notes Comp. Sci. 26, 153-160 (1975).

[PSG] Bibel, W. and Schreiber, J.: Proof search in a Gentzen-like system of first-order logic. Proc. Int. Comp. Symp. (ICS'75), North-Holland, 205-212 (1975).

[MB] Bibel, W.: Maschinelles Beweisen. Jahrbuch Überblicke Mathematik, B.Fuchssteiner, U.Kulisch, D.Langwitz, R.Liedl (eds.), BI Wissenschaftsverlag, 115-142 (1976).

[UTP] Bledsoe, W.W. and Tyson, M.: The U.T. Interactive Prover. Memo ATP-17, Math. Dept., Univ. Texas, Austin (1975).

[LTP] Chang, C.-L. and Lee, R.C.-T.: Symbolic Logic and mechanical theorem proving. Academic Press (1973).

[RAH] Joyner, W.H., Jr.: A resolution analogue to the Herbrand theorem. Presented at the conference on Automatic Theorem Proving, Oberwolfach (1976).

[ITP] Overbeek, R.: An approach to the implementation of theorem proving systems. Presented at the conference on Automatic Theorem Proving, Oberwolfach (1976).

STRUKTUR VON PROGRAMMBÜNDELN

B. Schinzel

I. EINLEITUNG

Die Kategorie der Sprachen und Übersetzer wird untersucht.

Dafür werden Sprachen für partiell rekursive Funktionen, rekursiv aufzählbare Mengen u.s.w. als Programmbündel betrachtet, deren Fasern aus allen äquivalenten Worten der Sprache bestehen. Übersetzer sind dann effektive fasertreue Abbildungen zwischen Sprachen.

Der Halbverband der Numerierungen der 1-stelligen partiell rekursiven Funktionen $\mathbb{P}_1$ [5] ist der der Kategorie der Numerierungen (ohne Syntax) unterliegende Halbverband. Einige Eigenschaften insbesondere der Gödelnumerierungen [5] erscheinen in der Kategorie der Programmbündel in neuem Lichte.

Die Struktur der Kategorie wird besonders im Hinblick auf eine Zerlegungstheorie untersucht: es wird gezeigt, daß die Gödelbündel in Friedbergbündel zerfallen.

II. PROGRAMMBÜNDEL

Definition 1:

Ein Programmbündel $B = (L,s,A)$ über A besteht aus

(i) der Sprache oder der Menge der Algorithmen L

(ii) der Basis A, die die Semantik darstellt

(iii) der Projektion des Bündels $s: L \longrightarrow A$, die die Semantikabbildung darstellt.

Zu jedem $f \in A$ heißt $s^{-1}(f)$ die Faser über f.

Die Betrachtung von Sprachen als Programmbündel hat folgende Vorteile:

1. Die klare Trennung zwischen Syntax und Semantik, zwischen Algorithmus und berechneter Funktion.
2. Der Begriff der Faser, der das Programmbündel in Mengen äquivalenter Programme zerlegt.
3. Programmbündel sind ohne Gödelisierung eingeführt; das entspricht der Praxis, wo dies für Sprachen

auch nicht geschieht. Sie können jedoch (vorausgesetzt, die Sprache ist rekursiv aufzählbar) leicht numeriert werden. So erfassen Programmbündel die Wirklichkeit besser als Aufzählungen.

Insbesondere gilt das für Komplexitätsbetrachtungen, da die (Blumsche) Schrittzählfunktion eine Invariante der Algorithmen, die Programmgröße eine Invariante der Programme ist. Die Sprache ist hier entscheidend.

Definition 2:

Bündelmorphismen zwischen zwei Programmbündeln $B_1 = (L_1, s_1, A_1)$ und $B_2 = (L_2, s_2, A_2)$ sind Paare (T,p), so daß mit der partiellen effektiven Abbildung $T: L_1 \longrightarrow L_2$ die partielle Abbildung $p: A_1 \longrightarrow A_2$ so verknüpft ist, daß das Quadrat kommutativ ist:

$$\begin{array}{ccc} L_1 & \xrightarrow{T} & L_2 \\ {\scriptstyle s_1}\downarrow & & \downarrow{\scriptstyle s_2} \\ A_1 & \xrightarrow{p} & A_2 \end{array}$$

d.h. $s_2^{-1}(p(a)) \supset T(s_1^{-1}(a))$ für alle $a \in A_1$, für die p definiert ist und für die T auf mindestens einem Programm von $s_1^{-1}(a)$ definiert ist.
Die Faser über $a \in A$ wird durch einen Übersetzer (T,p) in die Faser über $p(a)$ transportiert.

Ein Subbündel B_1 eines Programmbündels B ist in üblicher Weise durch einen totalen Übersetzer $(\subseteq, \subseteq)$ erklärt. Durch eine Äquivalenzrelation auf der Basis A wird ein Quotientenbündel induziert.

Definition 3:

Ein Schnitt eines Programmbündels (L,s,A) ist eine Abbildung $q: A \longrightarrow L$, so daß $s \cdot q = 1_A$ und das Bild von q in L aufzählbar ist.

Wir interessieren uns hauptsächlich für die Unterkategorie der Programmbündel über einer fixen Basis, meistens $\mathbb{P}_1$. Übersetzer sind dann (partielle) effektive Abbildungen T, so daß $s_1 = s_2 \cdot T$ für alle Programme von L_1, auf denen T definiert ist.

Definition 4:

Eine Gödelisierung ist eine bijektive effektive Abbildung $g: L \longrightarrow \mathbb{N}$. Dann ist für $s: L \longrightarrow A$ $\phi = s \cdot g^{-1}: \mathbb{N} \longrightarrow A$ eine Aufzählung der Objekte in A.

Programmbündel mit Gödelisierung heißen numerierte Programmbündel. (Die Effektivitätsforderung schränkt die numerierten Programmbündel auf diejenigen ein, deren Sprache rekursiv aufzählbar ist.) Ein Übersetzer $T: L_1 \longrightarrow L_2$ von numerierten Programmbündeln überträgt sich dann wie eine Koordinate auf eine partiell rekursive Funktion $f: \mathbb{N} \longrightarrow \mathbb{N}$, so daß

$$\phi_1 = s_1 \cdot g_1^{-1} = s_2 \cdot T \cdot g_1^{-1} = \phi_2 \cdot g_2 \cdot T \cdot g_1^{-1} = \phi_2 \cdot f$$

für $f = g_2 \cdot T \cdot g_1^{-1}$ [4].

Ein Gruppoid in der Kategorie der Programmbündel über einer Basis A ist durch ein Theorem von Myhill [3] charakterisiert:

Gibt es zu zwei Aufzählungen ϕ und ψ von A injektive totale Übersetzer f und g, so daß $\phi = \psi \cdot f$ und $\psi = \phi \cdot g$, dann sind ϕ und ψ rekursiv isomorph.

III. Die Unterkategorie der Gödelbündel

Es wurde festgestellt, daß jedes numerierte Programmbündel eine aufzählbare Sprache hat. Für Programmbündel über $\mathbb{P}_1$ heißt das, daß das Aufzählungstheorem (i) erfüllt ist.

(i) Es gibt eine partielle universelle rekursive Funktion, die die einstelligen partiell rekursiven Funktionen aufzählt, also

$$\exists\, x : \phi_x(y,z) = \phi_y(z) \quad \forall\, y,z .$$

Die Unterkategorie der Gödelbündel besteht aus allen Programmbündeln, zu denen es einen Übersetzer vom Bündel der Kleene-Charakterisierung gibt und umgekehrt.

Für Aufzählungen ausgedrückt: Jede Gödelnumerierung [5] ist charakterisiert durch die Eigenschaften

(i) Aufzählungstheorem und

(ii) s_n^m - Theorem: Jede m+n-stellige partiell rekursive Funktion läßt sich mittels einer totalen m+1-stelligen s_n^m-Funktion durch eine Mengen von n-stelligen partiell rekursiven Funktionen darstellen:

$$\forall\, m,n : \exists\, s_n^m \in \mathbb{R}_{m+1} \text{ , so daß } \forall\, x,y_1,..,y_m,z_1,..,z_n :$$
$$\phi_x^{(m+n)}(y_1..y_m,z_1..z_n) = \phi \cdot s_n^m(x,y_1..y_m)(z_1..z_n) \text{ .}$$

Eigenschaften der Gödelbündel:

1. Die Gödelbündel sind schwache Endobjekte in unserer Kategorie, da es von jedem numerierten Programmbündel einen Übersetzer in jedes Gödelbündel gibt.

2. Nach Rogers [5] sind alle Gödelnumerierungen rekursiv isomorph. Daher folgt: Die Unterkategorie der Gödelbündel bildet ein zusammenhängendes Gruppoid in der Kategorie der Programmbündel.

3. Jeder Retrakt $f(B)$ eines Gödelbündels B ist akzeptabel.

4. Jede Faser ist unendlich und nicht rekursiv aufzählbar, genauer nach H. Walter [7] produktiv. Das Komplement der Faser über der nirgends definierten Funktion ist kreativ, die Komplemente aller anderen Fasern sind produktiv [7] .

5. Zu jedem Gödelbündel gibt es einen globalen Schnitt: Friedberg [1] zeigte die Existenz bijektiver Aufzählungen von $\mathbb{P}_1$. Eine solche Friedbergnumerierung τ definiert in jedem Programmbündel, in das es einen Übersetzer f von τ gibt (und das ist wegen des Aufzählungstheorems von τ für alle Gödelbündel der Fall) einen globalen Schnitt $f \cdot \tau^{-1}$:

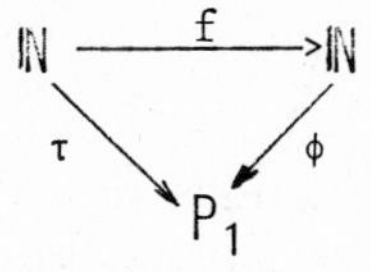

denn $f \cdot \tau^{-1} = 1_{\mathbb{P}_1}$ und das Bild von $f \cdot \tau^{-1}$ ist gerade das Bild von f und daher aufzählbar.

Bemerkung:

Nicht jedes Programmbündel über $\mathbb{P}_1$ hat einen globalen Schnitt: Es gibt Aufzählungen ψ , in die kein Morphismus von irgendeiner Friedbergnumerierung existiert. Für die dazugehörigen Programmbündel gibt es keinen globalen Schnitt q , sonst wäre das Bild von q aufzählbar und

IV Zerlegung von Gödelbündeln in Friedbergbündel

Definition 5:

Gegeben eine rekursiv aufzählbare Familie von (numerierten) Programmbündeln mit $\{\phi^i\}_{i\in N}$, dann ist die direkte Summe $\bigoplus_{i\in N} \phi^i = \pi$ definiert durch

$$\phi^i_x = \pi_{h(i,x)} \quad \text{für } i,x = 0,1,..$$

$$\text{mit } h(i,x) = \frac{(x+i)(x+i+1)}{2} + i \, .$$

Diese Definition erfüllt die universelle Eigenschaft von Summen in unserer Kategorie. Daher folgt: Der Halbverband der Numerierungen ist ein σ-Halbverband.

Satz 1:

Jedes Gödelbündel zerfällt auf dem Komplement der Faser über der nirgends definierten Funktion in eine Summe von Friedbergbündeln ohne die Fasern über der nirgends definierten Funktion.

Beweis:

siehe [6] .

Zwei Programmbündel heißen unvergleichbar, wenn kein totaler Übersetzer zwischen ihnen existiert.

Satz 2:

Jedes Gödelbündel ist Summe von Friedbergbündeln. Zusätzlich kann erreicht werden, daß diese alle unvergleichbar sind. Das wird für Aufzählungen numerierter Programmbündel bewiesen, also

$$\phi = \bigoplus_{i=0}^{\infty} \tau^i \quad \text{mit } \tau^i \not\leq \tau^j \quad \text{für } i \neq j \, .$$

Beweisandeutung:

Mit Prioritätsargumenten destilliert ein Algorithmus aus der Gödelnumerierung eine Aufzählung unendlich vieler Friedbergnumerierungen, und zwar so, daß jedes Programm der Gödelnumerierung mindestens als das erste Programm einer Friedbergnumerierung vorkommt.

die Identität auf $q(\mathbb{P}_1)$ ein Übersetzer von $q(\mathbb{P}_1)$ in ψ mit $\psi: q(\mathbb{P}_1) \longrightarrow \mathbb{P}_1$ Friedbergnumerierung.

Die Menge der Programmbündel zu einer Aufzählung

Ψ ist gegeben durch die Menge aller totalen Morphismen, die von ψ ausgehend in beliebige Programmbündel existieren. ψ hat in jedem Gödelbündel $B = (L, \phi \cdot g^{-1}, \mathbb{P}_1)$ eine eineindeutig zugeordnete Aufzählung von Programmen, da der Übersetzer s_1^1 wegen der produktiven Fasern von ϕ injektiv gemacht werden kann.

Die Menge aller Programmbündel zu einer Aufzählung (sogar innerhalb eines Kalküls) ist nicht aufzählbar. Das kann man durch Diagonalisierung der Übersetzer feststellen.

Die Menge aller Programmbündel zu einer Gödelnumerierung ist charakterisiert durch die Automorphismengruppe, die aus dem gleichen Grund nicht rekursiv aufzählbar und daher nicht endlich erzeugt ist.

Der von Rogers [5] eingeführte Halbverband der Numerierungen wird definiert durch die Halbordnung ($\phi \leq \psi \Longleftrightarrow \exists f \in \mathbb{R}_1 : \phi = \psi \cdot f$) induziert auf die Äquivalenzklassen von Numerierungen ($\phi \equiv \psi \Longleftrightarrow \phi \leq \psi$ und $\psi \leq \phi$). Das einzige maximale Element darin ist die Klasse der Gödelnumerierungen. Jede Friedbergnumerierung ist Repräsentant für eine minimale Klasse.

Es gibt jedoch minimale Aufzählungen, die nicht äquivalent zu irgendeiner Friedbergnumerierung sind.

Die Kategorie der Programmbündel mit totalen Morphismen ist die durch den Halbverband der Numerierungen induzierte Kategorie. Sie hat jedoch eine wesentlich reichere Struktur, ihre Objekte sind genau die Numerierungen, die Morphismen genau die Übersetzer.

Man kann sich also vorstellen, daß die Friedbergnumerierungen an der Gödelnumerierung aufgereiht werden. Der Algorithmus enthält eine Diagonalbedingung, die die Unvergleichbarkeit der Friedbergnumerierungen sichert. Diese Bedingung kann ohne Schaden für die Wirksamkeit des Algorithmus weggelassen werden.
Dann wird die Summe aller dieser Friedbergaufzählungen $\bigoplus_{i \in \mathbb{N}} \tau^i = \pi$ gebildet.
Es gibt einen injektiven Übersetzer von der Summe in die Gödelnumerierung. Umgekehrt läßt sich ein injektiver Übersetzer g von ϕ in π angeben, da das erste Programm jeder Friedbergnumerierung τ^i gleich dem i-ten Programm der Gödelnumerierung ist:

$$g(i) = h(i,0) = \frac{i^2+3i}{2}, \text{ so daß } \phi_i = \tau_0^i = \pi_{g(i)} .$$

Daher folgt mit dem erwähnten Verfahren von Myhill [3], daß ϕ und $\bigoplus_i \tau^i$ rekursiv isomorph sind, was sich auf die dazugehörigen Programmbündel überträgt.

Korollar 1:

Es gibt eine effektive Aufzählung von unendlich vielen unvergleichbaren Friedbergbündeln. (Khutoretskii zeigt in [2] die Existenz unendlich vieler unvergleichbarer Friedbergaufzählungen.)

Korollar 2:

Jeder totale Übersetzer zwischen Gödelbündeln zerfällt effektiv in partielle Übersetzer auf den Friedbergbündeln, deren Bilder wieder Friedbergsubbündel des Bildbündels sind.

Korollar 3:

Jede Gödelnumerierung ist Summe von Atomen des Halbverbandes der Numerierungen.

An dieser Stelle möchte ich Herrn Prof. Dr.H. Walter für seine Unterstützung dieser Arbeit herzlich danken.

LITERATUR:

[1] FRIEDBERG, R.: Three theorems on recursive enumeration. J. Symbolic Logic 23 (1958), 309 - 316.

[2] KHUTORETSKII, A.: On the reducibility of computable enumeration. Algebra i Logica Vol 8, No 2 (1969), 251 - 264.

[3] MYHILL, J.: Creative Sets. Zeitschrift für Math. Logik und Grundlagen d. Mathematik 1 (1955), 97 - 108.

[4] MYHILL, J. - SHEPHERDSON, J.C.: Effective Operations on Partial Recursive Functions. Zeitschrift f. Math. Logik und Grundlagen d. Mathematik 1 (1955).

[5] ROGERS, H.: Gödelnumberings of partial recursive functions. J. Symbolic Logic 23, 1958, 331 - 341.

[6] SCHINZEL, B.: Decomposition of Gödelnumberings into Friedbergnumberings. Zeitschrift f. Math. Logik und Grundlagen d. Mathematik, Mitte 1977.

[7] WALTER, H.: Beobachtungen über die Struktur von Fasern akzeptabler Aufzählungen. Memorandum AFS 4-1976, Fachbereich Informatik der Technischen Hochschule Darmstadt.

Bemerkungen zu den Übergangshalbgruppen linear realisierbarer Automaten

L. Eichner

§1 Einleitung

Ein endlicher Automat a ist ein Tripel $a = (S_a, X_a, \delta_a)$, wobei S_a, X_a endliche nichtleere Mengen sind (resp. Zustands-, Eingabealphabet) und $\delta_a: S_a \times S_a \longrightarrow S_a$ eine Abbildung ist (Übergangsfunktion). Sind S_a, X_a endliche Vektorräume über einem endlichen Körper K und ist δ_a eine K-lineare Abbildung des Vektorraumes $S_a \times X_a$ in S_a, dann heißt a K-linearer Automat. Ein Homomorphismus μ eines Automaten a in einen Automaten b ist ein Paar $\mu = (\mu_S, \mu_X)$ von Abbildungen $\mu_S: S_a \longrightarrow S_b$, $\mu_X: X_a \longrightarrow X_b$ mit der Eigenschaft $(s,x)\delta_a\mu_S = (s\mu_S, x\mu_X)\delta_b$, $s \in S_a$, $x \in X_a$. Sind μ_S und μ_X injektiv (surjektiv usw.), so heißt auch μ injektiv (surjektiv usw.). Ein Automat a heißt K-linear realisierbar, wenn es einen K-linearen Automaten l und einen injektiven Homomorphismus $\mu: a \longrightarrow l$ gibt.

In /3/ wird ein Verfahren entwickelt, mit dem in endlich vielen Schritten für gegebenes a entschieden werden kann, ob a GF(2)-linear realisierbar ist. In /12/ wird dieses Verfahren für beliebige GF(p) und in /13/ für beliebige endliche Körper (und Ringe mit Einselement) verallgemeinert. In /13/ wird ferner gezeigt, daß ein K-linear realisierbarer Automat auch K'-linear realisierbar ist, wenn K und K' die gleiche Charakteristik haben. Wir definieren daher: a heißt linear realisierbar oder p-linear realisierbar, i. Z. $a \in LRA_p$, wenn es einen Körper K mit der Charakteristik p gibt, so daß a K-linear realisierbar ist. In /6/ wird gezeigt, daß entweder die Menge der Primzahlen, für die a linear realisierbar ist, oder die Menge der übrigen Primzahlen endlich ist und effektiv berechnet werden kann. Die Berechnung erfolgt anhand eines ganzzahligen Gleichungssystems, welches mit Hilfe der Übergangsfunktion von a hergestellt wird. In /7/ wird gezeigt, daß ein endlicher Automat, der für einen Körper der Charakteristik 2 und einen Körper der Charakteristik $\neq 2$ linear realisierbar ist, total (d.h. für alle Primzahlen) linear realisierbar ist.

Die genannten Arbeiten machen alle Gebrauch von gewissen Eigenschaften der Abbildungen aus der Übergangshalbgruppe von a. Sei X_a^+ die freie Worthalbgruppe über X_a. Dann wird δ_a zunächst vermöge der Festsetzung $(s,wx)\delta_a := ((s,w)\delta_a,x)\delta_a$, $s \in S_a$, $x \in X_a$, $w \in X_a^+$, zu einer Funktion δ_a: $S_a \times X_a^+ \longrightarrow S_a$ erweitert. Sodann wird jedem $w \in X_a^+$ eine Abbildung δ_a^w: $S_a \longrightarrow S_a$ mit $s\delta_a^w := (s,w)\delta_a$, $s \in S_a$, zugeordnet. Zusammen mit der Hintereinanderausführung als Verknüpfung - es gilt $\delta_a^{uv} = \delta_a^u\delta_a^v$ für alle u, $v \in X_a^+$ - bilden die δ_a^w, $w \in X_a^+$, eine Transformationshalbgruppe auf S_a, die sogenannte Übergangshalbgruppe U_a von a.

Es liegt die Frage nahe, inwieweit sich linear realisierbare Automaten durch Eigenschaften ihrer Übergangshalbgruppen charakterisieren lassen. Antworten hierauf sind sicherlich nicht nur für Probleme der linearen Realisierbarkeit, sondern auch im Zusammenhang mit Fragen über erkennbare Wortmengen und Zerlegbarkeit von Automaten von großem Interesse.

Def. Eine Halbgruppe H heißt linear A-darstellbar oder p-linear A-darstellbar, i.Z. $H \in LDH_p$, wenn es ein $a \in LRA_p$ mit $H \cong U_a$ gibt.

Im einzelnen stellen sich folgende Fragen:

1.1. Kann man bei gegebener Primzahl p entscheiden, ob eine willkürlich vorgelegte Halbgruppe H p-linear A-darstellbar ist?

1.2. Kann man bei gegebener Halbgruppe H entscheiden, ob es eine Primzahl p mit $H \in LDH_p$ gibt, und wenn ja, kann man die in Frage kommenden Primzahlen angeben?

1.3. Durch welche algebraischen Eigenschaften lassen sich p-linear A-darstellbare Halbgruppen charakterisieren?

1.4. Durch welche algebraischen und abbildungstheoretischen Eigenschaften lassen sich die Übergangshalbgruppen p-linear realisierbarer Automaten charakterisieren?

Tatsächlich liegen für spezielle Fälle auch schon Antworten auf diese Fragen vor. In /4/, /5/, /11/, /14/ werden die Fragen 1.1, 1.2 und 1.3 für Gruppen geklärt, in /11/ die Frage 1.4 für transitive Permutationsgruppen.

Im vorliegenden Vortrag sollen einige weitergehende Ergebnisse vorgestellt werden. 1.1 und 1.2 werden vollständig beantwortet. Für Halbgruppen H (Transformationshalbgruppen U) mit $H - HH = \emptyset$ (bzw. $U - UU = \emptyset$) kann 1.3 (bzw. 1.4) ebenfalls geklärt werden; dagegen für Halbgruppen H mit $H - HH \neq \emptyset$ (bzw. Transformationshalbgruppen U mit $U - UU \neq \emptyset$) nur teilweise.

Def. Mit H wird im Folgenden stets eine endliche abstrakte

Halbgruppe bezeichnet. Mit H^1 wird die durch Adjunktion eines Einselementes an H entstandene Halbgruppe bezeichnet, falls H kein Monoid ist, und $H^1 = H$ sonst gesetzt. Weiter sei I_H die Menge der Idempotenten von H, Q_H der Kern und G_H^e die zum Idempotent e gehörende maximale Untergruppe von H. Die von einer Teilmenge $V \subseteq H$ erzeugte Unterhalbgruppe wird mit $\langle V \rangle$ bezeichnet.

Def. Seien T, V Teilmengen von H mit $TV \subseteq T$. Dann ist der Automat $\gamma = \gamma(T,V)$ wie folgt erklärt: $S_\gamma := T$, $X_\gamma := V$, $(s,x)\delta_\gamma := sx$ (Multiplikation in H) für $s \in S_\gamma$, $x \in X_\gamma$.

1.5. Satz. (vgl. /9/) $H \in LDH_p \iff$ H enthält eine Teilmenge E mit $H = \langle E \rangle$ und $\gamma(H^1,E) \in LRA_p$.

Nach /6/, /8/ kann man die Menge der Primzahlen, für die $\gamma(H^1,E)$ linear realisierbar ist, oder die Menge der übrigen Primzahlen effektiv berechnen. Da H endlich ist, gibt es zu H nur endlich viele Automaten der Art $\gamma(H^1,E)$. Damit sind 1.1 und 1.2 im Prinzip beantwortet.

Def. $E \subseteq H$ heißt (ein für p) ausgezeichnetes Erzeugendensystem von H $:\iff H = \langle E \rangle$ und $\gamma(H^1,E) \in LRA_p$.

In den nächsten Abschnitten wird u.a. eine vollständige Charakterisierung der ausgezeichneten Erzeugendensysteme gegeben. Dabei werden wir Wege kennenlernen, wie man sich verhältnismäßig gezielt (d.h. ohne "Durchprobieren" aller Teilmengen einer Halbgruppe) eventuell vorhandene ausgezeichnete Erzeugendensysteme beschaffen kann. Dies wird im Fall der Halbgruppen H mit $H - HH \neq \emptyset$ sehr einfach sein (es kommt hier nur die Menge H - HH in Frage), dagegen im Fall H - HH = $\emptyset$ gelegentlich sehr kompliziert.

§2 Allgemeine Struktureigenschaften

Von sehr weitreichenden Konsequenzen erweist sich ein einfaches, auf /10/ zurückgehendes und in der hier angegebenen allgemeineren Form von Stucky /13/ stammendes Lemma.

2.1. Lemma. Sei a ein linear realisierbarer Automat; sei $E_a := \{ \delta_a^x \mid x \in X_a \}$. Es gilt:

(1) $\bigwedge_{n \in N} \bigwedge_{u,u' \in E_a^n} \bigwedge_{s \in S_a} (su = su' \Longrightarrow u = u')$;

(2) $\bigwedge_{n \in N} \bigwedge_{u,u' \in E_a^n} \bigwedge_{s,s' \in S_a} (su = s'u \Longrightarrow su' = s'u')$;

($E_a^n := \{ \xi_1 \xi_2 \dots \xi_n \in U_a \mid \xi_i \in E_a$ für $i = 1,2,\dots,n\}$; N = Menge der natürlichen Zahlen ohne Null).

Geht man zu linear A-darstellbaren Halbgruppen über, dann folgt leicht:

2.2. Lemma. Sei H eine linear A-darstellbare Halbgruppe und E ein ausgezeichnetes Erzeugendensystem von H. Dann gilt:

(1) $\bigwedge_{n \in N} \bigwedge_{h_1,h_2 \in E^n} \bigwedge_{h \in H} (hh_1 = hh_2 \Longrightarrow h_1 = h_2)$;

(2) $\bigwedge_{n \in N} \bigwedge_{h_1,h_2 \in E^n} \bigwedge_{h,h' \in H^1} (hh_1 = h'h_1 \Longrightarrow hh_2 = h'h_2)$.

Eine Reihe halbgruppentheoretischer Überlegungen führen dann von 2.2 zu den beiden folgenden Sätzen:

2.3. Satz. Sei H eine linear A-darstellbare Halbgruppe. Es gilt:
(1) Die Menge I_H der Idempotenten von H ist eine Rechtsnullen-Halbgruppe.
(2) Die maximalen Untergruppen von H sind die Teilmengen He für $e \in I_H$. Sie sind alle isomorph.
(3) Der Kern Q_H von H ist eine Rechtsgruppe mit $Q_H = eH$ für jedes $e \in I_H$. Außerdem gilt $Q_H = \bigcup_{e \in I_H} He$.

2.4. Satz. Sei $H \in LDH_p$. Es gilt:
(1) Im Fall $H - HH \neq \emptyset$ ist $E := H - HH$ einziges für p ausgezeichnetes Erzeugendensystem (und folglich ist E für alle Primzahlen ausgezeichnet, für die H linear A-darstellbar ist), und es gibt eine ganze Zahl $r > 1$ mit folgenden Eigenschaften: Die Mengen $E, E^2, \ldots, E^{r-1}, Q_H$ sind paarweise disjunkt, und ihre Vereinigung ist H.
(2) Im Fall $H - HH = \emptyset$ gilt $H = Q_H$, und folglich ist H eine Rechtsgruppe.

Zu den Beweisen vgl. /9/. Die Aussagen 2.3(1) und 2.4(1) sind Verallgemeinerungen einiger von Ecker in /5/angegebenen Aussagen über die Übergangshalbgruppen nilpotenter linearer Automaten. Für diese Automaten gilt natürlich $I_H = Q_H$. In /5; 6.8/ wird jedoch auch behauptet, daß 2.2(1), 2.3(1), 2.4(1) (mit I_H anstelle von Q_H) und $|E| = p^n$ hinreichend dafür seien, daß H isomorph zur Übergangshalbgruppe eines nilpotenten linearen Automaten ist. Diese Behauptung ist falsch. In /9/ wird ein Gegenbeispiel angegeben.

Def. Die Zahl r aus 2.4(1) heißt Index von H, i.Z. Ind(H), der im Fall $H - HH = \emptyset$ gleich 1 gesetzt wird.

Der Index spielt eine Rolle bei der Frage, wann eine Halbgruppe isomorph zur Übergangshalbgruppe eines streng zusammenhängenden linear realisierbaren Automaten ist (vgl. §5).

Aus den algebraischen Eigenschaften lassen sich abbildungstheoretische Folgerungen für die Übergangshalbgruppen ziehen. Sei a ein endlicher Automat. Wir bezeichnen mit I_a die Menge der Idempotenten, mit Q_a den Kern und mit G_a^e die zum Idempotent $e \in I_a$ gehörende maximale Untergruppe von U_a. Sei a ein p-linear realisierbarer Automat und q irgendein Element aus Q_a. Wir erklären auf S_a eine Äquivalenz π_a durch: $(s,s') \in \pi_a \;:\Longleftrightarrow\; sq = s'q$ für $s,s' \in S_a$. Da Q_a eine Rechtsgruppe ist, hängt π_a nicht von der Wahl eines speziellen $q \in Q_a$ ab (vgl. /2/). Man zeigt leicht, daß π_a eine Automaten-Kongruenz ist.

2.5. Lemma. Sei $a \in LRA_p$. Dann ist a/π_a ein p-linear realisierbarer Permutationsautomat mit einer zu G_a^e, e beliebig aus I_a, isomorphen Übergangsgruppe. (Def. von a/π_a: $S_{a/\pi_a} := S_a/\pi_a$, $X_{a/\pi_a} := X_a$, $([s],x)\delta_{a/\pi_a} := [(s,x)\delta_a]$.)

Zum Beweis von 2.5 vgl. /9/. Aus 2.5 folgt: Die maximalen Untergruppen p-linear A-darstellbarer Halbgruppen sind ebenfalls p-linear A-darstellbar; ist E ein für p ausgezeichnetes Erzeugendensystem von H, so ist Ee ein für p ausgezeichnetes Erzeugendensystem von G_H^e, $e \in I_H$. Aus den bekannten Sätzen von Ecker, Hartmanis und Walter (/4/, /11/, /14/) folgt somit:

2.6. Satz. Ist G_H^e maximale Untergruppe einer p-linear A-darstellbaren Halbgruppe H, dann enthält G_H^e einen elementarabelschen Normalteiler Δ vom Exponenten p (d.h. Δ ist ein Normalteiler, dessen

Elemente mit Ausnahme des Einselementes sämtlich die Ordnung p haben) und ein Element v mit $G_H^e = \langle v\Delta \rangle$. Ist E ein für p ausgezeichnetes Erzeugendensystem von H, dann lassen sich v und Δ so wählen, daß $Ee \subseteq v\Delta$ gilt. Ee ist ein für p ausgezeichnetes Erzeugendensystem von G_H^e.

Sei a ein linear realisierbarer Automat und sei S_a^e das Bild von S_a unter der Abbildung $e \in I_a$. Die Abbildungen aus U_a führen die Mengen S_a^e bijektiv ineinander über. Dies sieht man folgendermaßen ein: Zu $u \in U_a$ und $e \in I_a$ gibt es wegen 2.3(3) ein e' mit $eu \in G_a^{e'}$, woraus $(S_a^e)u = (S_a)eu = (S_a)e' = S_a^{e'}$ folgt. Darüberhinaus erweisen sich die Mengen S_a^e für $e \in I_a$ als paarweise disjunkt. Denn aus $s \in S_a^e \cap S_a^{e'}$ folgt se = s = se', und damit see' = se'e. Diese Beziehung liefert wegen 2.1(1) e' = ee' = e'e = e. Insgesamt läßt sich zeigen (vgl. /9/):

2.7. Lemma. (1) Sei a ein linear realisierbarer Automat. Dann sind die Mengen S_a^e, $e \in I_a$, paarweise disjunkt. Jedes S_a^e hat mit jeder Klasse aus π_a genau ein Element gemeinsam.
(2) Sei a streng zusammenhängend und p-linear realisierbar. Dann gilt $S_a = \bigcup_{e \in I_a} S_a^e$, und die Mengen S_a^e, $e \in I_a$, sind die Klassen einer Automaten-Kongruenz ε_a. a/ε_a ist ein kombinatorischer, streng zusammenhängender und p-linear realisierbarer Automat. Darüberhinaus ist auch a/π_a streng zusammenhängend.

p-linear realisierbare Automaten können Faktorautomaten besitzen, die nicht p-linear realisierbar sind (vgl. /10/). Die p-lineare Realisierbarkeit von a/π_a und a/ε_a beruht im wesentlichen auf folgenden Tatsachen: Ist 1 ein K-linearer Automat, dann sind die

Klassen von π_1 (ε_1) die Nebenklassen eines Untervektorraumes von S_1, und $1/\pi_1$ (bzw. $1/\varepsilon_1$) ist wieder K-linear; für jeden Unterautomaten a von 1 sind die Klassen von π_a (bzw. ε_a) die Durchschnitte von S_a mit Klassen aus π_1 (bzw. ε_1) (vgl. /9/).

Wir kommen in §5 auf a/π_a und a/ε_a zurück.

§3 Der Fall H - HH = ∅

Wie wir aus dem vorigen Abschnitt wissen, handelt es sich bei einer linear A-darstellbaren Halbgruppe vom Typ H - HH = ∅ um eine Rechtsgruppe, also um eine Halbgruppe, die isomorph zu einem direkten Produkt einer Gruppe G mit einer Rechtsnullen-Halbgruppe I ist. Hierbei gilt $I \cong I_H$ und $G \cong G_H^e$ für alle $e \in I_H$. Die Rechtsnullen-Halbgruppen und Gruppen sind spezielle Rechtsgruppen.

Sei I eine Rechtsnullen-Halbgruppe. I enthält keine echte Teilmenge, die I erzeugt. Ohne größere Schwierigkeiten zeigt man - entweder wie in /9/ oder anhand des charakteristischen Gleichungssystems (vgl. /8/) -, daß $\gamma(I,I)$ total, d.h. für alle Primzahlen, linear A-darstellbar ist. Damit haben wir:

<u>3.1. Satz.</u> Sei I eine Rechtsnullen-Halbgruppe. Dann ist I total linear A-darstellbar. I selbst ist einziges und somit für alle Primzahlen ausgezeichnetes Erzeugendensystem von I.

Für Gruppen gilt nach /4/ und /11/:

<u>3.2. Satz.</u> Sei G eine Gruppe. G ist genau dann p-linear A-darstell-

bar, wenn G einen elementarabelschen Normalteiler Δ vom Exponenten p und ein Element v enthält mit $G = \langle v\Delta \rangle$. Ein Erzeugendensystem E von G ist genau dann für p ausgezeichnet, wenn sich Δ und v so wählen lassen, daß $E \subseteq v\Delta$ gilt.

Sei $H = G \times I$, wobei G eine Gruppe und I eine Rechtsnullen-Halbgruppe bezeichnet. Ist $E \subseteq H$ ein Erzeugendensystem von H, dann sind $(E)pr_1$ und $(E)pr_2$ Erzeugendensysteme von G bzw. I (pr_i bezeichnet die Projektion auf die i-te Komponente). Da I keine echte Teilmenge als Erzeugendensystem besitzt, gilt $(E)pr_2 = I$. Sei $e := (1_G, e')$, wobei 1_G das Einselement aus G und e' ein Element aus I bezeichnet. Die Zuordnung σ: $h \longrightarrow he$ für $h \in H$ ist dann ein surjektiver Homomorphismus von H auf die maximale Untergruppe $G_H^e = G \times \{e'\}$ von H. Sei η die Einschränkung von pr_1 auf G_H^e. Dann gilt $pr_1 = \sigma \circ \eta$. Nun wissen wir aus 2.6: Wenn E ein für p ausgezeichnetes Erzeugendensystem von H ist, so ist Ee ein für p ausgezeichnetes Erzeugendensystem von G_H^e. Aus der Isomorphie-Eigenschaft von η folgt dann weiter: $(E)pr_1$ ist ein für p ausgezeichnetes Erzeugendensystem von G. Insgesamt haben wir damit folgenden Sachverhalt gezeigt: Ist E ein für p ausgezeichnetes Erzeugendensystem der Rechtsgruppe $H = G \times I$, dann ist $(E)pr_1$ ein für p ausgezeichnetes Erzeugendensystem von G; darüberhinaus gilt $(E)pr_2 = I$. Wir zeigen noch die Umkehrung dieses Sachverhaltes. G möge ein für p ausgezeichnetes Erzeugendensystem E_G besitzen. Sei E eine Teilmenge von H mit $(E)pr_1 = E_G$ und $(E)pr_2 = I$. Wir behaupten: E ist ein für p ausgezeichnetes Erzeugendensystem von H. Zunächst überzeugt man sich leicht, daß E die Halbgruppe H erzeugt. Sodann denken wir uns die Elemente von E durchnumeriert, etwa $E = \{(\gamma_i, e_i) \mid i = 1,2,\ldots,n\} \subseteq G \times I$ und setzen $X := \{1,2,\ldots,n\}$. Wir erklären Automaten a_G, a_I wie folgt: $S_{a_G} := G$, $X_{a_G} := X$, $(g,i)\delta_{a_G} := g\gamma_i$ für

$g \in G$, $i \in X$; $S_{a_I} := I$, $X_{a_I} := X$, $(e,i)\delta_{a_I} := ee_i$ für $e \in I$, $i \in X$.
Aus der p-linearen Realisierbarkeit von $\gamma(G,E_G)$ und $\gamma(I,I)$ folgt sofort die p-lineare Realisierbarkeit von a_G und a_I. Sei $a := a_G \circ a_I$ das X-direkte Produkt von a_G mit a_I (Def.: Das X-direkte Produkt $b \circ c$ ist für Automaten b und c mit $X_b = X_c$ wie folgt erklärt: $S_{b\circ c} := S_b \times S_c$, $X_{b\circ c} := X_b = X_c$, $((s_1,s_2),x)\delta_{b\circ c} := ((s_1,x)\delta_b, (s_2,x)\delta_c)$ für alle $(s_1,s_2) \in S_{b\circ c}$ und $x \in X_{b\circ c}$.) Mit a_G und a_I ist auch a p-linear realisierbar. Ferner ist die Zuordnung

$$\delta_a^{i_1 i_2 \ldots i_k} \longrightarrow (\xi_{i_1},e_{i_1})(\xi_{i_2},e_{i_2})\ldots(\xi_{i_k},e_{i_k}) \text{ für } i_1 i_2 \ldots i_k \in X^+$$

ein Isomorphismus von U_a auf H, wobei $E_a = \{\delta_a^i \mid i \in X\}$ in E übergeht. Damit haben wir:

<u>3.3. Satz.</u> Sei $H - HH = \emptyset$. Es gilt:
$H \in LDH_p \iff$ H ist Rechtsgruppe mit einer p-linear A-darstellbaren maximalen Untergruppe. $\iff$ H ist isomorph zum direkten Produkt einer Rechtsnullen-Halbgruppe mit einer p-linear A-darstellbaren Gruppe.

<u>3.4. Satz.</u> (1) Sei $H = G \times I$, wobei G eine Gruppe und I eine Rechtsnullen-Halbgruppe ist. H ist genau dann p-linear A-darstellbar, wenn dies für G gilt. $E \subseteq H$ ist genau dann ein für p ausgezeichnetes Erzeugendensystem von H, wenn $(E)pr_1$ ein für p ausgezeichnetes Erzeugendensystem von G ist und außerdem $(E)pr_2 = I$ gilt.
(2) Sei H eine Rechtsgruppe, G_H^e eine maximale Untergruppe von H und E ein Erzeugendensystem von H. Dann gilt: E ist ein für p ausgezeichnetes Erzeugendensystem genau dann, wenn G_H^e einen abelschen Normalteiler Δ, dessen Elemente mit Ausnahme des Einselementes sämtlich die Ordnung p haben, und ein Element v besitzt mit $E \subseteq \bigcup_{e \in I_H} v\Delta e$.

Durch diese Sätze ist die Struktur der linear A-darstellbaren Halbgruppen vom Typ $H - HH = \emptyset$ vollständig geklärt. Zugleich ist das Bestimmen der ausgezeichneten Erzeugendensysteme für diese Halbgruppen auf das Bestimmen der ausgezeichneten Erzeugendensysteme für Gruppen zurückgeführt. Über die dabei auftretenden Situationen wird uns der nächste Abschnitt Klarheit verschaffen.

§4 Total linear A-darstellbare Halbgruppen

Ein endlicher Automat, der für die Primzahl 2 und eine weitere Primzahl linear realisierbar ist, ist total linear realisierbar (vgl. /7/, /8/). In einfacher Weise läßt sich hieraus eine analoge Aussage für die lineare A-Darstellbarkeit von Halbgruppen mit $H - HH \neq \emptyset$ ableiten. Sei $E := H - HH$. Falls $H \in LDH_2$ und $H \in LDH_p$, $p \neq 2$, dann folgt $\gamma(H^1,E) \in LRA_2$ und $\gamma(H^1,E) \in LRA_p$ und damit $\gamma(H^1,E) \in LRA_q$ für alle Primzahlen q, d.h., H ist total linear A-darstellbar. Es gibt Automaten und Halbgruppen, die für alle Primzahlen $\neq 2$ und nur für diese linear realisierbar bzw. A-darstellbar sind (vgl. /9/).

Die obige Schlußweise ist nicht auf Halbgruppen mit $H - HH = \emptyset$ übertragbar, da eine Halbgruppe dieses Typs verschiedene Erzeugendensysteme besitzen kann, die für jeweils nur eine Primzahl ausgezeichnet sind (vgl. /9/). Überraschender Weise gilt nun:

<u>4.1. Satz.</u> Sei H eine Halbgruppe mit $H - HH = \emptyset$. Folgende Aussagen sind gleichwertig:

(1) H ist für zwei verschiedene Primzahlen linear A-darstellbar;

(2) H ist total linear A-darstellbar;

(3) H ist isomorph zum direkten Produkt einer Rechtsnullen-Halbgruppe mit einer zyklischen Gruppe.

Die Zahl 2 spielt hier also keine ausgezeichnete Rolle. Wegen 3.3 ist 4.1 eine Folgerung des nachfolgenden Sachverhaltes.

4.2. Satz. Sei G eine Gruppe. Folgende Aussagen sind gleichwertig:

(1) G ist für zwei verschiedene Primzahlen linear A-darstellbar;

(2) G ist total linear A-darstellbar;

(3) G ist zyklische Gruppe.

Beweis. "(3) $\Longrightarrow$ (2)": Sei $G = \langle c \rangle$. Dann ist $\gamma(G,c)$ ein autonomer Automat und bekanntlich total linear realisierbar. "(2) $\Longrightarrow$ (1)" ist trivial. "(1) $\Longrightarrow$ (3)": Sei G p- und q-linear A-darstellbar. Nach einem Satz von Ecker /5/ ist dann G abelsch, und es gibt Zahlen $n,n' \in N \cup \{0\}$, $m,m' \in N$ mit $G \cong Z_p^n \times Z_m \cong Z_q^{n'} \times Z_{m'}$. ($Z_k$ bezeichnet die zyklische Gruppe der Ordnung k, Z_k^n das direkte Produkt aus n Exemplaren Z_k.) Da Z_m und $Z_{m'}$ zyklisch sind, folgt $n \leq 1$, $n' \leq 1$. Falls $n = 0$ oder $n' = 0$, dann wären wir fertig. Sei $n' = 1 = n$. Da Z_m zyklisch ist und $p \neq q$ gilt, folgt: q und m' sind teilerfremd. Daher ist G zyklisch. Q.e.d.

Aus 4.2(3) und 3.4(2) ergibt sich, daß eine total linear A-darstellbare Halbgruppe mit $H - HH = \emptyset$ ein für alle Primzahlen ausgezeichnetes Erzeugendensystem besitzt. Weiter erhalten wir:

4.3. Satz. Eine Halbgruppe H ist genau dann total linear A-darstellbar, wenn sie für die Zahl 2 und eine weitere Primzahl linear A-darstellbar ist. Eine für wenigstens zwei verschiedene Primzahlen linear A-darstellbare Halbgruppe besitzt nur zyklische Untergruppen.

Wir wollen uns kurz der Frage zuwenden, inwieweit man anhand der Multiplikationstabelle einer endlichen Halbgruppe erkennen kann, ob es sich um eine linear A-darstellbare Rechtsgruppe handelt. Die Vorgehensweise wird durch die Sätze 3.3 und 4.2 nahegelegt. Sei

(+)

	...	h	...	e	...
.		.		.	
.		.		.	
.		.		.	
h'	...	h'h	...	h'e	...
.		.		.	
.		.		.	
.		.		.	
				↑	
				He	

die Multiplikationstabelle einer Halbgruppe H. H ist genau dann eine Rechtsgruppe, wenn in jeder Zeile von (+) sämtliche Elemente von H auftreten. Denn eine endliche Halbgruppe ist genau dann eine Rechtsgruppe, wenn sie rechtseinfach ist, d.h., wenn für alle $h \in H$ die Beziehung $hH = H$ gilt (/1; 7.1.26/, /2; 1.11/). Sicherlich kann man aus (+) unmittelbar I_H ablesen.

Sei H als Rechtsgruppe erkannt. Dann stehen in der e-Spalte, $e \in I_H$, gerade die Elemente der maximalen Untergruppe He. Sei e ein für die weiteren Überlegungen fest gewähltes Idempotent. Sei $G := He$. Nach 3.3 haben wir nur noch G zu betrachten. Hierbei sind drei Fälle zu unterscheiden:

1. Fall: G ist eine zyklische Gruppe. Dann ist G (und damit H) total linear A-darstellbar. Für jedes erzeugende Element c von G ist $E_H := cI_H$ ein für alle Primzahlen ausgezeichnetes Erzeugendensystem von H.

In den anderen beiden Fällen ist G für höchstens eine Primzahl linear A-darstellbar.

2. Fall: G ist eine abelsche, nichtzyklische Gruppe. Wenn G p-linear A-darstellbar ist, so muß G isomorph zu $Z_m \times Z_p^n$ sein, wobei $n \geq 1$ und $p \mid m$ ("p teilt m") angenommen werden kann. (Falls p nicht m teilt, so gilt $Z_m \times Z_p^n = Z_{pm} \times Z_p^{n-1}$ mit $n \geq 2$, da G nicht zyklisch sein sollte.) Wie prüft man nach, ob G bis auf Isomorphie die Gestalt $Z_m \times Z_p^n$ mit $p \mid m$ und $n \geq 1$ hat? Zunächst bestimmt man ein Element c von höchster Ordnung, etwa k, bestimmt die Primteiler von k, etwa $p_1, p_2, \ldots, p_j$, und bildet die Mengen $G(p_i) := \{g^{p_i} \mid g \in G\}$, $i = 1,2,\ldots,j$. Es muß genau ein i_o geben, so daß $G(p_{i_o})$ zyklische Untergruppe von G ist. Andernfalls ist G nicht linear A-darstellbar. Sodann bestimme man ein n mit $kp_{i_o}^n = |G|$. Gibt es ein solches n nicht, so ist G nicht linear A-darstellbar. Schließlich hat man $G \cong Z_k \times Z_{p_{i_o}}^n$ zu zeigen. Gelingt dies, dann ist G und damit H als p_{i_o}-linear A-darstellbar erkannt. Ein ausgezeichnetes Erzeugendensystem wird dann gemäß 3.4.(2) hergestellt.

3. Fall. G ist nichtabelsche, nichtzyklische Gruppe. Man bestimmt zunächst die Kommutatoren von G, indem man sich anhand von (+) Elemente $h_i, h_i' \in G$ mit $h_i h_i' = e$ $(i = 1,2)$ sucht und $[h_1,h_2] := h_1 h_2 h_1' h_2'$ bildet. Sind die Ordnungen aller Kommutatoren nicht alle gleich einer und derselben Primzahl, so kann G (und damit H) nicht linear A-darstellbar sein. Denn der durch 3.2 charakterisierte Normalteiler liefert eine zyklische, also abelsche Faktorhalbgruppe G/Δ, weshalb Δ die Kommutatorgruppe von G enthalten muß. Besitzen

alle Kommutatoren die gleiche Primzahlordnung p, dann muß die Existenz eines elementarabelschen Normalteilers Δ vom Exponenten p und eines Elementes v mit $G = \langle v\Delta \rangle$ nachgewiesen werden. Gelingt dies, dann ist H als p-linear A-darstellbar erkannt. Ein ausgezeichnetes Erzeugendensystem erhält man anhand von 3.4(2).

Nun noch zwei halbgruppentheoretische Charakterisierungen total linear A-darstellbarer Halbgruppen. Die erste folgt aus einem Satz aus /7/.

4.4. Satz. Sei H eine Halbgruppe, E ein Erzeugendensystem von H. H ist genau dann eine total linear A-darstellbare Halbgruppe mit E als einem für alle Primzahlen ausgezeichneten Erzeugendensystem, wenn gilt:

(1) $\bigwedge_{n \in N} \bigwedge_{h_1,h_2 \in E^n} \bigwedge_{h,h' \in H^1} (hh_1 = h'h_2 \Longrightarrow h_1 = h_2)$;

(2) $\bigwedge_{n \in N} \bigwedge_{h_1,h_2 \in E^n} \bigwedge_{h,h' \in H^1} (hh_1 = h'h_1 \Longrightarrow hh_2 = h'h_2)$.

Der folgende Satz ist für die Bestimmung erkennbarer Wortmengen von total linear realisierbaren Automaten von Bedeutung.

4.5. Satz. Sei X eine endliche Menge und R eine Kongruenzrelation auf der freien Worthalbgruppe X^+. Es gilt: $H := X^+/R$ ist total linear A-darstellbar mit $E := X/R$ (= Menge der $x \in X$ enthaltenden Klassen aus X^+/R) als einem für alle Primzahlen ausgezeichneten Erzeugendensystem genau dann, wenn gilt:

(1) $\bigvee_{m \in N} \bigwedge_{\substack{w \in X^+ \\ |w|=m}} \bigvee_{\substack{w' \in X^+ \\ |w'|<m}} (w,w') \in R$;

$$(2)\quad \bigwedge_{\substack{w,w'\in X^+\\ |w|=|w'|}} \bigwedge_{u,v\in X^*} ((uw,vw')\in R \Longrightarrow (w,w')\in R);$$

$$(3)\quad \bigwedge_{\substack{w,w'\in X^+\\ |w|=|w'|}} \bigwedge_{u,v\in X^*} ((uw,vw)\in R \Longrightarrow (uw',vw')\in R).$$

(Hierbei bezeichnet X^* das freie Monoid über X.)

Die erste Bedingung des Satzes erzwingt die Endlichkeit der Halbgruppe H. Die anderen beiden Bedingungen folgen aus 4.4.

§5 Der streng zusammenhängende Fall

Def. Eine Halbgruppe H heißt streng zusammenhängend p-linear A-darstellbar, i.Z. $H \in ZLDH_p$ $:\Longleftrightarrow$ H ist isomorph zur Übergangshalbgruppe eines streng zusammenhängenden Automaten $a \in LRA_p$.

Eine Rechtsnullen-Halbgruppe I ist stets streng zusammenhängend linear A-darstellbar. Wenn eine Gruppe G p-linear A-darstellbar ist, so ist sie auch streng zusammenhängend p-linear A-darstellbar (denn $\gamma(G,E)$ besitzt für jedes Erzeugendensystem E von G eine transitive Übergangsgruppe). Die Aussage bleibt auch noch für Rechtsgruppen richtig, wie wir unten sehen werden. Für Halbgruppen mit $H - HH \neq \emptyset$ ist eine analoge Aussage jedoch nicht gültig. Gegenbeispiele findet man in /9/. Wir werden ein notwendig und hinreichendes Kriterium dafür angeben, wann aus $H \in LDH_p$ die Beziehung $H \in ZLDH_p$ folgt. Wir betrachten zuerst den kombinatorischen Fall.

In /5; 8.5/ wird behauptet: Ist $Y \in LDH_p$ eine kombinatorische Halbgruppe mit $E = Y - YY \neq \emptyset$, so gilt $Y \cong U_\gamma$ mit $\gamma = \gamma(I_Y,E)$.

Dies ist i. allg. nicht richtig (Gegenbeispiel in /9/). Tatsächlich gilt:

5.1. Satz. Sei $Y \in LDH_p$ eine kombinatorische Halbgruppe. Sei E ein ausgezeichnetes Erzeugendensystem von Y. Folgende Aussagen sind gleichwertig:

(1) $Y \in ZLDH_p$;

(2) $Y \cong U_\gamma$, $\gamma := \gamma(I_Y,E)$;

(3) für je zwei Elemente $h_1,h_2 \in Y$ gilt: Gibt es ein Idempotent e mit $eh_1 = eh_2$, so folgt $h_1 = h_2$.

Beweis. (Bem.: Eine kombinatorische Halbgruppe $Y \in LDH_p$ besitzt stets genau ein ausgezeichnetes Erzeugendensystem. Im Fall $Y - YY = \emptyset$ ist nämlich Y eine Rechtsnullen-Halbgruppe.) "(2)$\Longleftrightarrow$(3)" ist klar. Zu "(2)$\Longrightarrow$(1)": $\gamma(I_Y,E)$ ist streng zusammenhängend und als Unterautomat von $\gamma(Y^1,E)$ auch p-linear realisierbar.

Zu "(1)$\Longrightarrow$(2)": Sei a ein streng zusammenhängender, p-linear realisierbarer Automat mit $Y \cong U_a$. O.B.d.A. sei a X-reduziert (d.h. $\delta_a^x = \delta_a^{x'} \Longleftrightarrow x = x'$ für $x, x' \in X_a$). Zu jedem $s \in S_a$ gibt es ein $w \in X_a^+$ mit $s\delta_a^w = s$. Eine Potenz von δ_a^w liegt sicherlich in I_a. Hieraus folgt: Jedes $s \in S_a$ ist Fixpunkt eines $e \in I_a$. Wegen $I_a = Q_a$ folgt dann weiter: Zu jedem Paar $s,s' \in S_a$ gibt es ein $e \in I_a$ mit $se = s'$. Da I_a Rechtsnullen-Halbgruppe ist, läßt sich dann aber zeigen: Jedes $e \in I_a$ besitzt genau einen Fixpunkt. Setzt man jetzt $E_a := \{\delta_a^x \mid x \in X_a\}$, so folgt leicht $a \cong \gamma(I_a,E_a)$. Wegen $\gamma(I_a,E_a) \cong \gamma(I_Y,E)$ folgt dann (2). Q.e.d.

Zur Formulierung des allgemeinen Sachverhaltes benötigen wir folgende Definition.

Def. Sei $H \in LDH_p$. Auf H wird eine Relation ρ_H wie folgt erklärt:
$$(h_1,h_2) \in \rho_H \;:\Longleftrightarrow\; \bigwedge_{e \in I_H} Heh_1 = Heh_2, \text{ wobei } h_1,h_2 \in H.$$

In /9/ wird gezeigt: ρ_H ist Kongruenz; H/ρ_H ist kombinatorisch; $H/\rho_H \in ZLDH_p$; ist E ein für p ausgezeichnetes Erzeugendensystem von H, so ist E/ρ_H ein für p ausgezeichnetes Erzeugendensystem von H/ρ_H. Darüberhinaus wird in /9/ gezeigt:

5.2. Satz. Sei $H \in LDH_p$. Es gilt: $H \in ZLDH_p \Longleftrightarrow Ind(H) = Ind(H/\rho_H)$.

Dieser Satz besagt zugleich: Wenn H für mehrere Primzahlen p_1, $p_2,\dots$ linear A-darstellbar und für eine Primzahl streng zusammenhängend linear A-darstellbar ist, dann ist H für alle $p_1,p_2,\dots$ streng zusammenhängend linear A-darstellbar. Im kombinatorischen Fall folgt 5.2 aus der Gleichwertigkeit von 5.1(1) mit 5.1(3). Ist H eine linear A-darstellbare Rechtsgruppe, dann ist H/ρ_H eine Rechtsnullen-Halbgruppe, also ebenfalls eine Rechtsgruppe. In beiden Fällen ist der Index gleich 1; folglich ist H streng zusammenhängend linear A-darstellbar. Nach 3.3 ist H ferner in ein direktes Produkt einer kombinatorischen Halbgruppe mit einer Gruppe zerlegbar. Dieser Sachverhalt läßt sich verallgemeinern:

5.3. Satz. Sei H eine endliche Halbgruppe. Es gilt: $H \in ZLDH_p$ $\Longleftrightarrow$ Es gibt eine Gruppe $G \in LDH_p$ und eine kombinatorische Halbgruppe $Y \in ZLDH_p$ mit folgenden Eigenschaften: (i) H ist subdirektes Produkt von $G \times Y$ (zur Def. vgl. /1/); (ii) H besitzt ein Erzeugendensystem E, so daß $(E)pr_1$ und $(E)pr_2$ für p ausgezeichnete Erzeugendensysteme von G bzw. Y sind.

<u>Beweis:</u> " $\Longrightarrow$": Sei a ein streng zusammenhängender, p-linear realisierbarer Automat mit $H \cong U_a$. Für jedes $s \in S_a$ gilt $\{s\} = [s]_{\pi_a} \cap [s]_{\varepsilon_a}$ (vgl. §2). Die Zuordnungen $\mu_S : s \longrightarrow ([s]_{\pi_a}, [s]_{\varepsilon_a})$ für $s \in S_a$ und $\mu_X := id_{X_a}$ definieren dann einen Isomorphismus von a auf das X-direkte Produkt $a/\pi_a \circ a/\varepsilon_a$. Für G wähle man eine maximale Untergruppe von U_a, Y sei die Faktorhalbgruppe von U_a nach ϱ_{U_a}. G ist isomorph zur Übergangshalbgruppe von a/π_a, Y zur Übergangshalbgruppe von a/ε_a (vgl. /9/). Beachtet man jetzt noch, daß die Zuordnung $u \longrightarrow ue$, $u \in U_a$, ein surjektiver Homomorphismus von U_a auf G ist, falls e das Einselement von G, dann folgt (i). Die Eigenschaft (ii) folgt ebenfalls aus der Isomorphie $a \cong a/\pi_a \circ a/\varepsilon_a$.

" $\Longleftarrow$": Sei H subdirektes Produkt von $G \times Y$. Sei $E \subseteq H$ ein Erzeugendensystem von H derart, daß $(E)pr_1$ und $(E)pr_2$ für p ausgezeichnete Erzeugendensysteme von G bzw. Y sind. Zum Beweis des Satzes werden zwei streng zusammenhängende, p-linear realisierbare Automaten a_1 und a_2 mit $X_{a_1} = X_{a_2}$ definiert, deren X-direktes Produkt ebenfalls streng zusammenhängend und p-linear realisierbar ist und für die $U_{a_1} \cong G$, $U_{a_2} \cong Y$, $U_{a_1 \circ a_2} \cong H$ gilt.

Nach 3.2 besitzt G einen elementarabelschen Normalteiler Δ vom Exponenten p und ein Element v mit $(E)pr_1 \subseteq v\Delta$. Sei C eine zyklische Untergruppe von G, die außer dem Einselement 1_G keinen Normalteiler von G enthält und für die $C \cap \Delta = \{1_G\}$ gilt. Dann sei S_{a_1} die Menge der Rechtsnebenklassen von G nach C, $X_{a_1} := E$, $(Cg, \xi)\delta_{a_1} := Cg((\xi)pr_1)$. Nach /11/ ist a_1 streng zusammenhängend und p-linear realisierbar. Sodann setze $S_{a_2} := I_Y$, $X_{a_2} := E$, $(e, \xi)\delta_{a_2} := e((\xi)pr_2)$. Nach Voraussetzung über Y ist a_2 streng zusammenhängend und p-linear realisierbar und es gilt $U_{a_2} \cong Y$.

Mit a_1 und a_2 ist auch $a_1 \circ a_2$ p-linear realisierbar (/13/). Der strenge Zusammenhang ergibt sich nach folgendem Hilfssatz: Sei b ein Permutationsautomat und c ein kombinatorischer, p-linear realisierbarer Automat mit $X_b = X_c$. Sind b und c streng zusammenhängend, so gilt dasselbe für $b \circ c$. Wir beweisen diese Behauptung. Seien (s_1,s_2), $(s_1',s_2') \in S_{b\circ c}$. Es gibt ein $w_1 \in X_b^+$ $(=X_c^+)$ mit $s_1' = (s_1,w_1)\delta_b$. Setze $s_2'' := (s_2,w_1)\delta_c$. Es gibt ein $w_2 \in X_c^+$ mit $\delta_c^{w_2} \in I_c$ und $s_2' = (s_2'',w_2)\delta_c$ (vgl. Beweis zu 5.1). Ferner gibt es ein $k \in N$ mit $(\delta_c^{w_2})^k = id_{S_b}$. Somit gilt: $((s_1,s_2), w_1w_2^k)\delta_{b\circ c} = ((s_1, w_1w_2^k)\delta_b, (s_1, w_1w_2^k)\delta_c) = (s_1',s_2')$.

Aus der Eigenschaft $((Cg,e),\gamma)\delta_{a_1 \circ a_2} = (Cg((\gamma)pr_1),e((\gamma)pr_2))$ folgt dann $U_a \cong H$. Q.e.d.

5.4. Bemerkung. Die im zweiten Teil des Beweises angegebene Konstruktion liefert bei geeigneter Wahl von E und C bis auf Isomorphie jeden X-reduzierten, streng zusammenhängenden, p-linear realisierbaren Automaten a mit $U_a \cong H$ (vgl. /9/).

5.5. Bemerkung. Direkte Produkte p-linear A-darstellbarer Halbgruppen brauchen nicht p-linear A-darstellbar zu sein. Sei G eine Gruppe und Y eine kombinatorische Halbgruppe. Beide mögen p-linear A-darstellbar sein. Wir nehmen ferner an, Y sei keine Rechtsnullen-Halbgruppe. Wäre $W := G \times Y$ p-linear A-darstellbar, dann wäre $E := W - WW = G \times (Y - YY)$ ein ausgezeichnetes Erzeugendensystem. Für jedes Idempotent $e \in W$ gilt aber $Ee = We$ $(\cong G)$, d.h., die maximale Untergruppe We stimmt mit einem ihrer ausgezeichneten Erzeugendensysteme überein. Dies kann sicherlich nicht gelten, wenn G beispielsweise eine zyklische Halbgruppe ist, deren Ordnung keine Primzahl ist.

§6 Übergangshalbgruppen

Sei S eine Menge und U eine Transformationshalbgruppe auf S. Die Frage, ob es eine Primzahl p und ein $a \in LRA_p$ mit $U_a = U$ (und $S_a = S$) gibt, läßt sich im Fall $U - UU \neq \emptyset$ wie folgt beantworten: Sei $E := U - UU$. Dann definiert man ein a durch $S_a := S$, $X_a := E$, $(s,x)\delta_a := sx$, wobei sx das Bild von $s \in S$ unter $x \in E$ bezeichnet. Wenn es überhaupt einen linear realisierbaren Automaten a mit $U_a = U$ gibt, dann ist es der eben konstruierte (abgesehen von Automaten, die durch X-Reduktion auf a zurückgeführt werden können). Ob a linear realisierbar ist, und wenn ja, für welche Primzahlen, stellt man mit der in /6/ (vgl. auch /8/) angegebenen Methode fest. Die in den vorigen Abschnitten entwickelten Ergebnisse können hierbei gelegentlich nützliche Entscheidungshilfen liefern (z.B. 2.7(1)). Im Fall $U - UU = \emptyset$ wird man vielleicht zunächst ausgezeichnete Erzeugendensysteme von U bestimmen (vgl. die Überlegungen im Anschluß an 4.3), wobei U als abstrakte Halbgruppe aufgefaßt wird, dann Automaten wie oben konstruieren und diese gemäß /6/, /8/ auf lineare Realisierbarkeit untersuchen. Andere Möglichkeiten werden durch die folgenden Sätze nahegelegt, die zugleich Antworten auf die Frage 1.4 im Fall $U - UU = \emptyset$ darstellen. Wir wissen bereits, daß ein linear realisierbarer Automat a mit einer Übergangshalbgruppe vom Typ $U_a - U_aU_a = \emptyset$ ein Rechtsgruppen-Automat ist (d.h. U_a als abstrakte Halbgruppe aufgefaßt ist eine Rechtsgruppe).

<u>6.1. Satz:</u> Sei a Rechtsgruppen-Automat. a ist genau dann p-linear realisierbar, wenn eine (und damit jede) maximale Untergruppe G_a^e von U_a einen elementarabelschen Normalteiler Δ vom Exponenten p und ein Element v mit folgenden Eigenschaften enthält:

(i) $E_a := \{\delta_a^x \mid x \in X_a\} \subseteq \bigcup_{e \in I_a} v\Delta e$;

(ii) Δ induziert auf S_a^e eine halbreguläre Permutationsgruppe, d.h., außer e besitzt kein Element aus Δ einen Fixpunkt;

(iii) $S_a^e \cap S_a^{e'} = \emptyset$ für $e, e' \in I_a$ mit $e \neq e'$.

Kor. 1: Ein Gruppen-Automat a ist genau dann p-linear realisierbar, wenn U_a einen elementarabelschen Normalteiler Δ vom Exponenten p und ein Element v enthält mit

(i) $E_a \subseteq v\Delta$;

(ii) außer dem Idempotent $e \in U_a$ besitzt kein Element aus Δ einen Fixpunkt.

Kor. 2: (vgl. /11/) Sei a ein streng zusammenhängender Permutationsautomat. Sei s_o irgendein Element aus S_a und $C := \{u \in U_a \mid s_o u = s_o\}$. Es gilt: a ist p-linear realisierbar genau dann, wenn U_a einen elementarabelschen Normalteiler Δ vom Exponenten p und ein Element v mit folgenden Eigenschaften enthält:

(i) $E_a \subseteq v\Delta$;

(ii) $\Delta \cap C = \{1\}$.

Die Beweise der vorangehenden und nachfolgenden Sätze finden sich in /9/.

6.2. Satz. Sei a ein Rechtsgruppen-Automat. a ist für zwei verschiedene Primzahlen linear realisierbar $\Longleftrightarrow$ a ist total linear realisierbar $\Longleftrightarrow$ es gelten die beiden Aussagen:

(i) $S_a^e \cap S_a^{e'} = \emptyset$ für $e, e' \in I_a$ mit $e \neq e'$;

(ii) der Automat b mit $S_b := S_a$, $X_b := X_a$, $(s,x)\delta_b := ((s,x)\delta_a)e$

ist autonom.

Kor. Sei a ein Gruppen-Automat. Folgende Aussagen sind gleichwertig:

(1) a ist für zwei verschiedene Primzahlen linear realisierbar;

(2) a ist total linear realisierbar;

(3) a ist autonom.

Literatur

/1/ M. Arbib (Ed.): Algebraic theory of machines, languages, and semigroups, Acad. Press, New York (1968).

/2/ A.H. Clifford, G.B. Preston: The algebraic theory of semigroups, Vol. I, Amer. Math. Soc., Rhode Island (1961).

/3/ W.A. Davis, J.A. Brzozowski: On the linearity of sequential machines, IEEE Trans. EC-15, 21-29 (1966).

/4/ K. Ecker: On the semigroup of a linear nonsingular automaton, Math. System Theory 6, 353-358 (1972).

/5/ - : Algebraische Eigenschaften linearer Automaten, GMD-Bericht Nr. 87, Bonn (1974).

/6/ L. Eichner: Lineare Realisierbarkeit endlicher Automaten über endlichen Körpern, Acta Informatica 3, 75-100 (1974).

/7/ - : Total lineare Realisierbarkeit endlicher Automaten, Acta Informatica 3, 385-397 (1974).

/8/ - : Homomorphe Darstellungen endlicher Automaten in linearen Automaten, EIK 9, 587-613 (1973).

/9/ - : Die Übergangshalbgruppen linear realisierbarer endlicher Automaten, eingereicht.

/10/ J. Hartmanis, W.A. Davis: Homomorphic images of sequential machines, IEEE Trans. EC-14, 781-786 (1965).

/11/ J. Hartmanis, H. Walter: Group theoretic characterization of linear permutation automata, J. Comp. Syst. 7, 168-188 (1973).

/12/ B. Reusch: Lineare Automaten, Bibliographisches Inst., Mannheim (1969).

/13/ W. Stucky: Linear realisierbare Automaten, Universität Saarbrücken, Dissertation (1969).

/14/ Y. Zalcstein: On the semigroups of linear sequential machines, Intern. J. of Comp. and Inf. Sciences 2, 25-28 (1973).

DECIDABILITE DE LA FINITUDE DES DEMI-GROUPES DE MATRICES

G. Jacob

Introduction.

Divers articles de Schützenberger [16,17] ont introduit l'étude des séries formelles rationnelles et algébriques en variables non commutatives, entre 1961 et 1963. Elles y sont présentées comme une généralisation naturelle des langages réguliers et context-free. Dans un article publié avec Chomsky [2] en 1963, il montre qu'elles sont le cadre adéquat pour le calcul des multiplicités des dérivations produites par une grammaire context-free.

L'étude des séries rationnelles s'est montrée des plus fructueuses. On peut les définir en termes d' "expressions rationnelles" (Eilenberg [3]), mais c'est la définition en termes d' "automates avec multiplicités" (Eilenberg [3]), ou de "représentations matricielles" (Schützenberger [16,17], Fliess [6], Salomaa [15], Jacob [7]) - c'est-à-dire de "demi-groupes de matrices" - qui s'est révélée la plus féconde. On doit à Schützenberger [16] et à Fliess [6] des caractérisations et méthodes de calcul de la "représentation minimale" d'une série rationnelle. Ils fournissent ainsi des outils algébriques généraux pouvant contribuer à résoudre certains problèmes de décision les concernant (voir en particulier Fliess [4,6]).

Les séries formelles rationnelles posent certains problèmes nouveaux non triviaux, liés à l'introduction du semi-anneau A des coefficients. Rappelons qu'on appelle série formelle sur un alphabet fini X à coefficients dans A - ou A-sous-ensemble de X^*, suivant Eilenberg [3] - toute application du monoïde libre X^* dans A. On la note comme une somme formelle

$s = \sum \{(s,f)\ f\ ;\ f \in X^*\}$, où l'on a noté (s,f) le coefficient de f, ou multiplicité de f dans la série s, c'est-à-dire la valeur en f de la fonction s. Le support d'une série est l'ensemble des mots de X^* dont le coefficient est non nul.

Ainsi, le changement de semi-anneau de $\mathbb{N}$ à $\mathbb{Z}$ amène à se demander si les séries $\mathbb{Z}$-rationnelles à coefficients entiers positifs sont aussi $\mathbb{N}$-rationnelles. Il n'en est rien. Le problème est donc de pouvoir en décider. Dans un article tout récent de Soittola [20] , il est donné un procédé effectif permettant de décider - dans le cas où X est réduit à une seule lettre - si une série $\mathbb{Z}$-rationnelle à coefficients positifs est $\mathbb{N}$-rationnelle. Bien que restrictif, ce cas prend tout son intérêt en raison du lien profond entre les séries rationnelles sur une lettre et les systèmes de Lindenmayer (cf. Berstel [1]). Sur plusieurs lettres, ce problème de décision est un problème ouvert.

D'autre part, il est bien connu que le support d'une série $\mathbb{N}$-rationnelle est un langage régulier. Ce n'est plus vrai sur l'anneau $\mathbb{Z}$. A fortiori, c'est faux pour une série K-rationnelle, où K est un corps quelconque. Or une condition suffisante pour qu'une série K-rationnelle ait pour support un langage régulier est que cette série soit cofinie, c'est-à-dire ait un nombre fini de coefficients distincts (d'image finie dans [1]). Nous donnons ici un algorithme permettant de décider si une série K-rationnelle - donnée par l'un quelconque des procédés de définition déjà cités - est une série cofinie. Cet algorithme utilise la représentation minimale, qui joue alors le rôle d'un automate fini: en effet, une série K-rationnelle est cofinie si et seulement si sa représentation minimale est finie.

Notre algorithme consiste donc à décider si un demi-groupe de matrices est fini. Nous ne pouvons ici qu'en dessiner les grandes lignes, renvoyant pour développements et justifications à deux articles à paraître [9,10].

La technique employée met en évidence certains "groupes caractéristiques" du demi-groupe étudié, en lesquels on peut trouver toute l'information concernant sa finitude. Nous rejoignons ainsi certains travaux reliant les langages réguliers et leurs monoïdes syntactiques [12,21,18]. C'est cette étude de structure, inspirée de Schützenberger [18], que nous av ons ébauchée dans [8], où nous décid ons de la finitude du support d'une série rationnelle, en montrant l'existence dans les demi-groupes de matrices d'une bonne généralisation de la notion de boucle dans les automates finis.

Nous recevons à l'instant de Sao Paulo un article ronéotypé, d'Imre Simon et Arnaldo Mandel [22], présentant des résultats et méthodes très voisins des nôtres. Ils y étudient les séries rationnelles cofinies et les demi-groupes finis de matrices, à coefficients dans $\mathbb{N}$ ou dans un sous-semi-anneau de $\mathbb{Q}$.

NOTATIONS.

Appelons type d'un demi-groupe H le plus petit cardinal d'un système de générateurs de H.

Appelons largeur de H pour S (si H est engendré par S), le plus petit entier $j = \mathrm{larg}_S(H)$, vérifiant :

$$S^j \subset S \cup S^2 \cup S^3 \cup \ldots \cup S^{j-1}$$

Si un tel j n'existe pas, la largeur de H pour S est infinie.

La largeur de H est définie par :

$$\mathrm{larg}(H) = \sup \{\mathrm{larg}_S(H) \ ; \ S \text{ engendre } H\}$$

Notons qu'un demi-groupe de type fini est fini ssi il est de largeur finie.

I. - DEMI-GROUPES LINEAIRES.

Il s'agit ici des demi-groupes de matrices de dimension finie, ou encore, des demi-groupes d'endomorphismes d'un espace vectoriel de dimension finie sur un corps.

Théorème 1. [9,10] Soit H un demi-groupe linéaire sur un corps commutatif, engendré par un ensemble S.

On peut effectivement calculer un entier N, ne dépendant que du cardinal de S et de la dimension, qui majore le cardinal de H, à condition qu'il soit fini.

Ce résultat s'établit en deux étapes, que concrétisent les théorèmes 2 et 3 suivant. Leur énoncé nécessite quelques notations.

Définition 1. Nous appelons Im-noyau d'un demi-groupe linéaire tout sous-demi-groupe de type fini formé d'endomorphismes ayant tous la même image.

Définition 2. Nous appelons groupe caractéristique d'un Im-noyau $\mathcal{N}$ (notation $G(\mathcal{N})$), le groupe engendré par les automorphismes d'espace vectoriel qui sont induits par les éléments de $\mathcal{N}$ sur leur image commune.

Interprétons : un sous-demi-groupe d'un demi-groupe de matrices H en est un Im-noyau si et seulement si toutes ses matrices peuvent s'écrire, moyennant le même changement de base et la même décomposition par blocs, sous la forme :

$$A \quad , \text{ ou : } \quad \begin{pmatrix} A & 0 \\ B & 0 \end{pmatrix}$$

où A est une matrice carrée inversible. Le groupe caractéristique de cet Im-noyau est alors le groupe engendré par les matrices A. (On notera que nous avons fait opérer les endomorphismes à droite sur les vecteurs).

Théorème 2. [9] Soit H un demi-groupe linéaire, engendré par un ensemble S, sur un corps commutatif.

On peut effectivement calculer une fonction β de $\mathbb{N}$ dans lui-même, telle que , pour tout entier s, l'entier $\beta(s)$ majore la largeur des groupes caractéristiques finis de type s de H.

La fonction β dépend de la dimension, du cardinal de S, et de la caractéristique du corps de base, et du degré d'algébricité sur le sous-corps premier du corps engendré par les coefficients des matrices de S.

En caractéristique 0, β est une fonction constante.

Ce théorème précise un résultat obtenu en 1968 par Kopytov [11]. Y. Zalcstein nous a informé qu'il avait obtenu un résultat semblable indépendamment de nous, utilisant les méthodes de [12].

Théorème 3. [10] Soit H un demi-groupe linéaire sur un corps quelconque (skewfield).

Si pour tout entier s il existe un entier $\beta(s)$ qui majore la largeur des groupes caractéristiques (finis) de type s de H, alors on peut calculer un entier $T(\beta)$ qui majore la largeur de H (à supposer qu'elle soit finie).

L'entier $T(\beta)$ dépend de la fonction β, de la dimension, et de la largeur de H.

Corollaire (théorème de Burnside; - McNaughton et Zalcstein [12]).

Tout demi-groupe de matrices périodiques à coefficients dans un corps commutatif est fini. (Pour le cas non commutatif, voir [10]).

II. - UNE METHODE COMBINATOIRE.

Nous présentons ici les techniques développées dans [10] pour établir le théorème 3.

Nous appellerons phrase sur un demi-groupe M toute suite finie $w = (f_1, f_2, \ldots, f_k)$ d'éléments de M. Une phrase $w = (f_1, f_2, \ldots, f_k)$ sur un demi-groupe libre X^+ sera dite extraite d'un mot f de X^+ si et seulement si le produit $w = f_1 f_2 \ldots f_k$ est un sous-mot du mot f.

Définition 3. On appelle rang sur un demi-groupe M toute application ρ de M dans $\mathbb{N}$ vérifiant:

$$\forall f,g \in M, \qquad \rho(fg) \leqslant \inf(\rho(f), \rho(g))$$

Il est dit majoré par un entier m ssi pour tout "mot" f de $\rho(f)$ est inférieur ou égal à m.

Il est dit constant sur une phrase $w = (f_1, f_2, \ldots, f_k)$ ssi:

$$\forall\ 0 \leqslant i < j \leqslant k, \qquad \rho(f\ ) = \rho(f_{i+1}, f_{i+2}, \ldots, f_j)$$

Théorème 4. (Théorème du rang constant). [8].

Soit X un ensemble (non nécessairement fini).

Pour toute fonction ν de $\mathbb{N}$ dans $\mathbb{N}$, il existe une fonction $R(\nu)$ de $\mathbb{N}$ dans $\mathbb{N}$ telle que, si ρ est un rang sur X^+ majoré par un entier m, et si f est un mot de X^+ de longueur $R(\nu)(m)$, on puisse extraire de f une phrase w sur laquelle le rang ρ est constant, vérifiant:

il existe un entier s tel que l'on ait:

$$w = (f_1, f_2, \ldots, f_{\nu(s)})$$

chacun des mots f_j est de longueur au plus s.

Notons $R(\nu)(m) = R(\nu, m)$. La fonction R à deux arguments ainsi obtenue se calcule ainsi (justification dans 8).

$$R(\nu, 0) = \nu(1)$$

$$R(\nu, m+1) = (m+1) . R(\nu, m) . \nu(R(\nu, m))$$

Inspiré du théorème de Ramsey, ce résultat ne peut s'en déduire. [14]. (sauf dans le cas où ν est une fonction constante).

Définition 4. Nous appelons ensemble ordonné à degré la donnée d'un d'un couple (Δ, δ) où Δ est un ensemble ordonné, et δ, le "degré", est une application strictement croissante de Δ dans $\mathbb{N}$.

<u>Définition 5.</u> Nous appelons <u>Image à droite</u> sur un demi-groupe M à valeur dans un ensemble ordonné à degré (Δ,δ) la donnée d'une application Im de M dans Δ vérifiant:

$$\text{Im } f = \text{Im } g \implies \text{Im } fh = \text{Im } gh \quad \text{(stabilité à droite)}$$

$$\text{Im } fh \leqslant \text{Im } h \quad \text{(décroissance à gauche)}$$

$$(\rho \circ \text{Im})\ fh \leq (\rho \circ \text{Im})\ f \quad \text{(décroissance à droite mod. le degré)}$$

Pour un demi-groupe de matrices, on prendra pour image à droite d'une matrice, son image comme opérant à droite sur des matrices lignes.

Nous donnons [10] une interprétation de ces notions en termes de représentations ordonnées à droite.

<u>Définition 6.</u> Soit M un demi-groupe muni d'une application ordonnée à degré. Une <u>phrase</u> sur M sera dite <u>Im-régulière</u> ssi les"mots"qui la composent engendrent un sous-demi-groupe sur lequel l'application Im est constante.

Les <u>Im-noyaux</u> de M sont exactement les sous-demi-groupes de M engendrés par les"mots"d'une même phrase Im-régulière.

<u>Théorème 5</u>. (théorème de la phrase Im-régulière [10]).

<u>Soit X un ensemble fini.</u>

<u>Pour toute fonction</u> β <u>de $\mathbb{N}$ dans $\mathbb{N}$, il existe une fonction</u> $T(\beta)$ <u>de $\mathbb{N}$ dans $\mathbb{N}$ telle que, si Im est une image à droite sur X^+ de degré majoré par un entier m, et si f est un mot de X^+ de longueur</u> $T(\beta)(m)$, <u>on puisse extraire de f une phrase Im-régulière w, vérifiant</u>:

<u>il existe un entier s tel que l'on ait</u>:

$$w = (g_1, g_2, \ldots, g_{\beta(s)})$$

<u>chacun des mots</u> g_j <u>est de longueur au plus s.</u>

Dans le cas des demi-groupes linéaires, ceci démontre le théorème 3. On trouvera des interprétations plus générales dans [10].

Nous donnons à présent le système d'équations récurrentes per mettant de calculer $T(\beta)$. Soit donc d le cardinal de X, et soit dim un entier majorant le degré de l'image. (Pour les demi-groupes de matrices, on prendra la dimension).Nos équations utilisent à plusieurs reprises la fonction R à deux arguments définie après le théorème 4.

$T(\beta) = R(\nu, \dim)$ où ν est défini par:

$\forall z \in \mathbb{N}$ $\nu(z) = R(\mu_z, \tau(z))$

$\tau(z) = d + d^2 + \ldots + d^z$

μ_z est la fonction de $\mathbb{N}$ dans $\mathbb{N}$ définie par:

$$\forall t \in \mathbb{N} \qquad \mu_z(t) = 1 + \beta(\tau(z.(2t-1)))$$

III. UN ALGORITHME DECIDANT SI UNE SERIE RATIONNELLE PEUT ETRE RECONNUE PAR UN AUTOMATE FINI.

Soient A un semi-anneau, et X un alphabet fini.

Rappelons qu'on appelle A-X-automate la donnée $B = (N, \mu, i, t)$

d'un entier N, appelé la dimension de B

d'une représentation μ de X^+ dans le demi-groupe $\mathcal{M}_N(A)$ des matrices de dimension N sur A.

d'une matrice ligne i et d'une matrice colonne t de dimension N sur A.

Le comportement de B est alors la série formelle définie par:

$(b, \Lambda) = 0$ où Λ est le mot vide de X^*.

$\forall f \in X^+$ $(b, f) = i(\mu f)t$

On sait que toute série formelle s sur X peut s'écrire de façon unique comme une somme:

$$s = (s, \Lambda)\cdot\Lambda + s'$$

où s' a son support contenu dans X^+. On appelle terme constant de s la série $(s, \Lambda)\cdot\Lambda$, dont le support est réduit au mot vide de X^*.

Rappelons le résultat bien connu:

Théorème 6. de Kleene-Schützenberger (Schützenberger [17], Eilenberg [3])
Une série formelle sur X est A-rationnelle ssi elle est la somme d'un terme constant et du comportement d'un A-X-automate B. On dit alors que cette série est définie, ou reconnue, par B.

Proposition 1. Si une série est reconnue par un A-X-automate fini, alors la série s est cofinie.

Si $B = (N, \mu, i, t)$ est un A-X-automate fini, le demi-groupe formé des matrices μf est fini. Il est donc clair que l'ensemble des coefficients $i(\mu f)t$ est fini. C.Q.F.D.

Noter que l'automate fini obtenu par la donnée d'un tel A-X-automate fini permet de reconnaître, pour tout élément u de A, le langage régulier:

$$L_u = \{ f \ ; \ i(\mu f)t = u \}$$

En particulier, le support de s est alors un langage régulier.

La construction de la représentation minimale permet d'obtenir la réciproque de la proposition 1.

Définition 7. Le rang sur A d'une série A-rationnelle est le plus petit entier $\hat{n}$ tel que cette série puisse être définie par un A-X-automate de dimension $\hat{n}$.

On appelle A-X-automate minimal pour une série s tout A-X-automate dont la dimension est égale au rang de s sur A. La représentation matricielle qui définit cet A-X-automate est appelée représentation minimale pour s.

Théorème 7, de la représentation minimale. (Schützenberger 16 , Fliess 6)

Soit s une série K-rationnelle de rang $\hat{n}$ sur un corps K commutatif. On peut calculer la représentation minimale pour s (unique à similitude près) comme une combinaison linéaire de la forme:

$$\forall f \in X^+ \qquad \mu f = \sum_{i,j=1}^{\hat{n}} m_{ij}(s, g_i f d_j)$$

où les m_{ij} sont $\hat{n}^2$ matrices de $\mathcal{M}_N(A)$ linéairement indépendantes sur K, et où les mots g_i et d_j sont des mots fixés de longueur inférieure ou égale à $\hat{n}$, tels que la matrice d'entrées $(\sigma f)_{ij} = (s, g_i d_j)$ soit inversible.

Théorème 8. Soit s une série A-rationnelle, où A est sous-semi-anneau d'un corps K, commutatif. Alors s est cofinie si et seulement si son K-X-automate minimal (resp. sa représentation minimale) est finie.

Théorème 9. ALGORITHME DE DECISION.

Soit s une série A-rationnelle, où A est sous-semi-anneau d'un corps K commutatif.

On peut décider si la série s est cofinie, i.e. si elle peut être définie par un automate fini.

Le théorème 7 nous permet, connaissant le rang de s, d'en construire la représentation minimale $\hat{\mu}$. (Noter que la connaissance d'un entier majorant le rang suffit à la construction. Elle peut donc se faire si s est donnée par une expression rationnelle [3], ou par un système d'équations linéaire à droite [5]).

Nous pouvons alors décider, grâce au calcul de T(β) (cf. théorème 3) si la représentation $\hat{\mu}$ est finie, i.e. si le demi-groupe des matrices $\hat{\mu}f$ est fini. En effet, il suffit de tester la "largeur" du demi-groupe. Si elle est inférieure à T(β), le demi-groupe est fini. Si elle est au moins égale à T(β), il est infini.

Donnons un exemple: dans le cas de 2 matrices de dimension 3 sur $\mathbb{Q}$, T(β) est égal à 21^{27}. Si le demi-groupe est infini, il faut donc pour en décider calculer des produits de 21^{27} matrices de dimension 3. Ce n'est pas réalisable. Mais il faut noter qu'en cas de demi-groupe fini, notre algorithme ne fait que les calculs "utiles": si le demi-groupe est de largeur n, il ne calcule que des produits de n matrices.

Nous donnons en [9] une description complète de l'algorithme, sous forme d'un programme en algol 68. On trouvera en [10] les interprétations de ces résultats en termes de structure des demi-groupes de matrices.

BIBLIOGRAPHIE.

[1] BERSTEL J. Contribution à l'étude des propriétés arithmétiques des langages formels; Thèse Sc. Math.,Univ. Paris VII, 1972.

[2] CHOMSKY N., SCHUTZENBERGER M.P., The algebraic theory of context-free languages; in "Computer programming and formal languages" (P. Brafford & D. Hirschberg, edit.) p. 118-161, North-Holland, Amsterdam, 1963.

[3] EILENBERG S. Automata, languages and machines; Academic Press, vol. **A** (1974) New-York, London.

[4] FLIESS M. Deux applications de la représentation matricielle d'une série rationnelle non commutative; J. Algebra 19 (1970) 344-353

[5] FLIESS M. Séries reconnaissables et algébriques; Bull. Sc. Math. 94 (1970)

[6] FLIESS M. Matrices de Hankel; J. Math. Pures Appl. 53 (1974)

[7] JACOB G. Sur un théorème de Shamir; Inf. Control, 27 (1975) 218-261.

[8] JACOB G. Un théorème de factorisation des produits d'endomorphismes de K^N; J. Algebra, à paraître.

[9] JACOB G. Un algorithme calculant le cardinal des demi-groupes de matrices sur un corps commutatif; Theoretical Computer Science, à paraître.

[10] JACOB G. La finitude des représentations linéaires est décidable; soumis au Journal of Algebra.

[11] KOPYTOV Solvability of the problem of occurence in finitely generated soluble groups of matrices over the field of algebraic numbers; Algebra and logic, 7 (1968) 388-393. Translated from Russian.

[12] Mc NAUGHTON R. and ZALCSTEIN Y. The Burnside théorem for semigroups; J. Algebra 34 (1975) 292-299.

[13] NIVAT M. Transductions des langages de Chomsky; Ann. Inst. Fourier, 18 (1968) 339-456.

[14] RAMSEY F. P. On a problem of formal logic; Proc. London Math. Soc. 30 (1930) 264-286.

[15] SALOMAA A. Formal Languages; Acad. Press, (1973) New-York, London.

[16] SCHUTZENBERGER M.P. On the definition of a family of automata; Inf. Control 4 (1961) 245-270.

[17] SCHUTZENBERGER M.P. On a theorem of Jungen; Proc. Amer. Math. Soc. 13 (1962) 885-890.

[18] SCHUTZENBERGER M.P. Finite counting automata; Inf. Control 5 (1962) 91-107.

[19] SHAMIR E. A representation theorem for algebraic and context-free power series in non commuting variables; Inf. Control 6 (1963) 246-264.

[20] SOITTOLA M. Positive rational sequences; Theoretical Computer Science, 2 (1976) 317-322.

[21] ZALCSTEIN Y. Syntactic semigroups of some classes of star-free languages; in Automata, Languages and Programming (Nivat M. edit.) North-Holland, Amsterdam, 1973.

[22] MANDEL A. and SIMON I. On Finite Semigroups of Matrices; Instituto de Matematica e Estatistica, Universidade de Sao Paulo, Sao Paulo, Brasil.

part of the results of this paper were presented at the IV Escola de Algebra, Sao Paulo, July 1976.

CODES ET SOUS-MONOIDES POSSEDANT DES MOTS NEUTRES

D. Perrin - M.-P. Schützenberger

Introduction

Dans tout ce travail, A^* (resp. $A^+ = A^* \setminus 1$) désigne le monoïde libre (resp. le semigroupe libre) engendré par l'ensemble fixe non vide A et on considère un sous-monoïde X^* de A^* dont l'ensemble générateur minimal est $X = X^+ \setminus X^+X^+$, où $X^+ = X^* \setminus 1$. Une série de recherches se sont attachées à l'étude des rapports entre X, le sous-monoïde X^* et le monoïde syntaxique $S = A^*\xi$ de X^* ; en particulier, celles de J-F. Perrot [8], de R. Mc Naughton [7] et de G. Lallement [5] ont montré l'intérêt de la nature des groupes contenus dans S et de la structure des idéaux de ce monoïde. Le cas particulier où X engendre librement X^* (c'est-à-dire où X est un *code*) présente un certain intérêt supplémentaire en raison, notamment, de son interprétation en théorie de l'information et de ses rapports avec les processus stochastiques associés ; il pose divers problèmes algébriques non résolus.

Nous nous occupons ici du cas où X^+ admet des *mots neutres*, c'est-à-dire où il existe des mots $h \neq 1$ ayant même image syntaxique $h\xi$ que le mot vide 1 ; celle-ci est évidemment l'élément neutre du monoïde syntaxique S. Par conséquent, il existe des mots neutres non triviaux dès que S a une sous groupe U (des éléments inversibles ou unités) non-trivial. Formellement, h est un mot neutre ssi les relations $ab \in X^*$ et $ahb \in X^*$ sont équivalentes pour chaque paire de mots a, b de A^*. Cette hypothèse a une signification intuitive immédiate dans le cadre de la théorie du signal puisqu'elle exprime que le bruit sur la ligne est tel qu'on ne peut pas détecter la présence de segments égaux à h qui se trouveraient à l'intérieur des messages. En particulier, le mot $h = c^p$, où p est positif et c est une lettre, est neutre quand les dispositifs physiques ont la propriété que la longueur d'un segment $c \ldots c \ldots c$ formé de la répetition de cette lettre, ne peut être déterminée que modulo p (on pourrait dire qu'il s'agit d'un "bruit modulo p"). L'étude de ce problème se rattache aussi à la théorie des polynômes cyclotomiques.

Notre résultat principal concerne la reconnaissabilité de X^*, au sens de S. Eilenberg [4], c'est-à-dire la finitude de son monoïde syntaxique S . Comme on le sait, le théorème de Kleene affirme que X et X^* sont simultanément reconnaissables ou non. Nous établissons ici que, quand X admet des mots neutres non triviaux, *il est reconnaissable ssi l'un de ceux-ci,* soit h , *n'est pas complétable dans* X , c'est-à-dire si l'intersection de X avec A^*hA^* est vide. Un résultat plus fort, basé sur l'existence d'un mot $h \neq 1$ (non nécessairement neutre) tel que l'idéal à gauche A^*h rencontre le stabilisateur de chacun des états de l'automate minimal de X^*, nous a paru trop technique pour que sa preuve mérite d'être donnée ici. On remarquera que, de façon générale, si X^* est reconnaissable, il existe au moins un mot incomplétable dans X mais que, réciproquement, cette hypothèse implique seulement que si tout mot est complétable dans X^*, la densité asymptotique de ce dernier (au sens de Berstel [1] soit non nulle pour toute distribution de probabilités positive sur A .

Il est clair que l'existence de mots non complétables est assurée dans le cas particulier où X est *localement fini,* en ce sens que pour chaque sous-alphabet fini B de A , il n'y a qu'un nombre fini de mots de X dont toutes les lettres sont dans B^*. Dans ce cas, le sous-monoïde X^* est donc reconnaissable dès qu'il possède des mots neutres ; un phénomène curieux est que, si *aucun* des mots neutres n'est complétable dans X (donc en particulier si X est localement fini), le sous-groupe U de S est nécessairement cyclique. Cette situation algébrique correspond à celle du "bruit modulo p" perturbant la détermination des longueurs des segments c...c...c comme on l'a indiqué plus haut et où le paramètre p est évidemment l'ordre de U .

La technique de preuve fait intervenir la représentation de A par un monoïde de relations (c'est-à-dire un automate non déterministe) possèdant un sous groupe *transitif* sur les états. Réciproquement tout monoïde fini de ce type est monoïde syntaxique d'un sous-monoïde X^* ayant des mots neutres incomplétables dans X . Le cas des codes correspond à celui où le monoïde de relations est non-ambigu, au sens de J.M. Böe [2].

Notre second résultat affirme que si X^* (admettant des mots neutres) est engendré librement par un ensemble X localement fini, *le maximum des longueurs des mots de* X *est précisément l'ordre* p *du groupe cyclique* U . Une illustration de ce fait est fournie par la très remarquable famille de codes découverte par A. Restivo, à partir d'hypothèses toutes différentes [9].

Enfin un argument de comptage très simple donne une caractérisation des sous-monoïdes X^* (possèdant des mots neutres) qui sont engendrés par un code X *maximal* (c'est-à-dire qui ne soit pas contenu dans un autre code) : une condition nécessaire et suffisante pour que X ait ces propriétés est que chacune des relations du monoïde construit plus haut ait exactement p entrées non vides, où p est le nombre des états sur lesquels les relations sont définies. Ceci constitue une généralisation d'un fait qui serait banal si l'hypothèse qu'il existe des mots neutres non-triviaux était remplacée par celle que X soit un code préfixe. Cette remarque a une application immédiate au problème de la transmission sur une ligne affectée d'un "bruit modulo p".

Monoïdes de relations

1. Transitivité.

Soit Q un ensemble fini et R le monoïde des relations binaires sur Q ; il est commode d'appeler *états* les éléments de Q . Un monoïde de relations sur Q est un sous-monoïde de R ; en particulier son élément neutre est l'égalité sur Q . On remarquera qu'un sous-semigroupe de R peut être un monoïde (i.e. possèder un élément neutre) sans être, dans notre terminologie, un monoïde de relations ; nous dirons que c'est un semigroupe de relations.

Un monoïde M de relations est *transitif* si pour tout couple (q,q') d'états il existe au moins un m dans M contenant (q,q'). On dit que M est *très transitif* si il existe une *permutation* m dans M contenant (q,q') ; un monoïde de relations M est donc très transitif ssi son sous-groupe est transitif. La proposition suivante montre qu'on n'obtient pas une définition très différente en considérant des semigroupes de relations et sera utile pour la suite :

Proposition 1. Soit S *un semigroupe de relations sur un ensemble fini* Q *possèdant un élément neutre* e *et dont le sous-groupe est transitif. Alors* e *est une équivalence et* S *induit sur le quotient de* Q *par* e *un monoïde de relations très transitif isomorphe à* S .

Démonstration. Tout d'abord la relation e est transitive du fait que e est idempotent: si (q,q') et (q',q") sont dans e , alors (q,q") est dans $e^2 = e$.

Maintenant pour tout q dans Q , il existe un élément inversible s de S contenant (q,q) ; comme Q est fini, l'élément s est d'ordre fini, soit n ;

on a alors : $(q,q) \in s^n = e$, et ceci montre que e est réflexive. Enfin, si $(q,q') \in e$, soit s un élément inversible de S tel que $(q,q') \in s$; si n est l'ordre de s, on a alors $(q',q) \in s\,s^{n-1} = e$, puisque $(q,q) \in es = s$. Ceci montre que e est symétrique et démontre la propriété.

2. Stabilisateurs.

Soit M un monoïde de relations sur Q ; le *stabilisateur* d'un état q de Q est le sous monoïde P de M formé des relations qui contiennent le couple (q,q).

Proposition 2. Si M *est un monoïde de relations très transitif, il est le monoïde syntaxique de chacun des stabilisateurs des états.*

Démonstration. Soit P le stabilisateur de q et supposons que deux éléments m et n de M aient même image dans le monoïde syntaxique de P. Si un couple (q_1, q_2) d'états est dans m, soient g_1 et g_2 des éléments inversibles de M tels que $(q, q_1) \in g_1$ et $(q_2, q) \in g_2$. Alors (q,q) appartient à $g_1 m g_2$ et donc à $g_1 n g_2$; mais ceci implique que $(q_1, q_2) \in n$ et nous avons ainsi montré que $m = n$, ce qui signifie que M est le monoïde syntaxique de P.

Cette proposition montre que si ξ est une représentation de A^* par un monoïde de relations très transitif alors le monoïde syntaxique du stabilisateur dans A^* d'un état est égal à $A^*\xi$.

3. Ambiguité.

Reprenant la terminologie introduite par J.M. Böe, on dira qu'un monoïde de relations M sur un ensemble Q est *non-ambigü* si pour chaque m et n dans M et chaque couple (q,q') dans mn, il existe un *unique* état q'' tel que $(q,q'') \in m$ et $(q'',q') \in n$. Cette condition est évidemment remplie en particulier par les monoïdes d'applications et donc par le sous-groupe d'un monoïde de relations.

On sait que si ξ est une représentation de A^* par un monoïde de relations transitif, l'image réciproque par ξ du stabilisateur d'un état est un sous-monoïde *libre* X^* ssi ce monoïde de relations est non-ambigü.

4. Exemple.

Quand $\mathrm{Card}(Q) = 2$, le monoïde de relations M (resp. M') engendré par les deux permutations de Q et une relation ayant une seule entrée non vide (resp. une seule entrée vide) est très transitif par construction. On notera que M et M' sont des monoïdes isomorphes mais qu'ils ne sont pas équivalents en tant que monoïdes de relations ; de plus M (mais non M') est un exemple de relations non-ambigü.

Le cas général

Reprenant les notations utilisées dans l'introduction, nous établissons l'énoncé suivant, où on dit que X^* est reconnu par un monoïde de relations pour exprimer qu'il existe une représentation de A^* par un monoïde fini de relations telle que X^* soit le stabilisateur d'un état.

Théorème 1. *Une condition nécessaire et suffisante pour que* X^* *soit reconnu par un monoïde très transitif est l'existence d'un mot neutre incomplétable dans* X.

Démonstration. Supposons d'abord que X^* soit le stabilisateur de l'état 0 pour une représentation ξ de A^* par un monoïde de relations très transitif M, sur l'ensemble $Q = \{0, 1, \dots, p-1\}$. Notons G le sous-groupe de M et définissons par récurrence les mots $w_o, w_1, \dots, w_p$ en posant : $w_o = 1$ et $w_{i+1} = w_i u_i$, où u_i est un mot non vide de $G\xi^{-1}$ tel que : $(i,0) \in w_{i+1}\xi$. Le mot $f = w_p$ est alors incomplétable dans X puisque tous g,h dans A^*, si gfh est dans X^*, alors $(0,0) \in gfh\xi$ et il existe donc i et j dans Q tels que : $(0,i) \in g\xi$, $(i,j) \in h\xi$ et $(j,0) \in h\xi$. Mais on a : $h = w_{i+1}r$ et, comme $(i,0) \in w_{i+1}\xi$, et que $h\xi \in G$, on obtient $(0,j) \in r$; ceci montre que les mots gw_{i+1} et rh sont dans X^* et donc que gfh ne peut être dans X. Maintenant comme G est fini, f a une puissance, soit f^n, qui est l'élément neutre de G. Le mot f^n est alors un mot neutre incomplétable dans X.

Pour établir la réciproque, nous supposons l'existence d'un mot neutre $f \in X^*$ qui est incomplétable dans X, et nous notons R (resp. L) l'ensemble des facteurs droits (resp. gauches) propres de f.

Associons à tout mot u de A^* la partie $u\rho$ de $R \times L$ définie par :

$$(r, l) \in u\rho \Leftrightarrow r u l \in X^*$$

Notons maintenant π la partie de $L \times R$ définie par :

$$(l, r) \in \pi \Leftrightarrow l r = f$$

et démontrons la formule suivante, où les points notent des produits de relations :

$$\forall u, v \in A^*, \; uv\rho = u\rho . \pi . v\rho$$

Tout d'abord, si (r,l) appartient à $u\rho . \pi . v\rho$, il existe par définition (l', r') dans π tels que : $r u l', r' v l \in X^*$ et $f = l'r'$; on a alors $r' u f v l' \in X^*$, d'où $r u v l \in X^*$, du fait que f est un mot neutre, et enfin (r,l) appartient à $uv\rho$. Maintenant, si (r,l) appartient à $uv\rho$, alors $r u v l \in X^*$ et donc aussi $r u f v l \in X^*$; mais comme f est incomplétable dans X, cela implique l'existence d'une factorisation de f en : $f = l'r'$ telle que : $r u l', r' v l \in X^*$, ce qui exprime le fait que $(r,l) \in u\rho . \pi . v\rho$.

Ceci montre que l'application $\xi : u \in A^* \to \pi . u\rho$ (resp. $u\rho\pi$) est un homomorphisme de A^* sur un semigroupe de relations sur l'ensemble *fini* L (resp. R). Le monoïde $M = \xi A^*$ est donc fini et ξf est son élément neutre (mais n'est pas en général l'égalité sur L) ; le sous-groupe (des éléments inversibles) de M est de plus transitif : remarquons en effet tout d'abord que, du fait que M est fini, tout conjugué $g = r l$ de $f = l r$ est encore dans X^* puisqu'ils ont même image par ξ ; ainsi, pour tous l, l' dans L, si $f = l r = l' r'$, alors $r l r' l'$ est dans X et le couple (l,l') appartient donc à $l r' \xi$, qui est inversible dans M. Ainsi, d'après la proposition 1 la relation $f \xi$ est une équivalence et le monoïde de relations N induit par M sur le quotient de L par cette équivalence est très transitif. Enfin, l'image réciproque par ξ du stabilisateur de la classe de $1 \in L$ est égale à X^* puisqu'un élément de M stabilise 1 ssi il stabilise tous les éléments de sa classe.

L'énoncé suivant donne des conditions, en apparence beaucoup plus faibles, qui équivalent en fait à celles du théorème précédent. Leur intérêt nous semble être le fait qu'elles ne portent que sur des sous-alphabets finis de A et que chacune d'elles est, en un certain sens, unilatérale ; nous ommettons d'en donner ici la preuve.

Proposition 3. Une condition nécessaire et suffisante pour que X^* *soit reconnu par un monoïde très transitif est l'existence d'un mot* $h \in A^+$ *tel que pour tout sous alphabet fini* B *de* A *satisfaisant* $h \in B^*$ *les conditions suivantes soient remplies :*

(1) L'idéal à gauche B^*h *rencontre le stabilisateur de chacun des états de l'automate minimal reconnaissant* $Y^* = X^* \cap B^*$: $\forall\, b \in B^*, \exists g \in B^*: bb' \in Y^* \Leftrightarrow bhgb' \in Y^*$

(2) Pour tout $b \in B^*$, *il existe un entier* n *tel que* bh^n *soit incomplétable à droite dans* X : $bh^n B^* \cap X = \emptyset$.

Remarque 1. Le théorème 1 implique, sous l'hypothèse supplémentaire que X est un code, que X peut être reconnu par un monoïde de relations non-ambigu isomorphe à son monoïde syntaxique. Cet énoncé est, en fait, vrai de tous les codes reconnaissables, suivant le très important théorème de [3].

Sous monoïdes finiment engendrés

Nous en venons maintenant au cas où l'ensemble X est localement fini, c'est-à-dire que l'intersection de X avec B^* est finie pour tout sous alphabet fini B de A. Tout d'abord, d'après le théorème 1, X^* est alors reconnaissable s'il possède des mots neutres ; en effet, si $h \in A^+$ est un mot neutre il possède une puissance, soit h^n qui est incomplétable dans X, et h^n est encore lui-même neutre. On pourra donc, sans perte de généralité, supposer que A est fini ainsi que X.

Nous établissons le résultat suivant, dans lequel U désigne le sous-groupe (des éléments inversibles) du monoïde syntaxique de X^* et $|X|$ la borne supérieure des longueurs des mots de X :

Théorème 2. Si X *est fini,* U *est cyclique d'ordre au plus égal à* $|X|$.

Démonstration. Tout d'abord, les hypothèses du théorème 1 étant satisfaites, il existe une représentation ξ de A^* par un monoïde M de relations très transitif reconnaissant X^* ; d'après la proposition 2, M est isomorphe au monoïde syntaxique de X^* et U est donc isomorphe au groupe transitif formé des permutations contenues dans M. Notons B l'intersection de l'alphabet A avec $U\xi^{-1}$; la restriction de ξ à B^* est une représentation de B^* par un monoïde de relations qui est évidemment non ambigu et qui reconnaît l'intersection de X^* avec B^* ; la preuve suivra du lemme ci-dessous, dont nous ferons encore usage plus bas :

Lemme. Soit ξ *une représentation de* B^* *par un monoïde transitif de relations non ambigu sur un ensemble* Q *et* Y^* *le stabilisateur de l'état* 0 . *Alors* Y *est fini ssi il existe un ordre sur* Q *tel que pour toute lettre* $a \in A$, *on ait :* $(q,q') \in a\xi$ *seulement si* $q \leq q'$ *ou si* $q = 0$.

Démonstration. La condition est évidemment suffisante puisqu'elle implique que tout mot de Y ait une longueur au plus égale à $\mathrm{Card}(Q)$. Réciproquement, il nous suffit de vérifier que la relation sur $Q\backslash 0$ définie par $(q,q') \in a\xi$ pour au moins une lettre a A a une fermeture transitive antisymétrique. Supposons donc qu'il existe $q_1,\ldots, q_k \in Q\backslash 0$ et $a_1,\ldots, a_k \in A$ tels que : $(q_1, q_2) \in a_1\xi,\ldots, (q_k, q_1) \in a_k\xi$; soient $f,g \in A^*$ deux mots tels que : $(q,q_1) \in f\xi$, $(q_1, q) \in g\xi$ et que cette relation ne soit vraie pour aucun facteur droit (resp. gauche) de f (resp. g). On a alors $f(a_1 a_2\ldots a_k)^* g \subset Y$ puisque le monoïde $A^*\xi$ est non ambigu, en contradiction avec l'hypothèse que Y est fini.

D'après le lemme, toutes les permutations $b\xi$, pour b dans B doivent être égales à une même permutation circulaire de l'ensemble de tous les états ; ceci montre que le groupe U est cyclique d'ordre $p = \mathrm{Card}(Q)$ et que B^p est inclus dans X , ce qui achève de prouver le théorème.

Dans le cas où X est un code, l'énoncé précédent peut être précisé ainsi :

Corollaire. Si X *est un code fini, le groupe* U *est cyclique d'ordre* $|X|$.

Démonstration. En effet, d'après le lemme précédent, tout mot de X est de longueur au plus égale à $p = \mathrm{Card}(Q)$ et si b est une lettre dont l'image syntaxique est dans U , on a $b^p \in X$.

Remarque 2. Si X n'est pas un code, il peut contenir des mots de longueur supérieure strictement à l'ordre de U comme le montre l'exemple suivant : soit $A = \{a, b\}$ et $X = a^p \cup \{ a^i b a^j \mid 0 \leq i,j \leq p-1 \}$; on a alors $X = (a^p)^* \cup A^* b A^*$,

a^p est un mot neutre pour X^*, le groupe U est cyclique d'ordre p et $|X| = 2p-1$. Il serait intéressant de donner une borne à la longueur des mots de X en fonction de p .

Une propriété des monoïdes de relations non ambigus

Nommons Valence d'une relation r sur un ensemble Q son cardinal (en tant que partie de $Q \times Q$) ; un monoïde de relations sur Q peut être non-ambigu sans que tous ses éléments non-nuls aient la même valence ; cependant, dans le cas des monoïdes très transitifs, on obtient le résultat suivant :

Théorème 3. Soit M *un monoïde de relations très transitif sur* Q *ne contenant pas la relation vide. Alors* M *est non-ambigu ssi tous ses éléments ont une valence égale à* Card(Q).

Démonstration. On nommera valence d'une matrice m à éléments dans N la somme de tous ses éléments, notée $|m|$, et, pour toute relation r sur Q , on notera $\bar{r}$ la matrice à éléments dans $\mathbb{N}$ égaux à 0 ou 1, indexée par Q dont le support est r ; la valence de r est encore égale à $|\bar{r}|$.

Supposons d'abord que tous les éléments de M aient la même valeur p et montrons que M est non-ambigu : cela revient à montrer que pour tous éléments m,m' de M , la matrice $\bar{m}\,\bar{m}'$ n'a que des éléments égaux à 0 ou 1. Supposons donc par l'absurde que $\bar{m}\,\bar{m}'$ a au moins un élément égal à 2 et calculons la somme $s = \sum_{u \in U} |m u m'|$, où U est le sous-groupe de M ; d'une part $s = p\,\mathrm{Card}(U)$ puisque chacun des $m u m'$ a une valence égale à p . D'autre part, s est strictement inférieur à la somme $t = \sum_{u \in U} |\bar{m}\,\bar{u}\,\bar{m}'|$ puisque : $|m\,m'| < |\bar{m}\,\bar{m}'|$.
Or, on a aussi $t = |\sum_{u \in U} \bar{m}\,\bar{u}\,\bar{m}'| = |\bar{m}\,K\,\bar{m}'|$ où K est la matrice dont tous les éléments sont égaux à $q = \frac{1}{p}\,\mathrm{Card}(U)$, puisque U est transitif. Ceci montre que $t = p\,\mathrm{Card}(U)$, en contradiction avec le fait que $s < t$.

La réciproque est conséquence directe du lemme ci-dessous :

<u>*Lemme*</u>. *Soit* M *un monoïde de relations très transitif sur un ensemble* Q . *Si* M *contient un élément de valence strictement inférieur à* $p = \mathrm{Card}(Q)$, *alors* M *contient la relation vide.*

Si M *contient un élément de valence strictement supérieur à* p , *alors* M *est ambigu.*

<u>*Démonstration*</u>. Soit m un élément de M et K la matrice dont tous les éléments sont égaux à 1. Nous évaluons de deux manières la valence de la matrice $(K\bar{m})^n$, pour un entier n quelconque. D'une part : $|(K\bar{m})^n| = p|m|^n$ puisque $|K\bar{m}| = p\,|m|$ et que $(K\bar{m})^2 = |m|\,K\bar{m}$.

D'autre part : $|(K\bar{m})^n| = \sum_{u_i \in U} \frac{1}{q^n} |\bar{u}_1 \bar{m} \ldots \bar{u}_n \bar{m}|$ puisque la matrice K est égale à $\frac{1}{q} \sum_{u \in U} \bar{u}$.

Tout d'abord, si M ne contient pas la relation vide, chacun des termes de la forme $\bar{u}_1 \bar{m} \ldots \bar{u}_n \bar{m}$ a une valence non nulle et cela implique que $|(K\bar{m})^n| \geq p^n$; on en déduit que l'inégalité $|m|^n \geq p^{n-1}$ est vraie pour tout entier n et cela implique que $|m| \geq p$.

Maintenant, si M est inambigu, chacun des termes de la somme a une valence au plus égale à p^2 et ceci implique que $|(K\bar{m})^n| \leq p^{n+2}$; on en déduit que l'inégalité $|m|^n \leq p^{n+1}$ est vraie pour tout entier n , ce qui implique $|m| \leq p$.

Nous revenons maintenant à un sous monoïde X^* de A^* possèdant des mots neutres incomplétables dans X c'est-à-dire, d'après le théorème 1 que X^* est reconnu par un monoïde M de relations très transitif sur un ensemble Q ; on notera p, comme ci-dessus, le cardinal de Q et on désignera par $|f|$ la valence de la relation sur Q définie par le mot $f \in A^*$.

<u>*Corollaire 1*</u>. *Tout mot de* A^* *est complétable dans* X^* *ssi* $|f| \geq p$ *pour tout mot* $f \in A^*$.

En effet, pour que tout mot soit complétable dans X^*, il faut et il suffit que le monoïde M ne contienne pas la relation vide et cet énoncé est donc une reformulation de la première assertion du lemme.

Corollaire 2. Si X^* *est librement engendré par* X *, on a* $|f| \leq p$ *pour tout* $f \in A^*$.

Cet énoncé est une reformulation de la deuxième assertion du lemme puisque X^* est librement engendré par X ssi le monoïde M est non-ambigu. Enfin, on sait que si X est un code reconnaissable, alors tout mot de A^* est complétable dans X^* ssi X est un code maximal (on en trouvera une preuve en [4] ou [6]). On peut donc reformuler le théorème 3 de la façon suivante :

Corollaire 3. X *est un code maximal ssi pour tout* $f \in A^*$, *on a* $|f| = p$.

Cet énoncé a une forme plus frappante dans le cas où X est un code fini puisque, dans ce cas, si a est une lettre dont une puissance est un mot neutre, la valeur de $f \in A^*$ est le nombre de mots de la forme $a^i f a^j$ qui sont dans X^* avec $0 \leq i,j \leq p-1$. Cette formulation fournit une analogie remarquable avec le cas particulier des codes préfixes maximaux où la condition que le nombre de mots de cette forme soit égal à p est trivialement vérifiée.

Références

1 BERSTEL, J.- Sur la densité asymptotique des langages formels, in *Automata Languages and Programming* (M. Nivat ed.) North Holland (1972) 345-58.

2 BOE, J.M.- *Représentations des monoïdes : applications à la théorie des codes*, Thèse de 3ème cycle, Univ. des Sciences et Techniques du Languedoc (1976).

3 BOE, J.M., BOYAT, J. CESARI, Y., LACHENY, A. et M. VINCENT, Automates et monoïdes syntaxiques des sous-monoïdes libres, à paraître dans *Information and Control*.

4 EILENBERG, S.- *Automata, Languages and Machines*, Vol. A, Academic Press (1974).

5 LALLEMENT, G.- On regular semigroups as syntactic monoids of prefix codes, à paraître dans *Theoretical Computer Science*.

6 NIVAT, M.- Eléments de la théorie générale des codes, in *Automata Theory* (E.R. Caianiello ed.) Academic Press (1966).

7 Mc NAUGHTON, R. and PAPERT, S.- *Counter-Free Automata*, MIT Press (1971).

8 PERROT, J-F.- *Contribution à l'Etude des Monoîdes Syntaxiques et de Certains Groupes Associés aux Automates Finis*, Thèse, Paris (1972).

9 RESTIVO, A.- On codes having no finite completions, in *Automata, Languages and Programming* (S. Michaelson ed.) Edinburgh University Press (1976) 38-44.

A POLYNOMIAL-TIME TEST FOR THE DEADLOCK-FREEDOM OF COMPUTER SYSTEMS

T. Kameda

Abstract

We call a system of n processes sharing m reusable resources deadlock-free, if and only if the allocation policy which automatically grants any request that can be granted with currently free resource units never leads to a deadlock. The best known test for deadlock-freedom is essentially enumerative. We present a test employing a network-flow technique, which works in time bounded by $O(n^3m)$.

A Polynomial-Time Test for the Deadlock-
Freedom of Computer Systems

1. Introduction

Consider a system consisting of $n(\geq 2)$ processes, $P_1, P_2, \ldots, P_n$, sharing $m(\geq 1)$ resources (or resource types), $R_1, R_2, \ldots, R_m$, which are serially reusable [6]. r_j will denote the number of available units of R_j $(1 \leq j \leq m)$. The so-called deadly embrace or deadlock problem was pointed out by Dijkstra [3] and has since been investigated under different assumptions [2, 8]. A deadlock can occur in a system in which processes do not release the resources they hold unless their pending requests for additional resource units are granted. It is a situation where the progress of a set of processes is blocked forever

*Department of Electrical Engineering, University of Waterloo, Waterloo, Ontario, Canada N2L 3G1. This work was supported by the National Research Council of Canada under Grant No. A4315.

because of the lack of resource units to satisfy the request of any process in the set. In order to prevent deadlocks one could invoke an avoidance algorithm such as that of Habermann [5] or Holt [8], each time a new request occurs, to make sure that all processes can run to completion. One can do without an avoidance algorithm, granting requests, if possible, as they occur, provided there are sufficient number of resource units. If this allocation policy never causes a deadlock, we call such a system deadlock-free (or secure [8]). As in [5] we shall assume that the maximum resource requirement of each process is known a priori. This is a reasonable assumption, particularly, on system processes, and for the set of system processes the deadlock-freedom is a very desirable feature, dispensing with the need for deadlock avoidance algorithm or recovery from deadlock [2]. Let c_{ij} be the maximum number of units of R_j that are going to be used by P_i at some time. If they satisfy

$$\sum_{i=1}^{n} c_{ij} \leq r_j \quad (1 \leq j \leq m) \tag{1}$$

then any request can be granted automatically and therefore the system is deadlock-free [9]. The condition (1) is thus a sufficient condition for deadlock-freedom. Shaw [10] states that no nonenumerative algorithm is known for testing if a given system is deadlock-free. (His terminology for deadlock-free is safe.) We present below an algorithm which works within time $O(n^3m)$. For the meaning of the O( ) notation, the reader is referred to [1].

2. Deadlock

Let $N = \{1, 2, \ldots, n\}$ and $M = \{1, 2, \ldots, m\}$ be the sets of indices of the processes and resource types, respectively. At any given time a_{ij} will denote the number of units of R_j allocated to P_i, where $i \varepsilon N$ and $j \varepsilon M$. Let b_{ij} be a non-negative integer indicating the number of additional units of R_j requested by P_i. Then by the definition of c_{ij}, we have

$$a_{ij} + b_{ij} \leq c_{ij} \quad (i \varepsilon N \text{ and } j \varepsilon M) \tag{2}$$

Note that the number of currently free units of R_j is given by $r_j - \Sigma_{i\varepsilon N}\, a_{ij}$. In a given state represented by $\{a_{ij}\}$ and $\{b_{ij}\}$, the system is said to be deadlocked (or the state is a deadlock state) if for each $i\varepsilon N$, either

(i) P_i is completed (in this case $a_{ij} = b_{ij} = 0$), or

(ii) there exists $j\varepsilon M$ such that $b_{ij} > r_j - \Sigma_{k\varepsilon N}\, a_{kj}$

and there is at least one non-completed process. The condition (ii) above means that the process P_i is requesting more units of R_j than are currently free. In this case we say R_j is involved in the deadlock. We assume that the progress of a process is blocked as long as it has a pending request for additional resource units.

Example: Consider a system consisting of two processes, P_1 and P_2, and one type of resource, R_1. Let $r_1 = c_{11} = c_{21} = 5$. Suppose the system has entered a state where $a_{11} = 1$, $a_{21} = 3$, $b_{11} = 3$, and $b_{21} = 2$. Since there is only $r_1 - (a_{11} + a_{21}) = 1$ free unit and both b_{11} and b_{21} are larger than 1, the system is deadlocked in this state and therefore it is not deadlock-free.

Since our test of deadlock-freedom will involve a search for a deadlock state, it will be helpful to restrict the scope of search. In the above example we can "absorb" the free unit into P_1 by changing the state to $a_{11} = 2$, $a_{21} = 3$, $b_{11} = b_{21} = 2$, and can further reduce the number of additional units requested to $b_{11} = b_{21} = 1$, without changing the fact that the resulting state is still a deadlock state. The following lemma can be proved by generalizing and formalizing the above argument.

LEMMA 1: For any positive integers n and m, a system of n processes and m resource types is not deadlock-free iff it has a deadlock state in which there is no free unit of any resource involved in the deadlock, and each non-completed process has a pending request for exactly one additional resource unit.

Proof: The "if" part is trivial. In order to prove the "only if" part, let a deadlock state be represented by $\{a_{ij} | i\varepsilon N,\ j\varepsilon M\}$ and $\{b_{ij} | i\varepsilon N,\ j\varepsilon M\}$. For each non-completed process P_i in this state, pick an index $j = f(i)$ such that $b_{ij} > r_j - \Sigma_{k\,\varepsilon N}\, a_{kj}$. If $x = r_j - \Sigma_{k\,\varepsilon N} a_{kj} > 0$, then increas a_{ij} by x and change b_{ij} to 1, unless $b_{ij} = 1$ already. Finally, change $b_{ij'}$ to 0 for all j′ such that $j' \neq f(i)$ for any $i\varepsilon N$. It is easy to see that the resulting state is a deadlock state since each non-completed process P_i has a request for one more unit of $R_{f(i)}$. The order in which the above modification is carried out influences the resulting state, but the resulting state is always a deadlock state. Q.E.D.

3. Formulation as Network Flow Problem

We now view the problem as a network flow problem [4], as illustrated in Fig. 1. There is a node for each process P_i ($i\varepsilon N$) and for each resource R_j ($j\varepsilon M$), in addition to the source and sink nodes. There is an arc from each "resource node" R_j to each "process node" P_i, where $i\varepsilon N$ and $j\varepsilon M$. Further, there is an arc from each "process node" to the sink, and also from the source to each "resource node". The capacity of the arc from R_j to P_i is 1 if $c_{ij} > 0$ and 0 otherwise. The capacities of the other arcs depend on the set of non-completed processes under consideration as described below.

Let $I \subset N$ be the index set of non-completed processes. We define the deficiency of R_j associated with I by

$$d_j(I) = \max\,\{0,\ \Sigma_{i\varepsilon I} c_{ij} - r_j\}$$

Let $y = |\{P_i |\ i\varepsilon I \text{ and } c_{ij} > 0\}|$ be the number of processes indexed by I, which may request R_j. If $d_j(I) \geq y$, then a maximum of y processes of $\{P_i |\ i\varepsilon I \text{ and } c_{ij} > 0\}$ may be blocked due to lack of units of R_j.

This "maximum blocking" situation arises if $a_{ij} = c_{ij} - 1$ and $b_{ij} = 1$ for each $i\varepsilon I$ such that $c_{ij} > 0$. If, on the other hand, $d_j(I) < y$, then a maximum of $d_j(I)$ processes out of $\{P_i | i\varepsilon I$ and $c_{ij} > 0\}$ may be blocked due to lack of units of R_j.

Now for a given index set $I \subset N$, the capacity of the arc from each "process node" $P_i(i\varepsilon I)$ to the sink in Fig. 1 is 1. Other arcs to the sink all have capacity 0. The capacity of the arc from the source to each "resource node" R_j is $d_j(I)$.

THEOREM 1: The system under consideration is not deadlock-free if there is an index set $I \subset N$ such that the maximum integral flow in the network of Fig. 1 is $|I|$.

Proof: Suppose the maximum deficiency flow is $|I|$ and consider a maximum flow pattern. For each $i\varepsilon I$, there exists exactly one $j\varepsilon M$ such that there is a flow of 1 unit from the "resource node" R_j to the "process node" P_i. This corresponds to a situation where P_i is blocked due to the pending request for $b_{ij} = 1$ unit of R_j.

We now turn to the proof of "only if" part. By Lemma 1 we may assume that there is a deadlock state in which $b_{if(i)} = 1$ and $b_{ij} = 0$ $(j \neq f(i))$ for each $i\varepsilon I$ and $\Sigma_{i\varepsilon I}\, a_{ij} - r_j = 0$ for each R_j involved in the deadlock. This state corresponds to a maximum flow pattern such that there is a unit flow from node $R_{f(i)}$ to node P_i for each $i\varepsilon I$. The flow out of node R_j is:

$$
\begin{aligned}
|\{i\varepsilon I|\ f(i) = j\}| &= \Sigma_{i\varepsilon I}\, b_{ij} \\
&= \Sigma_{i\varepsilon I}\, b_{ij} + (\Sigma_{i\varepsilon I}\, a_{ij} - r_j) \\
&= \Sigma_{i\varepsilon I}\, (b_{ij} + a_{ij}) - r_j \\
&\leq \Sigma_{i\varepsilon I}\, c_{ij} - r_j = d_j(I)
\end{aligned}
$$

Therefore this flow pattern is feasible. Q.E.D.

The following theorem is useful in order to perform efficient test for deadlock-freedom.

THEOREM 2: Suppose the maximum flow in the network of Fig. 1 is less than $|I|$ and no flow passes through a node P_i $(i\varepsilon I)$ in a maximum flow pattern. Then no set $I' \subset I$, where $i\varepsilon I'$, can be the index set of the non-completed processes of a deadlock state.

Proof: The case $I' = I$ follows from Theorem 1 and therefore we take I' to be a proper subset of I. Assume, contrary to the assertion of the theorem, that in the network with capacities determined by the set I' there is a flow pattern F_1 with flow equal to $|I'|$ and that a maximum flow pattern F_2 in the network with capacities determined by the set I has flow less than $|I|$. We shall show that this leads to a contradiction by demonstrating that F_2 cannot be a maximum flow pattern. Now eliminate from F_2 all flows (from source to sink) that pass through any P_i $(i \varepsilon I')$ and replace them by the flow pattern F_1. We want to show that the new flow pattern F_3 thus obtained is a feasible flow pattern with flow larger than that of F_2. To this end we must show that at each "resource node" R_j, there is enough "supply" of deficiency flow from the source to take care of all the flow out of R_j. Recall that $d_j(I')$ is

either 0 or $d_j(I') = \Sigma_{i \varepsilon I'} c_{ij} - r_j$. If $d_j(I') = 0$, then there **is** no flow out of R_j in F_1, and therefore the above modification of flow pattern does not require additional "supply" of $d_j(I)$. So we now assume $d_j(I') > 0$. In the network with capacities determined by I, the capacity of the arc from the source to the node R_j is

$$\begin{aligned} d_j(I) &= \Sigma_{i \varepsilon I} c_{ij} - r_j \\ &= d_j(I') + \Sigma_{i \varepsilon I-I'} c_{ij} \end{aligned}$$

In F_1 the flow out of R_j is no more than $d_j(I')$ and in F_2 the flow from R_j to the nodes $\{P_i | i \varepsilon I-I'\}$ is no more than $\Sigma_{i \varepsilon I-I'} c_{ij}$. Therefore F_3 is a feasible flow, since R_j can supply up to $d_j(I)$ units of flow. Since a flow passes through each node P_i $(i \varepsilon I')$ in F_3, therefore F_3 has a larger flow than F_2, a contradiction. Q.E.D.

4. Algorithm

In this section we shall present an algorithm for testing the deadlock-freedom of any given system, based on Theorems 1 and 2. We assume that the reader is familiar with methods for finding a maximum flow in a network [4]. We start with the network of Fig. 1 with $I = N$. We assume the arcs with capacity 0 have been eliminated.

Algorithm: (Initially $I = N$.)

1. Find a maximum integral flow pattern in the network. If the maximum flow is equal to $|I|$, then stop (the system is not deadlock-free).
2. Eliminate the process nodes through which there is no flow, together with arcs entering or leaving them. For each $j \varepsilon M$ change the capacity of the arc from the source to node R_j to $d_j(I)$, where I is redefined to be the index set of the remaining processes. Eliminate the arcs out of the source with capacity 0.
3. If there is no remaining arc out of the source, then stop (the system is deadlock-free). Otherwise go to step 1.

Examples: Consider a system with three processes, $\{P_1, P_2, P_3\}$, and two resource types, $\{R_1, R_2\}$, where there are $r_1 = 1$ and $r_2 = 2$ units of R_1 and R_2, respectively. The maximum requirements are given by $c_{11} = c_{21} = c_{22} = 1$ and $c_{32} = 2$ (all other $c_{ij} = 0$). For the initial index set $I_o = N = \{1, 2, 3\}$, we have the network of Fig. 2(a). Following step 1 of the Algorithm, we find a maximum flow pattern which is indicated in Fig. 2(a) by the thick lines. Since there is no flow passing through the process node P_3, step 2 generates the network shown in Fig. 2(b), corresponding to the index set $I_1 = \{1,2\}$. The test in step 3 is negative, so we go back to step 1. A maximum flow pattern found by step 1 is indicated in Fig. 2(b). Step 2 now eliminates node P_1, generating the network of Fig. 2(c). Since there is no arc out of the source the system has been determined to be deadlock-free (step 3).

Now let us modify the system slightly by changing c_{12} from 0 to 1. The corresponding network is shown in Fig. 3 for $I = \{1, 2, 3\}$. In this case step 1 finds a maximum flow pattern with flow equal to $|I| = 3$, indicating the existence of a deadlock state. In fact the system can get deadlocked in the state defined by $a_{11} = a_{22} = 0$, $a_{12} = a_{21} = a_{32} = 1$, $b_{12} = b_{21} = 0$, and $b_{11} = b_{22} = b_{32} = 1$.

Analysis of the Algorithm

Suppose there are e arcs in the initial network, where $I = N$. The time required to find an augementing path [4] is bounded by $O(e)$. In order to find a maximum flow pattern in step 1 of the Algorithm we must find at most n augmenting paths. Therefore each time step 1 is invoked, we need to spend at most $O(ne)$ time. The worst case, as far as the time requirement is concerned, occurs when process nodes are eliminated by step 2, one at a time, until only one is left. In this case, step 1 will be invoked (n-1) times. Thus the time requirement of the Algorithm is bounded by $O(n^2e)$. Note that $e \leq nm + n + m < (n+1)(m+1)$, hence $O(n^2e) \leq O(n^3m)$.

Concluding Remark

H.M. Abdel-Wahab of the University of Waterloo has pointed out to the author that if for some $j \varepsilon M$

$$d_j(N) \geq |\{P_i| \; i \varepsilon N \text{ and } c_{ij} > 0\}|,$$

then the system is not deadlock-free. It is seen that in this case step 1 will immediately find a flow equal to $|N|$. For the special case of one resource type ($|M| = 1$), this is known to be a necessary and sufficient condition for a system not to be deadlock-free [7, p. 71].

If we consider the deficiency as a commodity, our problem is a special case of the classical transportation problem. We feel that a more efficient algorithm could be found, taking advantage of the special properties of the problem.

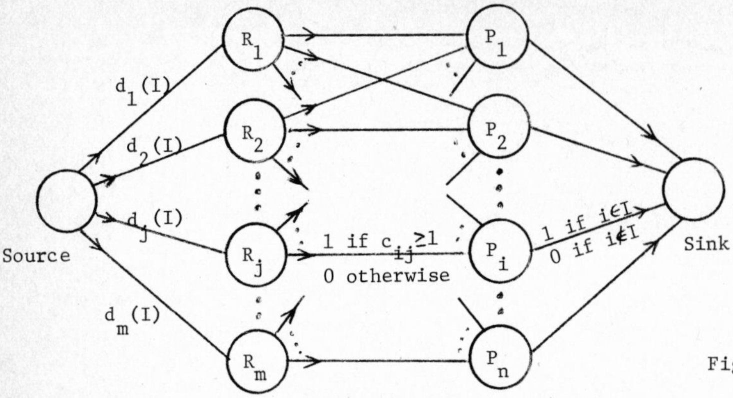

Fig. 1. A network model

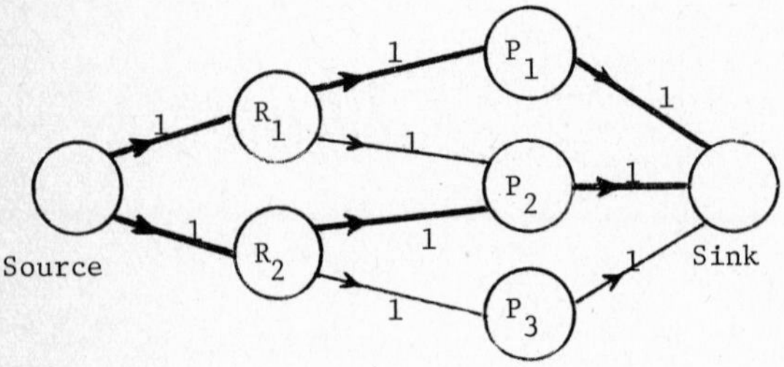

(a) $I_0 = \{1, 2, 3\}$

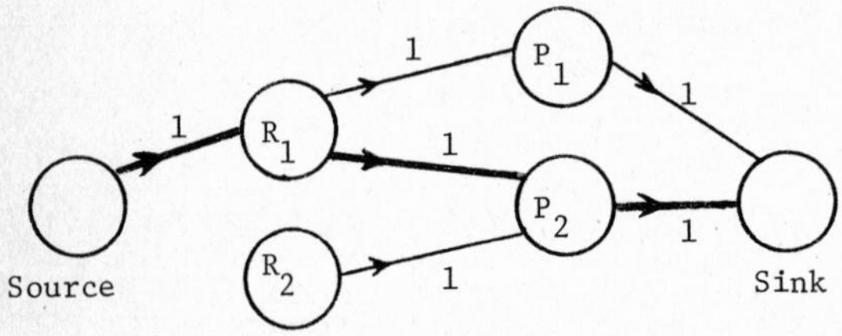

(b) $I_1 = \{1, 2\}$

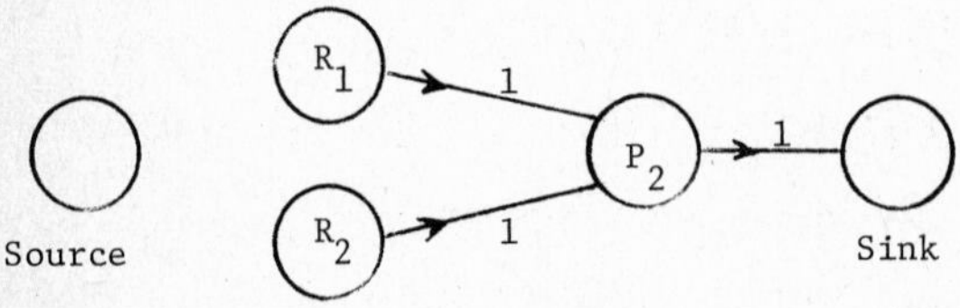

(c) $I_2 = \{2\}$

Fig. 2. Deadlock-free system

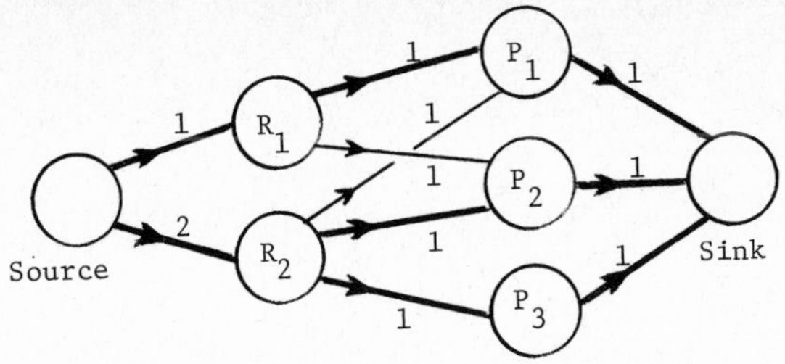

Fig. 3. Non-deadlock-free system

1. Aho, A.V., Hopcroft, J.E. and Ullman, J.D. The Design and Analysis of Computer Algorithms. Addison-Wesley, Reading, Mass., 1974.

2. Coffman, E.G. Jr., Elphick, M.J. and Shoshani, A. System deadlocks. Computing Surveys 2, 4 (June 1971), 67-78.

3. Dijkstra, E.W. Cooperating sequential processes. EWD 123, Math. Dept., Technological Univ., Eindhoven, The Netherlands, 1965. Also in "Programming Languages" (Genuys, F. Ed.), Academic Press, New York, 1968, 43-112.

4. Ford, L.R. and Fulkerson, D.R. Flows in Networks, Princeton University Press, Princeton, 1962.

5. Habermann, A.N. Prevention of System deadlocks. Comm. ACM 12, 7 (July 1969), 373-377, 385.

6. Havender, J.W. Avoiding deadlock in multi-tasking systems. IBM Systems J. 2, 7 (July 1968), 74-84.

7. Holt, R.C. On deadlock in computer systems. Tech. Rept. CSRG-6, Univ. Toronto, Jan. 1971.

8. Holt. R.C. Some deadlock properties of computer systems. Proc. Third Ann. Symp. Oper. Syst. Principles, Stanford, Oct. 1971, 64-71. Also Computing Surveys 4,3 (Sept. 1972), 179-196.

9. Reiter, A. A resource-allocation scheme for multi-user on-line operation of a small computer. Proc. AFIPS 1967 Spring J.C.C. Vol. 30, Thompson Book Co., Washington, D.C., 1-7.

10. Shaw, A. The Logical Design of Operating Systems, Prentice-Hall Englewood Cliffs, N.J., 1974, p. 230.

ASPECTS OF UNBOUNDED PARALLELISM

G. Gati

Abstract

The parallel program schemata, introduced by Karp and Miller [1], are considered for an unbounded number of operations and their decidability, result for determinacy is extended to this case under certain restrictions on the nature of the conflicts. The work of Keller [2] on maximal parallelism is discussed and an alternative approach to this problem is proposed which leads to a simple and fast solution algorithm for the general scheduling problem for unbounded parallelism. In contrast to this the general scheduling problem for bounded parallelism is NP-complete as proven in Ullman [3].

1. Unbounded Karp- and Miller-Schemata

Karp and Miller [1] have considered a formal model for parallel algorithms which only features the control structure and the memory locations of the domains and ranges of the operations.

Definition 1.1. An unbounded Karp- and Miller-schema (UKMS) $S = \{Op, T, D, R, H\}$ consists of a set of operations $Op = \{o(i) \mid i \in \mathbb{N}\}$ indexed by the natural numbers. To each operation $o(i)$ we assign an initiation symbol $\overline{o(i)}$ and H(i) termination symbols $o_1(i), \ldots, o_{H(i)}(i)$, where $H : \mathbb{N} \to \mathbb{N}$. We write $\underline{o(i)}$ instead of $o_j(i)$, $1 \leq j \leq H(i)$, when the value of j is irrelevant. Call $F(\mathbb{N}) \subset 2^{\mathbb{N}}$ the set of finite subsets of $\mathbb{N}$. Then $D, R : \mathbb{N} \to F(\mathbb{N})$. It is assumed that the i - th operation takes its operands from the memory locations whose addresses are in D(i) in the moment of its initialization and stores its results into the memory locations of R(i) in the moment of its termination. Also a decision with H(i) possible outcomes is made in the moment of its termination. We call $O := \overline{O} \cup \underline{O}$ the alphabet of the schema S, where $\overline{O} := \{\overline{o(i)} \mid i \in \mathbb{N}\}$ is the set of initiation symbols and $\underline{O} := \{\underline{o(i)} \mid i \in \mathbb{N}\}$ is the set of termination symbols. The control $T = (Q, q_o, t)$ consists of a (possible infinite) set of states Q, an initial state $q_o \in Q$ and a partial transition function $t : Q \times O \to Q$ which is total on $Q \times \underline{O}$. We shall also write t for the natural extension of t to $Q \times O^*$.

Operations are uninterpreted. To simulate concrete computations we have to specify all the data on which the operations can operate, their effect on the data and the decisions. This is done by interpretations.

Definition 1.2. An interpretation $I = (U, u_o, F, G)$ of an UKMS S consists of a universe U, an initial assignment $u_o \in U^{\mathbb{N}}$ of the memory and two families of maps $F = (F_i)_{i \in \mathbb{N}}$, where $F_i : U^{\mathbb{N}} \to U^{\mathbb{N}}$ specifies the action of the i - th operation, and $G = (G_i)_{i \in \mathbb{N}}$, where $G_i : U^{\mathbb{N}} \to \{1, \ldots, H(i)\}$ specifies the outcome of the decision associated to the i - th operation. We shall write I(S) for the class of all interpretations of a schema S.

Having defined interpretations of schemata one can define the set C (S,I) $\subset 0^*$ of computations contained in the "behaviour" of the automaton T because one requires certain additional conditions for the computations, e.g. that each prefix of a computation x $\in$ C(S, I) contains for each operation o(i) at least as many initiation symbols $\overline{o(i)}$ as termination symbols o(i); cf. [1]. We shall write P (S,I) for the set of prefixes of computations in C (S,I).

A computation x $\in$ (S,I) induces a sequence Z(x) of value assignments to the memory locations via the family of maps F starting with the initial assignment and on each single memory location j $\in \mathbb{N}$ a sequence Z (x,j) of value assignments. The elements of Z (x,j) are the intermediate and final values of the memory location j during the computation.

Definition 1.3. A UKMS S is determinate if $(\forall I \in I(S)) (\forall x,y \in C(S, I)) (\forall j \in \mathbb{N}) (Z(x,j) = Z(y,j))$.

For determinacy not only the final but also the intermediate values of all computations have to be equal.

2. Decidability of the Determinacy

We shall first introduce some notation for conflicts.

Definition 2.1. We call $\underline{K}(i,j) := (D(i) \cap R(j)) \cup (D(j) \cap R(i)) \cup (R(i) \cap R(j))$ the domain of conflict of two operations o (i) and o (j). We define a conflict relation $K := \{(i,j) \in \mathbb{N} \times \mathbb{N} \mid \underline{K}(i,j) \neq \emptyset\}$ and a "cross-section" $K(i) := \{j \in \mathbb{N} \mid K(i,j) \neq \emptyset\}$. We call $\underline{K} := \cup_{(i,j) \in \mathbb{N} \times \mathbb{N}} \underline{K}(i,j)$ the set of conflict locations of a UKMS.

Definition 2.2. A UKMS is called locally finite, if $(\forall_i \in \mathbb{N})$ ($|K(i)|$ is finite). A UKMS is called compact if $|\underline{K}|$ is finite.

We note that a locally finite schema does not have to be compact; e.g. consider the maps $D(0) := R(0) := \{0\}$; $D(i) := R(i) := \{i-1, i, i+1\}$, $i = 1, 2, 3, \ldots$ On the other hand a compact schema need not be locally finite, e.g. $D(i) := R(i) := \{0\}$, $i \in N$.

We shall now define a class of UKMS which can be considered as an extension of the parallel flowcharts of [1] to an unbounded number of operations.

Definition 2.3. The reachability set $R(\underline{W})$ of a r - dimensional VAS $\underline{W} = (d,W)$, where $d \in \mathbb{N}^r$ and W is a finite subset of Z^r, is the smallest subset of W^r which fulfills the following conditions:

(1) $d \in R$ ($\underline{W}$);

(2) if $v \in R$ ($\underline{W}$), $w \in W$ and $v + w \geq 0$ then $v + w \in R(\underline{W})$,
where $x \geq 0$ means $x_i \geq 0$, $1 \leq i \geq r$.

<u>Definition 2.4.</u> A UKMS over a r-dimensional VAS $\underline{W} = (d,\underline{W})$ (short: <u>SVAS</u>) is a UKMS S = (Op, T, D, R, H) where the control T is specified by:

$T = (Q, q_o, t)$;

$Q := R$ ($\underline{W}$);

$q := d$.

To specify the transition function t we shall furthermore assume a "finite presentation" of the control

(1) the existence of a finite partition $N_1, \ldots N_n$ of $\mathbb{N}$;

(2) that W consists of two disjunct subsets W_+ and W_- with

(a) $|W_+| = |W_-| = n$,

(b) each vector in W_+ has only coordinates from {0, + 1},

(c) each vector in W_- has only coordinate {0, - 1},

(d) if the i - th coordinate of a vector in W_- is - 1 then all other vectors in W_- have as i - th coordinate 0,

(3) the existence of two bijective maps $g_{\pm}$: {1, ... h} → $W_{\pm}$.

Then we can specify the transition function t in the following way:

If $q \in R$ ($\underline{W}$) and $1 \in N$; then t (q, $\overline{o(1)}$) is defined if and only if $q + g_-(i) \geq 0$ and then t (q, $\overline{o(1)}$) := $q + g_-(i)$;
t (q, $\underline{o(1)}$) := $q + g_+(i)$.

We shall repeat two technical terms from [1].

Definition 2.5. A UKMS is lossless if $R(i) \neq \emptyset$ $\forall i \in \mathbb{N}$. A UKMS S is repetitionfree if $x\ o(i)\ v\ o(i)\ w \in C(S, I) \Rightarrow (\exists\ \underline{o(j)} \in v)\ (R(j) \cap D(i) \neq \emptyset)$.

We shall now extend the main result from [1] to UKMS:

Theorem 2.1. It is decidable whether a locally finite, compact, lossless, repetitionfree SVAS S is determinate.

Outline of the proof: One immediately sees that the following characterization of [1] also holds for UKMS: A UKMS S is not determinate iff
$(\exists\ I \in I(S))\ (\exists\ \chi \in P(S,I))\ (\exists\ (i,j) \in K)\ (\chi\ \overline{o(i)} \in P(S, I) \wedge y\ o(j) \in P(S, I))$.

Now assume that $|\underline{K}| = m$, $h : K \rightarrow \{1, \ldots, m\}$ is a bijection and consider the following $(r + 2m)$ - dimensional VAS $\underline{V} = (d', V')$ where $\underline{W} = (d, W)$ is the r - dimensional VAS for S: $d' = (d, 0, \ldots, 0)$ and each operation $o(i)$ with $i \in \mathbb{N}_1$ induces two vectors in V of the form $(q_{\pm}(1), s_{\pm}(i))$ where the k - th component $(s_{\pm}(i))$ is ∓ 1 whenever $k \in h\ [D(i) \cap \underline{K}]$ or $k - m \in h\ [R(i) \cap \underline{K}]$ and 0 otherwise. Because of the local finiteness and compactness of S we thus get a finite dimensional, effectively constructable VAS. It is now obvious that S is not determinate iff $(\exists\ y \in R(\underline{V}))\ (\exists\ i \in \{1, \ldots, m\})\ (y \geq (0_r, 0_m, 2\delta_{ij}) \vee y \geq (0_r, \delta_{ij}, \delta_{ij}))$ where 0_r, resp. 0_m, are r -, resp. m -, dimensional zero vectors and δ_{ij} is the Kronecker - Delta.

3. A Parallel Complexity Measure

After Karp and Miller have demonstrated the usefulness of their schemata for obtaining decidability results Keller [2] has tried to solve another important problem in the framework of schemata, that of obtaining the maximal parallel form of an algorithm. Given an unbounded amount of parallel computer capacity this maximal parallel form should execute in shorter time than the sequential forms of the algorithm. To make this notion precise Keller has defined a complexity measure on the set $P(S) := \cup_{I\in I(S)} P(S, I)$, i.e. roughly spoken given a schema S and a function $v : Op \to \mathbb{N}$, the execution time, the measure gives the parallel execution time of the prefix (a precise description of Keller's model would be much more involved). Now Keller's complexity measure is not well defined on all $x \in P(S)$, not even on all $x \in C(S) := \cup_{I\in I(S)} C(S, I)$. A computation $x \in C(S)$, on which his complexity measure yields a well defined value for a certain execution time is called <u>consistent</u> with the execution time by Keller. Now Keller considers two (equivalent, determinate) schemata S, S' with equal Op, D, R and H but different control and calls the schema S' <u>faster</u> than the schema S if for each execution time there exists a $x' \in C(S')$ consistent with v which is faster than all $x \in C(S)$ consistent with v. Keller's theorem then is that the maximal parallel schema is also the fastest in his sense.

The following considerations should be viewed as a critical discussion of Keller's work. First it is immediate that the set of all non - sequential computations of a schema which are consistent with every execution time is empty. This suggests that one should change the definition of the complexity measure so that it is well defined on all computations of a schema for every execution time. Second one is mostly interested in few execution times and not in all. This suggests that one should only consider one execution time and call a schema S' faster than a schema S if the fastest computation of S' is faster than the fastest computation of S. Also one should have an algorithm for constructing the fastest computation of a schema without having to enumerate all computations. This is because a determinate schema for a relatively small algorithm like Strassen's algorithm for multiplication of 2 x 2 matrices [4] has more than $1{,}4 \cdot 10^{10}$ computations. In the following we propose to execute these tasks.

We shall start by presenting a complexity measure that is welldefined on all computations of a UKMS.

Notation 3.1. Let $x\,\underline{o(l)} \in P\,(S)$, where S is a UKMS. Then we write $l(x)$ for the substring $y\,\overline{o.(l)}$ of x where the mentioned occurence of $\overline{o\,(l)}$ is the initiation symbol corresponding to the mentioned occurence of the termination symbol $\underline{o(1)}$ in $x\,\underline{o(1)}$.

Definition 3.1. Let S be a UKMS and $v : Op \to \mathbb{N}$ the execution time. Then a parallel complexity measure $m : P(S) \to \mathbb{N}$ is recursively defined by:

$m(\lambda) := 0$, where λ is the null string,

$m(x\,\overline{o(1)}) := m(x)$;

$m(x\,\underline{o(1)}) := \max\{m(x), m(l(x)) + v(o(1))\}$.

Example 3.1. Consider the computation

$x := o(1)\ o(3)\ \underline{o(1)}\ o(2)\ \underline{o(3)}\ \underline{o(2)}$.

If $v(o(1)) = t_1$, $v(o(2)) = t_2$, $v(o(3)) = t_3$ then $m(x) = \max(t_1 + t_2, t_3)$. Assume $t_1 + t_2 < t_3$. Then x is not consistent with Keller's complexity measure.

4. Scheduling for Unbounded Parallelism

We shall now present an iterative algorithm which finds the fastest computation of a schema. For this we shall make two additional assumptions: that the control is specified in the form of a precedence graph which is induced by a partial order. The first assumption is trivial for SVAS. The second assumption is necessary to reduce the problem to a scheduling problem. The general form of a scheduling problem is similar to the following: Given a finite set of operations $Op := \{o(1), \ldots, o(n)\}$, a partial order $\prec$ on Op, an execution time: $v : Op \to \mathbb{N}$ find a function $f : Op \to \mathbb{N}$ with

(1) $o(i) \prec o(j) \Rightarrow f(o(i)) + v(o(j)) \leq f(o(j))$

(2) for any other function $g : Op \to \mathbb{N}$ which satisfies (1) we have $\max \{f(o(i)) \mid 1 \leq i \leq n\} \leq \max \{g(o(i)) \mid 1 \leq i \leq n\}$.

This problem is the general scheduling problem for unbounded parallelism. In the following we shall write o, o' for operations instead of o (i), o(j). We shall now informally describe the idea of our iterative algorithm.

In a procedure, called "NEXT" the following action is taken. Into the set C operations which are treated in the current iteration are read in. As in critical path algorithms the earliest possible initiation times e (o) of all $o \in C$ are computed. Then the set T of operations which have not yet terminated and the set I of operations, which have not yet initiated are augmented by the elements of C. We shall assume that the precedence graph has been completed by a START and a HALT-Operation in the obvious way. After the obvious initialization of the sets Y, T, I the procedure NEXT is called for the first time to input the first operations.

The main part of the algorithm consists of a repeat-loop. First the set T' of all operations which have to be terminated in this iteration is constructed by:

$T' := \{o \in T \mid o \text{ has already initiated} \wedge m(x_{\underline{o}}) \leq \min \{e(o') \mid o' \in I\}\}$. After the termination of the operations in T' the procedure NEXT is called again because new operations might be enabled. Then the set I' of all operations which have to be initiated in this iteration is constructed by

$I' := \{o \in I \mid e(o) = \min \{e(o') \mid o' \in I\}\}$.

This finishes the contents of the repeat-loop. This loop is executed until $I = \emptyset$.

The interested reader finds our algorithm programmed in Pidgin - PASCAL in the appendix.

We have executed our algorithm on the precedence-graph of the Strassen-Winograd-algorithm for multiplication of 2 x 2 - matrices [4] and found a schedule which is shorter by two parallel additions than the parallel schedule suggested by the sequential execution.

The proofs of the following attributes of the algorithm are straightforward:

Lemma 4.1. No operation is initiated unless all of its predecessors in the precedence graph have terminated.

Lemma 4.2. At each call of the procedure NEXT the set C is augmented by at least one element.

Lemma 4.3. In each call of the mentioned repeat-loop at least one operation is initiated.

Corollary 4.1. The mentioned repeat-loop is passed through at most n times.

Theorem 4.1. The algorithm finds a computation with minimal schedule time after at most n passes through the repeat loop.

Because of Theorem 4.1. the algorithm can be considered linear. This is interesting because the analogous scheduling problem for bounded parallelism has been proved NP-complete in [3].

It is furthermore immediate that the algorithm is equally well suited for precedence graphs with an unbounded number of operations. This is because the scheduling algorithm can be executed simultaneously with the execution of the operations.

Acknowledgement

I gratefully acknowledge that Prof. Dr. E. Engeler has posed this problem and that any new ideas are due to him. I am, however, the only one to be blamed for any shortcomings or errors in their carrying-out.

Appendix

Algorithmus "FASTCOMP".

```
procedure NEXT;
begin     L := C;
          C := {o ∈ V-Y | ∅ ≠ {o' ∈ V | (o',o ∈ E}  Y};
          ∀ o ∈ C : e (o) := max {e(o')+v(o') | (o',o)   E};
          Y := Y ∪ C;
          T := T ∪ C;
          I := I ∪ C;
end;
begin comment initialization; Y := C :=  START ;
                              x := λ;
                              T := I := ∅;
                              e(START) := 0;
                              NEXT;
      comment main part;
          repeat T' := {o ∈ T | ō ∈ x
                          m (xo) ≤ min {e(o') | o' ∈ I}} ;
                 T := T-T';
                 while T' ≠ ∅ do begin take o out of T';
                                       x := xo;
                                 end;
```

```
        NEXT;
        I' := {o ∈ I | e(o) = min {e(o') | o' ∈ I}}
        I := I-I';
        repeat take o out of I';
               x := xō
        until  I' = ∅;
    until  I = ∅
end.
```

References

[1] Karp, R.M. and Miller, R.E. Parallel program schemata. Journal of Computer and System Sciences, 3, 147 - 195 (1969).

[2] Keller, R.M. Parallel program schemata and maximal parallelism. Journal of the ACM, 2o, 514 - 537 and 696 - 71o (1973).

[3] Ullman, J.D. NP-complete scheduling problems. Journal of Computer and System Sciences, 1o, 384 - 393 (1975).

[4] Aho, A.V., Hopcroft, J.E. and Ullman, J.D. The Design and Analysis of Computer Algorithms. Reading, Mass. (1974).

Eigenschaften färbbarer Petri-Netze

R. Prinoth

1. Zusammenfassung

Der Begriff der Färbbarkeit führt zur Klassenbildung innerhalb der Petri-Netze; die Klassen zeichnen sich dadurch aus, daß die zu ihnen gehörenden Netze in spezieller Weise durch Zustandsmaschinen und/oder Synchronisationsgraphen überdeckbar sind. Sie machen deutlich die Einschränkung der Zustandsmengen im dynamischen Ablauf und zeigen alternative Ereignisfolgen auf.

2. Problemstellung

Der Einsatz von DV-Anlagen bedingt die Lösung organisatorischer Probleme zur Vermeidung widersprüchlicher Anforderungen an Systemkomponenten und zur wirtschaftlichen Nutzung des Gesamtsystems.

Widersprüchliche Anforderungen können den Stillstand des Gesamtsystems oder einzelner Systemkomponenten bewirken; ein Mangel an Resourcen kann die gleiche Situation hervorrufen oder zu Engpässen führen, die den Nutzen des Gesamtsystems mindern.

Läßt man alle Fälle außer acht, die mit dem Optimieren von Systemkonfigurationen zu tun haben, so bleiben u. a. die Probleme, die mit den kausalen Abhängigkeiten der Anforderungen an das System und der dazu notwendigen Systemstruktur verbunden sind.

Die von Petri eingeführten Netze ermöglichen eine mathematische Darstellung von Organisationsstrukturen, in der sich u. a. die Fragen des Stillstandes des Gesamtsystems oder von Teilkomponenten behandeln lassen (Lebendigkeit); hierbei ergeben sich Forderungen in Bezug auf die Vielfachheit vorhandener Resourcen (Sicherheit). Ausgehend von Zustands- und Ereignismengen der betrachteten Systeme werden die kausalen Zusammenhänge zwischen den 'Bedingungen, die erfüllt sein müssen, damit ein Ereignis eintreten kann' und dem betreffenden Ereignis (Vorbedingungen) und dem Ereignis und den 'veränderten Bedingungen nach Stattfinden des Ereignisses' (Nachbedingungen) modelliert, wobei alternativ bzw. parallel zu durchlaufende Zweige auftreten können. Hierbei kristallisieren sich Grundstrukturen heraus, die in engem Zusammenhang zu Synchronisationsgraphen bzw. Zustandsmaschinen stehen.

Diese Grundstrukturen ermöglichen eine sinnvolle Einschränkung der Petri-Netze auf die Klassen der stark 1-färbbaren bzw. stark 2-färbbaren Netze, die sich durch eine Reihe von Eigenschaften auszeichnen.

3. Stark färbbare Petri-Netze

Def.: Ein Petri-Netz (= PN) ist ein Quadrupel (S, T, V, N), wobei S und T disjunkte, endliche, nicht leere Mengen sind und V, N binäre Relationen:

$$V \subseteq S \times T \quad \text{und} \quad N \subseteq S \times T \quad \text{mit } V \cap N = \emptyset$$

und keine 'isolierten' Elemente der Mengen S und T existieren.

Die Elemente $s \in S$ heißen Stellen (oder Zustände), dargestellt durch Kreise, die Elemente $t \in T$ heißen Transitionen (oder Ereignisse), dargestellt durch Stäbe, die Elemente $k \in V \cup N$ heißen Kanten. V ist die Menge der Vorbedingungen, N die Menge der Nachbedingungen. $V \cap N = \emptyset$ schließt Nebenbedingungen aus. Abkürzend wird ein PN auch mit (S, T) statt (S, T, V, N) benannt.

Beispiel 1:

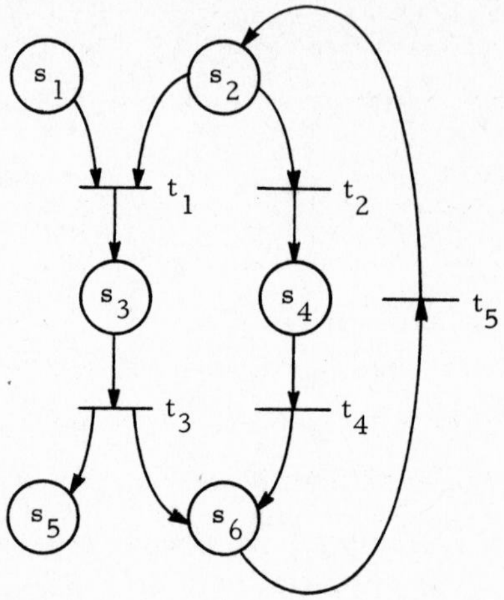

$S = \{s_1, s_2, s_3, s_4, s_5, s_6\}$

$T = \{t_1, t_2, t_3, t_4, t_5\}$

Für $A \subseteq S$ und $B \subseteq T$ werden definiert:

$$^{\bullet}A = \{t \in T \mid \exists\ s \in A : (s,t) \in N\}$$
$$A^{\bullet} = \{t \in T \mid \exists\ s \in A : (s,t) \in V\}$$
$$^{\bullet}B = \{s \in S \mid \exists\ t \in B : (s,t) \in V\}$$
$$B^{\bullet} = \{s \in S \mid \exists\ t \in B : (s,t) \in N\}$$

Für $s \in S$ wird auch die Schreibweise $^{\bullet}s, s^{\bullet}$ statt $^{\bullet}\{s\}$, $\{s\}^{\bullet}$ benutzt, für $t \in T$ auch $^{\bullet}t, t^{\bullet}$ statt $^{\bullet}\{t\}$, $\{t\}^{\bullet}$

Wird im Beispiel 1 $A = \{s_2, s_3\}$ gewählt, so ergibt sich $^{\bullet}A = \{t_1, t_5\}$ und $A^{\bullet} = \{t_1, t_2, t_3\}$.

<u>Def.:</u> Gegeben sei ein PN (S, T). Eine <u>Markierung</u> ist eine

Funktion $M : S \longrightarrow N_o$.

Eine Transition $t \in T$ eines PN (S, T) kann unter der Markierung M schalten, wenn alle $s \in {}^{\bullet}t$ (Eingabestellen) mindestens eine Marke tragen: Nach dem Schalten ist die Markenzahl jeder Eingabestelle um eins erniedrigt, die Markenzahl jeder Stelle $s \in t^{\bullet}$ um eins erhöht.

Durch das Schalten einer Transition $t \in T$ geht M in die Markierung M' über, was durch $M\ [t\rangle\ M'$ bezeichnet werden soll; M' heißt Folgemarkierung von M.
Eine Schaltfolge σ ist eine nicht leere Kette von Transitionen, die in der angegebenen Reihenfolge geschaltet werden. Die Schreibweise $M\ [\sigma\rangle\ M'$ bedeutet, daß eine Schaltfolge σ M in M' überführt.

Ein PN ist lebendig markierbar, wenn es mit einer Markierung M versehen werden kann derart, daß unter den Folgemarkierungen es immer wieder einmal möglich wird, jede Transition zu schalten.

Falls es unter M und allen Folgemarkierungen niemals vorkommen kann, daß die Markenzahl einer Stelle über alle Grenzen wächst, so heißt M beschränkt, übersteigt die Markenzahl jeder Stelle insbesondere niemals den Wert 1, so heißt M sicher.

Def.: Ein PN (S, T) heißt Zustandsmaschine (= ZM), falls

$$\forall_{t \in T} \quad |{}^{\bullet}t| = |t^{\bullet}| = 1 \quad \text{gilt,}$$

es heißt Synchronisationsgraph (= SG), falls

$$\forall_{s \in S} \quad |{}^{\bullet}s| = |s^{\bullet}| = 1 \quad \text{gilt.}$$

Def.: Sei ein PN (S, T) gegeben. $A \subseteq S$ heißt Trap, falls $A^{\bullet} \subseteq {}^{\bullet}A$ gilt, A heißt Deadlock, wenn ${}^{\bullet}A \subseteq A^{\bullet}$ gilt.

Ein Trap (Deadlock) heißt minimal, wenn er keinen nicht leeren Trap (Deadlock) echt enthält.

Def.: Gegeben sei ein PN (S, T, V, N) mit $m = |S|$ Stellen und $n = |T|$ Transitionen. Die Inzidenzmatrix C des PN ist eine (mxn)-Matrix mit:

$$\underset{s \in S}{\forall} \quad \underset{t \in T}{\forall} \qquad C(s,t) = \begin{cases} -1, & \text{falls } (s,t) \in V \\ +1, & \text{falls } (s,t) \in N \\ 0 & \text{sonst} \end{cases}$$

Das zu einem PN (S, T) umgekehrte PN (S', T') entsteht aus dem ersten durch Umorientierung aller Kanten.
Das zu einem PN (S, T) duale PN (S', T') entsteht aus dem ersten dadurch, daß jede Stelle in eine Transition und jede Transition in eine Stelle verwandelt wird.
Das zu einem PN (S, T) umgekehrt duale PN (S', T') entsteht aus dem ersten dadurch, daß die Operationen 'umkehren' und 'dualisieren' nacheinander ausgeführt werden.

Nachfolgend werden wir uns mit Netzen befassen, deren Kanten in geeigneter Weise gefärbt sind. Jede einzeln erkennbare Farbe heißt hierbei Grundfarbe.

Def.: Ein PN(S, T) heißt stark 1-färbbar, wenn alle Kanten derart (mit einer oder mehreren Grundfarben) gefärbt werden können, daß für jede Stelle $s \in S$ die Regel S1 und für jede Transition $t \in T$ die Regel T1 gilt:

S1: Alle Kanten, die mit der Stelle s inzidieren, tragen die gleiche Farbkombination.

T1: Jede Grundfarbe kommt auf der Eingangsseite der Transition höchstens einmal vor.
Jede Grundfarbe kommt auf der Ausgangsseite der Transition höchstens einmal vor.
Jede Grundfarbe, die auf der Eingangsseite vorkommt, kommt auch auf der Ausgangsseite vor und umgekehrt.

Bemerkung: S1, T1 erfüllende Grundfarben sind durch Stellenmengen eindeutig gekennzeichnet. Grundfarben, die S1, T1 erfüllen, werden auch 1-Grundfarben genannt. Ist f 1-Grundfarbe, so bezeichnet $U_f \subseteq S$ die durch f gekennzeichnete Stellenmenge.

Beispiel 2:

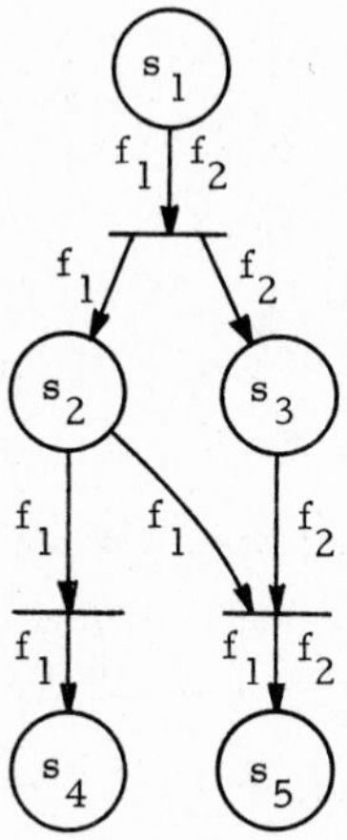

Das PN ist stark 1-färbbar. Die 1-Grundfarben f_1 und f_2 überdecken das gesamte PN.

$U_{f_1} = \{s_1, s_2, s_4, s_5\}$

$U_{f_2} = \{s_1, s_3, s_5\}$

Def.: Ein PN (S, T) heißt stark 2-färbbar, wenn alle Kanten derart (mit einer oder mehreren Grundfarben) gefärbt werden können, daß für jede Transition $t \in T$ die Regel T2 und für jede Stelle $s \in S$ die Regel S2 gilt:

T2: Alle Kanten, die mit der Transition t inzidieren, tragen die gleiche Farbkombination.

S2: Jede Grundfarbe kommt auf der Eingangsseite der Stelle höchstens einmal vor.

Jede Grundfarbe kommt auf der Ausgangsseite der Stelle höchstens einmal vor.

Jede Grundfarbe, die auf der Eingangsseite vorkommt, kommt auch auf der Ausgangsseite vor und umgekehrt.

Bemerkung: S2, T2 erfüllende Grundfarben sind durch Transitionsmengen eindeutig gekennzeichnet. Grundfarben, die S2, T2 erfüllen, werden auch <u>2-Grundfarben</u> genannt. Ist g 2-Grundfarbe, so bezeichnet $W_g \subseteq T$ die durch g gekennzeichnete Transitionsmenge.

Beispiel 3:

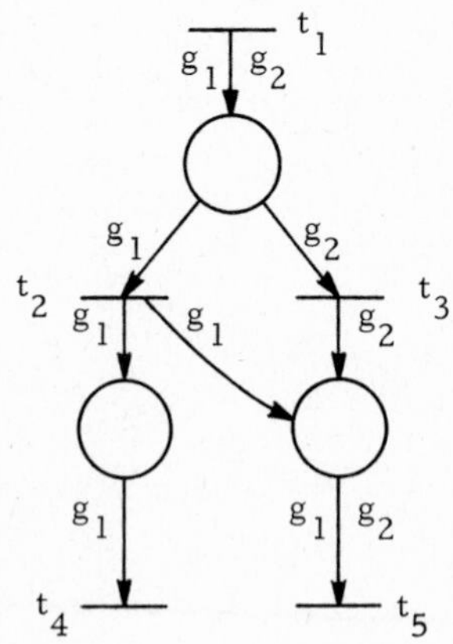

Das PN ist stark 2-färbbar.
Die 2-Grundfarben g_1 und g_2 überdecken das gesamte PN.

$$W_{g_1} = \{t_1, t_2, t_4, t_5\}$$

$$W_{g_2} = \{t_1, t_3, t_5\}$$

4. Eigenschaften stark 1- und/oder 2-färbbarer Netze

Die nachfolgend aufgeführten Eigenschaften stark 1-färbbarer und/oder stark 2-färbbarer PN sind ohne Beweis gegeben. Sie stellen lediglich eine Auswahl dar.

1. Ist ein PN stark 1-färbbar (stark 2-färbbar), so ist auch das dazu umgekehrte PN stark 1-färbbar (stark 2-färbbar).
   Ein PN ist genau dann stark 1-färbbar, wenn das dazu (umgekehrt) duale PN stark 2-färbbar ist.

2. In einem stark 1-färbbaren PN definiert jede 1-Grundfarbe eine ZM, in einem stark 2-färbbaren PN definiert jede 2-Grundfarbe einen SG. Ein von ZM überdeckbares PN ist jedoch nicht notwendig stark 1-färbbar und ein von SG überdeckbares PN ist nicht notwendig stark 2-färbbar.

3. In einem stark 1-färbbaren PN ist jede Folgemarkierung, die sich aus einer endlichen Anfangsmarkierung ergibt, beschränkt. In einem stark 2-färbbaren PN ist jede 2-Grundfarbe lebendig markierbar.

4. In einem stark 1- und 2-färbbaren PN ist der Durchschnitt einer 1-Grundfarbe mit einer 2-Grundfarbe ein Kreis oder er ist leer.

5. Die Restriktion eines stark 1- und 2-färbbaren PN auf eine 1-Grundfarbe ist stark 2-färbbar, die Restriktion auf eine 2-Grundfarbe ist stark 1-färbbar.

Beispiel 4:

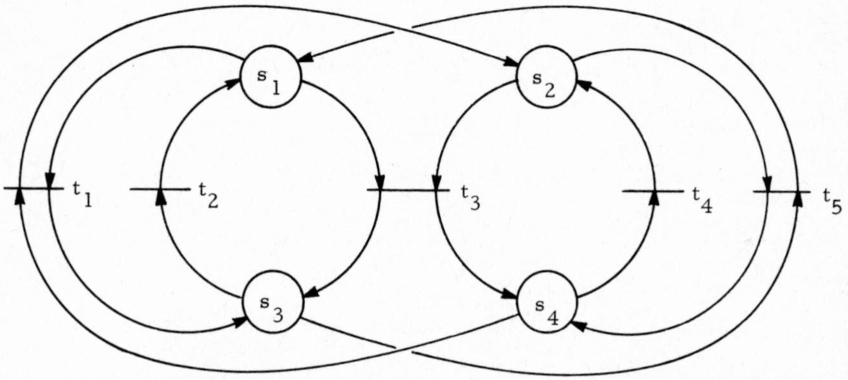

Das angegebene PN ist stark 1- und 2-färbbar. Eine Überdeckung mit 1-Grundfarben ist durch f_1, f_2 mit $U_{f_1} = \{s_1, s_3\}$, $U_{f_2} = \{s_2, s_4\}$ gegeben, eine Überdeckung mit 2-Grundfarben durch g_1, g_2 mit $W_{g_1} = \{t_1, t_5\}$, $W_{g_2} = \{t_2, t_3, t_4\}$ gegeben.

Der Durchschnitt der Grundfarben f_1 und g_1 etwa liefert den durch s_1, t_1, s_3, t_5 festgelegten Kreis, die Restriktion des PN auf f_1 (es ergibt sich ein PN (S', T') mit $S' = \{s_1, s_3\}$, $T' = \{t_1, t_2, t_3, t_5\}$ und den Kanten, die aus den Elementen S' und T' gebildet werden können) ist stark 2-färbbar: g_1 und g_2 sind mit jeweils einem Kreis vertreten.

6. Jede Stellenmenge $U = U_f$ einer 1-Grundfarbe f eines stark 1-färbbaren und stark zusammenhängenden PN definiert einen minimalen Deadlock und einen minimalen Trap.

7. In einem stark 2-färbbaren und stark zusammenhängenden PN (S, T) bilden alle 2-Grundfarben, die mit den Stellen eines Deadlock $D \subseteq S$ inzidieren, mindestens einen Kreis in D; unter den gleichen Voraussetzungen bilden alle 2-Grundfarben, die mit den Stellen eines Trap $W \subseteq S$ inzidieren, mindestens einen Kreis in W.

An Hand der Inzidenzmatrix $\mathcal{C}$ des PN in Beispiel 4 soll die Algebraisierung des Grundfarbenkonzepts skizziert werden:

$\mathcal{C}$ (S ↓, T →)

S \ T	1	2	3	4	5
1	-1	1	-1		1
2	1		-1	1	-1
3	1	-1	1		-1
4	-1		1	-1	1

Die Lösung des Gleichungssystems

$$\mathcal{C}' * \mathfrak{y} = \mathfrak{o}$$

führt auf den allgemeinen Lösungsvektor

$$\mathfrak{y} = a \begin{pmatrix} 1 \\ 0 \\ 1 \\ 0 \end{pmatrix} + b \begin{pmatrix} 0 \\ 1 \\ 0 \\ 1 \end{pmatrix}, \quad a, b \in R$$

Dabei geben $\begin{pmatrix}1\\0\\1\\0\end{pmatrix}$ und $\begin{pmatrix}0\\1\\0\\1\end{pmatrix}$ die Vielfachheit der Stellen $\begin{pmatrix}s_1\\s_2\\s_3\\s_4\end{pmatrix}$ in

der Lösung an.

Ein Vergleich mit U_{f_1} und U_{f_2} zeigt, daß durch den Vektor $\begin{pmatrix}1\\0\\1\\0\end{pmatrix}$

gerade die 1-Grundfarbe f_1 und durch $\begin{pmatrix}0\\1\\0\\1\end{pmatrix}$ die 1-Grundfarbe f_2

identifiziert wird.
Die Lösung des Gleichungssystems $\mathfrak{C} * \mathfrak{t} = \mathfrak{o}$ identifiziert in gleicher Weise 2-Grundfarben und Vektoren, deren Komponenten die Vielfachheit anzeigen, mit der Transitionen in Lösungen vertreten sind.

8. Existiert in einem stark zusammenhängenden PN (S, T) eine 1-Grundfarbe f mit $U_f \subseteq S$, so gibt es unter den Lösungen des Gleichungssystems $\mathfrak{C}' * \mathfrak{y} = \mathfrak{o}$ ($\mathfrak{C}$ ist die Inzidenzmatrix des PN (S, T)) einen Vektor $\mathfrak{y}_f = (y_1, \dots, y_{|S|})'$, dessen Komponenten nur die Werte 0 oder 1 annehmen und für den gilt:

$$(s_i \in U_f) \Longleftrightarrow (y_i = 1) \quad , \quad 1 \leq i \leq |S| \quad .$$

9. Existiert in einem stark zusammenhängenden PN (S, T) eine 2-Grundfarbe g mit $W_g \subseteq T$, so gibt es unter den Lösungen des Gleichungssystems $\mathfrak{C} * \mathfrak{t} = \mathfrak{o}$ einen Vektor $\mathfrak{t}_g = (t_1, \dots, t_{|T|})'$,

dessen Komponenten nur die Werte 0 oder 1 annehmen und für den gilt:

$$(t_j \in W_g) \Longleftrightarrow (t_j = 1) \quad , \quad 1 \leq j \leq |T| \ .$$

10. Die zu den 1-Grundfarben gehörenden Vektoren (vgl. 8.) gehören zu den 1-elementaren Lösungen des Gleichungssystems $\mathcal{C}' * \mathfrak{y} = \mathfrak{o}$. Diese Lösungen charakterisieren minimale Stellenmengen, für die das Schalten beliebiger Transitionen keinen Einfluß auf die Gesamtmarkenzahl einer derartigen Lösung hat. Die Marken sind dabei mit der durch die 1-elementare Lösung angegebenen Vielfachheit entsprechender Stellen zu zählen.

11. Die zu den 2-Grundfarben gehörenden Vektoren (vgl. 9.) gehören zu den 2-elementaren Lösungen des Gleichungssystems $\mathcal{C} * \mathfrak{x} = \mathfrak{o}$. Diese Lösungen charakterisieren minimale Transitionsmengen die – zu Schaltfolgen angeordnet – Markierungen reproduzieren, falls eine derartige Schaltfolge realisierbar ist, d. h. die dort aufgeführten Transitionen in der angegebenen Reihenfolge schalten können.

12. Ein stark zusammenhängendes PN, das aus einer 1-elementaren Lösung besteht und minimaler Deadlock ist, ist genau dann lebendig und sicher markierbar, wenn die 1-elementare Lösung 1-Grundfarbe ist.

13. Hinreichende Bedingung für die Existenz einer lebendigen und sicheren Markierung eines stark 1-färbbaren PN, das aus einer 2-elementaren Lösung besteht ist, daß jeder Deadlock einen Trap enthält.

14. Hinreichende Bedingung für die Existenz einer lebendigen und beschränkten Markierung eines stark 1-färbbaren PN, das von 2-elementaren Lösungen überdeckt wird ist, daß jeder Deadlock einen Trap enthält.

15. Hinreichende Bedingung für die Existenz einer lebendigen und sicheren Markierung eines stark 1-färbbaren PN, das von 2-elementaren Lösungen überdeckt wird ist, daß jeder minimale Deadlock 1-Grundfarbe ist.

Beispiel 5:

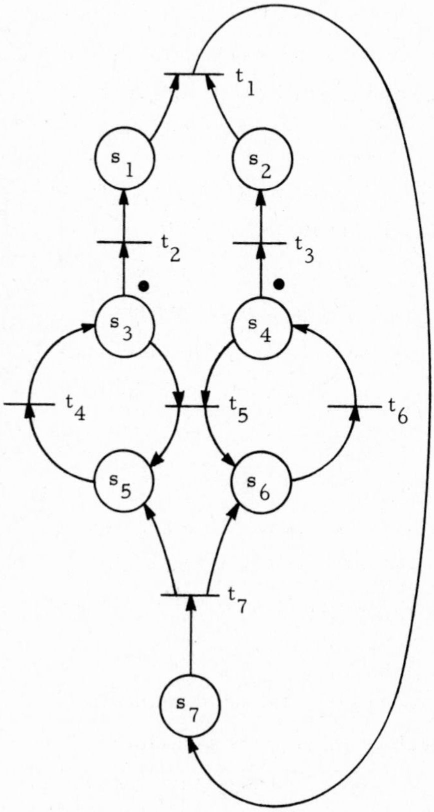

Das PN dieses Beispiels erfüllt alle Voraussetzungen des Punktes 15.

Sind f_1, f_2 1-Grundfarben, dann gilt:

$U_{f_1} = \{s_1, s_3, s_5, s_7\}$

$U_{f_2} = \{s_2, s_4, s_6, s_7\}$

Das PN ist also von 1-Grundfarben überdeckbar, also stark 1-färbbar.

Sind g_1, g_2 2-Grundfarben, dann gilt:

$W_{g_1} = \{t_4, t_5, t_6\}$

$W_{g_2} = \{t_1, t_2, t_3, t_4, t_6, t_7\}$

Die Überdeckung des PN mit 2-elementaren Lösungen ist gesichert, da das PN sogar stark 2-färbbar ist.

Es gibt zwei minimale Deadlocks: $D_1 = \{s_1, s_3, s_5, s_7\}$ und $D_2 = \{s_2, s_4, s_6, s_7\}$. Da jeder minimale Deadlock 1-Grundfarbe ist, ist das PN nach Punkt 15 lebendig und sicher markierbar (vgl. eingezeichnete Markierung).

Literaturverzeichnis

[1] H. J. Genrich, K. Lautenbach
Synchronisationsgraphen
Acta Informatica 2, 1973, 143-161

[2] M. H. T. Hack
Analysis of production schemata by petri nets
MAC-TR-94; MIT, 1972

[3] K. Lautenbach
Exakte Bedingungen der Lebendigkeit für eine
Klasse von Petri Netzen
Berichte der GMD, BMFT-GMD-82, 1973

[4] K. Lautenbach
Wegsysteme in Petri-Netzen
GI/GMD-Fachtagung über Ansätze zur Organisationstheorie
rechnergestützter Informationssysteme, 1974

[5] K. Lautenbach
Lebendigkeit in Petri-Netzen
Interner Bericht 02/75-4-1, 1975

[6] C. A. Petri
Concepts of net theory
Proceedings of symposium and summer school
High Tatras, 1973

[7] E. Raubold
Interpretierbare Netze
GMD, IFV-intern, 1975

[8] Project MAC conference on concurrent systems
and parallel computation
ACM, 1970

On the rationality of Petri net languages

R. Valk - G. Vidal

In this paper we study a class of concurrent systems having a rather regular flow of control. The following parallel program uses instructions as 'meet', 'split', 'branche' and 'await'. Any part of the program which is executed in a strictly sequential way is represented by a single arrow. (cf[Ko]) The flow of control of this program can be described by the given Petri net as well.

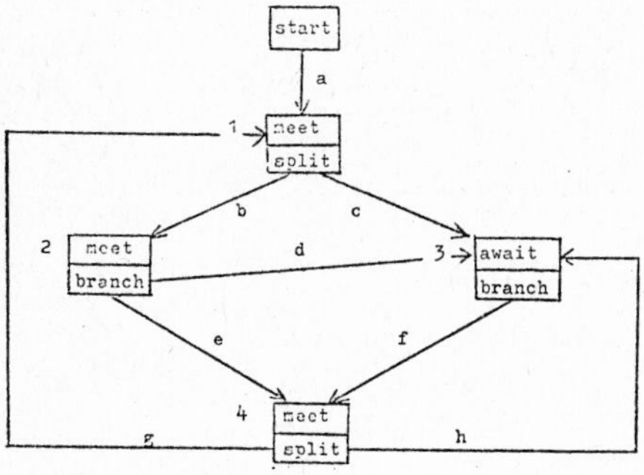

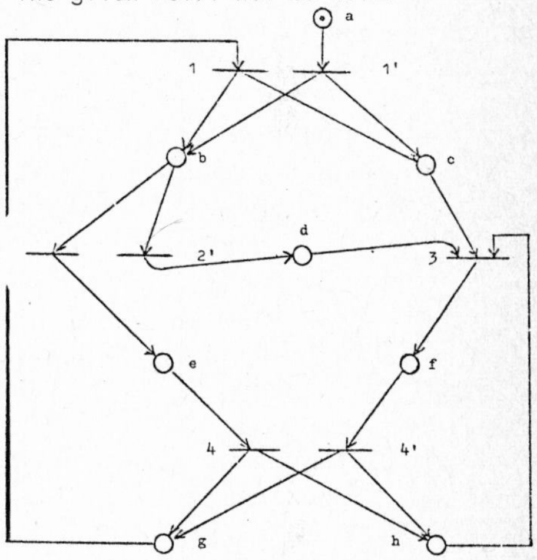

Since the net is not bounded important questions like liveness and detection of deadlocks cannot be answered by inspection of the associated case graph, which is infinite. Nevertheless, since the language of the net, which is the set of all possible firing sequences, is a rational set all such questions can be answered by the construction of the accepting finite automaton. (In this example only by firing transitions 1' and 2' from the beginning a deadlock can occur.) We shall show that rationality for ordinary Petri nets is decidable, but that the same question becomes undecidable for nets where different transitions can have the same label and which have terminal markings. This question is mentioned as an open problem in [Pe] .

Def 1: A Petri net $N = (P,T,E,S,M_o)$ is defined by a set $P = \{p_1,\ldots,p_r\}$ of places , a set $T = \{t_1,\ldots,t_s\}$ of transitions and maps E and S from $P \times T$ into $\mathbb{N}$ and the initial marking $M_o \in \mathbb{N}^r$. (Sometimes E and S are interpreted as matrices as well as markings $M \in \mathbb{N}^r$ are written as maps $M : P \to \mathbb{N}$.)

For markings $M, M' \in \mathbb{N}^r$ and a transition $t \in T$ the firing relation

$M \xrightarrow{t} M' :\Leftrightarrow M \geq Et \wedge M' = M + (S-E)t$ is recursively extended to firing sequences $w \in T^*$. ($t \in T$ is identified to the corresponding unit vector $t \in \mathbb{N}^s$). $[M\rangle := \{M' \mid \exists w \in T^* : M \xrightarrow{w} M'\}$ is the set of reachable markings from M.

Def 2: $L(N) := \{w \in T^* \mid \exists M : M_o \xrightarrow{w} M\}$ is the language of N . For a given finite set $\mathfrak{M}_t \subset \mathbb{N}^r$ of terminal markings $L(N, \mathfrak{M}_t) = \{w \in T^* \mid \exists M \in \mathfrak{M}_t : M_o \xrightarrow{w} M\}$ is the terminal language of M .

Def 3: A Petri net $N = (P,T,E,S,M_o)$ together with a labelling function h $h : T \rightarrow H$ is called a labelled Petri net. In this case in L(N) and $L(N, \mathfrak{M}_t)$ any symbol $t \in T$ is substituted by h(t) . Nets which have no labelling function as in Def 2 are sometimes called ordinary Petri nets.

The advantage of using a labelling function lies in the fact that we can model a single event by several transitions, and thus represent the case of an event which may occur under different circumstances ([Ha]) ; e.g. :consider 1 and 1' etc. in the example as identical labels.

Def 4: Let be $\hat{P} \subset P$ a set of places and $U_{\hat{P}} \in \mathbb{N}^r$ be defined by $U_{\hat{P}}(p) = 1$ if $p \in \hat{P}$ and $U_{\hat{P}}(p) = 0$ if $p \notin \hat{P}$.

Then we say, that

a) $\hat{P}$ is majorized for M if $\exists k \in \mathbb{N}\ \forall M_1 \in [M\rangle \exists \hat{p} \in \hat{P} : M_1(\hat{p}) \leq k$

b) $\hat{P}$ is minorized for M if

$\exists k \in \mathbb{N}\ \forall n \in \mathbb{N}\ \forall M_1 \in [M+nU_{\hat{P}}\rangle\ \exists \hat{p} \in \hat{P} : M_1(\hat{p}) \geq M(\hat{p}) + n - k$

c) $\hat{P}$ is uniformly majorized for M and uniformly minorized for M , respectively, if the second existential quantifier in a) and b), respectively, is replaced by an universal quantifier.

Lemma 1: a) If $\hat{P}$ is uniformly majorized for M, then $\hat{P}$ is majorized for M.

b) $\hat{P}$ uniformly minorized for M implies $\hat{P}$ minorized for M

c) $\hat{P}$ is uniformly majorized if and only if $\{p\}$ is majorized for all $p \in \hat{P}$.

d) If P is uniformly minorized, then $\{p\}$ is minorized for all $p \in \hat{P}$.

The proof follows immediately from the definition. In the net $N := (\{p_1,p_2,p_3\}, \{t_1,t_2,\dots,t_6\}, E, S, M_o)$ defined by

$$E := \begin{pmatrix}100100\\012000\\000012\end{pmatrix} \quad S := \begin{pmatrix}000000\\121000\\000121\end{pmatrix} \quad M_o = \begin{pmatrix}1\\0\\0\end{pmatrix}$$

the set $\hat{P} := \{p_2,p_3\}$ is minorized and majorized for M_o but not uniformly minorized and not uniformly majorized. In the net $N' := (\{p_1,p_2\}, \{t_1\}, \binom{1}{1}, \binom{0}{0}, M_o)$ the sets $\{p_1\}$ and $\{p_2\}$ are minorized for any M_o but $\hat{P} = \{p_1,p_2\}$ is not uniformly minorized for any M_o. These examples show that equivalence in statements a), b) and d) of Lemma 1 would be false.

Def 5: A place $p \in P$ of a net $N = (P,T,E,S,M_o)$ is bounded if $\{p\}$ is majorized for M_o and N is bounded if P is uniformly majorized for M_o.

Def 6: Let be $\hat{P} \subset P$, $\hat{P} \neq \emptyset$, $M_o \in \mathbb{N}^r$

a) $\hat{P}$ is not majorized for M_o with context $\hat{M} \in \mathbb{N}^r$ if $\hat{M}(p) = 0$ for $p \in \hat{P}$ and $\forall k \exists M_1 \in [M_o\rangle$ $(\forall p \in \hat{P} : M_1(p) \geq k \wedge \forall p \notin \hat{P} : M_1(p) = \hat{M}(p))$

b) $Con(\hat{P},M_o) := \{M \mid \hat{P}$ is not majorized for M_o with context $M\}$

c) $\hat{M} \in Con(\hat{P},M_o)$ is maximal if $\hat{\hat{M}} \in Con(\hat{\hat{P}},M_o)$, $\hat{\hat{M}} \geq M$ and $\hat{\hat{P}} \supset \hat{P}$ imply $\hat{\hat{M}} = \hat{M}$ and $\hat{\hat{P}} = \hat{P}$.

Lemma 2 : For any $\hat{M} \in Con(\hat{P},M_o)$ there are $\hat{\hat{M}}$ and $\hat{\hat{P}}$ such that $\hat{\hat{M}} \in Con(\hat{\hat{P}},M_o)$ is maximal and $\hat{\hat{M}} \geq \hat{M}$ and $\hat{\hat{P}} \supset \hat{P}$.

Proof: Let be $\hat{M} \in Con(\hat{P},M_o)$. On $\mathfrak{M} := \{(P',M') \mid M' \in Con(P',M_o)$ and $P' \supset P$ and $M' \geq M\}$ a partial ordering $\preccurlyeq$ is defined by $(P',M') \preccurlyeq (P'',M'') :\Leftrightarrow P' \subset P'' \wedge M' \leq M''$. Assume that $\mathfrak{M}$ contains no maximal element. Since P is finite there must be a subset $P_m \subset P$ such that $(P_m,M_m) \in \mathfrak{M}$ for some M_m and $P_m \subset P'$ implies $P_m = P'$. By the assumption there is an infinite sequence $(M_i)_{i \geq 1}$ of pairwise different markings such that $M_1 = M_m$ and $M_i \leq M_{i+1}$, $(P_m,M_i) \in \mathfrak{M}$ for all $i \in \mathbb{N}$. Now for $P_1 := \{p \mid card\{M_i(p) \mid i \geq 1\}$ infinite $\}$ we conclude $P_1 \neq \emptyset$ and $P_1 \cap P_m = \emptyset$. Since $\{M_i(p) \mid p \notin P_1, i \geq 1\}$ is bounded there is a subsequence $(M_{i_j})_{j \geq 1}$ such that $M_{i_j}(p) = M_{i_1}(p)$ for all $p \notin P_1$ and $j \geq 1$. For $\tilde{P} := P_m \cup P_1$ and $M \in \mathbb{N}^r$ defined by $M(p) := M_{i_1}(p)$ if $p \notin \tilde{P}$ and $M(p) := 0$ if $p \in \tilde{P}$ we obtain $M \in Con(\tilde{P},M_o)$. But $P_m \subsetneq \tilde{P}$ is in contradiction to the definition of $\tilde{P}$.

We briefly recapitulate the definition of the coverability graph of a net (cf. the complete coverability tree in [Ha]).

Def 7: The coverability graph of a net $N = (P,T,E,S,M_o)$ has nodes from the set $\mathbb{N}_\omega^r := (\mathbb{N} \cup \{\omega\})^r$. We extend the operation + and the relation < on $\mathbb{N}$ to $\mathbb{N}_\omega := \mathbb{N} \cup \{\omega\}$ (and consequently to $\mathbb{N}_\omega^r$) by $\omega + \omega = \omega + n = n + \omega = \omega$ and $n < \omega$ for all $n \in \mathbb{N}$. For $Q \in \mathbb{N}_\omega^r$ and $M \in \mathbb{N}^r$ we define $Q^{-1}(\omega) := \{p \in P \mid Q(p) = \omega\}$ and $Q \underset{fin}{=} M :\Leftrightarrow \forall p \notin Q^{-1}(\omega) : M(p) = Q(p)$

The coverability graph is defined by the following procedure :

a) $Q_o := M_o$ is the initial node.

b) If $Q \in \mathbb{N}_\omega^r$ is a node already constructed then we establish a labelled edge $Q \xrightarrow{t} Q'$ iff there is a marking $M \in \mathbb{N}^r$ having the following properties:

1. $Q \underset{fin}{=} M$
2. $M \xrightarrow{t} M'$ is in the firing relation for some marking M'.

   Define $P_1 := Q^{-1}(\omega) \cup \{p \mid S(p,t) > 0$ and $\forall p' : E(p',t) > 0 \Rightarrow p' \in Q^{-1}(\omega)\}$
3. If there is a note $\hat{Q} \in \mathbb{N}_\omega^r$ already constructed and a path going from $\hat{Q}$ to Q (possibly $\hat{Q} = Q$) such that $M'(p) \geq \hat{Q}(p)$ for all $p \notin P_1$.

then $Q'^{-1}(\omega) = P_1 \cup \{p \mid M'(p) > \hat{Q}(p)\}$ and $Q' \underset{fin}{=} M'$
else $Q'^{-1}(\omega) = P_1$ and $Q' \underset{fin}{=} M'$

We recall that a net is bounded iff $Q^{-1}(\omega) = \emptyset$ for all nodes Q of it's coverability graph. The following graph is the coverability graph of the net given in the introduction. Any node $Q = (n_1, \ldots, n_8) \in \mathbb{N}_\omega^8$ is represented as a word $a^{n_1} b^{n_2} \ldots h^{n_8}$. Letters having zero exponents are omited.

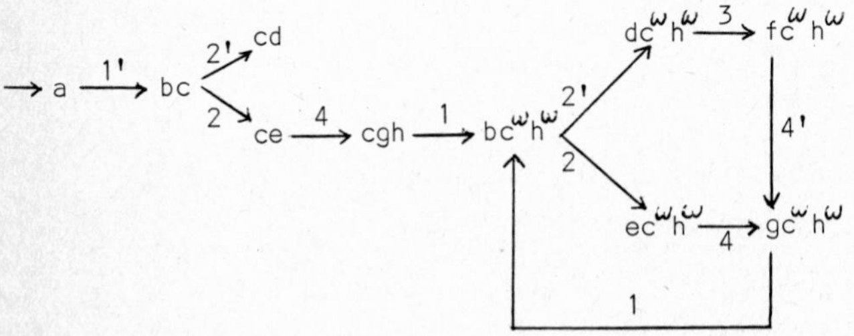

<u>Def 8</u>: A node $Q \in \mathbb{N}_\omega^r$ in the coverability graph of a net is <u>maximal</u> if $Q' \geq Q$ implies $Q' = Q$ for all nodes Q' of the graph.

<u>Lemma 3</u>: A set of places $\hat{P}$ is not majorized for M_o with maximal context $\hat{M}$ if and only if the coverability graph contains a maximal node Q having properties $P = Q^{-1}(\omega)$ and $M \underset{fin}{=} Q$.

Proof: Assume that Q is a maximal node in the coverability graph such that $Q^{-1}(\omega) \neq \emptyset$. Then $\hat{P} := Q^{-1}(\omega)$ is not majorized with context $\hat{M}$ for M_o where $\hat{M}(p) = 0$ if $p \in \hat{P}$ and $\hat{M}(p) = Q(p)$ if $p \notin \hat{P}$. $\hat{M}$ is maximal since Q is maximal.
On the other hand, assume that $\hat{M} \in Con(\hat{P}, M_o)$ is maximal, i.e.

$$\forall k \in \mathbb{N}\ \exists w_k = t_{k_1} t_{k_2} \ldots t_{k_{r_k}} \in T^* \exists M_k : M_o = M_k^o \xrightarrow{t_{k_1}} M_k^1 \xrightarrow{t_{k_2}} M_k^2 \longrightarrow \cdots \longrightarrow M_k^{r_k} = M_k$$

and $\forall p \in \hat{P} : M_k(p) \geq k$ and $\forall p \notin \hat{P}: M_k(p) = \hat{M}(p)$.

Now we prove the <u>assertion:</u> $\{M_k^j(p) \mid k \geq 0,\ 0 \leq j \leq r_k,\ p \notin \hat{P}\}$ is bounded by an integer $b \in \mathbb{N}$.

Assume that the set is not bounded. Then there is a place $\check{p} \notin \hat{P}$ such that for any $q \in \mathbb{N}$ there exist h_q and i_q with $M_{h_q}^{i_q}(\check{p}) \geq q$.

But the sequence $(M_{h_q}^{i_q})_{q \geq 0}$ contains a subsequence $(M_{k_q}^{j_q})_{q \geq 0}$ such that

$$M_{k_q}^{j_q} \leq M_{k_{q+1}}^{j_{q+1}} \text{ and } M_{k_q}^{j_q}(\check{p}) \lneq M_{k_{q+1}}^{j_{q+1}}(\check{p}) \text{ and } M_{k_q}^{j_q}(\check{p}) \geq q \text{ for all } q \geq 0.$$

Hence, considering decompositions $M_o = M^o_{k_q} \xrightarrow{\overline{w}_{k_q}} M^{j_q}_{k_q} \xrightarrow{\overline{\overline{w}}_{k_q}} M^{r_{k_q}}_{k_q} = M_{k_q}$ of the firing sequences $w_{k_q} = \overline{w}_{k_q}\overline{\overline{w}}_{k_q}$ the new firing sequences $\overline{w}_{k_{q+1}}\overline{\overline{w}}_{k_q}$ can be started in M_o : $M_o \xrightarrow{\overline{w}_{k_{q+1}}\overline{\overline{w}}_{k_q}} \overline{M}_{k_q}$ yielding $\overline{M}_{k_q} \geq M_{k_q}$ and $\overline{M}_{k_q}(\check{p}) \ngeq M_{k_q}(\check{p})$.
Define $P_1 := \{p \mid \text{card}\, \{\overline{M}_{k_q}(p) \mid q \geq 0\}$ infinite $\}$ and $\hat{\hat{P}} = \hat{P} \cup P_1$. Since $\{\overline{M}_{k_q}(p) \mid p \notin \hat{\hat{P}}\}$ is bounded there is a subsequence $(\overline{M}_{k_{q_i}})_{0 \leq i}$ and $\hat{\hat{M}}$ such that $\forall p \notin \hat{\hat{P}} : \overline{M}_{k_{q_i}}(p) = \hat{\hat{M}}(p)$ and $\forall p \in \hat{\hat{P}} : \hat{\hat{M}}(p) = 0$. By this $\hat{\hat{P}}$ is shown to be not majorized for M_o with context $\hat{\hat{M}}$. Since $P_1 = \emptyset$ implies $\hat{\hat{M}} \ngeq \hat{M}$ we have $\hat{\hat{P}} \supsetneq \hat{P}$ or $\hat{\hat{M}} \ngeq \hat{M}$ in contradiction to the maximality of $\hat{M}$. Thus the assertion is true.

From all sequences $M_o = M^o_k, M^1_k, \ldots, M^{r_k}_k = M_k$ we select subsequences $(M^{i_j}_k)_{0 \leq j \leq r_k}$ of maximal length such that $M^{i_j}_k(p) < M^{i_{j+1}}_k(p)$ for all $p \in \hat{P}$.
By our assumption the length of these subsequences is not bounded and from the assertion we know that for all subsequences of length greater than b we can find $i_j < i_{j'}$ such that $\forall p \in P - \hat{P} : M^{i_j}_k(p) = M^{i_{j'}}_k(p)$. Let $u,v,w \in T^*$ be firing sequences with $M_o \xrightarrow{u} M^{i_j}_k \xrightarrow{v} M^{i_{j'}}_k \xrightarrow{w} M_k$. Then $M^{i_j}_k \leq M^{i_{j'}}_k$ and $M^{i_j}_k(p) < M^{i_{j'}}_k(p)$ for all $p \in \hat{P}$. From this we can conclude that a path labelled by uvw can be found in the coverability graph leading from the initial node M_o to some node Q with $\hat{P} \subset Q^{-1}(\omega)$ and $Q \underset{fin}{=} \hat{M}$.
If $\hat{P} \neq Q^{-1}(\omega)$ then $Q^{-1}(\omega)$ is not majorized for M_o with context $\hat{\hat{M}}$ defined by $\hat{\hat{M}}(p) = \hat{M}(p)$ for $p \notin \hat{\hat{P}}$ and $\hat{\hat{M}}(p) = 0$ if $p \in \hat{\hat{P}}$. But this is in contradiction to the assumption that $\hat{M}$ is maximal. Hence, $\hat{P} = Q^{-1}(\omega)$ and the lemma is proved, since Q is maximal if $\hat{M}$ is maximal.

We are now ready to establish our first main result.

<u>Theorem 1</u>: The language L(N) of an ordinary Petri net is not rational if and only if there is a non empty set of places $\hat{P}$ and a marking M such that

a) $\hat{P}$ is not majorized for M_o with context M and M is maximal in $Con(\hat{P},M_o)$ and

b) $\hat{P}$ is not uniformly minorized for M.

Proof: Assume that the condition is not satisfied i.e. $\forall \hat{P} \subset P\ \forall M$: $M \notin Con(\hat{P},M_o)$ or M is not maximal or $\hat{P}$ is uniformly minorized for M.

To prove the rationality of L(N) we show that there is an integer k such that the number of tokens in any place cannot be reduced more than k. In this case the net can be simulated by an automaton having a finite number of k-bounded counters, which implies that the language is rational.

Thus we have to prove: $\forall \hat{p} \in P\ \exists k \in \mathbb{N}\ \forall M \in [M_o\rangle\ \forall M' \in [M\rangle : M'(\hat{p}) \geq M(\hat{p})-k$

Assume the contrary: $\exists \hat{p} \in P\ \forall k \in \mathbb{N}\ \exists M_k \in [M_o\rangle\ \exists M'_k \in [M_k\rangle : M'_k(\hat{p}) < M_k(\hat{p})-k$

The sequence $(M_k)_{o \leq k}$ such defined contains a subsequence $(M_{k_i})_{o \leq i}$ which satisfies $M_{k_i} \leq M_{k_{i+1}}$ for all $i \in \mathbb{N}$. The set of places $\hat{P} := \{p \in P \mid \forall m \exists i : M_{k_i}(p) \geq m\}$ contains $\hat{p}$ and $\{M_{k_i}(p) \mid i \geq 0 \wedge p \notin \hat{P}\}$ is bounded by an integer n. Therefore there is a subsequence $(M_{k_{i_j}})_{o \leq j}$ and a marking $\hat{M}$ such that $\forall p \notin \hat{P}\ \forall j \geq 0 : M_{k_{i_j}}(p) = \hat{M}(p)$ and $\hat{M}(p) = 0$ for all $p \in \hat{P}$.

Now it is easy to verify that $\hat{P}$ is not majorized for M_o with context $\hat{M}$ and furthermore some calculations show that $\hat{P}$ is not uniformly minorized for $\hat{M}$. Using lemma 2 for $\hat{M} \in Con(\hat{P},M_o)$ there must be a maximal marking $\hat{\hat{M}} \in Con(\hat{\hat{P}},M_o)$ such that $\hat{M} \leq \hat{\hat{M}}$ and $\hat{P} \subset \hat{\hat{P}}$. It follows that $\hat{\hat{P}}$ is not majorized for M_o with context $\hat{\hat{M}}$ and that $\hat{\hat{P}}$ is not uniformly minorized in contradiction to our initial assumption.

On the other hand we assume that the condition holds and that $\hat{P} \neq \emptyset$ satisfies a) and b), i.e. $\hat{P}$ is not majorized with a maximal context $M \in Con(\hat{P},M_o)$. By lemma 3 the coverability graph contains a maximal node Q such that $\hat{P} = Q^{-1}(\omega)$ and $M \underset{fin}{=} Q$. Since $\hat{P}$ is not uniformly minorized for M there is a place $\hat{p} \in \hat{P}$ satisfying

$\forall k \in \mathbb{N}\ \exists n_k \in \mathbb{N}\ \exists M_k \exists \hat{p}_k \in \hat{P} : M+n_k U_{\hat{P}} \xrightarrow{w_k} M_k$ and $M(\hat{p}_k)+n_k-M_k(\hat{p}_k) \geq k$.

Since the coverability graph is finite and the set of w_k is infinite, there must be a path starting at Q: $Q \xrightarrow{t_{i_1}} Q_1 \xrightarrow{t_{i_2}} \ldots \rightarrow Q_p \xrightarrow{t_{i_{p+1}}} \ldots \xrightarrow{t_{i_{p+q}}} Q_{p+q}$

such that a) $Q_p = Q_{p+q}$

b) $\left(\sum_{j=p+1}^{p+q} (S-E)t_{i_j}\right)(\hat{p}) < 0$

c) $t_{i_1} \ldots t_{i_{p+q}}$ is prefix of a word w_k.

Define $\hat{\hat{P}} := Q_p^{-1}(\omega)$, $v := t_{i_1} \dots t_{i_p}$ and $w := t_{i_{p+1}} \dots t_{i_{p+q}}$.

By the definition of the coverability graph there are words $\{w_1, w_2, \dots w_{n+1}\} \subset T^*$, $\{v_1, \dots v_n\} \subset T^+$ such that

$$\forall k \; \exists q \; : \; M_o \xrightarrow{w_1 v_1^q w_2 \dots w_n v_n^q w_{n+1}} \hat{M}_k \text{ and } \forall p \in \hat{\hat{P}} : \hat{M}_k(p) \geq k \; \wedge$$

$\forall p \notin \hat{\hat{P}} : \hat{M}_k(p) = Q(p)$. It follows that the language

$L_1 := L(N) \cap w_1 v_1^* \dots w_n v_n^* w_{n+1} v w^*$ is not rational. By firing $w_1 v_1^{q_1} \dots w_n v_n^{q_n} w_{n+1}$ we can accumulate a certain unbounded number of tokens in the places $p \in \hat{\hat{P}}$. For an infinity of such markings w can be fired repeatedly. But since each firing of w reduces the number of tokens in p by at least one the number of possible firings of w is bounded and the bound depends on $q_1, \dots, q_n$. Thus L_1 and consequently L(N) are not rational.

<u>Def 9</u>: Petri nets N and $(N, \mathfrak{M}_t)$ are <u>rational</u> if their language L(N) and $L(N, \mathfrak{M})$, respectively, are rational.

Clearly, every bounded net is rational and the coverability graph of a bounded ordinary net can be considered as a finite automaton accepting this language.

<u>Corollary 1</u>: Given an ordinary Petri net N, it is decidable whether N is rational.

Proof: By theorem 1 a net N is rational iff for all maximal nodes Q of its coverability graph and M defined by $M(p) = 0$ if $p \in Q^{-1}(\omega)$, $M \underset{fin}{=} Q$ the set $\hat{P} := Q^{-1}(\omega)$ is uniformly minorized for M. From the proof of the theorem we conclude that this condition can be tested by verifying that there is no

cycle $Q_1 \xrightarrow{t_{i_1}} \dots \xrightarrow{t_{i_n}} Q_{i_n} = Q_1$ starting at $Q = Q_1$ such that

$\left(\sum_{j=1}^{n} (S-E) t_{i_j}\right)(p) < 0$ for at least one $p \in Q_1^{-1}(\omega)$.

<u>Corollary 2</u>: Let N be an ordinary Petri net.

a) If N is rational then a finite automaton accepting L(N) can be effectively constructed.

b) It is decidable whether N is live and rational.

Proof: a) If N is rational then the procedure of corollary 1 gives a k such that no place can loose more than k tokens. Restricting step b)3. in Def 6 to paths of length at least k we obtain anautomaton accepting L(N) taking all nodes as terminal states.

b) First decide whether N is rational. If so we construct an accepting automaton for L(N) and decide whether the net is live or not.

As an example we consider the net N given in the introduction. The net is rational and in this case the coverability graph is a finite automaton accepting L(N). Inspection of this graph shows that the net is not live, but it becomes live for M'_o := ce as initial marking, if transition 1' is deleted from the net.

The same results do not hold for labelled Petri nets. Petri nets can be considered as weak counter automata having several weak counters in the sense of [Bo] or [Hö]. Under this interpretation ordinary Petri nets are deterministic weak counter automata whereas labelled Petri nets are non-deterministic.

Def 10: A program machine PM is given by a finite set $R = \{r_1,\dots,r_p\}$ of registers, a finite set $Q = \{q_o,\dots,q_f\}$ $(f > 1)$ of labels and a finite set of instructions. PM has one instruction q_o : START GOTO q_1, one instruction q_f : HALT, and all other instructions are of the form

q_s : $r_i \leftarrow r_i + 1$ GOTO q_m $\quad (1 \leq i \leq p)$ and

q_s : IF $r_i = 0$ THEN GOTO q_m ELSE $r_i \leftarrow r_i - 1$ GOTO $q_{m'}$.

A computation of PM can be denoted by a word

$$w = q_o 1^{k_1^1} 0 1^{k_1^2} 0 \dots 0 1^{k_1^p} q_1 1^{k_2^1} 0 1^{k_2^2} 0 \dots 0 1^{k_2^p} \dots q_{i_r} 1^{k_r^1} 0 1^{k_r^2} 0 \dots 0 1^{k_r^p} q_f$$

over $\Sigma := Q \cup \{0,1\}$ where q_{i_j} is the label of the instruction executed in step j and k_j^s is the content of register r_s at that step (before the execution of q_{i_j}).

Let be $L(PM) := \{ w \in \Sigma^* \mid w \text{ denotes a computation of PM} \}$.

Lemma 4: L(PM) is rational if and only if L(PM) is finite.

Proof: If L(PM) is not finite then there is an inifinity of words $w_i = q_o 1^{j_i} 0 \dots q_1 1^{j'_i} 0 \dots q_f$ denoting a computation of PM and $j_i = j'_i$.

Since the infinite language $L' = \{ 1^{j_i} 0 1^{j_i} \mid i \geq 0 \}$ is the image of L(PM) by some rational transduction, L(PM) cannot be rational.

Theorem 2: For any program machine PM a labelled net N with terminal marking set $\mathfrak{M}_t$ can be constructed such that $L(N, \mathfrak{M}_t) = \Sigma^* - L(PM)$.

Proof: Without loss we may assume that PM is a program machine with two registers. To test a word $w \in \Sigma^*$ whether it is in $\Sigma^* -$ L(PM) we have to check

a) whether it is not in $q_0 1^* 0 1^* q_1 1^* 0 1^* (Q 1^* 0 1^*)^* q_f$ or whether it contains a subword

$v = q_i 1^{k^1} 0 1^{k^2} \bar{q}_i 1^{\bar{k}^1} 0 1^{\bar{k}^2}$ where

b) $\bar{q}_i$ is not the correct next label or

c) $\bar{k}^1$ or $\bar{k}^2$ do not denote the correct contents with respect to instruction q_i of PM.

All these tests can be made by a net N with terminal marking $\mathfrak{M}_t = \{\begin{pmatrix} 0 \\ \vdots \\ 0 \end{pmatrix}\}$

in a nondeterministic way. Tests a) and b) can be executed by a finite automaton whereas for tests of form c) we need an unbounded place. For instance if we want to test whether $\bar{k}^1 \neq k^1-1$ we check nondeterministicly $\bar{k}^1 < k^1-1$ or $\bar{k}^1 > k^1-1$. The first test can be made in N in the following way:

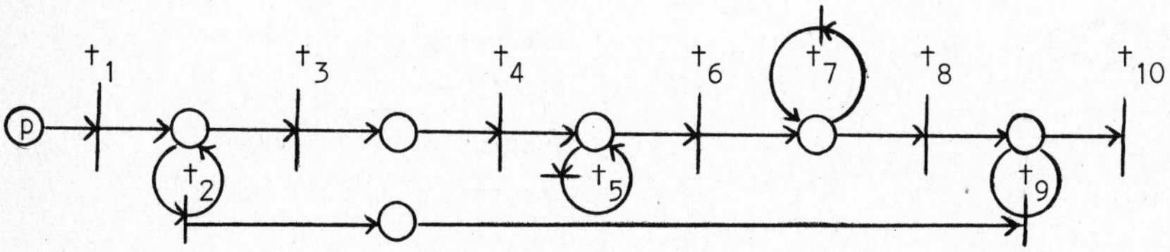

where $h(t_1) = q_i$, $h(t_8) = \bar{q}_i$, $h(t_2) = h(t_3) = h(t_4) = h(t_5) = h(t_7) = h(t_9) = 1$, $h(t_6) = h(t_{10}) = 0$. Now assume that by firing w in N we reach nondeterministic ly the subword v having one token in p. Then v is "read" by firing transitions $t_1, t_2, \ldots, t_{10}$ where the number of firings of t_2, t_5 and t_9 is n_1, n_5 and n_9, respectively. It follows $n_1+2+n_5 = k^1$, $n_9 = \bar{k}^1$, $n_5 \geq 0$, $n_1 \geq n_9$ and we reach the zero marking of $\mathfrak{M}_t$ if and only if $n_1 = n_9$, i.e. $\bar{k}^1+2+n_5=k^1$ and $\bar{k}^1+1 < k^1$. All other tests work in a similar way.

<u>Corollary 3</u>: Given a labelled Petri net N with terminal marking set $\mathfrak{M}_t$, it is undecidable whether $L(N, \mathfrak{M}_t)$ is rational.

Proof: Assume that the problem is decidable. Then for any program machine PM by theorem 2 we can construct a labelled Petri net N with terminal marking set $\mathfrak{M}_t$ such that $L(N, \mathfrak{M}_t) = \Sigma^* -$ L(PM). By lemma 4 the following statements are equivalent:

a) $L(N, \mathfrak{M}_t)$ is rational,

b) $\Sigma^* - L(N, \mathfrak{M}_t) =$ L(PM) is rational

c) L(PM) is finite

But since program machines have the power of Turing machines problem c) cannot be decidable.

In the proofs of theorem 2 and corollary 3 labelled nets with only one unbounded place are used. Therefore the corollary even holds for this subclass of nets. By similar methods it is possible to show that even for this subclass of labelled nets equivalence for terminal languages is undecidable.

In contrast to [Ha] this stronger result is obtained without reducing it to the undecidability of Hilbert's Tenth Problem. For this and more details of the present paper we refer to [VV].

References:

[Bo] BOASSON, L. Paires Itérantes et Langages Algébriques, Thèse de Doctorat, Université Paris VII, 1974

[Ha] HACK, M. Decidability questions for Petri nets, MIT, Laboratory for Computer Science, Techn. Rep. 161,1976

[Hö] HÖPNER, M. Über den Zusammenhang von Szilardsprachen und Matrixgrammatiken, Bericht Nr. 12 des Inst. für Informatik, Univ. Hamburg Hamburg 1974

[Ko] KOPP, H. Bemerkungen über die Struktur paralleler Programmschemata, non published paper

[Pe] PETERSON, J.L. Computation Sequence Sets, Journal of Comp. and Syst.Sci. 13 (1976), 1-24

[VV] VALK,R., VIDAL-NAQUET,G., Sur la Décidabilité de la Rationalité des Langages associés aux Réseaux de Petri Publ. de l'Inst. de Programmation, Univ. Paris VI, Paris 1976

AN ALGORITHM FOR TRANSITIVE CLOSURE WITH LINEAR EXPECTED TIME

C.-P. Schnorr

Abstract: An algorithm for transitive closure is described with expected time $O(n+m^*)$ where n is the number of nodes and m^* is the expected number of edges in the transitive closure.

1. Introduction

Algorithms that construct the transitive closure of a given directed graph have obtained considerable attention. Warshall (1962) proposed an algorithm which works in $O(n^3)$ steps, where n is the number of vertices. In 1970 four Russians published an algorithm with time bound $O(n^3/\lg n)$. M. Fischer and A.R. Meyer (1971) applied Strassens fast matrix multiplication. This yields an algorithm for transitive closure with time bound $O(n^{2.81})$.

Recently Bloniarz, Fischer and Meyer proposed an algorithm for transitive closure with average time $O(n^2 \lg n)$. We propose an improved algorithm with expected time $O(n+m^*)$ where m^* is the expected number of edges in the transitive closure. Moreover the event that this algorithm takes more than cn^2 steps has probability less than 2^{-cn} for some $c > 0$. These bounds hold for all those graph distributions where the probability of a graph only depends on its number of edges and on its number of vertices. This for instance is true whenever the n^2 possible edges of the random graph with n vertices (i.e. whether there is an edge $i \to j$ or not) are identical and independent random variables. The above class of graph distributions is only slightly smaller than the one which is used by Bloniarz, Fischer, Meyer. They require that the probability of a graph only depends on the set of out-degrees of its edges. This latter class of graph distributions is not preserved under the transformation which associates to each graph its edge reversal (the edge $i \to j$ is replaced by $j \to i$ by this transformation). Requiring that the class of graph distributions is closed with respect to the transformation of edge reversal leads to our smaller class of distributions.

2. The algorithm

Our machine model will be the RAM machine with unit costs and addition/subtraction by 1. This model is linear-time-equivalent to the Kolmogorov-Uspensky machine (1958, 1963) and to the machine which was proposed by Schönhage (1970), see Schnorr (1974) for the equivalence proofs.

We suppose that the input graph has node set $\{1,2,\ldots,n\}$ and is given by its adjacency lists $L_i = \{j \mid \exists$ edge from i to j$\}$ for $i = 1,\ldots,n$. Let $m = \Sigma_{i=1}^{n} \|L_i\|$ be the number of edges of the given graph. Let $L_i^r = \{j \mid \exists$ edge from j to i$\}$ $i = 1,\ldots,n$ be the adjacency lists of the edge reversed graph. By standard methods L_i^r $i = 1,\ldots,n$ can be constructed from L_i $i = 1,\ldots,n$ within $O(n+m)$ RAM-steps. j is called a <u>successor</u> of i, if there is a path from i to j. In this case, i is called a <u>predecessor</u> of j.

Informal description of the algorithm

The algorithm has 3 stages. In stage 1 we associate in breadth first search manner to each vertex i a list S_i of successors such that either (1) or (2) holds

(1) $\|S_i\| < \lceil n/2 + 1 \rceil$ and S_i is the complete list of successors of i

(2) $\|S_i\| = \lceil n/2 + 1 \rceil$

Stage 2 of the program is similar to stage 1. We associate to each vertex i a set P_i of predecessors such that either (1) or (2) holds with P_i substituted for S_i.
In stage 3 we adjoin all edges $i \to j$ with $\|S_i\| = \|P_j\| = \lceil n/2+1 \rceil$ to those edges of the transitive closure which have already been found in stages 2 and 3.

It will suffice to describe stage 1 of the algorithm which constructs S_i $i = 1,\ldots,n$ in breadth first search manner. Let stack 1 and stack 2 be two push-down-stacks. The lists Q_j $j = 1,\ldots,n$ are supposed to be initially empty.

stage 1 of the algorithm

```
for i = 1 step 1 until n do
begin S_i : = {i}, stack 1 : = i, stack 2 : = Ø
      counter : = 1, mark i
      while stack 1 ≠ Ø and counter < ⌈n/2 + 1⌉ do
            j : = top node of stack 1
            while counter < ⌈n/2 + 1⌉ and L_j ≠ Ø do
                  a : = first node of L_j
                  L_j : = L_j - {a}, Q_j : = Q_j ∪ {a}
                  if a is not yet marked then
                  [push a at the bottom of stack 1,
                  mark a, S_i : = S_i ∪ {a},
                  counter : = counter + 1]
```

```
        end
        remove j from top of stack 1
        push j on the top of stack 2
    end
    for all j on stack 2
    [unmark j, L_j := L_j ∪ Q_j, Q_j := ∅]
end
```

Comments on the algorithm

Consider the procedure for fixed i. Whenever node j is visited for the first time then j is pushed on the bottom of stack 1. The inner while loop exhausts the adjacency list L_j under examination. As soon as the inner while loop that exhausts L_j is finished then j is removed from stack 1 and pushed on stack 2.

3. Correctness and analysis of the algorithm

Theorem 1

The complete algorithm correctly computes the transitive closure.

Proof: The outer while-loop in stage 1 either finishes because stack 1 = ∅ or because counter = $\lceil n/2 + 1 \rceil$. If it finishes since stack 1 = ∅ then S_i is the complete list of successors of node i. If the while loop finishes with stack 1 ≠ ∅ then counter = $\lceil n/2 + 1 \rceil$ and this means $\|S_i\| = \lceil n/2 + 1 \rceil$. This proves that stage 1 associates to each node i a set of successors S_i such that either (1) or (2) above hold. Stage 2 of the algorithm works exactly as stage 1 with L_i replaced by L_i^r and S_i replaced by P_i.

It remains to prove that for each edge $i \to j$, $i \to j$ is in the transitive closure of the input graph if and only if

$[j \in S_i$ or $i \in P_j$ or $\|S_i\| = \|P_j\| = \lceil n/2 + 1 \rceil]$

"<=" obviously, if $j \in S_i$ or $i \in P_j$ then the edge $i \to j$ is in the transitive closure. If $\|S_i\| = \|P_j\| = \lceil n/2 + 1 \rceil$ then $S_i \cap P_j$ cannot be empty since this would imply $\|S_i \cup P_j\| > n$. However $S_i \cap P_j \neq \emptyset$ implies that $i \to j$ is in the transitive closure.
"=>" if $j \to i$ is in the transitive closure and either $\|S_i\| < \lceil n/2 + 1 \rceil$ or $\|P_j\| < \lceil n/2 + 1 \rceil$ then the correctness conditions (1), (2) of stages 1 and 2 of the algorithm imply that S_i is the complete set of successors of i provided $\|S_i\| < \lceil n/2 + 1 \rceil$ and that P_j is the complete set of predecessors of j provided $\|P_j\| < \lceil n/2 + 1 \rceil$. ∎

<u>Theorem 2</u>

Suppose that the probability of a graph is a function of its number of nodes n and edges m. Then the expected running time of the algorithm is $O(n+m^*)$, where m^* is the expected number of edges in the transitive closure.

<u>Proof:</u> We first consider those parts of the algorithm which are not affected by the distribution. At the very beginning we have to compute L_i^r $i = 1,\dots,n$ from L_i $i = 1,\dots,n$ which takes $O(n + m)$ steps with $m = \Sigma_{i=1}^n \|L_i\|$. Next we consider stage 3 of the algorithm which does the following:

$$\text{construct } P_i^r = \{j \mid i \in P_j\} \quad i = 1,\dots,n$$
$$L_i^* := S_i \cup P_i^r \quad i = 1,\dots,n$$
$$S := \{i \mid \|S_i\| = \lceil n/2 + 1 \rceil\}$$
$$P := \{j \mid \|P_j\| = \lceil n/2 + 1 \rceil\}$$
$$\text{for all } i \in S, \text{ for all } j \in P : L_i^* := L_i^* \cup \{j\}$$

This yields the adjacency lists L_i^* of the transitive closure and stage 3 can clearly be done within worst case run time $O(n + \Sigma_{i=1}^n \|L_i^*\|)$.

It remains to bound the expected run time of stage 1 of the algorithm. Each examination of a node $a \in L_j$ within the inner while loop of stage 1 is said to be a handling of the edge $j \to a$. The number of steps in stage 1 is clearly proportional to the total number of handlings of edges within the construction of S_i $i = 1,\dots,n$. The following Lemma is standard in probability theory.

Lemma 1

Let $A \subset \{1,\dots,n\}$ with $\|A\| = k$ be fixed and let $a_1, a_2, \dots, a_i, \dots$ be independent random variables which are uniformly distributed over $\{1,2,\dots,n\}$. Then $\min \{i \mid a_i \notin A\}$ has the expected value $1 + k/(n-k)$.

Proof: $\text{Prob}\ [a_1,\dots,a_r \in A \text{ and } a_{r+1} \notin A] = (k/n)^r (1-k/n)$

Hence the expected value of $\min \{i \mid a_i \notin A\}$ is

$$1 + \Sigma_{r=1}^{\infty}\ r(k/n)^r (1-k/n). \quad \text{Obviously}$$

$$\Sigma_{r=0}^{\infty}\ r\ \alpha^{r-1} = (1/(1-\alpha))' = 1/(1-\alpha)^2.$$

Hence

$$\Sigma_{r=1}^{\infty}\ r(k/n)^r (1-k/n) = (k/n)/(1-k/n) = k/(n-k).$$

This proves Lemma 1. ∎

Lemma 2

Let $a_1, a_2, \dots, a_i, \dots$ be independent random variables which are uniformly distributed over $\{1,2,\dots,n\}$. Then for $k \le n/2$: $\min\{i \mid \|\{a_1, a_2, \dots, a_i\}\| \ge k\}$ has expected value $\le 1.5k + O(1)$.

Proof:

According to Lemma 1 the expected value of $\min\{i \mid \|\{a_1, a_2, \dots, a_i\}\| \ge k\}$ is bounded by $\Sigma_{\nu=1}^{k} (1+\nu/(n-\nu)) \le 1.5k + O(1)$ provided $k \le n/2$. ∎

Now let $a_1, a_2, \dots, a_j, \dots \in \{1,2,\dots,n\}$ be the sequence of nodes which are examined in the inner while loop during the construction of S_i. Let a_j $j = h(\nu),\ldots,h(\nu+1)-1$ exhaust the ν-th adjacency list $L_{\sigma(\nu)}$ under examination, i.e. $L_{\sigma(\nu)} = (a_{h(\nu)},\ldots,a_{h(\nu+1)-1})$. Here $h:N \to N$ is a function that depends on the input graph and the start vertex i. Let $S_i(t) = \{i,a_1,\ldots,a_t\}$ be the set S_i after examining the first t nodes. We like to apply Lemma 2 in order to bound the expected value of $\min\{j > t \mid a_j \notin S_i(t)\}$. This is the number of handling of edges that is required in order to increase $S_i(t)$ by one element. However, the sequence $(a_\mu \mid \mu = 1,2,\ldots)$ is not independent.

The segments $a_{h(\nu)},\ldots,a_{h(\nu+1)-1}$ that represent the adjacency list $L_{\sigma(\nu)}$ are obtained by two steps from a sequence of independent random variables.

(1) by eliminating elements which previously occurred and
(2) by a subsequent permutation of this sequence.

Obviously $\min\{j > t \mid a_j \notin S_i(t)$ does not increase by eliminating elements a_μ which previously occurred. On the other hand a permutation of the sequence a_μ might well increase the expected value of $\min\{j > t \mid a_j \notin S_i(t)\}$ provided $S_i(t)$ is fixed. This is for instance the case if $S_i(t) = \{j,j+1,\ldots,n\}$ and $a_{t+1},\ldots,a_{t+r},\ldots$ is ordered such that all a_μ with $a_\mu \geq j$ come first. However, a permutation of the sequence a_μ does not change the expected value of $\min\{j > t \mid a_j \notin S_i(t)\}$ provided $S_i(t)$ is randomized in a way such that the events $a \in S_i(t)$ for $a \in \{1,\ldots,n\}$ are independent and have the same probability.

It follows by induction on ν that for random variable $t = h(\nu)-1$ the events $a \in S_i(t)$ are independent and uniformly distributed for $a \in \{1,2,\ldots,n\} - \{i\}$. (Observe that t is a random variable since h is a random function depending on the input graph). In order to apply Lemma 2 it is sufficient that the sets $S_i(t)$

for $t = h(\nu)-1$ are uniformly randomized over $\{1,2,\ldots,n\}$. Moreover the effect of $\mathrm{Prob}[i \in S_i(t)] = 1$ can be eliminated by taking the average with respect to i. This altogether proves

Lemma 3

Let $F(i,k)$ be the expected value of $\min\{t \mid \|S_i(t)\| \geq k\}$ then $\frac{1}{n}\Sigma_{i=1}^{n} F(i,k) \leq 1.5k + O(1)$, provided $k \leq n/2$.

Let s be the expected and let $\|S_i\|$ be the actual size of S_i upon completion of stage 1. Obviously $s = \Sigma_{k=1}^{\lceil n/2+1 \rceil} k \cdot \mathrm{Prob}(\|S_i\|=k)$ Observe that s does not depend on i. Let Q be the expected total number of handled edges during the construction of S_i $i = 1,\ldots,n$.

Lemma 4

$$Q \leq 1.5\, ns + O(n)$$

Proof:

$$Q \leq \Sigma_{i=1}^{n} \Sigma_{k=1}^{\lceil n/2+1 \rceil} \mathrm{Prob}(\|S_i\| = k) F(i,k)$$

by Lemma 3

$$\leq \Sigma_{k=1}^{\lceil n/2+1 \rceil} \mathrm{Prob}(\|S_i\| = k)(1.5kn + O(n))$$

$$\leq 1.5ns + O(n)$$ ▨

Because of Lemma 4 and $ns \leq m^*$ the total number of handled edges during stage 1 and 2 of the algorithm is bounded as $3m^* + O(n)$ and this finishes the proof of theorem 2. ▨

Our algorithm not only has a linear expected running time but the event that the running time exceeds cn^2 for some fixed c has probability less than 2^{-cn}. We shall use the following fact from probability theory, see e.g Erdös, Spencer (1974).

Lemma 5

Let X_i $i = 1,\ldots,k$ be independent random variables with $\mathrm{Prob}(X_i = 1) = \mathrm{Prob}(X_i = -1) = 1/2$. Then

$$\mathrm{Prob}(\Sigma_{i=1}^{k} X_i > \lambda) \leq e^{-2\lambda^2/k}.$$

Let $A_{n,q}$ be the event that there are more than n^2q handlings of edges within stage 1 of the algorithm. Set $X_i = 1$ if the i-th handling of an edge leads to some node which is already in the set S_j under construction. Otherwise set $X_i = -1$. Obviously $\mathrm{Prob}(X_i = 1) \leq 1/2$ and $\mathrm{Prob}(X_i = -1) \geq 1/2$, this follows from $\|S_i\| < \lceil n/2 + 1 \rceil$.

Lemma 4 holds a fortiori in this case, provided that the X_i are independent. However, this is not true since the same edges are handled during the construction of S_j and S_ν. On the other hand the event $A_{n,q}$ implies that nq edges are handled during the construction of some S_j, and the random variables X_i which correspond to those edges are independent (more precisely: this sequence of edges is obtained from a sequence of independent random variables by transforming pairwise disjoint segments of length $\leq n$ as follows:

(1) by eliminating elements which previously occurred in the segment

(2) and by a subsequent permutation of this segment).

Therefore Lemma 5 can be applied and for $k = nq$ and $\lambda = (q-2)n$ this yields $\mathrm{Prob}(A_{n,q}) \leq n\, e^{-2(q-2)^2 n/q}$.

This clearly proves

Theorem 3

There is some $c > 0$ such that the event, that the algorithm takes more than cn^2 steps, has probability less than 2^{-cn}.

Acknowledgement:

I thank M. Fischer for valuable comments.

References

[1] Arlazarov, V.L., Dinic, E.A., Kronod, M.A., Faradzev, I.A.: On economical construction of the transitive closure of an oriented graph. Dokl. Acad.Nauk,SSSR, 11 (1970), 1209-1210

[2] Bloniarz, Fischer, Meyer: A note on the average time to compute transitive closures. In: Automata Languages and Programming. Ed.: Michaelson and Milner, Edinburgh University Press 1976

[3] Erdös, Spencer: Probabilistic methods in combinatorics. New York: Academic Press (1974)

[4] Fischer, Meyer: Boolean matrix multiplication and transitive closure. Twelfth Annual IEEE. Symposium on Switching and Automata Theory, East Lansing, Michigan, 1971, 129-131

[5] Kolmogorov, Uspenskij: On the definition of an algorithm. Uspecki mat. Nauk 13,4 3-28 (1958), English translation in: Amer.math.Soc. Transl.II Ser.29, 217-245 (1963)

[6] Schnorr, C.P.: Rekursive Funktionen und ihre Komplexität. Teubner, Stuttgart 1974

[7] Schönhage, A.: Universelle Turingspeicherung. In: Automatentheorie und formale Sprachen. Ed.: Dörr, Hotz. B.I. Mannheim Wien Zürich, 1970

[8] Warshall, S.: A theorem on Boolean matrices. J. ACM 9 (1962), 11-12

THE LBA-PROBLEM AND THE TRANSFORMABILITY OF THE CLASS $\mathcal{E}^2$

B. Monien

1. Definitions and basic results

The relationships between the classes defined by deterministic and nondeterministic tape complexity (denoted by TAPE (f(n)) and NTAPE (f(n)), respectively) have been of considerable interest in the last years. Several authors ([2],[4],[8],[9]) showed that NTAPE(log n) = TAPE(log n) holds if and only if certain subclasses of the context free languages (linear languages, one-way one-counter languages) are contained in TAPE(log n).

In this paper we consider the original LBA-problem, that is the problem whether NTAPE (n) = TAPE (n). We show how to get equivalent problems by transformations within the class $\mathcal{E}^2$.
By using this method we show in section 2 that NTAPE(n) is equal to TAPE(n) if and only if each languages $L \subset \dashv \{1\}^* \vdash$,which is acceptable by some nondeterministic two-way one-counter automaton whose counter length is bounded by the length of its input, is contained in TAPE(log n).

Now let $\mathcal{E}^2$ be the class defined by A.Grzegorczyk in [3].

Definition: An $\mathcal{E}^2$-acceptor is a 6 tuple $A = (k,\pi,\alpha,T,\omega,\beta)$ where $k \in \mathbb{N}$ and $\pi: \mathbb{N} \to \{0,1\}, \alpha,\beta: \mathbb{N} \to \mathbb{N}^k$, $T: \mathbb{N}^k \to \mathbb{N}^k, \omega: \mathbb{N}^k \to \{0,1\}$ are functions belonging to $\mathcal{E}^2$ such that $T^y\alpha(x) \leq \beta(x)$ holds for all $x,y \in \mathbb{N}$.

$t_A(x) = (\mu y)[\pi T^y \alpha(x) = 0]$ is called running time of A and

$L_A = \{x \in \mathbb{N} \mid \omega T^{t_A(x)} \alpha(x) = 0\}$ is the language accepted by A.

Definition: An $\mathcal{E}^2$ acceptor type is a 6-tuple $\mathfrak{A} = (M,F_0,F_1,F_2,F_3,F_4)$, where $M \subset \mathbb{N}$ and $F_i \subset \mathcal{E}^2$ for all $i = 0,\ldots,4$.

An acceptor $A = (k,\pi,\alpha,T,\omega,\beta)$ belongs to the type $\mathfrak{A}$ iff $k \in \mathbb{N}$ and $\pi \in F_0, \alpha \in F_1, T \in F_2, w \in F_3, \beta \in F_4$.

We set $\hat{\mathcal{E}}^2 = (\mathbb{N}, \mathcal{E}^2, \mathcal{E}^2, \mathcal{E}^2, \mathcal{E}^2, \mathcal{E}^2)$.

It is clear that a language is accepted by an $\mathcal{E}^2$ acceptor iff its characteristic function belongs to $\mathcal{E}^2$ (and its binary coding belongs to TAPE(n), respectively).

<u>Definition</u>: Let $\mathcal{A}$, $\mathcal{B}$ be $\mathcal{E}^2$ acceptor types. $\mathcal{B}$ is <u>transformable</u> to $\mathcal{A}$ if there exists a sequence of natural numbers k_i, $i \in \mathbb{N}$, and two sequences of functions $\phi_i : \mathbb{N} \to \mathbb{N}$, $\kappa_i : \mathbb{N}^i \to \mathbb{N}^{k_i}$, $i \in \mathbb{N}$, each of the functions belonging to $\mathcal{E}^2$, such that to every acceptor $A = (i,\pi,\alpha,T,\omega,\beta)$ of the type $\mathcal{B}$ there exists an acceptor $A' = (k',\pi',\alpha',T',\omega',\beta')$ of the type $\mathcal{A}$ such that the following holds:

(0) $k' = k_i$

(1) $$\bigwedge_{z\in\mathbb{N}^i} \bigvee_{y\in\mathbb{N}} [T'^{y}\kappa_i(z) = \kappa_i T(z) \wedge \bigwedge_{0<\tilde{y}<y} [T'^{\tilde{y}}\kappa_i(z) \notin \kappa(\mathbb{N}^i)]]$$

(2) $$\bigwedge_{x\in\mathbb{N}} \bigvee_{y\in\mathbb{N}} [T'^{y}\alpha'\phi_i(x) = \kappa_i\,\alpha(x) \wedge \bigwedge_{0<\tilde{y}<y} [T'^{\tilde{y}}\alpha'\phi_i(x) \notin \kappa(\mathbb{N}^i)]]$$

(3) $$\pi'(y) = 0 \iff \bigvee_{z\in\mathbb{N}^i} [y = \kappa_i(z) \wedge \pi(z) = 0]$$

(4) $$\omega'(y) = 0 \iff \bigvee_{z\in\mathbb{N}^i} [y = \kappa_i(z) \wedge \omega(z) = 0]$$

Note that these 4 conditions guarantee that the acceptor A' simulates (apart from the coding ϕ of the input) every step of the acceptor A in a finite number of steps. A' halts (accepts) iff A halts (accepts).

<u>Definition</u>: A <u>nondeterministic $\mathcal{E}^2$ acceptor</u> is a 6-tuple $A = (k,\pi,\alpha,F,\omega,\beta)$ where $k,\pi,\alpha,\omega,\beta$ have the same meaning as in the deterministic case and where $F \subset \{f \in \mathcal{E}^2 \mid f: \mathbb{N}^k \to \mathbb{N}^k\}$ is a finite set.

A defines for each $x \in \mathbb{N}$ a relation $R_A(x)$ on $\mathbb{N}^k$ by

$$y\,R_A(x)\,z \iff \pi(y) = 0 \wedge z = y$$
$$\vee\ \pi(y) \neq 0 \wedge z \leq \beta(x) \wedge \bigvee_{f\in F} [z = f(y)]$$

Let $R_A^*(x)$ be the transitive closure of $R_A(x)$. Then the language L_A accepted by A is defined in the following way:

$$L_A = \{x \mid \bigvee_{z\in\mathbb{N}^k} [\alpha(x)\,R_A^*(x)\,z \wedge \pi(z) = 0 \wedge \omega(z) = 0]$$

Definition: Let $\mathfrak{A} = (M, F_o, \ldots, F_n)$ be an $\mathcal{E}^2$ acceptor type. A nondeterministic $\mathcal{E}^2$ acceptor $A = (k, f_o, f_1, F, f_3, f_4)$ belongs to the type $\mathfrak{A}$ if $k \in M$, $F \subset F_2$ and $f_i \in F_i$ for $i = 0,1,3,4$.

Definition: An $\mathcal{E}^2$-acceptor type is called deterministic (nondeterministic) total if for every (nondeterministic) $\mathcal{E}^2$-acceptor A there exists a (nondeterministic) $\mathcal{E}^2$-acceptor if the type $\mathfrak{A}$ such that $L_A = L_{A'}$ holds.

Now we will prove our basic result.

Theorem 1: Let $\mathfrak{A}, \mathfrak{B}$ be $\mathcal{E}^2$ acceptor types. Let $\mathfrak{B}$ be nondeterministic total and transformable to $\mathfrak{A}$. Then NTAPE(n) = TAPE(n) holds iff the characteristic function of every language, acceptable by some nondeterministic acceptor of the type $\mathfrak{A}$, belongs to $\mathcal{E}^2$.

Proof: Let Σ be an alphabet and let the mapping $c_\Sigma : \Sigma \to \mathbb{N}$ be defined by

$$c_\Sigma(a_1 \ldots a_n) = \sum_{i=1}^{n} c(a_i) \cdot |\Sigma|^{i-1}, \quad \text{where } c: \Sigma \to \{1, \ldots, |\Sigma|\} \text{ is a bijective}$$

mapping.

Consider some $L \subset \Sigma^*$. $L \in$ TAPE(n) (or NTAPE(n), respectively) if and only if $c_\Sigma(L)$ is accepted by some $\mathcal{E}^2$-acceptor (nondeterministic $\mathcal{E}^2$-acceptor, respectively) of the type $\mathfrak{B}$.

Now let $A = (i, \pi, \alpha, F, \omega, \beta)$ be an arbitrarely chosen nondeterministic $\mathcal{E}^2$-acceptor of the type $\mathfrak{B}$. Set $r = |F|$ and suppose $F = \{T_1, \ldots, T_r\}$. Since $\mathfrak{B}$ is transformable to $\mathfrak{A}$ there exist $k_i \in \mathbb{N}$ and function $\phi_i : \mathbb{N} \to \mathbb{N}, \kappa_i : \mathbb{N}^i \to \mathbb{N}^{k_i}$ such that to each acceptor $A_j = (i, \pi, \alpha, T_j, \omega, \beta)$, $j = 1, \ldots, r$, there exists an acceptor $A'_j = (k_i, \pi'_j, \alpha'_j, T'_j, \omega'_j, \beta'_i)$ of type $\mathfrak{A}$ such that conditions (1)-(4) hold.

Because of (3) and (4) $\pi'_1 = \pi'_j$ and $\omega'_1 = \omega'_j$ hold for all $j = 1, \ldots, k$.

Now set $\tilde{A} = (k_i, \pi'_1, \alpha'_1, F', w'_1, \beta')$ where

$F = \{T'_1, \ldots, T'_r\}$ and $\beta'(x) = \max\{\beta'_j(x) \mid j \in \{1, \ldots, r\}\}$.

Then the following holds:

$x \in L_A \iff \exists\, t \in \mathbb{N}$ and $x_o, \ldots, x_t \in \mathbb{N}$:

$$x_o = \alpha(x) \wedge \pi(x_t) = \omega(x_t) = 0 \wedge \bigwedge_{\nu=0}^{t-1} \bigvee_{f \in F} [f(x_\nu) = x_{\nu+1}]$$

$\iff \exists\, t \in \mathbb{N}$ and $z_o, \ldots, z_t, y_o, \ldots, y_{t-1} \in \mathbb{N}$:

$$z_o = T_1'^{\,y_o} \alpha' \emptyset_i(x) \wedge \pi'(z_t) = \omega'(z_t) = 0$$

$$\wedge \bigvee_{\nu=0}^{t-1} \bigvee_{f \in F'} [f^{y_i}(z_\nu) = z_{\nu+1}]$$

$\iff \emptyset_i(x) \in L_{\tilde{A}}$

Now let g_A and $g_{\tilde{A}}$ be the characteristic functions of A and $\tilde{A}$, respectively. Then $g_A = g_{\tilde{A}}\emptyset$. Therefore $g_{\tilde{A}} \in \mathcal{E}^2$ implies $g_A \in \mathcal{E}^2$.

We will show in section 2 how this theorem can be applied in order to prove the new equivalence result mentioned in the beginning of this section.

We defined the notion of transformability in a quite general manner because the author believes that future investigations concerning the LBA problem should concern not only "classical" automata. The essential condition in the definition of the transformability is the first part of condition (1). If the κ_i, $i \in M$, are injective mappings then this condition is fulfilled if a class $F \subset \mathcal{E}^2$ is given such that to every $T \in \mathcal{E}^2$, $T\colon \mathbb{N}^i \to \mathbb{N}^i$, there exists a $T' \in F$ such that

$$\bigwedge_{z \in \mathbb{N}^k} \bigvee_{y \in \mathbb{N}} [T(z) = \kappa_i^{-1} T'^y \kappa_i(z)]$$

Therefore the structure of the class $\mathcal{E}^2$ has to be studied.

On the other hand only little attention has been payed to the study of very simple cases of nondeterminism. It is known that the $\mathcal{E}^2$-acceptor type $\mathfrak{A} = (\{1\},\{\psi\},\{id\},\mathcal{E}^2,\{\psi\},\mathcal{E}^2)$

where

$$\psi(x) = \begin{cases} 0, & \text{if } x = 0 \\ 1 & \text{otherwise} \end{cases}, \quad id(x) = x$$

is nondeterministic total.

<u>Question</u>: Does the 0-1-function which is computed by the nondeterministic $\mathcal{E}^2$-acceptor $A = (1,\psi,id,\{f,g\},\psi,id)$

where

$$f(x) = \begin{cases} \frac{x}{2} & \text{, if } x \equiv 0 \bmod 2 \\ x & \text{, otherwise} \end{cases}, \quad g(x) = \begin{cases} \frac{x+1}{3} & \text{, if } x \equiv 2 \bmod 3 \\ x & \text{, otherwise} \end{cases}$$

belong to $\mathcal{E}^2$?

2. The new equivalence result

We consider two-way k-counter automata which are defined in the following way (see f.e. [1]).

Definition: A two-way k-counter automaton $M = (S,X,\delta,s_o,F)$ consists of a finite memory (S - set of states, $s_o \in S$ - starting state, $F \subset S$ - set of final states), k counters and an input tape (X - set of input symbols) with a two-way read-only head. $\delta: S \times X \times \{0,1\}^k \to 2^{S \times \{-1,0,+1\}^{k+1}}$ is the transition function.

A configuration of M is a (k+3) - tuple $(s,w,i,n_1,\dots,n_k) \in S \times X^* \times \mathbb{N}^{k+1}$. In the usual way δ defines a relation $\to$ on the set of configurations. $\overset{*}{\to}$ is the transitive closure of $\to$. M is called deterministic if each image under δ has at most one element. Otherwise M is called nondeterministic.

We denote by $\mathcal{C}_k, k \in \mathbb{N}$, the class of all languages acceptable by nondeterministic two-way k-counter automata whose counter lenghts are bounded by the lenght of the input. More formally,

$L \in \mathcal{C}_k$.

<=> There exists a nondeterministic two-way k-counter automaton M with the following properties:

1. $w \in L$ = $\exists\ t \in F;\ i,n_1,\dots,n_k \in \mathbb{N}$:

$$(s_o,w,0,0,\dots,0) \overset{*}{\underset{M}{\to}} (t,w,i,n_1,\dots,n_k)$$

2. For all $w \in L$ there exists a sequence of configutations leading to acceptance such that all counter lenghts are bounded by $\ell(w)$.

Now suppose that a nondeterministic two-way k-counter automaton operates only on unary input strings (that means that the input strings are of the form $\dashv 1^n \vdash$, $n \in \mathbb{N}$.). In this case we can associate to A an $\mathcal{E}^2$ acceptor $B = (k+3,\pi,\alpha,T,\omega,\beta)$ in a quite natural way.

Note that we can identify the set S with the set $\{0,\ldots,q\}$ for $q = |S|-1$. Let us assum that $|F| = 1$ and that s_o and F are identified with 0 and $\{q\}$, respectively. Furthermore we identify each input string $\dashv 1^n \vdash$ with the number n. Then to each configuration of A there corresponds an element of $\mathbb{N}^{k+3}$. The functions π,α,ω,β are defined by

$$\pi(n) = \omega(n) = 0 \iff n \in \{q\} \times \mathbb{N}^k$$

$$\alpha(x) = (0,x,0,\ldots,0)$$

$$\beta(x) = (x+1,x+1,\ldots,x+1)$$

The function $T: \mathbb{N}^{k+3} \to \mathbb{N}^{k+3}$ maps a tuple $(s,x,z_o,\ldots,z_k)$ with $s \leq q$ onto a tuple $(s',x,z_o+\eta_o,\ldots,z_k+\eta_k)$ where

(1) $s' \leq q, \eta_\nu \in \{-1,0,+1\}$ $\quad\forall\, \nu = 0,\ldots,k$

(2) $z_o + \eta_o \leq x+1, z_\nu + \eta_\nu \leq 0$ $\quad\forall\, \nu = 0,\ldots,k$

(3) s' and $\eta_o,\ldots,\eta_k$ are determined uniquely by s and the predicates $z_o = x+1$, $z_\nu = 0$ $(\nu=0,\ldots,k)$.

Let $\mathcal{L}$ be the acceptor type defined in this way for arbitrary k and let $\mathcal{L}_1$ be the acceptor type defined by k = 1.

Let us denote by $\mathcal{C}_k^1$ (TAPE(...), respectively) the class of all languages $L \in \mathcal{C}_k$(TAPE(...), respectively) such that $L \subset \dashv \{1\}^* \vdash$.

Then the main result of this paper is the following

Theorem 2: NTAPE(n) = TAPE(n)
$\iff \mathcal{C}_1^1 \subset \mathrm{TAPE}^1(\log n)$

Theorem 2 follows immediately from theorem 1 and the following two lemmas.

Lemma 1:

(1) $\mathcal{L}$ is nondeterministic total

(2) $L \in \mathrm{TAPE}^1(\log n) \iff g_L \in \mathcal{E}^2$

where
$$g_L(x) = \begin{cases} 0, & \text{if } \dashv 1^x \vdash \in L \\ 1, & \text{otherwise} \end{cases}$$

Proof: It follows from the definition of the Grzegorczyk classes [3] that $f \in \mathcal{E}^2 \iff L = \{x \mid f(x) = 0\}$ is accepted by some $\mathcal{E}^2$-acceptor

Now let Σ be some alphabet. Set $r = |\Sigma|$. Let $c_r : \Sigma \to \{1,\dots,r\}$ be some bijective function and let us denote by c_r also the extension $c_r : \Sigma^* \to \mathbb{N}$ defined by

$$c_r(\mathcal{E}) = 0$$

$$c_r(a\,v) = c_r(a) + r \cdot c_r(v) \qquad \forall\, a \in \Sigma, v \in \Sigma^*.$$

c_r is a bijective mapping.

Let $L \subset \Sigma^*$ be some language. It is wellknown ([6],[7]) that the following holds:

$c_r(L)$ is accepted by some $\mathcal{E}^2$-acceptor (nondeterministic $\mathcal{E}^2$-acceptor)

$\iff L \in TAPE(n)$ ($NTAPE(n)$, respectively)

$\iff \{\dashv 1^{c_r(v)} \vdash \mid v \in L\} \in TAPE^1(\log n)$ ($NTAPE^1(\log n)$, respectively)

Therefore $g_L \in \mathcal{E}^2$

$\iff \{x \mid g_L(x) = 0\}$ is accepted by some $\mathcal{E}^2$-acceptor

$\iff L = \{\dashv 1^x \vdash \mid g_L(x) = 0\} \in TAPE^1(\log n)$

We still have to prove (1). With the same method which was used in [1] in order to prove a similar result it can be seen easily that $NTAPE(\log n) = \bigcup_{k \in \mathbb{N}} \mathcal{C}_k$. Furthermore it is clear that for every set $M \subset \mathbb{N}$ M is accepted by some nondeterministic $\mathcal{E}^2$-acceptor of the type $\mathcal{B}$ iff $\{\dashv 1^n \vdash \; n \in M\} \in \bigcup_{k \in \mathbb{N}} \mathcal{C}_k$. Therefore (1) follows.

$\square$

Lemma 2: $\mathcal{L}$ is transformable to $\mathcal{L}_1$.

Proof: For each $k \in \mathbb{N}$ we have to define functions $\phi_k : \mathbb{N} \to \mathbb{N}$ and $\kappa_k : \mathbb{N}^{k+3} \to \mathbb{N}^{\psi}$ in such a way that to every acceptor $A = (k+3,\pi,\alpha,T,\omega,\beta)$ of the type $\mathcal{L}$ there exists an acceptor $A' = (4,\pi',\alpha',T',\omega',\beta')$ of the type $\mathcal{L}_1$ such that the conditions (1) - (4) hold. Note that $\pi',\alpha',\omega',\beta'$ are determined uniquely by the fact that A' is an acceptor of the type $\mathcal{L}_1$.

Let $\kappa_k^{\nu} : \mathbb{N}^{k+3} \to \mathbb{N}^{k+3}$, $\nu = 1,\ldots,4$ be the four functions defining κ_k. Since every acceptor of the type $\mathcal{L}_1$ can be interpreted as a two-way 1-counter automaton κ_k^1 computes the state, κ_k^2 the input number, κ_k^3 the head position and κ_k^4 the number stored by the counter of the automaton A'.

Therefore condition (2) can hold only if

$$\kappa_k^2(s,y,z_o,\ldots,z_k) = y \qquad \forall s,y,z_o,\ldots,z_k \in \mathbb{N}.$$

We define κ_k^1 in such a way that for every acceptor $A = (k,\ldots)$ of the type $\mathcal{L}$ the function κ_k^1 maps the "set of states" of A injective into the "set of states" of the associated automaton A' of the type $\mathcal{L}_1$. Formally we set

$$\kappa_k^1\ (s,y,z_o,\ldots,z_k) = 2\,s \qquad \forall s,y,z_o,\ldots,z_k \in \mathbb{N}$$

Furthermore we set

$$\kappa_k^4(s,y,z_o,\ldots,z_k) = 0 \qquad \forall\ s,y,z_o,\ldots,z_k \in \mathbb{N}$$

and $$\kappa_k^3(s,y,z_o,\ldots,z_k) = Q_k(y,z_o,\ldots,z_k)$$

with some function $Q_k : \mathbb{N}^{k+2} \to \mathbb{N}$ which we still have to define.

The main difficulty in proving this theorem is to find pairing functions $P_q : \mathbb{N}^q \to \mathbb{N}$ which belong to $\mathcal{E}^2$ (especially they must be polynomially bounded) and which have the property that given some number $m = p_q(n_1,\ldots,n_q)$ the test "which of the n_v, $v = 1,\ldots,q$, is equal to 0" and the operations $m \to P_q\ (n_1 + \eta_1,\ldots,n_q + \eta_q)$, $\eta_v \in \{-1,0,+1\}$, can be performed by a two-way one-counter automaton.

Essentially we define the functions $P_q, q \in \mathbb{N}$, in such a way that given some numbers $n_1,\ldots,n_q \in \mathbb{N}$ the 3-way decomposition of $P_q(n_1,\ldots,n_q)$ is $2\,b(n_1)2\ldots2\,b(n_q)$. Here $b\colon \mathbb{N} \to \{0,1\}^*$ denotes the mapping which associates to each natural number its binary decomposition. Because of technical reasons we modify the notion of a pairing function a little and we define the functions $P_q\colon \bigcup_{n \in \mathbb{N}} \{0,\ldots,2^{\ell(b(n))}-1\}^q \times \{n\} \to \mathbb{N}$ in such a way that for all $m_1,\ldots,m_q,n$ with $m_1,\ldots,m_q < 2^{\ell(b(n))}$ the 3-nary decomposition of $P_q(m_1,\ldots,m_q,n)$ is $2\,\mathcal{S}_1\,2\ldots2\,\mathcal{S}_q\,2$ with $\ell(\mathcal{S}_v) = \ell(b(n))$ and $\mathcal{S}_v = 0\ldots0\,b(m_v)^R$ for all $v = 1,\ldots,q$. (Here ℓ denoted lenths of a 0-1-string and ^{R} its reversal).

The definition of κ_k, $k \in \mathbb{N}$ is brought to an end by setting

$$Q_k(y,z_o,z_1,\ldots,z_k) = P_{k+2}(z_1,\ldots,z_k,z_o,y+1-z_o,y+1)$$

Note that the length of the 3-nary decomposition of $Q_k(y,z_o,\ldots,z_k)$ depends only on y (as long as $Q_k(y,z_o,\ldots,z_k)$ is defined). This length is given by $r_k(y) = (k+2)\cdot\ell(y+1)+k+3$. Here ℓ denotes the function $\ell\colon\mathbb{N}\to\mathbb{N}$ defined by $\ell(x) = \ell(b(x))$.

The functions $\emptyset_k, k \in \mathbb{N}$, are defined in the following way: For every $x \in \mathbb{N}$ the 3-nary decomposition of $\emptyset_k(x)$ is

$$\underbrace{0\ldots0}_{r_k(x)}\;2\;\underbrace{\underbrace{0\ldots0}_{\ell(x+1)}\;2\ldots2\;\underbrace{0\ldots0}_{\ell(x+1)}}_{k+1}\;2b(x+1)^R\;2\;\underbrace{0\ldots0}_{r_k(x)}\;1$$

Note that

$$\emptyset_k(x) = 3^{r_k(x)}\cdot P_{k+2}(0,\ldots,0,x+1,x+1)+3^{r_k(x)+1}$$

We have to show that to every acceptor $A = (k+3,\ldots)$ of the type $\mathcal{L}$ there exists an acceptor $A' = (4,\ldots)$ of the type $\mathcal{L}_1$ such that (1) and (2) are fulfilled.

Condition (2) stated that A' can compute $h = P_{k+2}(0,\dots,0,x+1,x+1)$ starting from $h = \emptyset_k(x)$ and $c = 0$. (Let us denote by h the head position and by c the content of the counter of the automaton A').

A' operates in the following way.

1. $h \leftarrow \max\{3^j \mid 3^j \leq \emptyset_k(x)\}$, $h \leftarrow \emptyset_k(x) - h$

   (afterwards $h = 3^{r_k(x)} \cdot P_{k+2}(0,\dots,0,x+1,x+1)$)

2. While $R_3(h) = 0$ do $h \leftarrow D_3(k)$

   (afterwards $h = P_{k+2}(0,\dots,0,x+1,x+1)$)

[Here $D_3, R_3 \colon \mathbb{N} \to \mathbb{N}$ denote the functions $R_3(x) = x \bmod 3$, $D_3(x) = (x - R_3(x))/3$.]

We now have to define A' in such a way that also the condition (1) is fulfilled. Let A' start with $h = P_{k+2}(z_1,\dots,z_k,z_o,y+1-z_o,y+1)$ and $c = 0$ with $y \in \mathbb{N}$ and $z_o,\dots,z_k < 2^{\ell(y)}$. We divide the operations of A' into two parts.

I. A' escamines which of predicates $z_o = y+1$ and $z_\nu = 0, \nu = 0,\dots,k$, hold.

II. A' computed $h = P_{k+2}(z_1 + \eta_1,\dots,z_o+\eta_o, y+1-z_o-\eta_o, y+1)$ for arbitrarely given $\eta_\nu \in \{-1,0,+1\}$, $\nu = 0,\dots,k$.

I. A' operates in the following way

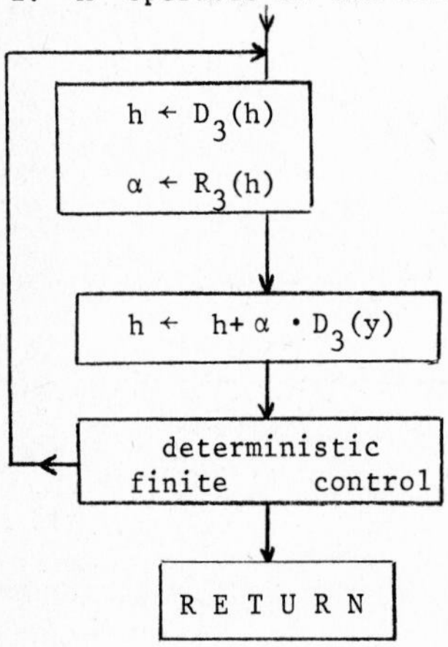

The finite control goes to its RETURN-exit, if α has the value 2 for the (k+3)-th time.

It is not difficult to see that if at the beginning $h = \sum_{\nu=0}^{r-1} a_\nu 3^\nu$ then in the ν-th run of this algorithm α has the value $a_{\nu+1}$.

Therefore by performing this algorithm A' computes which of the predicates hold. Afterwards $h = \sum_{\nu=0}^{r-1} a_\nu D_3^{r-\nu}(y)$.

II. Starting now with $h = \sum_{\nu=0}^{r-1} a_\nu D_3^{r-\nu}(y)$

A' operates in the following way

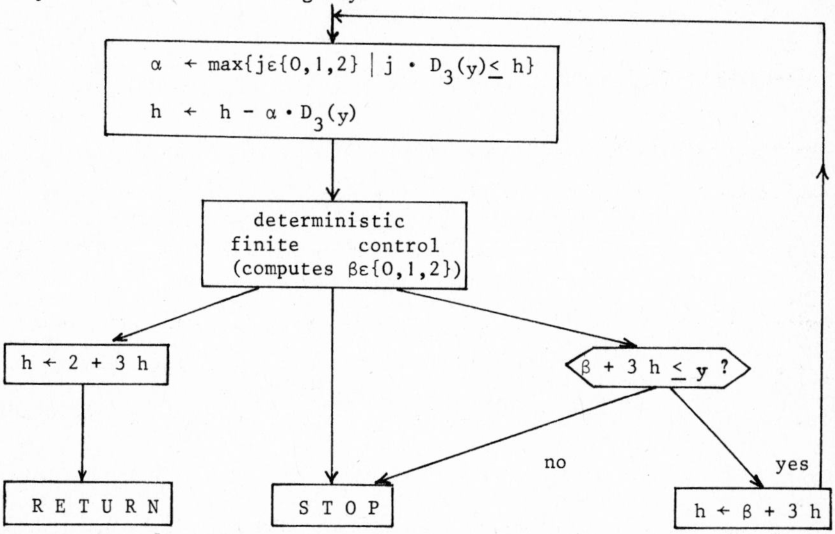

Again it is not difficult to see that the value of α computed in the ν-th run, $1 \leq \nu \leq r$, of this algorithm is $a_{r-\nu}$. The deterministic finite control simulates in this case a finite automaton which adds 1 or 0 or −1 to an 0-1-string enclosed by the symbol 2.

In this way A' reaches the head positions

$P_{k+2}(z_1+\eta_1,\ldots,z_k+\eta_k,z_o+\eta_o,y+1-z_o-\eta_o,y+1)$

and condition (2) is fulfilled.

For a more detailed version of this algorithm and for a proof of the correctness see [5].

□

References

1. Fischer,P.C.,Meyer,A.R. and Rosenberg,A.L.: Counter Machines and Counter Languages, Math. Systems Theory 2, 265-283,1968

2. Galil,Z.: Two Way Deterministic Pushdown Automaton Languages and some open problems in the Theory of Computation, 15-th Ann.Symp. Switch.Autom.Theory, 170-177,1974

3. Grzegorczyk,A.: Some classes of recursive functions, Rozprawy Matematyczne 4, 1-46, 1953

4. Monien,B.: Transformational Methods and their Application to Complexity Problems, Acta Informatica 6, 95-108, 1976

5. Monien, B.: The LBA-problem and the deterministic tape complexity of two-way one-counter languages over a one-letter alphabet, submitted for publication

6. Ritchie, R.W.: Classes of predictably computable functions, Trans.American Math. Soc. 106,139-173, 1963

7. Savitch,W.J.: A note on multihead automata and context-sensitive languages, Acta Informatica 2, 249-252, 1973

8. Sudborough, I.H.: A Note on Tape-Bounded Complexity Classes and Linear Context-Free Languages, J.Ass.Comp.Mach. 22, 499-500, 1975

9. Sudborough,I.H.: On Tape-Bounded Complexity Classes and Multihead Finite Automata, J.Comp. Systems Sciences 10, 62-76, 1975

Das Normalisierungsproblem und der Zusammenhang mit der Zeitkomplexität der kontextsensitiven Analyse

M. Stadel

Eines der schwierigen und bisher noch ungelösten Probleme der Komplexitätstheorie ist, eine Antwort auf die Frage, ob NSPACE(n) $\subset \mathbf{P}$ ist, zu finden.

In der vorliegenden Arbeit soll keineswegs eine Antwort auf obige Frage gegeben werden. Es soll vielmehr versucht werden, den Kern des Problems herauszuschälen. Ich folgte dabei einer Idee von Herrn Prof. Dr. G. Hotz:

Wir definieren eine kontextsensitive Grammatik G wie in [2]. Die Produktionen können wir dann als kontextfreie Produktionen auffassen, die jedoch nur dann angewandt werden dürfen, wenn gewisse Kontextbedingungen erfüllt sind. Die Produktionen sind dabei keineswegs vom strikten Erweiterungstyp. Es ist auch nicht möglich, durch Übergang zu einer äquivalenten Grammatik die Produktionen der Form $A \to B$ (A, B Nichtterminalzeichen) durch Produktionen vom strikten Erweiterungstyp zu ersetzen, da im allgemeinen die Kontextbedingungen nicht richtig zusammenpassen würden.

Es ergibt sich nun folgende Frage: Wie beeinflussen die Kontextbedingungen die Zeitkomplexität des Wortproblems (kontextfreie Sprachen sind ja in Polynomzeit analysierbar)?

Nehmen wir an, wir machen zunächst eine kontextfreie Analyse, indem wir die Kontextbedingungen unberücksichtigt lassen. Dann untersuchen wir, ob ein gefundener Ableitungsbaum auch unter Berücksichtigung der Kontextbedingungen zu einer Ableitungsfolge bezüglich der gegebenen kontextsensitiven Grammatik G führt. Diesen Test nennen wir "Normalisierungsproblem".

Das Ziel der vorliegenden Arbeit ist es nun, zu untersuchen, ob die Zeitkomplexität des Normalisierungsproblems wesentlich zur Beantwortung der Frage, ob NSPACE(n) $\subset \mathbf{P}$ ist, beiträgt. Wir werden sehen, daß es kontextsensitive Grammatiken gibt, für die das Normalisierungsproblem **NP**-vollständig ist. Andererseits gibt es zu jeder kontextsensitiven Sprache L eine kontextsensitive Grammatik G, die L erzeugt und für die das Normalisierungsproblem in Polynomzeit lösbar ist. G wird eine Grammatik in linkskontextsensitiver Normalform sein.

Wir haben uns allerdings damit noch nicht überlegt, wie die Anzahl der verschiedenen Ableitungsbäume für ein Terminalwort w bezüglich des kontextfreien Kerns der Grammatik G die Zeitkomplexität des Wortproblems beeinflußt. (Es kann exponentiell viele verschiedene Ableitungsbäume geben!) Beim Übergang zur linkskontextsensitiven Normalform erhöht sich im allgemeinen die Mehrdeutigkeit des kontextfreien Kerns (sie wird exponentiell!). Die folgende Frage ist unter anderem auch deshalb von Interesse: Ist es möglich, das Normalisierungsproblem parallel für alle kontextfreien Ableitungsbäume eines Terminalwortes w in Polynomzeit zu lösen?

Einige einfache Resultate zu dieser Frage können in [6] nachgelesen werden.

Ich möchte an dieser Stelle Herrn Prof. Dr. G. Hotz für die Anregung zu dieser Arbeit und für die zahlreichen Diskussionen herzlichst danken.

DIE **NP**-VOLLSTÄNDIGKEIT DES NORMALISIERUNGSPROBLEMS.

Zunächst wollen wir das Normalisierungsproblem definieren.

Die Definitionen der elementaren Begriffe wie "Grammatik", "kontextfreie Grammatik", "Ableitungsbaum für eine kontextfreie Grammatik", etc. entnehmen wir [3]. Wir definieren jedoch ähnlich wie in [2]:

DEFINITION 1.

Eine Grammatik G = (N, T, P, S) *heißt kontextsensitiv, falls gilt:*

$$P \subset \{\alpha A\beta \to \alpha\gamma\beta : \alpha,\beta \in (N \cup T)^*, \gamma \in (N \cup T)^+ \text{ und } A \in N\}.$$

Die von kontextsensitiven Grammatiken erzeugten Sprachen heißen kontextsensitive Sprachen.

DEFINITION 2.

Sei G = (N, T, P, S) *eine kontextsensitive Grammatik. Dann heißt* G^{cf} := (N, T, P^{cf}, S) *mit*

$$P^{cf} := \{A \to \gamma: \exists \alpha, \beta \in (N \cup T)^{*} \text{ mit } (\alpha A \beta \to \alpha\gamma\beta) \in P\}$$

der kontextfreie Kern von G.

Um das Wortproblem für eine kontextsensitive Sprache, die von einer kontextsensitiven Grammatik G = (N, T, P, S) erzeugt wird, zu lösen, kann man wie folgt vorgehen:
Man löst zunächst das Wortproblem für G^{cf}. Dabei ermittelt man zu vorgegebenem $w \in T^{*}$ alle möglichen Ableitungsbäume bzgl. G^{cf}. Für jeden dieser Ableitungsbäume testet man dann, ob es eine Ableitungsfolge $S \overset{*}{\underset{G}{\longrightarrow}} w$ gibt, deren "kontextfreier Kern" gerade diesen Ableitungsbaum besitzt. Demnach definieren wir formal:

DEFINITION 3.

Sei G = (N, T, P, S) *eine kontextsensitive Grammatik und* $w \in L(G^{cf})$. *Dann sei:*

$$\text{NORM}(G, w) := \Big\{ \tau \text{ Ableitungsbaum bzgl. } G^{cf} \text{ und } w\text{:}$$

$$\exists \text{ Ableitungsfolge } S \underset{G^{cf}}{\longrightarrow} \alpha_1 \underset{G^{cf}}{\longrightarrow} \alpha_2 \underset{G^{cf}}{\longrightarrow} \ldots \underset{G^{cf}}{\longrightarrow} w$$

$$(\alpha_i \in (N \cup T)^{*}) \text{ mit zugehörigem Ableitungsbaum } \tau, \text{ so daß}$$

$$S \underset{G}{\longrightarrow} \alpha_1 \underset{G}{\longrightarrow} \alpha_2 \underset{G}{\longrightarrow} \ldots \underset{G}{\longrightarrow} w \Big\},$$

$$\text{NORM}(G) := \bigcup_{w \in L(G^{cf})} \text{NORM}(G, w).$$

Um zu testen, ob ein Wort $w \in L(G^{cf})$ mit Ableitungsbaum τ bzgl. G^{cf} in L(G) ist, muß jetzt also nur noch das Wortproblem für NORM(G) gelöst werden, also $\tau \in$ NORM(G) überprüft werden. Wenn wir dies tun, so sagen wir, "wir lösen das Normalisierungsproblem für τ und w".

Versucht man auf die oben beschriebene Weise das Wortproblem für eine kontextsensitive Sprache zu lösen, so gibt es drei Dinge, die wahrscheinlich sehr zeitaufwendig sind:

(i) Es gibt zu viele verschiedene Ableitungsbäume für $w \in L(G^{cf})$.

(ii) Da P^{cf} im allgemeinen Produktionen der Form $A \to B$ mit $A, B \in N$ enthält, kann die Tiefe (und damit die Kodierung) eines Ableitungsbaumes für G^{cf} sehr groß werden.

(iii) Die Zeitkomplexität des Wortproblems für NORM(G) ist zu groß.

In dieser Arbeit wird gezeigt:
Es gibt eine kontextsensitive Grammatik G_0 für die NORM(G_0) **NP**-vollständig ist (Theorem 4).

Andererseits kann jede kontextsensitive Sprache von einer Grammatik in linkskontextsensitiver Normalform erzeugt werden (s. [5]), und für diese läßt sich das Normalisierungsproblem in Polynomzeit lösen (s. [6]).

THEOREM 4.

Es gibt eine kontextsensitive Grammatik $G_0 = (N, T, P, S)$, *für die* NORM(G_0) **NP**-*vollständig ist.*

BEWEIS.

Wir geben zunächst die Grammatik G_0 an. Es sei:

$$N := \{S, T, \ddagger, A_0, A_i, B, B', C_i, D_i, E_i, F_i : i=1,2,3\},$$

$$T := \{a\},$$

P enthalte die folgenden Produktionen. Dabei durchlaufe $X_1, X_2, \ldots, X_6$ die Nichtterminalen $C_1, C_2, C_3, D_1, D_2, D_3, E_1, E_2, E_3, F_1, F_2, F_3$ und i,j durchlaufe die Zahlen 0,1,2,3.

(1)
- (i) $S \to \ddagger T \ddagger$
- (ii) $T \to TT$
- (iii) $T \to B'C_1C_2C_3E_1E_2E_3B'$

(2)
- (i) $B \to a$
- (ii) $D_i \to a \quad i \neq 0$
- (iii) $F_i \to a \quad i \neq 0$
- (iv) $\ddagger \to a$

(3)
- (i) $\ddagger\, B\, X_1X_2X_3X_4X_5X_6B \to \ddagger\, B'X_1X_2X_3X_4X_5X_6B$
- (ii) $B'B\, X_1X_2X_3X_4X_5X_6B \to B'B'X_1X_2X_3X_4X_5X_6B$
- (iii) $B'X_1X_2X_3X_4X_5X_6B\, B \to B'X_1X_2X_3X_4X_5X_6B'B$
- (iv) $B'X_1X_2X_3X_4X_5X_6B\, \ddagger \to B'X_1X_2X_3X_4X_5X_6B'\ddagger$

(4)

(i) $\ddagger\ B'X_1X_2X_3X_4X_5X_6B' \rightarrow \ddagger\ A_jX_1X_2X_3X_4X_5X_6B'$

(ii) $A_iB'X_1X_2X_3X_4X_5X_6B' \rightarrow A_iA_jX_1X_2X_3X_4X_5X_6B'$

(iii) $A_iX_1X_2X_3X_4X_5X_6B'B' \rightarrow A_iX_1X_2X_3X_4X_5X_6A_jB'$

(iv) $A_iX_1X_2X_3X_4X_5X_6B'\ddagger \rightarrow A_iX_1X_2X_3X_4X_5X_6A_j\ddagger$

(5)

(i) $\ddagger\ A_oX_1X_2X_3X_4X_5X_6A_i \rightarrow \ddagger\ B\ X_1X_2X_3X_4X_5X_6A_i$

$\ddagger\ A_1C_1X_2X_3X_4X_5X_6A_i \rightarrow \ddagger\ B\ C_1X_2X_3X_4X_5X_6A_i$

$\ddagger\ A_2X_1C_2X_3X_4X_5X_6A_i \rightarrow \ddagger\ B\ X_1C_2X_3X_4X_5X_6A_i$

$\ddagger\ A_3X_1X_2C_3X_4X_5X_6A_i \rightarrow \ddagger\ B\ X_1X_2C_3X_4X_5X_6A_i$

(ii) $B\ A_oX_1X_2X_3X_4X_5X_6A_i \rightarrow B\ B\ X_1X_2X_3X_4X_5X_6A_i$

$B\ A_1C_1X_2X_3X_4X_5X_6A_i \rightarrow B\ B\ C_1X_2X_3X_4X_5X_6A_i$

$B\ A_2X_1C_2X_3X_4X_5X_6A_i \rightarrow B\ B\ X_1C_2X_3X_4X_5X_6A_i$

$B\ A_3X_1X_2C_3X_4X_5X_6A_i \rightarrow B\ B\ X_1X_2C_3X_4X_5X_6A_i$

(iii) $B\ X_1X_2X_3X_4X_5X_6A_jA_i \rightarrow B\ X_1X_2X_3X_4X_5X_6B\ A_i$

(iv) $B\ X_1X_2X_3X_4X_5X_6A_j\ddagger \rightarrow B\ X_1X_2X_3X_4X_5X_6B\ \ddagger$

(6)

(i) $A_iX_1X_2X_3X_4X_5X_6A_o\ddagger \rightarrow A_iX_1X_2X_3X_4X_5X_6B\ \ddagger$

$A_iC_1X_2X_3X_4X_5X_6A_1\ddagger \rightarrow A_iC_1X_2X_3X_4X_5X_6B\ \ddagger$

$A_iX_1C_2X_3X_4X_5X_6A_2\ddagger \rightarrow A_iX_1C_2X_3X_4X_5X_6B\ \ddagger$

$A_iX_1X_2C_3X_4X_5X_6A_3\ddagger \rightarrow A_iX_1X_2C_3X_4X_5X_6B\ \ddagger$

(ii) $A_iX_1X_2X_3X_4X_5X_6A_oB \rightarrow A_iX_1X_2X_3X_4X_5X_6B\ B$

$A_iC_1X_2X_3X_4X_5X_6A_1B \rightarrow A_iC_1X_2X_3X_4X_5X_6B\ B$

$A_iX_1C_2X_3X_4X_5X_6A_2B \rightarrow A_iX_1C_2X_3X_4X_5X_6B\ B$

$A_iX_1X_2C_3X_4X_5X_6A_3B \rightarrow A_iX_1X_2C_3X_4X_5X_6B\ B$

(iii) $A_iA_jX_1X_2X_3X_4X_5X_6B \rightarrow A_iB\ X_1X_2X_3X_4X_5X_6B$

(iv) $\ddagger\ A_jX_1X_2X_3X_4X_5X_6B \rightarrow \ddagger\ B\ X_1X_2X_3X_4X_5X_6B$

(7)

(i) $A_1C_1 \rightarrow A_1D_1$

(ii) $A_2X_1C_2 \rightarrow A_2X_1D_2$

(iii) $A_3X_1X_2C_3 \rightarrow A_3X_1X_2D_3$

(8)

(i) $C_1X_2X_3X_4X_5X_6A_1 \rightarrow D_1X_2X_3X_4X_5X_6A_1$

(ii) $C_2X_3X_4X_5X_6A_2 \rightarrow D_2X_3X_4X_5X_6A_2$

(iii) $C_3X_4X_5X_6A_3 \rightarrow D_3X_4X_5X_6A_3$

(9) $C_iX_{i+1}X_{i+2}F_i \rightarrow D_iX_{i+1}X_{i+2}F_i \quad i \neq 0$

(10) $D_iX_{i+1}X_{i+2}E_i \rightarrow D_iX_{i+1}X_{i+2}F_i \quad i \neq 0$

(11)

(i) $E_1E_2 \rightarrow F_1E_2$

(ii) $E_2E_3 \rightarrow F_2E_3$

(iii) $E_1X_5E_3 \rightarrow E_1X_5F_3$

Damit ist $G_0 = (N, T, P, S)$ eine kontextsensitive Grammatik im Sinne der Definition 1.

Wir bezeichnen mit SAT(3) das Erfüllbarkeitsproblem für boolsche Ausdrücke in konjunktiver Normalform mit höchstens drei Literalen pro Klausel (s. [2], [4]). $\propto$ bezeichne die Relation "Reduktion in Polynomzeit", wie sie in [4] definiert wurde. Unser Ziel ist es, SAT(3) $\propto$ NORM(G_0) nachzuweisen. Wir wissen, daß SAT(3) **NP**-vollständig ist ([2], [4]). Ferner ist klar, daß NORM(G) $\in$ **NP** für eine kontextsensitive Grammatik G: man muß lediglich eine Ableitungsfolge

$$S \xrightarrow[G^{cf}]{} \alpha_1 \xrightarrow[G^{cf}]{} \alpha_2 \xrightarrow[G^{cf}]{} \cdots \xrightarrow[G^{cf}]{} w$$

zu dem gegebenen Ableitungsbaum nichtdeterministisch raten und dann überprüfen, ob

$$S \xrightarrow[G]{} \alpha_1 \xrightarrow[G]{} \alpha_2 \xrightarrow[G]{} \cdots \xrightarrow[G]{} w$$

gilt. Wenn wir also SAT(3) $\propto$ NORM(G_0) gezeigt haben, ist Theorem 4 bewiesen.

Sei also a ein boolscher Ausdruck in konjunktiver Normalform mit höchstens drei Literalen pro Klausel. Ohne Einschränkung können wir annehmen, daß keine Variable mehrfach in einer Klausel vorkommt. Es seien $x_1, x_2, \ldots, x_l$ die Variablen, die in a vorkommen, und $a = \kappa_1 \wedge \kappa_2 \wedge \ldots \wedge \kappa_k$, wobei κ_i $(1 \leq i \leq k)$ die Klauseln von a sind. Wir konstruieren jetzt zu a einen Ableitungsbaum τ_a bzgl. G^{cf} und zeigen dann:

$$\tau_a \in \text{NORM}(G_0) \Leftrightarrow a \in \text{SAT}(3).$$

1) Konstruktiion von τ_a.

Zunächst wird mittels der Produktionen (1i) und (1ii) aus S die Satzform

$$\ddagger T^{(1)} T^{(2)} T^{(3)} \ldots T^{(k)} \ddagger \quad \dagger$$

erzeugt (vgl. Figur 1). Dann wird (1iii) angewandt und die Satzform

$$\ddagger B'^{(1,1)} C_1^{(1)} C_2^{(1)} C_3^{(1)} E_1^{(1)} E_2^{(1)} E_3^{(1)} B'^{(1,\bar{1})} \ldots$$

$$B'^{(k,1)} C_1^{(k)} C_2^{(k)} C_3^{(k)} E_1^{(k)} E_2^{(k)} E_3^{(k)} B'^{(k,\bar{1})} \ddagger$$

erzeugt. $B'^{(\mu,1)}$ wird wie folgt weiter abgeleitet:

$$B'^{(\mu,1)} \xrightarrow[G^{cf}]{} A_{i_{\mu,1}}^{(\mu,1)} \xrightarrow[G^{cf}]{} B^{(\mu,1)} \xrightarrow[G^{cf}]{} B'^{(\mu,2)} \xrightarrow[G^{cf}]{} \ldots$$

$$\xrightarrow[G^{cf}]{} B'^{(\mu,l)} \xrightarrow[G^{cf}]{} A_{i_{\mu,l}}^{(\mu,l)} \xrightarrow[G^{cf}]{} B^{(\mu,l)} \xrightarrow[G^{cf}]{} a \qquad (1 \leq \mu \leq k)$$

und analog wird $B'^{(\mu,\bar{1})}$ abgeleitet:

$$B'^{(\mu,\bar{1})} \xrightarrow[G^{cf}]{} A_{i_{\mu,\bar{1}}}^{(\mu,\bar{1})} \xrightarrow[G^{cf}]{} B^{(\mu,\bar{1})} \xrightarrow[G^{cf}]{} B'^{(\mu,\bar{2})} \xrightarrow[G^{cf}]{} \ldots$$

$$\xrightarrow[G^{cf}]{} B'^{(\mu,\bar{l})} \xrightarrow[G^{cf}]{} A_{i_{\mu,\bar{l}}}^{(\mu,\bar{l})} \xrightarrow[G^{cf}]{} B^{(\mu,\bar{l})} \xrightarrow[G^{cf}]{} a \qquad (1 \leq \mu \leq k).$$

Die Indizes $i_{\mu,\nu}$ werden dabei wie folgt definiert:

$$i_{\mu,\nu} := \begin{cases} 0 & x_\nu \text{ kommt in } \kappa_\mu \text{ nicht vor} \\ i & y_i = x_\nu \quad \kappa_\mu = (y_1 \vee y_2 \vee y_3) \\ & \qquad\qquad \text{bzw. } \kappa_\mu = (y_1 \vee y_2) \\ & \qquad\qquad \text{bzw. } \kappa_\mu = (y_1). \end{cases} \qquad (1 \leq \nu \leq l,\ 1 \leq \mu \leq k)$$

---

† Die oberen Indizes an den Nichtterminalen dienen im folgenden nur zur Unterscheidung der einzelnen Knoten mit gleichem Label.

Der erste Index durchläuft die Zahlen 1, ..., k und kennzeichnet eine Zugehörigkeit zu der entsprechenden Klausel. Der zweite Index (falls vorhanden) durchläuft die Werte $1, \ldots, l, \bar{1}, \ldots, \bar{l}$ und kennzeichnet eine Zugehörigkeit zu der entsprechenden Variablen bzw. ihrer Negation.

Analog:

$$i_{\mu,\bar{\nu}} := \begin{cases} 0 & \overline{x_\nu} \text{ kommt in } \kappa_\mu \text{ nicht vor} \\ i & y_i = \overline{x_\nu} \quad \kappa_\mu = (y_1 \vee y_2 \vee y_3) \\ & \text{bzw. } \kappa_\mu = (y_1 \vee y_2) \\ & \text{bzw. } \kappa_\mu = (y_1). \end{cases} \qquad \begin{matrix}(1 \le \nu \le l, \\ 1 \le \mu \le k)\end{matrix}$$

Die restlichen Ableitungen sind:

$$C_i^{(\mu)} \xrightarrow[G^{cf}]{} D_i^{(\mu)} \xrightarrow[G^{cf}]{} a, \qquad E_i^{(\mu)} \xrightarrow[G^{cf}]{} F_i^{(\mu)} \xrightarrow[G^{cf}]{} a \qquad \begin{matrix}(1 \le \mu \le k, \\ 1 \le i \le 3),\end{matrix}$$

$$\ddagger \xrightarrow[G^{cf}]{} a.$$

Der durch diese kontextfreie Ableitung definierte Ableitungsbaum sei τ_a. In Figur 2 ist τ_a für den boolschen Ausdruck $a = (x_1 \vee \bar{x}_2 \vee x_3) \wedge (x_2 \vee \bar{x}_3 \vee \bar{x}_4)$ als Beispiel aufgezeichnet.

Wir vermerken an dieser Stelle:

τ_a hat die Tiefe $3l + k + 1 \le 5|a|$.

τ_a erzeugt das Terminalwort $a^{8k + 2}$.

Eine natürliche Kodierung von τ_a hat die Länge $O(|a|^2)$ und kann aus a leicht (d.h. in Polynomzeit) berechnet werden.

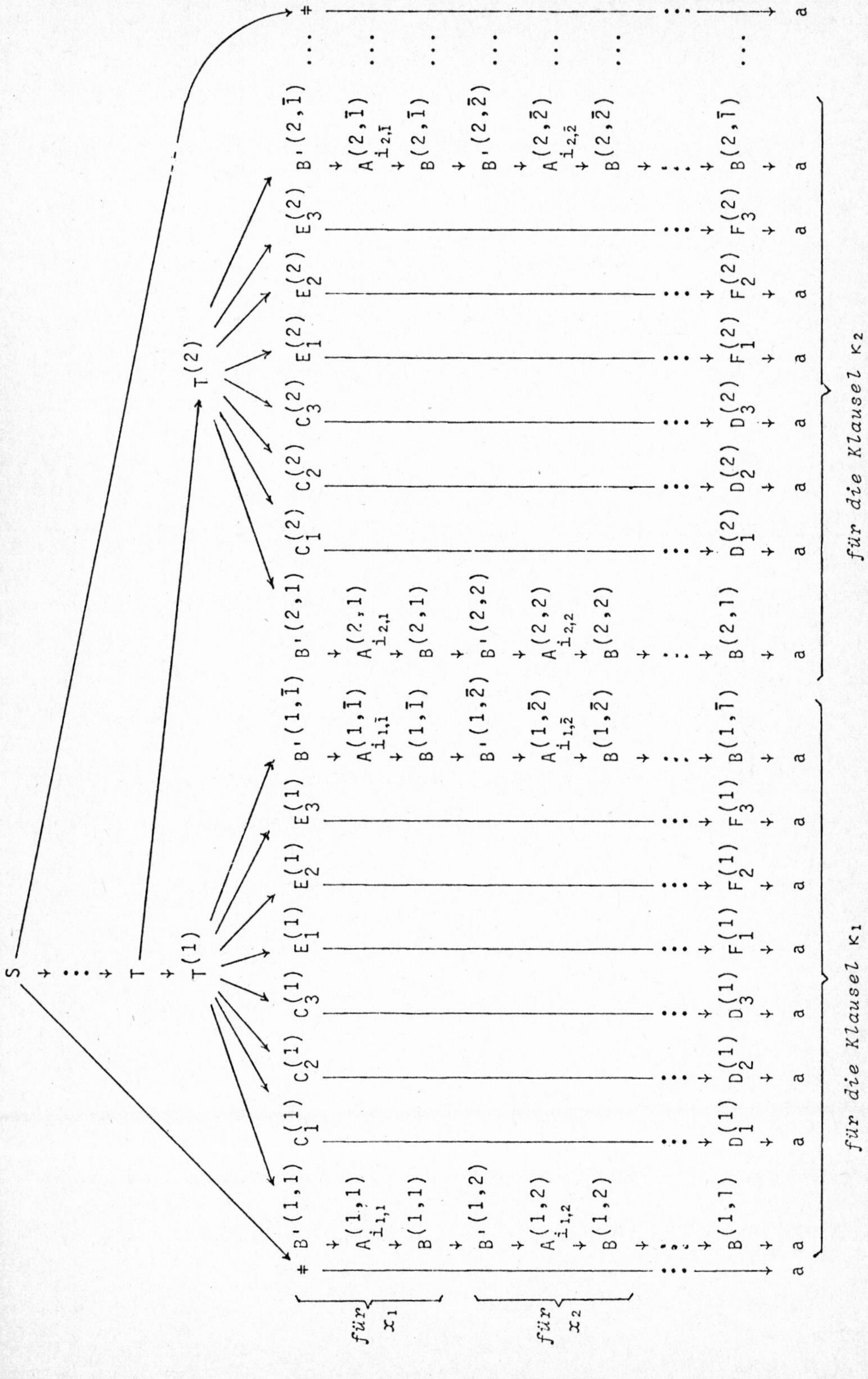

Figur 1

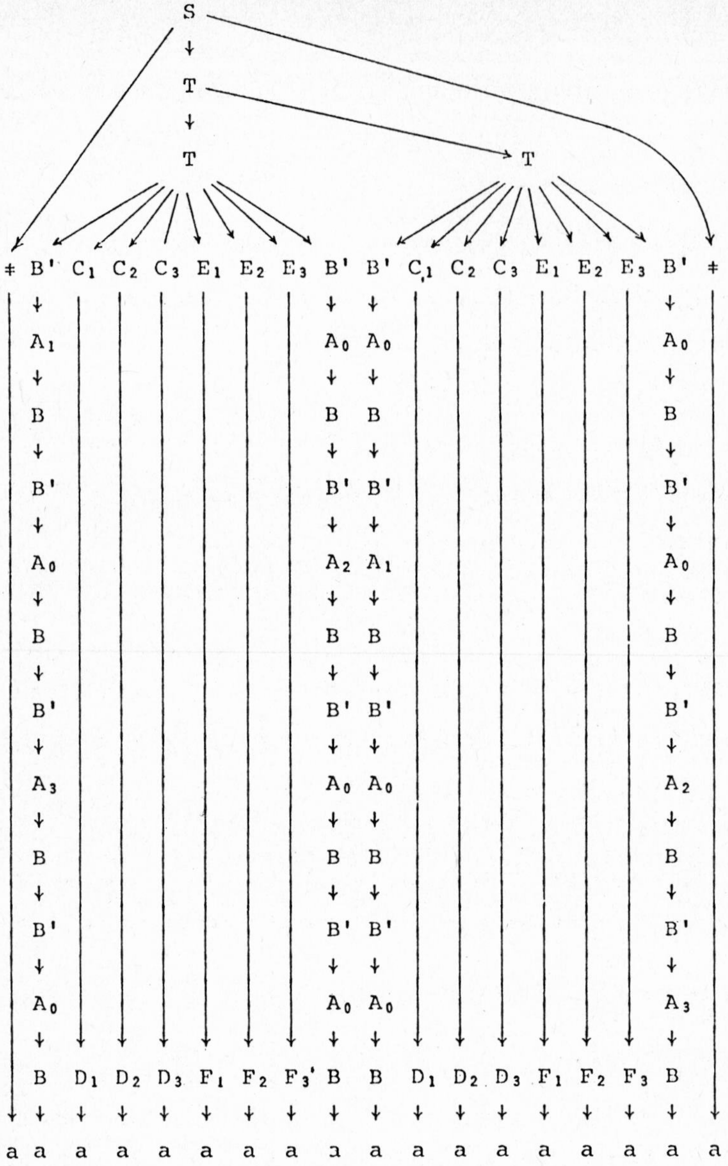

$a = (x_1 \vee \bar{x}_2 \vee x_3) \wedge (x_2 \vee \bar{x}_3 \vee \bar{x}_4)$

Figur 2

2) $a \in SAT(3) \Rightarrow \tau_a \in NORM(G_0)$.

Sei $x_\nu = \xi_\nu$ mit $\xi_\nu \in \{0,1\}$ $(1 \leq \nu \leq l)$ eine Einsetzung, die $a = 1$ macht. Wir erzeugen zunächst durch "leftmost Ableitung" aus S die Satzform

$$\ddagger B'^{(1,1)} C_1^{(1)} C_2^{(1)} C_3^{(1)} E_1^{(1)} E_2^{(1)} E_3^{(1)} B'^{(1,\bar{1})} \ldots B'^{(k,\bar{1})} \ddagger$$

gemäß τ_a. Wir gehen dann induktiv wie folgt vor und nehmen an, wir hätten die Satzform

$$\ddagger B'^{(1,\nu)} \ldots\ldots B'^{(1,\bar{\nu})} B'^{(2,\nu)} \ldots\ldots B'^{(2,\bar{\nu})} \;\ldots\; B'^{(k,\bar{\nu})} \ddagger$$

schon erreicht. Unter Benutzung der kontextsensitiven Produktionen (4) können wir die B' von links nach rechts zu A_i ableiten (i gemäß τ_a) und erhalten so die Satzform

$$\ddagger A_{i_{1,\nu}}^{(1,\nu)} \ldots\ldots A_{i_{1,\bar{\nu}}}^{(1,\bar{\nu})} A_{i_{2,\nu}}^{(2,\nu)} \ldots\ldots A_{i_{2,\bar{\nu}}}^{(2,\bar{\nu})} \;\ldots\; A_{i_{k,\bar{\nu}}}^{(k,\bar{\nu})} \ddagger .$$

Ehe wir die A_i weiter ableiten, werden jetzt einige der C_j abgeleitet. Wir unterscheiden dazu die beiden Fälle $\xi_\nu = 0$ und $\xi_\nu = 1$.

$\xi_\nu = 0$			$\xi_\nu = 1$		
$i_{\mu,\bar{\nu}}$	Produktion	angewendet auf	$i_{\mu,\nu}$	Produktion	angewendet auf
1	(8i)	$C_1^{(\mu)}$	1	(7i)	$C_1^{(\mu)}$
2	(8ii)	$C_2^{(\mu)}$	2	(7ii)	$C_2^{(\mu)}$
3	(8iii)	$C_3^{(\mu)}$	3	(7iii)	$C_3^{(\mu)}$
anschließend Ableitung der A_i zu B von <u>links nach rechts</u> mittels der Produktionen (5)			anschließend Ableitung der A_i zu B von <u>rechts nach links</u> mittels der Produktionen (6)		

Zum Abschluß des Induktionsschrittes benutzen wir die Produktionen (3), um von links nach rechts die B zu B' abzuleiten. Wir erreichen dann die Satzform

$$\ddagger B'^{(1,\nu+1)} \ldots\ldots B'^{(1,\overline{\nu+1})} B'^{(2,\nu+1)} \ldots\ldots B'^{(2,\overline{\nu+1})} \;\ldots$$
$$B'^{(k,\nu+1)} \ldots\ldots B'^{(k,\overline{\nu+1})} \ddagger .$$

Wenn wir auf die oben beschriebene Weise vorgehen, erreichen wir die Satzform

$$\ddagger B^{(1,1)} U_1^{(1)} U_2^{(1)} U_3^{(1)} E_1^{(1)} E_2^{(1)} E_3^{(1)} B^{(1,\bar{1})} \ldots$$

$$B^{(k,1)} U_1^{(k)} U_2^{(k)} U_3^{(k)} E_1^{(k)} E_2^{(k)} E_3^{(k)} B^{(k,\bar{1})} \ddagger,$$

wobei $U_i^{(\mu)} = C_i^{(\mu)}$ oder $U_i^{(\mu)} = D_i^{(\mu)}$ ist, je nachdem, ob $C_i^{(\mu)}$ schon zu $D_i^{(\mu)}$ abgeleitet wurde oder nicht.

Ist $U_1^{(\mu)} = D_1^{(\mu)}$, so wenden wir der Reihe nach die Produktionen (11ii), (11iii), (10) an.

Ist $U_2^{(\mu)} = D_2^{(\mu)}$, so wenden wir der Reihe nach die Produktionen (11iii), (11i), (10) an.

Ist $U_3^{(\mu)} = D_3^{(\mu)}$, so wenden wir der Reihe nach die Produktionen (11i), (11ii), (10) an.

Nachdem wir mittels der Produktionen (9) die restlichen $C_i^{(\mu)}$ zu $D_i^{(\mu)}$ abgeleitet haben, haben wir die Satzform

$$\ddagger B^{(1,1)} D_1^{(1)} D_2^{(1)} D_3^{(1)} F_1^{(1)} F_2^{(1)} F_3^{(1)} B^{(1,\bar{1})} \ldots$$

$$B^{(k,1)} D_1^{(k)} D_2^{(k)} D_3^{(k)} F_1^{(k)} F_2^{(k)} F_3^{(k)} B^{(k,\bar{1})} \ddagger$$

erreicht (vgl. auch Fig. 1). Die Terminalproduktionen (2) machen hieraus a^{2+8k}. Wir haben damit $\tau_\alpha \in \mathrm{NORM}(G_0)$ nachgewiesen.

3) $\tau_\alpha \in \mathrm{NORM}(G_0) \Rightarrow \alpha \in \mathrm{SAT}(3)$.

Sei $S \xrightarrow[G^{cf}]{*} a^{2+8k}$ eine Ableitungsfolge, wie sie nach Definition 1.3 zu $\tau_\alpha \in \mathrm{NORM}(G_0)$ existiert. Führt man die in dieser Ableitungsfolge vorkommenden Produktionen (1) zuerst aus, so erhält man eine Ableitungsfolge

$$S \xrightarrow[G^{cf}]{*} \alpha_1 \xrightarrow[G^{cf}]{} \alpha_2 \xrightarrow[G^{cf}]{} \dots \xrightarrow[G^{cf}]{} a^{2+8k}$$

mit $\alpha_i \in (NUT)^*$ für $i = 1,2,\dots$ und

$$\alpha_1 = \ddagger B'^{(1,1)} C_1^{(1)} C_2^{(1)} C_3^{(1)} E_1^{(1)} E_2^{(1)} E_3^{(1)} B'^{(1,\bar{1})} \dots B'^{(1,\bar{k})} \ddagger .$$

Ordnet man jedem Nicht-Endknoten K von τ_a diejenige Produktion aus P^{cf} zu, die in K angewandt wird, um die Nachfolger von K zu erzeugen, so kann man auf der Menge der Nichtendknoten von τ_a eine lineare Ordnung "<" wie folgt definieren:

Sind K_1, K_2 Nichtendknoten von τ_a, so sei

$K_1 < K_2$:⇔ Die zu K_1 gehörige Produktion wird in $S \xrightarrow[G^{cf}]{*} \alpha_1 \xrightarrow[G^{cf}]{} \dots \xrightarrow[G^{cf}]{'} a^{2+8k}$ zeitlich früher angewandt, als die zu K_2 gehörige Produktion.

Wir gliedern den Rest des Beweises in drei Lemmata.†

---

† Man kann sich den Ableitungsbaum τ_a ganz grob wie folgt veranschaulichen:

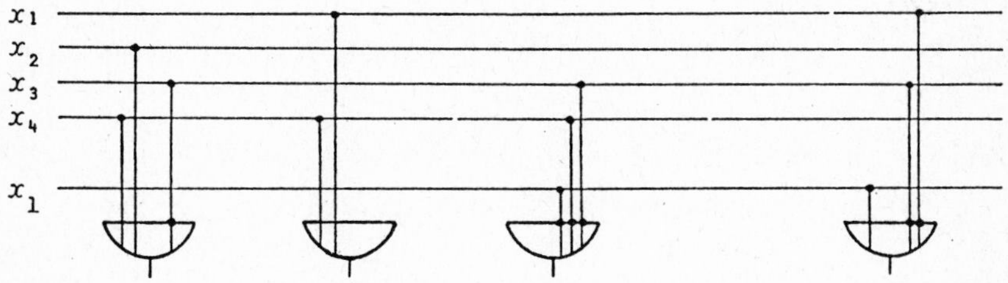

Figur 3

In dieser Zeichnung stellen die waagrechten Linien Leitungen dar (für jede Variable eine Leitung). Für jede Klausel von a wurde ein "Odergatter" eingezeichnet.

Im Lemma 5 zeigen wir, daß zwischen den Leitungen für die einzelnen Variablen keine "Kurzschlüsse" auftreten können. Lemma 6 besagt, daß jede Leitung nur zwei verschiedene "Zustände" haben kann und garantiert den richtigen Anschluß der "Odergatter". Die beiden Zustände traten im Teil 2) des Beweises schon auf, als wir die A_i von <u>links nach rechts</u> bzw. von <u>rechts nach links</u> zu B abgeleitet haben.

Das Lemma 7 zeigt, daß die "Odergatter" richtig funktionieren, daß also a erfüllbar ist.

LEMMA 5.

(i) $\alpha_i = \ldots B'^{(\mu,\nu_1)} \ldots\ldots B'^{(\mu,\overline{\nu_2})} \ldots$ *oder*

$\alpha_i = \ldots B'^{(\mu,\overline{\nu_1})} B'^{(\mu+1,\nu_2)} \ldots \quad \Rightarrow \nu_1 = \nu_2.$

(ii) $\alpha_i = \ldots A^{(\mu,\nu_1)}_{i_{\mu,\nu_1}} \ldots\ldots A^{(\mu,\overline{\nu_2})}_{i_{\mu,\overline{\nu_2}}} \ldots$ *oder*

$\alpha_i = \ldots A^{(\mu,\overline{\nu_1})}_{i_{\mu,\overline{\nu_1}}} A^{(\mu+1,\nu_2)}_{i_{\mu+1,\nu_2}} \ldots \quad \Rightarrow \nu_1 = \nu_2.$

(iii) $\alpha_i = \ldots B^{(\mu,\nu_1)} \ldots\ldots B^{(\mu,\overline{\nu_2})} \ldots$ *oder*

$\alpha_i = \ldots B^{(\mu,\overline{\nu_1})} B^{(\mu+1,\nu_2)} \ldots \quad \Rightarrow \nu_1 = \nu_2.$

(iv) $\alpha_i = \ldots A^{(\mu,\nu_1)}_{i_{\mu,\nu_1}} \ldots\ldots B^{(\mu,\overline{\nu_2})} \ldots$ *oder*

$\alpha_i = \ldots A^{(\mu,\overline{\nu_1})}_{i_{\mu,\overline{\nu_1}}} B^{(\mu+1,\nu_2)} \ldots \quad \Rightarrow \nu_1 = \nu_2.$

(v) $\alpha_i = \ldots B^{(\mu,\nu_1)} \ldots\ldots A^{(\mu,\overline{\nu_2})}_{i_{\mu,\overline{\nu_2}}} \ldots$ *oder*

$\alpha_i = \ldots B^{(\mu,\overline{\nu_1})} A^{(\mu+1,\nu_2)}_{i_{\mu+1,\nu_2}} \ldots \quad \Rightarrow \nu_1 = \nu_2.$

(vi) $\alpha_i = \ldots B'^{(\mu,\nu_1)} \ldots\ldots B^{(\mu,\overline{\nu_2})} \ldots$ *oder*

$\alpha_i = \ldots B'^{(\mu,\overline{\nu_1})} B^{(\mu+1,\nu_2)} \ldots \quad \Rightarrow \nu_1 = \nu_2+1.$

(vii) $\alpha_i = \ldots A^{(\mu,\nu_1)}_{i_{\mu,\nu_1}} \ldots\ldots B'^{(\mu,\overline{\nu_2})} \ldots$ *oder*

$\alpha_i = \ldots A^{(\mu,\overline{\nu_1})}_{i_{\mu,\overline{\nu_1}}} B'^{(\mu+1,\nu_2)} \ldots \quad \Rightarrow \nu_1 = \nu_2.$

BEWEIS durch Induktion nach i. ∎

LEMMA 6.

Für $1 \leq \nu \leq 1$ *gilt entweder (0) oder (1), wobei*

(0) *(i)* $A^{(\mu,\nu)}_{i_{\mu,\nu}} < A^{(\mu,\bar\nu)}_{i_{\mu,\bar\nu}}$, $\quad \forall\mu,\ 1 \leq \mu \leq k.$

(ii) $A^{(\mu,\bar\nu)}_{i_{\mu,\bar\nu}} < A^{(\mu+1,\nu)}_{i_{\mu+1,\nu}} \quad \forall\mu,\ 1 \leq \mu < k.$

(iii) $A^{(\mu,\nu)}_{i_{\mu,\nu}} < C^{(\mu)}_{i_{\mu,\nu}} \quad \forall\mu,\ 1 \leq \mu \leq k$ mit $i_{\mu,\nu} \neq 0.$

(1) *(i)* $A^{(\mu,\nu)}_{i_{\mu,\nu}} > A^{(\mu,\bar\nu)}_{i_{\mu,\bar\nu}} \quad \forall\mu,\ 1 \leq \mu \leq k.$

(ii) $A^{(\mu,\bar\nu)}_{i_{\mu,\bar\nu}} > A^{(\mu+1,\nu)}_{i_{\mu+1,\nu}} \quad \forall\mu,\ 1 \leq \mu < k.$

(iii) $C^{(\mu)}_{i_{\mu,\bar\nu}} > A^{(\mu,\bar\nu)}_{i_{\mu,\bar\nu}} \quad \forall\mu,\ 1 \leq \mu \leq k$ mit $i_{\mu,\bar\nu} \neq 0.$

BEWEIS indirekt durch Fallunterscheidung. ■

LEMMA 7.

Sei $\kappa_\mu = (y_1 \vee y_2 \vee y_3)$ *mit Literalen* y_1, y_2, y_3, $1 \leq \mu \leq k$.
Dann gilt :

(i) $y_1 = 0 \Rightarrow E_2^{(\mu)} > E_1^{(\mu)}$,

(ii) $y_2 = 0 \Rightarrow E_3^{(\mu)} > E_2^{(\mu)}$,

(iii) $y_3 = 0 \Rightarrow E_1^{(\mu)} > E_3^{(\mu)}$.

Ist $\kappa_\mu = (y_1 \vee y_2)$ *bzw.* $\kappa_\mu = (y_1)$, *so gilt ebenfalls (i), (ii) und (iii), wenn man* $y_3 := 0$ *bzw.* $y_2 := y_3 := 0$ *setzt.*

Da nicht gleichzeitig $E_2^{(\mu)} > E_1^{(\mu)} > E_3^{(\mu)} > E_2^{(\mu)}$ gelten kann, muß also κ_μ den Wert 1 haben. Dies gilt für alle Klauseln in α, also hat α den Wert 1, was zu zeigen war. ■

BEWEIS des Lemmas 7.

Wir zeigen (iii), die anderen Aussagen beweist man analog. Wir unterscheiden dazu drei Fälle:

1. Fall: $y_3 = x_\nu$ für ein ν, $1 \leq \nu \leq l$.

Es folgt $i_{\mu,\nu} = 3$, $i_{\mu,\bar\nu} = 0$, $i_{\mu,\nu_1}, i_{\mu,\bar\nu_1} \neq 3 \ \forall \nu_1 \neq \nu$.

Wegen $y_3 = 0$ folgt aus Lemma 6 $C_3^{(\mu)} > A_3^{(\mu,\nu)}$. Für $C_3^{(\mu)} \longrightarrow D_3^{(\mu)}$ stehen die Produktionen (7iii), (8iii) und (9) zur Auswahl. (8iii) kommt wegen $i_{\mu,\bar\nu} \neq 3$ nicht in Frage. (7iii) verlangt $A_3^{(\mu,\nu)} > C_3^{(\mu)}$. Es bleibt also nur (9) übrig. Dann muß aber $F_3^{(\mu)} > C_3^{(\mu)} > E_3^{(\mu)}$ sein. $E_3^{(\mu)} \longrightarrow F_3^{(\mu)}$ ist nur durch (10) oder (11iii) möglich. (10) verlangt $D_3^{(\mu)} > E_3^{(\mu)} > C_3^{(\mu)}$, was nicht sein kann. Aus (11iii) folgt schließlich die Behauptung $E_1^{(\mu)} > E_3^{(\mu)}$.

2. Fall: $y_3 = \bar x_\nu$ für ein ν, $1 \leq \nu \leq l$.

Es folgt $i_{\mu,\bar\nu} = 3$, $i_{\mu,\nu} = 0$, $i_{\mu,\nu_1}, i_{\mu,\bar\nu_1} \neq 3 \ \forall \nu_1 \neq \nu$.

Wegen $y_3 = 0$ folgt aus Lemma 6 $C_3^{(\mu)} > A_3^{(\mu,\bar\nu)}$. Für

$C_3^{(\mu)} \longrightarrow D_3^{(\mu)}$ scheidet die Produktion (7iii) wegen $i_{\mu,\nu} \neq 3$ aus und die Produktion (8iii) verlangt $A_3^{(\mu,\bar{\nu})} > C_3^{(\mu)}$. Der Rest geht wie im 1. Fall.

3. Fall: $\kappa_\mu = (y_1 \vee y_2)$ bzw. $\kappa_\mu = (y_1)$.
Es folgt $i_{\mu,\nu}, i_{\mu,\bar{\nu}} \neq 3 \ \forall \nu=1,2,\dots,l$. Für $C_3^{(\mu)} \longrightarrow D_3^{(\mu)}$ kommt daher nur die Produktion (9) in Frage. Der Rest geht dann wieder wie im 1. Fall. ■

OFFENES PROBLEM

Gibt es eine kontextsensitive Grammatik $G_1 = (N, T, P, S)$ *vom strikten Erweiterungstyp, für die* NORM(G_1) NP-*vollständig ist?*

Versucht man aus der Grammatik G_0 durch einfache Modifikation der Produktionen eine Grammatik vom strikten Erweiterungstyp zu machen, so wächst der einem boolschen Ausdruck α zugeordnete Ableitungsbaum τ_α exponentiell an, oder aber eine zu Lemma 6 analoge Aussage läßt sich nicht mehr beweisen.

Literaturverzeichnis

[1] Aho, A. V., Hopcroft, E. H., Ullman, J. D.: *"The Design and Analysis of Computer Algorithms"*, Addison-Wesley, Reding (mass.), 1974.

[2] Hotz, G., Claus, V.: *"Automatentheorie und formale Sprachen, III Formale Sprachen"*, BI, Mannheim, 1972.

[3] Hopcroft, E. H., Ullman, J. D.: *"Formal Languages and their Relation to Automata"*, Addison-Wesley, Reading (Mass.), 1969.

[4] Karp, R. M.: *"Reducibility among Combinatorial Problems"* in Miller, R. E., Thatcher, J. W. (ed.): *"Complexity of Computer Computations"*, Plenum Press, New York, 1972.

[5] Penttonen, M.: *"One-Sided and Two-Sided Context in Formal Grammars"*, IC 25, 371-392 (1974).

[6] Stadel, M.: *"Das Normalisierungsproblem und der Zusammenhang mit der Zeitkomplexität der kontextsensitiven Analyse"*, Dissertation, Saarbrücken, 1976.

ÜBER NETZWERKGRÖSSEN HÖHERER ORDNUNG UND DIE MITTLERE ANZAHL DER IN NETZWERKEN BENUTZTEN OPERATIONEN

C. Reynvaan - C.-P. Schnorr

Abstrakt Aufbauend auf dem Begriff der Größe eines Netzwerkes ß führen wir weitere Komplexitätsmaße für Netzwerke ein, welche die strukturelle Kompliziertheit eines Netzwerkes ausdrücken. Angewandt auf Boolesche Funktionen drücken diese Komplexitätsmaße neue interessante Eigenschaften aus, welche eng mit der Größe und der Rechenzeit von Turing-Programmen zusammenhängen.

Wir beschreiben ein Netzwerk ß durch eine Funktion g, die jedem Knoten ν von ß seine Operation und seine Vorgängerknoten zuordnet. g wird als Boolesche Funktion kodiert und hat somit eine wohldefinierte Netzwerkgröße $C_1(g)$. Die Netzwerkgröße $C_1(ß)$, $C_1(f)$ von Netzwerken und Booleschen Funktionen f kann man nun wie folgt iterieren:

$$C_{k+1}(ß) = \min\{C_k(g) \mid g \text{ beschreibt } ß\}$$

$$C_{k+1}(f) = \min\{C_{k+1}(ß) \mid ß \text{ berechnet } f\}$$

Wir zeigen für n-stellige f: $C_{k+1}(f) \leq C_k(f)(1+o(n)/n)$.
Für jedes Turing-Programm P, welches f berechnet, gilt:

$$C_k(f) \leq O(\|P\| + \lg^{k-1} T_P).$$

Dabei ist $\|P\|$ die Anzahl der Anweisungen und T_P die Rechenzeit von P. $\lg^k$ ist der k-fach iterierte Logarithmus.

Zu einem Netzwerk ß sei AV(ß)die Anzahl der im Mittel (average) bzgl. aller Eingaben benutzten Knoten. Zu einer Booleschen Funktion f betrachten wir die minimale Anzahl der im Mittel bei einem Netzwerk zu f benutzten Knoten:
$AV(f) := \min\{AV(ß) \mid ß \text{ berechnet } f\}$. AV(f) steht in enger Beziehung zur mittleren Rechenzeit von Turing-Programmen.

1. Einleitung

Die Netzwerkgröße C(f) einer Booleschen Funktion f hat sich als ein fundamentales Komplexitätsmaß für Boolesche Funktionen erwiesen. C(f) drückt (mit Abweichungen) das minimale Produkt aus Größe und Rechenzeit eines f berechnenden Turingprogramms aus, siehe M. Fischer [1] und C.P. Schnorr [7].

Andererseits werden viele Komplexitätseigenschaften Boolescher Funktionen f durch die Netzwerkgröße nicht berücksichtigt. Z.B. haben alle Permutationen Boolescher Variablen die Netzwerkgröße null, obwohl es offensichtlich sehr einfache und sehr komplizierte Permutationen gibt. Die Kompliziertheit dieser Permutationen kommt nicht in der Netzwerkgröße, sondern nur in einer komplizierten Netzwerkstruktur zum Ausdruck. Netzwerke mit gleicher Knotenzahl können nämlich sehr regulär sein, wie z.B.

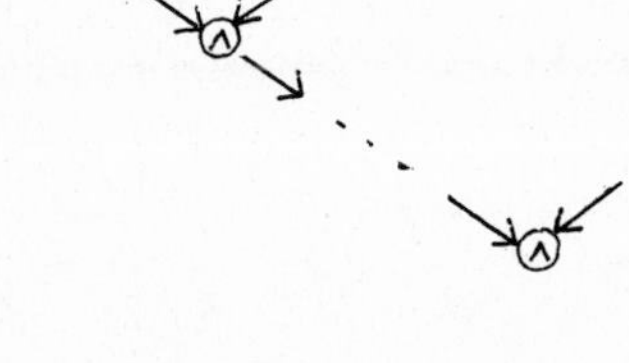

oder aber keine erkennbaren Regularitäten aufweisen. Unregelmäßige Netzwerke können mehr Information in ihrer Netzwerkstruktur speichern.

Das Maß für den Informationsgehalt eines Netzwerkes wird die Netzwerkgröße einer Funktion sein, die dieses Netzwerk beschreibt. Durch Iteration gelangt man zu Netzwerkgrößen höherer Ordnung einer Funktion f. Um ein Netzwerk durch eine Funktion eindeutig zu beschreiben, numerieren wir die Knoten des Netzwerkes durch. Berechnet ein Netzwerk ß die Funktionen $f_1,\dots,f_r$, so soll die Reihenfolge der f_i, welche auf die Netzwerkgröße keinen Einfluß hat, in die höheren Netzwerkgrößen von $f_1,\dots,f_r$ eingehen. Um dies zu erreichen, markieren wir die Ausgabeknoten und ordnen sie.

2. Netzwerkkomplexitäten höherer Ordnung

Sei $N = \{1,2,\dots\}, B = \{0,1\}, [r] = \{1,2,\dots,r\}$.

Sei x_i eine Boolesche Variable, dann sei

$x_i^1 = x_i$ und $x_1^0 = \neg x_i$. Sei $B^* = \bigcup_{n\in N} B^n$

Zu $f: B^n \to B^m$ sei $f_j : B^n \to B$ die j-te Komponente von f, $1 \le j \le m$. Wir schreiben $f = (f_1,\dots,f_m)$.

Definition 2.1

Ein logisches Netzwerk ß ist ein gerichteter, azyklischer Graph mit beschrifteten Knoten derart, daß

(1) jeder Knoten ν entweder den indegree 0 hat (dann wird er Eingang genannt) oder ν zwei einlaufende Kanten $\nu^1 \to \nu$, $\nu^2 \to \nu$ hat, $\nu^1 \to \nu$ ist die erste und $\nu^2 \to \nu$ die zweite einlaufende Kante.

(2) jeder Eingang ist mit einer Variable op(ν) aus $\{x_i \mid i \in N\}$ beschriftet, jeder Knoten, der nicht Eingang ist, (Nichteingang) ist mit einer binären Booleschen Operation op(ν) beschriftet.

Jedem Knoten ν von ß wird eine Boolesche Funktion $res_ß^\nu$ zugeordnet, die von den Variablen von ß abhängt:

Für alle Eingänge ν:

$$res_ß^\nu := op(\nu)$$

Hat ν die einlaufenden Kanten $\nu^1 \to \nu, \nu^2 \to \nu$, dann sei

$$res_ß^\nu := op(\nu)[res_ß^{\nu^1}, res_ß^{\nu^2}]$$

Wir sagen ß berechnet $f = (f_1,\ldots,f_m)$ (oder: ß ist ein Netzwerk für f), falls es für jedes j mit $1 \le j \le m$ einen Knoten $\nu_j \in ß$ gibt mit $res_ß^{\nu_j} = f_j$. Der Knoten ν_j heißt dann j-ter Endknoten von ß bei der Berechnung von f.

Die Netzwerkgröße $C_1(ß)$ von ß sei die Anzahl aller Knoten in ß. Die Netzwerkgröße von $f:B^n \to B^m$ sei $C_1(f) = \min\{C_1(ß) \mid ß$ berechnet $f\}$.

Unsere von der üblichen Konvention abweichende Vereinbarung, daß Eingänge bei der Netzwerkgröße mitzählen, wird die folgende Darstellung der höheren Netzwerkgrößen $C_k(ß)$ und $C_k(f)$ vereinfachen.

Wir wollen ein Netzwerk ß, welches die Boolesche Funktion f berechnet, durch eine Boolesche Funktion g beschreiben. g soll zu jedem Knoten ν von ß die Vorgängerknoten in geordneter Reihenfolge und die Operation op(ν) angeben.

Weil g eine Boolesche Funktion sein soll, ist es im folgenden zweckmäßig anzunehmen, daß die Knoten des Netzwerkes binäre Folgen gleicher Länge sind; falls notwendig, kodiere man die Knoten geeignet. g soll ferner zu jedem ν angeben, ob ν Endknoten ist. Damit die Reihenfolge der Endknoten ebenfalls aus g hervorgeht, verlangen wir, daß die Endknoten bzgl. der lexikographischen Reihenfolge auf den Knoten (endliche binäre Folgen) geordnet sind.

Definition 2.2

Sei ß ein Netzwerk zur Berechnung von $f:B^n \to B^m$. Dann heißt $g:B^r \to B^r \times B^r \times B^4 \times B$ Beschreibung von ß falls für $g = (g_1, g_2, g_3, g_4)$ folgendes gilt:

(1) die Knoten von ß sind in B^r.

(2) für alle Nicht-Eingänge ν von ß mit einlaufenden Kanten $\nu^1 \to \nu$, $\nu^2 \to \nu$ gilt:
$g_1(\nu) = \nu^1, g_2(\nu) = \nu^2, g_3(\nu) = \text{Kode}(\text{op}(\nu))$

(3) für alle Eingänge ν von ß mit $\text{op}(\nu) = x_i$ gilt
$g_1(\nu) = g_2(\nu) = \text{Kode}(i)$

(4) $g_4(\nu) = 1 \iff \nu$ ist Endknoten

(5) Es gibt m Endknoten, $\nu_1 < \nu_2 \ldots < \nu_m$ in lexikographischer Reihenfolge, so daß $res_ß^{\nu_i} = f_i \quad i = 1,\ldots,m$.

Dabei seien $\text{Kode}(\text{op}(\nu)) \in B^4$ in (2) und Kode(i) in (3) geeignete binäre Kodierungen. g in 2.2 kann mehrere Netzwerke beschreiben, welche sich jedoch nur um für die Berechnung von f wirkungslose Knoten unterscheiden. Zur Kennzeichnung der Eingänge sei in 2.2 (2) und (3) noch vorausgesetzt, daß die beiden Vorgänger eines Nicht-Eingangs verschieden sind.

Im Gegensatz zu der mehr technischen Vereinbarung 2.2 ist die folgende Definition grundlegend.

Definition 2.3

Ausgehend von der Netzwerkgröße $C_1(\beta), C_1(f)$ von Netzwerken β und Booleschen Funktionen f, definieren wir induktiv:

$$C_{k+1}(\beta) = \min\{C_k(g) \mid g \text{ beschreibt } \beta\}$$
$$C_{k+1}(f) = \min\{C_{k+1}(\beta) \mid \beta \text{ berechnet } f\}.$$

α heißt 2-tes Netzwerk zum Netzwerk β, wenn α eine Boolesche Funktion berechnet, die Beschreibung zu β ist. α heißt (k+1)-tes Netzwerk zu β, wenn α eine Beschreibung eines k-ten Netzwerkes zu β berechnet. Berechnet β die Funktion f, so heißt jedes k-te Netz zu β auch k-tes Netz zu f. Es gilt dann

$$C_k(\beta) = \min\{C_1(\alpha) \mid \alpha \text{ ist k-tes Netz zu } \beta\}$$
$$C_k(f) = \min\{C_1(\alpha) \mid \alpha \text{ ist k-tes Netz zu } f\}.$$

Satz 2.4

(1) Für alle β gilt: $C_2(\beta) \leq C_1(\beta)(1+o(C_1(\beta))/C_1(\beta))$

(2) Für alle $f:B^n \to B^m$: $C_2(f) \leq C_1(f)(1+o(n)/n)$

Beim Beweis benutzen wir die asymptotische Schranke von Lupanov-Shannon:

$$\max\{C_1(f)/f:B^n \to B\} \leq 2^n/n \ (1+o(n)/n)$$

Diese Schranke kann man leicht wie folgt verallgemeinern. Sei F(n,s) die Klasse der Funktionen $f:B^n \to B$ mit $f(x) = 0$ für alle $x \in B^n$, die nicht zu den s-lexikographisch kleinsten Folgen in B^n gehören. Dann gilt

<u>Lemma 2.5</u>

$\max\{C_1(f) \mid f \in F(n,s)\} \leq s/\lg s\ (1+o(n)/n)$

<u>Beweis von 2.4</u> Offenbar folgt (2) aus (1) und es genügt (1) zu beweisen. Sei $C_1(ß) = s$ und $r = \lceil \lg s \rceil$. Dann identifiziere man die Knoten von ß mit den s lexikographisch kleinsten Knoten in B^r. Dies liefert als Beschreibung von ß eine Funktion $g:B^r \to B^r \times B^r \times B^4 \times B$, deren 2r+5 Komponentenfunktionen $g:B^r \to B$ alle in der Klasse F(r,s) liegen. Nach 2.5 gilt für jede dieser Komponentenfunktionen $C_1(g) \leq s/\lg s(1+o(r)/r)$. Daraus folgt $C_1(g) \leq 2s(1+o(r)/r)$. Den Faktor 2 können wir noch sparen, indem wir die Identifizierung der Knoten von ß mit den s lexikographisch kleinsten Folgen in B^r so vornehmen, daß für den ersten Vorgänger $g_1(\nu)$ bzgl. der lexikographischen Ordnung < gilt:

<u>2.6</u> $\nu < \mu \Rightarrow g_1(\nu) < g_1(\mu)$ für alle Nichtendknoten ν, μ.

Die Voraussetzung 2.6 impliziert

<u>2.7</u> $C_1(g_1) \leq O(s/\lg s) = o(s)$

<u>Beweis von 2.7</u> Wir beschränken uns auf den Fall, daß die Anzahl der Endknoten in ß klein ist im Verhältnis zu $C_1(ß)$. Dann kann man o.B.d.A. annehmen, daß 2.6 für alle Knoten ν, μ gilt, weil die wenigen Endknoten die Netzwerkgröße von g kaum beeinflussen.

Sei $g_1(x_1,\ldots,x_r) = y_1,\ldots,y_r$. Wegen 2.6 ist $y_1 = y_1(x_1,\ldots,x_r)$ eine Schwellenwertfunktion mit einem Schwellenwert $z_0 \in B^r$ bzgl. der lexikographischen Ordnung < auf B^r:

$$y_1(x_1,\dots,x_r) = \begin{cases} 0 \text{ falls } x_1x_2\dots x_r < z_0 \\ 1 \text{ sonst} \end{cases}$$

$y_{i+1}(x_1,\dots,x_r)$ ist bei festem $y_1,\dots,y_i$ ebenfalls eine Schwellenwertfunktion $S_{y_1\dots y_i}(x_1,\dots,x_r)$.

Wegen $y_j^{z_j} = 1$ genau dann, wenn $y_j = z_j$ gilt:

$$y_{i+1} = \bigvee_{z_1z_2\dots z_i \in B^i} y_1^{z_1}y_2^{z_2}\dots,y_i^{z_i}S_{z_1\dots z_i}(x_1,\dots,x_r)$$

mit geeigneten Schwellenwertfunktionen $S_{z_1\dots z_i}$.

Offenbar gilt

$\max\{C_1(S_{z_1\dots z_i}) \mid z_1\dots z_i \in B^i\} \leq O(r)$

und somit

$C_1(y_1,\dots,y_{i+1}) \leq C_1(y_1,\dots,y_i) + O(2^i r)$.

Es folgt

$C_1(y_j \mid j = 1,\dots,r-\lceil \lg r\rceil^2) \leq O(\sum_{i=1}^{r-\lceil \lg r\rceil^2} r2^i$

$\leq O(r2^{r-\lceil \lg r\rceil^2}) = O(2^r/r) = o(s)$

Andererseits folgt aus 2.5

$C_1(y_j \mid j = r-\lceil \lg r\rceil^2 + 1,\dots,r) \leq \lceil \lg r\rceil^2 2^r/r(1 + o(r)/r)$

$\leq o(2^r) = o(s)$.

Damit ist 2.7 bewiesen.

Für jede der Komponentenfunktionen $\bar{g}:B^r \to B$ von g gilt wegen 2.5 $C_1(\bar{g}) \leq s/_{\lg s}(1 + o(r)/r$. Zusammen mit 2.7 ergibt dies $C_2(\beta) \leq C_1(g) \leq s(1+o(r)/r) \leq C_1(\beta)(1+o(r)/r)$. ▨

Korollar 2.8

(1) Für alle ß gilt: $C_{k+1}(\beta) \leq C_k(\beta)(1+o(C_k(\beta))/C_k(\beta))$

(2) Für alle $f:B^n \to B^m$: $C_{k+1}(f) \leq C_k(f)(1+o(n)/n)$.

Beweis: Wieder genügt es (1) nachzuweisen, weil (2) aus (1) folgt.

Es ist

$$C_k(\beta) = \min\{C_1(\alpha) \mid \alpha \text{ ist } k\text{-tes Netz zu } \beta\}$$

Sei α k-tes Netz zu ß und $C_1(\alpha) = C_k(\beta)$. Sei δ 2-tes Netz zu α mit $C_1(\delta) = C_2(\alpha)$. Dann ist δ (k+1)-tes Netz zu ß und es gilt

$$C_{k+1}(\beta) \leq C_1(\delta) \leq C_1(\alpha)(1 + o(C_1(\alpha))/C_1(\alpha))$$
$$\overset{2.4}{=} C_k(\beta)(1 + o(C_k(\beta))/C_k(\beta))$$ ▨

Aus Korollar 2.8 folgt sofort, daß die obere Schranke von Lupanov-Shannon auch für C_k gilt:

$$C_k(f) \leq 2^n/n(1 + o(n)/n) \text{ für } f:B^n \to B$$

Die untere Schranke von Lupanov-Shannon für C_1 gilt ebenfalls für C_k, weil das dabei benutzte Abzählargument sich auf C_k in derselben Weise anwenden läßt wie auf C_1. Daher gilt

Korollar 2.9

$$\|\{f:B^n \to B \mid C_k(f) \leq 2^n/n\}\|/2^{2^n} \to 0 \text{ für } n \to \infty$$

Das asymptotische Verhalten von $C_k(f)$ entspricht also weitgehend dem von $C_1(f)$. Andererseits ist zu erwarten, daß für viele Funktion f gilt: $C_{k+1}(f) \ll C_k(f)$. Aus den Beziehungen von $C_2(f)$ zur Rechenzeit von Turing-Programmen, die wir im nächsten Kapitel behandeln, folgt, daß $C_2(f) \ll C_1(f)$ für viele Boolesche Funktionen f. Denn $C_2(f)$ verhält sich wie der Logarithmus der Rechenzeit von Turing-Programmen und $C_1(f)$ wie die Rechenzeit selbst.

3. Netzwerkkomplexitäten höherer Ordnung und Programmgröße

Wir betrachten im folgenden Ein- oder Mehrband-Turingmaschinen über einem festen Alphabet, etwa $\{0,1,\square\}$. Als Programmanweisungen lassen wir Verschiebe-, Druck- und Testanweisungen zu, die stets einen Kopf bzw. ein beobachtetes Feld betreffen. Ist die Resultatfunktion res_P des Programms P auf B^n gleich $f:B^n \to B^m$, so sagen wir, P berechnet f.

T_P^n sei die maximale Rechenzeit von P auf Eingaben aus B^n, $T_P(x)$ die Rechenzeit von P bei Eingabe x. $\|P\|$ sei die Anzahl der Anweisungen von P. Zu $k \in N$ sei $lg^k x$ der k-fach iterierte Logarithmus von x. Es ist bekannt ([1], [7]), daß sich die Netzwerkgröße $C_1(f)$ einer Funktion $f:B^n \to B^m$ für jedes Turingprogramm P, welches f berechnet, durch $C_1(f) \leq O(\|P\|\ T_P^n \lg T_P^n)$ abschätzen läßt.

Satz 3.1

Das Turingprogramm P berechne die Funktion $f:B^n \to B^m$, dann gilt für alle $k \geq 2$:

$$C_k(f) \leq O(\|P\| + lg^{k-1} T_P^n).$$

Beweisskizze: Wir führen eine Induktion über k durch und konstruieren zu einem k-ten Netz zu f ein k+1-tes. Wir benutzen dabei, daß die so kontruierten Netzwerke β_k stets aus einem Teil Π bestehen, dessen Größe durch $O(\|P\|)$ beschränkt werden kann, und Addierwerken τ_i ($i \in \{1,2\}$ für $k \geq 3$ und $i \in \{1,...,4\}$ für k=2). Für $k \geq 3$ addiert τ_i zu einer Eingabe $x_1 \ldots x_s$ den Wert $e_i \in \{0,1\}$, wobei e_i von Π berechnet wird.
Wir konstruieren τ_i aus s Einheiten $E_1,...,E_s$:

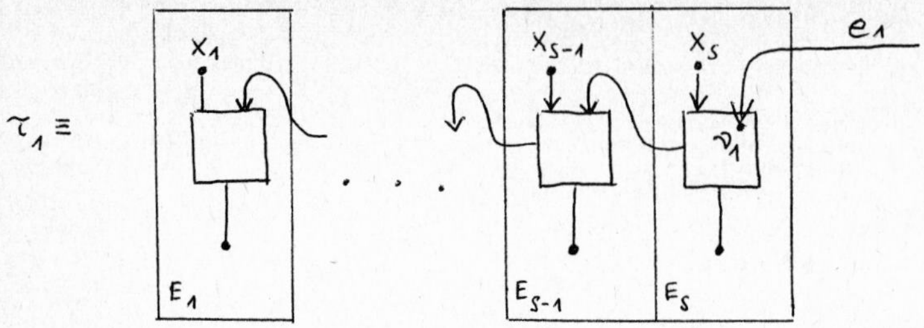

τ_2 sei analog aufgebaut (e_2 anstelle von e_1 und ν_2 anstelle von ν_1). Allerdings sollen die Eingabeknoten nicht auch zu τ_2 gehören, damit die Netzteile Π, τ_1, τ_2 das Netz β_k in disjunkte Knotenmengen zerlegen.

Bemerkung:

Offenbar liegen die Vorgänger eines Knotens $\nu \neq \nu_i, \nu \in E_j$ in E_j oder E_{j+1}. Für ν_i liegt ein Vorgänger in E_s, der andere in Π.

Wir schreiben abkürzend für ein Netzwerk τ der obigen Gestalt:

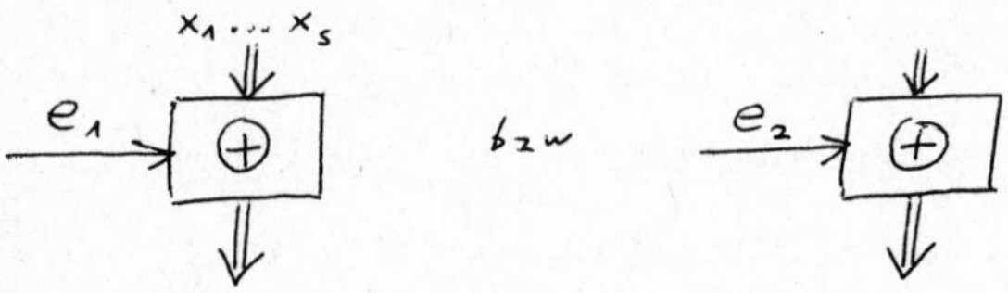

Wir zeigen, daß man zu jedem $k \geq 3$ ein β_k mit der folgenden Struktur angeben kann:

(1)

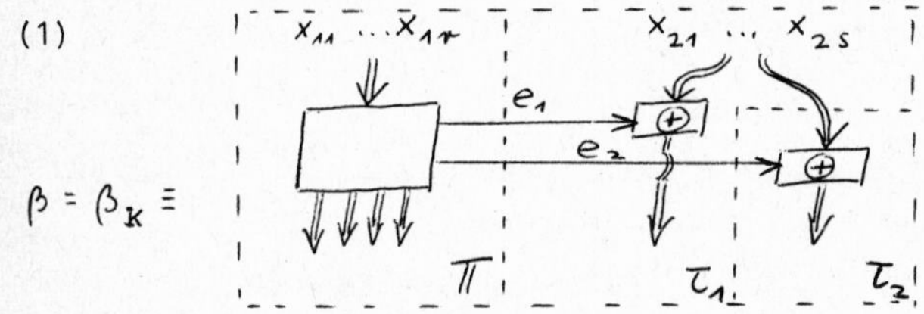

(2) $C_1(\Pi) \leq O(\|P\|)$

(3) $s \leq O(\lg^{k-1} T_P^n)$

Wir betrachten zunächst den Induktionsschritt:

Es ist zu zeigen, daß es unter den Voraussetzungen (1) bis (3) ein 2-tes Netzwerk ß' zu ß gibt, welches (1), (2) und

(3') $s \leq O(\lg^k T_P^n)$ erfüllt.

Die Knoten ν in ß erhalten zwei duale Nummern $a(\nu)$, $b(\nu)$. $a(\nu)$ charakterisiert, ob ν in Π, τ_1 oder τ_2 liegt und ob ν einer der ausgezeichneten Knoten ν_1, ν_2 ist (3 Dualstellen). Außerdem bezeichne $a(\nu)$ die Stellung von ν innerhalb Π bzw. der Einheit E_j, in der ν liegt ($O(\lg\|P\|)$ Dualstellen).

$b(\nu)$ ist die Nummer der Einheit E_j, in der ν liegt:

$$b(\nu) := \begin{cases} j & \text{falls } \nu \in E_j \\ s & \text{sonst} \end{cases}$$

$b(\nu)$ benötigt nur $\lceil \lg s \rceil \leq O(\lg^k T_P^n)$ Dualstellen.

Seien ν^1, ν^2 die Vorgänger von $\nu \in$ ß. $op(\nu)$, $a(\nu^1)$, $a(\nu^2)$ und, ob ν Endknoten ist oder nicht, hängen nur von $a(\nu)$ ab. Wesentlich ist, daß auch $b(\nu^1) - b(\nu) =: e_1(\nu)$ und $b(\nu^2) - b(\nu) =: e_2(\nu)$ nur von $a(\nu)$ abhängen und nur 0 oder 1 sein können, was aus der obigen Bemerkung und der Definition von $b(\nu)$ folgt.

Eine Beschreibung $g := (g_1,\dots,g_4)$ von ß läßt sich daher darstellen durch:

$g_1(a(\nu),b(\nu)) = (g_1'(a(\nu)),\ e_1(\nu) + b(\nu))$

$g_2(a(\nu),b(\nu)) = (g_2'(a(\nu)),\ e_2(\nu) + b(\nu))$

$g_3(a(\nu),b(\nu)) = g_3'(a(\nu))$ $\qquad$ $(op(\nu))$

$g_4(a(\nu),b(\nu)) = g_4'(a(\nu))$ $\qquad$ (ν ist Endknoten?)

mit geeigneten Funktionen g_1' bis g_4'.

Daraus folgt, daß ein

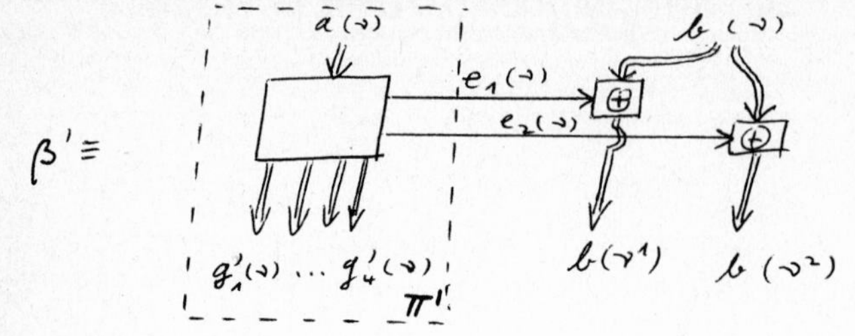

die Behauptungen (1), (2) und (3') erfüllt:

(1) und (3') gelten nach Konstruktion. Da Π' nur O(lg‖P‖) Eingänge und O(lg‖P‖) Ausgänge hat, benötigt Π' nach der Schranke von Shannon-Lupanov nur O(‖P‖) Knoten und damit gilt (2).

Es bleibt noch die Induktionsverankerung zu sichern: Dazu simuliere man einen Schritt von P durch ein Netzwerk mit $O(\|P\| T_P^n)$ Knoten und T_P^n Schritte durch T_P^n solcher Netze, die hintereinander geschaltet werden. Mit der gleichen Technik wie im Induktionsschritt konstruiert man ein Netzwerk ß', welches das simulierende Netzwerk ß beschreibt, der Gestalt:

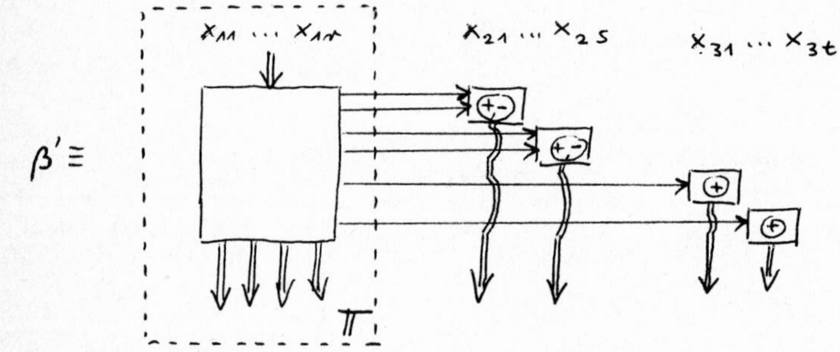

mit $C_1(\Pi) \leq O(\|P\|)$

$s,t \leq O(\lg T_P^n)$ und

Netzteilen $\boxed{+,-}$, die wie $\boxed{\oplus}$ aus Einheiten E_j aufgebaut sind, aber entsprechend den beiden von n übermittelten Werten die Eingabe konstant lassen, 1 hinzuzählen oder 1 subtrahieren. Wieder auf die gleiche Weise konstruiert man dann zu ß' ein beschreibendes ß", welches die Induktionsvoraussetzung erfüllt. ▨

Für k = 2 folgt aus Satz 3.1:

Korollar 3.2

(a) $C_2(f) << C_1(f)$ für jede Funktion f mit großer Netzwerkkomplexität $C_1(f)$, falls f auf der Turingmaschine durch ein kleines Programm mit ungefähr $C_1(f)$ Rechenschritten berechnet werden kann.

(b) Ist $f_i : B^i \to B$ eine Folge von Funktionen mit mindestens linear in i wachsendem $C_2(f)$, so wächst die Rechenzeit jedes Programms für $f : B^* \to B$ mit $f|_{B^i} := f_i$ exponentiell in der Eingabelänge.

Wir beweisen nun eine Umkehrung zu Satz 3.1: (zunächst für k = 2, in 3.5 für $k \in N$)

Satz 3.3

Das Netzwerk ß berechne die Funktion $f : B^n \to B^m$, dann gibt es ein Programm P für f mit (1) und (2):

(1) $\|P\| \le O(C_2(\beta))$

(2) $T_P^n \le O(C_2(\beta) \cdot C_1(\beta)^{2+\varepsilon}) \le O(2^{c \cdot C_2(\beta)})$

Beweis:

Sei α ein zweites Netz zu ß mit $C_1(\alpha) = C_2(\beta)$. Code (α) sei eine binäre Kodierung von α, den Endknoten von α und ihrer

Reihenfolge. Aus Code (α) läßt sich Code (ß) berechnen und damit auch f. Um aus Code (α) die Folge Code (ß) zu erzeugen, benötigt ein Turingprogramm fester Größe $\leq O(C_1(ß) \cdot C_2(ß)^{2+\varepsilon})$ Rechenschritte. Zur Berechnung von f mittels Code (ß) benötigt das Programm $\leq O(C_1(ß)^{2+\varepsilon})$ Schritte, $\varepsilon > 0$. Das folgende Lemma 3.4 sichert, daß ein Turingprogramm mit $O(C_2(ß))$ Anweisungen in der Zeit $O(C_2(ß)^2)$ die Folge Code (α) erzeugen kann. Damit folge (1) und $T_P^n \leq O(C_2(ß) \cdot C_1(ß)^{2+\varepsilon})$. Da $C_2(ß) \geq \lg C_1(ß)$ ist auch (2) erfüllt. ▨

Lemma 3.4

Ist C eine binäre Folge der Länge $n \cdot \lceil \lg n \rceil$, so gibt es ein Programm P mit (1) bis (3).

(1) $\|P\| \leq O(n)$

(2) P berechnet C

(3) Die Rechenzeit von P ist $\leq O(n^2)$

Beweis: Sei $C = C_1 \ldots, C_n$ mit $C_i \in B^{\lceil \lg n \rceil}$. P besteht aus den Teilen $P_{11}, \ldots, P_{1n}, P_2, P_3$. Zum Drucken von C_i wird durch P_{1i} die Anweisung mit der Nummer C_i in P_2 angesprochen. P_2 enthält zu jedem $x \in B^{\lceil \lg n \rceil}$ eine Anweisung mit Nummer x und druckt, wenn diese angesprochen wird, die Folge x aus. P_3 bewirkt den Sprung zu P_{1i+1}. Wir skizzieren P_2: Wird die Anweisung mit der Nummer x in P_2 angesprochen, so werden nacheinander die Folgen 0....0,0...01,...,x erzeugt und x wird ausgegeben. Dies wird geleistet durch:

```
1...1    k:= k + 1
1..10    k:= k + 1
  .        .
  .        .
  .        .
0..01    k:= k + 1
0...0    print k then P3
```

Dabei sei $k := k+1$ ein Programm, welches eine Folge x in die lexikographisch nächste überführt. Für P gilt offenbar (1) und (2). Da P_2 n mal angesprochen wird und P_2 nur O(n) Schritte benötigt, folgt auch (3). ▨

Mit den Bezeichnungen

$$\|f\| := \min\{\|P\| \mid P \text{ berechnet } f\}$$

$$\|k\| := \min\{\|P\| \mid P \text{ berechnet die Konstante } k\}$$

$$\|T_f\| := \min\{T_P^n \mid P \text{ berechnet } f\}$$

ergibt sich analog zum Beweis von 3.3

<u>Satz 3.5</u> Für jedes $k \in N$ gibt es eine Konstante c, so daß

(1) $\|f\| \leq O(C_k(f) + \|k\|)$

(2) $\|T_f\| \leq O(\underbrace{2^{2^{\cdot^{\cdot}}}}_{(k\,-\,1 \text{ Zweien})}{}^{2^{c \cdot C_k(f)}})$

<u>Beweis:</u> Ist α ein k-tes Netz zu f mit $C_k(f)$ Knoten, so erzeuge man den Kode eines f berechnenden Netzwerks aus Code (α), durch k-1fache Anwendung eines festen Programms.

4. Der mittlere Aufwand von logischen Netzwerken

Analog zu der Abschätzung

$$C_1(\mathrm{res}_P^r) \leq O(\|P\| T_P^r \cdot \lg T_P^r)$$

wird eine Abschätzung für die mittlere Turing-Zeit gegeben. Mit Hilfe der iterierten Netzwerkkomplexität formulieren wir eine Umkehrung dieser Abschätzung. Zur technischen Vereinfachung betrachten wir nur Funktionen $f:B^n \to B$.

Zu gegebenem $f:B^n \to B$ werden wir für jedes $x \in B^n$ und jedes ß, welches f berechnet, B(ß,x) definieren als die Zahl der in ß zur Berechnung von f(x) auszuführenden Operationen. Damit können wir den mittleren Aufwand von Netzwerken (Funktionen) folgendermaßen einführen:

Definition 4.1

Sei w eine Wahrscheinlichkeitsverteilung auf B^n. Wir bezeichnen

$$AV_w(ß) := \sum_{x \in B^n} w(x) \cdot b(ß,x)$$

$$AV_w(f) := \min\{AV_w(ß) \mid ß \text{ berechnet } f\}$$

als mittleren Netzwerkaufwand von ß (bzw. f).

Zur Definition von B(ß,x) geben wir einen Algorithmus b(ß,x) an, der in einem depth-first-search Verfahren Knoten in ß markiert, so daß f(x) mit den markierten Knoten aus ß zu bestimmen ist. Die Anzahl der markierten Nichteingänge setzen wir als B(ß,x). Ein Knoten ν ist genau dann markiert, wenn $\mathrm{res}_\nu^ß(x)$ im Verlauf von b(ß,x) bereits berechnet wurde.

Sei $res^{\beta}_{\nu_o} = f$. $b(\beta,x)$ setze das Resultat der Eingänge von β entsprechend der Eingabe x fest und markiere die Eingänge. Dann werde $res^{\beta}_{\nu_o}(x)$ durch das Programm "Berechne res^{β}_{ν}" bestimmt.

Das Programm "Berechne res^{β}_{ν}" nutzt aus, daß der Wert an einem Knoten μ oft schon festliegt, wenn einer der Vorgänger einen bestimmten Wert hat. Wir bezeichnen mit $\nu^+(\nu^-)$ den größeren (bzw. kleinsten) der beiden Vorgänger von ν bzgl. der lexikographischen Ordnung. Wir sagen, μ hat den Typ a b c d B^4, wenn

$$res^{\mu^+}_{\beta}(x) = a \rightarrow res^{\mu}_{\beta} = b \quad \text{und}$$

$$res^{\mu^-}_{\beta}(x) = c \rightarrow res^{\mu}_{\beta} = d.$$

Wir definieren rekursiv:

<u>Procedure</u> Berechne res^{β}_{ν}
<u>begin</u> <u>if</u> ν ist markiert <u>then</u> <u>stop</u>
    <u>if</u> ν hat keinen Typ
    <u>begin</u> Berechne $res^{\beta}_{\nu^+}$, Berechne $Res^{\beta}_{\nu^-}$
        $res^{\beta}_{\nu}(x) := op(\nu)[res^{\beta}_{\nu^+}(x), res^{\beta}_{\nu^-}(x)]$
        markiere ν, <u>stop</u>
    <u>end</u>
    <u>if</u> ν hat den Typ a b c d
    <u>begin</u> <u>if</u> ν^+ ist bekannt und $res^{\beta}_{\nu^+}(x) = a$
        <u>then</u> [$res^{\beta}_{\nu}(x) := b$, markiere ν, <u>stop</u>]
        <u>if</u> ν^- ist markiert und $res^{\beta}_{\nu}(x) = c$
        <u>then</u> [$res^{\beta}_{\nu}(x) := d$, markiere ν, <u>stop</u>]
        Berechne $res^{\beta}_{\nu^+}$
        <u>if</u> $res^{\beta}_{\nu^+}(x) = a$
        <u>then</u> [$res^{\beta}_{\nu}(x) := b$, markiere ν, <u>stop</u>]
        Berechne $res^{\beta}_{\nu^-}$
        $res^{\beta}_{\nu}(x) := op(\nu)[res^{\beta}_{\nu^+}(x), res^{\beta}_{\nu^-}(x)]$
        markiere ν, <u>stop</u>
    <u>end</u>
<u>end</u>

Vorbereitend zu den Abschätzungen über die mittlere Turing-Zeit führen wir die folgenden Vereinbarungen ein:

Zu $g:B^n \to R$ sei $E_w(g) := \sum_{x\in B^n} w(x)\cdot g(x)$ der Erwartungswert von g.

Sei $T_{P,n}$ die Rechenzeit von P eingeschränkt auf B^n.

<u>Satz 4.2</u>

Das Turing-Programm P berechne $f:B^n \to B$. Dann gibt es ein Netzwerk ß. welches f berechnet, mit (1), (2) und (3):

(1) $AV_w(ß) \leq O(\|P\|\cdot E_w(T_{P,n}\cdot \lg T_{P,n}))$

(2) $C_2(ß) \leq O(\|P\| + \lg T_P^n)$

(3) $C_1(ß) \leq O(\|P\|\cdot T_P^n \lg T_P^n)$

<u>Beweis:</u> Zu P betrachten wir das Netzwerk ß aus Satz 3.1. ß berechnet f und erfüllt (2) und (3). Wir fügen zu ß einige Knoten hinzu, so daß (2) und (3) nicht verletzt werden und dann auch (1) erfüllt ist. Wir ergänzen ß mit Netzteilen $A_t, t \in [T_P^n]$, die an Knoten α_t die Funktionen

$$Res_t(x) = \begin{cases} 1 & \text{falls } T_P(x) \leq t \text{ und } f(x) = 1 \\ 0 & \text{sonst} \end{cases}$$

berechnen. Die A_t sind untereinander gleich und A_t wird an den Netzteil $ß_i$ von ß gehängt, nach welchem t Schritte von P simuliert sind. Vor α_t liegen dann bezüglich der natürlichen Halbordnung auf dem Netz nur $O(\|P\| t \lg t)$ Knoten. Wir verknüpfen die α_t disjunktiv:

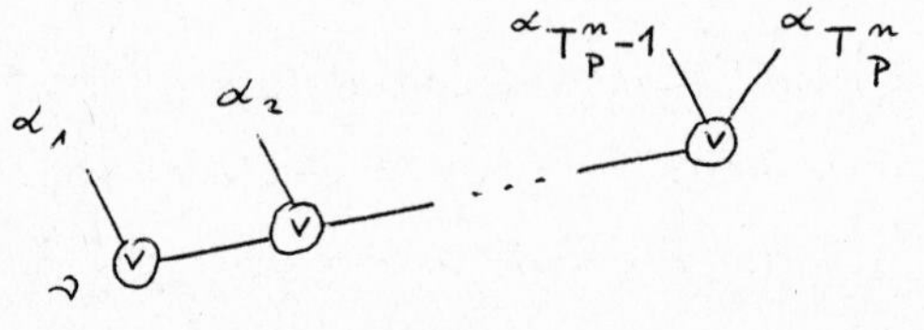

Das so ergänzte Netz nennen wir wieder ß. ß berechnet f am Knoten ν. Bei geeigneter Bezeichnung der Knoten durch binäre Folgen ist für ein x mit $T_P(x) = t$ dann $B(ß,x) \leq O(\|P\| t \lg t)$ und damit folgt die Behauptung (1). ▨

Sei $E_w(T_{P,n})$ der Erwartungswert der Rechenzeit zur Verteilung w auf den Eingaben in B^n. Es gilt folgende Umkehrung zu 4.2:

Satz 4.3

Das Netzwerk ß berechne $f:B^n \to B$. Dann gibt es ein Turing-Programm P, welches f berechnet, mit (1), (2) und (3):

(1) $E_w(T_{P,n}) \leq O((C_2(ß)^{2+\varepsilon}+n)E_w(B(ß,.)^2))$ mit $\varepsilon > 0$

(2) $\|P\| \leq O(C_2(ß))$

(3) $T_P^n \leq O(C_2(ß) \cdot C_1(ß)^{2+\varepsilon})$

Beweis: Zu ß betrachten wir das Programm P aus Satz 3.3 P erfüllt (2) und (3). Wir ändern P ab, so daß auch (1) erfüllt ist. Das abgeänderte Programm heißt wieder P. Wie im Beweis zu 3.3 erzeuge P den Kode eines geeigneten zweiten Netzwerkes α zu ß. P Berechne den Wert von f nach dem Algorithmus b(ß,.). Vorgängerknoten und Operationen werden im Verlauf von b(ß,.) durch Simulation von α berechnet. Die Knoten von ß haben eine binäre Darstellung der Länge $\leq C_2(ß)$ und daher haben die bei der Durchführung von b(ß,x) auftauchenden Listen eine Länge $\leq O(B(ß,x) \cdot C_2(ß) + n)$. Der Zusatzterm n wird durch die Eingabeliste $x_1,\ldots,x_n$ verursacht. Da die Listen nur O(B(ß,x)) mal durchlaufen werden, läßt sich die dazu nötige Rechenzeit durch $O((C_2(ß) + n)B(ß,x)^2)$ abschätzen. Hinzu kommt O(B(ß,x)) mal ein Aufwand $O(C_2(ß)^{2+\varepsilon})$ für die Simulation von α. P benötigt also bei der Eingabe x

$$T_P(x) \le O((C_2(ß) + n)B(ß,x)^2 + C_2(ß)^{2+\varepsilon}B(ß,x))$$
$$\le O((C_2(ß)^{2+\varepsilon} + n)B(ß,x)^2)$$

Rechenschritte. Damit erfüllt P neben (2) und (3) auch (1). ▨

Der mittlere Netzwerkaufwand $AV_w(f), f:B^n \to B$ wächst höchstens linear mit n:

<u>Satz 4.4</u> Für jede Funktion $f:B^n \to B, n \ge 2$ ist $AV_w(f) \le 3n-5$ für jede Wahrscheinlichkeitsverteilung w.

<u>Beweis:</u> Wir setzen:$MAV_w(n):\max\{AV_w(f) \mid f:B^n \to B\}$.

Sei $f:B^{n+1} \to B$, dann gibt es $f_1, f_2:B^n \to B$ mit:

$f = x_{n+1}f_1(x_1,\ldots,x_n) \vee \neg x_{n+1}f_2(x_1,\ldots,x_n)$

für i = 1,2 sei $ß_i$ ein Netzwerk, welches f_i berechnet, mit $AV_w(ß_i) \le MAV_w(n)$.

Wir betrachten das zu obiger Darstellung von f gehörige Netz ß:

Der Knoten $y \, (\wedge\neg) \, x$ berechne die Operation $y \wedge \neg x$. Die lexikographische Ordnung der Knoten entspreche der Ordnung der Nummern in Klammern.

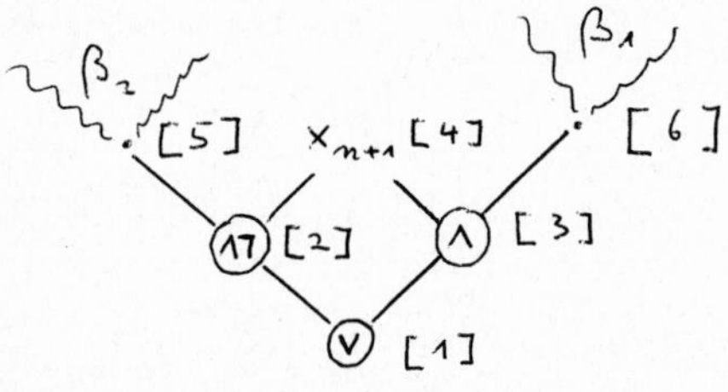

Ist $x_{n+1} = 1$, so ist $B(ß,x) = 4 + B(ß_1,(x_1,\ldots,x_n))$.

Ist $x_{n+1} = 0$, so ist $B(ß,x) = 4 + B(ß_2,(x_2,\ldots,x_n))$.

Also $MAV_w(n+1) \le 3 + MAV_w(n)$ mit der Anfangsbedingung $MAV_w(2) = 1$.

Damit folgt die Behauptung. ▨

Für viele Funktionen ist $AV_w(f)$ sogar unabhängig von der Eingabelänge. Z.B. ist für eine Konjunktion (Disjunktion) f stets $AV_{w_o}(f) \leq 2$, wobei w_o die Gleichverteilung bedeute.

<u>Satz 4.5</u>

Sei $S_n : B^n \to B$ die Summe modulo 2 auf n Variablen. Es ist $AV_w(S_n) = n-1$.

<u>Beweis:</u> $AV_w(S_n) \leq n-1$ ist klar. Andererseits muß bei jeder Eingabe x ein Algorithmus, der $S_n(x)$ berechnet, Information von jeder der n Komponenten von x verarbeiten. Da ein Netzwerk n-1 Nichteingänge benötigt, um n Knoten zusammenzufassen, folgt $AV_w(S_n) \geq n-1$ und damit die Behauptung. ▨

Der folgende Satz ist das Analogon der unteren Schranke von Shannon Lupanov für $C_1(f)$:

Sei $A_n := \{f \mid f : B^n \to B\}$

<u>Satz 4.6</u>

Für jedes $\varepsilon > o$ gilt

$$\frac{|\{f \in A_n \mid AV_w(f) \leq (1-\varepsilon)n\}|}{|A_n|} \to 0$$

für $n \to \infty$.

<u>Beweisskizze:</u> Eine k-Fläche in B^n sei die Teilmenge aller Folgen $x_1,\ldots,x_n \in B^n$, die an n-k festen Stellen die gleichen Werte $C_1,\ldots,C_{n-k}$ ($C_i \in B$) haben. Ist $f : B^n \to B$ auf keiner k-Fläche konstant, so ist $AV_w(f) \geq n-k$, denn bei jeder Eingabe x muß Information von n-k Stellen durch das Netzwerk zusammen-

gefaßt werden. Ist $k(n) \geq \varepsilon \cdot n$ $(\varepsilon > 0)$, so geht die Wahrscheinlichkeit für ein zufälliges f auf keiner k-Fläche konstant zu sein gegen 1. ▨

Diese Arbeit wurde auf Anregung und unter der Leitung von Herrn Prof. C.P. Schnorr angefertigt. Herr H. Bremer war durch wertvolle Diskussionsbeiträge beteiligt.

Literaturverzeichnis

[1] Fischer, M.J.: Lectures on Network Complexity. Preprint Universität Frankfurt

[2] Lupanov, O.B.: Complexity of Formula Realisation of Functions of Logical Algebra. Prob. Cybernetics Vol.3 (1962)

[3] Paul, W.J.: Realizing Boolean Functions on Disjoint Sets of Variables. Theoretical Computer Science, Vol.2 Number 3, September 1976

[4] Pippenger, N.: Information Theory and the Complexity of Boolean Functions. Preprint 1976

[5] Pippenger, N. and Fischer, M.J.: Relations Among Complexity Measures. IBM, New York; University of Washington,Preprint

[6] Savage, J.E.: Computational work and time on finite machines. J. ACM 19, 1972

[7] Schnorr, C.P.: The Network Complexity and the Turing Machine Complexity of Finite Functions. Acta Informatica 7, 1976

Ein vollständiges Problem auf der Baummaschine

H. Bremer

> Jeder Baum, der keine gute
> Frucht bringt, wird umgehauen
> und ins Feuer geworfen.
> (Mt 7.19)

Einleitung

Die Baummaschine ist ein anschauliches Maschinenmodell, das unbeschränkte Parallelität von Rechenprozessen zuläßt. Die Baummaschine ist, (was hier nicht gezeigt wird) polynomial zeitäquivalent zur Vektor RAM, (Pratt, Stockmeyer, Rabin) bzw. zur RAM mit Multiplikation, (Hartmanis, Simon).
Über kombinatorische Probleme, die selbst für Maschinenmodelle mit unbeschränkter Parallelität schwierig sind (im Sinne von voraussichtlich nicht in polynomialer Rechenzeit entscheidbar) ist bisher wenig bekannt. Probleme in der Klasse NP der auf der Turingmaschine in nicht-deterministischer, polynomialer Zeit entscheidbaren Prädikate kommen dafür nicht in Betracht, ebensowenig wie die Prädikate in der Meyer-Stockmeyer-Hierarchie, welche NP fortsetzt. Denn alle diese Prädikate lassen sich offensichtlich auf Maschinen mit unbeschränkter Parallelität in polynomialer Zeit bewältigen.

Wir geben hier ein kombinatorisches Problem an, welches das Erfüllbarkeitsproblem der Aussagenlogik erweitert und das voraussichtlich auch für Maschinen mit unbeschränkter Parallelität nicht in polynomialer Zeit zu bewältigen ist. Unser Nachweis eines solchen Problems besteht in der Angabe eines Prädikats, welches vollständig in der Klasse NP_B der auf der nicht-deterministischen Baummaschine in polynomialer Zeit entscheidbaren Prädikaten (bzgl. Transformationen in polynomialer Zeit) ist. Die Struktur der Baummaschine erlaubt es in natürlicher Weise eine nicht-deterministische Baummaschine einzuführen, und dieses nicht-deterministische Modell ist voraussichtlich wesentlich effizienter als das entsprechende deterministische Modell.

Im Verlauf der Arbeit sollen zunächst die deterministische und die nicht-deterministische Baummaschine definiert werden. Danach wird die Klasse NP_B der auf der nicht-deterministischen Baummaschine in polynomialer Zeit berechenbaren Funktionen untersucht, d.h. es wird ein vollständiges Problem darin angegeben, nachdem zuerst geklärt wurde, wie dieses aussehen könnte.

Die Baummaschine

Eine Baummaschine ist eine baumartige Verbindung gleicher endlicher Automaten, wie es die Abb.1 zeigt:

Abb.1

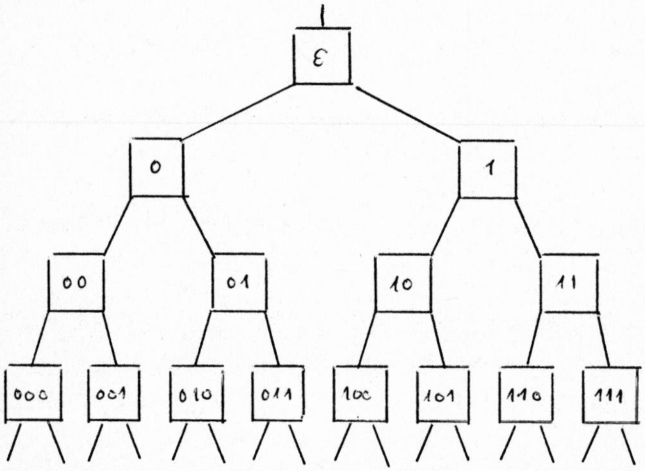

Die Teilautomaten werden mit Elementen aus B^* bezeichnet, wie es in der Abb.1 angegeben ist. Natürlich ist $B = \{0,1\}$. Die Zustandsmenge eines jeden Teilautomaten sei oBdA B^l. Ein Teilautomat speichert also bis zu l bit. s_i^t sei der Zustand der i-ten Teilmaschine zur Zeit t. Die Übergangsfunktion f ist für alle Teilautomaten gleich. Sie bildet den eigenen Zustand, den des Vorgängers und die der beiden Nachfolger auf einen neuen Zustand ab. f ist also eine Abbildung von B^{4l} in B^l mit

(1) $$s_i^{t+1} = f(s_i^t, s_{io}^t, s_{i1}^t, s_{i'}^t).$$

io geht aus i natürlich durch Anhängen einer o hervor, ebenso i1, und i' entsteht aus i durch Weglassen der letzten Stelle, was natürlich nur geht, wenn $i \neq \varepsilon$. Denn für den Kopfautomaten gibt es keinen Vorgänger. An dessen Stelle tritt die Eingabe. OBdA sei auch jedes Eingabeelement aus B^l, d.h. jeder Eingabewert e^t zur Zeit t hat l bit. Für den Kopfautomaten gilt dann

(2) $$s_\varepsilon^{t+1} = f(s_\varepsilon^t, s_o^t, s_1^t, e^{t+1}).$$

Die Ausgabe werde durch eine Funktion $g:B^l \to B$ gebildet. Und zwar ist die Ausgabe a^t zur Zeit t gegeben durch

(3) $$a^t = g(s_\varepsilon^t).$$

Der Automat beginnt die Berechnung stets mit der trivialen Anfangskonfiguration

(4) $$s_i^o = (o,\dots\dots,o) \quad \text{für alle } i \in B^*.$$

Es folgt noch eine formale Definition der Baummaschine:

Definition: (l,f,g) heißt Baummaschine, wenn $l \in N$, $f:B^{4l} \to B^l$ und $g:B^l \to B$ ist.

Setzt man $f:B^{4l} \to B$ fort zu einer Abbildung $F:(B^l)^{B^*} x B^l \to (B^l)^{B^*}$ durch

(5) $$F((s_i)_{i \in B^*}, e) = (f(s_i, s_{io}, s_{i1}, s_{i'}))_{i \in B^*},$$

worin $s_{o'} = e$ sein soll, so kann die Ausgabefolge $(a^t)_{t=1,2,\dots}$ auf die Eingabefolge $(e^t)_{t=1,2,\dots}$ wie folgt beschrieben werden:

(6) $$a^t = G(F(F(\dots\dots F(F((o,\dots\dots,o)_{i \in B^*}, e^1), e^2)\dots, e^{t-1}), e^t))$$
mit $G((s_i)_{i \in B^*}) = g(s_\varepsilon)$

Die nicht-deterministische Baummaschine

Eine nicht-deterministische Maschine entsteht aus einer deterministischen, indem man die Übergangsfunktion durch eine Relation ersetzt. Auf der Baummaschine kommen aber nur auf allen Teilbäumen gleiche Relationen infrage. Es bleiben zwei Möglichkeiten:

1. Im Falle einer nicht-deterministischen Entscheidung zwischen zwei Möglichkeiten entscheiden sich alle Teilautomaten für die eine oder alle für die andere Möglichkeit.

2. Jeder Teilautomat entscheidet sich unabhängig von den anderen für eine der Möglichkeiten.

Die erste Art von Nicht- Determinismus führt nicht wesentlich über die deterministische Baummaschine hinaus. Deshalb soll nur die zweite Art betrachtet werden. Hier können in einem Verzweigungsschritt bis zu 2^n verschiedene Folgezustände möglich sein, wenn gerade n Maschinen nicht im Ruhezustand sind.

Anstelle einer Funktion $f:B^{4l} \to B^l$ wird also eine Relation $r:B^{5l} \to B$ betrachtet. Und zwar ist nun ein Folgezustand genau dann zulässig, wenn

(7) $$r(s_i^{t+1}, s_i^t, s_{io}^t, s_{i1}^t, s_{i'}^t) = 1$$

ist. Wenn auf eine Eingabe $e^1, e^2, \ldots$ jemals die Ausgabe 1 erscheinen kann, so akzeptiert die nicht-deterministische Baummaschine. Ausgabe 1 heißt, daß die Kopfmaschine im Zustand 1 = (1,...,1) ist.

Analog zu anderen Maschinenmodellen kann man nun Raum-, Zeit- und auch Tiefenklassen definieren. Da im folgenden aber nur eine Klasse behandelt wird, soll nur sie angegeben werden. Es ist die Klasse der nicht-deterministisch auf der Baummaschine in polynomialer Zeit berechenbaren (o,1-wertigen) Funktionen NP_B.

(8) NP_B = {f | $\exists$ nicht-deterministische Baummaschine M: M berechnet f, Rechenzeit $T_M(x)$ auf Eingabe x ist polynomial in (x) beschränkt}

Einige Komplexitätsklassen

Im vorangehenden Abschnitt ist unter Punkt 1 eine schwache Art von Nichtdeterminismus angegeben, wo sich alle Teilmaschinen in einem Verzweigungsschritt gleich verhalten. Dieser schwache Nichtdeterminismus aber läßt sich leicht deterministisch nachbilden, da die Baummaschine ja sehr gut geeignet ist, um Verzweigungen in nur zwei Wege zu simulieren. Wenn also Klassenbezeichnungen wie NTime, NSpace usw. auftreten, so sollen sie sich immer auf den starken Nichtdeterminismus beziehen, wo sich in einem Rateschritt alle Teilmaschinen unabhängig verhalten.

Die Raum- und Zeitklassen auf der Baummaschine werden analog zu denen auf der Turingmaschine gebildet. Der Index B steht für Baummaschine, der Index TM für Turingmaschine. So sind z.B. in $\mathrm{Space}_{TM}(S)$ alle Probleme, die sich auf der Turingmaschine im Raum S erledigen lassen, und in $\mathrm{NTime}_B(T)$ sind alle Probleme, die auf einer nichtdeterministischen Baummaschine höchstens die Zeit T brauchen. Weitere Abkürzungen sind P(polynomiale Zeit auf der Turingmaschine), NP (polynomiale Zeit auf der nichtdeterministischen Turingmaschine), P_B (polynomiale Zeit auf der Baummaschine), NP_B (polynomiale Zeit auf der nichtdeterministischen Baummaschine), PSpace (polynomialer Raum auf der Turingmaschine).

Indem man sich Bänder einer blinden Turingmaschine in die Baummaschine hineindenkt, erhält man

(9) $$\mathrm{NTime}_{TM}(T) \subset \mathrm{Time}_B(\log T)$$

und insbesondere

(10) $$NP \subset P_B.$$

Liegt eine Turingmaschine vor, so kann man versuchen, einen Weg von der Anfangskonfiguration zu einer Endkonfiguration binär zu raten. Simuliert man so die Turingmaschine auf der Baummaschine, so erhält man

(11) $$\mathrm{Space}_{TM}(S) \subset \mathrm{Time}_B(S^2)$$

und insbesondere

(12) $$\mathrm{PSpace} \subset P_B.$$

Durch Simulation der Baummaschine auf der RAM erhält man leicht die Beziehung

(13) $$\mathrm{Time}_B(T) \subset \mathrm{Space}_{TM}(T)$$

und insbesondere

(14) $$P_B = \mathrm{SPace}.$$

Es wäre also zu untersuchen, was es nützt, daß man auf der deterministischen Baummaschine stets Informationen Richtung Wurzel schicken kann, im Gegensatz zur nichtdeterministischen Turingmaschine, die man sich ja auch als einen Baum vorstellen kann, in dem keine Information zurück kann, dessen Teilmaschinen aber nicht nur endliche Automaten sind, sondern ganze Turingmaschinen.

Wenn man also der Anschauung folgt, daß Nichtdeterminismus um eine Zweierpotenz schwieriger ist als Determinismus, d.h. daß eine nichtdeterministische Maschine mit Laufzeit T auf einer entsprechend deterministischen nur in der Zeit 2^T simuliert werden kann, und wenn man ebenso der Anschauung folgt, daß die Raumklassen um eine Zweierpotenz schwieriger sind als die Zeitklassen, d.h., daß eine Maschine, die im Raum S arbeitet, auf einer ebensolchen nur in der Zeit 2^S simuliert werden kann, dann erkennt man, daß die Baummaschine wegen (14) und (10) um eine Zweierpotenz schwieriger ist als die Turingmaschine, d.h. daß eine Baummaschine, die in der Zeit T oder im Raum S fertig wird, auf einer Turingmaschine nur in der Zeit 2^T oder im Raum 2^S simuliert werden kann.

Wenn also schon P_B=PSpace ist, was ist dann NP_B? Nun, NP_B ist vielleicht um eine Zweierpotenz schwieriger als P_B bzw. PSpace. Ein vollständiges Problem in PSpace ist die Menge aller wahren Booleschen Ausdrücke mit beliebig vielen Quantoren (Meyer, Stockmeyer).

(15) $$\exists x_1 \forall x_2 \ldots . Qx_n : A(x_1, \ldots, x_n)$$

Will man den Wahrheitswert einfach durch Probieren herausbekommen, so muß man 2^n Fälle durchprobieren. Ersetzt man die x_i durch n-stellige Funktionen f_i, so entsteht

(16) $$\exists f_1 \forall f_2 \ldots . Qf_n : A(f_1, \ldots, f_n).$$

Zum Durchprobieren muß man schon $\left(2^{2^n}\right)^n = 2^{n2^n}$ Fälle durchprobieren. Das ist ungefähr eine Zweierpotenz mehr, und in dieser Richtung wäre ein vollständiges Problem für NP_B zu suchen. Davon handelt der Rest dieses Aufsatzes.

Ein vollständiges Problem in NP_B

Es liegt nahe, daß auf der nichtdeterministischen Baummaschine alle Klassen gegenüber der nichtdeterministischen Turingmaschine um eine Zweierpotenz schwieriger sind, daß also in NP_B ein Problem vollständig sein könnte, in dem nicht nur über einzelne Variable, sondern über Funktionen quantifiziert wird. D.h. es geht um die Entscheidung von Ausdrücken der Art

(17) $$\exists f_i : A(f_i).$$

Wie diese Ausdrücke ganz konkret auszusehen haben, ergibt sich aus der Notwendigkeit, daß jedes Problem in NP_B polynomial in einen solchen Ausdruck überführt werden muß, und aus der Notwendigkeit, daß dieses Problem selbst in NP_B zu liegen hat.

Es ist also nötig, die Zustände der Baummaschine geeignet durch Funktionen zu beschreiben. Das geschieht etwa in jeder Tiefe k des Baumes, zu jedem bit j des Zustandes der Teilmaschinen und jedem Zeitpunkt t durch eine Funktion $S_{kj}^t : B^k \to B$. Ist

(18) $$s_i^t = (s_{i1}^t, \dots, s_{il}^t),$$

so wird S_{kj}^t definiert durch

(19) $$S_{kj}^t(x_1, \dots, x_k) = s_{(x_1, \dots, x_k), j}^t$$

Nun lassen sich mit den Funktionen S_{kj}^t leicht Ausdrücke bilden, die korrektes Arbeiten, Anfangs- und Endbedingungen beschreiben. Dazu sind neben stellenweisen Operationen auf diesen Funktionen nur Unter- und Oberfunktionsbildungen nötig.

Hier entsteht jedoch ein Problem. Zwar möchten wir aus Schönheitsgründen alle Unterfunktionen direkt bilden können, doch ist dann nicht zu sehen, wie das Problem noch in NP_B sein soll. Diese Schwierigkeit führt dazu, daß nur Unterfunktionen gebildet werden, die durch Festsetzen der letzten Variablen entstehen. Ebenso wird nur die eine Oberfunktion gebildet, die durch das Anfügen einer weiteren Variablen ohne Einfluß entsteht.

Die Entscheidung eines vorgelegten Ausdruckes kann etwa so vor sich gehen: Kommen m Funktionen mit maximal n Variablen in einem Ausdruck vor, so stehen in der Tiefe n+ldm genügend Plätze zur Verfügung, um in einem einzigen Rateschritt die Wertebelegung der m Funktionen zu raten. Wie das geschehen soll, stellt die Abb. 2 genauer dar.

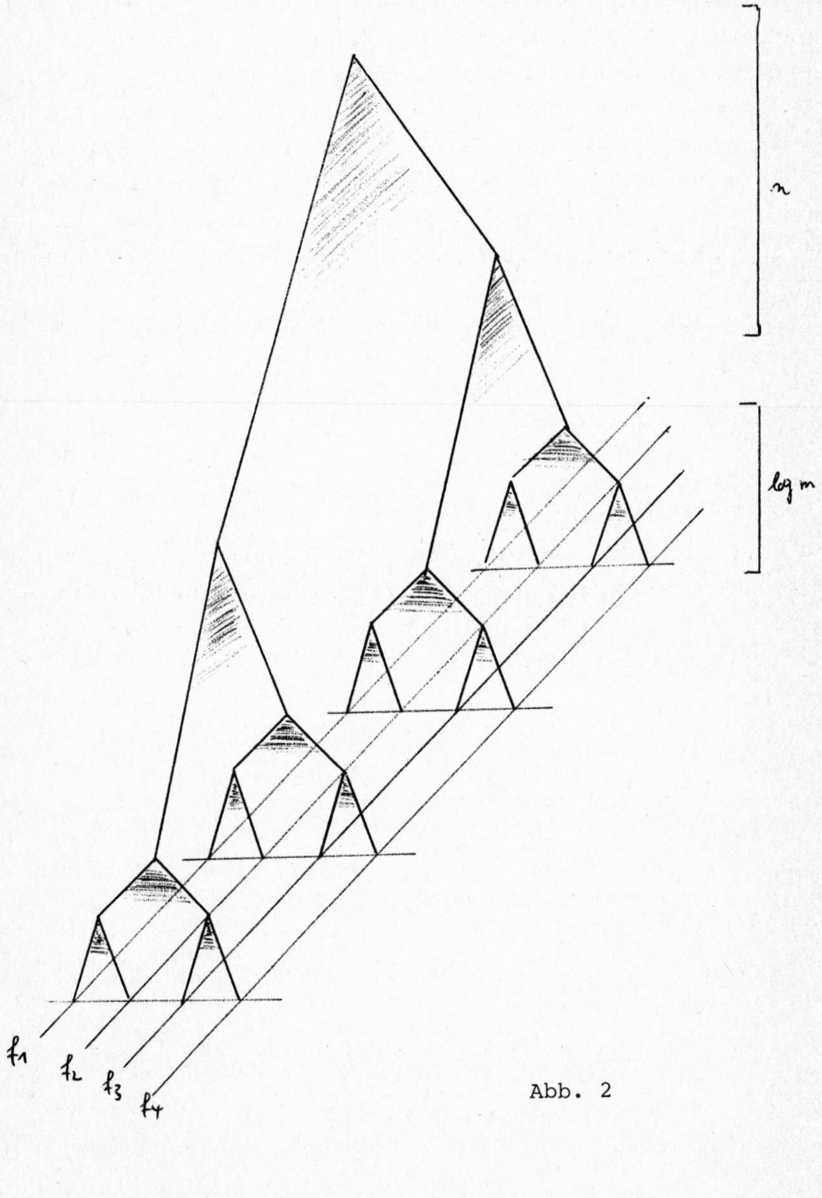

Abb. 2

Funktionen mit n Variablen belegen bei der Lage wie in Abb.2 alle vorgesehenen Plätze, Funktionen in weniger Variablen jeden 2., 4.,... Platz. Man sieht sofort, daß mit dieser Lage der Funktionen stellenweise Operationen sehr schnell, nämlich parallel, ausgeführt werden können. Ebenso kann man auch schnell feststellen, ob zwei Funktionen gleich sind. Und man kann leicht Unterfunktionen bilden, wenn man sich auf solche beschränkt, in der die letzte Variable o oder 1 gesetzt wird. Setzt man sie o, so braucht man gar nichts zu ändern. Die Funktion wird einfach als eine mit einer Stelle weniger interpretiert. Setzt man die letzte Variable gleich 1, so muß man die entsprechenden Werte nach vorne an die richtige Stelle schaffen. Das geschieht aber ebenfalls parallel. Abb. 3 verdeutlicht den einfachen Informationsfluß, wenn man eine Unterfunktion durch Festsetzen der letzten Variablen bildet.

Abb. 3

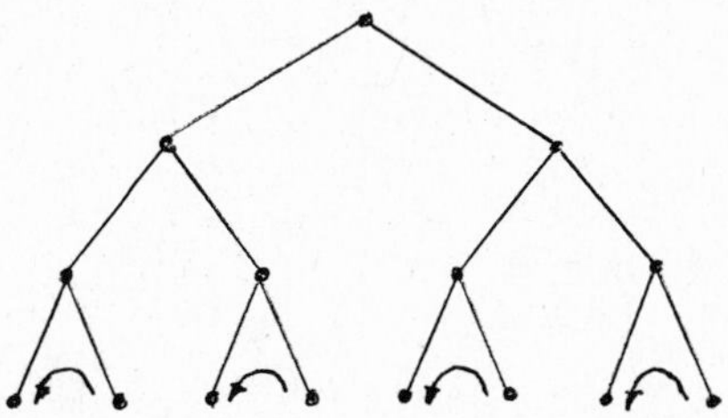

Abb. 4 dagegen zeigt, wie weit die Wege sind und wie Engpässe entstehen, die paralleles Arbeiten verhindern, wenn man etwa die Unterfunktion bilden will, die durch Festsetzen der ersten Variablen entsteht.

Abb. 4

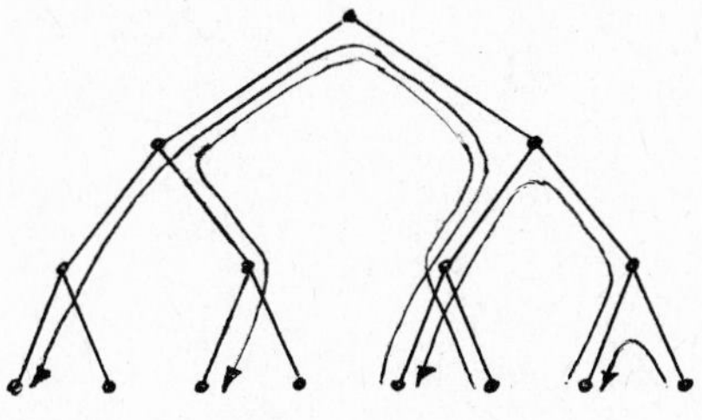

Alle diese Überlegungen führen zu der nun folgenden Definition der Funktionenausdrücke.

Definition des Funktionenproblems

F_n sei die Menge der Booleschen Funktionen von B^n nach B, und F sei die Vereinigung aller F_n mit n = o,1,2,.. s(f) ist die Stellenzahl von f.

Die zwei Unterfunktionsoperatoren u_o und $u_1 : F \nrightarrow F$ sind def. durch

(20)
$$\begin{aligned} Def(u_o) &= Def(u_1) = F - F_o \\ s(u_of) &= s(u_1f) = s(f) - 1 \\ (u_of)(x_1,\dots,x_{s(u_of)}) &= f(x_1,\dots,x_{s(u_of)},o) \\ (u_1f)(x_1,\dots,x_{s(u_1f)}) &= f(x_1,\dots,x_{s(u_1f)},1) \ . \end{aligned}$$

Der Oberfunktionsoperator $o : F \rightarrow F$ ist definiert durch

(21)
$$\begin{aligned} s(of) &= s(f) + 1 \\ (of)(x_1,\dots,x_{s(of)}) &= f(x_1,\dots,x_{s(of)-1}) \ . \end{aligned}$$

Die Konjunktion und Adjunktion sind als stellenweise Fortsetzung definiert. $\wedge, \vee : F^2 \nrightarrow F$,

(22)
$$\begin{aligned} Def(\wedge) &= Def(\vee) = \bigcup_{i=o}^{\infty} F_i^2 \\ s(f \wedge g) &= s(f \vee g) = s(f) = s(g) \\ (f \wedge g)(x_1,\dots,x_{s(f)}) &= f(x_1,\dots,x_{s(f)}) \wedge g(x_1,\dots,x_{s(f)}) \\ (f \vee g)(x_1,\dots,x_{s(f)}) &= f(x_1,\dots,x_{s(f)}) \vee g(x_1,\dots,x_{s(f)}) \ . \end{aligned}$$

Analog ist die Negation definiert. $\neg : F \rightarrow F$,

(23)
$$\begin{aligned} s(\neg f) &= s(f) \\ (\neg f)(x_1,\dots,x_{s(f)}) &= \neg f(x_1,\dots,x_{s(f)}) \ . \end{aligned}$$

Es folgt die Gleichheit $= : F^2 \nrightarrow B$ definiert durch

(24)
$$Def(=) = \bigcup_{i=o}^{\infty} F_i^2$$

$$(f = g) = \begin{cases} 1, & \text{falls } \forall x_1,\dots,x_{s(f)} : f(x_1,\dots) = g(x_1\dots,), \\ o & \text{sonst.} \end{cases}$$

Es bleiben die Konstanten o_i und 1_i aus F_i mit i = 1,2,3,... zu definieren:

(25) $o_i(x_1,\dots,x_i) = o \quad , \quad 1_i(x_1,\dots,x_i) = 1 \ .$

Nun zur eigentlichen Definition der Ausdrücke.

1. $f_1, f_2, f_3, \ldots$ heißen Funktionen.
2. Sind f, g, h Funktionen, so sind $u_o f=h$, $u_1 f=h$, $of=h$, $\neg f=h$, $f \wedge g=h$, $f \vee g=h$, $o_i=h$ und $1_i=h$ elementare Ausdrücke. Diese elementaren Ausdrücke entsprechen den Klauseln bei Satisfiability.
3. Sind $\alpha_1, \ldots, \alpha_k$ elementare Ausdrücke, sind $g_1, \ldots, g_l$ die in ihnen vorkommenden Funktionen und sind weiterhin $j_1, \ldots, j_l$ natürliche Zahlen, so ist

(26) $$(j_1, \ldots, j_l \; ; \; \exists \; g_1, \ldots, g_l \; : \; \alpha_1, \ldots, \alpha_k)$$

ein Ausdruck.

Ein Ausdruck heißt korrekt, wenn die Stellenzahlen $j_1, \ldots, j_l$ zu den Operationen passen. Die Kodierung der Zahlen $j_1, \ldots, j_l$ erfolgt unär, der Rest wird binär kodiert, so daß die Gesamtlänge des Ausdrucks größer als die maximale Stellenzahl ist, was sehr wichtig wird.

Nun kann das Problem "Funktionenerfüllbarkeit" (kurz: Fkterf) definiert werden.

Definition: Fkterf ist die Teilmenge von B^* gegeben durch

(27) $$\text{Fkterf} = \{ i \in B^* \mid i \text{ ist Kodierung eines korrekten Ausdrucks und dieser Ausdruck ist logisch wahr} \}.$$

Der Rest dieses Aufsatzes beschäftigt sich nun mit dem Nachweis der Vollständigkeit von Fkterf in NP_B, d.h. es wird der folgende Satz bewiesen:

Satz: Fkterf ist vollständig in NP_B bzgl. polynomialer Reduktion auf der Turingmaschine.

Polynomiale Reduktion von NP_B auf "Fkterf"

Es liege ein Problem A aus NP_B mit der Rechenzeit $T:N \to N$ vor. Nun soll zu diesem Problem A eine Funktion $\varphi:B^* \to B^*$ angegeben werden, die auf der Turingmaschine und damit auch auf der Baummaschine nur polynomiale Rechenzeit braucht und für die gilt:

(28) $\varphi(x) \in \text{"Fkterf"} \leftrightarrow x \in A$

Um φ zu konstruieren, nimmt man eine nichtdeterministische Baummaschine her, die A in polynomialer Zeit entscheidet. Diese Maschine werde von der Relation $r:B^{51} \to B$ erzeugt. Es geht nun darum, das korrekte Arbeiten einer Baummaschine, die Eingabe und den Schlußtest in einen Funktionenausdruck zu überführen.

r beschreibt die Korrektheit des Überganges an einem Teilautomaten. Es wird übergeführt in eine Funktion R_k^t, die die Korrektheit des Überganges in einer Tiefe k des Baumes zur Zeit t darstellt.

$$R_k^t : F_k^{21} \times F_{k+1}^1 \times F_{k-1}^1 \to F_k \quad \text{def. durch}$$

(29)
$$R_k^t(S_{k1}^{t+1},..,S_{kl}^{t+1},S_{k1}^t,..,S_{k+1,1}^t,..,S_{k-1,1}^t,..)(x_1,..,x_k)$$
$$=r(S_{k1}^{t+1}(x_1,..,x_k),..,S_{k1}^t(x_1,..,x_k),..S_{k+1,1}^t(x_1,..,x_k,o)$$
$$S_{k+1,1}^t(x_1,..,x_k,1),...,S_{k-1,1}^t(x_1,..,x_{k-1}),...)$$

für t = 1,2,3,...,T-1 und k = 1,2,3,...,T-1.

R_o^t muß etwas anders definiert werden, da der Automat anstelle eines Vorgängers ja die Eingabe hat:

$$R_o^t(S_{o1}^{t+1},..,S_{o1}^{t+1},S_{o1}^t,..,S_{o1}^t,S_{11}^t,..,S_{11}^t)$$
$$=r(S_{o1}^{t+1},..,S_{o1}^{t+1},S_{o1}^t,..,S_{ol}^t,S_{11}^t(o),..,S_{1l}^t(o),S_{11}^t(1),..$$
$$..,S_{1l}^t(1),e_1^{t+1},..,e_l^{t+1})$$

für t = 1,2,3,...,T-1.

Auch R_T^t muß etwas anders definiert werden, da ja die Teilautomaten der Tiefe T+1 nicht mehr betrachtet werden. Auch muß noch R_k^o für den korrekten Beginn (alle Automaten im Zustand o) und R_o^T (es erscheint Ausgabe 1) definiert werden. Die übrigen R_k^T können

beliebig gewählt werden, da sie ohne Bedeutung sind. Das alles geschieht wie in den Formeln (15) und (16).
Jedes dieser R_k^t läßt sich nun durch Ober- und Unterfunktionen, durch Konstanten und durch stellenweise Operationen ausdrücken. Dazu sei $r_k: F_k^{51} \to F_k$ die stellenweise Fortsetzung von r, definiert durch

(31) $r_k(f_1,..,f_{51})(x_1,..,x_k)=r(f_1(x_1,..,x_k),..,f_{51}(x_1,..,x_k))$.

Aus (29) folgt nun ohne weiteres

(32) $R_k^t(S_{k1}^{t+1},...............,S_{k-1,l}^t)$

$=r_k(S_{k1}^{t+1},..,S_{kl}^{t+1},S_{k1}^t,..,u_oS_{k+1,1}^t,..,u_1S_{k+1,1}^t,..,oS_{k-1,1}^t,..)$

Ebenso folgt aus (3o):

(33) $R_o^t(S_o^{t+1},.................,S_{11}^t)$

$=r_o(S_{o1}^{t+1},..,S_{o1}^t,..,u_oS_{11}^t,..,u_1S_{11}^t,..,e_1^{t+1},..)$

Und für R_T^t braucht man auch die Konstanten:

(34) $R_T^t(S_{T1}^{t+1},................,S_{T-1,l}^t)$

$=r_T(S_{T1}^{t+1},..,S_{T1}^t,..,o_T,..,o_T,..,oS_{T-1,1}^t,..)$

Ebenso ist es bei den übrigen R_k^t. Damit ist nun gezeigt, daß die Arbeitsweise, die Eingabe und der Schlußtest der Baummaschine mit den zur Verfügung stehenden Operationen beschrieben werden kann, denn außer den r_k kommen nur Ober- und Unterfunktionen und die Konstanten vor. r_k aber ist stellenweise gebildet und kann in elementare Ausdrücke zerlegt werden. Nur ein Beispiel:

Statt $f\wedge(g\vee oh)=1$ schreibt man $\exists$ h',g':oh=h',g∨h'=g', f∧g'=1 .

So lassen sich alle Ausdrücke R_k^t zerlegen, und zwar alle R_k^t glm. mit evtl. Vereinfachungen. R_k^t zerfalle in die elementaren Ausdrücke $A_{k1}^t,..,A_{kN}^t$, wobei zusätzlich über die Variablen $H_{k1}^t,..,H_{kM}^t$ quantisiert werden muß. Dann sieht der Gesamtausdruck wie folgt aus:

(35) $((k)_{t,k,j},(k)_{t,k,m}; \exists\, (S_{kj}^t)_{t,k,j},(H_{km}^t)_{t,k,m}:(A_{kn}^t)_{t,k,n})$

Dabei durchlaufen die Indizes die folgenden Werte:

t=o,1,..,T, k=o,1,..,T, j=1,2,..,l, m=1,2,..,M, n=1,2,..,N.

Der Ausdruck hat die Länge $O(T^3)$. Den Hauptterm bilden die Stellenzahlen. Er läßt sich auch in $O(T^3)$ Schritten hinschreiben.

"Fkterf" ist in NP_B

Abb. 2 zeigte schon, wie die Funktionen gespeichert werden sollen. Man bestimmt anhand des vorliegenden Ausdruckes die maximale Stellenzahl n und die Zahl m der Funktionen. In der Tiefe $n+\lceil ld(m+1)\rceil$ ist dann genügend Platz, um m Funktionen raten zu können. Der Rateprozeß eliminiert den Existenzquantor, so daß danach nur noch auf deterministische Weise nachgeprüft werden muß, ob die hinter dem Doppelpunkt des Quantors stehenden Ausdrücke mit der geratenen Belegung erfüllt sind.

Die Funktionswerte einer n-stelligen Funktion werden in der üblichen Reihenfolge auf den vorgesehenen Plätzen festgehalten. Bei einer (n-i)-stelligen Funktion werden nur die Plätze $1,\ 2^i+1,\ 2.2^i+1,\ 3.2^i+1,\ldots,2^n-2^i+1$ belegt. Damit man Funktionen verschiedener Stellenzahlen auch unterscheiden kann, ist es nötig, Register für die Stellenzahlen einzuführen. Um weiterhin die Korrektheit eines Ausdrucks festzustellen und um die Einleitung und Ausführung der verschiedenen Phasen zu gewährleisten, ist noch ein Organisationsteil nötig. Außerdem wird noch ein Rechenregister benötigt, weshalb ja auch m+1 und nicht m Funktionsregister geschaffen wurden. Der Gesamtbaum könnte etwa so aussehen:

Abb. 5

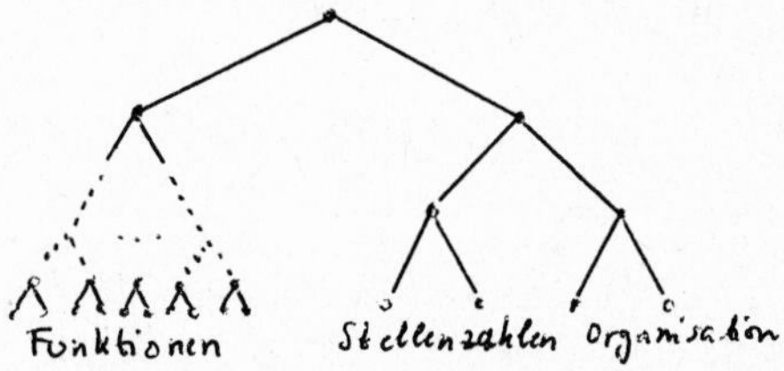

Nun muß man sich nicht mehr überlgegen, wie der Gesamtausdruck entschieden wird, sondern man muß nur noch die einzelnen elementaren Ausdrücke durchgehen. Dazu ist es nur nötig, sich Klarheit über den Informationsfluß zu verschaffen.

Zum Testen von Ausdrücken wie $u_o f=h$, $f \wedge g=g$, $1_i=h$ u.ä. erstellt man zunächst im Rechenregister die linke Seite l der Gleichung. Steht sie einmal da, so braucht man nur noch l=h zu testen. Das ist aber parallel zu erledigen.

Es bleibt also nur noch zu klären, wie die linken Seiten in das Rechenregister gelangen. Für stellenweise Operationen ist das trivial, da es parallel und überall gleich geht. Ebenso sind die Konstanten leicht zu erzeugen, so daß nur noch Ober- und Unterfunktionsbildung bleiben.

Bildet man die Unterfunktion $u_o f$, so schreibt man einfach f in das Rechenregister ab und vermerkt die Stellenzahl von $u_o f$, die um eins geringer ist als die von f.

Die Unterfunktion $u_1 f$ ist schon schwieriger. Dabei muß bei einer (n-k)-stelligen Funktion der $2i2^k$-te Platz von f auf den $(2i-1)2^k$-ten Platz des Rechenregisters. Sieht man sich diese Platzzahlen an, so erkennt man sofort, daß die Wege, auf denen die Information fließen muß, sich nicht kreuzen, so daß die Operation u_1 parallel ausführbar ist. Das macht auch die Abb. 6 deutlich:

Abb. 6

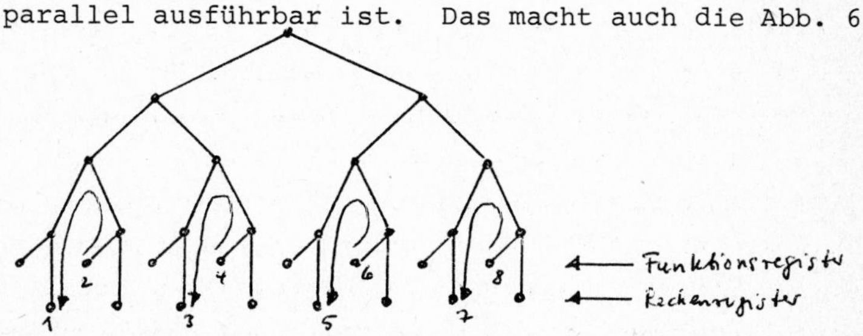

Bei der Oberfunktionsbildung ist es ebenso. Der $i2^k$-te Platz von f muß auf den $i2^k$-ten und den $(i+1/2)s^k$-ten Platz des Rechenregisters. Auch das geht parallel,wie die Betrachtung der Platznummern oder des Bildes 7 lehrt.

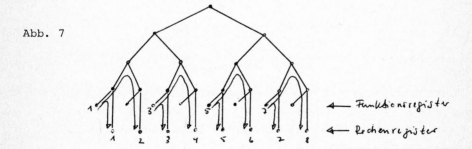

Abb. 7

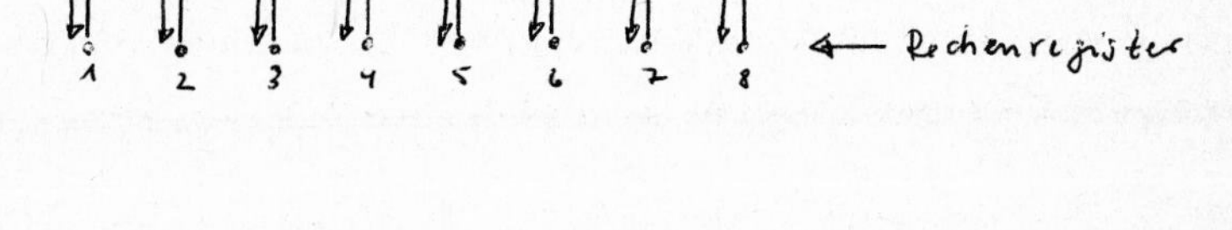

Zum Abarbeiten eines elementaren Ausdrucks braucht man nur ein O von der Weglänge des Weges, der von der Information zurückgelegt werden muß und der zur Einleitung der Operation und zur Organisation nötig ist. Diese Weglänge ist sicher $O(n+ldm) = O(L)$, worin L die Länge des vorgelegten Ausdrucks ist. Hier ist wichtig, daß $n \leq L$ ist, weshalb die Stellenzahlen unär kodiert wurden. Die Gesamtzeit ist somit $O(L^2)$, so daß Funktionenausdrücke in polynomialer Zeit entschieden werden können.

Damit ist der Beweis des Satzes von Seite 12 abgeschlossen, und damit ist Fkterf polynomial vollständig in NP_B.

Ich danke den Herren Conrad Reynvaan und Prof. Dr. C.P. Schnorr für die Anregungen und die Betreuung dieser Arbeit.

Literatur

1. A. Borodin: On Relating Time and Space to Size and Depth 1976

2. S. Cook: The Complexity of Theorem-proving Procedures, 3rd ACM Symp., S. 151-158

3. Juris Hartmanis, Janos Simon: On the Power of Multiplication in Random Access Machines. 15th Annual Symposium on Switching and Automata Theory, New Orleans, 1974, S. 13-23

4. V. Pratt, L. Stockmeyer, M.O. Rabin: A Characterization of the Power of Vektor Machines. 6th ACM Symp., S. 122-134

5. L.J. Stockmeyer, A.R. Meyer: Word Problems Requiring Exponential Time. Proceedings of 5th Annual ACM Symposium on Theory of Computing, Austin, Texas 1973, S. 1-9

ÜBER DIE LÄNGE EINER BERECHNUNG BEI LINEARER PARAMETERABHÄNGIGKEIT DER OPERATIONSZEIT

R. Schauerte

In STRASSEN [3] werden " Berechnungen " (d.h. Programme ohne Verzweigungen) in partiellen Algebren definiert, denen dann als Komplexitätsmaß " Länge " ihre Rechenzeiten bei serieller Ausführung zugeordnet werden. Ist dann eine endliche Teilmenge E dieser partiellen Algebra gegeben, so wird die Länge von E durch die Länge einer optimalen Berechnung von E gemessen. Das setzt jedoch voraus, daß von jeder Operation der entsprechenden partiellen Algebra die Ausführungszeiten auf einem gegebenen Rechner bekannt sind. Oft sind aber die genauen Werte unbekannt und damit auch die tatsächliche Länge einer Berechnung. Hier wird nun gezeigt, daß bei linearer Abhängigkeit der Operationszeit von einem Parameter $x \in D$ (dem positiven Kegel des $\mathbb{R}^n$) die Länge von E eine stetige Funktion von x ist und D so in endlich viele konvexe Polyeder zerlegt werden kann, daß auf jedem dieser Polyeder eine Berechung optimal ist.

Gegeben sei eine Menge Ω von Operationen. Dabei werden Konstanten als nullstellige Operationen betrachtet. Unter einer <u>Berechnung</u> werde dann ein Algorithmus ohne Verzweigungen verstanden, d.h. eine endliche Folge von <u>Rechenschritten</u>, wobei im i-ten Rechenschritt genau eine Operation $\omega_i \in \Omega$ ausgeführt wird, deren Argumente Ergebnisse vorhergehender Rechenschritte sind (eine exakte Definition liefern etwa die Berechnungen oder die Ω-Mengen in STRASSEN [3] für homogene bzw. die Δ-Mengen in ZINN [4] für heterogene partielle Algebren).

Ist nun für jede Operation $\omega \in \Omega$ eine nichtnegative reelle Zahl als Ausführungszeit gegeben, so kann man einer Berechnung B ihre Rechenzeit L(B) zuordnen. Zu einer endlichen Menge E, die mit Operationen aus Ω berechnet werden kann, ist dann eine " optimale Berechnung " gesucht, d.h. eine Berechnung B_o mit der Eigenschaft

$$L(B_o) = \inf \{L(B) \mid B \text{ berechnet } E\}.$$

Dazu werde definiert (vgl.STRASSEN [3]):

<u>Definition 1:</u> Eine Abbildung $z : \Omega \longrightarrow [0,\infty)$ heißt <u>Operationszeit</u>, wenn $z(\Omega)$ mit der von $[0,\infty)$ induzierten Ordnung wohlgeordnet ist.
Ist B eine Berechnung mit k Rechenschritten, so ist die <u>Länge von B</u> definiert durch

$$L(B) := \sum_{i=1}^{k} z(\omega_i).$$

Ist E eine endliche Menge, die mit Operationen aus Ω berechnet werden kann, und

$$W := \{B \mid B \text{ berechnet } E\},$$

so ist die <u>Länge von E</u> definiert durch $L(E) := \min_{B \in W} L(B)$.

Daher läßt sich die Bestimmung der Länge L(E) in gewisserweise als " Optimierungsproblem" auffassen: " Minimiere die Zielfunktion L(B) auf der Menge W." Das legt es nahe, die Operationszeit in linearer Abhängigkeit von n unabhängigen Parametern zu definieren, und zwar ähnlich wie beim Parametrisieren der Zielfunktion in der linearen parametrischen Optimierung (vgl.z.B. DINKELBACH [1]):

<u>Definition 2:</u> Sei $n \geq 1$ und D der positive Kegel des $\mathbb{R}^n$ (in der komponentenweisen Halbordnung). Sind dann $z_o, z_1, \ldots, z_n$

Operationszeiten, so werde gesetzt:

$$z : \Omega \times D \longrightarrow \mathbb{R},\ z(\omega,x) := z_o(\omega) + \sum_{i=1}^{n} x_i z_i(\omega).$$

Wegen Lemma 4 in STRASSEN [3], S.326 ist dann $z(.,x) : \Omega \longrightarrow \mathbb{R}$ für alle $x \in D$ eine Operationszeit. Bezeichnet dann $L_i(B)$ bzw. $L_i(E)$ die Länge bzgl. z_i für $0 \le i \le n$ und $L(B,x)$ bzw. $L(E,x)$ die Länge bzgl. $z(.,x)$ für $x \in D$, so gilt:

Satz 3: Für alle $x \in D$ und jede Berechnung B ist

$$L(B,x) = L_o(B) + \sum_{i=1}^{n} x_i L_i(B).$$

Daraus ergibt sich sofort eine untere Abschätzung für $L(E,x)$:

Satz 4: Für alle $x \in D$ gilt:

$$L(E,x) \ge L_o(E) + \sum_{i=1}^{n} x_i L_i(E).$$

Mit den Mitteln der konvexen Analysis kann man nun zeigen, daß $L(E,x)$ auf D stetig ist. Zur Vereinfachung späterer Beweise wird dabei jedoch etwas allgemeiner vorgegangen:

Definition 5: Sei M eine beliebige nichtleere Menge von Berechnungen. Dann werde gesetzt:

$$L_M : D \longrightarrow \mathbb{R},\ L_M(x) := \min_{B \in M} L(B).$$

Ein konvexes Polyeder im $\mathbb{R}^n$ ist definiert als Durchschnitt endlich vieler abgeschlossener Halbräume. Damit gilt:

Lemma 6: Sei $P \subseteq \mathbb{R}^n$ ein konvexes Polyeder und M eine nichtleere Menge stetiger konvexer Funktionen $f : P \longrightarrow \mathbb{R}$.

Ist dann

$$g : P \longrightarrow \overline{\mathbb{R}},\ g(x) := \sup_{f \in M} f(x)$$

für alle $x \in P$ endlich, so ist g eine konvexe Funktion, die auf P stetig ist.
Zum Beweis vgl. ROCKAFELLAR [2], S.35,78,84 und 184.
Daraus folgt:

Satz 7: L_M ist eine isotone, konkave und stetige Funktion auf D. Insbesondere ist damit auch $L(E,x)$ isoton, konkav und stetig auf D.

Weiter kann man nun zeigen, daß es endlich viele Berechnungen $B_1, \ldots, B_k$ und eine Zerlegung von D in konvexe Polyeder $P_1, \ldots, P_k$ gibt, so daß B_i auf P_i optimal ist. Dazu werde für $B \in W$ gesetzt:

$$O(B) := \{x \in D \mid L(E,x) = L(B,x)\}.$$

Dann gilt:

$$O(B) = D \cap \bigcap_{C \in W} \{x \in \mathbb{R}^n \mid \sum_{i=1}^{n} x_i(L_i(C) - L_i(B)) \geq L_o(B) - L_o(C)\}.$$

Bei den folgenden Überlegungen kann man sich im wesentlichen auf solche Berechnungen $B,C \in W$ beschränken, für die

$$H_{B,C} := \{x \in \mathbb{R}^n \mid \sum_{i=1}^{n} x_i(L_i(C) - L_i(B)) = L_o(B) - L_o(C)\}$$

eine Hyperebene ist. Denn sind $B,C \in W$ mit $L_i(B) = L_i(C)$ für $1 \leq i \leq n$, so ist im Fall $L_o(B) < L_o(C)$ bzw. $L_o(B) > L_o(C)$ nämlich $O(C) = \emptyset$ bzw. $O(B) = \emptyset$, im Fall $L_o(B) = L_o(C)$ aber $O(B) = O(C)$.
Nach ROCKAFELLAR [2], S.45/46 gilt:

Lemma 8: Für konvexe Mengen $M,N, \subseteq \mathbb{R}^n$ gilt:

a) Ist $M \neq \emptyset$, so ist auch ri $M \neq \emptyset$.
b) Ist $M \subseteq N$ und $M \not\subseteq$ rr N, so gilt ri $M \subseteq$ ri N.

Dabei bezeichne ri M das relative Innere und rr M den relativen Rand von M.

Damit kann man nun zeigen:

Satz 9: Für alle $B \in W$ ist $O(B)$ ein konvexes Polyeder.

Beweis: Ist $O(B)$ leer, $O(B) = D$ oder die Menge

$$K := \{H_{B,C} \mid C \in W \ \&\ H_{B,C} \text{ Hyperebene}\}$$

endlich, so ist $O(B)$ trivialerweise ein konvexes Polyeder.
Sei nun

$$M := \{H \in K \mid O(B) \subseteq H\}$$

die Menge aller Hyperebenen $H_{B,C}$, die $O(B)$ enthalten.
Da die Mengen $z_i(\Omega)$, $0 \leq i \leq n$ wohlgeordnet sind, kann man leicht zeigen, daß M endlich ist. Ist nun

$$N := \{H \in K \setminus M \mid O(B) \cap H \neq \emptyset\}$$

die Menge aller eigentlichen Stützhyperebenen $H_{B,C}$ von $O(B)$, so gilt:

$$O(B) \subseteq D \cap \bigcap_M H \cap \bigcap_N H^+,$$

wobei H^+ den zur Hyperebene H gehörigen positiven Halbraum bezeichnet.
Sei nun $x \in (D \cap \bigcap_M H) \setminus O(B)$. Setzt man dann

$$S := \{C \in W \mid H_{B,C} \in K \setminus M\},$$

so gilt:

$$L_S(x) = \min_{C \in S} L(C,x) < L(B,x).$$

Wegen Lemma 8 ist $\text{ri}\, O(B) \neq \emptyset$, und für beliebiges $y \in \text{ri}\, O(B)$ gilt:

$$L_S(y) > L(B,y).$$

Da L_S wegen Satz 7 stetig auf D ist, existieren $C_o \in S$ und $z \in O(B)$ mit

$$L(C_o,z) = L_S(z) = L(B,z).$$

Damit ist H_{B,C_o} Stützhyperebene von $O(B)$ mit $x \notin H^+_{B,C_o}$.
Daraus folgt

$$O(B) = D \cap \bigcap_M H \cap \bigcap_N H^+.$$

Da die Mengen $z_i(\Omega)$, $0 \leq i \leq n$ wohlgeordnet sind, kann man leicht zeigen, daß auch N endlich ist. Daher ist $O(B)$ ein konvexes Polyeder.

Satz 10: Es gibt endlich viele Berechnungen $B_1,\dots,B_k \in W$ mit $\bigcup_{j=1}^{k} O(B_j) = D$ und $\dim O(B_j) = n$ für $1 \le j \le k$.

Beweis: Sei $x \in D$ und

$$M := \{B \in W \mid L(B,x) = L(E,x)\}.$$

Definiert man auf M eine Äquivalenzrelation R durch $(B,C) \in R$ genau dann, wenn $L_i(B) = L_i(C)$ für $o \le i \le n$ gilt, so kann man leicht zeigen, daß M/R endlich ist, da die Mengen $z_i(\Omega)$ wohlgeordnet sind.

Im Fall $M = W$ ist x trivialerweise innerer Punkt von $\bigcup_M O(B) = D$ in der Relativtopologie von D.

Im Fall $M \neq W$ sei $N := W \setminus M$.

Dann gilt:

$$L_N(x) = \min_{B\in N} L(B,x) > \max_{B\in M} L(B,x).$$

Wegen der Stetigkeit von $L_N(x)$ und $\max_{B\in M} L(B,x)$ ist x dann ebenfalls innerer Punkt von $\bigcup_M O(B)$ in der Relativtopologie von D.

Daher gibt es ein $B \in M$ mit $\dim O(B) = n$, da sonst $\bigcup_M O(B)$ nirgends dicht wäre in der Relativtopologie von D.

Weiter kann man leicht zeigen, daß die Menge

$$\{O(B) \mid \dim O(B) = n\}$$

endlich ist, da die Mengen $z_i(\Omega)$ $(o \le i \le n)$ wohlgeordnet sind.

Eine Seite eines konvexen Polyeders P ist definiert als Durchschnitt von P und einer Familie von Stützhyperebenen.

Nach ROCKAFELLAR [2], S.164 gilt:

Lemma 11: Ist P eine konvexes Polyeder und $S \neq P$ eine Seite von P, so gilt $S \subseteq rr\, P$ und damit $\dim S < \dim P$.

Daraus folgt:

Satz 12: Sind $B,C \in W$, so ist $O(B) \cap O(C)$ eine gemeinsame Seite von $O(B)$ und $O(C)$.
Ist insbesondere $\dim O(B) = \dim O(C) = n$ und $O(B) \neq O(C)$, so gilt

$$\text{ri}\, O(B) \cap \text{ri}\, O(C) = \emptyset.$$

Literatur:

[1] Werner DINKELBACH:
" Sensitivitätsanalysen und parametrische Programmierung"
Springer, Berlin 1969.

[2] R.Tyrrell ROCKAFELLAR:
" Convex Analysis "
Princeton University Press, Princeton (N.J.) 1970.

[3] Volker STRASSEN:
" Berechnung und Programm I/II"
Acta Informatica 1 (1972), 320 - 335 & 2 (1973),64 - 79.

[4] Rainer ZINN:
" Untersuchungen zur Komplexität von Berechnungen mit Verzweigungen"
Dissertation, Göttingen 1975.

ANSCHRIFT DER AUTOREN

AE, T.
Hiroshima University, Department of Electronics
Faculty of Engineering
Senda-machi 3-8-2, Hiroshima 730, Japan

Alt, H.
Universität des Saarlandes, Fachbereich 10
6600 Saarbrücken

Autebert, J.-M.
Université Paris, Institut de Programmation
4, Place Jussieu, 75230 Paris Cédex 05, France

Berman, L.
Cornell University, Department of Computer Science
Ithaca, NY

Bibel, W.
Technische Universität München, Institut für Informatik
8000 München

Boasson, L.
Université de Picardie, U.E.R. de Mathématiques
33, rue St-Leu, 80039 Amiens Cédex, France

Brandenburg, F.-J.
Universität Bonn, Institut für Informatik
Wegelerstr. 6, 5300 Bonn

Bremer, H.
Universität Frankfurt, Fachbereich Mathematik
Robert-Mayer-Str. 6-10, 6000 Frankfurt/M.

Claus, V.
Universität Dortmund, Lehrstuhl Informatik II
Postfach 50 05 00, 4600 Dortmund 50

Courcelle, B.
IRIA-LABORIA, Domaine de Voluceau
78150 Rocquencourt, France

Damm, W.
RWTH Aachen, Lehrstuhl für Informatik II
5100 Aachen

Dieterich, E.-W.
Technische Universität München, Institut für Informatik
8000 München

Eichner, L.
Universität Freiburg, Institut für Angew. Mathematik
Hermann-Herder-Str. 10, 7800 Freiburg i.Br.

Estenfeld, K.
Universität des Saarlandes, Fachbereich Informatik
6600 Saarbrücken

Gati, G.
Seestr. 83, CH-8702 Zollikon, Switzerland

Hartmanis, J.
Cornell University, Department of Computer Science
Ithaca, NY

von Henke, F.W.
Gesellschaft für Mathematik und Datenverarbeitung Bonn
5205 St. Augustin 1

Huwig, H.
Universität Dortmund, Lehrstuhl Informatik II
Postfach 50 05 00, 4600 Dortmund 50

Jacob, G.
Université Lille I, Laboratiore d'Informatique Théorique
et Programmation (C.N.R.S., laboratoire associé 248)

Kameda, T.
University of Waterloo, Faculty of Engineering
Department of Electrical Engineering
Waterloo, Ontario, Canada, N2L 3G1

Kikuno, T.
Hiroshima University, Department of Electronics
Faculty of Engineering
Senda-machi 3-8-2, Hiroshima 730, Japan

Kott, L.
Université Paris VII, U.E.R. de Mathématiques
2, place Jussieu, 75005 Paris, France

Loeckx, J.
Universität des Saarlandes, Fachbereich 10
6600 Saarbrücken

Lohberger, V.
Universität Dortmund, Abteilung Informatik
4600 Dortmund

Monien, B.
Universität Dortmund, Lehrstuhl Informatik
4600 Dortmund-Hombruch, Postfach 500

Paterson, M.S.
University of Warwick, Department of Computer Science
Coventry CV4 7AL, England

Perrin, D.
Université Paris VII, Laboratoire CNRS d'Informatique
Théorique et de Programmation

Perrot, J.-F.
Université Paris VI et C.N.R.S., Institut de Programmation,
Laboratoire d'Informatique Théorique et Programmation

Prinoth, R.
GMD, Institut für Datenfernverarbeitung
Rheinstraße 75, 6100 Darmstadt

Reynvaan, C.
Universität Frankfurt, Fachbereich Mathematik
Robert-Mayer-Str. 6-10, 6000 Frankfurt/M.

Rodriguez, F.
E.N.S.E.E.I.H.T. et Université PAUL SABATIER,
Toulouse, France

Schauerte, R.
J.W. Goethe-Universität, Fachbereich Mathematik
Robert-Mayer-Str. 6-10, 6000 Frankfurt/M.

Schinzel, B.
Technische Hochschule Darmstadt, Fachbereich Informatik
Magdalenenstr. 11, 6100 Darmstadt

Schnorr, C.-P.
Universität Frankfurt, Fachbereich Mathematik
Robert-Mayer-Str. 6-10, 6000 Frankfurt/M.

Schützenberger, M.P.
Université Paris VII, Laboratoire CNRS d'Informatique
Théorique et de Programmation

Stadel, M.
Universität des Saarlandes, Fachbereich 10
Im Stadtwald, 6600 Saarbrücken

Tamura, N.
Hiroshima University, Department of Electronics
Faculty of Engineering
Senda-machi 3-8-2, Hiroshima 730, Japan

Valk, R.
Universität Hamburg, Institut für Informatik
Schlüterstr. 70, 2000 Hamburg 13

Vidal, G.
Université Paris VI, Institut de Programmation
4 Place Jussieu, 75005 Paris, France